MEGASAGA

by

WALTER JESSON
(Author of 'Betwixt Ribbel and Moerse')

Front cover and title page illustration taken from the Bayeux Tapestry.

ISBN 0 9514040 1 6

First Edition
First Impression October, 1991

Copyright © Walter Jesson, 1991

Published and Printed by
Crompton & Little,
61a Linaker Street, Southport, Merseyside, PR8 5DQ
Telephone: (0704) 542177   Fax: (0704) 533499

All rights reserved. Any copying of the text or photographs in this book by any means whatsoever is strictly prohibited without express written consent from the author, Walter Jesson.

FOREWORD

Whilst this book is in no way a sequel to 'Betwixt Ribbel and Moerse' it does however contain much of the original text from it, omitted in condensing it from a proposed Lancashire Archival Educational project, to render it readable and viable commercially, induced by the change in the Boundaries, and the subsequent economical environment prevailing at the time of publication.

The references given, in this volume, of text and photos contained in 'Betwixt Ribbel and Moerse', although they are helpful, are not imperative, but the original book is still in print, or is available on loan at all Sefton Libraries, as shelf issues or reference copies.

This treatise is not primarily an historical project, but a 'Saga' or story, which attempts to trace the origins of one family, the Rimmers, not only in their one thousand year occupation of local territory, but back to Nordic, and even Biblical eras.

In this process, it does however, present a geneological, chronicled, historical record, which will bear a considerable amount of critical scrutiny, of the Rimmer's connections through inter-marriage with other families, coming to occupy the area, for many centuries past.

These names are all of over 100 families, directly related to, or connected with the Rimmers, who appear in this book, listed alphabetically, but not chronologically: Abram, Ashcroft, Aspinall, Ainscough, Aindow, Alty, Anderson, Aughton, Baker, Ball, Barton, Balshaw, Baxendale, Baxter, Bibby, Blundell, Blenkinsop, Bold, Bond, Boothroyd, Bradshaw, Brookfield, Breakill, Butler, Carr, Cadwell, Charnley, Comstive, Cookson, Coulton, Cropper, Dandy, Dickinson, Fairclough, Fleetwood, Franklin, Gorstage, Grayson, Gregson, Green, Grimes, Halsall, Hesketh, Hodge, Hoscar, Howard, Hunt, Harrison, Hall, Hooton, Jacson, Jackson, Johnson, Jolley, Jump, Kitchen, Leadbetter, Linaker, Lawson, Lloyd, Leatherbarrow, Marshall, Masters, Milner, Moss, Nixon, Orrell, Parr, Pearson, Peet, Rainford, Rigby, Riding, Russell, Robinson, Rowbottom, Scarisbrick, Sedgwick, Segar, Shorlicar or Sherlicar, Spencer, Sutch, Sutton, Sumner, Tasker, Todd, Thomasson, Threlfall, Thwaites, Tomlinson, Waring, Watkinson, Wignall, Whiteside, Wright. Their family records, coupled together with the Rimmer's activities overseas in many lands, and their connection with the tribe of Dan, constitute therefore, not just a 'saga' or story, but a 'MEGASAGA'.

DEDICATION

This book is dedicated to my grandfather, Robert Rimmer, 1864-1936.

CONTENTS

Page

CHAPTER 1
NORDIC SEASAGA — 'THE COMING' 7

CHAPTER 2
'THE PROMISED LAND' 23

CHAPTER 3
NORTH AND SOUTH MEOLS —
HIGH PARK'S "LOST VILLAGE" 35

CHAPTER 4
RECUSANTS — SMUGGLING —
SEA COPS — FLOODS & PLAGUE 53

CHAPTER 5
MARSHSIDE —
'LITTLE IRELAND' AND 'LITTLE LONDON' 71

CHAPTER 6
THE RIMMERS IN BIRKDALE —
AINSDALE AND FORMBY 81

CHAPTER 7
GENEOLOGIES OF RIMMER'S RELATIVES 115

CHAPTER 8
THE RIMMERS AND SOUTHPORT 129

CHAPTER 9
THE LLOYD — PEET — GREEN DYNASTY 139

CHAPTER 10
THE ORIGIN OF SPECIES —
KING ARTHUR — ROBIN HOOD 161

CHAPTER 11
RIMMERS AND DAN — GENESIS —
EXODUS — NUMBERS — REVELATIONS? 179

PHOTOGRAPHS 193

MEGASAGA

A VOYAGE BACK IN TIME

CHAPTER 1

NORDIC SEASAGA — 'THE COMING'

The encyclopaedic and lexical definition of 'SAGA' is 'SEGJA' — 'what is said or told'; Icelandic, medieval prose narrative, embodying the history of Scandinavian Expansion, or Nordic King story of heroic achievement or adventure, and long family Chronicles'. Although originally considered to be imaginative reconstructions of the past, oral tradition of individuals, they are now regarded as conceptions of accurate Ethnology and folklore combined. Sagas were told by Skalds or Court Poets.

My 'saga' of the Rimmers begins about seventy years ago, when they had already completed over a thousand years of local settlement.

In Bispham Road, in the High Park district of Southport, especially in winter, we used to complain about the biting wind, causing liberal applications of 'Snowfire' salve, to chapped legs and knees.

My grandfather Robert Rimmer, fisherman and Independent Methodist lay preacher, told us that the wind came across "T'Pool fra Siberia". As our general knowledge, including geography, increased, so did the question. "Siberia that's in Russia?". "Ay' th's reet," he said. When pressed later on with the question "Where did your lot come from?" his enigmatic reply was "We coo'med with wind." (he always pronounced this as in wind = 'to turn'). "You mean the Rimmers came from Russia?" "Aye, and the'er abouts." was his reply to that. "If that's so," I said to him, "how come my mam's always on about how the Rimmers were 'Rymers', 'singers', and 'musicians', and they came from Norway?" "Ay that's reet an'aw." "So now we're coming to it," I said, "The Vikings, that burning and pillaging lot of thieves and robbers?" "Nay, not so," was his reply, "We was a'fore and after them." "Well then what about the Rimmers being found living on the rim of the Mere?" "We do now," he said, "don't we, we've a'lus lived on't edge of watter." "You weren't on the edge of the sea inside Russia surely?" "Ay, we were an a'w," was his reply to that. By the time I had given up trying to make sense out of these bouts of cryptic badinage, I was beginning to write out notes for him, for his weekly sermons. On one occasion I said to him sarcastically, "I suppose you'll be telling me next that your lot came out of Noah's Ark?" "Appen not," he said, "But we've bin near about the'er."

Over the years he continued to throw out all sorts of snatches of enigmatical information, which didn't necessarily refer, or appear to concern Rimmers, or their origins. When, for instance, in reply to a question concerning what direction the Rimmers had come from, he said "Tha mo'n look out for Th' Northern Leets." I thought he was referring to the Blackpool Illuminations! Like many of his ilk, he was a great believer in the medicinal properties of herbal preparations, and home-made concoctions, such as a hot onion for earache, and toothache, and a weird object he called the "saut bag", which consisted of a long sock, full of rock salt, which, when heated up in the oven, was considered to be the cure for many ailments. He was a frequent consultant with a man called Luke Morris, herbalist, who had a surgery in Hill Street. I think many people even today, will remember him. One item however which stands out above the rest, and is pertinent to this saga, was a herbal plant. It is still grown in profusion locally, known by the name of 'KNIT BONE' = Comfrey, used mainly for external application, still available today, and when infused, produced a vile greenish, evil smelling concoction, which could be taken internally, specifically for the treatment of tubercular diseases. When my grandad was questioned about his affection for this plant he said, "We brought it wi'us." It was this innocent reference which was to start, in later years, a chain of inquiry into the mystery of the Rimmer's origin.

One thing the Rimmers, and many other dwellers in the northern parts of Britain, were affected by, were constant language variations. Old Norse, was the language spoken by the North Germanic or Scandinavian people, when the two languages became separated, from about 100 A.D. Subsequently, to this, the Scandinavian, or so-called 'Viking' invasion of Britain, was followed by settlements of a permanent nature. In the north of England, Scotland and Scottish islands, the Anglo-Saxon, old English, and Scottish languages, became infused, in the Viking period from 750 to 1050, with traditions, and speech, from at least seven different Norse dialects. Also to these, Old Icelandic, Old Swedish, and Old Danish languages, which themselves had broken away from the Germanic language of the Burgundians, Goths, and Vandals, as far back as 200 B.C., were added. It is small wonder therefore, that such a profusion of language variations have been retained in the topography of place names of the north-west. So too, did the intermingling of language, and dialect, have influences that can be detected, even now, in our everyday speech.

A few examples of this language infusion can be given, mostly in West Norse. AT in west Norse is THAT pronounced UT "I saw ut he were asleep": BRU = Hill slope or brow. "I wer going upt' broo (BRU): EKKI = not, used by us today "Will I heck as like." BRUNT = Burn't, "I brunt me hond." (I burned my hand). GAUM attention or heed, "He warn't tekkin na' gaum.": LAUSE — Loose, let go, "Loyse thee ow'd on it.": LYGI = untruth — used by us in our schooldays "He's a right "LIGGER" = Liar: FORRUT — Forewards: BUCKERT — Backwards: SINN = time, "It were long sinn." (Long ago): NU — now, pronounced 'noo': EGGJAR = urge or exhort — still used = to "Egg on". DEAG to sprinkle = pronounced Degg.

We used to call a watering can, "Degging Can": WEINDT pronounced "wint" = passage or entry, still in general use.

These terms were, and are in general use in this north west corner of England, and were only kept together as a patios, when a section of the Rimmer clan moved to Marshside, after they had first settled at Bank Nook, which was on higher ground than the marsh, which only began to be occupied in the second half of the 18th century. They were a tight knit community, and retained their own dialect, until inter-marriage gradually eroded it, into what is loosely termed as the "Marshside dialect" of recent years.

A second cousin of mine, who contacted me recently after the newspaper article on my uncle Bob, however, agreed with me that a language, spoken by the original Rimmers was, on occasions, totally different to the so called "Marshside dialect" which we both could speak, and understand. She told me that, as a young girl, she had occasion to visit our house in Bispham Road, when there had been a large catch of shrimps, and all my family, and relatives, had gathered around a large wooden table to assist in the "shilling" or picking of the shrimps, and that the whole bunch of Rimmers were conversing together in a lingo which was totally incomprehensible to her!

She was also able to clear up the mystery of an "Auntie Betty" of Bank Nook. The reason why I could not remember her was because, around about the year 1911, she had been knocked down by a horse in Manor Road. She was taken to relatives in High Park, from where she originated, on a milk float, and died there the next day. My grandad had three brothers, and four sisters, amongst the High Park Rimmers, one of whom, Tom, who lived with his sister Esther Ellen, in Old Park Lane, was a lifeboatman and fisherman. As a small boy, I can remember visits to the Lifeboat House, and playing in the Lifeboat, which used to be open to visitors, and the lifeboat custodian, in full rig of cork lifejacket and "sou'wester". He used to breed canaries in a loft above the boat. My mother carried a photograph of him, around with her, in this full rig. He was referred to, by her, as "Grandfather Rigby", from my granny's side of the family. As the lifeboat station was closed down in 1926, he was probably the last custodian. The lifeboat would probably be the John Harling, which later on, my grandad helped to convert into a pleasure boat on the Marine Lake.

On the corner of Devonshire Road, and in Old Park Lane, is a small Gospel Hall, still flourishing. This used to be known simply as 'The Room'. Many of the High Park Rimmers attended this Hall, which administered the simple, but very strict doctrines of The Plymouth Brethren. It had none of the trappings of organised religion, you just declared your faith in front of the 'Table' and that was it. Whether it was first established by the Rimmers is not clear, as it was later associated with many of the families who were intermarried with the Rimmers, the Rigbys, Wrights, and also relatives of 'Old Duke' Sutton himself. My grandad, even when he was an Independent Methodist Minister, spoke there on many occasions.

I mention this Hall, because, to me, it has another bearing on my

Grandad's remarks concerning the Rimmer's origin. In 1807 there came to North Meols a missionary, the Rev. George Greatbatch, to bring to the people the message of the Non-Conformist movement, which was the subject of much opposition in the area. The theory that the 'Room' in Old Park Lane was the site of, or near, land that was given to him by some farmers, can be added to support the account of the Rev. George Greatbatch being refused permission to build a place of worship in the Parish of Churchtown. So I believe that the chapel which was built for him, was erected somewhere in High Park. Greatbatch's first contact with North Meols was from Ormskirk. The main route into North Meols, was by way of Foul Lane and Wennington Road (Long Lane), then a short distance down Bispham Road, into Old Park Lane. He was welcomed in High Park, and his self appointed protector, or 'minder' was a Hooton, from Old Park Lane (who also happened to be a relative of the Rimmers). This leads me to think about the remark what was made when the 'chapel' was completed, that it looked like "Noah's Ark", which has stuck in my mind, as being similar to other enigmatical hints made by grandad Rimmer!

To obtain some idea as to the origin of this mysterious people, tribe or clan, or whatever we wish to call them, we can first of all go back to the early part of the 10th century. In the year 912 A.D. Ethelfreda, daughter of King Alfred, 'Lady of the Mercians', established a monastery at Brombrough, in the Wirral. The Mercians, by the defeating of the Northumbrian Danes by King Athelstan in 937 A.D., then pushed the North border of the Mercian Kingdom to the River Ribble. I have referred to the site of this battle, which took place at an undiscovered place called Brunanburgh, (also being the site of King Arthur's last battle), as being Bamber Bridge, both contentions of which were supported by at least one eminent historian, and confirmed by the discovery of the Anglo Saxon and Danish Treasure Hoard, at Cuerdale in 1840. The treasure hoard story was given credence in a TV programme by Bob Smithies, just recently in 1990, (see "Betwixt" Page 14 and Map Page 15).

In the wake of the Viking raids, the Rimmers had come to England as peaceful settlers, but it's recorded that one of Skald Grimm's two sons, was killed at the Battle of Brunanburgh.

Skald Grimm's or (Rimmers), Nordic name, was Egil Skallagrimson, who had become both the liegeman, and 'Skald' (story teller) of Athelstan, as well as the navigator on board. This was the only way of recording events before written records. 'Skalds' were used as court poets, as well as recording family, and historical events. It is from them, that we get the description of the Rimmers being the Nordic 'Rymers.'

For the Nordic history of the Rimmers I used, in conjunction with literally hundreds of other sources of reference, two other sources of information, Landnamabok and Islendingabok, which were written in the three centuries from 1120—1400, covering the history of the Saga Age, which lasted from about 900—1050 A.D. The two 'Boks' or Books, many volumed, and of enormous length, contained Historical Research — Lives of Kings, and Geneaologies of all the Nordic races before the Saga Age, and also settlements abroad. I used them in reference to many localities, as evidenced in the reference to Crossens as Krossa-Ness, 'Cross on the ness' or 'headland' (page 37 of Betwixt).

Long before the Rimmers came to the Nordic countries, however, there are references to part of their origins, in earlier sagas, such as the Ynglinga Saga, which gives the history, or origin, of the Rimmers as a dynasty, which was in existence from 400 B.C., to approximately 400 A.D. They were referred to as the tribe of Dan, and were supposed to be devotees of the pagan religion of Odinism. They were then residents of the coast of the Black Sea, in the Caucasus. Some of grandfather Rimmer's 'hints' now become clearer, as the place they were, on the 'rim of the sea', is only a few miles from Mount Ararat, where the remains of Noah's Ark was photographed! So the Rimmers had dwelt on the rim of an inland sea, in Russia. Another of his 'hints' also turned out to be true, as I found out that his beloved Comfrey was 'indigenous to the Caucasian mountains,' in flora lore! They were also, then, not a great distance from Siberia, where the 'wind came from', which astonishingly enough is on the same latitude as the greater part of Northern England, including Martin Mere, and Bispham Road! The remark about the Rimmers being "round about theer", was also true, as it states in the Ynglinga Saga that, in a period covering many generations, an 'Odin' moved his 'tribe' from the region of Don, in early Anno Domini, to avoid Roman Conquest. From around 200 B.C., the Rimmers had been on the move to avoid confrontations with Burgundians and Goths, and the Vandals. Some of these warlike tribes originated in Sweden, who was the 'mother' of all Scandinavian peoples. From the beginning of history, Sweden had instigated a career of conquest in the South. From Sweden came the Danes, and the Norwegians. Sweden was the home of the oldest culture, and traditions, of the Norse peoples. Subsequently there came a great linguistic change when all these different peoples adopted their own dialects, and national traditions. The true Scandinavian expansion came during the Viking period, from 750 to 1050 A.D. The Vikings were not only Norse, or Norwegian, but also Danish, and Swedish. The word 'Viking', is found in texts earlier than the Norse Viking raids. Even in Old English-Anglo Saxon, the word 'Wicing' was used, to denote 'Pirate'. Shortly after the commencement of the Viking raids, the Swedes established a kingdom around Novgorod, and moved on later to form another Kingdom around Kiev, went up the Dyna by boat, then by land to the Dneipr, and into the Black Sea. They swept on to Constantinople and became the founders of Russia, where the Swedes were known as 'Rus'. This Kingdom of Rus was mainly Slavonic, and these Swedes eventually lost their Scandinavian traditions and language.

According to the many Sagas subsequently written, the Swedes established friendly relationships with the Rimmers, who eventually moved back with them to Sweden, no doubt being employed by them as 'Skalds', for the recording of Nordic history. The Rimmer skalds were also used for the composition of Runic Songs, and inscriptions on Runic stones.

The Rimmers also had a more practical application in the construction and the inscripting of these Runic stones. They were originally thought to have been introduced by the Goths on the North Coast of the Black Sea. It has been recorded however in one 11th century Saga, that, when the Swedish Vikings contacted the Rimmers on the Eastern side of the Black Sea, which was the furthest Eastern penetration of the Vikings, the Rimmers erected and inscribed, a Runic grave vault stone, with a skull and crossbone motif, for the Swedes at Berezanji, now thought to be Batumi, which approximates to the location of the Rimmer settlement, under the shadow of Mount Ararat. My grandad told me that when his family were connected with the (Old Duke) Sutton's, in the stonemason trade, their trade mark was a skull and crossbones, which many people wrongly associated with pirates, particularly at St. Cuthbert's churchyard. It would be an astonishing flight of fancy to assume that it had been used to mark a Viking 'pirates' grave, so long ago, and so far away. Long before that however, the skull and crossbones sign, has been used in the Kidron Valley near Jerusalem, at Golgotha, 'The place of the Skull', a Jewish Cemetery.

When the Rimmers eventually moved into the Nordic area, they settled, probably by friendly invitation, in East Gotland. It is not to be assumed that the Rimmers erected all the Scandinavian Runic stones, but it seems more than coincidence that Sweden had the highest number. There are more than 2000 still in existence there, including probably the most noted of them all, The Stone of Rök, from east Gotland, stated as being "fashioned by 'Warin' (Rimmer), in memory of his dead son." This stone also records the history covering nine generations of Rimmers, and their association with the Goths.

How long the Rimmers remained in East Gotland is not certain, but eventually they moved further west, in about 400 A.D. It is interesting to note that Warin Rimmers, or Rymers as they were then known, are recorded in the Calendar Patent Rolls in Yorkshire in 1229, having moved across the Ribble, as Preston was then within the boundary of Yorkshire.

Although the Rimmers spoke the language, and inscribed Runic stones through many countries, also employing the countries own language, it was said that, when they left, the Rimmers still retained an undefined language of their own. Their name had changed from 'Odin', to Dan, then 'Halfdan'. Landnamabok mentions 'Odda', son of Grim, as the first settler in North Meols. The Scandinavians called them Grimr. The Danish, before moving from Sweden to Denmark called them 'Hrimr', or Giant, as did the Swedes. The Saxons confused the issue later on, by asserting that Grim, the "masked one", was one of the names of Woden, High God of the Saxons.

One of the Rimmers greatest Skalds took the 'mickey' out of many of these conjectures, by writing a Saga-poem called Prymskvida, in the style of later English Ballads, in which he ridiculed the idea of the Rimmers being associated with Gods, Scandinavian or otherwise, and confused them still further by referring to the Rimmers as 'Hryma' and 'Prymr' and 'Grymr', all in half a dozen sentences. Although this was written about the year 900, I have seen a facsimile of this Saga-poem, printed on vellum, many years later. The reference, in the Scandinavian language to 'Skrymir', like many others, is open to different interpretations, consistent with the country, and time, and change, and can be used to indicate 'huge one', but in later Danish-Swedish interpretations, both 'Skrymir' and 'Hrimr' are both quoted as, "to take up great space, or "seem big", and in the context of the Rimmers, merely means that they were "a large body of people, requiring much space".

The myths and legends concerning the Rimmers being associated with Gods and Giants, can also be dispelled by perusing a Norse cosmograph termed 'Yggdrasil', which is depicted as the "Ash Tree (Ash for Apple), on which the structure of the universe is based", and was taken from the Ynglingla saga of the Rimmers. The tree, symbolic of the tree of good and evil in Eden, is described as the Ash tree, "which is the greatest of all trees and the noblest, its limbs spread out all over the worlds, and stands above heaven." It has two roots Askr = Man and Embla = Woman, depicting man's origin. Another root is stated as spreading out amongst the frost giants or 'Skrymir'. 'YGG', in this graph is referred to as 'Odin', "The Allfather, creator of all, who sits in the high seat in the Hall of Many Doors" (In my father's house there are many mansions), and looks out over the world, and sees every man's acts. There are many references in this graph, to places such as Niflheim (Hell), and Valholl (Heaven), or as we know it, Valhalla. There is also a reference to a place where another root is found. This place was where once, before Creation, was the 'Yawning Gap', among the frost giants, who were referred to as 'Skrymir', the name meaning, in modern Norwegian, as 'huge one', and in Swedish 'Skrymma' "to take up great space — seem big". These references doubtless led to the legend of the Rimmer's connection with giants, which persisted into the time when North Meols was associated with the Rimmers. The connection however, between the 'Yggdrasil', and its account being related by the Rimmer Saga named 'Ynglinga', promotes the contention that the Rimmer's connection with 'Odinism', is Biblical in aspect. The Norse derivation of Odin, 'Ygg' in 'Ynglinga', is God, singular Creator of All, and nothing to do with the Nordic worship of Gods. The Rimmers therefore, brought this faith with them, and it appears that wherever they settled, they had a profound influence on other people's religious beliefs, to the effect that by the year 1000, the whole of the Scandinavian territory was Christianised. The 'Ynglinga' Sagas were associated with the tribe of Dan and Odinism, in Norse Cosmology, by references to Freya and Freyr, god and goddess, male and female. Their father was 'Njoror' God of the sea. It is quoted in Norse mythology "He rules the course of the wind, and stills the sea and fire: on him shall men call for fortune, in voyages and fishing,": attributes which the Norse people associated the Danites, and, Odinism, as possessing. Freyr was also referred to as 'Snot Saka' a 'maid of battles'. In this context 'Snot' was referred to as 'Lady'. Therefore 'Snotr' could be used in several different deviations, and was so used by the Danites or Rimmers in later centuries. Freyr was also called 'Yngvi', ruler of peace, fertility and sunshine, which gave the name to the sagas. In other references in varied Norse language, she is named as daughter of 'Njord', associated with Odin, and the sea giant

'Gymir', also known as 'Hrymir', a deviation, which finally crept into 'Rimmer' adoption as a tribal name. In one instance the single name Freyr, was used to denote a god of fertility, and especially agriculture, equating with Adam, whose biblical name means 'earth'. The whole essence of Norse Cosmology or mythology, seems therefore, to be centred around the Genesis story of creation, and many other civilizations have incorporated it into their historical mythology, and cosmology, in the same manner. Certainly in the case of Nordic cosmology, the arrival of a tribe expounding the idea of a single deity, appealed to them, particularly by the later arrival of the Danites, or Hrimrs, or Rimmers, as they promoted verbal accounts of their ancestors experiences, reaching back virtually to Creation itself. They could show evidence of the fulfilment of phrophecies, divinely inspired by God himself, through the Prophets, even including their own experience of the Crucifixion, and the ultimate destruction of Jerusalem in 70 A.D., which led to their own exile, as being also one of the very prophecies they were relating.

There is therefore another puzzle to answer, concerning the Nordic or Scandinavian peoples. Why did they, so suddenly after the arrival of a Nomadic wandering tribe, so quickly embrace the Christian conception of Creation into their cosmology, and promote the acceptance of Christianity in the whole of Scandinavia by the year 1000 A.D. Another aspect presented an ethnological enigma. What was a race of large statured, white skinned, blonde haired people doing, in a region totally composed of dark skinned asiatic, and slavic races, smaller and squatter than the Scandinavians in general appearance?

The answer has been debated for many centuries, until a conjectural contention came from the Norse people themselves. In 1914 Thor Heyerdahl a 'latter day Norwegian Viking', was born in Larvik, Norway, not a long way from the Rimmer Kingdom of Hoederland. He studied at Oslo University, and after many field researches in Natural Science in all parts of the world, including excavation in British Columbia, finally came to the conclusion that the Norse people had come from the South. He took up the theory that Plato's story of the lost city of Atlantis being in the Atlantic, and lost in cataclysmic upheaval, was credible, that some survivors had gone north, and others across to found civilisation in the Americas. He went to places in the middle east, Africa and Egypt and built balsa wood, and papyrus reed rafts in the same manner, and locations, that the Danites had built similar vessels. His expeditions of thousands of miles journeys, including two across the Atlantic via the Canary Islands, which he contended were the tops of mountains of Atlantis, have been well documented in writings, and on television. His later expedition in 1977, was to construct and sail, a papyrus reed raft around the Persian Gulf, to visit all the Biblical sites from the Garden of Eden, to the ghost city sites of Ur and Babylon, in the Euphrates. Only recently have the modern, oceanic, seismographical surveys shown that the split in the ocean bed which destroyed the discredited city of Atlantis, stretched all the way to Iceland. More incredible than the Rimmer-Dan 'saga' would you think?

Where the Rimmers really originated, is therefore, still a tantalizing mystery. That they were of ancient Biblical origin, can be proved by the reference in the 'Ynglinga', quoting from the Book of Tobit V1.V18, one of the seven Apocryphal books that were part of the Bible, when it was first compiled, gives a distinct reference to the Rimmers being concerned in an 'Exodus'. It also states, that with reference to the statement in Genesis Chapter 6, Verse 4 (King James Version), that "there were giants in the earth at this time," did not refer to the Danites as being physical giants. I found out by cross reference, that the 'giants' connected with the Danites, were Nephilm, of the Anak tribe, see Numbers 13.V.33, the giants were indeed physical giants, who died out with the death of Goliath. This was in the time of Enoch, whom "God took up alive", and that was after Creation, at the time when Enoch was born to Cain's wife. The 'Yggradasil' is an account of the Creation, so we cannot go further back than that. No wonder when I asked my Grandad about Noah, he wasn't having me on when he said, "It's 'aw in't Bible." Talk about "Seek and ye shall find!"

It is thought that the Rimmers moved into East Sweden about the year 300 A.D., the real date is uncertain, but the Runic Stone of Rok, already referred to, testifies to their presence and activity there.

The European Exodus of the Rimmers continued when, about the year 400, they moved over to the West of Norway, and took over, or were granted establishment, of a small Kingdom, in land which was ruled over by King Byorgyn, after whom Bergen was named. This Kingdom was known as Hoederland or Hordaland, situated around the Hardanger Fiord. The area granted to the Rimmers was on, and around, the Sogne Fiord, to the North West of Hardanger Field. These areas are easily identifiable today, from any atlas. There is also a contention, that the area was originally called "Oddaland', as 'Odda' was another name for Odin. Dan had been a leader of the Rimmers on the move from the region of the River Don (another conjection), in early Anno Domini, 'Halfdans' were also 'leaders'. The West Norse people referred to 'Odda', as the son of Grimr, who they wrongly associated with Grim, 'the masked one', the counterpart of Woden in Scandinavia. All these attendant confusions were gradually sorted out, but the name of Rimmer survived, even after Landnamabok referred to 'Odda, son of Grim', when recording him as the first Norse settler in North Meols. There is no literal record in the West Norse language however, showing the gutteral pronunciation 'Grim', as a basic reference to these people from the East. As I have explained again later on, that although a gutteral pronunciation such as the 'Grim', for instance from the Danish Vikings, has been retained when they established Grimsby, the gutteral sound could not be pronounced in the Old Norse languages of Sweden, or in West Norway especially, so the nearest they could get to it in expression was 'Hrimr' which I think is the true origin of the name 'Rimmer'. Generally speaking if, in the case of the Rimmer's Nordic adventures, you read the 'Grimr' deviation as 'Rimmer', you will not be far off the mark. The influence on the West Norse people, once again, proved to be favourable, as can be indicated by the fact that a Runic stone, discovered at Eggjum in Sogne, during World War I, was raised about the year 800. This was about the time that it was recorded that the Principal Hersir, or Earl of Sogn (Sogne) was Wether Grimr. It is not clear if he caused it to be raised, or if it was a tribute to him, but the riddle concerning it, is the fact that the inscription was made in Icelandic, or at least the translation is. One sentence reads, "Which of the rune-horde has come here to the land of men?" It ends "Let no man make this stone naked, nor let bold or senseless men throw it down." It is possible that one of the rune maker Rimmers returned after they left Norway for Iceland. It has survived however, intact for over 1000 years. This equates with the Biblical exhortation "Remove not the landmarks thy forefathers hath set up." One other place that has maintained its identity over the years, is Grimstad, near Kristiansend, on the south east corner of Norway, and simply means, Grim's home.

Although the main expansion of the Scandinavians took place from 750 A.D. onwards, bands of these piratical adventurers, in large enough numbers to be called 'armies', sailed overseas, not only in search of plunder, but also to win land for settlement. Piracy had long been an honourable form of enterprise among seafaring Germanic races. As far back as the years between 512 and 520, it was recorded, in Frankish annals, and the Anglo Saxon poem 'Beowulf', a Swedish King, Hugleik, made a raid on the Rhineland, from which he never returned. Norwegian Vikings, before 700 A.D., had made settlements in the Shetlands. Towards the end of the 8th century, attacks were made on the shores of England, Ireland, Friesland and France. Christian Europe was an easy prey for the Norsemen, but the Scandinavians had become increasingly disturbed by the destruction of the naval power of the Friesians, who had been the Norseman's rival on the sea, by Charlemagne, who then commenced military operations in the north of Germany, by a movement to invade Denmark. Much of Scandinavia had been overpopulated, and when Harald Fairhair took over the Kingdom of Hoederland, or Hordeland, from his father, Halfdan The Black, about the year 860, the Rimmers were apparently in trouble, as Harald Fairhair subjugated all the smaller Kingdoms, and declared himself King of Norway. He interfered with rights of sovereignty and ownership, imposing heavy taxes, killing and outlawing all objectors. This, together with many political changes, drove many Scandinavians abroad into exile. The struggles of rival princes for the throne of Denmark was another factor which led to two main courses of Viking expeditions. To the East, they were mainly Swedish and Danish, to the West the Norwegians took the route to Ireland, around the North of Scotland to the Isle of Man, and our own shores. Most of the Viking invaders along the East Coast of Britain were Swedish and Danish. Thus the Viking raids eventually encircled Europe.

However as Harald Fairhair was the rightful heir to the region, or Kingdom, in which the Rimmers had established themselves, they continued with their comparatively peaceful and undisturbed existence. There is no doubt that this had a steadying influence on Harald Fairhair, but his conquest of Norway continued until a great naval victory over the Kings of South West Norway in 872, gave him complete possession of the whole realm. A romantic sideline to these events is in the story, by another Rimmer Skald, that Harald's aspirations only took form when his paternal Kingdom, in South East Norway, in the Grimstad area, was small. He sued for the hand of Gyda, daughter of another small Kingdom ruler, but she said she would "Not waste her maidenhead for a King who only ruled a few counties." She commented on the fact that King Gorm was sole ruler of Denmark, and Eirik was King at Uppsala in Sweden, but there was "No King who could make Norway his own." Thereupon Harald declared he would not comb, or cut, his hair until he had won Norway for his own. He kept his vow, thus earning for himself the cognomen (fancy word for 'nickname') of 'Harald Fairhair', and completed his triumph by marrying his beloved Gyda. (It was never recorded whether he made a visit to the a barber!).

In the eyes of the Nordic literary historian, Iceland is the most important, for it was here that the greater part of Old Norse literature which survives today, was written. Harald Fairhair (to give him his full title Konungr-Harald ins Harfagr Halfdanarsonar ins Svarta, which reads "King Harald Fairhair, son of Halfdan the Black'), illustrates the type of verbal geneology, used in our time, by the Rimmers and associated families. He was intent on bringing Norway and Iceland under his control. He represented the forces that were bringing the old heroic society to an end, and the colonisation of Iceland was therefore not just an ambitious venture, but an attempt to weld the Nordic Kingdoms together, to resist the threat of invasion from the Germanic forces.

Iceland was first discovered in 860, by a Swede, living in Denmark, who was blown off his course in a storm, and the first settler was a Norwegian in 874. Many of the great men of Norway fled to the Orkneys and the Shetlands, and took to Viking life in the West, wintering in the Scottish islands and harrying the coast of Norway in the summer, so eventually Harald took a fleet and cleared the isles. This was about the time when Iceland was discovered, and colonised by many of the exiled chiefs. Landnamabok gives the names, and origin, of about 400 settlers, who were determined to maintain their old freedom, and heroic order of society. They were the best of Norwegian aristocracy, and lovers of freedom. About two thirds of them came direct from Norway, and surprisingly enough, about 115 from the British Isles, some of whom were English, with a few Rimmers scattered amongst them, who, apart from their Skaldic proclivities, had by now proved to be expert seaman, and navigators.

Many of the Rimmers joined the exodus to Iceland in the wake of the exiles, and their navigational aids had told them from experience, of the existence of the warm Gulf stream, which runs along our own shores, and the Scottish coasts, and the western coasts of Norway and Iceland. They were therefore able to assist in what subsequently proved to be a successful, and peaceful, settlement in Iceland, which, at that time, had a population of approximately a quarter of what it is today.

The Scandinavian countries had by now, owing to their non-gutteral intonation, accepted the pronunciation of 'Hrimr', for the Rimmers, which was seduced to 'Grim' now pronounced 'Hrim', in Icelandic Sagas, retained in place names such as "Grim was the name of the man who took settlement from Gills to Grimsgill" (a gorge or ravine). A 'Steingrim' lived at Steingrimstead, now Sigmustead, on Steingrimr Fiord, in the North West of Iceland. Modern spelling gives us Grimsey Island to the North of Iceland, on the Arctic Circle. Nearer home of course, we have Grimsboer = Grimsby, Lincs, which shows the contradiction in the various Nordic languages, as 'Boer' means farmstead, or house, in Old Norse. It was quite likely that the dipthong was dropped in favour of the Danish, BY, which is the derivation I have kept to, in Chapter 8 of 'Betwixt Ribbel and Moerse', when describing Formby, which means "possessed by the Danes". Here again you can get lost in a maze of contradiction as, Fornebei, Fornebi and Fornebra, are given in the 12th century, for Formby, in 'Old Swedish'! A further anomally occurs, if we assume that Grimsby was founded by 'Grim', a Rimmer who was a West Norse Viking, and gave it a Danish Viking prefix. I think this only points to the fact that the Rimmers belonged to one race, their own, but collaborated, and integrated, into any society they contacted on their 'Exodus'. It is certainly a curious fact to consider that, not so very long ago, at the middle, to the end, of the 19th century, Southport was second only to Grimsby, as having the largest fishing fleet in the Kingdom.

The influence of the Rimmers in Iceland was progressive, and as far as historical records from sagas and poems go, permanent, and pertinent to this day, as many of them maintained places of residence which have survived to the present. The composition of the sagas, and the Landnambok and Islendingabok which took over three centuries to compile, added to this permanency.

Since writing these notes concerning the Rimmers in Iceland, a TV travel programme presenter in August 1990, commented on research he had conducted in Iceland, that he was quite astonished to find that the Icelanders were not all the large 'Nordic Blonde' type of individuals he had expected to see, but many of them were smaller and darker in complexion, could it be that they were a small 'remnant' left behind by the Rimmers Exodus? He found the inhabitants were most hospitable, and the country quite equable in climate and scenery. He was informed by local people that the 'Vikings' had, long ago, put it about that Iceland was cold and remote, to prevent it being over-run by immigrants!

One of the greatest of the Rimmer Icelandic Skalds closely connected with the history of England, was the Egil Skallagrimson, referred to earlier, who was involved with our own local history, with the events at Brunanburgh (Bamber Bridge) in 935 A.D. His life story was recounted in one of the greatest of the Sagas. It was written probably around the year 1220, while the author was living at Egil's old home in the West of Iceland, at Borg near Reykjavik.

The final stage of the Rimmer's adventures in Nordic regions before the discovery of America, was the discovery of Greenland. It is very difficult to place all these events in strict chronological order, as for instance, I found in some old records that 'papar' or Irish monks, had been in Iceland prior to

800 A.D., which was before the Norsemen landed there! I have therefore had to confine this narrative strictly to the movement of the Rimmers, and keep also to the name they finally retained in North Meols.

Norway was the first of the Scandinavian lands in which Christianity obtained a firm footing, and the earliest Christian teachers were English, who had adopted one style of writing from the Irish, and also a Frankish style, used for writing Latin. This was fully illustrated by the Rimmer Saga 'Prymskvida' a facsimile of which is preserved on vellum, in the Codex Regius in the Royal Library at Copenhagen. Another of the most important sagas, that of Egil Rimmers son, or 'Skallagrimson', is preserved in manuscripts on vellum, and known as the Wolfbuttel Manuscript, in Germany.

The last Nordic expansion before the discovery of America, was officially made by Eirik the Red, who was exiled from Iceland for manslaughter in 981. He sailed west, to look for some rockly islets he had been told about, which had been seen some seventy years previously by an Icelander named Gunnbjorn.

These islets have since been charted and named 'Gunnbjarnasker'. Eirick the Red never found these islets, but he discovered Greenland, the largest island in the world. A landing on the east coast was impracticable, so he around the southern extremity, to the firth indented, western side. He weathered three years of exploration, before returning to Iceland, where he gave what was probably an exaggerated, attractively optimistic account of this new land. In 985 A.D., twenty five ships struck out across the ice strewn, western sea. These voyages of discovery were all made in open boat, some ships had a small cabin at either end, many had no decks or shelter of any kind. Only fourteen ships survived the journey. Two colonies were formed, on the west coast near Godthaab. The probable population of the colonies never exceeded 5000, so eventually, when communications between Iceland and Norway were disrupted in the fourteenth century, the general effects of climate, and limited diet, caused the inevitable evacuation. The Eskimos, who had left before the settlements were made, then returned, and took over the territory.

The Rimmers do not appear to have had much recorded history in Greenland, apart from a vague reference to a Runic stone, from the island of Kingiktorsoak, Baffin Bay, off Greenland, which, apart from a venturesome journey to the 'cold edge of the world' to Svalbard, probably Spitzbergen, was the Norsemen's furthest northern discovery. The Greenlanders however, did produce many of their own sagas, one of which made reference to Odin's influence on their geneology. This saga also infers that, through this connection, the descendants of the 'Odin' people, possessed the powers of prophecy, equivalent of the modern 'spirit medium', and clairvoyancy, which has still been manifested today, in recent fortune telling, and clairvoyancy establishments in various arcades, avenues, and on Southport Pleasure Fairground, and in some less professional pursuits such as 'tea leaf' readings! A poem by Rimmer 'Grimnismal', referring to 'The Sibyl's Prophecy' connected with 'The Prophetess of Greenland', concerns the statement that "Odin knew from this, that disaster was prophesised for the mythical gods of the Norsemen." Which again is Biblical, if 'Odin' equates with 'Jehovah', the one true God-Creator of the Universe.

There were no trees in Iceland, so timber, and even cattle, were transported by ship to Greenland. Timber was also transported by the Greenlanders from Markland, now known as Newfoundland. These journeys were only accomplished by astounding feats of seamanship, in the fearful, storm ridden northern seas. Many of us are doubtless aware of the 'Maelstrom Whirlpool', of the Lofoten Islands in Norway, but one Greenland Saga refers to the marvel of the 'Hafgerdingar' where the "seas, and tempests meet into three huge waves, higher than the mountains", the backwash of which reaches the shore of Greenland. These climatic upheavals were probably caused by seaquakes, but when you consider that a normal storm in these regions produced waves higher than Nelson's Column, and even in relatively calmer condition further south, the experiences on the oil rigs, can testify to the courage of the Norsemen's contribution to navigation. Progress by rowing, would only cover about twenty miles per day, even when assisted by the use of the single mainsail each ship possessed. So other navigational aids had to be employed, knowledge of astronomy, and also the progression, and utilization, of the various sea currents, such as the North Atlantic Drift, the Labrador Current and the Gulf Stream, also seasonal rainfalls, and temperatures, and wind drifts, such as the Westerlies and Horse Latitudes. In this respect the Rimmers had acquired much skill, and were included in voyages, not merely as navigators, skalds or rymers, but also in one other aspect. The Norsemen were steeped in centuries of mythology, and superstition, and "King's Luck" and a skald's approval, of any enterprise, was greatly valued. They knew by now, from many sagas, such as the one concerning 'The Prophetress of Greenland', that the Rimmers exercised powers of divination, very similar to that of many ancient Nordic cosmographers, so that their approval, and presence of any of them, on any undertaking, was widely sought, and approved.

There are two versions of the Norseman's discovery of America, but there is now no doubt that it was discovered by them, some 500 years before Columbus, who incidentally, never set foot on the mainland of America. It is generally credited to Leif Ericksson, but the saga concerning him quotes that he 'sighted' America in the year 1000. Another saga states that Bjarni Herjolfsson 'discovered' America in 986.

Reverting however to the Runic Stone found on the island of Kingiktorsoak in Baffin Bay, it is thought that the Bjarni inscripted on the stone, was Bjarni Grimolfson, son of one of the Grim's, or Rimmers, who took an expedition into the Arctic regions of North America. The stone is not dated, but it is believed to precede both of the other dates. The same Bjarni Grimolfson, is recorded as being the captain of one of two vessels, who made a journey to Vinland, or Wineland, as the American mainland came to be known. Of the Arctic expeditions that Bjarni made, it is not certain whether they reached Labrador, Newfoundland, or Nova Scotia, but all the voyages were from Greenland, and all were approved by the 'Goddess of Greenland', also with the 'King's Luck' which was transferable, and came down to them from King Harald, 'the Rimmer King'.

The mainland of America was named Wineland, the wild vines producing grapes from which the Scandinavians made wine, also wild corn grew there. It matters little that the grapes were no larger than peas, it proved that landings had been made on the mainland, if there are no proofs available that settlements were made. Later explorers confirmed that these facts were correct, Cartier, Champlain, and Hudson, confirmed the Viking's landings at Cape Ann, Cape Cod, Branstaple Peninsular, and even one conjectural location Hop, as being around New York Harbour. I think the Hopi Indians are still suing the Americans for several hundred billions of dollars for the return of their territory, but there is no indication whether these are in any way connected. There is some factual evidence of early landings, and concord, with the Red Indians of North America, with very detailed accounts being given in the Sagas. A normal expedition would number 160 men, and many interchanges, and comparisons in conditions, and equipment took place. Red and white shields were used by the Norsemen, and on occasions, red and white striped sails, symbolical of peace and war, were used on the Viking ships. It was recorded in the Sagas, that the Indians used red and white as symbolic of peace and war, and that later on, the Indians of the prairies carried small flags, one of white bison's hide, the other of reddened leather, in the same way that the red and white shields were used by the Norsemen. Another interchange of ideas, was in the use of the Indian spear, or lance, with similar decorations, being plunged into the ground as a declaration of territorial rights, or war. This was similar to the 'Stake of Scorn' as used by the Skald Egil Skallsgrimssonar against Eirik, son of King Harald Fairhair. This was described in the Ynglinga Saga II, 'as being erected, crowned with a mutilated mare's head, turned towards the victim's home or lands.' Magic formulas were uttered, and runes cut on the stakes. It was set against the spirits of the lands. This particular one was set to drive out King Eirik, and Queen Gunnhild within two years, which it did. There are many other later references to people who wore 'white clothes, and uttered loud cries and carried poles, and went about with flags'. The white clothes were probably buckskin, the loud cries Indian war-whoops, and the Indian flags are well known. Whether carried out by West Norse, Icelandic or Greenland Vikings, the majority of the expeditions set off from a place called Brattahlid, meaning 'steep slope', which can now be identified as being Cape Farewell, at the Southernmost tip of Greenland. It is also recorded that 'Landnamabok' quotes the transportation of cattle from Norway, Greenland, and later, both cattle, and women, went on voyages to America, then known as Vinland.

One of the main reasons I have, in quoting references of the Rimmer connection with America, is that when I wrote, in 'Betwixt Ribbel and Moerse', about the archeological discoveries made after the draining of Martin Mere, I made a reference to the discovery of canoes, hollowed out of tree trunks. One of these, was the one recovered from Martin Mere by the

Rev. W. E. Bulpit, which was eventually placed in the Botanic Museum after its discovery in 1899.

What I did not quote, was the essence of a report, made at the Harris Museum in Preston, where the canoe was examined by an expert, who declared that it was of a type of canoe, the construction of which was only carried out by the Red Indians of North America!

There was no explanation then, nor is there now, of the possibility of this being given any sort of credence, except that the connection between the Norse people, and Britain, and America, goes a lot further back than anyone could possibly conjecture.

There is no doubt that this connection, particularly with the Eastern seaboard of North America, as well as British Columbia on the west coast, is being sustained and increased, by the volume of enquiry concerning the Rimmers, now coming across the Atlantic from both East and West coastlines.

CHAPTER 2

THE PROMISED LAND

The main theme of this (long winded?) Saga is now emerging, the landing on these shores, and the thousand years settlement of the Rimmer tribe.

Many members of the tribe accompanied the Vikings on the early raids as Skalds, and navigators, through all the Scottish Islands and coasts, and the Isle of Man, and the coast of Ireland and Wales. The main body of the Rimmers came as a peaceful settlement, setting off from the Kingdom of 'Oddaland" or Hordaland, in the Sogne Fiord, in the Hardanger region of Western Norway. From the early bases in the Isle of Man, our coastline had been thoroughly reconnoitred and the River Douglas, named the Askyr or the Yggdrasil; the whole of Martin Mere area was declared a sacred area according to Norse Cosmology, and eminently suitable for the followers of 'Odda, son of Grim'. The portents were favourable, in spite of the fact that the region consisted of bog and marshlands, and that the area was also then, under the control of the Northumbrians. The powers of divination declared that the time, and the place, were correct.

Indeed, by the time that the Rimmers had landed, and settled, the assistance rendered by Egil Skallagrim, at the battle of Brunanburg (Bamber Bridge), led to Ethelfreda being able to push the borders of the Mercian Kingdom to the River Ribble. The Christian tendencies, and record of the Rimmers, also impressed Ethelfreda into granting them a permanent settlement in the area. The Rimmers, although by now a hardy seafaring race, always preferred coastal regions, be it sea, river, or mere. They could harvest the offerings of sea and shore, and the land, they could construct their own dwellings and boats, and could handle livestock, and thrive in a region which was considered by earlier settlers, as unfit for human habitation. They utilized the very ground they walked on, for 'TORF' (West Norse for Turf), was used for building purposes, and bank enclosures, and peat for fuel. They were aware of the healing properties of the sphagnum, and bog mosses. Their divining propensities could, and probably had, in the past, found 'water in the deserts'. They fished the Mere, once larger than Windermere, and were virtually cut off from the rest of England by marsh, and bog, from the East. From the North they were protected by a great forest, mostly comprising of oak trees, with some Birch, Hazel, Pine and Fir, which stretched from the elevated land at 'Kross Ness' (Crossens) to Rufford ('Rough Ford') and Burscough ('Birch Wood by the water, or on the ridge'). To the west, they were confined by settlements already allocated in earlier Viking landings.

All these events, and subsequent historical data are contained in the opening chapters of 'Betwixt Ribbel and Moerse'. Owing to the condensing of the book into its present size, the details of the Rimmers, which is a separate account anyway, had to be omitted.

When the Rimmers reached these shores, around about the years 940 to 950 A.D., they sailed up a water course running from a huge bay. This river was situated between what is now Marshside, and the Sluice at Crossens. It ran under Preston New Road, through what is now the 'Stray', and through what is now the Botanic Gardens, where it was subsequently dammed to form the lake. It still runs through Meols Hall Grounds, under Moss Lane, and alongside the Devonshire Road Recreation Ground, where it divided into two water courses, one running to the East, into Martin Mere, and the other continuing on to Scarisbrick, where it was eventually dammed to form the present lake in Scarisbrick Hall grounds. Another tributary flowed west, to form the boundary later on, of Southport and Birkdale. This is Sandy Brook, which still flows on through Birkdale and Ainsdale, where another stream flows into White Otter Mere. It terminates in the lake in Formby Hall grounds. The stream running on to Scarisbrick Hall, was also known as Sandy Brook. They can all be clearly seen on the copy of the first Ordnance Survey made in 1848, which is reproduced between pages 94-95 of 'Betwixt Ribbel and Moerse'. In the middle of the drought of the summer of 1989, when I did some research to find the 'Pool' which once was near the site of the Firework Factory, I found that a large clump of Willow trees had grown up around the 'Pool', which is still there, where the two streams once divided. Although this ditch, which we called 'Seccy River' or 'Seccy Ditch' was only a muddy morass, it is still flowing now, as evidenced by the locals having placed stepping stones across it, at the rear of the new Bishop Shepherd School (All Saints), to take 'doggies for walkies' on the Old Links Golf Course. Many of the other smaller water courses, and the Pool beyond, have been drained into Fine Jane's Brook which is linked up with Crossens Sluice. This was once called 'Three Pools', and then subsequently reduced from 'Two Pool's, into a single water course. It was then that the original Pool became known as the second pool, or 'Seccy' River, or ditch, 'Seccy' of course being slang for 'second'. If this is confusing, consider also that, at the North Meols end, the 'Old Pool' becomes the 'New Pool', which is now the Botanic Lake. This course was again diverted, to make a new windmill, to replace the medieval watermill which stood on a island, where the Pool was divided into two streams. The new mill gave its name to Mill Lane, and was subsequently run by the Thwaites family. The old mill was adjacent to Goorhey Cover, in Meols Hall grounds.

This water course, or River, was given the name of Otterspool, by Domesday recorders, but the original name given to it by the Rimmers, who settled along its banks, was derived from the West Norse, Snotr, which means 'to run', as in a stream or river, a running boundary — hence 'Snotrpul', or 'Snoterpool', which ran from the Scarisbrick area to the sea.

To support this contention, there was also a mention of a 'Snoterpool' in a boundary dispute in the middle of the 14th century, to establish the northern boundary of North Meols, as running from the 'Snoterpool', which was a natural stream, to the 'Snoterstone', a limestone boulder, which was also used to define the boundary of the Hundreds of West Derby and Leyland. The connection with the Rimmers, and the land appertaining to this boundary at Hundred End, goes back from the present day, to when they were first granted it by Ethelfreda. The Norse derivation of 'Snoterstone' as a boundary, was referred to by the Rev. W. E. Bulpit who claimed to have found it, also with the Rimmer family mark on a 'half stake', a Norse tradition.

There was an abortive field study carried out probably by the Southport Historic Society, around the late 1940's, based from the Botanic Museum, it was in the time anyway, of a great friend of mine John Scholes, who was the curator, to try to find this 'Snoterstone'. I didn't join in this merry romp, as I knew from historian Farrer's records, and also Meols Hall records, that the indefatigable Reverend, and a team of workers, had worked for several weeks, boring and probing the silt, before they found the stone. In a similar fashion to the verbal geneology used in the district, it had been passed down, that the stone was there, but had not been seen for perhaps a hundred years or more. Encouraged by this fact, their patience was finally rewarded and the stone, and the stake, were found, about nine feet down in the mud. The stone was impossible to move, and is still there. Nothing more was even said about the 'stake' which, by description, could have been a Runic Stone, or a boundary marking. The 'Snoterstone' itself was probably just one of the many glacial boulders brought down in the iceflow from Dumfriesshire, similar to the one at the Crossens Sewage works, found in 1956 (Photo No. 4). The two boulders in Crossens Churchyard (Photos 1, 2) were one of sharp granite, and one of carboniferous limestone, which were dug up near the church, at a depth of 17 feet. The Gypsum Boulder, at Crosby, is probably the largest, and most interesting (Photo No. 3). I was fortunate to find one myself, when a cottage opposite the Weld Blundell Hotel, at the entrance to Ince Blundell Woods, was demolished (Photo No. 37), about 30 years ago, in 1960.

The nearest thing we have to a Runic Stone, is the incised stone in St. Luke's Churchyard, Formby. It was stated that this was probably pre-Christian as the pagan burial rite of moving three times around it in a clockwise direction, had been connected with it. It was also known locally, as 'The Godstone'. If it was a Runic Stone, it could be either Christian or pre-Christian. The only inscription I could find was chalked in by me, and appears to be something between a stepped, and Celtic Cross. A local world wide traveller, produced a picture off the wall of his house in Hillside, to indicate that it has the appearance of the Egyptian Ankh, the ancient symbol of life! You pays your money, and takes your choice with this one

(Photo No. 34). Old Orme, the Corsair, plunged his Raven standard into the sand near this spot, marking the Boundary of Ravenmeols and Formby (see poem page 45). There is a modern boundary stone, which I found in the sand, about a quarter of a mile north of the Lifeboat House, which was still in existence at that time. This was in 1960, when I took the photo of the site of Cop Cross in Kirklake Round. Up to the very day when this site was cleared, the Formby Council still ignored both personal, and former newspaper correspondence, concerning this historic relic (see pages 101-102 and Photo No. 36). Although, according to the Roman map maker, or cartographer, Ptolomy, there was no River Ribble or Mersey, in the 2nd Century (Ref. map on page 9 or reference map on enclosed sketch — revised) but there was a huge bay which he called Belisama, situated approximately in the region of modern Southport. There is only one indentation in this bay indicating the presence of a water course or river, and this I believe is the 'Snotrpool', on which the Rimmers settled in the 9th century. This bay had, by then, become the bay referred to in 'Landnamabok', above which was the headland 'Krossaness' (Crossens). There was then no Churchtown, or Marshside, and a huge lake eventually developed off Southport. Subsequent silting of the estuary had resulted in the Belisama becoming the Ribble estuary, leaving the only other watercourses with outlets to the sea as being the 'Snoterpool', and the sacred river named by earlier Vikings as the 'Askyr', or as we know now it the River Douglas.

All the accounts of the history of this region are documented in the earlier chapters of Betwixt Ribbel and Moerse, but the whole story of the Rimmers will never be correctly authenticated because of their reticence, and reserve, in their dealings with any peoples they came into contact with in their wanderings.

All the foregoing activities took place before the written word replaced saga, and song, to record their heroic and hardy migration, or 'Exodus', through many lands and seas, until finally the historical 'Book of Settlements', 'Landnamabok' records their arrival on these shores, in what was to prove their final colonisation as a collective people, or tribe.

'Landnamabok' is quoted as the authority stating that the first settlers were led by 'Odda' the son of Grim, or at least a descendant of Odda, a Marc de Melis. Both of these contentions are incorrect, for by now the Rimmers had put behind them all pretensions of belonging to a land owning, ruling class, and had settled down to being simply a fishing-cum farming, group of people, wresting a living from land and sea. They spread out along the 'Snoterpool', and eventually, probably with the help of other Nomadic settlers, built a wharf for sea going purposes. Not very long ago according to relatives, who lived there, this wharf was found in an excavation at the beginning of the 20th century, about 100 years ago, at Meols Hall gates. The excavation was made only at one end of the cottages in which they were living, and was abandoned because of the danger to them. A platform was uncovered about 12 feet under the surface, which, in turn, was about 20ft. above the level of low tide. This platform has been alluded to as being part of

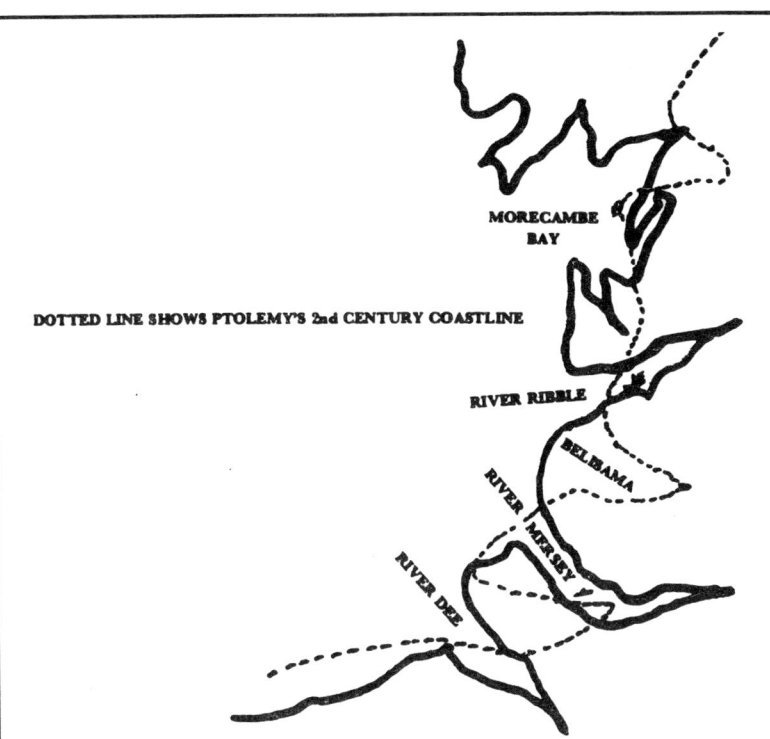

THE RIDDLE OF BELISAMA

Belisama was the name given by Ptolemy, the Roman cartographer or map maker of the 2nd Century, in an eight volumed work on geography that first showed a spherical world instead of flat maps.

His demarcation of this coastline shows no Ribble or Mersey. The mouth of the Mersey was then marshy ground, until the sea forced a passage through to the River Dee, which it joined just below Chester. The Dee with its port, the Roodee, now the Racecourse, was the first Roman river to be named. 'Belisama' was probably derived from the Celtic 'Bel' or mouth and 'Sama' from a Celtic deity, The Great Bay, where the Rimmers landed was Belisama. As stated in 'Landnamabok, it stretched from the sandstone cliffs at Kross Ness (Crossens) to Formby Point. The only watercourse at this time was the 'Snoterpool'. The Ribble estuary was later formed, and also the Douglas, or Askyr, of the Vikings, when the Great Bay eventually silted up.

a ship building wharf, or a bridge, across the Pool, or a sluice to keep back the tide, or parts of all three. My Uncle George Coulton, who lived as a boy in one of these cottages (he was responsible for those scary ghost stories connected with the Hall) told me that, at least the stones upon which the structure, or other subsequent wooden erections were built, had been put there by the Rimmers when they came there, "hundreds of years ago".

The evidence concerning the discovery also, of eel trap remains, could have little to do with these early activities, as fishing rights for one section of the Pool, had been granted to Evesham Abbey, later on, in 1113. Robert, son of the Earl of Chester, bought the entire eel fishing rights in 1278.

The Rimmers however, had no dealings with Abbey or Manor, apart from Cop building, as it is my belief that they moved on, down the Snoterpool, still maintaining contact with the sea, and the Mere. Where I think historians have been confused is indicated on the map, found between pages 94-95 in 'Betwixt Ribbel and Moerse' where the 1848, first Ordnance Survey, shows that the upper part of the 'Snoterpool', passing through North Meols, is indicated as being the *New* Pool, whilst the branch off at the Firework Factory site is listed as being the *Old* Pool, which flowed into Martin Mere, thus affording the Rimmers with two sources of fishing, and some excellent farm land, where the mere had receded. This was the true 'Snoterpool', flowing from sea to mere. The branch off to Scarisbrick running through Snape Green, and Scarisbrick Park, where the Lake was formed is Sandy Brook, not to be confused with the other Sandy Brook, another offshoot to Formby Hall, which is the Southport Boundary. It is interesting to note that the Scarisbrick Sandy Brook, has surfaced again, and made an excellent Fishing Reserve at Hurlston Hall, where Sandy Brook has been renamed Hurlston Brook. This is only a short distance from the 14th century 'Fisherman's Cottage' at Diglake, which has long been the object of research, and possible conservation.

In the early days of the Rimmer settlement before the Domesday survey, a number of the Rimmers had established themselves at places along these waterways, for fishing and agricultural purposes. There are still some excellently renovated cottages, built in later years, such as the ones at Pinfold, Scarisbrick, and many farm establishments, which testify to the permanency of occupation they gained over the succeeding centuries. The stone effigy of the man in the prow of a boat, on the side of Halsall Church, is a testimony to the fishing of the many meres which surrounded them.

From the village of 'Scarisbric' as it was known in 1200, from 'Brekka', West Norse for Slope — 'Village on the Slope', through the village later known as Berchecar in 1331 or Bescar, and lying in between the lower reaches of the Snoterpool now called Sandy Brook, is the spot where a number of Rimmers settled, around the year 1000. This tiny hamlet was named Drombalsdale in 1546, taken from the Scandinavian nickname 'Drumbe' which means 'drummel or lout', by early historians.

I have always been in contention with the historians concerning this derivation, as the 'Snoterpool' Rimmers came here direct from West Norway, and I prefer the West Norse translation of 'Draumrsdalr' which comes from 'Draumr' (dream) and 'Dalr' (dale), hence Drummersdale, or 'Dream Vale'. This district, even today covers quite a large area overlooking Martin Mere, and historically, is quite close the the area, still listed on Ordnance maps, as Batloom, or Battle Holme, the site of King Arthur's battle on the shores of Martin Mere. My grandfather in his days as a Methodist lay preacher, had quite an affinity with the Rimmers, and other inhabitants of the district, and would think nothing of walking from the nearby New Lane station, to the Drummersdale Mission, to fulfil his 'circuit' duties. The Mission is still quite a thriving affair, judging by recent refurbishing, but I mention this area as the furthest connection, going back perhaps 1000 years, between the 'Snoterpool' and the Rimmers.

The last link in this long chain can quite easily be traced on today's Ordnance maps, which is the reason for mentioning this area. It is called the Drummersdale Drain, running from here to the sea for the full length of the 'Snoterpool', and its tributaries, as part of the great draining system, introduced to supplement previous draining of Martin Mere which is not totally successful, even in this advanced technical age. There have been strenuous efforts for over 500 years, to drain off the Mere, notably the efforts of Thomas Fleetwood of Bank Hall, Bretherton, who cut a sluice between Crossens and Banks, to the sea, controlled by floodgates.

The Drummersdale Drain utilized all the water courses of the 'Otterspool', as it was then known, picking up the Sandy Brook at Scarisbrick, and Snape Green and Bescar Lane, and the Black Brook, which ran into it from New Hall Farm, at the Isolation Hospital. It also connected up the Old Pool, with the tributaries from Pool Hey, and Wyke Farms. Then it was part of Fine Jane's Brook at Moss Lane, passing to the right of the 'Snoterpool', which ran through Meols Hall grounds, and the Botanic Gardens. The Drummersdale Drain is still shown on ordnance maps, skirting the edge of Crossens, and emptying into the sluice. It is not known where the 'Otterspool' (or Rimmer Snoterpool) entered the sea, as it can only be traced as far as the 'Stray' on Preston New Road.

Historically, but inadvertently, the Rimmer's adoption of the word 'Snoterspool', and 'Snoterstone', later became the accepted term in Lancashire to denote boundaries, and locally in the designation of Cemetery Road, as being the former 'Snuttering Lane', linking Birkdale, via an ancient Roman-British trackway, to North Meols, marked by an ancient cross, known as a 'Breeing Stone', which stood beside an old windmill. The other stone cross was the Shore Cross, $\frac{3}{4}$ of a mile away in a North Westerly direction, and has the distinction of being named officially in a deed, dated 1529, concerning the land and sea boundaries appertaining to Richard Aughton, then Lord of the Manor 'A cruce in le Hose (or Haws) in Villa de North, Mylls asque ad Snotstan'. The only other official reference recorded in the pre-conquest description of Otegrimele (North Meols), was the existence of five manors, by five Thanes, one of whom was, according to 'Landnamabok', Marc de Melis, who was believed to be a descendant of a Norse settler 'Odda', the son of Grim. This is the only historical reference to the settlement of the Rimmers in this part of England. After the years 979, and up to the Norman Conquest, during the reign of Ethelred the Unready, most of England, including the lands 'betwixt Ribbel and Moerse', were subject to a tax known as Danegeld. The land was later added to the Kingdom of Mercia, but the marshy state of the ground in these districts caused them to have special consideration. Thanes were generally fighting men, and villeins, serfs, freemen, sokemen and cottars, were general terms for people who held land. In the West Derby Hundred, there were fifty one manors assessed for rent, fifteen were exempt from rent, but paid Danegeld, when the Domesday Survey was completed in 1086. The full history of all these historic events is fully and I might add, accurately, documented in chapter three of 'Betwixt Ribbel and Moerse', and has no bearing on this 'saga', because nowhere, in all the records, I have seen of the population of the West Derby Hundred, which in the Domesday Survey numbered less than 4000 people, can you find record of the subsequent activities of the Rimmers, who had by then discarded all references to Odin, Odda, Halfdans, Dans, Hrimrs, Grimrs, etc. From the fancy title of OTEGRIMELE they stripped off the 'OTEG', which only denoted that it was a place, and 'MELE' for sandhill, and thus became plain or common 'RIMMERS'. North Meols therefore got its subsequent title from Mele, by which it was known after the Domesday Survey.

There is a contradiction also, in the Domesday Survey, as when the land passed to Count Roger of Poictou, who received it from the King, and subsequently was held by his knights, North Meols in the Barony of Penwortham, consisted of Thanage of free farms of 3 caracates. A caracate was a quantity of land as might be tilled with one plough, in a year and a day, approximately 60 acres, varying in size according to team lands, total 180 acres. The Danegeld records show that 'OTEGRIMELE' paid half a hide, three plough lands, approximately valued at 10/- for 60 acres. Roger of Poictou took over the land in 1102, but the Barony of Penwortham was only created by Henry 1st at the beginning of the 12th century, when he held the Hundred of Lailand (Leyland) but there is no mention, naturally of North Meols, which was in the Derbei (Derby) Hundred. There is an entry in the Domesday Book which I have not seen, listed as follows: QUINQUE TAINI TENEBANT OTEGRIMELE IBI DIMIDIA HIDA VALEBAT X SOLIDAS, which translated reads "Five Thanes held Otegrimele. There is half a hide, the value was 10/-." It would appear therefore, that the Domesday Survey Commissioners did very little checking, and adopted the original Danegeld records. Also in the process they mistakenly recorded the 'Snoterpool', as 'Otterpool'. The Domesday Survey was only concerned with places, not names, so there are no records of the inhabitants, as the Thanes, by degree of social evolution, forfeited their rights, or became free tenants under the Count's knights.

Although the Domesday Survey was generally seen to be a thorough if ruthless Survey, there is no doubt that the wild, inhospitable region, of this coastal plain, caused the Commissioners to accept any scanty previous Danegeld records, and present them as up to date assessments of their own.

On the title page of "Betwixt Ribbel and Moerse" are the four lines:
'When all England is aloste,
Where so safe as in Chrysts Croft,
Where do you think Chrystes Croft be,
But between Ribbel and Moerse'.

This is a Domesday Doggerel, 'a verse of irregular metre, sometimes semi-comical. It appears to be, on the surface, trivial or inferior.' That is the dictionary definition. It is not quite as simple in meaning when you give it a second glance. It is true that all England was 'aloste', and being put to the flame, and sword, at that time. A 'croft' was a small enclosed piece or arable land, or small farm. One version quotes not 'alost', but 'aloft', which can indicate turmoil and strife, and could be a seafaring term for being up in the rigging, at the mast head, possible in a storm. It could have been written by a god-fearing, former sea-going 'Rymer', to indicate secretly, to any would be fugitives from the Norman wrath, that there was a safe haven in Christes Cross (God's House), in the region 'Betwixt Ribbel and Moerse'.

In the period of the Norman Conquest, and for a considerable time afterwards, the Rimmer continued to occupy the region of the 'Snoterpool' for sea-fishing and mere fishing. What there was of Churchtown, or North Meols, was by the sea. Bankfield Lane marks the high watermark in those days, and even as late as the middle of the 16th century, a boat was wrecked, and named after its cargo, as Sugar Hillock, exactly on No. 18 Sunny Road, so the high water mark would be even further inland in those early days. The only other landmark in the area, could have been perhaps, a small wooden cross on a mound, where St. Cuthbert's Church now stands, to mark the spot where the Saint's body was rested on his removal for sanctuary, some 200 years after his death at Lindisfarne in AD 687. This could only have been a few years before the Rimmers settled here, and no doubt they, and any other inhabitants of the area, respected this spot, as is evidenced by their future friendly relationships with the monks of Sawley Abbey, who traded with the Rimmers for supplies of fish, and grazing rights for cattle, along the 'Snoterpool', in the region of the 'Stray' on Preston New Road. They also made salt pits, building great banks of sods near St. John's Church, Crossens, at a place called Le Hythe. The evaporated sea water was used for salting and preserving fish, and the cattle, which were killed and salted for use in the winter. The Le Hythe, was a wharf, similar to the one at Meols Hall. A watering pit known as Wolf's Pit, was in the vicinity of the Plough Hotel, and a part of the land off Crossens referred to as 'Le Warsch' was obtained by the monks later on, and after a period of settling into the district they built a sea embankment along Bankfield Lane, early in the 13th century (pages 37-38).

Part of the fishing rights of the Chapel of Mele, as North Meols was then known, had been granted to Evesham Abbey. Mele changed its name several times, until Robert De Coudray was granted a market at Melys, by Henry III, in the 13th century, and an annual fair on the Eve of St. Cuthbert, March 19th and 20th. The earliest possible Saxon family at Meols Hall was probably the De Demeles, or De Meols, in 1149, but it dwindled in size until the De Coudray's took over in 1195, in the reign of King John, who had been the former Governor of the town of Domfront in Normandy. In 1326 Robert, descendant of William De Coudray, married Joan De Meols, descendant of the earlier Saxon family owners of the Manor. The title passed, by marriage of his daughter, to Richard Aughton, who died in 1543, leaving two daughters. The Manor was divided in 1547, one half including Meols Hall, descending to the Heskeths, and the other to the Bolds of Bold. In 1842, the whole of the Bold moiety, and about half of the Hesketh moiety, were purchased by Charles Scarisbrick. Two thirds of the property which he thus acquired, is still in the ownership of his descendants. Much of the property, such as Hesketh Golf Links, the Marsh, and foreshore at Marshside and opposite the centre of the town, were purchased by Southport Corporation in the 1930's. Meols Hall ceased to be a Manor House in the 18th century, and became the home of the Linakers for a hundred years, as resident agents. In 1761, when Peter Bold MP for Lancashire died, his 3rd daughter Frances, became the wife of Fleetwood Hesketh. Fleetwood took Meols in exchange for land at Rossall, in the Fylde. Eventually, the 1825 Act of Parliament, divided the two estates, the Hesketh portion going to Bold Fleetwood Hesketh, who was succeeded by Robert Hesketh in 1819, and he was succeeded by his son, Sir Peter Fleetwood Hesketh. It was purchased from him by the Rev. Charles Hesketh, Rector of North Meols. He was succeeded in 1886 by his son, Col. Edward Fleetwood Hesketh, then by the late Roger Fleetwood Hesketh (Lieut. Colonel). Known affectionately, to us, as the 'Young Colonel' of the ('Doyley's), Duke of Lancs Own Yeomanry.

Around the year 1835, Meols Hall had become a farmhouse, occupied for a period of forty years, by a well known local farmer Thomas Baker, who has a memorial tablet in St. Cuthbert's Church. The full details of the history of Meols Hall, and its occupants can be seen in Chapter Six of 'Betwixt Ribbel and Moerse", and I can state categorically that all the records and deeds listed, were produced and the whole chapter verified, at Meols Hall, by the later Lieut. Col. Roger Fleetwood Hesketh. I only mention these details to illustrate the lack of any documentation connecting the Rimmer family with these places and events.

Although there were no parish records for some considerable time after the Domesday settlement, there was the national reference to the plague, the Black Death, which came across from the Continent in 1348. This eventually reached Lancashire, but because perhaps, of its isolation, the area around North Meols seemed to escape contagion, also by its proximity to the open sea, and freedom from the overcrowding prevalent in medieval living conditions. The Rimmers no doubt, would point to divine intervention and protection that had prevailed in all their migrations. So the Rimmer pursued their peaceful existence along the 'Snoterpool', and the Mere, not forgetting their extensive excursions by sea, gradually merging and intermarrying with other local inhabitants, and settlers, but still adhering to the strict biblical tenets to which they had clung to all through their many wanderings. Another factor also, had promoted co-operation with the inhabitants of this north west area. In the 13th century, the skill which the Rimmers had displayed, cooperating with the men of North Meols and Crossens and Banks, in the construction of the Monks Embankment at Bankfield Lane, and other various pits and cops, at the seaward entrance to the 'Snotrpool', had been extended to other districts, particularly at the inland connection of the 'Snoterpool' with 'BLA VIK' the 'dark bay', on the shores of Martin Mere, later corrupted to Le Wyk, and eventually Blowick, as it is now known. The Rimmers were commissioned to construct a dyke around the middle of the 14th century, to drain the water into the 'Snoterpool', and eventually, into the sea. It was completed about half a century later. The agricultural land created, resulted in increased prosperity, and the water flowing through the 'Snoterpool' created more power to the Millers 'elbow'.

Most people will be able to identify this water course as 'Fine Janes Brook', coupled together with other drainage dykes, draining the Meres. At the Churchtown end, it can be associated with Fine Jane's Bridge which was swept away in the floods in 1720. No one had ever been able to confirm that 'Fine Jane' was a lady who ended her life by drowning herself in the brook.

Neither was there any confirmation that, owing to the skill of the Rimmers, and the water table being known as the 'ream' their name originated because they were known as 'reamers'. As verbal records show from the Rimmers of our family, there was some substance on both assumptions.

After the Mere was drained, and became rich land, there was discussion, if not dispute, between the Aughtons of North Meols, and the Scarisbricks, as to whom the land belonged. Later the Heskeths entered the lists, and contention reigned for centuries. Even today, several roads in High Park, such as Warren Road, Lawson Street, High Park Road, Old Park Lane, pay ground rents, some on each side of the road, to the Hesketh and Scarisbrick Estates, separately.

CHAPTER 3

NORTH AND SOUTH MEOLS —
HIGH PARK'S LOST VILLAGE

As you will see from "Betwixt Ribbel and Moerse" and any other historical documentary, I have constantly bombarded long suffering readers with, I have always tried to present events in strict chronological order. Thus "Betwixt" starts two hundred million year ago, and ends in the present twentieth century. Occasionally however, as in this instance, I am perforce to fluctuate between dates to present a complete picture of certain events.

In this respect let us peruse a Lancashire Record Deed, DDSC 56/9, if you want to be precise. This is supposed to be a 'Saga', or story, not an historical round up, but it is pertinent to the story, so I quote, in full: Dated January 1488/9 it states that "A close called Londheye, in North Melys which Hugh Aghton Squyer, let to Hugh Schau of Scaresbrek for the annual rent of 1111S, payable at the festy's of the Annunciation of our Lady Virgin, and Sayn't Michael ye Archangell."

This deed, dating from the 15th century, ultimately affects the fortunes of some of the Rimmers, at least in our family, up to the late 19th century, and must be recorded because of subsequent events. Remember the mention of the Rimmer's sea going voyages from the 'Snoterpool'? Well, one of their routes was to, and from Walney Island near Barrow-in-Furness to transport wool, sometimes up the River Astland, or the Viking 'Askyr', or River Douglas as we now know it, to collect wool from the monks of Walney. Although farming and fishing, constituted the mainstay of local industry, with the draining and reclaiming of the land, it also led to an increase in wool production. It is assumed that 'Londheye' or 'Little London', was named after the London wool merchants, or their agents, who came to collect wool, to be subsequently treated, and woven, for the Continental market. Presumably it was routed through Liverpool, probably by ship, in similar fashion to the wool deposited at a port on the River Douglas, probably the port called Mylthorp, used by King Arthur in earlier days. This was also from Walney, and in later years, the old course of the River Douglas became part of the Leeds and Liverpool Canal, and a direct link with Liverpool. In the meantime, the wool at Little London was stored in a Tithe Barn, presumably situated in the region of Tithebarn Road, near St. Luke's, as 'Little London' was later called.

I will connect all these events with the later activities of the Rimmers, and other families, in my Grandad's time in this area.

It is a curious fact that, in all the volumes of historical local research, very little has been written about the Rimmers collectively, neither amongst all the relatives geneological, and family tree records. They were very reticent to commit to written records, any details of their activities. They had been officially granted a 'Kingdom' by Nordic royalty, but they appointed no 'King' or superior official, they still operated the closely knit, almost tribal system, they had used since arriving in Nordic regions from the Holy Land. They carried no fancy escutcheons, or coats of arms. Perhaps, because of their considerable numbers, it would have been impossible to maintain any system to replace their verbal chronology, so we can only rely on subsequent odd dates in Parish records, and various Deeds and Documents. I can guarantee however, that in every family tree, of all the prominent inhabitants of at least the North West Lancashire coast, since written records commenced, that there are Rimmers or their relatives, lurking in every corner. The present increasing volume of enquiry, from many parts of the world, points to the intensity of the desire for Rimmers, and their off-shoots, to discover their roots.

By the beginning of the 16th century the Rimmers had become well integrated into other families, but still maintained their tightly knit community, intensely Biblical in outlook, with no creed but the Bible, and its laws, for the guidance they had needed in all their long 'Exodus'. We can therefore glean only small glimpses of their activities, from the record of their very few instances of deviation from their very strict code. Land deeds, and church, and Manor records, in this respect give us general information, but individual records of the Rimmers as a community, are so scarce as to be largely non-existent, except perhaps for records of geneology in the inevitable family Bibles.

For instance in 1533, in a boundary settlement in Birkdale it was agreed that William Rymer, in his capacity as reamer, together with several others, 'would set stakes on the boundary from the stone cross in the Hawes, and on to the high water mark on the Warthe (beach), and following the south channel to the sea'. This is fully recorded, and still available for inspection at the Lancashire Record Office in Preston, just ask for DDIN 45/6. I updated these records in 1990, whilst a furore was going on, amongst local historians, and dignitaries, concerning the stone wall containing the Boundary stone marking of Birkdale, and North Meols in Lord Street West. They were puzzled as to the lettering on the Boundary stone set into the wall. The initials R.B. are of course Robert Blundell who set the stone up. Underneath is the letter W. which caused the confusion. This however only means that it was the 'WARTHE' boundary stone, replacing the wooden posts. There is no mystery about the 'Birkdale Wall', as the wall itself is built of bricks of a later period, and the stone is from another, original location close by.

Another document, recorded in 1547, in connection with the Rimmer's occupation of land at the Northern end of the Derby Hundred, stated that the boundary would begin at a stone called the 'Snoterstone', and the

Snoterpool, or Walding Pool, and that "No Turves should be cut or delved, or ditches dug, within the space of a hundred feet, on either side of the boundary."

The most significant events concerning the development in the North Meols district took place from 1500 onwards. The most important factor for the Rimmers was the gradual silting up of the great bay, and subsequently along the 'Snoterpool'. In the middle of the 16th century the population of North Meols was estimated at about five hundred, with only three tenant farmers, from about 25 being Rimmers, and these were from far apart as Thomas Rymer of Blowyke, to William Rymer of Crossens. There were however, by now, many independent Rimmer establishments around "Bankefielde, Crossens Common, and Kyrktowne Moss" which was mostly wasteland, also 'Pyttes', which later became Pitts House Lane, and which had taken its name from the salt pits of the 13th century constructed for the monks of Sawley. The Rimmers also established farms long Moss Lane, adjacent to the 'Snoterpool' and the ancient water mill, situated on the length of the river, divided to allow the mill to be driven by water power. This was north of Meols Hall, and not to be confused with the windmill, which was later erected in Mill Lane. They had also cultivated the mossland, along the 'Snoterpool' Northwards, and eastwards to the Mere.

Although this is only a Rimmer 'saga' I must mention, before they descend upon me with violent recrimination, that there were many other families who intermarried with the Rimmers. Indeed for instance, at least a couple of these families could be the subject of research into even Viking connections. The Bonds, or 'Bondis', as they were known in West Norway, were independent, hereditary entailed, landowners, but also known to be raiders and also builders and suppliers of boats. The latter crafts and skills they brought with them, as evidenced by the boat building activities still employed along the Douglas, opposite the bend in the river where King Arthur established, or took over? an existing port for his own use.

Another family, the Ball's, were also of Norse origin, descendants of Scallgrimr Baldi (the Bald). When you throw in all the Anglo Saxon families, I can guarantee I can produce evidence to the show the Rimmer's connections with any local family tree that has been draw up since the 13th century. Small wonder isn't it that no historian could possibly plot the geneology of this incredible people?

With the Rimmer's influence and settlement, stretching from the Hundred End Boundary to Birkdale, and beyond to Ainsdale and Formby, there is now the matter of a somewhat population explosion, to be considered. The estimation of their being only a population of 500 in North Meols seems to be rather sparse, but this was only for *North* Meols, and given before Church records of the Parish, which have not survived prior to 1594. There is some doubt as to whether records had been kept, even before then, and some speculation as to whether the church itself would survive, in the middle of the century.

In the light of these somewhat distressing circumstances would it not now be pertinent to enquire what about *South* Meols?

Similar to the history of the Rimmers, there is not much record of South Meols as such, and certainly no indication of its location.

The laugh is certainly on me in this instance, because on page 40 of 'Betwixt Ribbel and Moerse' I stated that I had been unable to trace a portion of land mentioned as 'The Wray'. I discovered its location when I began to use notes and records, which I had to cut out of the book when it was reduced from about half a million words, to just over fifty thousand. It was whilst using these records to compile this saga of the Rimmers, that I found, that, not only was I born within sight, and sound, of 'The Wray' and went to school near it, I had crossed and re-crossed it, a thousand times, played on it, and, after a period of some 20 years, seen its disappearance, except for a few tiny fragments, under the property developers hammer in 1927.

I am referring to of course to the 'STEELES' (correct spelling) an area of ground which originally formed a rough square mile of Roe Lane, Bibby Road, Cambridge Road, and back to Roe Lane, via Hesketh Drive. There was a cinder footpath in our day, which ran diagonally across it from Roe Lane, to join up with the present Churchgate Path to the Old Smithy in Botanic Road. This footpath was an ancient Roman Vistula-British trackway, which in the North, ran on from Churchtown, across the River Douglas, to link up with the Priory at Penwortham. Southwards, it ran across the Fisher Drive fields, down Grange Road, Marsden Road, St. Lukes Road, Snuttering Lane (now Cemetery Road), Eastbourne Road, across Birkdale Common, then across the Moss to link up the two churches of St. Cuthberts in Halsall, and Churchtown. There has been much contention between historians and clergy, concerning this theory (see page 32 of 'Betwixt Ribbel and Moerse), but I think I am safe in asserting that the present 'Churchgate' path, is the only remaining portion of this ancient track, which once ran from Penwortham to the Roman Road at Warrington. We certainly didn't care much who made the track, when we were given 15 minutes to get from All Saints School, in Wennington Road, to Churchtown School, for woodwork class!

Around the middle of the 16th century, the Rimmers were granted a plot of land, rather marshy, and not of good quality described as 'The Wray' or The 'Rowe', which was landward of Churchgate, and North of what is now Wennington Road. Between the years 1550, the Rimmers built cottages and tenements, and established farms and fields well into the 1700's. The 'Wray' or 'Wroe', changed its name many times in this period. In 1605, Robert Rymer was farming in New Row, and served as a juror in North Meols in 1643, when it was New Rowe. A John Rimmer, farmed Row Hay field, and by the early 1700's it had become Row or Roe Lane. The Rookery Cottage No. 81 Roe Lane was started as a farmhouse, as did No. 85, which is almost in Hesketh Drive, and another one presumably No. 83, which was a dairy farm, can all still be seen on the Roe Lane, Hesketh Road corner. A friend of mine, Ivor Russell, lived at one time in the cottage coverted from the dairy farm. Several years ago, we took my Mam, as prospective purchaser, to see the Rookery end of Rookery cottage, which was empty at the time, but backing on to Bibby's Wood, and with so low bedrooms ceilings that you couldn't stand upright at the windows. It constituted a gloomy aspect, and anyway the selling price of about £1,600 was too exhorbitant to consider it as a propspect for purchase. My brother, Albert, and his wife, Dorothy, have brought up a daughter, Susan, in a couple of Churchtown cottages, and as far as I'm concerned they are alright for picture postcards, and paintings, but not for living in. Whilst we are in this 'corner of the wood', to coin a phrase, the Bibby-Hesketh Wood I mentioned, used to stretch from Roe Lane to the Railway. What was left of it, became a horse sanctuary, and a bungalow was built on it by a Miss Vera Wheeler, who used to give out essay prizes at All Saints School for Cruelty to Animals and Vivisection subjects. I can remember my brother Bernard (the Head-master, Austin Lloyd, called him 'Bernado Del Carpio', whoever that was), winning a book prize called 'Tich and Jock', the story of two dogs. We went to the bungalow on several occasions, and always got permission, at the 'Conker' season, to gather horse-chestnuts from the grounds. Soaked in vinegar, they were as hard as rocks, and unbeatable in the school playground. I cannot remember the soldiers on the 'Steeles', only some tents about 1919, but I distinctly remember that Hesketh Road was only a rough cart track to the Railway bridge. Although it was made of red brick, it was called the White Bridge. It is castellated on the top, and you were 'chicken' if you didn't walk across the top at least once. We also, at one time, started to cross the electric railway line for a dare, until one of our mob got singed in the process, he still has a slight stammer in his speech to this day. We used to call for a drink of water at Thorn Tree Cottage, on the corner of Coudray Road and Hesketh Drive. This area was just being converted into modern houses, from being Carriers Lane. The little old lady who lived there, never seemed to grow any older in our time. She was certainly there when I was born, and was either a Rimmer, or an offshoot, according to my mam.

This cottage was roughly the seaward limit of the 'Steeles' as we knew it. If you turned right here, from Hesketh Drive, you entered Carriers Lane, running behind Cambridge Road. It contained a couple of cottages with long gardens, and a plot of land at the side. My granny fancied having one of these at one time, when one became empty, In think this was Daisy Cottage. This lane joined an iron railway bridge which we called the 'Red Bridge'. The area of Silverthorne Drive — Coudray Road estate, was all open space, and would have been part of the original 'Steeles'. Over the railway bridge, and into what is now Beresford Drive is White Lodge, the old dairy farm, the farmhouse is still there, No. 63. The field in front of this was always wet and boggy, and we very seldom crossed it, and the 'natives were hostile' as the saying goes. I can remember there was a large bath in the field, full of drinking water for the cows, from which we beat a hasty retreat when very nearly getting caught, larking about on it. King's Hey Drive is built on it now. The farm, and part of Beresford Drive, mark the line of Carrier's Lane which continued, turning left from the railway bridge, in the direction of Denmark Road. There is still a row of cottages on the corner of Beresford Drive, before turning right into Chase Heys. Tommy Howard, nicknamed

'Roots', lived in the corner cottage. The Leatherbarrows (Peggy, I think) lived in one cottage. There was a passage between the cottages, leading to the back of Chase Heys. Alongside the bungalow at 84 Beresford Drive, there is still a gate, now closed, but the entry is still there. Out of the row of cottages, at what is now 88, there have been some cottages renovated in 1989, and made into two, modernized dwellings, but still retaining the old style. The end cottage, and the one next to it are, in 1990, as I write, still the original ones, similar to those on Chase Heys. Although there are now officially only five cottages, there were quite a number of cottages comprising the Beresford Drive, or Carrier's Lane row. As is the case in many areas, small cottages have been joined together, to make one large dwelling.

The cottages in Beresford Drive comprise one side of a three part complex, which was called Chase Heys, and not Carrier's Lane, although one part or arm, was in Carrier's Lane, now Beresford Drive. No. 5 Chase Heys is now called Corner Cottage. The row of cottages I have described along Bibby Road, Nos. 2.3.4., have been made up of a row of cottages, including the front parlour sweet shop. Around the corner is another row of cottages, making up three parts of a square. The first is the only cottage with a second floor. This is No. 15, which has the date 1772, incribed on the second floor gable. Number 14 is now Apple Tree Cottage, whilst numbers 10 and 12, together with number 14, have been made up out of a row of cottages. Between No. 4 and the 'Corner' cottage, is a 'back jigger' leading to numbers 5 and 7, a couple of steps down from the road. There appears to be now no sequence on the numbers, as No. 8 also appears to be down the steps. Nos. 2 and 4 Chase Heys, was once a row of small cottages leading to the tiny, front roomed, sweet shop. No. 4 was occupied by two of my Aunties in succession, Auntie Esther (Rimmer), married a 'foreigner', Steve Baxter, a 'Bonkser', railway signal man. We spent many a happy hour on Churchtown station when he was a porter, then helping to 'throw' the signals at Blowick Signal Box. When they moved to Parbold, Auntie Annie, (Rimmer), and Uncle Albert Wright, as newlyweds, took over. I remember when Auntie Esther's cat arrived at Chase Heys after walking 'home' from Parbold. There was only one bedroom to the cottage then, and the back gardens were across the lane, backing onto the huge field, where the Annual Churchtown Fair was held in August. Chase Heys is now in Bibby Road, which in those days only started at the junction of Peets Lane, and the old Churchgate Trackway. This completed the square of our 'Steeles', as Bibby Road, and Rectory Road went on to Roe Lane, and the Rectory, all built in that corner. There were railings across three openings onto the 'Steeles', with swing gate stiles, built into them, which has lent credence to the theory, that the 'Steeles' were named after them, but further historical evidence will shortly put all conjectures to rest, with the truth, a little further on in this story. The Churchtown Fair was held on the large meadow at the side of Bold House in Manor Road, built about 1554, and occupied by John Bold. Now, only quite recently, has there been an enquiry concerning a ditch running at the side of the Telephone Exchange and behind Rose Cottage, in

Botanic Road. When my brother Albert worked at Meols Hall, one of his tasks was to keep this clear. It was probably at one time connected with the water courses, and the Pool at Thwaites Mill. This ditch ran under Botanic Road, along Peets Lane, then both lane and ditch ran parallel to Peets Farm, which stood approximately in the middle of the 'Steeles'. The lane, still Peets Lane and ditch, then crossed the 'Steeles' past the farm, which gave its name to the Lane that ran beside it, until they went past the end of Bibby's Wood, along what is now Henley Drive. Both then disappeared under the railway line at Hesketh Park station, but the ditch carried on underground, until it was eventually run into the lake at Hesketh Park.

On the 'Steeles' where this ditch passed the large, boggy meadow, was a large, reedy pool, serving as a drainage system for the meadow, which stretched across to Beresford Drive White Lodge Farm, and the railway footbridge. This was the ditch, and pool, where we spent many hours catching newts, frogs, and gathering frog spawn and tadpoles, and jacksharps etc. The lane was wide enough to take farm traffic, and went alongside the ditch for its whole length from the Peets Lane — Churchgate — Bibby Road junction, right to Hesketh Park station, where it ended as a footpath to the station. It also formed a connection with Hesketh Road, at the foot of the White Bridge, so, apart from the Churchgate path which ran diagonally across the 'Steeles', it was the most important line of communication from Churchtown to the Hesketh Park area.

The reason I have given all this detailed information lies in the fact that in the year 1560, North Meols had two resident squires, Barnaby Kitchen, and John Bold, who were brothers-in-law, who didn't see eye to eye. In a dispute concerning land to the rear of Bold House, Barnaby sued John Bold for trespassing on a meadow called 'Shylds', and a water course called 'Water Dyche'.

It is therefore my contention that, in similar fashion to 'The Wray' changing its name several times over 100 years, and becoming eventually Roe Lane, (which is a mis-spelling in any case), so too, the 'Shylds' eventually became known as the 'Steeles'.

Whilst we are on the subject of dealings concerning John Bold, when the subject frequently cropped up concerning the identity of the lady who ended her unhappy life by drowning herself in what later became known as 'Fine Janes Brook', my mother used to say that she flung herself into the Botanic Lake from the bridge in Bankfield Lane. Also that 'Fine Jane' meant that she was named Jane, the 'Fine' that she was a lady of breeding from the Manor House, which could have been Bold House, and not Meols Hall. The bridge referred to was, in the 18th century, known as 'Fine Jane's Bridge', spanning the 'Otterspool', as it was then known. The lake of course would not have been there then, but it would have been an ideal spot, being only a short distance from Bold House. Plus also, an unsubstantiated story, that the John Bold mentioned, had been the husband of the Jane in question, but the records of the Aughton family, from whom both John Bold and Barnaby Kitchen were descended, do not seem to confirm this. There was an Elizabeth, who died in 1558, who had two husbands, the second one being a

John Bold. Her sister married the Barnaby Kitchen, who could have been brother-in-law to John Bold, as she was an Aughton, Ann, who died in 1572, aged 45. Elizabeth was only 36 when she died, so it is possible that John Bold could have re-married, 10 years later, the daughter of a Matthew Travers, in 1582, the 'Jane' of 'Fine Jane's Brook'.

I could have checked this possibly at Meols Hall through the Hesketh-Bold family connection, but at the time I think I was still brainwashed into thinking that the 'Fine Jane' was a bit of local folklore. I used to think that Fine Janes 'bridge' was the one in Foul Lane, by the railway crossing, but as I found out later, there are at least ten 'Fine Jane Bridges', two at Foul Lane, one in Meols Cop Road, one in Scarisbrick New Road, two in Town Lane, (one near Bentham's Way), one each in Moss Road, New Cut Lane, and Segar's Lane, and of course the Bankfield Lane-Botanic Garden one. I think that my mother really put it about, that the brook, especially at Foul Lane, was haunted, to keep us away from playing about on the railway lines, that criss-crossed at this spot. It was very handy for us, particularly when the General Strike was on in 1926, as we used to trespass on the embankment that carried the line from Meols Cop, down to the main line, waiting for the engine crew to toss out lumps of coal. 'Fine Janes' was at various times a 'brook' then a 'ditch' and finally the 'Dyke' when it was constructed as such, and joined to the Drummersdale Drain at Crossens. It has always been referred to, on ordnance survey maps, as 'Fine Janes Brook'. There is only one bridge named on it as 'Fine Janes Bridge', and that is the one in Meols Cop Road. This is the one that has the reputation now of being haunted, so, as the Foul Lane Bridge is only a matter of yards away, perhaps my mam was not exactly conning us with the 'ghost of Foul Lane Bridge' after all. There is another bridge, at the moss end of Crowland Street, by the cement works, where the 'Brook' was known to us as one of the 'three pools'. This bridge is shown on the ordnance survey map as Brook Farm Bridge. The Brook Farm shown alongside it, now swallowed up by the cement works, was always know to us as 'Todds Farm'. The firework factory was built in the corner of their farm land, and the 'Seccy Ditch' or 'Snoterpool' of the Rimmers went into the 'Bla Vik', on Martin Mere, at this point.

In the Dyke connotation my mother had another 'fairy story', of the little boy in Holland, who put his finger in the Dyke, to prevent the land being flooded, a story which curiously enough has survived in folk lore through the years. She seemed to impute that, in some obscure sense, to childish minds, there was some connection between Dykes, and Holland, and the Rimmers. Later on we did hear of a place called Downholland, which could be reached by 'Altcar Bob', from Meols Cop, or Butts Lane, or Kew Stations, but that didn't seem to be the real Holland of the Dykes. I did learn later also, that my mother had relations in Warrington on my father's side, but they were nothing to do with the Rimmers, although she used to visit them. This would be well over 70 years ago.

The sequel to this, is the fact that, only just recently, have I been informed by a person, unconnected with the Rimmers, that, not less than a quarter of a century ago, a Rimmer, curator of a Warrington Museum, during research, had information that a group of people in Holland called Van Rhymers, had definite family connections with Rimmers, not only in this area, but specifically in Downholland, and also Upholland. The implications of this information have yet to be clarified, but it does show how even a chance remark from any Rimmer source, must be taken seriously, however bizarre or incredible it would appear to be on the surface.

The original Bold House is not the present house still standing in Manor Road, although it stands on the same site. It was occupied by the Bold family from 1554 to 1612, and subsequently used as a farmhouse, but it was rebuilt in 1802, by Peter Bold Esq, MP, for use when the family visited Southport. This spot is historic however, for it is near the ancient smithy, at the top of Churchgate, at Botanic Road. Manor Road and the 'Place' overlooked by the smithy, were once known as 'Cock Clod'. This is the 'Place', opposite to the row of cottages, which are still in existence, that formed the ancient approach to Meols Hall, built by Robert de Coudray in the 13th century. It was here that Sir Richard Aughton, of North Meols, knighted in July 1533, at the Coronation of Henry the Eighth and Ann Boleyn, was called upon to muster troops at the 'Place' in 1536, to join the Earl of Derby's contingent at Sawley Abbey Cistercian Monastery. A proper 'con' this by Old Henry, as he appointed quite a number of knights at the Coronation, who were required to raise troops in time of war. Hard luck on the 36 unfortunate rustics who were chosen. This wasn't the Cromwellian-Roundhead Civil War, which was in the next century, but a rising called the 'Pilgrimage of Grace', and when it reached Lancashire from Lincolnshire, via Yorkshire, it was known as the 'Northern Rebellion'. The monks of Sawley were very industrious in stirring things up, but the thing fizzled out on Clitheroe Moor, when a truce was called. It appeared that some of the 36 from North Meols, were in sympathy with the rebels, some of whom were hanged by the roadside and in the market places. It is not recorded how many of the 36 returned to North Meols. I remember gathering these facts, and that, when I was fortunate to get four 'wheels' (car) instead of 'two' (bike), it was my practice to always see every place I wrote about, including Sawley Abbey. When I went to view the Abbey, that figures so much in our local history, one of its arches spanned the road, quite a unique experience, especially so, as the site where the ruins stand, is called Southport!

It is quite a debatable point, that when the Rimmers spread out from the 'Snoterpool' area in the sixteenth century, owing to the gradual silting up of the river and the great bay, they only began to develop land which had been granted to them in the 10th century by Queen Ethelfreda, comprising mostly of mossland and marshland. It would include the very area upon which the future village of North Meols was to be formed. This land had been wrested from them by the Conquest, so it would appear to be a complete anacronism, that when they were granted land in the 'Rowe' or 'Wray', district, they were only being given back land which was granted to them in the first place!

It also poses the question that, if the statement made at the time, that the area of land was to be 'landward of the Churchgate, and Northward of the

Row' was true, how much of the property developed, such as the whole of Peets Lane, and many of the cottages at the southern end of Mill Lane, were actually in *South* Meols and not *North* Meols!

To support this contention, there were cottages or farm dwellings, some of which only disappeared in our day, at the corner of Mill Lane and Roe Lane, which formed one part of the area now known as High Park Place, which stands at the junction of Roe Lane, Mill Lane, Moss Lane and Old Park Lane. In our day, when it was a tram terminus, with a cab stand and toilets, it was known, and still is by many, as 'Four Lane Ends', eventually shortened to 'Lane Ends'. At the junction of Old Park Lane and High Park Road, on the site of the former Conservative Jubilee Hall, now Church Close, there stood an ancient row of tenement cottages, contemporary with the construction of similar buildings in the 'Row' (Roe Lane) in the 17th century. These cottages were depicted in a picture postcard, one of a stack which appeared when my Auntie Esther lived at a railway house at Hoscar. After Uncle Steve died, she operated hand signals from a small cabin by the main Manchester to Southport line. The postcards were all old local views, which she used to send to my mam, to let her know when she was coming to High Park, but sad to say, they must have been lost over the passage of time. I also remember that, when my mam visited Auntie Esther, she used to, even when she was well over 80, take a short cut from Burscough Junction station to the railway house, along the main railwayline!

Wherever she was stationed, my Auntie Esther used to cycle to the nearest connection with Meols Cop, to attend Norwood Avenue Baptist Church, making it four of my Aunties, at least two of which were married there, who were members.

I found another curious connection with High Park Place, whilst I was getting in touch with another stalwart of Norwood Avenue Church, a second cousin, also named Esther Ellen, who gave me information about our family when she was a small girl watching the shrimps being picked, I mentioned her earlier. She wishes to remain anonymous, typical Rimmer reticence. I can say that she and her husband are still well, and active, and thoroughly deserve the many awards, and appreciation, they have gained over the years in church and choir matters.

What I did discover was that, at the junction of High Park Road, and High Park Place, the pair of houses number 8 and 10 Old Park Lane, are called 'Road View'. The next pair of houses, number 12 and 14, are called 'Park View'. The pair of houses next to them, number 16 and 18, are called 'High View'. The next pair of houses on the corner of Old Park Lane, and Chester Road, are numbered 141 and 143 Chester Road, and they are called 'Old View'. On the corner of Chester Road and Old Park Lane, on the other side of the road, number 20 now comprising two business complexes, was once Garrison's Cycle Shop. Then next door, number 22, was formerly Jagger's Removal, and furniture shop. Then opposite Old Park Lane Independent Methodist Church, is a house number 22a, next to Jagger's old shop.

This church is now the Southport Methodist Church 'Ebenezer with Zion' so named after the Zion Church in St. Lukes Road was closed, and merged with Old Park Lane in 1984. It has two Ministers, Mrs. H. Wright of Old Park Lane Church, and Mrs. J. Rimmer formerly of Zion. Mrs. J. Rimmer, formerly Jennie Rigby, was married to Tommy Rimmer, whose family were related to us in Bispham Road.

I wanted to solve a mystery here, which is pertinent to local history of several hundred years, possibly even a thousand years ago. It was last year, in the long hot summer of 1989, that I solved the puzzle of the names of the houses and the locations. Over the front wall of 'High View' number 18 Old Park Lane, I got into conversation with a gentleman pottering about in the garden.

He turned out to be Bill Wright, aged 92, retired railway man, brother of Grocer John, who ran the shop in High Park Place, on the corner of Moss Lane for many years.

Bill Wright told me he was born on a farm in Moss Lane. He told me that the 141-143 Chester Road pair of houses, were formerly in Old Park Lane, and had to be demolished to make space for the Chester Road junction, which had led to the re-numbering confusion. He also told me all the houses concerned, were built on 'Poverty Field', which backed on to Roe Lane.

The conclusion I have drawn from the names of these houses is that 'Road View' appertains to High Park Road, and 'Park View' to the 'Deer Park' attached to Meols Hall in the 1300s. 'High View' is also referring to the High Park Road area. The west pair of houses 'Old View', were built facing an area, after which, Old Park Lane was named.

To me this infers that there was a much older Park, most probably the 'high park' that was inhabitated by the Rimmers when they settled along the 'Snoterpool', and along to the Wyke or Bla-Vik, which later became Blowick, when the area was drained off by the 'Reamers' or Rimmers.

The main road, or trackway, the first roadway made from Ormskirk to North Meols, was along Red Lane and Foul Lane, and Wennington Road, turning off at Bispham Road, then along the 'Old Park' Lane, to what we now know as High Park Place, or Lane Ends, then to North Meols. This supports my contention therefore, that Four Lane Ends, High Park Place, and the whole of High Park, as it was then, comprises the area of South Meols, and was the first fully inhabited district, older than North Meols. Later on, Wennington Road (Long Lane), was extended as far as Roe Lane, before it was developed, and a roadway was then made from this junction, along what we now know as Manchester Road, to the small cluster of buildings at South Hawes, which later became Southport.

My mother was born on a farm, which was at the corner of Wennington Road, and subsequently lived at 149 Bispham Road, reputably the oldest house in Bispham Road and appropriately named 'Ellen's Home'. She was Ellen Rimmer before she married my father Walter Jesson. This was where we carried on the shrimping business, six miles from the sea.

When it was demolished in 1966, to make way for a builders showroom, my mother, who was then 80 years of age, and myself, sorted through the rubble, and removed the name stone, and placed it in the front garden of 85 Newton Street, round the corner. It is still there, eleven years after she died in 1979, at the age of 92, after being involved in a road accident in Bispham Road at the age of 90. The house in Bispham Road had always belonged to my Granny's family, the Rigby's, and the Comstives, until it was turned into a garage. My younger brother Albert, was born at 149, whilst my elder brother Bernard, and I, were born at No. 80. My birth certificate states that I was born in North Meols, the Registry being at Ormskirk, not 'North Meols, so High Park probably started in the region of Wennington Road, and, over the years, has lost its identity as being even in South Meols, or part of it.

When Southport was developed, High Park finally lost its identity, and claim, to be the earliest development in the area. If Southport became, as it was once described, the 'Montpelier of the North', and the 'Ship of State', High Park became a suburb comprising its 'Power House', as Southport's gas works were removed to Crowland Street, and the Electricity Works were built in Russell Road. The main Corporation Tram Depot, and Repair Depot and the adjoining Corporation Refuse Disposal Depot, and Repair Depot were built in Canning Road. They did however, have the good grace to establish Canning Road Baths, in the middle of this complex. The fresh water swimming bath was free of charge, and the 'Slipper' baths ('2 pence a go, bring your own soap'). None of the surrounding houses had bathrooms, until the establishment of the Canning Road housing estate. The influx of people also from the Liverpool area, and the earlier nineteenth century immigration of workers, from as far away as East Lancashire, who came to work in the Railway Engineering Depot established at Meols Cop, made a thriving lively community, and completely obliterated High Park's claim as a village.

It seemed a complete anacronism that a 'fishing' industry was carried out in the middle of all this bustle, at 149 Bispham Road, until the late 1920s. There was even a fishing boat built in the back garden. It was lifted over the wide entry of the next door dairy, and conveyed to the sea on Tommy Rimmer's coal cart! Some of the shrimps were hawked around, but the bulk of them were taken for processing to Wright's in Marshside Road. It still amuses me to think that I was complimented on the excellent quality, and size, of our products, as being superior to those of the Marshside shrimpers, and had been included in many consignments of breakfast delicacies for the regular voyages of the Transatlantic Liners, especially when I think of the old clothes washing boiler, in the wash house, in which the shrimps were boiled!

My grandad always conformed to the Rimmer's strict shrimping code, of 'raddling' or 'riddleing' small shrimps back into the sea, and never taking any in 'spawn'. It was the cessation of this method, and the general silting up of the fishing grounds, which led to the decline, as he had forecasted, of the shrimping industry. The boats had disappeared about the 1950s, and today there are only a few individual mechanized vehicles to be seen at the Weld Road shore entrance to the beach.

Our connection with the activities at sea, ceased completely in 1927, when my grandad's only son, my Uncle Bob was tragically drowned, within sight of Southport Pier at the age of 22, an incident from which we, and many others, particulary my grandad, never fully recovered. It constitutes a strange, and tragic parallel with the experience of the Icelandic forefather of my grandad, the Skald Poet, and adventurer, Egil Skallagrimson, whose efforts, I have described, when assisting King Athelstan at Brunenburgh, led to the granting of the area of ground by Queen Ethelfreda to the Rimmers on the 'Snoterpool' Estuary, and so to the eventual establishment of North Meols. Egil Skallagrimson's greatest poem the 'Sonatorrek', considered to be one of the greatest of the Nordic poems, describes his grief at the death by drowning, of his only son, an event connected by only a few miles in location, but nearly one thousand years in time, with my Grandfather's experience.

Before returning to the activities of the Rimmers in South Meols, and elsewhere, I would like to make it clear that the name of Rimmer was particular to them only. The confusion, in all Nordic references to the gutteral pronunciation of 'Grimr', as in 'Grims Fairy Tales' is misleading, as this sound cannot be pronounced in West Norse. The English consonant 'G' is softly spoken, as it would be in 'gad about'. The nearest Scandinavian derivation of Rimmer, as I have explained, was the Swedish 'Hrimr', which still comes out as Rimmer, and was never altered wherever they chanced to be. They obviously picked up phrases from any language they encountered, even the so called 'Marshside dialect' but retained many odd expressions throughout their long exilian exodus. When my grandad for instance, would say "tak off thi' shuffen, thi' feet mon be witchet" this could be well understood in the local lingo, although different to it, "Take of your shoes, your feet must be wet").

Only just recently, for another instance, when describing our youthful activities referring to games and general concourse, I subconsciously used the expression, "we had plenty of 'tal' in those days". There will probably be only a few oldies like myself, who would remember this word. I don't think anyone knew where it originated, but the West Norse dictionary gives the definition of 'tal' as 'talk, consultation, reckoning or general gathering, enjoying fun". I dug that one out of an 'Islandingabok' report of a 'Krists', or Christian meeting, attended by the Rimmer's ancestors, Halfdan the Black, written in 870 AD, the equivalent of the annual Sunday School outings of our youth!

In the school playground you might be told not to 'frigg', or 'mess about', from the same source. The West Norse derivation of 'snotr' could be equally applied to a running nose, as well as to indicate 'something running' as applied to a water course, such as the 'Snoterpool', is certainly self evident, and could not have originated as a local North Meols, or Marshside, expression.

Another factor in the ability of the Rimmer clan to adapt to changes in language, and contact, with strange people, can be illustrated by the visits I can recall when very young, to the Gypsy caravans, which arrived at the same time every year, at the top of Foul Lane. I can remember sitting on the steps of one caravan of the real, original, horse drawn outfit type, talking to one old woman in particular, dressed in the traditional costume seen in story books. I can still see the bangles, and hear the jingling of those tiny, shiny medallions they used to wear round their headbands, but this was an everyday outfit, not some gaudy showpiece for the benefit of fairground customers. When my mother went into the caravan, I heard them conversing in a language I had never heard before, or since, certainly not a local dialect. Years later, I began researching the Rimmer's history, when I learned of their connection with the inhabitants of the shores of the Black Sea. I formed the opinion that the language I heard on that occasion, was that of the Romany Gypsies, who originated from the shores of the same sea, the Black Sea, where the Rimmers had spent many years during their 'Exodus'. Originally Gypsies were of a wandering race of Indian extraction. All gypsies or gipsies, were Nomadic in character, but retained very strong traits, and customs, which would doubtless appeal to the Rimmer's aspect of life in those days. I have mentioned earlier, the affinity some of the Rimmer and their relatives had with the 'fortune telling' fraternity.

Exercising the penchant that the old have for recalling incidents from their younger days, I do remember that when my mother, then a widow, finally emerged from the caravan in the gathering dusk, the Manchester to Southport express was thundering over the Foul Lane railway crossing, with its occupants mostly comprising of businessmen, sharply silhouetted against the dark background, in their brightly illuminated compartments. The Gypsy woman, standing on the step of the caravan looked at the train, and said, "There they go, off to wives waiting for them, but you and I, dearie, have no husbands waiting at home for us to come home to, have we?" Probably an inspired guess no doubt, but one which made a lasting impression on a young mind. There used to be a couple of vans tucked away just off the road in the shelter of a farm building on the Shore Road, near the Hundred End Boundary, which arrived there for many years at the same time, stayed for the same length of time, and then moved silently away before dawn, leaving no trace, or mess, behind them. Many years ago I was informed by a lady in Formby, that whilst walking her dog along Broad Lane, she had found a boundary stone hidden in the grass verge. As described on page 48 of 'Betwixt Ribbel and Moerse", this was the ancient Danesway track, leading from Scarisbrick to a port on the River Alt, used by the Derbys of Lathom Hall in the 12th century, and by the Gypsies, and other travellers, for much longer than that. This was confirmed by the occupants of the caravans, who had always parked in the verge alongside the boundary stone, for as long as anyone could remember.

By another of the strange coincidences that occur whenever I put pen to paper, the state of Rumania, bordering on the Black Sea, home of the original Romany's, today, Easter Sunday 1990, as I write, is celebrating its first day of independence from the conquerors yoke, which it has suffered under for so long.

As this is a saga or story, I am allowed to diverge into these personal 'random reminiscences', so before I go back to the chronological order of the

Rimmer Saga, and whilst we are in Foul Lane, let me point out to you the water meadow which still lies on the Pool Hey side of Foul Lane, opposite to where the caravans have been arriving and departing for many generations gone by.

This boggy area referred to, is one of the last areas in the district containing, apart from many varies species of wild flowers, according to my brother Albert, a very rare species of wild orchid. That's a note to keep the naturalists interested.

For the conservationists, another example of municipal vandalism, is the closing of Foul Lane to make a rubbish refuse depot. I am too upset to make the observation, "What a 'Foul' thing indeed", to add to the 'sell out' at the Kew Woods Lake Conservation Project.

We can now return to the Rimmers, and others in the 'Rowe' or Roe Lane, via Foul Lane, and under the railway bridge into Red Lane, past a small un-named farm on the left, against the railway embankment. Although 'Red Lane' was not officially separate, it was part of Foul Lane, running from Wennington Road to Foul Lane railway crossing. No-one knows why, or who named it as such. On the corner of Wennington Road, and still in Red Lane, are 'Fairclough's farm buildings, although this was the name still there in 1990, the farm was originally Hall farm. To the left was Butt's Lane Halt, Railway Station, and 'Coggy' Blundell's outfit, no place for him in the official genealogical records, but real top class in our affections. Butt's Lane derivation has never been pinpointed, it could be from 'Byte' the 'butting' or digging by hand, when turning plough horses in the restricted area of arable ground, wrested from Martin Mere.

The suggestion that Butts Lane could possibly have been named after archery "butts" should be considered seriously however, because of its proximity to High Park, which was a Deer Park in the 13th century, presumably for Meols Hall. In the middle ages it was compulsory for a parish to maintain an acre for archery practice. It is known that Homer Green Farm, within the Ince Blundell estate, contained a field in the settlement, called 'Long Shoot' for this purpose. At Churchtown also, there was a field on Peets Lane Farm called "Lung Hey" or 'Long Field' which comes into contention also in this respect, for the training of military conscripted bowmen. Longbows are discussed elsewhere in the account of Robin Hood's possible presence in the area. It was a decree by King Henry VIII, that herons which nested only in tall trees, could only be shot down by Longbows, to protect them as a species, which has lasted until today. There are still protected heronries at Formby and Ince Blundell. Herons are still plentiful on the mosses in the area, and could be survivors from the great woods that existed in medieval middle ages. Proceeding towards Roe Lane I remember Todd's Dairy Farm, on the left, stretching to the railway embankment. There was also a football pitch, and a cricket pitch, where the Cash and Carry complex of buildings now stands, opposite the former Progressive Laundry on Crowland Street. The football pitch was used by High Park football team, before they moved to Russell Road. Perhaps this field was the situation of the archery butts, as all the other areas across the lane would be then part of Martin Mere. There was a railed off footpath along the railway embankment we used, to get to the Butt's Lane Halt Station, and Haig Avenue Football Ground. On the right of Wennington Road, opposite Todd's Farm was Mark Halsall's farm, which stretched right across to Canning Road. It contained a large pond, which we were chased away from, on many occasions, with 'Old Mark' waving his stick in impotent ire. This area, behind Cobden Road, was later dubbed the 'Blowick Alps', on account of the huge mounds of cinders from the Gas Works being deposited there. This was recent enough in time as to be deplored as a hindrance to television reception.

Part of Cobden Road and Wennington Road, from just past Milton Street was new development in our day, and completely built over when the Canning Road Estate was built in the 1930's on 'Pop' Lloyds Field, on the Wennington Road side, with Mr. Blenkinsop's Field on the other side of Canning Road. 'Pop' Lloyd, with the club foot, kept his cows in Heysham Road, and Mr. Blenkinsop kept his in Bispham Road, near to Wennington Road, and the farm which I don't remember on the corner of Bispham Road and Wennington Road, where my mother was born. Between the grocers shop on the corner of Milton Street, formerly operated by the Greenall's, and the Blenkinsop's Field, there was a detached house, Number 27, and then the two houses No.s 23-25 which have been reconditioned. One of these was occupied by the Cobb family. The detached house No. 27, had to be demolished, because they were all standing in the corner of Blenkinsop's Field, which in our time was just a reedy, boggy mass, stretching over what is the north end of Cobden Road, to Russell Road. This area, part of Martin Mere, was so boggy, that the detached house, and the semi No. 23-25, were known as the 'lean-to houses'. They all sank into the Mere, to the extent that the roofs were almost touching. Blenkinsop's meadow was fed by a stream, coming from the Snoterpool, through a valley, now Russell Avenue, which also contained a farm. This was one of a network of tributaries which ran across Pop Lloyd's field, and fed old Mark Halsall's duck pond. Some went underground into Kew Lakes, which were always full of fish, and one joined Sandy Brook, near the Isle of Wight Farm, to become the Southport Boundary, near to the source of the River Nile in Charnley's Hills. Before the draining off, of many of the rivulets, into Drummersdale Drain and Fine Jane's Brook, the sea, and Martin Mere, were always in close proximity and contact with each other, from Mere Brow to Woodvale. Carrying on up Wennington Road we pass Poulton Court, the site of our old school 'All Saints'. The only open area between here, and Roe Lane was the Fisher Drive field, covering all the ground on which Griffiths Drive and Chester Avenue now stands. The 'Church Gate' trackway ran across this area, diagonally from Grange Road, and Norwood Avenue, with a right of way clean through Merlewood Farm, which stood on the corner of Wennington Road and Roe Lane.

I have previously described the cottages on the Roe Lane-Hesketh Drive corner which were built in the 1700s, so we will now catch up with the farming and building activities in Roe Lane from the 1550s until then.

From 1410, until 1554, there had been dispute between various parties concerning the glebe and tithe land, between the Bolds and Scarisbricks, and Kitchens. One of these affairs was over a meadow called Baldemeryhokes or the 'Wykes', previously owned by the Meols family, who were connected with the Scarisbricks in the early part of the 14th century. At a trial held in 1554, several Rimmers were called as witnesses, Nicholas, Peter and Richard Rimor of Birkdale, plus a James Rymor, and father and son, Thos. Rymer of North Meols, were also involved. This indicates the difficulty when names are changed in the process of time. It was never defined whether this meadow was actually in Blowick, or Scarisbrick, hence the dispute. Subsequently however, meadows were granted in Row Lane. Ridings and Todds and Balls joined John Rimmer, who was farming a field called Row Hey. These were on the Scarisbrick side of the 'Row' as there are records of the Aughtons, who had fields on the Hesketh side. There is a record of a 'pinder', assistant to the burleyman, or 'by law man', officially responsible for the upkeep of field boundaries and water courses. One of the 'pinders' was a Richard Rimmer who operated on the Hesketh side of Row Lane, who was responsible for the upkeep of an area called 'The Wite Hill' in the 'Shyld' or Steeles area in 1640. I have often wondered if this had a connection with the railway bridge area of Hesketh Road because, although the Railway Bridge is made of red brick, we always referred to it as The White (or Wite?) Bridge. The building expansion continued well into the 16th century, and as Parish Registers are not available before 1594, we have to have recourse to County Court records, and the like for news in the early, and middle part of the 16th century.

CHAPTER 4

RECUSANTS — SMUGGLING — SEA COPS — FLOOD AND PLAGUE

The Rimmers were, by now, well integrated into the community, and intermarriage was beginning to intrude upon their strict codes of family and religious life, and indeed from about 1625 onwards, there appeared to be somewhat of a religious furore developing in North Meols. There had been very little persecution recorded in the area, but in 1580, recusant families had become well organised, and manor houses had private chapels and priest holes. There well well known Catholic families, such as the Blundells of Little Crosby, who are well documented in Chapter 13 "The Way to the Cross" in 'Betwixt Ribbel and Moerse'. I even threw in a plea for Church Unity (see page 105) when I found that Little Crosby Park Cross had been used for both Catholics and Protestants alike! (Photo No. 41).

North Meols was, like Scarisbrick, involved in recusant activities in Queen Elizabeth's reign. In North Meols it was quite an open affair, until Mrs. Hesketh of Meols Hall, living with the family of Barnaby Kitchen, was arrested, and taken to the New Fleet, to join her father, Sir John Southworth, of Salmesbury Hall. This was at the time when the Jesuit Priest, Edmund Campion, had preached quite openly in Churchtown in 1580, and was said to have been hiding in Meols Hall. I was told that the diamond shaped brickwork, with a white insert, built into the top of the south wing, was an indication that the occupants were sympathetic to the Catholic cause. I spent quite a lot of time around Meols Hall whilst my brother was working there, and one day in 1938, Lieut. Colonel Roger Fleetwood Hesketh (The Young Colonel), called me into the Hall, and said I would be interested in something they had uncovered during alterations. This proved to be a small cupboard like recess, which corresponded with a location where Campion was reputed to have been hiding, over 350 years ago, as Campion was hanged in 1581.

Whilst the Rimmers, and other families, were systematically improving their lot in South Meols, in North Meols the plight of the Protestants was becoming worse than the Catholics, as, apart from the Campion episode, there was little persecution, but poorer families suffered when fines were imposed for non-attendance at church. The church itself, according to a survey in 1552, seemed to be in a sorry state. There was a timber framed nave, and a steeple with two bells, to which a hand bell was added for use at funerals. The Bishop of Sodor and Man, Thomas Stanley, Rector from 1557, had other incumbencies, and rarely visited North Meols, and the Church by 1598, had deteriorated until the chancel roof was caving in, no glass in the windows, and the churchyard in disrepair. St. Cuthbert's at this time had never had a communion book, or even a Bible! The locals were utterly confused, changing from Catholic to Protestant, and back again, following the neglect of the Kitchen and Bold families, in their various, changeable, religous allegiancies.

There were therefore, no parish registers, prior to 1594, and until they were required by law to be maintained, but even then, there are no records of baptisms until 1595.

Around about 1550, there seemed to be evidence of the Rimmers moving into the community, as evidenced by Tenant Farmer records, listing William Rymer in North Meols, and Thomas Rymer of Crossens, and Thomas Rymer of Blowycke.,

Further afield however, the Rimmers had already spread to all parts, as well as into North Meols, due to the action of sea and sand. They had reached into Scarisbrick by land, and water, making use of the 'Snoterpool', and the Mere, and along the Ormskirk trackway from Foul Lane. There are still old fishing cottages at Pinfold, Scarisbrick, and the 'Fisherman's Cottage' at Diglake, has been well documented. I have long held the belief that a row of cottages in Hillock Lane, Scarisbrick, opposite St. Elizabeth's Catholic Church have more to do with fishing on the Mere, than farming, as they ran down the slope — 'Brekka' in Norse — 'Scares Brekka', Scarisbrick, 'Village on the Slope', towards Drummersdale and Martin Mere. Only just recently I was in touch with Jim Orrell, a Southport architect, now living in Scarisbrick, in Hillock Lane. A few years ago he renovated one of these cottages, which is now a listed building, and found evidence of stonework, as in the case of the Diglake Cottage, to indicate that this little lane on Bescar Brow, had once been a thriving fishing community. Incidentally, he was the architect concerned with the erection of the modern bungalow, opposite the east entrance to Scarisbrick Hall in Damwood Lane. The stone which was found, which I still have in my garden, was delivered to me by him, is believed to be the 'Cymrostone' connected with Cymrostone Field, probably a 'Mass' field. It is described as being connected with Cliffe Wood Cross, parts of which were last seen in 1877, and still constitutes an unsolved mystery (see pages 112-113 and the 1848 Ordnance Survey Map facing page 94 of 'Bewtixt Ribbel and Moerse'). The architect in question, is also the unfortunate 'local architect' ref. pages 67-68, who was inveigled into going down the underground passage at Lathom House.

Chronologically, we are still in the 15th to 16th century, with the Rimmers moving slowly into the local community. In the farming aspect, it is pertinent to clarify the information, given on page 32 of 'Betwixt Ribbel and Moerse', concerning the sugar boat, which was wrecked on a sandbank site, (situated in Churchtown, at No. 18 Sunny Road), in 1565. It has been claimed that the first potatoes to be grown in England, were done so in Formby, but it has since been established by an outside source, no less than the Scottish Potato Federation, that the first potatoes came off the Sugar Boat wreck in Churchtown, and were grown there locally. Subsequently it was established that the first potatoes to be grown *commercially*, were indeed from Formby.

In 1542, the population in North Meols, was only listed as being about 500, but by the time some sort of Parish records were established in 1594, no doubt the population in North Meols, and district had increased. The general delapidation of the Church, which was systematically neglected by both the Bolds and the Kitchen families, from the years 1552 to 1598, had resulted in no records at all being kept.

Round about the year 1600, even some of the Rimmers were getting into the records, not necessarily in an apostate sense, as it was difficult to reject a faith which was purely Biblical in concept, but anyone who did not attend the Church of England regularly, when living in a Parish governed by State authorities, was considered recusant. Even so if they had no particular inclination for religious affairs. Most people managed to keep clear of the authorities, who only made infrequent official visitations, so it was hard luck on the unfortunate Ellis Rimmer, who was the only recusant recorded in 1601. The rector at the time, a young man who had taken his BA degree at the age of 17, at Balliol, Oxford, and had come as rector, was only 20 years of age, and married, when he took over at North Meols. He was noted for his liberal approach to the locals, but the authorities looked askance on his attitude. This young man, Matthew French, had a disastrous time in North Meols, at his personage at Crossens, as his wife, in the hard winter of 1608, died, and left him with three children. He remarried a Preston woman, and had more children, and afterwards, things improved in the Parish, especially after he had been called upon to witness, and draw up the will of Barnaby Kitchen at Meols Hall, who unfortunately died the following day. Kitchen had been Lord of the Manor for over 50 years, including the whole of the reign of Queen Elizabeth I. These facts are only relevant because Kitchen's daughter married Hugh — son of Sir Thomas Hesketh of Rufford, thus creating a succession which has existed to the present day. These events are only worth recording because the early records did not come from the inconsistent sequence of Church Parish Records, but from the Lancashire Records Office at Preston. The 'Wills and Inventories' of Matthew French, dated 1615, after his death in 1614, are a fully documented record of goods, chattels and property, which afford a fascinating insight into the conditions appertaining to this period in time. If any student or researcher wishes to check these details, they can be found in the Lancashire Records Office at Preston.

The Rimmer's connection with the Heskeths, does not show up until John Hesketh, who was born in 1715 and died in 1753, married Ellen Rimmer. They had four children before he died, aged 38. The only other connection, a very tenuous one, is that "Aunty Betty' of Bank Nook, was married to "Fleetwood Robin", but there are no records of the Fleetwood Heskeths to connect these two events. Bank Nook is quite a literal description of a place, still shown on Ordnance Maps (Ref. SD31) at the Fleetwood Road Corner of Radnor Drive. There are still quite a few fishermen's cottages, indicative of the former thriving shrimping industry, nestling in the 'Nook', formed by the huge 'bank', protecting it from the south westerly winds coming off 'Angry Brow' and Faircloughs Lake, which ran alongside Fleetwood Road, as far as the present Prince of Wales Hotel. The Homeopathic Cottage Hospital, which still stands on this high bank is still there, but gone now is the tall building alongside it, also built on this huge bank, facing Fleetwood Road. This was variously a Rimmer-Fleetwood venture, known by various names, such as 'Fleetwood Inn' — 'New Inn'. This area was on the edge of the 'Great Bay', which was the first landfall for the Rimmer tribe who sailed up the 'Snoterpool' anchorage, so it holds a claim to be amongst the venues for the first settlers, arriving in the wake of the Viking longboats, over one thousand years ago.

We must continue however, with the activities of North Meols residents in the early 16th century, as records were now catching up with the events of the day. When a church visitation was made in 1625, they made a more diligent search into recusant activities. The Rector, Henry Wright, also held the living of Leyland, and was unable to cover up all the 'goings on' in the Parish. Non-communicants were listed, and fined, and some rather unsavoury activities at Meols Hall came to light. William Hesketh gentlemen, and his 'supposed wife', were accused of a secret marriage, and, amongst the Rimmers involved, were Cuthbert Rimmer, son of the former named Ellis, accused of 'seducing good Protestants'. Richard Rimmer and Thomas Rimmer, were also named amongst many others, as being concerned in secret marriages, and producing 'illegitimate' children, but the biggest crime would seem to have been absence from church, as Peter Rimmer and his wife Mary, were excused, "because of her advanced pregnancy". Quite a few of the Rimmers, from Churchtown, Crossens, Banks, Row and Newe Row, were members of the North Meols Jurors, at the Court Leet, and Court Baron in the records between 1640 and 1643, as well as 'pinders', and parish constables. One Rimmer was actually fined for fighting, and Thomas Rimmer coneyman, or rabbit keeper, also got into the records. Richard Rimmer was fined 3/4d for 'annoying' the neighbours, who had mares in heat. His only offence was keeping a 'stoned horse', one that had not been gelded!

During the Civil War, which started in 1642, North Meols took advantage of its isolated situation, and there is, as far as I can gather, no evidence of the Rimmers being involved.

There was a brief skirmish, when Prince Rupert's cavalry, defeated at Marston Moor, fled down the Ribble, and attempted to cross over by the guide road from Freckleton. The pursuit was taken up by a force of Roundheads, under Col. Assheton, at Hesketh Bank. They passed through Banks, and made a last stand at Brade Street, Crossens, before being routed on Aughton Moss. Some cannon balls and musket shot, which were found during the rebuilding of houses in Brade Street, many years later, were included in the artefacts, maps and manuscripts, connected with the publication of 'Betwixt Ribbel and Moerse', and were included in an exhibition at the Atkinson Library in 1983. All literary material was subsequently presented to, and kept for reference, at the Botanic Museum, Churchtown. However, there is no conclusive evidence to support the claim that the military artefacts were from the skirmish at Crossens. There was a report that troops had passed through North Meols, and along Foul Lane, for the last stand on Aughton Moor, near Halsall Church, in 1644 (page 30). The second siege of Lathom House is covered by Chapter Eleven of 'Betwixt Ribbel and Moerse'.

The estates of William Hesketh, Cavalier 1616-43, who died in the service of Charles I, were sequestered by Parliament, and as a consequence, no rents were collected for many years by his heirs, prior to the first half of the 17th century.

When records became established, we find that Nicholas, and John Rimmer, two of the churchwardens, had to provide a Table of Degrees, and a book, for church accounts, as it had been too dangerous to maintain any sort of registers during the Civil War, because of their kinship with landowners who had supported the Crown. Apart from this obvious difficulty for local historians to maintain any continuity, it is particularly frustrating for even a member of the Rimmer clan, to obtain any continuity of a people who were only used to the method of passing down geneology, or other records, strictly by word of mouth. This was the obvious procedure adopted after the 'Skald' storytelling saga, and poem era, preceeding any written records. It still obtains to a certain degree today, when many generations of Rimmers can be accounted for in a few spoken sentences.

Although the main body of the Rimmers kept to their main activities, now stretching from South Meols to Formby, there is some evidence that some of them were making their presence felt in North Meols, as evidenced by Hearth Tax recordings, which became due on Lady Day. For every hearth, except for houses valued at one pound per annum, and people in receipt of poor relief, a tax of 2/- per hearth, was levied. Meols Hall had six, and Bold House four. From the records in 1664, which are in the Public Record Office E179/250/11, we find that, of the Rimmers by the year 1666, those hearth taxes recorded, were, by now, very much diversified. William Rimmer paid one in Churchtowne, which we assume to be North Meols. Robert Rymer and Jo Rymer paid one each in Banks. John Rymer and Robert Rymer once each in Crossens. Thos Rymer and Ric Rymer, one each in Hawes, and John Rymer, one in Blowicke. There appears to have been quite a large expansion westwards, as in Birkdale there was one each, to Jo and Ellis Rymer, William Rymmer Jun, John Rymmer Jun, Dorothy Rymer, Nick Rymer, James Rimmer, Gilbert Rymmer, Richard Rimmer and Thos Rymmer Sen. In Ainsdale, Elizabeth Rimmer and Gilbert Rimmer, each paid one hearth tax. The Rimmers in Formby were more isolated, in a fastly developing district, and need a separate record, as there were other districts in between such as the lost ghost town of Argameols, and places such as, Meanedale and Elreslete, which have been dealt with Chapters Seven and Eight of 'Betwixt Ribbel and Moerse'.

The significant factor of quoting these records, lies in the instance of the varying derivations of the Rimmer names, engendered by the increase in their prestige, and importance, and also intermarriage of those who "have got on a bit", as the common or garden Rimmer would be wont to express. I myself, like the contrasting instance of the two Rimmer brothers, who found a porpoise on the shore at Birkdale, and took it to Salwick near Preston, where Sir Cuthbert Halsall, then Lord of the Manor, was residing, and insisted on carrying it up to his bedroom to show it to him! That sounds more like the 'Roaring Rimmers' to me. There was always an underlying vein of humour underneath their strictly pious and moral code.

There was no more singular feature affecting the fortunes of the Rimmers, than the construction of Crossens Sluice, which is referred to on Thomas Fleetwood's memorial in St. Cuthbert's Church. In the late 17th century, Thomas, of Bank Hall, Bretherton, took lease of land between Crossens and Banks, and cut a channel 24 feet wide, and a mile and a half long through the marsh to the sea. The high watermark, at the spring tide, was ten feet above the level of Martin Mere. Drainage was done solely on gravity, and a pair of floodgates were erected, to be closed when the tide came in. This was undoubtedly to prove the salvation of the fishing Rimmers who were losing the access to the sea along the Snoterpool, due to silting up of the Great Bay. The prediction that the drainage scheme would "convert the immense mere of Martin into firm dry land", did not completely materialize, but sufficient areas of mereland were transformed, around the edges, to create arable land from the fenny pasturages. For the land based 'Reamers', there was work enough created, together with the continuity engendered by the continual construction of the sea cops, for the next three hundred years, including the transference of the shrimping, fishing fleets, from Southport's silted pier anchorage in the 1920's, to the Sluice.

The main body of the Rimmers kept pressing on, increasing their industrious occupations, and development of the new tillage afforded by the draining on the Mere, and keeping their fundamental religious basic faith, which had enabled them to exist amongst the various diversely religious people they had lived peacefully alongside for the past centuries.

There were of course, even amongst the most isolated peoples, as evidenced, even by the Children of Israel on their forty years wandering in the wilderness, apostates to any cause. We have seen evidence of Rimmers being apostates, and recusants in the various activities in connection with Church and Manor, in North Meols. The pendulum propensity, in religious activities in Tudor times, took a swing in 1694, when Roger and Mary Hesketh were involved in the Jacobite Movement, and as supporters, through the succession of heirs through James II, were held in prison, in Manchester. Catholic support was not very enthusiastic in the North Meols district, and support for any cause was certainly non-existent in the Rimmers of South Meols and district. By 1695, when William and Mary came to the throne, it had become legal to hold Protestant Dissenters meetings, which however, had to be registered at the quarter sessions.

During research on other matters, I have inspected a Lancashire Records Office (number QSP 766/15) document dated 1695, which states that "The dwelling house of William Rymmer, senior, of North Meoles, and Thomas Brakills of the same, are intended for meeting houses for an assembly of Protestants, dissenting from the Church of England, and desires that they may be recorded accordingly." I don't think that these dissenter meetings were anything but peaceful ones, and cannot be linked with the accusation that they were involved in the charge of storage of arms, at Meols Hall, levelled at Roger and Mary Hesketh, in the previous year. The Heskeths seemed to have learnt a lesson from these events, as by the time the next century dawned, they had embraced the Protestant faith, and did not support risings of the Old, or Young Pretenders.

The Rimmers involved in these events were connected to the Breakill family by marriage in 1602, and down through several generations through Robert Rymer in 1678, and Ellin Rymer in 1705, to descendants in Eccleston, Ormskirk and Prescot, which in those days represented a considerable area. It does however, indicate some support for the Rimmer's primary intention of keeping their own counsels, and beliefs, and not becoming involved in affairs of state, manor, or church.

Such isolation could not prevail, as commerce and trading had always been the main activity of the seafaring Rimmers. They had come from West Norway, via the Shetlands, and the Isle of Man and, inevitably, many of them had remained behind, in most of the places they had contacted. Even in my day, my grandad maintained links by sea fishing, and passenger sailings, with Rimmers in the Isle of Man, and Barrow, and other scattered residents along the coast, northward through Lancashire. To the south, the Rimmers spread along the coast, and many of them joined the larger vessels plying the trading routes from Liverpool, to all parts of the world. Ironically, some were Arctic whaling vessels, plying the waters in areas where their ancestors originated.

The Rimmers had congregated in fairly large communities around Formby, in the centuries preceding 1740, in the belief that Formby would be established as the chief dockland of Liverpool, but silting of the Formby Channel put paid to that idea. Rimmers were not original settlers in Formby, which was 'possessed' by the Danish Vikings. Liverpool was only a comparatively new port, so was the Mersey itself, as Lancashire and Cheshire were once connected, until they were separated in the fifth century by an earthquake. The Ribble and the Dee, are older, but the Ribble estuary was originally the Great Bay, between Southport and Crossens, which contained the 'Snoterpool'. Liverpool had its own 'Snoterpool', (now Otterspool), long before the 'Lyver Pool' appeared, in the marshes which are now Liverpool. Chapters One and Seven of 'Betwixt Ribbel and Moerse' explains all this, and how squirrels 'skipped from tree to tree, from Formby Point to Hilbre'.

This forest stretched from Pembrokeshire, and far enough North to foul my grandad's fishing nets, off Formby. It's not one of my grandad's stories that these submerged forests were evidence of the Mosaic or Noah's deluge, and were referred to long ago as 'Noah's Woods' (see Geological Survey Preface to Chapter 1).

In the north, the Rimmers in their 'reaming' capacity had, subsequent to the foundering of the sugar boat in 1565, built another sea bank to keep the tide away from North Meols. This followed roughly the line of the former railway embankment from Churchtown Station, to Crossens. I am not able to confirm that the railway was built on it, but it was probably utilized to create the rise over the roadway at Churchtown Station. The line of this bank can also be roughly defined by a cottage, 'Matts Cottage', which is in an area called 'Matts Brow'. It is at the bottom of the left side of Sunny Road, approximately where the railway embankment ran from Churchtown to Crossens. This was therefore, quite probably another sea embankment, 'Brow'. Another sea bank was constructed, in the 17th century, for Nicholas Abram, nearer the sea, which was named 'Nabb's Cop', doubtless after him. This cop ended in the south, in the sandhills near Bank Nook, after running along Knob Hall Lane, across Marshside Lane (Road) along Shellfield Road to Fairhaven Road. Various other sea cops were constructed up to the nineteenth century, and only recently have the Hesketh Golf Links been extended to the sea cop, running to Marshside and Crossens. There were three sea banks standing behind one another, between Crossens and Hesketh Bank. I have to relate the story of the terrible tragedy which occurred in 1720, when the sea broke through 'Nabb's Cop', but as I write these notes, the recent flooding at Towyn in North Wales, illustrates the ever repeated folly of building development taking place, when property is built, inside sea defences, at a lower level than sea level. We have locally, the incidence of flooding occurring in 1970 when the tide broke through the sea bank at Crossens, and inundated the new housing estate in the Skipton Avenue, and Harrogate Way area. The new estates at Marshside are also in a similar situation, and the proposal to eventually build inside the coast road area, seems to be compounding the folly of construction below sea level, without adequate defence. The fact that Massams Slack, near Formby Golf Links, loses 12ft. of land by sea erosion each year, illustrates the danger of complacency. At very low tides it was possible (as at Morecambe), to cross over the estuary of the Ribble, and indeed, when I worked at Whitesides, this feat was achieved in a 'Bull Nosed' Morris Cowley, which had a high running board that just cleared the water level.

On October 1st 1835, the Rev. Charles Hesketh, after his appointment as Rector of North Meols, left Bispham near Blackpool, with a carriage and gig, with his wife, and two other ladies, and several carts loaded with furniture and livestock. They crossed the Ribble at the Hesketh Bank Ford, where the cart containing the livestock, presumably by its weight, got stuck in the bed of the river, but was extricated just in time. This record I obtained, was from the diary manuscript of Mrs. Charles Hesketh, which had been preserved at Meols Hall. It is quite possible, that in earlier times, a crossing could be made to the Crossens headland, where there are mentions of the cross, which was opposite the Plough Hotel, being used as a landmark for shipping, and people crossing the sands. In a 12th century charter there is mention of a hospice, or lodging house or 'hospitalitas', so it is possible that the Plough Hotel site is more ancient than has hitherto been considered. The Plough, in the 18th century, was occpupied by Hugh Gregson, whose daughter Jane, then aged 21, married William Sutton, 'The Old Duke' in 1776. William was then 24, and was encouraged by the Gregsons, to become an innkeeper, in the year of his marriage. William was of an artistic temperament, with no head for business, so in the history books his antics at the Black Bull in Churchtown, overshadowed The Plough, and Crossens, then described as a 'hamlet'. Generally speaking, Crossens became overshadowed in historical context by North Meols, in spite of the fact that it was more ancient, as evidenced by the 'Landnamabok' account of the Rimmer's arrival in the 'Great Bay', nearly 1000 years ago. Rimmers were always associated with Crossens, especially in later years, after their association concerning the sea embankment construction in the 13th century. When the ancient Pool at Crossens, and the Sluice from Martin Mere, came together, to make a common outfall over the marsh at Crossens to the sea, the Rimmers used the anchorage, as well as Southport Pier, until my grandad, and Uncle Bob's days, in the 20th century. There were always Rimmers in the district, even in farming activities, until almost the present day, in the naming of Bridge Will's Lane, formerly Dock Lane. 'Bridge Will' was tenant of Bridge Farm, which was near the crossing over Fiddler's Ferry into Ralph Wife's Lane. A William Rimmer was the tenant of the farm, probably in my grandad's time. Slutch, deposited on Crossens shore, led to Crossens being derisively referred to as 'Muckington on Slutch', but the last laugh was on the Crossens side, when Bold Fleetwood Hesketh, declared that the slutch was more durable for enriching the soil, than the marl from the Mere. Historically also, Crossens has the distinction of being the first 'Viking' settlement in the wake of the Viking raids, albeit that the 'Vikings' who settled there from West Norway, were not true Vikings at all, but a 'remnant' of the lost Biblical tribe of Dan, with a history stretching back to the very limits of recordable time! In the 1950s when I was a commercial traveller, visiting many local garages, there used to be a group of elderly gentlemen who used to gather round the stove at Dandy's Garage, which is still there, by the bridge, over the Douglas at Tarleton. It also served as the local barber's shop, and all sorts of discussions would take place. One old chap, who lived in a two storied cottage on the Shore Road at Hesketh Bank, used to harp on about "The Flood", which he said was imminent. He was the subject of much ridicule, but when he heard about my interest in local history, he took the trouble to explain to me that he had studied records, and that about every sixty five years, there was a confluence of high winds and tides, which caused flooding. This he explained, used to happen in the English Channel, causing the floods in Lincolnshire and Holland, before the dykes and drainage ditches were constructed. He maintained that this situation was due to occur in the Ribble Estuary, in spite of the silting that had increased over the years. When I mentioned the three sea banks protecting the coast, he said that the farmers had cut through a couple, and part of the third, to gain more arable land. There came one day when he was missing from his usual place by the stove, and when I enquired as to his welfare, they told me, amongst much ribaldry, that he was busy moving his furniture to the top floor of his cottage, as the time had come for winds and tide to meet. There was no derision when I made the next visit, as the tide had swept through the sea banks, forced on by a tremendous gale. All the cottages sustained flood damage, including the old chap's, but at least his furniture was intact. The subsequent damage to the land has taken many years to recover, and will probably never be quite the same. There was a water flood sign indicating the height in feet, standing for many years on the Shore Road and Guide Road corner, at Hesketh 'Brow', at the top of Station Road.

My mother for many years, predicted that the sea would return, and surround us, and it is not a quarter of a century ago, subsequent to the increased building in South Formby, and Altcar areas, where once again it was easily observed from the Abrahams Alt Bridge, on the Woodvale By-Pass, that on occasion, the level of the River Alt was higher than the land over the side of its banks.

When eventually, during a storm, accompanied by high winds, the river broke through the bank at Moss Side, the whole of the countryside, as far as Halsall was inundated. Accompanied by flooding in other areas, albeit it was only for a few hours, the roads to Ormskirk and Preston were flooded, and Southport was completely cut off. All this, in spite of the fact that I had predicted that one day, with a combination of silting and encroachment of plant life, that the Ribble Estuary would revert to its original state, and become dry land once more!

It cannot be said that Fairclough's Lake could compare with the volume of sea traffic that the ports of Preston and Liverpool could command. With the loss of the 'Snoterpool' to the Rimmers, as a seafaring enterprise, owing to the silting of the Great Bay, it resulted in the Rimmers becoming increasingly involved in the crewing of the many ocean going vessels from the larger ports. They were still actively involved in the local shipping on Fairclough's Lake, but for another reason, this time, the nefarious one of smuggling.

At low water, Fairclough's Lake was only a shallow anchorage, which in the nineteenth and twentieth century, became the 'Bog Hole' anchorage, north of Southport Pier, dominated by the Horse Bank, which today, employs the efforts of the sand removal plant on the Coast Road. Seabank Road also, affords an indication as to its location. The Prince of Wales Hotel, and Little King Street, were approximate limits to the South of the Lake, which was connected to the sea by a half mile wide channel, and would have been approximately two miles long. The vessels could get within half a mile of the shore, as the depth of water would be about 40 feet, but the anchorage was exposed to south westerly gales, and the constantly shifting sandbank approaches made navigation extremely hazardous.

At the northern end of the lake, there was a group of cottages, listed on navigation charts in the early 18th century as 'Sugar Houses'. These were used as a cottage industry, in the refining of the sugar cane, unloaded there by the slave trading vessels, after dropping their main cargoes at Liverpool. Although it is abhorrent to contemplate the generally law abiding, and pious attitude of the main body of the Rimmers, as even being connected with the slave trade, it would only be as members of the crews, that contained any of the Rimmer seafarers. Accounts become, over the years, elaborated, and exaggerated, as I have explained by the skull and crossbone pirate motif on gravestones, giving rise to the inference of piratical activities in North Meols. This was evidenced by the burial of poor old Thomas Rimmer in 1713, whose only crime was to be held captive in Barbary for sixteen years. Stories and rumours however, do persist, and lose nothing in their recounting. Even as recently as the 1950s, many people will remember the 'Goree Piazzas', in the Liver Building area of Liverpool, where huge rings were still embedded in the walls of the roadway, built on the site of the old quays, through which the traffic used to roar in a constant stream, as it still does. I had a hard time convincing the locals that these were not, as they strenuously asserted, 'for chaining slaves to', but were the iron rings to which the ships were anchored.

However it is true to say, that on many a moonlight night, in suitable conditions, the shallow, open beaches of North Meols would be dotted with the silent, puposeful figures of local inhabitants, busy with the conveyance, from ship to shore, of large quantities of contraband goods.

It is no mitigance of these nefarious activities, to state that such influential people as the Heskeths of Meols Hall, and the diarist, and Squire, of Little Crosby, Nicholas Blundell were involved, when trying to excuse the involvement of some of the Rimmers, especially considering their connection with 'piracy' for the past 800 years or more!

There were records of the Rimmer's involvement in smuggling over many years, as being a most profitable, and successful enterprise. There was little doubt that they were highly organised, and the 'Great Diurnal' of Nicholas Blundell, RS110, 112, 114 records, amongst other Rimmer activities, that on 30th March, 1710, he states, "My wife and I dined at John Rimers, and subsequently went on board the 'Betty', in North Meols."

There had been a customs officer appointed, but it seems to have made little difference, as smuggling had been going on long before 1677, when North Meols acquired him. There does not seem to be much evidence of interference in this traffic, as operations in an official capacity, were probably conducted from Preston. There was a case in 1688, when Barnaby and Bartholomew Hesketh, were accused by William Blake, customs officer, in a petition to the quarter sessions, for "obstruction with violence, whilst discharging his duties aboard the 'Mary', then being in Fairclough's Lake in North Meols." Barnaby and company were, apparently fraudulently, conveying large quantities of brandy, and tobacco, from several ships, and attempts to enter Barnaby's house, presumably then Meols Hall, were frustrated by "a company gotten there together." In the Sessions at Ormskirk, the magistrates, who were Mr. Hesketh's fellow Squires, with a poor opinion of Revenue officers, declared the accused, "discharged" and the warrant, "stayed and discharged." Small wonder there were very few accounts of smuggling activities.

Even then, fifty years later, it was alleged that, although North Meols was made a customs station, with four extra officers, sent to assist, there was a complaint that the local "waiter and searcher, had been made to lie down on deck, whilst goods were taken on shore." Could it be mere coincidence that the High Sherriff of Lancashire , in 1740, was none other than Roger Hesketh of Rossall, and North Meols!

North Meols was never officially recognised as a 'port', for it was first responsible to the Port of Poulton, and from 1680, the limits of the Port of Liverpool were defined to embrace the whole coastline betwixt 'Ribble and Mersey'. There appears to be little or no reference at any time, to the heinous crime of 'wrecking'. Salvage of goods from wrecked vessels occurred in 1825, when an accusation of looting was also made, but as it subsequently appeared that the captain, and crew, were all rescued by a fishing boat, no charges were levelled. The general rule of 'Flotsam and Jetsam', was usually applied when vessels were wrecked, as in the case of the Ann E. Hooper, wrecked in 1862. The boat was from Baltimore, an American freighter of 1145 tons, which, after the rescue of the crew, struck the pier. About 1500 barrels of flour were washed ashore, and saved, and many of the poorer people were prevented, by the wreck officers, from saving some of the dry flour in the centre of many of the damaged barrels, which were all washed away to sea. As a result, a great quantity of the articles saved, were smuggled and buried, at both ends of the town. Tobacco, bacon, and clockworks, were rescued. The bacon went bad, through being buried in the sand while wet. The tobacco was consumed, and it was said, by my grandad, that up to 20 years afterwards, clockworks were still stowed away in the thatches of old cottages. As my grandad was born in 1864, he could have had first hand information of at least the latter occurrence, the 'movement' of the clockworks, in his earlier years!

One other item I must mention, out of context, but concerned with smuggling, is the question posed many times, but never answered, was concerning the origin of the naming of Ralph's Wife's Lane, which runs from the Ferry at Crossens, to Banks. As nobody has ventured a reason, I will let my grandad answer it. "It was alus Ralph's Loo'an (Lane), cos he lived thear." One nee't, his wife wer waitin' fer Ralph to cum oo'am from smugglin', in't loo'an, an't cau'd weather wer too much fer 'er, and she died. So ar'ter that, they alu's cau'd it Ralph's Wife's Loo'an (Lane). It wer' sed that, 'arter that, she wer sen' (seen) in't looa'an, awaitin' fer Ralph, mon'y times, but that may be 'ony a tale.''

I have recorded the dates, on page 3 of 'Betwixt Ribbel and Moerse', of sand encroachment being consistent from about 1750, and records of dangerous storms given as, 1532, 1553, 1720, 1739, 1771, 1833, 1896 and 1927. On page 46, I referred to the old church of St. Luke's, in the sandhills, in Formby being swept away in the gale of 1739, which ironically, was the year that celebrations were held in North Meols, on the occasion of the reopening of St. Cuthbert's Church, at North Meols, after rebuilding was completed. It was also recorded, in this year that Thomas Rimmer, and Thomas Aughton, his brother-in-law, were said to have carried "sixty pounds weight of tea, to be hidden somewhere in the Meols." Also in the same year, William Rimmer of Scarisbrick arrived in Banks, and took away "eight half-anchors of brandy, on four horses," so it appears that smuggling persisted for at least two centuries, before giving way to the salvaging, flotsam and jetsam, beachcombing type, of shore activity.

    I have long been confused with the sequence of the building of the Sea Cops, and banks along the coast. The 'Monk's Embankment' of course, was the first, and so too have previous historians, consistent with the constant receding of the coastline, been subsequently at variance, with the sequence of construction since the 13th century 'Monk's' Bankfield Lane embankment. The next embankment was in the 16th century, identified previously as being the one approximately along the line of the railway, between Churchtown and Crossens. This was the 16th century Tudor one, as at that time the high water mark was believed to be from St. Cuthbert's Church's vicinity, past the Sugar Hillock — Sunny Road landmark, roughly along the line of the railway from Churchtown to Hesketh Park stations, then slightly seaward off Marlborough Road, and Hawesside Street, to Yellow House Lane. At this time also, the 'Ghost Town' of Argameols, once a part of Birkdale, also disappeared (see Chapter Seven). The third embankment of the three, identified by Bulpit, was supposed to be 'Nab's Cop', which ran from approximately the present Bank Nook, Knob Hall area, across Marshside Road, and along Shellfield Road to Crossens. This was built by Nicholas Abram in the 17th century, so 'Nab' was the obvious cognomen to employ for Nicholas, who lived close to it, probably in the Bakers Lane area. Shellfield Road was formerly called 'Danglus Lane', often identified with the Marshside bellman nicknamed 'Dangler'. It was under the water in the 17th century, and when it dried out, shells were found, embedded in the old marsh at the Fairhaven Road end. When the cottages, which are still there, were built, it became Shellfield Road for its full length. Nabb's Cop ran roughly along the line of Knob Hall Lane, from Bank Nook, and can still be traced, not only by old maps, but by contemporary street plans of Southport.

    The West Norse derivation of 'Bru' (Brow) is 'hill', or 'slope', and subsequent to the building of 'Nabb's Cop', cottages built near the sea banks were known as 'Brows', so 'Nabb's Bank', or 'Cop' can be traced by the presence of 'Cotty's Brow', 'Boss's Brow', 'Crostons Brow' etc. from Bank Nook to Marshside Lane (now Marshside Road). From here, 'Dangler's Brow' eventually known as 'Danglus Lane', then Shellfield Road, shows the full extent of 'Nabb's Cop'. Even then, as late as the 19th century, other 'Brows' such as 'Hoskers Brow', which was the name given to a row of cottages along Knob Hall Lane, appeared. Nicholas Blundell is variously said to have occupied a 'farmhouse' near 'Cottage Brow', which could be the present 'Cotty's Brow', and also could have been a place called 'Rabb Hall', possibly near Bakers Lane, and the old 'Clengers Brow', off Baker's Lane. I don't think 'Knobb was meant to imply 'Nob' in an elite connotation, but only as a corruption of 'Nab'. There was a Sea Cop, constructed in 1805, and a 'New Bank' in 1892, which ran on past Marshside, and continued past

Crossens. I do not know when the banks, which ran from Banks, to Hundred End, were built, as their construction would be consecutive, rather than continuous, in the time sequence. The construction of the Southport — Crossens Coast Road, has altered things, in the respect that the land has been made available for extension to the Hesketh Golf Club course, and the Municipal Golf Links. The proposal however, to utilize the marshy ground near Marshside, inland over the coast road, would, in view of recent flooding scares, appear to be a very hazardous project indeed, for the construction of a new housing estate. I think that Nabb's Cop to the south, would probably link up with the high sand banks that protected Bank Nook, and on which the Cottage Hospital was subsequently built. I have detailed the above sequence of the sea banks, which I hope are correct. They will at least correct the statements of two historians, that 'Nabb's Cop' was under construction in 1805, and was also the last bank to be constructed! I have kept up the reference to 'Nabb's Cop, because it constitutes the basis for a drastic, and very tragic sequence of events, which occurred in the early 18th century.

These events started in 1710, when a Robert Abram, and his family, living near 'Nabb's Cop', suffered a near tragedy, when a terrible gale demolished part of his house and outbuildings. The confluence, also of rain and high seas, washed away household goods, 46 sheep, and destroyed his crops. He had to shelter his wife, and eight small children in the chimney breast, as the sea broke down the door, and burst through the house. They were fortunate to escape with their lives. There is a record of this event in the Lancashire Records Office at Preston, Ref. QSP 1171/9, which does not state however, whether Robert was any relation of Nicholas. It is irrelevant in any case, as many of these records around this period makes harrowing reading.

There were the usual relief collections made in local churches, but apparently the Rimmer 'reamers', and other workers, had been complaining for some time that 'Nabb's. Cop' was in urgent need of reconstruction. It was however, only repaired, and despite many warnings, was virtually untouched for the next decade.

So it was, as explained to me over two hundred years later, by the old chap in the garage, at Tarleton, that in the year 1720, with the combination of wind, sea, and river overflow from the Pennines, there occurred, in the Ribble Estuary, the worst inundation of the Lancashire coast in recorded history. There was flooding on also the Fylde side of the Ribble, with Lytham, Cockerham, Pilling, and Marten Mere all suffering damage.

The worst damage however, was on the North Meols side of the Estuary, worsened by the fact, that, in spite of repeated warnings over a full decade ago, apart from the repairs necessary to 'Nabb's Cop', after the storm of 1710, it had been forgotten, and neglected, with the course of time, and apparent recession of the high water mark.

There had been, in December of 1720, a general period of heavy rain until the 10th, then a 'calm before the storm' period up to the 16th, then the heaviest spell of thunder and lightning, ever experienced at this time of the year, with the strongest wind, and heaviest seas, and highest tides in living memory, pounding away at the sea defences. Frantic efforts to strengthen the 'Cop', proved abortive, and the sheer horror experienced by the inhabitants, can only be imagined, as the tidal wave occasioned by the accumulation of the elements, tore through the breach in the 'Cop', ever widening with the weight of the sea pouring, and foaming through it. In this graphic description of the disaster Nicholas Blundell, the diarist, stated that the "sea had overflowed 6600 aikers of land, and washed down 157 houses, and dammifyed 200 more."

Even the official records at Preston, LR/ QSP 1171/9, and LRO QSP 1183/6, contain harrowing descriptions of the events up to, and including, the inundation. In North Meols alone, more than 5000 acres of land, probably over half the land under cultivation was under sea water, forty seven houses were destroyed, and many more were completely uninhabitable. Winter stocks of corn, hay, and fuel, were swept away, and household goods, and clothing ruined by salt water. Nine people in North Meols lost their lives, and very few livestock survived, people had to cling to the rafters of their ruined shells of houses and cottages. A thousand acres of wheat sown land, was flooded. The bridge, called Fine Janes Bridge, which carried the road over the 'Snoterpool', was swept away. The water fortunately, flooded down onto Martin Mere, which no doubt acted as a sponge, as the floodwater reached as far north as Hesketh Bank, and Tarleton. Two bridges on the River Douglas were damaged, one at Rufford. In the south, the Alt Bridge was damaged, and one at Little Crosby, but there was no land flooding there. Martin Mere reverted to what it had previously claimed to be, "the largest inland lake in the country."

It might only be coincidence, that the Church at North Meols, and the school were both rebuilt in 1739, as there is no record of any flood damage to either, the Church was in a state of disrepair long before the flood, probably the draining away of water onto the Mere, may have saved it anyway.

Not a very happy Christmas for the 135 families who suffered, a hundred of them being virtually ruined, and homeless. There does not seem to be any reference in general, to the activities of the Rimmers, during what my grandad would call, 'a big blow up'. Being a hardy lot, and conditioned to the sea and land disasters for generations past, they no doubt took to their boats and were able to render valuable assistance in rescue work, a voluntary activity they have maintained all through their long history until the 20th century. The only reference I have found, is that Oliver Rimmer was one of the fourteen organisers of a petition for losses of land and property, for flood victims. Oliver's only comment, when it was noted that his personal losses included eighty bushels of malt, was that he regretted ruefully, that he had already paid duty for malt, to the tax collectors!

There is a modern song which contains the lines "It's a long, long time from May to December' that would effectively describe the events in the same decade as the great inundation, for that was the period, in 1727, that there occurred another disaster, worse than that of the Black Plague, which fortunately had largely by-passed the sea coast area of North Meols. This was a fever type of distemper, a disease perhaps more largely associated with animals today, than human beings. Out of a population of little over 1000 in North Meols, there were 82 burials alone, at St. Cuthbert's, registered. This time it appeared that the coastal areas suffered the most. It is interesting to note that, when the area was visited by the Bishop of Chester, when he divided the parish into eight parts, no mention was made of the South Meols area, or High Park Place, and district, probably because they were unconnected with North Meols in ecclesiastic affairs. However, even in the Parish records of the two volumes published between 1594-1812, the surname of Rimmer is given as being the most common (4327), with Ball (2639), Wright (2507), as the next in proportion. In all records of population in the surrounding districts, such as Birkdale, there were always twice as many Rimmers, as any other two families put together. It is also interesting to note that the smallest family in North Meols, of any note was the Suttons, who have created the most comment, probably no doubt because of 'Old Duke Sutton', who is regarded as the founder of Southport. I have not included the 'Old Duke' in this saga, as we have had a celebration in May 1990, on the occasion of the Anniversary of the death of William Sutton 250 years ago, the accounts of which will be in a scrapbook of articles, which will accompany this epic, in the files at the Botanic Museum, for future posterity reference.

In spite of all the floods, plagues, 'war alarums, and excursions', and various other vicissitudes, attendant with their former nomadic existence, the Rimmers had managed to maintain a certain degree of equilibrium, and equanimity, in relationships with other peoples, but now, with a more static, and settled existence in prospect, they had to cope with the aspect of increasing concourse, and intermarriage, with other families. They still maintained their evangelical attitude towards religious matters, and even infused newcomers into their families, with their fairly strict, fundamental Biblical beliefs.

They were not however, without a strain of, sometimes caustic, wit in their make-up, as for instance, where a neighbour in the 'Rowe' had his holding on 'Poverty Field', quite a number of Rimmers, were in contrast, wont to dub their fields as 'Paradise', which became a fashionable name for fields in the 'Rowe', and district.

Many of the Rimmers, and their relatives, were notable for their longevity. In spite of many birth recordings proving to be inaccurate, geneology was confirmed by memory. Any age, over sixty, was remarkable in the 17th and 18th century. On one instance, the father of the 'Old Duke' William Sutton, remarked that of the eight persons in his company, all were over 60, and was also astonished to find that, about the year 1793, there were 199 people in North Meols, all above sixty years of age, at that time, one tenth of the population, and that of recent burials, Gilbert Rymer was 92, Anne Sutch 91, and Elizabeth Sutton 91, all intermarried with the Rimmers, as was Hannah Johnson, of South Hawes, who died at the age of 103. There had been a John Ball, a witness at the Baldermeryhokes trial in 1554, who was able to give evidence at his age, estimated to be about 106.

There was some doubt about William Blundell, in 1641, giving his mother's age as 100. 'Cockle Dick' Aughton, claimed to be 99, in his old age, when he was only 94. He was officially declared to be nearly 96 when he died. His wife, who was Isabell Blundell, was 90, when she died in 1819, they were childhood sweethearts. Shorlicars, of Birkdale, claimed to be a couple who were both 99, but their true ages were 94 and 84. It seems that although many of the 'Sandgrounders' were not as old as they claimed, possibly promoting the 'Oldest Inhabitant' theme, it would seem that their claim of longevity was true, in comparison with the national average. The age of Hannah Johnson, was however officially confirmed as being 103. It was not that the inhabitants themselves made false claims, but the incidence of legevity was promoted by later entrepreneurs, and other public bodies, stressing the claims of Southport as a popular place for retirement.

Some of the Rimmers had continued their connections with North Meols, as well as their expansion along the coast, as evidenced by an inscription on the south door of the former St. Cuthbert's Church, James Rimer, Thomas Rimer, Robert Ball, Churchwardens, with the date given as 1730. The rebuilding started in this year, was only completed by 1739.

CHAPTER 5

MARSHSIDE —
'LITTLE IRELAND' AND 'LITTLE LONDON'

Marshside has long been described as the epitome of a typical picturesque, little coastal fishing village, but compared to the historical record of the Rimmers, it is only a comparatively new venture, in view of the fact that being such a marshy area, with no sandhills, it was, in earlier times, used mainly for cattle pasturage, and salt pits, by the Rimmers, in their dealings with the Sawley monks in the 13th century, at the Crossens end, as most of it was under water until the 17th century. It was first mentioned in Parish records in 1662, as 'Marsh-Side, being the development taking place along Marshside Lane, now Marshside Road, running from North Meols seaward.' In 1736, Bankes' map, made for the Bold family, shows only scattered development, as far as the Baker's Lane area. There were not many Rimmers established here, except for the fishing community at Bank Nook, which, protected by the huge sandbank ridge, had been established for many years before Marshside.

In respect of this reference to Bank Nook, and Baker's Lane, I have received, whilst writing this account of Marshside, a photostat of the deeds of the Thorn Tree Cottage situated in Coudray Road, on the corner of the former Carrier's Lane. I will refer to this in a later account, but on the corner of the photostat map, is an area called 'Nabb's', which also shows the 'Bank' running from Bank Nook, where it ends on the marsh near Crossens, which featured as 'Nabbs Bank' in the 1720 inundation account I have just completed.

The population of Marshside built up gradually over the next 200 years, with the proportion of Rimmers being at all times, one in two, and always maintained, as stated, even in Parish Registers, as being 'Larger than any two of the other families residing there." Even today, when the proportion of Rimmers in the Bank Nook areas, is no larger than any of the other inhabitants, it is interesting to note that, in spite of the scattering of Rimmers north, and south of Southport, the number of Rimmers still in Southport and district, is larger than the number from the whole of Southport to Lancaster, whilst to Liverpool and the South, the Southport district contains three quarters of the number in size, equivalent to the total given for that region. A sad tailpiece to the constant reference I keep making, concerning the two to one ratio of Rimmers in the local population, has occurred in 1991. In the proposal of the Southport Project 1991 appeal fund, for the updating of names, for inclusion on the Southport War Memorial, of the casualties in World War II, 1939-45, the number of Rimmer names submitted, is twice as large as any other, and indeed is larger than any other two families put together. Whilst it is only a reflection of the size of the Rimmer tribe still in existence, and in due proportion to local population, it indicates that tragedy also, is commensurate with predominance in numbers. Another sad postscript to these statistics came in 1990, with the obituary of Lance Corporal Andrew Rimmer, R.E.M.E., who died on active service on July 18th, whilst serving with the United Nations Peace Force in Cyprus. Mourned by his Dad, Mum, brother Mick, also of the R.E.M.E, and his Grandparents, Alice and Harry Wright. Andrew Rimmer was 22 years of age. Grief and sorrow however, on land or sea cannot be quantified or rationalized, only endured. As John 15 V13, states, "Greater love hath no man than this, that a man lay down his life for his friends."

As this is only a 'saga' of the Rimmer tribe, I do not intend to give a history of Marshside, but only their numbers, and influence, they had on the district. The Mission Hall, similar to the one in Old Park Lane, built on the corner of Kirkham Road and Shellfield Road in 1869, alongside a ship building yard of the same period, was strictly tee-total. The 'Ship afloat on a sea of Temperance', is still inscribed on the emblem of a full rigged ship, built into the gable wall overlooking the front porch. This building does not appear to have any reference to the old 'Sugar Hillock' chapel on the corner of Sunny Road and Cambridge Road, or any Rechabite connections in Churchtown. The Rechabites had a biblical, tribal connection, but the Rimmers were of a different biblical descent. Nevertheless Marshside has to this day never succumbed, as have its neighbours in Crossens and Banks, to the introduction of a public house. As I explain later, the 'Shrimpers' public house, on the periphery of the Marshside Industrial Estate, does not qualify as an original 'village pub'. Neither does the 'Farmers Arms' guesthouse, which was half way down Hoole Lane, Banks, qualify, although it was supplied by Wilkin's Brewery. Owing to the strong Rechabite, and Methodist's allegiance to tee-totalism, the licence of the 'Farmer's Arms' was withdrawn in 1908. The news of these instances of abstinence in two villages, caused world wide comment. There was strong opposition much later, when an agricultural show proposed to introduce alcohol in 1945, to raise money for the Red Cross, and Welcome Home Fund, for the troops. The present pub, the 'Fleetwood House', was actually the previous private home, of magistrate Hugh Cropper. It was proposed to open this house as a pub in 1960, but planning permission was refused. It was finally passed at Ormskirk Session in January 1961, and opened on July 4th, 1962. The opening was the more remarkable when a whirlwind removed part of the roof. This was attributed to "Divine Intervention"!

There are many other Marshside stories I have covered in newspaper articles, which will be included with scrapbooks, accompanying this Rimmer 'saga'. They will all be placed in the Walter Jesson file in the Botanic Museum, in which all the photos, reference maps, original drafts of the book 'Betwixt Ribbel and Moerse' have been used, in the past, for reference for many different academic thesis, and for publications, and books, for other authors. I hope they will continue to be used in the future, but I would request that you bear in mind that, although these events will, in respect of historical fact, bear a considerable amount of critical scrutiny, you are now only perusing a 'saga', or story, and some of the conjectures and assumptions you are shortly to be asked to consider, will test your credence to the limit.

We cannot leave Marshside without a few personal observations however. There are many, many instances of people deploring the fact, that the mainly tee-total, God fearing folk of Marshside, became a too tighly knit community, with its fear of 'foreigners', and ostracism of many locals, who dared to marry 'outsiders', even from High Park, Blowick and Birkdale, not to mention Crossens and Banks. Some Churchtowners too were looked upon askance, even from the top of Marshside Road!

The necessity however, for instance, that of education, which was only available in Churchtown, and becoming subsequently compulsory, led to a great change in the attitude of the Marshsiders. Both North Meols and Marshside employed, what historical outsiders terms, "a mixture of idiomatic phraseology" of their own. Like many other places in Lancashire, and other parts of the country, they were, in conversation, "blunt and unaffected." The fact that so few surnames were shared, by so many people in Marshside, however, led to idiomatic phraseology in geneology, and occupations, and even places of abode. Throughout all the coastal region, from Crosby to Hesketh Bank, on Bankes Map of 1736, we find James Rimmer, Coneyman, John Rimmer, farmer, James Rimmer, Paradise, Thos Rymer Nics, as instances. One curious nickname, 'Bodger', surviving to the 20th Century, is actually derived from an Ancient Egyptian woodworking name for a primitive lathe operator!

The employment of nicknames therefore, served as a threefold development, geneological, vocational, and topographical. This has persisted throught the years. Even in my schooldays, when we attended Churchtown School for woodwork lessons, there were so many Rimmers attending, that nicknames were still employed, to distinguish one from another. In 1859, it was stated that many people would puzzle, before grasping who could be meant, by such a name as Wright in Marshside, even if he were their own parent, but would recognize him, if referred to as "Priscilla's John", for instance.

I can give a more recent and graphic illustration by recalling that, 70 years later in 1929, whilst still a schoolboy, I was given the task of taking fishing tackle, comprising nets, and other oddments, from Bispham Road, to Marshside. My Uncle Bob had been drowned a couple of years previously in a fishing boat accident, so by ancient unwritten code, it was customary to pass such items to the nearest seafaring relative. I was directed to proceed to Marshside Road and turn into, from memory, I think it was 'Cotty's Brow', ask for Mr. Wright, and hand over the 'tackle' to him. I was quite familiar with the district, 'Clengers Brow', 'Crostons Brow', 'Knob Hall Lane' — having frequently visited 'Bender' Watkinson's Bike Shop in Marshside Road, and the corner shop on Shellfield Road where I called for the wool, with which my grandad knitted his own 'Gansey's' (Guernsey Jerseys). It was the typical scene, row of thatched cottages with small gardens, but would you believe it, just one person in sight, a knarled old, ruddy faced seaman, in the traditional 'gansey', leaning on the wooden gate of a cottage. I stopped in front of him, struggling to maintain control of the slippery mass, balanced precariously on the bike handlebars. "I'm looking for Mr. Wright," I managed to gasp at last. He looked at me, then all around, with small, puzzled, shakes of his head, without uttering a word, I might have come from another planet, judging by his suspicious attitude. Then I said I had come to give these nets, and tackle to Mr. Wright, but still no response. In a last desperate flash of inspiration recall, I said, "My grannie said, that if I got into trouble, ask for "Sweet", not knowing what that meant, probably thinking it was to be some confectionery reward for my endeavours. His face broke into something resembling an astonished half smile, "Why, 'am Sweet", he said, "Oo art ta"? I told him the facts about my Uncle Bob, and the family, "Ah, that were a bad do." His face softened a little, I thought he seemed to have a far away look for a second or two. "E were Little Bob's, (grandad) Big Bob-Lob", (that meant my Uncle Bob, who was known as 'Big Bob', being taller than my grandad, and his nickname being 'Lob'). "Then tha' mon be Little Bob's, Nellies, lad," he said, my mother being formerly Ellen Rimmer. In a few sentences therefore you had geneology, mixed with vocation and comment, on locality, and events, if you could follow the gist of the 'idiomatic phraseology', referred to by historians.

Many nicknames have practical usage, and had existed for a long time. The nickname 'Tuffy' for instance, was introduced into local use by the Rimmers. As I have previously explained, 'Torf', is West Norse for Turf, and in later years, was used to denote anyone connected with the 'reamering' of turf, or sods, on the banks, or in the dykes, with the nickname of 'Tuffy'. This nickname, very prevalent in Marshside, was also used in places like High Park. There are many 'Tuffy' Rimmers, right up to the present day. One 'Tuffy' Rimmer, was still active in Meols Cop, in my day, 'reamering', as a part time occupation to his regular job. The sea washed turf from the marshes, had a short wiry growth, which never exceeed an inch or so in height, and was in popular demand locally, until the local nurseries took over. Sea washed turf remained popular until its present decline, which has been caused mainly by changes such as the sparta grass, now fouling up the estuary.

Marshside, as a community, did not exist until the middle of the 18th century. Today, with the fishing industry declining to a few mechanized outfits at the far end of Shellfield Road, the introduction of an industrial estate, and housing, on its periphery, including the inevitable 'Shrimpers' pub, it has now almost lost its identity as a village. It is very rare indeed to find any cottage, even with refurbishment, which pre-dates the middle of the 18th centuries. My younger brother Albert lived and worked in Churchtown, for a great number of years before, during, and after World War II. He was called up for National Service whilst working at Meols Hall early in 1938, and was still on it when the broke out.

I have referred elsewhere to the assistance afforded me by personal family contacts, and access to records at Meols Hall for well over half a century. This, combined with my brother's knowledge of the topography, and acquaintance with the inhabitants, and their antecedents geneology, of Churchtown, Marshside, Crossens and surrounding areas, has enabled me to compile information, not always available from written matter.

We have together re-traced many locations, right up to the autumn of 1990, when we made final forays, ending in the Marshside district, connecting the many 'Brows' and 'Nooks', associated with the progressive construction of the various sea bank, and cops.

To finalise this episode, we traced out one feature of Marshside which has always been there in our time, and so take for granted, as to be neglected in an historical context.

I refer to a landmark known officially as 'Ibbys Pad', in our days referred to as 'Dibby's Pad'. It is a passage-way, still very much used, which still stretches from Larkfield Lane (formerly known as Watkinsons Lane), through to Cleveleys Road, then continues from across the road in the same manner, via Shellfield Road, then parallel with Kirkham Road, to Lytham Road. Across the road from here, it passes Manx Jane's Lane, and the back of St. Anne's Road, and ends at Fylde Road, near Fleetwood Hesketh's Sports Ground. There is no indication of its age, but its presence near Manx Jane's Lane, is a Rimmer connection with the Isle of Man. It was used as a short cut by Marshsiders, to and from, Churchtown Station and later, when Preston New Road was built, also from the Regent Cinema, via Mallee Crescent. It is certainly older than Marshside Road, or Marshside Lane, as it was known. It was also connected with the centre of North Meols, at St. Cuthbert's Church via either 'Matts Brow', or St. Cuthbert's Road. It would not be there in the 15th century, as the area was covered by the tide, but it has been, for at least the last three centuries, a pathway to the sea, consistent with the receding of the high water line, and could possibly be an old land connection between the 'Snoterpool' and the sea. Whilst we are in this corner of the community it would be appropriate if we considered one other place, which has received very little attention by the historians.

My grandad has described walking through the sandhills to Bank Nook, calling, on many occasions, to a place known as 'Little Ireland'. This was situated on the southern end of the huge range of sandhills which contained Bank Nook, the 'New Inn', and the Homeopathic Cottage Hospital in later years.

'Little Ireland' was situated approximately on, and under, the shelter of the hill, that now holds the complex of buildings comprising the Hesketh Golf Club. For many years it was indicated by a single cottage, standing some little further north than the club house, clearly visible from Fleetwood Road. It has always been assumed that this small village, was only a "colony of outlawed, and nondescript hut dwellers, who were reputed to defy respectability (and the police) on the hinterland of the north shore", as a well known local poet, Wilfred Thorley, who was born at 25 Scarisbrick New Road, described them in his "Recollections of Southport" in the eighteen eighties. It is true to say that most of the inhabitants referred to at that time, were descendants of families driven out of Ireland, by the potato famine. The Southport Directory of 1876, describes 'Little Ireland' as a "Low, squalid-looking place, destitute of all sanitary arrangements, and consisting of 47 households, and a school." Old photographs however, show that, although there is an apparent aura of dilapidation, and destitution, amongst the inhabitants, it is no worse than other areas of that time. Indeed, one of the most frequently produced postcard photographs, purporting to show the 'demolition of the Little Ireland cottages', and shown very recently in the local press, was also wrongly published as being taken of old cottages being demolished in Churchtown, much later when the village of 'Little Ireland' was demolished in 1904. It was also said that the small community was unable to integrate with other local people, but my grandfather promoted a different story altogether, as he said that on many occasions, he had attended the small school-cum church services, and described how even as a boy, he had walked through the sandhills from 'Little London' to 'Little Ireland', and Bank Nook, as well as Marshside. He always said he felt sorry for the inhabitants, who were no doubt treated as 'foreigners' by the Marshsiders in the late 19th century. He was quite correct when he pointed out that Marshside itself, was comparatively a new place, as indeed it was, and made the somewhat startling observation that the Little Irelanders "had been there longer than them, (the Marshsiders), and "us" meaning the Rimmers!

These sort of observations of grandad Rimmer have stayed in my memory, and have formed the basis of many reseaches into local history. The apparent demise of 'Little Ireland' therefore, appears to have been completed when Southport's Municipal History commenced with the establishment of the Improvement Commission, when a period of improvements, included the boundary extension of 1865, of the Hesketh Park area to the north. Among the places taken in was "Little Ireland', "a colony of labouring people, among the sandhills of the north shore near the 'New Inn". The 'New Inn' was then described as being the "Fleetwood Arms, built around 1840, a favourite objective for walkers along the shore."

The Hesketh Golf Club was founded in 1885, but as the Little Ireland site was only cleared officially in 1904, or thereabouts, it could explain the incorporation of a couple of cottages in the golf complex. The great sandbank, on which the Hesketh Golf Club still stands at the southern end of the ridge, contains a large sandhill at its northern end, separated by a valley, which was cut through, to house various buildings, and equipment, for the links maintenance. On the isolated hill there is a two storeyed house, rather large for a greenkeeper's residence, for which purpose it now serves. It has no doubt been renovated several times, as it is in excellent condition. I visited this building in June 1990, and the lady of the house, without any prompting whatsoever, as they had only been in residence for about 3 years, told me she was given to understand that the building had formerly been a school. This then, would seem in some respect, to confirm my belief, handed down to me, by both my grandfather, and my mother, that this building was the school cum-church that my grandfather visited. The lady also said she knew that the area had once been a village, inhabited by Irish people, and again without any prompting, confirmed another story of my mother's, that a few yards across the first hole of the course, behind 'Cockle Dick's Cottage', there was a cottage still there, buried under a sandhill. The road to the Hesketh Club house is an offshoot of Cockle Dick's Lane. Also, whilst we are in this corner, I must mention that whilst we would meander through the sandhills after calling at 'Cockle Dick's', on the way to Bank Nook, my mother said there were strawberries growing wild at one time in the area. I'm sorry we didn't take all her stories for granted, but it has transpired since, that strawberries were grown there, in the middle of the 19th century, and were sold in Southport's first hotels, but this was when the Blundell's were in residence at Cockle Dick's Cottage. As the Botanic Gardens were once known as 'Strawberry Gardens', no wonder I was confused. The romantic story of 'Cockle Dick' and his wife being childhood sweethearts was also true. Unaware of the 200 year time gap, I had been scared of the tale that "Dick was crooked backed, and would wave a stick at anyone who called after him" didn't seem to fit either, but later information tells us that it was an attack of the old rheumatics, that had caused his disfigurement, due to hard work. He and his wife hawked the shrimps, and the cockles (the expertise in the procuring of the latter which gave him his cognomen), to Preston and Ormskirk markets. As one of our contemporaries, also humped back with hard work, said to us, "Hard work ne'er kilt' 'onybody, but it sure tarn's some o' us quare shapes!"

There is however the other 'little' community in the area, 'Little London', whose existence is well established, and documented, as I have quoted earlier, as being in official records in 1488/9. I have explained its foundation, and its function in the commercial activities of the north west area.

'Little London' was described as a hamlet, which grew up in the vicinity of St. Lukes Station, on the ancient Romano-British, bridle path trackway, known as 'Kirkgate' or Churchgate, in its full length from Birkdale to Churchtown. It was so named by the early North Meols settlers, probably the Rimmers, as the name is derived from the West Norse word 'gata' — a way, in the same way that Meanygate 'common way', occurs in many places, as a 'roadway', in the old Martin Mere area. Churchgate was a field path, which connected Birkdale, to Churchtown, by 'Snuttering Lane', (now Cemetery Road), which was so named by Birkdale Rimmers, from the North Meols 'Snoterpool' derivation. It also meant a 'boundary', in this case the Birkdale boundary, in the vicinity of Boundary Street, stretching to the shore, which was at one time skirted by the 'Kirkgate'. Although it changed its name in many places, it was an old Romano Vistula-British trackway, which, in its full length, ran from Warrington's Roman Road to Penwortham. In some places, even in my grandfathers time, it was only a narrow track between sandhills.

'Little London' was shown on Yates map of 1786, as being in existence before Southport's beginnings. Previously on Bankes' map of 1736, there appears to be no habitation, and no evidence of the Tithebarn, which was known to have been there. Early maps, in many instances however, are very unreliable, as Bankes' map only consisted of a survey of the Bold estate, so it must be assumed that 'Little London' was part of the Hesketh property. Next to the site of the St. Lukes railway station, there are still two houses named 'Rose Hill', and just behind, on the corner of Kensington Road, and Windsor Road, is the London Hotel, which was probably built on the site of an old fisherman's inn, which was demolished, in conjunction with some small cottages in the 1890s, to make way for new residential property. It has been generally supposed that the present Blue Anchor Inn, formerly the 'Anchor Inn', and the 'Rope and Anchor', was the first established Inn in 'Little London', but as the Rose Hill area was adjudged to be nearer to the 'Kirkgate', it is probable that the London Hotel is on the oldest site.

'Little London' once had its own place of worship, situated alongside the 'Kirkgate', which ran up St. Luke's Road, then through Marsden Road, and Grange Road. This 'Mission Hall' was probably the one replaced by St. Lukes Church, in 1878-80. As the Mission Hall was only built in 1869, it could have been built on the site of a more ancient place of worship. It is assumed that Marsden Road, was named after the Rev. W. N. Marsden, who was made vicar designate, in 1877, and held the living until 1903. He was notable for establishing St. Lukes as the most Anglo Catholic of Southport churches, with the creation of this new parish. As a composite village, Little London was doomed when it was decimated by the building of the Southport—Manchester railway, and St. Lukes Station in 1855. There seems to be little, or no, reference to the Tithebarn, which was one of several in the district. It was probably not of such worthy note as the others, which were mainly used for corn and hay. The 'Little London' Tithebarn, however was used mainly for the storage of the fleeces, sheared from the flanks of the sheep which grazed on the coastal marshes. This activity served to associate 'Londheye' with the London wool merchants, who came to collect the raw wool, to be dressed and woven for the European market, forerunner no doubt, of the present day, EEC. The tithebarn site has never been located, but I believe it was situated near the corner of Tithebarn Road, and Hawkshead Street, probably on the site of Outram's Bakery, which brings the area of Meols Cop into reckoning as a place of some importance, lying near the junction with Long Lane, (Wennington Road), then the main road to Ormskirk, and Liverpool. Meols Cop was then, only a very boggy track across the marsh, to Scarisbrick. Meols Cop seems to be another district largely ignored by historians, not being claimed to be in High Park, or Blowick, but it was an important junction for traffic in all directions. When the Rimmers started to move away from the 'Snoterpool', quite a number moved to 'Little London', which was by then a thriving community. Tithe Barn Road was originally Tithe Barn Lane, leading to Rose Hill, St. Lukes, to join 'Snuttering Lane'. The hub of the community would appear to be the part of 'Snuttering Lane', which became Barton Street, then afterwards St. Lukes Road. Many of the Rigby members of the family settled here, and along the lane that became Hart Street, which led to Blowick, and Ormskirk, via Foul Lane. They retained their sea-going activities however, and served as lifeboatmen. I have stated earlier, my Granny's connection with the lifeboat Rigby's. My grandad's side of the Rimmers did not move very far inland, as my mother was born on a farm at the corner of Wennington Road. They subsequently moved to what was thought to be the first, or one of the first houses built in Bispham Road, No. 149, from which they conducted their shrimping activities, six miles from the sea. My grandfather, as an Independent Methodist minister, was closely connected with the Zion Independent Chapel, on the corner of St. Lukes Road and Sussex Road, where his marriage took place. It was called the 'Fishermen's Chapel' and was built in 1874, to replace the original 'Fishermen's Chapel' in Hawkshead Street, which was built in 1862. The Zion Chapel was rebuilt in 1897, when a top was erected on the single storey chapel. My grandfather, and my mother, had lifelong connections with the Zion, my grandfather all his life, and my mother was in the choir, from the day the chapel was rebuilt, until the 1960s. The 'Little London' Rimmers inter-married with many other families, notably the Rigbys, Lloyds, Comstives, and Sutches. Also the Blundell family, who were scattered all over the north west district, were connected with 'Little London'. Gilbert Blundell, son of Miles Blundell, of Churchtown, who was born in 1710, lived in Little London, and Lytham, and married Hannah Rimmer, who died in 1751. It is certainly a true statement, that there is hardly a family in the north west area of Lancashire that does not contain a Rimmer in its ranks. No wonder the local historians gave them a wide berth in respect of geneology, they have to be considered separately in their connections with each individual family.

There was further extended expansion, and intermarriage, in the 18th century. For instance the Hooton family I have mentioned before as relatives, were outright 'foreigners', having originated from Patricroft. Thomas Hooton, a grandson of the William who first arrived in the district, was born in 1728, married Jane Rymer, of Marshside, who was born in 1733. They were married on the 21st January, 1753-54, when Thomas was described on the marriage certificate as a 'Weaver of Marshside'. It was their son John, however, who was born in 1758, who was credited with the introduction of handloom, weaving into North Meols during the 1790s. John was described in an obituary notice in 1836, when he died in Churchtown aged 78, as a man of "great ingenuity, and kindness" and, as the Preston Pilot newspaper went on, "who introduced cotton weaving into the parish of North Meols, about forty six years ago, and, although he had at the time much opposition to contend with, both from the farmers, and the landowners, he lived to see upwards of a 1000 looms at work, within his native parish." He received reassurance from Miss Bold, who was always known as 'Lady Bold', at North Meols, in the early stage of his work, that he had her approval, but opposition came from the Lords of the Manor of North Meols, banning the erection of any cotton mill in the area. In the implementing of this directive, which led to the decline of the cotton industry, I find that there is proof that the clause to this effect was only added, in ink, to the standard, printed leases, from about 1790 on, until, a few years later, it was embodied as a standard clause. It was John's wife, Ellen, who died aged 22, and is reputed to have stated on her death-bed, according to the historian Bland, that she would die happy because she was leaving behind her, "descendants, exactly the same in number, as those of Jacob, who accompanied the Patriarch into Egypt. Reach for your Bibles ye of little faith," this would appear to be an extraordinary statement unless, being well schooled by her Rymer mother-in-law, in Biblical history, she was referring to a long lost tribe, of which she was a member, who had once been led into Egypt by the Patriarch Abram, born in 2160 B.C., who as Abraham, grandfather of Jacob, became the "father of many nations."

Although the Hootons were associated with Patricroft, and John, no doubt, went there to gain experience, his baptism appears in the parish register, so there is no doubt that he was from a well established local family.

That family links can lie hidden for many years, and through many generations, can be indicated by my own personal experience, for when I was married in 1938, I was taken to task because I had not invited any member of the Hooton family, as a relative. I was acquainted, sure enough with a great number of High Park people, but on-one had ever told me they were relatives. This illustrates the difficulty anyone faces in tracing, even contemporary history, of such a taciturn bunch as the Rimmers, small wonder no-one has ever attempted to piece it together. I am doubly thankful therefore that this is only a 'saga', a story, and not an historical record.

CHAPTER 6

RIMMERS IN BIRKDALE — AINSDALE — FORMBY

Chapters seven and eight of 'Betwixt Ribbel and Moerse' afford perhaps a somewhat condensed history of Birkdale, Ainsdale, and Formby, from Scandinavian times. It is difficult to separate the development of all three places, but in later years, with the expansion of the Rimmers from the 'Snoterpool' areas, we can get a clearer picture by records that are available. Maps from the middle of the 16th century, until late in the 18th century, did not show the villages of Birkdale or Ainsdale. As stated on page 47 and 48, Bowens map of 1720, and the Morden map I had in my possession, show only the road to Formby, the old Danesgate (Deansgate). The Morden map incidentally, a genuine one, printed in 1700, I have presented to the Botanic Museum, as it is now 200 years old. None of these maps give more than an indication that the coastline consisted of anything but sandhills. Later maps and surveys, commissioned by the various landowners, are very deceptive, as they only show their individual holdings.

The intermingling of the Norse-Scandinavian and Anglo-Saxons, which took place in Birkdale, Ainsdale, and Formby area, in the later seventeenth, and eighteenth centuries, led to a more accurate record of the Rimmers, who, from their original Norse occupation of the 'Snoterpool' area, had previously lived in small hamlets, with fields enclosing their small farmsteads, dispersed over a wide area. They had no churches, or memorial halls, to form centres of villages. The Anglo Saxons, living further south, occupied larger, compact villages, with open fields. Birkdale and Ainsdale therefore, represented a more scattered nature of settlement, contrasting with North Meols, and Halsall, grouped around church, and manorial buildings.

With the improvement of communications and records therefore, we get a clearer picture of the Rimmer influence on the area, except for the ever present difficulty of distinguishing one Rimmer, Rymor, or Rimor, from another.

In case you might be of the opinion that I have hitherto presented a picture of the Rimmers as a pious, temperate, God fearing, Bible carrying, nomadic tribe (which they no doubt were, with quite a few exceptions), let me present one of the earliest records of their Birkdale activities. The earliest record of an ale house keeper in Birkdale, was William Rymer, who, in December 1627, was charged to appear at the Quarter Sessions, for "harbouring rogues, and receiving stolen goods." I can find no record however of the charge being substantiated, but it does appear that intermingling, and intermarriage, was having its influence of their fortunes and habits.

To illustrate the confusion that arises in the Rimmer surname, there appears a record of Gilbert Rymer, a Birkdale mariner, who died in, or about 1694, quoted as one of the wealthiest men in the village, with his inventory totalling £90, which was probably one of the largest recorded for 25 years. He had livestock, husbandry gear, and goods, considered to be in the luxury class. It is not clear whether he was the Gilbert Rymer who made up his will in 1739, disposing of a very large wardrobe of clothing. There is no record of his burial in local records, so it was presumed that he died on his journeys. However there is a record that there was the burial of a Gilbert Rymer, aged 92, which took place in or about 1793, which inadvertently confused historians, who also recorded another Gilbert Rymer, who died aged 91. There had also been another Gilbert Rymmer, who was listed as paying Hearth Tax in Birkdale in 1664. There was another Gilbert Rymer, who was making up an inventory in 1737, who was probably the 1739 Gilbert. So confusing were even the indexes in history books, that when I wrote 'Betwixt Ribbel and Moerse', although it appeared to be a new departure, I included no index for the text, and placed page references to all the photographs, which, especially in the case of the chapter on ancient stone crosses, proved to be very successful, especially in the case of field studies.

Another deciding factor, was the name of my grandfather Robert Rimmer. The task of tracing all the Roberts in the Rimmer tribe, would try the patience of Job.

Although Birkdale is not mentioned in the Domesday records, it was recorded in Cockersands Abbey Chartulary, round about 1200, and subsequently had its name changed several times. As I explain in chapter seven of 'Betwixt Ribbel and Moerse', it was known by its Scandinavian derivation of Birk (birki) — Birch copse, and Dalr — (dale), and was formerly part of a place called Erengermeles. Eringer was a Norse personal name, and Mel or Mels, is Icelandic for sand hills, overgrown with stargrass. This was later called Argarmeols, of which Birkdale was only a part. Argameols was reputed to have been washed away by the sea in the 14th century. When the Rimmers established communication by way of Snuttering Lane, Birkdale was pronounced variously, as Birtle, Bertel, and Berkel.

By the year 1680, the women were getting into the act, as Margaret and Katrine Rimmer, left clothes in wills, and in 1682, Margaret Rymer, also from Birkdale, left property to be preserved as family heirlooms in perpetuity. Furniture in particular, in those days, was highly prized, as were all goods and chattels. The furniture too, being made of solid oak, was practical, and if uncomfortable, very long lasting.

In 1684 Richard Rymer, a mariner, paid £20 for a new lease of a house, consisting of one bay and a down dubb, with outbuildings. It is not clear who looked after the land, as he often went to sea, combining the two occupations, because he was a bachelor. This farm appears to be across the southern boundary of Birkdale and Ainsdale, and covered approximately 6 acres.

Another factor, adding to the confusion occasioned by the Hearth Tax, was the Window Tax, which was imposed at the end of the 17th century. This explains why cottages had small sliding sash type windows, with small rectangular panes. Glass, including mirrors, was very expensive. Bay windows, and large mirrors, were largely the perogative of the wealthiest inhabitants. As early as 1699, almost as soon as the tax was in force, Thomas Rimmer, although he was living in North Meols, petitioned that he had been over-assessed for window tax on property he owned in Birkdale.

Rabbit warrens were another aspect of local industry, as an important agricultural improvement. It is not known exactly when they were introduced into Europe by the Normans, who intended to rear them in captivity, solely for profit. They were, from about the middle of the 17th century, established by the landowners of the north west, particularly in coastal areas, as a welcome, and natural source, of food and fur. The warrens were protected by ditches and fences, controlled by keepers, or 'coneymen' who acquired this cognomen from the animals they controlled. The original name 'rabbit', was only used to indicate a small animal, and the coney was full grown one. Over the subsequent years the names appear to have been completely reversed. Just as well, as it would have seemed rather incongruous to us, as youngsters, to refer to one of our own local characters as 'Coney' instead of 'Rabbit Lucy'! Further investigation into this aspect of the 'Warreners', has elicited the information that 'Rabbit' is a derivation from the French language, brought over and used by the Normans, subsequent to the Domesday survey. The derivation 'Coney' however was adopted by the Rimmers, directly from the Bible, from Proverbs Chapter 30 and verse 20 "The Conies are but a feeble folk, yet they made their houses in the rocks." The conies referred to in the Bible were small creatures, about the size of a rabbit called Lyrax, or 'rock badger' or 'dassie' which is Dutch for 'badger'. They seemed to be a mixture of several species, including the marmots, living in crevices of rocky outcrops of rocks, in the sandy desert. The term 'Rabbit' therefore was only used when wild coneys were cultivated.

Some warrens were leased out, for instance Thomas Rymer of Birkdale, in 1700, leased warrens for terms up to seven years, paying £8 per annum after the first year. He was required to supply 80 couples of coneys per year, to Henry Blundell. Quite a large number of Rimmers were listed on maps and deeds, in the subsequent years, as this was an occupation well within their capabilities, and liking for open air activity. They had the official title of 'Coneyman', being listed as such, on all official references. There was naturally, a great deal of poaching, with severe fines for stealing from a warren, instead of taking wild rabbits. However, when a claim, made in the early part of the 18th century, that killing rabbits that were consuming corn on the private farmland was justified, it put a different complexion on the whole of the industry, which began to decline after the 18th century.

There was a Thomas Rimmer, who was the builder of the Ash Tree Hotel, in the mid-eighteenth century, on the site of the present Portland Hotel, whose land to the south held, what was probably the largest, warren in the area. It is not clear whether his near relatives, or his immediate family held this warren, which appears to stretch to Carr Lane, and on to the Ainsdale Windmill, which lay across the Birkdale-Ainsdale boundary, but this warren was the furthest one east from the shore, lying just off Wham Lane, (Stamford Road) near the 'Isle of White' farm, on the peaty edge of Martin Mere.

One interesting connection with the Rimmers, and the warrens, appears in the changing of names. The hollows in the sandhills between the warrens are normally referred to today, as 'slacks'. The Rimmers formerly called these slacks, 'Branks' (changing at Formby Hall into the 'Bronc'), which was preserved in the name of a group of cottages running along a track across the warrens, at the southern end of Birkdale Common, to a group of cottages at Carr Lane. The name of the cottages was 'Brank's End', which name, although I have been unable to trace, I believe to be a Scandinavian derivation, introduced by the Rimmers.

On Bankes 1736 map, on the road or trackway, afterwards named Hawes Side Lane, running from the coastal sandhills, opposite an area called the 'New Marsh', which was later incorporated with South Hawes, into Southport, there is a large area ref. 6.0.29, on the north side of the track, designated 'James Rimer Coneyman'. On the whole, Birkdale, consisting of fifty per cent sandhills, contained perhaps the largest number of warrens. However, the area I have just described, was actually the one I saw listed at Meols Hall, in the handwriting, in a notebook, of Frances Hesketh, relating to the lease of the "Rabbit Warren" for twelve years, or a minimum of ten years, beginning on the 5th November 1784, for a rent of £25 11s 6d. This hamlet can be identified as Haws Side. A fragment of Hawes Side Lane, is Hawesside Street, which is only shown on Yates map of 1786. It was a continuation of Row Lane, through a settlement called 'Horse Houses', which appears on a headstone in St. Cuthbert's Churchyard inscribed "South Hawes W.B. 1728". There were other Rimmers connected with this area, as well as James Rimer. This is not very far from the hamlet of 'Little London'. Records show that, as is the general case in the district, the ubiquitous Rimmers, once again, comprised the larger numbers, when South Hawes subsequently became part of Southport.

Although the Rimmers were the most numerous of the population, spreading out along the North West coastline, and inland for a considerable distance, it has to be said that, with doubtless increasing prosperity, their self-contained, clannish attitude, and reluctance to become involved in outside current affairs, became increasingly mellowed as the centuries rolled on.

Although there can be found some Parish records of Poor Relief in the area, as far back as the 17th century, the overall impression gained, is that local parish support was of a very low order.

It is to the credit of the Rimmers, that I can find very little reference therefore, to an independent Relief for the poor, set up as Peter Rymers 'Benefaction for the Poor' of North Meols. What form it took, or how it was administered, I do not know, but reluctance on this score, would be typical of the Rimmers, with their biblical attitude to general existence. I am of the opinion that it was inaugurated to offset the Elizabethan Poor Act of 1601, which made a decree, that each parish was responsible for its poor.

By the middle of the 17th century, some funds were being raised in the various parishes, in the form of a 'poor rate'. The money was used to help the very poor, the sick, the old, and the orphans. No one however, who was likely to become chargeable to the parish, was allowed to settle, and was removed back to their own parish. By the end of the 17th century, further abhorrent measures were introduced.

It was then declared that paupers were to be identified by a large red or blue, letter P, on a badge, on the right shoulder, in some districts outside North Meols. I'm not sure whether this was in Birkdale, or Ainsdale, or Formby or all three, but I remember noting this when the Jews in Germany, prior to World War Two, were treated in a similar fashion, when pogrom, not poverty, was in vogue.

No doubt there are plenty of records of individual benefactors supplying funds for churches and schools, but I think the Rimmers would be disturbed, to say the least, that poor relief was so neglected. No doubt a tightly knit community, such as they had been, looked after their own, but now they had spread out along the coast, they became more conscious of conditions around them. From records which are scanty, but nevertheless provable, charitable funds had been appropriated, as in one instance, reported in the Quarter Sessions at Ormskirk in 1678, a churchwarden, thought to have been one of the Rimmer clan, sought to obtain an order to compel the Rector of North Meols, a man of substance, who had purloined funds in the region of £10 intended for poor relief, to make restitution to the community.

Although, generally speaking, the Biblical exhortation in respect of the giving of alms to "let not the left hand know what the right hand does", would be no doubt adhered to, probably incidents like the above, would tend to encourage a more official approach to charitable bequests, to ensure that charitable funds reached the lawfully appointed recipient. As an instance, after a few bequests had been made, Katrine Rymer, of Birkdale, in her will dated 1680, left the proceeds of the residue of her estate "to the poor of Birkdale".

There were many other cases of parish officials, affording low support to those in need, in the 17th Century, with cases of relief being delayed to aged people for instance, even when law threatened action, until in many cases, relief was only paid for a limited time. In one particular instance, an Ainsdale couple, in their nineties, residents for over 40 years, both blind, only received aid a few months before they died. In many cases in Ainsdale and Formby, relief was only available by the generosity of neighbours. Many cases were too harrowing for people to record. Against this sort of background, it was recorded that about 1775, at least eight men and women of Birkdale, were receiving money from Peter Rymer's North Meols Benefaction. Charity would appear to "begin at home" when Thomas Rymer, a tailor from Birkdale, was receiving money from Peter Rymer's Benefaction about 1778, but I only quote this to show that the Rimmer's had poverty problems amongst their own as well.

In the history relating to the Rimmers in Birkdale, it is interesting to note the sequence of events concerning four 'cottages for the poor', owned by the Birkdale Township, standing on 'Little Common'. Although now reduced to two cottages, these are still standing in Sandon Road, but the school, which succeeded the first 'own school house on the common' built with the aid of the villagers in 1769, has now been replaced by a house and modern building complex, Ashton Court.

Around the year 1814, it was reported that the cottages were in a state of great disrepair, but owing to the general increase in poor relief, they were not attended to, until about 1816, when only a small amount of a few pounds was spent on them. What does surprise me however, is the fact that in 1814, one of the cottages was occupied by two old women, one was Nancy Ball, and the other was the mother of James Rimmer, of the Ash Tree Inn built in 1790. Unless living accommodation at the Inn was limited, it is possible that he would have at least been required to assist her, because neither women received any weekly pay, but only rent, and probably turves, or coal, provided for heating. In some years they had received a weekly poor relief payment of about 1/6d, and shoes, and potatoes. I cannot reconcile the accounts entry, that a Margaret Rymer was provided with 'bedsteads and shifts costing 14s, is the same woman, because of the change in surnames, but this again was not an unusual thing. When the Poor Law Act Amendment came into force in 1830, the parishes of Lancashire, south west of the Ribble, came under the control of the Ormskirk Union, and the situation in Birkdale, as regards poor relief, deteriorated, as application had to be made to Ormskirk, and Birkdale was now in the Formby district, and we all know to this day, about the 'Ormskirk Workhouse'! I had to quote these particulars, not very long ago, to substantiate a statement, made by an inhabitant of North Birkdale, that it had once been a district of Formby.

Under this new ruling, legislation decreed that the cottages could no longer fulfil their original function. There is no record of their actual disposal, but certainly in her will made in 1840, a Mary Rimmer had bequeathed them to her children, but there is nothing to show that she actually occupied any of them.

By 1845, the four cottages were made into two, one of them being occupied by James Ball, a stonemason, with his daughter Alice, and son-in-law, Richard Bradshaw, who was the ninth child of the Bradshaws, who were living in the cottages in 1814. Don't go away now you've got this far, but the story gets worse, because James Ball himself, was the son of parents who were paupers of the then landlord of the Ash Tree Inn, Thomas Rymer.

Was it not true then, that his mother-in-law was in another of the cottages in 1814?

On top of all this, the next door neighbour to James Ball, was Henry Ball, who does not appear to be related to James Ball, but he was related to Richard Bradshaw by marriage. Richard lived in his cottage with his young wife, who seemed to be occupied as a servant in one of the local houses, and he also had his mother-in-law living with them, who was supposed to be a 'table mat maker'. All these various interchanges of families, and fortunes, would appear to 'cock a snook' at the prevailing rule in the Marshside area, at the other end of the district, that to marry a 'foreigner' was to incur the penalty of ostracism.

Certainly it is difficult to realise that the cottages today, splendidly refurbished and redecorated, were the worst on the 'Little Birkdale Common', nearly two centuries ago.

In 1789, Thomas Rymer, of Birkdale was classified as 'poor', which to me appears to be a complete anachronism for, as far as I can make out, he was the only blacksmith recorded in Birkdale. Carpenters and joiners, were recorded in Birkdale from the eighteenth century, to the nineteenth century, as is evidenced by tool inventories, taken at various times, for will bequests.

It becomes increasingly difficult, as time and records progress, to separate the various districts from one another. Take the millers for instance. In North Meols, records are clear and concise, with only two mills in their existence of several centuries, with their successive ownerships being well defined.

In Birkdale however, the mill does not appear to be as large, or as successful, as either the North Meols or Ainsdale Mill (run successfully at one time by the Rymers, I might add). Although very attractive in appearance, being a wooden sailed, post or peg mill, and no doubt a feature of the landscape, to travellers passing over the North Meols to Birkdale Boundary, along Snuttering Lane. It therefore became the subject of artists, of all ranks, because it stood on a sandhill, with open views of the surrounding countryside. It had to be decorated by a compulsory order, every year, and maintained its own lime kiln for this purpose, as were all the farms in the district. It was only a second hand mill, purchased from Kirkham in the Fylde, and was erected in about the period of 1750-1790. The miller turned the whole mill by hand, to face the wind, by means of a great long post, no mean task. The mill was situated, on, or near Snuttering Lane, near the corner of Mosley Street and Upper Aughton Road. There is apparently no connection with the Rimmers and this mill. The ouput of this mill, constructed for the inhabitants of old Birkdale, was inadequate, consistent with late development, and the Ainsdale Mill was employed to serve both communities.

In respect of the Rimmers I am interested in this area, because of the somewhat vague tradition of the preaching of John Wesley, on the nearby Birkdale Common. What can be established however, is the fact, that before the ban of non-conformists was lifted, there were meetings held in Nanny Ball's cottage, not far from the mill. James Rimmer and others, had preachings there, in the mornings, which concluded in time for them to get to North Meols, along the Churchgate, for public worship at St. Cuthbert's. This was before, and after, the period about 1765-70, when John Wesley was reputed to have held services in the district. I think this cottage was in the Grove Street area, which has many historic connections with Birkdale's history. It is also significant that my grandad had a strong connection with the Mission Hall on the Boundary Street-Fernley Road corner. Fernley Road was named after John Fernley, a great Southport benefactor (1797-1873), a native of Stockport, who came to Southport in 1859, due to his wife's ill health. She was the Eliza, of Lifeboat disaster fame, daughter of the prominent Manchester Methodist, James Wood. Within 25 years, Southport had nine Methodist churches. In this corner of Birkdale, John Fernley built, or contributed to the construction of, significantly enough the Wesley Church in Aughton Road, and the complete cost of Trinity Church in Duke Street, which had been preceeded by a 'Free Breakfast' Mission Centre at 'Ecclesfield', which was a district, or hamlet, in Fisher Lane, near St. Pauls Church. Ecclesfield was the name given to this Mission Church, the foundation of which was laid in 1862, in the barren sandhills near the River Nile bank, which was then still partly navigable. It flourished to a large congregation, before it was probably absorbed into South Hawes, the earliest reference to which, appears on the gravestone, at St. Cuthbert's in 1728, but it was listed in the Parish Register as early as 1617 as, Haws. Peter Hodge was a well known character, who had a cottage near St. Pauls Church, and the Rimmers, Howards, Balls, Jacksons and Wrights, also had cottages in the early 18th century. The Rimmers have remained in this area until the present day. These native cottagers were farmers, fishermen, coney catchers and fowlers, were amongst those whom Bulpit asserts were credited, with some part, in the foundation of Southport, as they were not averse to adapting their cottages to dispense hospitality to visitors.

All this activity connected with Non-Conformism in this area, certainly indicates that if John Wesley had preached on Birkdale Common, and elsewhere in the district, Nanny Ball's cottage would be a likely base to operate from. The former Wesleyan Methodist Church, in Brighton Road, on the way to the Common, had also been a former Mission Chapel.

As listed in the Hearth Tax of 1666, there were 21 'householders' increasing to 27, in 1673. The population would then be about 150. There was only one house with two hearths, the population was then consisting of more than half of them being Rimmers, and we have followed the accounts of these records of Birkdale, and their progress into the 17th century.

As Birkdale was, in itself, only a part of the lost town of Argarmeols, its development was slow but steady. It had no memorial hall, but this would not worry the Rimmers at all, as their tribe had no such dwellings, since their sojourn in Scandinavia. It would be all the more appropriate therefore, to assess their progress in what was to become a more pemanent settlement for the majority, and a tapering off of their nomadic wanderings.

So indeed, this process we can find, from the various inventories, wills and deeds, and some permanent records. Even so, how difficult it is to pin the

Rimmers down. Take Nicholas Rimmer for instance, who appears in the Baldermeryhokes trial as a Rimor witness from Birkdale. He or, of course another Nicholas, appears in the Hearth Tax returns of 1664 as Nic Rymer. By the early 18th century, another Nicholas Rymer again this time, appears as one of the wealthiest men in Birkdale, with a larger than average house containing upper rooms, and loft storage, the crowning glory being in the form of proper stairs to the upper rooms, instead of the usual ladder. In the year 1726, Nicholas made a special bequest of a 'thacking' ladder to his son John, and if it's the same Nicholas, furnishings and cutlery in luxury status, to his wife Elizabeth, and also to John again, a clock and chair, all items indicative of the very well off in those days. If you think this is complex, try sorting out the Robert Rimmers, but I warn you, before you've finished the men in white coats will be around to collect you!

There are several Richard Rimmers, in records going back to the early days. One of the Richard Rimmers I was interested in, is the one listed as being at Underhill Farm, Birkdale, in the early 18th century. There are more than two Underhill Farms in the district, one on Birkdale Common. When I came to live in Birkdale in the late 1940s, at No. 12 Nixon's Lane, I became very friendly with the Barton family, who farmed Anderson's Farm, which is in Nixon's Lane, but on the moss, over the Halsall side of the Sandy Brook boundary. Tommy Barton, who gave me a lot of detail concerning the area, particularly about Aughton Hall, where he was born, gave me information concerning quite a few Rimmers in the district. One of these, many years ago had farmland, which was in the area across Liverpool Road, opposite Nixon's Lane. I had seen a cottage or farmhouse, at the rear of Birkdale Cemetery, very near to the Southport and Ainsdale golf course, but before I had time to investigate, it was demolished to make way for the playing field extensions of Windy Harbour Road school, (now Birkdale High School). Tommy Barton told me that it had been Underhill Farm, but there was nothing left by then. I have assumed from an inventory that has survived intact, that this was a fairly average farmholding, as the inventory listed mainly farming implements, with the luxury of the ownership of a clock, valued at £1.5s. as being the most notable item. One of the witness of the inventory was a Thomas Rimer.

Also demolished, around this time, was a cluster of old cottages to make way for houses in Ryder Crescent, and Windy Harbour Road, opposite the school. I had at first associated this small hamlet with a story I wrote about the 'Lost Farm', but later investigation showed that the site of the farm is exactly under Greenbank High School, in Hillside, near to the 'Fisherman's Path', passing between Hillside and Birkdale Golf Clubs, which has been used for hundreds of years, along the coast between the Rivers Douglas and the Alt. I have always hoped that some day the pupils at Greenbank, will put on a play concerning the 'Lost Farm', at least the location would be correct!

Whilst we have got away from the inevitable, but boring quotation of endless dates and statistics, for a moment let's get a breath of fresh air on what is left of the 'Hump' at Hillside, opposite the 'Round House', and if it's a clear day, observe at least half a dozen surrounding counties, and as happened one day, the Mountains of Mourne, in Ireland. You can see the site of Underhill Farm and 'The Lost Farm', but you will have to conjecture where Balshaw's Farm was in 1750. This was a big 'spread' with many bays to the outbuildings, consisting of barns, stable, sheep house, shippon and hay loft. It was contemporary to the 'Lost Farm' being in existence in 1749, but further inland, between Windy Harbour, and the 'Lost Farm'. In 1789, appears the only record I can find of the fishing Rimmers in the district, when Robert Rymer of 'Hillside', was the possessor of one of only two boats in the Birkdale-Ainsdale area, fishing was mainly done, without boats, from the shore. Sea fishing was dangerous, and boats were expensive items.

Not far away from here, we can pinpoint where the cottage of one of the most colourful characters of the Rimmer clan stood. This was on the site of Bickerton House School, in Bickerton Road, and belonged to old Harry Rimmer, known as 'Fiddler Harry'. He lived from 1742 to 1828, and, even when he was 80, he was still entertaining people on the 'green' in front of the cottage. Consistent with the development of Southport as a bathing resort over the years, Harry became a celebrity with the visitors, who came to seek out the gradually disappearing site of the 'Lost Farm'. Many visitors to the Sutton 'Dukes Folly', also called at Harry's, as being a contemporary 'fiddler'. Sutton in 1824, then 72, was still plying his fiddle, when Harry died in 1828, at the age of 86. Harry's fame reached a peak, when he was featured in the 1820's in a rhyme entitled 'Southport, alias North Meols'. It was written by a well known literary figure of the day, John Gregson, who wrote under the name of 'Gimcrack'. The long poem, describing all the other attractions of the Southport he knew so well, put the town, fairly and squarely, on the map as a holiday resort, and brought fame, if not fortune to Harry, who cared little for either, only his visitors, who he endeavoured to make, like himself, free, open hearted and generous. 'Buttered Peas' and 'Lads Thrashing Barley', were favourite tunes of Harry's, especially in the evening gloaming, when the 'tripping on the green', and the dancing started in earnest.

Over the years, the 'Lost Farm' became overgrown with blown sand, and by 1832 it was becoming a legend, as there was a "tradition that there was a farm in the neighbourhood of Birkdale, which had been totally buried". In 1848, it is known that donkey parties would go in search for the 'Lost Farm', and for some time, the tops of some fruit trees which grew in the garden, could still be seen. John Roby, in his Traditions of Lancashire (1831), made the farm the scene of a romantic legend, together with the 'Phantom Voice', set in the "humble lonely dwellings in the desolate sandhills."

Round about one hundred years after these events, I investigated the legends concerning the 'Lost Farm' which concerned the 'Scarlet Pimpernel' — like activities, of the Earl of Derwentwater, and found the true facts. Confirmation of the amazing, and mysterious events, consistent with the 'Legend', came from none other than Lady Mary, wife of Roger Fleetwood Hesketh, daughter of the Earl of Scarborough. As a child she had been a near neighbour at Lumley Castle, of the Derwentwater's descendants, and had spent many hours searching for the 'treasure' referred to in the story. She had been married, and come to live at Meols Hall in 1952. I remember we had a protracted discussion, across the top of a van, when we both arrived, at the same time, at my brother's cottage at 52 Botanic Road, when he was still employed at Meols Hall. I had set the events at the farm in 1746, but Lady Mary was of the opinion that the Earl of Derwentwater could not have been in the sandhills with the Derwentwater treasure, as he had been executed for participating in the Jacobite Rebellion in the year before. Then I produced documents to show that the man in hiding at the 'Lost Farm', was not the first Earl of Derwentwater, but his brother, who was the 'Titular' inheritor of the Derwentwaters. The estates however, had been sequestered by the King, and the Earl was on the run. We agreed then, that all the events and sequences were in order, and she was astonished to find that the 'treasure' they had been looking for all those years ago, had turned up with the Earl, in a farmhouse, in the Birkdale sandhills.

The full story, approved by Lady Mary, and accompanied by her photo, was afforded a large feature by Alan Pinch, then editor of the 'Southport Visiter'. It is in the scrapbook, which will eventually be placed, with all other material, in the Botanic Museum. A weird, but true, sequence of events, occurring two centuries ago. I would like at this juncture to make a more expansive comment upon the assistance afforded to me throughout the years by the local press. The continuity of effort afforded by Alan Pinch, to support and promote the cause of local History in our region has been invaluable, and this is still maintained today by the "All Our Yesterdays" section in the Southport Visiter, by Sue Webster. I have been writing Local History features published in all the local papers, throughout the Southport Journal, and Guardian days, from the 1930s onwards. In the middle 1970s, there appeared the feature 'Southport, Then and Now', which occasioned another full scrap book of 'The Southport Weeklys' series on local history. In the late 1980s, this was replaced by the present Southport and Ormskirk Star. As chief reporter and Editress of the Star, Angela Birchall, has inaugurated and sustained 'Birchall's Beat', which has completely revitalized our local history interests. Her promotion of 'Bewtixt Ribbel and Moerse', in a series of articles, has led to world wide interest, and the publication of several new issues, until the present day. She encouraged and stimulated local interest by the presentation of souvenir 'Beat' editions, to various civic societies, and has also done much to sustain initial group efforts, by encouraging different local history enthusiasts, such as Friends of Botanic Museum, and Friends of the Stray, with lectures, presentations, and promotion of historical jubilee celebrations. In addition I have been supported from the early days of John Scholes, Curator of the Botanic Museum in the 1940s, by the academic, and also practical assistance, afforded by him, and his subsequent successors, Geoff Burrows, and Steve Forshaw, and finally, by Anthony K. Wray, B.A.(Hons.); (I always address him with his full qualifications). Without his expertise, above and beyond the call of duty, much of the content of this book could not have been written. I am therefore delighted at his recent promotion to Keeper of Art Galleries and Museums, for the Metropolitan Borough of Sefton.

It would not, I think, be out of order to mention the late Mr. C. Broadhurst, of C. K. Broadhurst's Bookshop in Market Street, and Jack Sankey and Lennie Hardman of that establishment, who have afforded me, not only patronage, but sound advice, for over the past decade. In similar fashion, so too have William Bailey, and the late Michael Walker, of the Bibliographic Services Department of the Metropolitan Borough of Sefton, dispensed something more than just patronage, in our negotiations.

Jean and Jim Borsey, Mike Griffin, Charles Bond and David Sallabanks of Crompton and Little, who are publishers, and printers of both books, have exercised not only experienced expertise, but great patience in my direction, but at least they have had some recompense in the recognition of their company now, as having achieved full publication and print status, in both national and international, areas of distribution, in the Standard Book Numbering Agency field. I make no apologies for breaking into this story in this unorthodox manner, as it is the usual practice to, quite deservedly so, make such acknowledgements separately.

I did not, in this instance, feel that I should confine them to the periphery of this book, but as a tribute to their combined efforts on behalf of Local History, between the Ribble and Mersey, place them where they rightly belong, in the centre.

So here we still are, in this story or 'saga', standing on the 'Hump' at Hillside. The 'Hump', now only a shallow sandhill, was in our early days, very large, the highest point in Southport. It was always associated, rather romantically in my memory, with a burial tumulus. I can remember sliding down the hill at considerable speed (tin tray if you hadn't got a tobaggan). There was much protracted discussion and drawing up of plans, before the Second World War, to erect some sort of a monument on the top, which would be a landmark to mariners in Liverpool Bay.

However the 'Round House' situated across the road, became the focal point instead. It was built by Luke Highton in 1924-25, and was memorable for an extraordinary collection of the worlds leading astronomers for the total eclipse of the sun in 1927, being one of the few spots in the world where it could be observed. It also had then, an observation dome. We had to make do with pieces of smoked glass, on the rubbish tip by the Aerodrome Hangars, at the top of Hesketh Road. I have been in this house several times, once during the war, when it was in a state of disrepair and empty. I was offered it for £1725, chance would be a fine thing! There was vegetation growing in the fireplace on the ground floor. We didn't think much of my mam's story that it had been built by a former sea captain, who being at sea most of his life didn't want to dwell in a building which had corners in the rooms! I believe the price dropped to a few hundred pounds, but it was only renovated after the war.

Just before we leave the 'hump', take a look north to the Ribble, and South to the Mersey. You are truly 'Betwixt Ribbel and Moerse' and let me expound to you, a not so wild theory concerning a never ending popular theme "What, or who, constitutes a Sandgrounder?" Answers range from being 'True Jannock' locals, as opposed to well to do 'incomelings, or outsiders'. Or were they just "born with sand in their shoes", or the qualification of "having *both* parents born in Southport?".

There is however one other derivation of a true 'Sandgrounder' when you cast your eyes upon the 'Fisherman's Path', which you can still tread to the North to Formby Point and the River Alt, as they did long ago, entirely through the sand, between the rabbit warrens and the sea. When the Rimmer clan came to these shores in the wake of the Vikings, they eventually spread to the North, as far as the River Douglas, and to the South eventually to link up with other Viking settlements around the River Alt, before the River Mersey was formed. The River Douglas was named by the Vikings as the 'Askr', after the 'sacred apples' (associated later with King Arthur on Martin Mere) which they always carried in their long boats.

In the course of time, the 'Askr', or 'Ash Tree', became the Astland, and through the centuries the area became well known as 'the sand land', and at places like Crossens and Banks, and eventually at Marshside. The number of sheep for instance was limited, according to a person's means. This method was also adopted gradually south, to Birkdale, Ainsdale, and Formby, as far as the River Alt, adopted by name from the term, 'Alet Fl' of Roman times.

So, according to old legend a 'Sandgrounder' must be born on sand, "Betwixt Alt and Astland". An interesting theory is it not? I don't know how far the Rimmers go in this one, but it wouldn't be surprising if it emanated from them, as they were the most prolific of the populations, of the areas mentioned.

I have for a long time had a romantic notion, that the visualization of the 'Fisherman's Path' being completely restored, in its entire length, between the Askyr in the North, to the Alt in the South, might one day become an established fact. I have promoted the idea of this project to various ecological, and conservationist bodies, at various intervals. Perhaps the time is not too far distant when this project, and the Martin Mere-Brow excavation, can be as successfully accomplished as the restoration of the lifeboat was, after over 60 years of campaigning.

There were quite a number of Rimmers who took up residence in the Everton Road (formerly Mill Street) — St. Peters Road (formerly Church Road) district known as 'Birkdale North End', but it has never been very clear to me as to the location of each Rimmer. The only building extant, and preserved as a listed dwelling, is the cottage on the corner of Crosby Road and Liverpool Road. It is a 15th century farmhouse of the usual cruck constructed, clan slap and daub, cum cow manure method, associated with many similar structures in the area. It has had a somewhat chequered existence, as a farm, and an Inn. There were several families in occupation, over the years, right up to the present, in 1973, when a James Rimmer was still in occupation. This is probably the oldest building in the district. Rimmers and Rymers, were two of the families. In the early 17th century it was recorded as being an Inn. I think I can recall when James Rimmer ran a taxi service, or some sort of a hire car concern, and Mrs. Catherine Rimmer was a midwife, or nurse of some description. They were notable as being somewhat eccentric, for they had no gas, electricty, and no water inside, as I think I can remember they had a water tap in the yard. How the taxi service operated with any degree of efficiency, is hard to conjecture, for it was only by virtue of the exigencies of Catherine's occupation, that a telephone had to be installed. As, quite naturally, they were some sort of relatives, I would only be about 15 years younger than Mr. Rimmer. Perhaps, with hindsight, considering the exhorbitant charges today, for the three main services, they were not so daft in resisting the march of 'progress', to the last possible moment, particularly as, having a well in the front garden, the erection of a mains water tap in the rear of the building would be a complete anachronism, as Catherine refused to have it installed inside the cottage.

The development which was taking place in the Birkdale area, and elsewhere, up the coast, along the length of the Churchgate, and Snuttering Lane trackway, was, when it reached Birkdale, more in the nature of rebuilding, because of the loss of three towns on the north west coast, in the 1328 earthquake, an account of which has been published, and will be added later to this story of the Rimmer tribe.

Still in the north end of Birkdale, there is a record, by virtue of his published will, of Thomas Rymer, in the middle of the 18th century, occupying North End House, which was the next farm to 'The Cottage' of James Rimmer in Liverpool Road.

In conjunction with Birkdale Mill, which reached the area by way of Mill Lane (now Everton Road) the North End area became quite a large development. Squire Henry Halsall had a Manor House/Farm, built in 1583, for his agent, Gilbert Rymer, which was rebuilt in 1861, and is thought to be the North End Farm later occupied by Gilbert Rimmer. This area was behind St. Peter's Road, round about where numbers 7-9 are today.

There was some sort of an extension or annexe, built in 1638, behind where Cookson's Nursery now stands, which could have been connected with 'The Cottage' on Liverpool Road, when it was an Inn. In the late 18th century there appears to be a record of a North Side Lane, being run between two Inn buildings, which later became the Liverpool Road link between 'Little London', and Birkdale Common. Claremont Road and Eastbourne Road, are also mentioned in connection with North End. Gilbert Rimmer who, in the 1841 census was stated as being at the 'house' at the corner of what is now Claremont Road and Everton Road, farmed land at the southern end of Everton Road. His wife would be Mary Rimmer, and they had two sons.

Just recently during the interchange of tenants of a shop next to Wood's Wine Merchants, on the corner of Everton Road and Claremont Road, I was asked about a discovery they had made, of a huge hole underneath the floor. I did not see the hole, which had by then been covered over, but I like to think that my assumption, that it could have been an old well on Gilbert Rimmer's premises, is as near enough in location anyway, to preserve the illusion, if not fact, that it was one more instance of 'past meeting present'.

Another haunt of the Rimmers, lies in the area at the corner of Everton Road, and Vaughan Road. The farm however which probably stood where

St. Teresa's Church now stands, was 'William Rimmer's Farm'. I do not know the date when it was built, but its interest for me lies in a small slice of contemporary history, as I have reason to believe that my grandad was there on more than one occasion.

About 70 years ago, when I was about five or six years old, I came home to Bispham Road, to find a rather quietly spoken, resplendently apparelled gentleman, sitting in the 'best chair' by the front door. I knew the visit must have been one of great import, because our front door was, in my memory, never opened (even the police sergeant bringing tickets for the poor kids 'do' at the Cambridge Hall on Boxing Day, had to 'come round the back'. I was somewhat impressed by his rather cheery, 'un-Rimmer' like greeting, and it was explained that he was, as I understood, my grandfather's cousin, who had come to visit us from Manchester, "Where he had a Brass Band." Later on it was explained by my mother, that, apart from running brass bands, he also wrote the music for the bands, for which he was quite well known. Apart from the High Park and 'Little London' and district connections, I have never been able to pin-point which of my grandad's ancestors he was linked to, but he was the William Rimmer whose name was placed on the scroll of notable personages of a Southport connection, at the recent foundation laying ceremony of the Winter Gardens Complex.

I have traced Bandsman William Rimmer's connection with 'William Rimmer's Farm', but only in the usual local idiomatic geneology. "He was my father's cousin," was the explanation given to me by one of the Vaughan Road, Birkdale Rimmers, Danny, whose family have been my near neighbours, and friends, for several years. There are surprises around every corner, when you try to sort the Rimmers out. There is a record of a Mr. Tom Rimmer and his band, playing at the first Formby Horticultural Show in 1886, but I'm not sure if there is any connection between these Rimmers, but bandsman William Rimmer's father, Thomas, was also a well known conductor.

There are indeed suprises in every corner whenever I delve into the Rimmer's activities. For instance on April 11th, 1991, as this book is being prepared to go into print, the Southport Star, in 'Birchall's Beat', has published an account of bandsman William Rimmer's activities I had written with the co-operation of Anthony Wray, who I have just mentioned a few sentences ago. Before I had even seen a copy of the article, 87 years old Hannah Wignall nee Rimmer, of Lytham Road, Marshside, has just contacted me. I had not seen this branch of the family since I used to call, when collecting the 'gansey' wool from their Shellfield Road corner shop. She has confirmed the family relationship through another cousin of my grandad's, John Rimmer, who was also a cousin of William Rimmer, the bandsman. She also called to mind that another relative, Peter Rimmer, John's son, was also connected, and other family relatives, with John Rimmer, who had the cobbler's shop on the corner of Shellfield Road. I am never quite certain about youthful recollections, especially when, in those days, every other person seemed to be a relative. In our time the shop was a hardware store. Grandfather John Rimmer was also concerned with the establishment of the Temperance Mission in Kirkham Road, built in 1869. A 'relatively' short discussion, and production of photographs left me, with the addition of several phone chats with Hannah, with enough material for another book. Hannah's sister, Vera, subsequently contributed several more photographs, and even a long poem entitled, 'The Marshside Temperance Hall', by grandfather John Rimmer, to engender a series of articles, photo's and comment, in the Southport Star, in July 1991.

From this one family complex alone therefore, there comes a mass of information which defies accurate classification, because it was a living example of the verbal, geneological, method which the Rimmers, and others have employed for centuries. There were eight Rimmer grandchildren, and three great grandchildren, with a bewildering array of connections with other families to try to sort out. With the Wrights of Bank Nook alone, who included grandmother Hannah, there were subsequent connections made. Peggy married a Comstive, Martha Wright married a Brookfield. There was an Alice, and Betty, a John and Jim, who went to Australia, Jeff was a 'Corpy' worker. When I mentioned 'Old Manty', on his three-wheeled cycle, opening the Preston New Road by-pass, captured on film, I was afforded a complete geneological connection with my grandad, and granny, which explained how I had come to be delivering the fishing tackle to Manty's son, many years ago. I have now half a dozen connections, leading to Manty, through other Rimmers, one of whom lived in Manty's house in Shellfield Road. When I was married in 1938, this was also the year of the Diamond Wedding of Grandfather John Rimmer and Hannah. Hannah Wignall, and her parents, left the boot shop, when she was four, and lived, until the age of 26, in a bungalow built I think by them, at the top of Marshside Road, in the 'Brow' of the Sea Cop, just opposite the Fog Bell. It had no main lighting, sewerage, or water supply, the water coming from a small running brook near the bungalow. Reminiscent of the 'Cottage', built in Birkdale, by the Rimmers, four centuries earlier, and indicative of the proclivity of the Rimmer tribe to adapt to conditions, and prosper, under any circumstances, in any period of time. Both cottage, and bungalow are still standing today, as a testimony to this adaptability.

I was, by now in possession of details between this one branch of Rimmers in Marshside, and the High Park, and Little London, Rimmers, directly related to my Grandad. Also from here, there were the inevitable relationships with Rimmers in Birkdale, Ainsdale, Formby, West Kirby, and also many places abroad including British Columbia! I was very interested also, in the number of Marshside Rimmers and relatives, who were connected with the Marshside Temperance Band over many consecutive years. All this from a chance remark concerning Bandsman William Rimmer. The cognomen of Rimmers being also 'Rymers', certainly applies in this instance.

Although there is some evidence that the Rimmers spread out north and south, and inland, before the Domesday Survey, it is only the records of the various Abbeys, from the 12th century onwards, which show some very sparse information concerning their movements, but as they were sea faring, as well as landowners, they were extremely mobile throughout the long period of their history. In this respect, they would not appear to have colonized North Meols, then moved on to Birkdale, Ainsdale, Formby and Altcar in the south, and Crossens, Banks, and Hesketh Bank to the Ribble in the North. They seemed to appear in all these places around about the same time. They still maintained contact with Rimmers they had left behind, in various stages of their movement from West Norway, all the way up the coast to Fleetwood, Lancaster, Walney Island and Barrow in Furness, Grange over Sands, The Isle of Man, and even the Shetland Islands.

Therefore, when examining immediate local history concerning such an elusive, nomadic tribe like the Rimmers, it becomes very difficult to segregate one district's connection with them, from another. This becomes evident when you consider the sequence of events between such areas, as Birkdale, Ainsdale, Formby, and Altcar on the coast, and Halsall and Scarisbrick, and Ormskirk and district, inland.

It would also be as well to remember that, in collating records, it is invariably only the 'well to do', who get mentioned, the very poor usually coming into account only as a statistic in civic records. When we look around today, we see only the refurbished, re-vamped and modernized dwellings, giving us the old fashioned, pretty pretty, impression of the 'roses round the door' thatched cottages of 'Ye old Merry England village life'. It is as well to remember therefore, that particularly in the area we are considering, there were a great number of small holdings, whose inhabitants waged a constant battle against the forces of nature, in the Anglo-Saxon, and Norman Era, before the coming of the Rimmers to North Meols. If I tend to paint a glowing picture of their influence in the progress that was made after their settlement, I am only stating facts, whilst relating a 'story' or 'saga', of their progression from a Nomadic, wandering tribe of unknown origin, into a solid, prosperous, communal integration, which has now survived for over a thousand years.

With their most recent 'Viking' experiences, as being a hardy sea going race preferring coastal regions, combined with a sustained knowledge of many centuries of overland existence, the Rimmers had been awarded the worst possible area, perhaps in the whole of Britain, an area of salt marshes and bogland, and mudflats, desolate and isolated, with a coastal region shaped by the forces of nature, so formidable in aspect, that the earliest settlers had completely ignored it. It was hardly a 'Promised Land' they had arrived at, after their 'Exodus'. They had to drain the land by natural banks, as well as constructed ones, construct dwellings from the turf, used also for fuel, then cut timber, and brushwood, for roof construction. They brought virgin land under cultivation. They knew also, the harvest which the sea provided in abundance. They also fished the great Martin Mere, and the lesser meres, Gettern, Barton, and White and Black 'Otter' pools, or 'Snotr' pools as they named them, utilizing the tidal navigable waters of their 'Snotrpool' river, for the connection with the Great Bay, where they made their first landfall from the Isle of Man, to the mainland of Britain, on their journey from West Norway, via the Shetland Isles.

Therefore, by the 16th century, they had become well established, along all the coast between Ribble and Mersey. The Mersey had only come into being, in their time. There had been a 'Liver' pool, and another 'Snoterpool' or Otterspool as it later became known, beyond the 'Liver' pool, but there had only been sporadic excursions up to there, and to the other great river concourse via the 'Roodee' of the Roman era, now the River Dee, and City of Chester, Roman Deva.

One other curious factor, but advantageous when I am writing a story, and not a historical recording, is the amount of random items that crop up from old notes, and records, discarded when reducing 'Betwixt Ribbel and Moerse" from a large 'tome' to a small book. Also linked with these notes from perhaps well over half a century ago, even today, items resurge which link up with past events.

For instance I have recorded in the development of the Rowe Lane area, the fact that, from there, Wennington Road, which was previosuly known as 'Long Lane', was connected by way of the old Red Lane, or Foul Lane, to the main road to Ormskirk. By the 19th century visitors were arriving by stage coaches from, not only Wigan, Manchester, Bolton, and many parts of Yorkshire, but also from Liverpool daily, as well as the other places having a three times weekly service. Most of the visitors arrived at Scarisbrick, by canal packet boats, then by coach to Southport, all via Foul Lane, Red Lane and 'Long Lane' to Roe Lane corner. They then turned left in the direction of Southport. The Liverpool coaches, which came in pairs, utilized the paved turnpike road from Liverpool to Ormskirk.

However, what puzzled me was a description of the last part of the journey from the Roe Lane — Long Lane (Wennington Road) corner to Southport, which was described by one eminent visitor as passing through a "diminutive mountain pass, in the sand hills, where sand lies drifted across the road, to such a depth that the utmost effort of the cattle, are required to drag the vehicle along." At the time, I had dismissed this item for further investigation as being the figment of a somewhat prolific imagination. Another record I had been also unable to confirm was that, in this area, there had been a rabbit warren in the vicinity, operated by a Rymer or Rimmer, in the 18th century, not apparently listed in any records.

These two items remained unconnected therefore, in miscellaneous notes for all these years, until I was in the process of penning this story, in the year 1990. One day in July of that year, I was talking to an acquaintance who referred to a local newspaper article I had written, and had been published, concerning the various interesting characters I had met, whilst working at Whitesides Garages in the 1930s. I had explained that the workshop of Whitesides had been in Manchester Road, in a First World War I Nissen Hut type of building, situated in a hollow, behind the Mount Pleasant Hotel. I was recounting an incident, not in the article, concerning a customer, I remember his name was Mr. Pegg, who had a blue, open sports car. He drove up the slope, out of the garage, and turned right to go down Manchester Road, towards Trinity Church, down a gentle slope in the road. A few minutes later he was back at the garage, without the car but with a remarkable tale. He had been driving slowly and leisurely along, when, as he reached the junction of Hawkshead Street, he saw, from the corner of his eye, a car wheel, coloured blue, rolling gently past him down the slight incline in the road. To his astonishment he then realized that it was the back wheel from the offside of his own car, which had overtaken him! He slowly applied his brakes, the car came gently to a halt, then sank slowly down to the ground at the rear end. The wheel rolled merrily on, until a slight bend in the road caused it to come to a halt, opposite the 'Rabbit Inn' public house, about a quarter of a mile down Manchester Road, on the corner of Mount Street, which appears to have some connection. The cause of the incident, a broken hub, which caused the wheel to shoot off the axle, and spin off under the impetus. Owing to the traffic being much lighter than it is today, no contact, or injury with, or to, any person or object was sustained.

This incident however, as I was recounting the details, quite suddenly brought two things clearly to mind. Firstly the Mount Pleasant Hotel has always been referred to as 'The Mount', and I realised that this had been the location of the "diminutive mountain pass", where the coaches had difficulty climbing over. Furthermore, when I took a closer look at Bankes Map of 1736, the 'Rabbit Inn' was built on the field, Ref. 6.0.29, which was the 'rabbit warren' of James Rimer, 'coneyman', which I had hitherto been unable to locate. The fact also, that amongst the many subsequent landlords of this unusally named 'Inn' there have been several Rimmers, and their offshoots, is purely coincidental, and offers no proof, but I am now satisfied that, after all these years, these two locations complement each other in the confirmation of yet one more aspect of local history, hitherto unsolved. The Mount Pleasant was listed on the 1848 Ordnance Survey map as being on the road from Manchester, via Meols Cop, made after the 'Long Lane' (Wennington Road) route, and was described as a meandering track, linking Roe Lane with Lord Street, made about 1836. At this time the area was believed to be the highest point in Southport. It is not known exactly when the hotel was built. The "mountain" of sand however was removed in 1853, when the sand was utilised at Burscough, for use in the building of the Southport to Manchester Railway.

Another thought also springs to mind is that, in later years, 'coneymen' were referred to as 'warreners', which no doubt accounts for the title given to Warren Road, High Park, which cuts through the Rimmer rabbit warren, which was located along the bank to the west of the 'Snoterpool'. As this area alternated, in ownership, between the Heskeths and the Scarisbricks, it is not clear who were the original owners, unless the Rimmers held it before the Norman Domesday Records in 1068.

In the early days of the Rimmer occupation of the North Meols area, in the 9th century onwards, the coastline, from the Great Bay, starting at Crossens, then along the line of Bankfield Lane to Churchtown, seaward of St. Cuthbert's Church, on the line of Sunny Road, then roughly along the line of the railway from Churchtown to Hesketh Park Railway Station, continued southwards slightly seawards of Marlborough Road, and Hawesside Street, to Yellow House Lane. This was generally accepted as being the high water mark, as late as the reign of Queen Elizabeth I. Subsequently it was also accepted, that the Rotten Row Embankment, was a high tide demarcation.

The destruction however, of three towns, probably in the 13th century, by earthquake, one of which was Argarmeols, makes the true definition of the actual coastline conjectural. The references in Chapter Seven of "Betwixt Ribbel and Moerse" refers to other lost lands, as well as Argarmeols. One area, between Formby and Argarmeols, called Elreslete, I identified as being between the two, and probably part of Ainsdale, as its was situated between Pinfold Lane, and Woodvale Bridge. The house subsequently named 'Elreslete', after my research, was actually built over the stream dividing the two areas. There are other areas mentioned in this chapter, as Aynesdale, or Anoldesdale, and the manor of Birkedale, were claimed to be part of Meandale, and the parish of Mele, which is now Ravenmeols. Disputes on those areas ranged over three centuries, from the 13th century onwards. Also, in Chapter Eight, there is reference to a Formby family deed of around 1282, to a bridge or causeway called Hyfin, connecting the Formby Mainland to an island, shown on Ptolemys 2nd century maps, as being opposite Formby Point. I thought this island might have been part of Argarmeols, so it is difficult to conjecture what the districts would have been like, before the sand encroachment, as there were no sandhills here before 1690.

So once again we have to rely on deeds, and wills, for indications of the Rimmer presence in the area. Once again we find that the Rimmers outnumbered any other family in the area, in double proportion. Indeed in a Directory, referring to Formby as an outlying part of the Parish of Walton-on-the-Hill, compiled in 1679, it shows that the Rimmers comprised over one quarter of the whole population, in an area which included Ainsdale as well. There had been an agreement drawn up in 1377, between Otes de Halsall, and William de Aughton, Lord of North Meols, regarding pasture in Northmeles, Aynaltesdale, Byrckdale, and Argarmeols. In the 16th century, the Halsall's appointed 'Keepers' and 'pinders', to round up cattle in Birkdale and Ainsdale, which were impounded in Halsall. There was also an eventual reciprocal agreement made with the inhabitants of Formby, round about the beginning of the 16th century. As we have seen, by the middle of the 17th century, the population of Birkdale was also comprised of nearly half being Rimmers, so at all stages of development in the area, their activities were very diversified.

Not only were they fishermen, and farmers 'reamers', bank and cop constructers, but also remaining fairly static as coneymen, or warreners, on the coasts, and inland as burleymen and pinders, constables attending Court Leets, from North Meols to Formby, and churchwardens, and Jurors. They were not averse however, to the carrying on of itinerant trades, such as travelling salesmen or peddlers, although anyone who was considered to be a vagrant was whipped out to the village boundary. There were cottage industries of weaving, cotton, and carding, and spinning, all involved in textile production, to supplement incomes from land and sea. The north west coast for cotton, and the south west for linen, were well known in the 16th and 17th centuries. Flax, and hemp, were grown locally, and I can remember mention of fustian trousers, by my grandad, which were a type of corduroy material. 'Higglers' were also itinerant dealers, and carriers of poultry or dairy produce, as well as farmers. James Rimmer of Hillside, had a holding of over 12 acres, pasture and arable, on a strip of land I can see from where I live. This was the 'Gorstile', changed now to Gorse Hill Farm, on New Cut Lane. Also visible from here, is land to the south of Anderson's Farm, Nixon's Lane, farmed by John Rymer, the miller at Ainsdale. In 1694 his inventory was produced, when the contents of the mill house were valued at well over £100, very high indeed for those times, but the mill itself had then been in operation since early in the 17th century. It was built to replace an earlier mill, which, together with the early Ainsdale settlement, had been washed away. It was originally similar to the Birkdale Mill, of timber post construction, used by both Birkdale and Ainsdale, as the boundary was said to run through the middle when it was rebuilt, as a brick tower mill, about the end of the 18th century. It was still in use, at least until after the Second World War, as many of us remember clattering over the mill's railway lines on Liverpool Road, on our way to Ainsdale Beach. The railway ran from Mill Road, diagonally across what is now the Natterjack Pub car park, then through where the laundry stood, which is now occupied by the block of Millhouse Lodge flats. Then down the rear of Burnley Road, to link up with the main railway line at Ainsdale. Somewhere around the early sixties it stopped operating, and the line was closed. Being in the motor trade, travelling around the garages, Councillor Wilkie Buckley, who owned the nearby Reliance garage, and myself, for obviously different reasons, hearing that a new garage was to be erected on the Mill site, were considerably perturbed. I was categorically assured that the mill would remain intact, being a listed building, and that the garage would be built alongside it. It certainly was built alongside, but every time I patronize the garage today, I can vividly recall the shocked horror I experienced, one day in 1970, when I arrived to find the Mill reduced to a heap of bricks and rubble! This old mill had been a landmark to us practically all our lives although living at the other end of the area. When I came to live in Nixons Lane in 1947, the mill was the only visible landmark, before the Heathfield Road estate was extended to Ainsdale. Far off to the south, we could see the Anglican Cathedral at Liverpool, above the Ince Blundell Woods, and also two remaining Tower Buildings of New Brighton, after fire had destroyed the Tower. The hills of North Wales, and even Snowdonia, could be seen on clear days, from the bedroom window.

The mill played its part in World War II, for fire watchers, and Home Guard personnel, used to keep in touch with our Home Guard station situated on the Promenade at the top of Leyland Road, by means of signalling to Wardens on top of Trinity Church Tower, from the roof of the mill. I well remember we were alerted one night, when a land mine, attached to a parachute, was reported to be drifting in our direction.

It passed by the horrified watchers on Trinity Church by a distance of feet only, descending in our direction. A slight shift of wind off the sea, caused it to veer off, to a landing in Leyland Road, where it gently drifted through the branches of a tree. Charlie Webb, who had been our manager at the Whitesides garage, behind the Mount Pleasant Hotel, described to me how he heard the breaking of the tree branches, and his horror when his flashlamp shone slowly up this huge cylindrical object, resting at a slight angle against the tree trunk! Whether it had a faulty fuse, or the tree branches had taken the weight, the land mine obviously didn't go off, or the Mount Pleasant, would not be the 'pleasant' sight it is today.

Before its demolishing, I can testify to the magnificent view across to Moss to Halsall and Parbold from the mill. I never saw the sails of course, which disappeared many years ago, together with the surrounding mill buildings. The driving shaft, weighing at least a ton was still in position, and so were the foot square oak beams, still supporting the four floors of the mill. The dome however, was then covered with tarpaulin, the wheels on it were still intact, as the whole dome used to turn on them, to face the wind. Grain was still being produced well into the 1960's, being ground by electrical machines. The line of the ever changing, Birkdale and Ainsdale boundary, is only defineable by the period in time. Chapter Seven of 'Betwixt Ribbel and Moerse' discusses this at length. Ainsdale Mill was formerly in the Parish of Halsall. In 1664 William Rymer described it as going through the mill, then along a 'Githorne Ditch' to the windmill, which probably stood at Mill House Farm, at Barton, near Halsall, which was a granary for the monks.

My Grandad was known to have walked to the Ainsdale Mill in his younger days, as there were descendants of his, who had lived there, and also of Thomas Rimmer the blacksmith, who ran the Smithy in Segars Lane (formerly Smithy Lane) who also lived at the mill in the middle of the 19th century.

Later on he covered the areas, in his preaching capacity as Methodism was then becoming a force to be reckoned with.

The miller Rymers who also farmed the land south of the mill would then be operating in three different districts. The mill, being in both Ainsdale and Birkdale, and the 'Gorstile' including Anderson's Farm, and Boundary Farm, from New Cut Lane to Segars Lane, is in Halsall, as the Sandy Brook Boundary, bisects Nixon's Lane, a few yards from where I am writing. There is a considerable incline to Anderson's Farm which lies on the moss, whereas, this house is on the higher drier, ground adjacent to the old Birkdale Farm school. The mossland, south of New Cut Lane, to Segars Lane, has been variously the property of the Church Commissioners, easily the largest landowners in the county, and other farming consortiums, who are, at this moment in time, busy closing all the ancient trackways and roads which cross the mosses, all the way to Formby Hall. On the moss, behind Anderson's Farm, is the Old Canal, which connects the drainage system to the Sluice at Crossens, utilizing Fine Janes Brook, and Drummersdale Drain in the process. That it is still tidal, can be proved by an experience several years ago at Rainbag Cover, near the site of Rainbag Farm, on Segars Lane, when a bread van left the road, and ended on its side in the Old Canal. No injuries were sustained, but the contents of the van occasioned much surprise when quite a few loaves turned up in the Sluice at Crossens! This Old Canal connects the three meres, White Otter, Black Otter, and Gettern, and the farms of those names, which for many years have been considered as much a part of Ainsdale, although being on Halsall Moss.

I have previously mentioned Anderson's Farm, and its situation at the end of Nixon's Lane, which is divided by the Sandy Brook Boundary stream. Anderson's Farm was doubtless named after people who were probably the first occupiers. I have mentioned also the Barton family living there. The most interesting development however, has just emerged concerning this area, in the fact that two prominent citizens of Ainsdale have just died in November 1990, within a week of each other. They are Mr. and Mrs. Eric Arcari, and his wife, ('Mollie' to us). They had lost their son Laurie, in the opening of the same year. It transpires that 'Mollie', before her marriage was Mary Ellen Nixon, who was born at Anderson's Farm in 1906, and that Nixon's Lane was named after her family. It has also transpired since, that Mary Ellen's brother, who was killed in World War I, had the family forename of Anderson, after which the farm was named, so the lane, and the farm, were associated with the same family. There are or were, members of the Nixon family still in Birkdale, so the window cleaner who claimed in 1974, when we moved in, that he was a Nixon, connected with the farm was probably right.

Another place which seems to have been of an indefinite location is 'Hawes House', the site of which lies on the seaward side of the railway line, on the Hillside Golf Links. It could be reached from Ainsdale from the S. & A. golf course club house, but it was also in line with the Underhill Farm of Richard Rimmer, on the part of Nixon's Lane which ran into the sandhills. I have no details of 'Hawes House', except that at some time, it was occupied by more than one of the Rimmer family in succession. It appears that it was only let, at one time with the 'holding' of a fishing 'stall' on the Birkdale sands, one of four 'stalls' staked out on the beach. In 1799, a Peter Rymer was known to have given, on oath, the description of the 'stall' boundary post being placed on a hill by the Rimmer family, round about the middle of the century. This was another Lancashire Record Office document found at Preston. This record I found very interesting, as it is the only one I found of the Rimmers using 'pitch nets', in this area, apart from 'putting', for shrimps and 'raddling' for cockles, as the latter were only found in the Marshside area, and north of the Pier.

I have no record of our family engaging in this type of fishing, but my old friend of many years standing, John Masters, 'Clerk of Works', showed me rough drawings of stake nets, used on Birkdale sands at the turn of the century. These were of a type used in quite a few places along the coast, as far as Morecambe Bay. They were simply stakes, about 7ft. long, driven into the sand, leaving about 4ft. of net above the surface, with the nets spread out between them, which caught fish in them as the tide receded. He had however information, that round about 1900 to 1902, there was a John

Rimmer, who lived in Kew Road, and Mark Robinson of Banastre Road, who were engaged in stake fishing, quite probably on the former Hawes House 'stall'. They were both lifeboatmen, whether on a permanent basis or stand-by, but they could combine both activities within the proximity of the Lifeboat station nearby. We thought they could have been related, as there was a Richard Robinson, who was coxswain of the lifeboat, 'Three Brothers' in 1902, but curiously enough there appears to be no records of this lifeboat's activities, as it only did two years service. The Rimmers were related to at least four of the families of the lifeboatmen who perished in the 'Eliza Fernley' disaster of 1886. Amongst the harrowing stories concerning this disaster, John Robinson was found, still alive, on the shore in the early hours of the morning after, and died in the arms of Thomas Rimmer, shortly afterwards.

I have been acquainted with the Masters' family for as long as I can remember, and always assumed that they were connected with the Rimmers somewhere along the line, a safe assumption indeed, as it would be far easier to list the families they were NOT related to, than those who were.

John Masters possessed a mass of local historical data, and well into his nineties, we were discussing ways and means of getting it into print. His pet topic was the disappearance of the Birkdale Coat of Arms Chairman's Chain of Office, which has never been found. When Gerard Swarbrick of Scarisbrick, called to see me in the early 1980s, concerning the proposed production of his Pictorial Map of Sefton, John Masters was eventually compensated, to a degree, by the inclusion of the depiction of the Chairman's Chain of Office, of the former Birkdale Urban District Council 1894-1912. Even when John Masters was housebound, we had many protracted telephone conversations, discussing the content of his 'proposed' memoirs.

I am constantly amazed by the wealth of information, and data, in the possession of local inhabitants, and like the lifeboat project, shall continue to press various authorities until a suitable research centre, probably at the Botanic Museum, is established for the deposit, and future reference, of all historical material, which will doubtless be gladly contributed by many local families.

The Ainsdale Mill was probably the most ancient possession of the community, but there were also established business premises by the beginning of the 18th century. There was a travelling salesman, or pedlar, resident in Ainsdale in the 17th century, but John Rymer, was a shopkeeper, who sold similar items, around about 1750. Other trades associated with local demands, had also become well established. There was one family of Rimmers who were butchers throughout the 17th and 18th centuries. There were quite a number of John and Thomas Rymers, who were blacksmiths, carpenters, joiners, and wheelwrights etc. They seemed to alternate their trades with Birkdale, so that, where there were joiners for instance in Birkdale, there were none in Ainsdale. When a water powered mill was established at Halsall, cottage spinning of cotton had declined from the mid-eighteenth century, and there was not enough work for the tailors of

Birkdale and Ainsdale, and there were applications, ironically, in one instance, by a Thomas Rymer for poor relief, from Peter Rymer's Benefaction before the end of the 18th century.

Besides the business of rabbit warrens, there were all sorts of other trades for which 'boons and rents', were payable to the landowners, in this instance the Blundells of Ince. Lands were held by tenants on leases, lasting the life of the tenant, and two members of his family. This three generation system, in the 17th and 18th centuries, for sums payable on the taking out of the lease, varied from about £4, up to £300, by the 18th century. In 1775, sheep 'boons' and 'shearing', were added to the lease of Richard Rimmer of Ainsdale. Varying gifts of produce were payable annually to the landlord, for instance Richard was obliged to supply, "one good sheep annually." Even when official documents can be traced, it is difficult to separate one Rimmer from another, and the habit of adding the trade description to a name, has proved to be the most efficient method, right up to our own times. A couple of illustrations, given by my grandad can be quoted as instances. The nickname of 'Tuffy' as a 'digger', or reamer of turf, is quite common amongst many other families as well as Rimmers, as referring to an occupation. These nicknames and appellations, to personalities, can be instanced, also when the Methodist Non-Conformists appeared on the scene as an alternative to the established Church, and the Roman Catholic religion. Meetings were mostly held in the open, and in cottages if wet. Therefore, in the 18th century there were quite a number of Non-Conformists, who were referred to as 'Methody' ie, James Rimmer, 'Methody' (from North Meols). James Rimmer 'Methody' from near Birkdale Mill in Snottering Lane. Thomas Ball (Methody Tommy), who was born in 1791, was a well known character. James ('Methody') Rimmer, from Little Altcar, was not averse to addressing a congregation from the Formby, Cable Street, mill platform in inclement weather. This mill was probably the brick windmill built in 1807. There was a large contingent of Rimmers who were early settlers in the Cable Street area. When I visited the many garages in the Formby area, in the course of travelling in the motor trade, it was fascinating to see the water ream coming up through the floor of the Nissen hut which served the purpose of a garage, at the top of Cable Street. It was probably the spring I referred to in 'Betwixt Ribbel and Moerse' (page 47), when referring to a house called Waterings, which was accessible by boat, as recently as 1860.

There was an abundance of records available when I spent many years researching the Rimmers of Formby. There were more Rimmers at the Watchyard Lane end of Cable Street, where Billy and Jim Rimmer, ran the Smithy Brow Farm. I could find no record of any families, so either they were bachelors, or had sold their wives from the market cross, at Cross Green, as was the custom at one time!

I was fortunate also, to trace a link between our Rimmer family of lifeboatmen, and the Formby lifeboatmen, in the Brewery Lane area. This was at Watt's Cottage, one of the most attractive cottages in Formby. The occupants at that time, in the late 1960s, could trace their descendancy to

Isabella Rimmer, whose father was an Aindow, and a coxswain of the Formby lifeboat. My satisfaction at forging this link, however was somewhat nullified by the demolition of the cottage shortly afterwards. There was some compensation however, that because of this incident, I was placed in touch with Edward Aindow, housebound, in a Gores Lane cottage by the loss of one foot, who gave me information concerning the shaft of Formby Cop Cross, which he had seen buried in a cop in Kirklake Road, 60 years before. He also confirmed the legend of the ancient stone coffin, buried in St. Lukes Churchyard as being correct, as he was present when it was partly exposed, and quickly covered up for some undisclosed reason. I was only able to photograph the cop before the whole lot was removed. (See page 91 and 101-102 and also photo No. 36 Betwixt Ribbel and Moerse). This, despite newspaper appeals and Friends of Formby attempts, also a personal appeal at Formby Town Hall (would there have been a Councillor Rimmer in office at that time)? Not one of my most successful projects, as Edward Aindow died shortly afterwards, and ironically enough, I was obliged to visit the garage, twice a week afterwards, which was built on Cross Cop site.

Rimmers in Formby in the 18th century are fairly easy to trace, except that, as is the case elsewhere, there seems to be so many of them, and of similar names and trades. The seemingly abstemious habits of their forefathers appeared to have gone slightly 'out of the window' too, with their connections with the various hostelries, and ale houses, from North Meols to Birkdale, and Ainsdale, in Formby also, by the establishment of the Brewery partnership of Dickinson and Rimmer in, predictably enough, Brewery Lane. This was in the early 19th century, and there is probably enough evidence to support the fact that they supplied ale to Duke's Folly, and other subsequent hotels in Southport's new township. Although it was a foul concoction called 'Jacky Water', probably inferring that it was made of ditch water containing 'jack sharps' and other obnoxious ingredients, it remained in great demand for many years, as the Brewery was only sold out to Tetley's in 1920, so the quality of its products must have improved, as many local people can testify even today. Locals have also inferred that the Brewery perhaps 'tapped' into the streams that flowed down Long Lane, from Kirklake, and Queens Road draining, as many others did, into the Downholland Brook, via a channel known as 'Dobbs Gutter', which contained a plentiful supply of jack sharps, or tadpoles! There were also 'forget me nots', my mother's favourite flower, and I remember the rows of willow trees along the stream, and the water cress, even as late as the 1950 era, when even goats could be seen in the fields. This was in the Ravenmeols Lane, and the old Cockle Lane (Coronation Avenue) area, where there were Rimmers in a cluster of fishermen's cottages. 'Old Spanker's' cottage with its name plate quite clearly visible from the main road was a key point, but the thing I remember most about Formby, were the banks dividing the various fields, cottages and farm holdings, and I have often wondered how many of these turf banks had been constructed by Rimmer ancestors.

Across the road from 'Old Spanker's', and other cottages, probably built from ships timbers, is the Royal Hotel, built by Tom Rimmer, behind which was another brewery built by him, mainly for brewing his own beer. This was called Reciprocity Brewery, which was sold to Threlfalls Brewery in 1896. The Royal Hotel was built in the 1870s.

Another place with strong Rimmer connections was Whitehouse Farm, in Kenyons Lane near to Queen's Jubilee Hall (1887). The farm was still there in the early 1970s, but I have no details of the Rimmers who lived there. Some local people will recall, no doubt, the wagonette, operated by Rimmers in Gores Lane, which made the weekly trip to Ormskirk, every Friday.

There were many Rimmers who took part in Council affairs. James Rimmer, was Chairman of the Council eleven times, which must constitute a record. Joseph Rimmer whose name made him easily recognized, was associated with the Formby Council of Social Welfare in 1949. When you come to examine the Court Leet of the Manor of Formby, that lasted until the year 1917, which appointed Pinders, Moss reeves, (Lookers) for sea activities, waifs and strays, house, wreck, cockle bed, and all other guardians of the Manor, chosen for the last time before the creation of the Urban District, you can take your pick of Rimmers concerned, John, or James, Nicholas and William.

The Formby family, and Formby Hall, appears to have been, as now, on the northern periphery of the village.

The main road to Liverpool, on which the Hall was built, has always been to the east of the village of Formby, as its boundary with Altcar runs down the middle of Hogshill Lane, and Liverpool Road. The Hall has always appeared to be somewhat isolated, as it was separated by a large area, known as the 'Bronc', or (Brank') as in Ainsdale and Birkdale. The 'Bronc' was a huge rabbit warren, the size of which can still be estimated by the expanse of Woodvale Aerodrome, the 'Bronc Farm' complex, part of the estate, lay approximately where the Control Tower of the aerodrome is now. The road from there, to the Hall, can still be traced from the by-pass road. The Rimmers seem to have been connected with activities on the 'Bronc' since the present Hall was built in the early 16th century. The Formby's have retained in their possession a letter, written on rough paper, which they alluded to in the family as "Jane Rimmer's Reminiscences." It was written in March 1868, and refers to Jane Rimmer's birth at the "Old Bronk House" at the end of the 18th century. Amongst the general activities she mentions, are new bonnets, made by Isabella Rimmer of Ainsdale, who seems to have supplied many other garments for people at the Hall, and in the villages. The letter was written when Jane Rimmer was "lying on her bed of affliction and suffering" and mentions "Old Bronk House whear I was Bourn", and refers to many members of the Formby family, with whom she had a lifelong association. She refers to her confirmation, at the age of 16, by the Rev. Richard Formby (1760-1832), in the same year as the Reverend Richard Formby died. She mentions her grandfather, sending her to the Hall, with birds called "Dotrals, shot in Spring", and receiving a reciprocal present of the first pair of "Parterages", shot in the season. Another member of the Formby family, alludes to vists to Jane Rimmer's grandmother, and records "I see it all — old age, venerable, and well cared for, the nicely sanded floor, the varnished clock, the open door, the garden, the blackcurrant bushes, the free stretch of sandhill, and the fresh wind blowing." An idyllic scene no doubt, until you see the rest of the description of the "dear old grandmother", who, crippled by rheumatism, was won't to sit, year by year, in an armchair by the fireside." According to my reckoning however, Jane Rimmer, lying on her bed of affliction and suffering, was only 51 when she wrote the letter!

In the middle of the 19th century, in a description of the view westward to the sea, there is a reference to the 'Bronc', which mentions the "bright yellow of the sandhill boundary." This was before the pine trees were planted in 1894. There is a mention also of two cottage homesteads, with thatched roofs. Even assuming that one of these is the 'Bronc' dwelling, which Jane Rimmer described as "Old Bronk House", there appears to be another cottage in the view from the Hall grounds, across the 'Bronc'. If it is not one belonging to the Rimmer's 'Bronk' House, it could be the one I was asked to investigate last year.

I wrote an article in the Southport Star on the 25th January, 1990, concerning this building, which was formerly known as Willowbank Caravan Site, which is down a lane on the northern edge of Woodvale Aerdrome. This lane has been severed by the building of the By-Pass Road but finishes up with the road that connects with the entrance to Formby Hall. The lane that passes Willowbank Farm, is marked on the 1953 Ordnance Map, by a series of Boundary Posts, which are shown as lying in a westerly direction, through the aerodrome, and the pine woods to the sea. Easterly, the boundary line is shown as running through the Formby House grounds. As Willowbank Farm is a listed building, being well over 200 years old, it could have been one of the cottages referred to by the Formbys. The fact that it was formerly known as 'Captain Rimmer's' cottage, also supports this contention. However, as the district, including the former Woodvale railway station, and the Cheshire Lines extension, was only opened in 1884, there has been some disagreement as to whether Willowbank Farm was in Southport, or Formby, as Woodvale aerodrome lies between the both.

There had been rumours that the company concerned in the Winter Gardens project in Southport, were going to build a hypermarket, and leisure complex, at Willowbank, and a by-pass to the coastal road. When I arrived at Willowbank, I found the farm had been the subject of extensive vandalism. The site was occupied by several caravan squatters, scattered over a large area. There was also a large luxury caravan parked near some wooden outhouse buildings on the edge of a clump of willow trees, just seaward of the cottage. Several children were playing in and out of the caravan. With my usual penchant for getting involved in unusual occurrences when I am engaged in historical research, I remarked to one of the other caravan occupants, there there appeared to be an increasing volume of smoke issuing from the largest of the wooden outbuildings. Another caravan occupant appeared from the direction of the buildings, in some agitation. From the gist of the subsequent conversation, I gathered that they had decided to call out the Fire Brigade, but hadn't much idea about doing this. I told them that the nearest phone was some considerable distance away, and the best thing they could do was to drag the caravans to a safe distance and make sure there were no children missing, and I would phone the Fire Brigade from the main road. I was unable to get through from the nearest phone box at Staveley Road corner in Ainsdale, so I went home to Nixon's Lane, and phoned from there. The operator enquired about the location which seemed to be causing confusion because of the old difficulty concerning the boundary situation, so I said the Formby Brigade were used to dealing with grass fires on the site, especially owing to the dry summer of 1989, and please hurry up, there are children on the site who could be in danger.

I was considerably perturbed by these events, and by the fact that it appears you cannot contact any essential services direct, but only through Liverpool. After several hours persistent badgering of various authorities, I eventually persuaded Hatton Garden Fire department to give me the Formby Fire Brigade's phone number. When eventually I made contact later in the evening, they told me that the Leading Fireman in charge of the incident, would not be back on duty until the next day. When I finally contacted him, I told him I had been worried about the children at the site of the fire, and although he was not supposed to discuss official business, it transpired that he was a Birkdale man, and an avid reader of historical events I write about in the 'Star' newspaper, particularly a recent account of a local newspaper vendor called "Enoch", well known to him, and many other people in the Southprt district. So, unofficially, I learnt from him, that they had arrived at Willowbank in a few minutes after receiving the alarm, and as they arrived, the whole of the outbuildings, probably shed and hen houses, had "gone up like a bomb", scattering burning debris over a wide area. Fortunately all the vans had been moved to safety, and no one was injured. He told me that, in spite of boundary difficulties, they had dealt with numerous fires at Willowbank in the previous dry summer, grass fires mainly, but also one due to the 'burning off' of scrap cable covering, to extract the copper wiring, which brought good prices on the scrap market. A new twist to the 'money for old rope' business we used to operate ourselves, from old rope we used to recover on our beachcombing expeditions, to flog to the scrap yard in Virginia Street. We had a chat about the difficulties of central control, concerning the essential services. I told him the original fire station was in Cable Street, when the firemen were called together by ringing a bell, and also I had been present, even after the new station was built on the main road nearby, on many occasions, when volunteers were summoned by siren, after the National Service Wartime outfit was handed over in 1947.

To show that things have not moved much over the years, I also recalled one incident that had all the markings of a 'Mack Sennett — Keystone Cop' film comedy theme. In 1899, the Fire Service was run from Crosby, when the Formby Golf Club caught fire. Messages went backwards and forwards to Crosby from Formby, and back again, giving the alert. In a one horse trap, a certain Captain Charters rushed around the village alerting the Fire Brigade volunteers by whistle. However, when the two wheeled cart, serving as a fire appliance, came to be loaded up, there was a delay, as some of the hoses, drying out in the yard, had to be rolled up. With this hold up, coupled with the distance they had to travel, it was no surprise that, when they arrived on the scene, the Golf Club was a smouldering ruin.

In the article I also mentioned that my Uncle Harry Spencer, who was a chemist, originally from East Lancashire, had listed and hand painted, all the species of plants in the area, many of them blown off grain ships coming into Liverpool.

By another of these strange supportive coincidences I always get if I commence any line of research, or field work, there appeared once again, as I was writing these events, a programme called 'Seaside' on BBC 2, presented by Geoffrey Lancaster, who is an authority on rare and tropical plants, which showed many of the plants still flourishing in the area which includes the Willowbank site.

Subsequently, there arose several conservationist projects, combined with local meetings of protest by Ainsdale, and Woodvale residents, which has served to delay the scheme. At the time of updating these notes in August, 1990, there has been no further development in the area, as the company proposing this project, and the Winter Gardens fiasco, has gone into the hands of the receivers. I am afraid however, that by the time these notes get into print, these projects, like the Kew Woods 'sell out', will have chopped another slice off our Green Belt heritage.

As in North Meols, the fluctuation between religious functions affected the Formby, and Crosby area for several centuries, the Formbys and the Blundells changing allegiance with the times. The Rimmers appeared on recusant lists from time to time, even using the graveyard of the old chapel, as did many other families, after the destruction of the chapel, for the burial of both Roman Catholics and Protestants. The church of St. Luke's afterwards took over from the chapel, which was shown to have been there, by Cockersands Abbey records, in the early 12th century. The chapel could have been built like the 'Harkirke' chapel, in Little Crosby grounds, following the Norse settlement, in the district, and promoted by Ethelfreda, from Bromborough, in the 9th and 10th centuries.

Mention of religious establishments such as Merevale, Stanlow and Cockersands, in connection with Altcar, Ravenmeols, and the Ince Blundell area, also leads to the conjecture that, as in the case of the co-operation of the Rimmers with the Monks of Sawley, in North Meols and Crossens in the 13th century, they were also actively concerned in the construction of river banks, and dykes, in the River Alt area, as it is inconceivable that the small contingent of monks, alloted by their respective abbeys, would be insufficient enough to enable them to cope with the fertility of the land, and the cultivation of the soil, as well as dealing with the construction of the river banks, and cops, necessary for the prevention of flooding along the River Alt. The Rimmers in their capacity as 'reamers', could also mediate in disputes, arising as they did, in the early 13th century, between the Abbey of

Stanlow, Cheshire, who received land to the south of the Alt, from the Blundells of Ince, and the Abbey of Merevale, in Warwickshire, who held the north side of the Alt and the Manor of Altcar. Ellel Grange, still in existence near Lancaster, also held land locally.

With the Rimmer's 'reamer' connection with the 12th century Burscough Priory, and the 'Snoterpool' and River Askyr (or Douglas), connections, and the granting of fishing rights to the monks of Burscough on Martin Mere, the Scarisbrick and Diglake connections through the smaller meres, White, and Black Otter Mere, and Gettern Mere, the Downholland Brook, and the Lydiate Brook, and the River Alt, the influence of the Rimmers, by sea and land, had completed the great circle of 'Betwixt Ribble' and Mersey. This was excepting, of course, that in the early days, there was no Mersey. Apart from the later 'Liver-pul', the furthest southerly point was beyond the lost port of Altmouth, which was shown on several maps as being south of the Alt. This point, the exact situation of which is not known, was a small hamlet, the ruins of which were found in sewerage operations. This was assumed to have been Moorhouses, where medieval pottery, found there, indicated that it was very old indeed. As the River Alt, however, which was known as a Roman River since the 2nd century, has changed its course several times in its history, the discovery of the remains of wharves, and quays, right up to the 20th century, are all probably connected with the once great river delta of the Alt.

I am sure that may people like myself, can still remember the old lighthouse on the River Alt, demolished in our time, perpetuated in name by the Lighthouse Restaurant in Altcar, on Liverpool Road, with a model of the Lighthouse on its roof.

The further expansion of the Rimmers, from Crosby into Waterloo, and Liverpool, developed mainly in the later centuries, from the loss of the towns on the coast due to earthquakes, and the silting up of the estuaries. The rejection of Formby, as the dockland area of the Mersey, was inevitable, so Formby never became a port. The arrival of the large sea-going vessels into Liverpool, also led to the dispersal of many of the Rimmers, as sea crews, to all parts of the world.

I have a final personal reminiscence of the Rimmer influence concerning Formby. I have in the course of research, unearthed many strange coincidences, and also many apparently inequatable factors in myth, legend, and factual details of events, past and present. During the research into Norse Cosmology, I wondered for instance how to equate the records of the supposed divinational, and prophetical properties, of the 'skalds', or story tellers, with their references to such seemingly improbable beings as the 'Goddess of Greenland', with the strict Biblical code of the Rimmers in their subsequent settlement in this part of the country. There again, this in turn, did not compare with the aspects of fortune telling proclivities, evident in local seaside, fairground, and avenue, and arcade activities.

I have mentioned in this respect, one instance of the curious proclivity of 'tea cup' readings by my Auntie Annie, which, in spite of some scepticism on my part, proved in many, in fact most instances, to be uncannily accurate. I have known relations come from many parts of the country, and receive predictions, proved subsequently to be accurate, down to the minutest detail. I myself was the subject on one occasion, whilst living out of town. The forecast of my return, and subsequent events, were correct to the smallest detail. I once asked her what she actually saw in the process, and she replied that she saw nothing, the facts just came. I considered that, in some way, telepathy was involved.

There was never, at any time, any monetary aspect concerned, as she was a person of strict religious upbringing, which however, was flexible enough for her to act as relief organist to any church requiring her services. My grandad, who was the fisherman cum-preacher attached to the Independent Methodist circuit, had no prejudices. He would visit, as I have recounted, any denomination or group. Two of his daughters were married at Norwood Avenue Baptist Church. Myself, and my two brothers, went on our own volition, probably largely because of convenience, to Canning Road Congregational Church, round the corner from where we lived with my mother, and grandparents.

So there was no restriction of belief, or any factor involved when, in the Formby district some years ago, I was afforded an instance of the latent psychic, predictive ability, or whatever other term you wish to call it, of this extraordinary people.

At that time, I will not give dates or names to save any family distress or embarrassment, I used to visit Turban Motors a garage, run by George Turner, which stood on the corner of Church Road, and School Lane. Many people will remember the garage mainly as the local cycle repair shop, standing next door to the Police Station on Church Road.

The incident I refer to was the unfortunate disappearance of a young boy, whilst picknicking on the sandhills with his mother and friends.

An intensive search was mounted, covering the sandhills and pinewoods, and as the boy was seen only a short time before he went missing, speculation became rife, that he had variously been kidnapped, (inevitably by gypsies of course), or person or persons unknown. Posters were placed in various locations, places, police stations, shops, and public buildings. The inevitable 'cranks', subsequent to mass publicity by the media, located him in places as far away as the Midlands, by such methods as swinging pendulums over maps. This Midlands location was also supported by a woman psychic from Holland, who had successfully assisted the police on previous occasions, but no trace of the boy was found.

Some time after this, on one of my weekly visits to my Auntie Annie, she told me she was very worried, as she had heard people talking about the little boy who had disappeared. When I asked why she was worried, she said "I have seen the little boy." When I asked her where, she told me, "He is under the sand of the hill he was playing on." I asked her to tell me all she knew. She described how he was dressed, in just shorts, and I think she said a striped shirt, and also what the colour was, and that the boy was very near where the mother had been sitting. She told me it was not a dream, and she had not seen any poster concerning the boy. The next time I was in the garage in Formby, it was with some diffidence, on account of all the attendent publicity, that I mentioned it to George Turner, the garage proprietor. He had been very upset, as the boy had been a customer of his, or at least the relations had, so he insisted that we contacted the police next door. All the police staff were well known to us, and the Sergeant in charge of the search was very sympathetic, but he said that the area had been thoroughly combed. Whether or not it was the prediction, that the boy, was under the hill, had worried the Sergeant or not, but some time later, when all other avenues had been investigated, and proved negative, they returned to the spot, and levelled the sandhill. The little boy was there, just as my Auntie had said he was. Apparently, he had gone just to the other side of the hill, and tunnelled his way into the sandhill, and the sand had shifted from the top, leaving no trace of what had happened.

I myself am inclined to think that my Auntie had probably noticed the poster, perhaps in the local post office subconsciously, but the incident is certainly remarkable, in any context.

CHAPTER 7

GENEOLOGIES OF RIMMER'S RELATIVES

Not one historian, and indeed it would be an impossible task to draw up a genealogical tree, has, to my knowledge, attempted a separate list of the Rimmer family connections locally, and it is therefore only by early deeds, and land grants, and also later, parish records, that any clear record emerges. It is only from family trees of people who have intermarried with the Rimmers, that some indication is observed of the extent of their influence on the community in general. In this respect, I find that it would be easier to detail the local families, stretching back for many generations, who were not connected with the Rimmers, rather than try to list the ones that are!

The Parish Register of the North Meols area list, in two published volumes covering the period 1594-1812, gives us, for instance, the most commonest surnames of that period as being: Rimmer (4327), Ball (2639), Wright (2507), Johnson (1408), Blundell (1216), Howard (918), Bond or Boond (902), Abraham or Abram (586), Hodges (568), Jackson (512), Aughton (479), Marshall (476), Brookfield (451), Halsall (388), Hunt (369), Hesketh (360), Wignall (353), Watkinson (326), Wareing (297), Sutton (271).

This was only from the North Meols records, and all these families were at some time intermarried with the Rimmers. Also, with expansion taking place, other families can be traced in connection with the Rimmers: Bartons, Breakhill, Boothroyds, Hootons, Leadbetters, Thomasson, Todds, Gregsons, Lloyds, Aindows, Jumps, Jolleys, Sutches, Altys, Robinsons, Aspinalls, Baxters, Butlers, Blenkinsops, Grayson, Green, Peets, Rigbys, Linakers, Shorlicars or Sherlicar, Harrisons, Comstives, Segars, Hoscars, Sumners, Sedgwicks, Lawsons, Bibbys, Taskers, Grimes, Ridings, Coultons, Dickinsons, Faircloughs, Ainscoughs, Rainfords, Andersons, Nixons, Orrells, Russells, Ashcrofts, Milners, Rowbottoms, Shaws, Carrs, Kitchen, Parrs, Bolds, Bibbys, Halls, Croppers, Fleetwoods, Franklin, Fairclough, Leatherbarrows, Scarisbricks, Thwaites, Balshaws, Bradshaws, Cadwells, Charnleys, Whitesides, Masters, Jacsons, Gorstage, Ashcrofts, Baxendales, Cooksons, Pearsons, Threlfalls, Bakers, Spencer, Moss, Tomlinsons. These are not all in alphabetical order, but only as they appear in records, and family trees, before these Parish Registers, back to the first landing of the Rimmers, apart from the scanty, mostly inaccurate records of the Domesday Survey in 1086, there is no record of the Rimmers. The apparent description of the 'Otegrimels' of the Danes, and Normans, and the references stated earlier to 'Odda', 'Grim', 'Hrimr', and other conjectural Norsemen, such as 'Audgrimr', (reduced, as was natural by the Rimmers, to the nickname 'Oudgrim' (Old grim), meant that little was known of their activities, until the connections were made with the various religious establishements in the area from the 11th century onwards. before the Parish Registers, there are only sketchy records, in the Court Rolls of the County of Lancaster, in the 13th century onwards, principally in the reign of Edward II, of even the North Meols area, and I can find no record of any Rimmer being called to account for any misdemeanor whatsoever, amongst the local inhabitants.

Whilst it is impossible to give a geneological sequence of all the Rimmer intermarriages, a few instances can be given from Parish Records, and other family trees, to illustrate the extent of their expansion after the move from the 'Snoterpool' into other areas.

From the 1550 line of Heskeths, we can trace the record, listed elsewhere, of Ellen Rimmer's marriage to John Hesketh, about the 1740s. John Hesketh was a descendant of Sir Thomas Hesketh, of Rufford, and the Kitchen family. The descendants of John and Ellen, can be traced through the Hesketh lineage, down to the Hesketh's of Meols Hall today. This was easily done from Meols Hall records.

From the Abram's of 1635, in Crossens, can be found Alice Rymer, married to Lawrence Abram in 1726. One of their four children, James, married a 'foreigner', Margaret Hall of Croston, in 1767. Another Margaret, daughter of John Abram, and Ann Bond, married Peter Rymer in 1737. In 1736, in another branch of the Abrams, Ellin Rymer was married to Robert Abram. There was a Thomas Rymer, married to Peggy, daughter of William Robinson and Ann Wright, in 1800, whilst Thomas's sister, Ellin Rymer, was married to Peggy's brother James in 1802.

The Aughtons were a very mixed bunch, with about nine branches to their family. They were 'reet foreigners' and no mistake, going back to a Saxon Thane in the Domesday survey. The male line can, however be traced back to Welsh descent. Aughtons were associated with Uplitherland, near Aughton, and Skelmersdale. They were Lords of the Manor of North Meols for about 200 years. I can only find the Rimmers being connected with them through Barnaby Kitchen, in the 16th century. In 1686, Isabell Rymer appears to have been the second wife of Thomas Aughton, whom she married on December 13th, 1686. They had a daughter, Issabell, of whom there is no record, but their son John, married Ellin Jacson, who appears to be connected with Formby Hall, in the 19th century, as one of the Formbys became Catherine Jacson, the authoress of several books on Formby and Europe. In another branch of the Aughtons, Margery Rymer was married to Robert Aughton in the 18th century, but nothing is known of Margery's wedding date, or death, as Robert was married a second time, to another

Margaret, a Shorlicor, but there is again no indication of her, or their marriage. As Robert would be 84 when he died, the fact of his marrying a second time would have created little comment.

In the line of Richard Aughton ('Cockle Dick'), born about 1729, there does not appear to be a Rimmer, until the branch off to Birkdale, when Margery Rymer was married on July 12, 1756, to Robert Aughton, who was Overseer of the Poor of North Meols, which duty he performed apparently from Birkdale, as he was listed as being from Birkdale Common. In 1796, he was also listed as being Parish Constable of North Meols. Margery Rymer died in March 1760, and Robert re-married on 14th April, 1761, Margaret Sherlicor, who died in 1807, aged 68. Robert died in 1808, so he must have been 76 when he re-married. In 1857, Alice Rimmer married James Aughton, and Ann Rimmer born 1837, died 1924, married Richard Aughton 1832-1922, they would be 87 and 90 years of age. They had seven sons, one of whom Richard 1880-1956, married Ellen Rimmer, no date given for births marriages or deaths, but they seemed to have had a daughter, Verna. Notable here, is the gradual shift from Rymer, into Rimmer. The Aughtons too, illustrate the shift in names, in this instance they only changed their name to Aughton, when they were granted land in Aughton, after being driven out of Wales in the 13th century. This shows how names can be taken from places, occupations, deed poll etc. Boteler, changed to Butler, was a butler for the Earl of Chester. Spencer, like my Uncle Harry, who coincidentally was a chemist, came from 'Dispenser' or Apothecary, to Spencer. Smiths did their own thing, 'Black' or otherwise, Wrights did their 'Wrighting', wheel, or ship. Rimmers did the lot apparently, picking up various derivations from all places and times, a proper 'Cook's Tour' of confusion, for historians, amateur or professional.

There is no way will I be persuaded to try to trace the connections between, for instance, the Balls and Wrights, especially with the Marshside Rimmers, for although they were a closely knit community, their relationships were so complex, with their verbal geneology, that there were, because of their early non-established church inclinations, very few records available, apart from Parish Records. Having connections with such places as the Temperance Mission in Marshside, and various other non-comformist's mission chapels, and churches springing up, meant that records were scattered over a wide area. In the last few hundred years, burials had to take place, and be recorded at Parish Churches, and then registered. Gravestones give dates, but time, and weather erosion have removed many traces, and in any case only limited geneology could be obtained from them, so it is little wonder that the verbal geneology, prevalent amongst the Rimmers most recent ancestors, actually increased, right up to our present time.

There are still, however, many instances of the Rimmer's intermarriages into the local communities, in all the districts 'Betwixt Ribbel and Moerse'.

The Blundells for instance, were another family with many branches, stretching from the 'Askyr to the Alt'. Their lineage goes back to the 13th century, when William de Coudray married Amabel Blundell in 1224. I have referred many times to the Blundell's influence in the area, especially William the Cavalier, and his grandson Nicholas, well renowned for his 'Diarist' achievements. I also gave an acknowledgement in 'Between Ribbel and Moerse', of Mr. B. M. Whitlock Blundell, of Little Crosby Hall, who not only gave me access to records, but also accompanied me on field excursions around the Hall, even when photographing the Harkirke Chapel, and the Park Crosses in the rain. We had much contact in the 1950s and 1960s privately, and then publicly, when we both deplored the acts of municipal vandalism committed by the Council, in the destruction of the Virgin Lane cottages, and Cross, (pages 106-107, photo 54-57). There has however been the subsequent result, after the deploring of a botched up attempt at the Harkirke Chapel, by a recent expert excavation of the Saxon foundations of the Chapel, which is still proceeding successfully. Of the other branches of the Blundell families, some contact with the Rimmers can be traced, when Gilbert Blundell 1710-55, of Little London, and Lytham, married Hannah Rimmer, who died in 1751. Their son Miles, of Blowick, 1748-1824, married Ann Rymer. They had two sons, Richard who married into the Wright family, and Gilbert, who married Alice Barton. They had also three daughters, Hannah, who married Robert Barton, Ellen, who married John Moss, and Alice, who married John Johnson. It was Richard and Gilbert, who each had a son, Miles in 1804, and 1815. Miles seems to have become a family name in this branch, for there had been a Miles Blundell in Crossens 1760-1821, who died without issue. A Miles, of Halsall, 1741-1823, married Mary Jump of Halsall in 1766, who died in 1833. Their son James 1767-1851, married, in 1794, a Jennet Rimmer. They lived at Weathercock Farm, presumably in Halsall. They again had a Miles, 1792-1872, who lived at Birkdale, who married a Rebecca Gorstage in 1815. They also had a Miles, amongst their three sons and a daughter. Another Miles, 1802-62 of Birkdale, and Ainsdale, married Margery Rimmer in 1826. They had four sons, one of them a Miles, but I cannot understand that one son is listed as being James Rimmer, of Gorse Hill Farm, Halsall 1831-1909. James Rimmer is also listed as being married to Mary, the daughter of the Birkdale Miles, who married Rebecca Gorstage. Mary and James, are presumably the parents of Miles Rimmer, 1870-1933 of Scarisbrick Hall Farm. I am on familiar ground here, if this branch of the family was also connected with Warren Farm, Ainsdale. In Halsall also, Blundells have been associated with Rimmers in business, for some considerable time. When we used to take another short cut to Bank Nook via Cockle Dick's Lane, or across the 'Strawberry Fields' I always associated 'Cockle Dick's Farm' with the Blundells, who still occupy it to this day, as 'Cockle Dick's Nurseries'. I have never clearly defined the relationship between the Rimmers and Blundells completely, as it would be as complex as the Balls and Wrights.

I had an auntie we called, Auntie 'Nin', and that was the name we called her until she died. She was a Jane Rimmer, who was married to a Norwood Road Barton. One Barton line started with John Barton marrying a Jane Blundell, in 1732, at Ormskirk. They had nine children, one of whom Robert, married Alice Threlfall in 1770. They had ten children. Robert's brother Thomas, married a Margaret Rimmer in 1764, and they also had ten children. This line also had a James Rimmer, who married Ellen, who was one of only eight children, in 1847. They eventually got mixed up with the Blundells, but along the way there was a Peter Leadbetter, who had eleven children by his second wife, Jane Todd whom he married in 1791. She was a daughter-in-law of Alice Rimmer, who was married to a Barton in 1765. Talk about the Bible exhortation to go forth and multiply! A few more instances of Rimmer connections with other families, shows how complex this issue is, for geneologists and historians alike.

In the Bond family, who had property locally, in the 'Rowe' in 1697, threre appears a Gilbert Rimmer, married to Ann Bond in 1768, and a James Rimmer, married in 1885. Another Bond, Ellen, sister of Ann, married to Gilbert Rimmer, was married to Martin Rimmer in 1768, a double wedding, which took place on 1st February. Neither of them had any children, but their sister-in-law Catherine, had eight children. Later on, in the 20th century, Rimmers in my family were related through the Baxters and Bonds, to several families in the Banks area. There was a James Rimmer, married on June 13th, 1885 to Elizabeth, who died in 1936, but I don't know where they fit in. This of course is only the North Meols record, and is incomplete, as the Bonds operated further north, as I have explained previously. I have made reference to contact between Rimmers and Breakills, but there was a Margery Rymer, who was married in, or about 1603, but it is not known whom she married. There was a Robert Rymer, married to Margery in 1678, and an Ellin Rymer, married to James, one of Margery's brothers, in 1705. Breakills also appear in records in Altcar, Eccleston, and Ormskirk, so it is very time consuming to pursue lines of enquiry, which are general, instead of specific.

Brookfield's records appear in 1612, but little is known of the Thomas Brookfield of Banks, whose first wife died in 1612, but in his two marriages there is no record of his birthday or death, nor of his wives' surnames, apart from the second wife's name Isabell, who died in 1662. Thomas had a son John baptised April 23rd, 1595, died 1671, who married, in 1621, Alice Rimmer, who was buried in 1676. They had four sons. This illustrates the difficulty in intermarriages, outside in country districts, and in different parishes. There is Ann Rimmer, married to John Brookfield in 1759, and another Ann Rimmer, the second wife of Edward Brookfield, who was married to him in 1762. She only lasted 8 years, as she died in 1770, and it is not recorded who his third wife was, but they had two children from this third marriage. Elizabeth Rimmer, who was married to John Brookfield in 1808, had two children by him, both born and buried in 1808, according to records. They had two more children, William and Margaret, in 1809 and 1812, given the same names as the two infants who died. There was also a Mary Rimmer, married to John's brother William, who was ten years older than John. They married in 1809, and had two children, Ann and Alice, born in 1810 and 1812. There is no record of the High Park Brookfields, well known to us, but here again, the absence of records could be due, as in many cases, to changes in religious convictions, to non-conformist principles, from the established church, as the records in the Wesleyan and Congregational, and other such religious bodies was, apart from of course regional registers, confined to Rolls of Honour, when scholars became members of the Church, after being enrolled in the Sunday Schools.

There is no very early connection between the Rimmers and the Gregsons, and contact would appear to be rather tenuous, as their line can be traced back to Hugh Gregson of Penwortham, and local records only show the date of his burial as being on 12th April, 1783. He does however seem to have had a great deal of interest locally, as his first wife was Mary Bond, who he married in 1742. She died in January, 1750, with one son, born in 1745, who died in his fourth year. They had a daughter Jane, who was born in 1743, and died when she was 8 years old. Their other son Robert, was born in 1747, and died in 1774. Mary Bond died in 1749, then in June 1750, Hugh married Ellen Hunt, also from North Meols, and they had eight children.

It is howver one of these children, their daughter Jane, born in 1755, upon whom history is largely centred, owing to her marriage to William Sutton (The Old Duke) on the 20th August,. 1776.

So much has been said of William Sutton, especially by 'out of town' historians, inferring in derogatory terms, that he was also an 'out of towner', originating from the Fylde area, and somewhat of an mountebank, and a buffoon, that I, along with many other locals, have spent much time and effort in research, to present the true picture of William Sutton.

There is no doubt whatsoever that William was the pivot and 'King Pin', of all historical events occurring, in both Churchtown and Southport, of which he was undoubtedly the founder. His birth in 1752, was a landmark in local history, and his death in 1840 was this year, 1990, celebrated, as an 150 year anniversary, by a tree planting ceremony, near the site of his 'Duke's Folly Hotel', acknowledged the fact that Churchtown was the 'Mother of Southport', and 'Duke Sutton' was the one and only founder of Southport. It was only after penning the history of the 'Duke', and attending the ceremony, that I realized how many people, and families were represented, from home and abroad, and what a prodigious task I had set myself to account for the Rimmers, who in North Meols alone, had originally outnumbered the Suttons by at least fifteen to one!

The Rimmers appear to have been connected with the Suttons through several families, including the Bonds, Gregsons, Linakers, Hunts, and in the Sutton family, to Kate Rimmer, who died in 1970, and also on my Granny's side through Rigby-Suttons, Comstives and Lloyds.

The Hunts originated from Much Hoole, through Henry Hunt, no record of birth or death, or his two wives. One son of his first marriage, was James 1647-1732 who was Parish Clerk of North Meols. Another James Hunt, who died in 1778, occupied Meols Hall for some time, and gave his name to Hunts Cottages standing on the edge of the Hall grounds, behind Botanic Road. My brother Albert, and his family, lived in one of these for some time in the 1960s whilst working at Meols Hall. In 1725 William Hunt 1701-1772, married Alice Rimmer in 1725. They had eight children, Jennet, who was born and died in 1726, was followed by another Jennet in 1730. Jennet appears to have been a family name by this time, probably replaced by Jane in later years. The Jennet born in 1730, was married to a John Rimmer, on December 29th, 1747, whilst her sister Ellen, (another family name), married a Richard Rimmer on February 27th, 1753. Another sister married a Blundell, and another brother, James, married Ann Wright, on December 17th, 1759. Of their three children, the daughter Alice, married William Rimmer, on December 4th, 1783. From another branch of the family, Margaret Rimmer was married on November 7th, 1727, to James Hunt, who was baptised in January, 1704. Margaret died in February 1729/30, and James remarried on 7th December, 1730. I do not know from which branch of the family he came, but James Hunt who died in 1778, occupied Meols Hall for a time, but it could have been the James who married Maragret Rimmer, or the James, married to Margaret Brookfield, but he built Hunts Cottages whilst in residence at Meols Hall, in the years of his occupation.

It was not uncommon that, although they are admired and sought after in these days, old manorial halls did not accord with eighteenth century conceptions of elegance. It is not surprising therefore, that whilst the Heskeths were living at Rossall, owing to the marriage of Roger Hesketh in 1733, to Margaret Fleetwood, Meols Hall was let off to various families. The building could have housed several families at once, the northern part, at one period, being sealed off as a cottage, from the main building. Records are rather confusing, as they state that Thomas Ball (died 1767), Henry Milner (living in 1771), and the aforesaid James Hunt, we listed as being 'at' or 'of' the hall. From 1780, the hall was occupied by the Linaker family, acting as the lord's agents, namely Henry, (died 1796), and his sons Richard, (drowned 1807) and John (died 1846).

Although not appearing in Parish Records as being in as great a number as other families with reference to North Meols, their influence, and activities, in all local areas, has lasted, at least officially, from the 16th century to the present day.

This family goes back as far as Henry Linaker of Crossens, who died in 1669. One of the most memorbale members was John Linaker (1709-1746), whose name appears on the remains of the village stocks still standing to the west of the Black Bull (Hesketh Arms), beside the Churchyard wall. The stocks were last used in 1860 for six hours, for a case of drunkenness, of one of the Rimmers. The inscription on the side posts, 'John Linaker 1741', barely legibile, over half a century ago, when I looked at it, probably referred to John Linaker being a constable, or steward of the Manor at that time. Undoubtedly one of the most outstanding historical events concerning the Linakers was the marriage of Robert, son of Henry Linaker and Jane Hoscar, who were married at Hoole in 1756. Robert, who was born in 1775, was married to Margaret (who was born in 1777), daughter of 'Duke' Sutton, of the Black Bull Inn. The 'Old Duke' as he was later called, had, in 1798, taken a lease from Miss Bold, around his house 'Dukes Folly', and built a new inn called the South Port Hotel. When his daughter Margaret (listed in the Sutton lineage as 'Peggy') was married in the same year, Sutton transferred the 'Black Bull' into the hands of Margaret (or 'Peggy'), and took up residence at his new hotel.

It is not recorded in the Sutton lineage, that Robert and Margaret, had two children, Jane, who was born in 1798, and Henry born in 1800. Henry died in 1814, but the untimely death of Robert Linaker, in June 1800, was a shattering blow to all concerned. I am not certain, but a chance remark I picked up from family conversation when we lost a Robert, my uncle, a fisherman aged 22, drowned in 1927, seemed to infer that Robert Linaker was also a relative who had been lost in similar circumstances. The fact that our Rimmer link with 'Duke Sutton' came from the Linaker relationship, supports this contention.

As far as I can trace, one of Henry Linaker's sons, John, (born 1684), married Ann Rimmer (born 1685). This was the first reference to an official link between the Rimmers and Linakers. The death of Richard, the agent for Meols Hall, who was drowned in 1807, made it a double tragedy for the Linakers, even although Richard was 49 when he was drowned. His wife, formerly Sarah Whiteside, died five years later. They however, left five sons, one of whom, Edward, (born 1797) married a Jane Rimmer. Their other son James (1805-88) married Jane Sutton. One of their grandsons, Edward (1838-1906), married Sarah Rimmer, and they had eight children, one, John (1879-1944) married Jane Sutton (1879-1968). One of their two sons was Henry Sutton Linaker, born 1899, who was the principle guest at the Tree Planting Ceremony in 1990.

A strange coincidence occurred when I wrote an article in the Southport Star, in the 17th May, 1990, prior to the tree planting ceremony commemorating the 150th anniversary of The 'Grand Old Duke's death in 1840. This ceremony took place, near the site of 'Dukes Folly' on Tuesday, May 22nd, and the article was coupled together with one from Henry Sutton Linaker, 90 years of age. The other senior member of the gathering of the Sutton clan, reported in the Star on 31st May, 1990, was Bert Ashworth also a nongenarian and a friend of long standing, from Yellow House Lane, where I worked for 32 years. I was invited to the tree planting ceremony as an observer, and thus included in the accompanying photo as such. I have only met Henry Sutton Linaker once, when I was a small boy, and did not remember him, but I have had many phone conversations with him, including one after the publishing of 'Betwixt Ribbel and Moerse' in which he told me he had written 60,000 words by then on the Linakers. It occured to me, as I watched the ceremony, and other proceedings, that, as my granny was also descended from the 'Old Duke' through the Rigby-Suttons, I could have presented, coupled with my grandad's stonemason connections with the 'Old Duke', a very strong claim to be included as a participant, and not as observer. Therefore the majority of the people who attended the ceremony were unaware that they were relatives of the 'Lost Tribe' of Rimmers, with a lineage not only stretching back to the 'Old Duke', but perhaps to Methusaleh, Enoch, Moses, and the time when the "Patriarch took the Tribe into Egypt!".

There is another connection with John (Village Stocks) Linaker, and the Rimmers, through their son Henry (1709-75), who married Alice Rymer on the 3rd of December, 1759. One of their three sons is described as being Robert Rymer (1764-94) of Ormskirk. Henry and Alice, coincidentally, had three more sons who died in infancy.

Although the Linaker connection with the Suttons is, without doubt, very strong indeed, we must not forget the scores of other families, spreading out over the area, in a gigantic web of genealogical connection, which has taken many families into years and years of research, but the more research I carry out over successive periods of time, confirms the contention that, because of its reticence, plus its great original numeracy, sustained and increased for over a thousand years, the Rimmer family or 'Tribe', in this area, is accordingly, the greatest, geneological, enigmatic task of all time. A few more instances of this diversity of connection with other families will surely suffice to illustrate, and support, this statement.

Still adhering mainly to North Meols Parish records, in alphabetical order after the Suttons, we can divert once again to Crossens, where records of the Thomasson family commenced with Thomas, who was buried in 1699, with no record obtainable of his birth, or marriage. There is a record however, of a son Richard (died February 1698), who was married to Lydia Ball, who was subsequently remarried to James Rimmer. They had a son Thomas (1684-1746), who was listed as being of the Roe Lane Rimmers. Another son John (1696-1729), married Elizabeth Wright in 1724. Their son Richard, (1725-62), who was from Banks, married Anne Rymer in 1749. One of their four sons John (1842-1901), married Alice Gorstage-Linaker (1846-1912) thus forging a link back to Catherine Gorstage (1797-1867), who was married to William (1796-1864), son of John Linaker (1766-1846), who was the brother of Robert Linaker who married Margaret (or 'Peggy'), daughter of Duke Sutton.

This geneology stunt is like unravelling the 'hanks' of wool I used to go for to the Marshside—Shellfield Road shop, to enable my grandad to knit his 'gansey's'. I you keep at it, it comes right out in the end, but there are some very curious patterns that emerge in the process.

Most families have some skeletons in their cupboards. Many minor offences do not get recorded, except in larger parishes.

The Leadbetter family for instance, quite respectable in our district, had quite a scattered history, which appears to have started, according to North Meols records, with a John Leadbetter, of Banks, who married Mary Wright on the 25th April, 1762. John died in 1798 at the age of 58. They had six children, one of whom, Peter, who married Mary Barton in October, 1786, had a son, John (1787-1841) who was convicted of forgery in 1820, and imprisoned in Lancaster Castle. However the lineage of the Leadbetters is very confusing, as there is also recorded a Peter Leadbetter (1733-1797), who was believed to be a native of Tarleton, and perhaps the brother of John Leadbetter of Banks. As I will illustrate later, prison charges are often very scanty, and misleading, causing injustice in many instances. When 'Duke Sutton' gave up his licence of the South Port Hotel in 1802, he is supposed to have let it, on a 21 years lease, to two people, William Hilton, and Henry Leadbetter. Sutton continued to run the Hotel, as he is later stated to be in debt to the Formby Brewery in 1803-6. The last delivery of ale was made in 1806, and in 1807, according to the accounts of the Brewery, one of the partners being Jno Rimmer, the sum of £214.17s.11d. was "secured upon Mortgage on South Port Premises etc." I have made reference to my Grandad having his fishing nets fouled by the remains of the submerged forest off Formby Point (page 8), and the boatbuilding yard, which stood at the end of Little King Street, on the site of the now demolished Trinity Hall, which stood in Duke Street, (page 10). I did not however, put much credence on his statement that the Rimmers once used to sail up the River Nile! But I have since found out that there was a wharf, or landing stage on the River Nile, near the boat yard, probably also connected, at one time, with Fairclough's Lake.

I have since discovered also, that the last delivery of ale, similar to the deliveries made to 'Duke' Sutton on previous occasions, was indeed, made by the seafaring relatives of the Rimmer partner, of Formby Brewery, from Formby, by sea, and up the River Nile, to the landing stage. The river was probably at least 10 feet wide then. Even before it reduced to being 'pole jumped' width, in later years, coal was conveyed to adjacent dwellings. The Nile was subsequently culverted, partly to make the lake at Victoria Park, but in my time I have seen the wooden blocks comprising the Lord Street surface at the old Glaciarium, which became Whitesides, and Kirby showrooms, lifted up by storm flood, 'backwater'. Earlier than that, I have seen the cellars at Rowntrees Bakery, where my Auntie Lois was employed, fill up with this backflow from the River Nile.

When cottages were first built on Lord Street, channels were made in front of the gardens to drain away surplus water. Even later than the middle of the 19th century, when Lord Street flooded after high tides, passengers were ferried across Lord Street by boat, at the southern end of the street.

At this moment in time, the old tradition regarding the 'Old Duke' being imprisoned in Lancaster Castle for debt, has never been proven. There appears to be some confusion whether 'Duke Sutton', or a Leadbetter, or neither, were ever imprisoned, or even charged, at Lancaster. Whether Tho Rimmer ever got any of his debt repaid, is not stated, as the South Port Hotel was still in business, according to the advertisment in the Liverpool Advertiser, in May 1809.

One of the Leadbetter's links came later, in 1898, when Ellen Rimmer married Thomas (1876-1958). From a marriage in September 1784, between Thomas Leadbetter (1762-1831), to Ann (Nally) Peet, came the youngest son Peter who married Mary Ashcroft, on the 14th March 1828. Peter was the last of twelve children born to Thomas and Ann. They were recorded as being the first fishing family to move from North Meols around 1843. The 1851 census at Fleetwood, gives them as having four children, aged from nine to seventeen, born at North Meols, and three children aged two, three, and seven, born in Fleetwood. Their actual relationship to Ellen Rimmer is not clear, but this is a case of the Rimmers still maintaining relationships with the descendants of the original 'Tribe' who remained there from the first landing, or an invitation by other Rimmers who had worked their way up the coast.

As this small account of these Rimmer connections seems to have taken alphabetical form, I should be now discussing the Rimmer connection with the Lloyde or Lloyd family, but I am leaving this one as a final round-up, as I have personal connections, leading right up to the present day, with them.

A couple of references will complete this account, which is mostly comprised of parish records, and land deeds and wills, and merely illustrates the connections made by the Rimmers, with all their subsequent marriages to other settlers, from their early days in the 9th century to the 20th century.

A brief but important connection with the Thomasson family was formed, when Thomas, of Crossens, is recorded as being buried, possibly at Crossens, in the middle of the year 1699. Their eldest son Richard, who died in 1698, married Lydia Ball, who was later married to James Rimmer. In turn their eldest son Thomas, appears (1684-1746) in Roe Lane. Another son John (1696-1729) married Elizabeth Wright in 1724, and their son Richard (1725-62) who was living in Banks, married Ann Rymer in 1749. She died in 1766, but their eldest son John, (1755-97) married Alice Gregson in 1784, and another of their four subsequent descendants, a great grandson John (1842-1901), married Alice Gorstage Linaker (1846-1912) thus linking half a dozen families in a long line of subsequent relationships.

A similar situation occurred just recently with the arrival, from British Columbia, of an enquiry, one of a constant stream of requests for information, I receive from the four corners of the globe, for antecedents of people who forsook these shores for unaccountable generations past. This enquiry was engendered by the appearance of a Woodland's schoolgirl's photograph, in the Southport Star. It was addressed to a sister-in-law, previously of the Todd family, but with no connection with the branch of the family in British Columbia.

Research on this enquiry, was from a previous student of Woodland Technical College in 1946-8, whose maternal grandmother was a Mary Carr, who married into the Todd family. Her grandmother, six times removed, was Jennet Todd, daughter of John and Mary Todd of Rowe Lane, who married William Carr in 1775. Ellen Carr, daughter of another William Carr, married a Paul Todd circa 1838, who farmed in Ainsdale, and sold beer from the farm, which comprised some 40 acres. Her father, William Carr, a son of Jennet Todd, and William Carr, was shown as being at Ainsdale Mill in the 1812 census.

The lady in question, Brenda Pearson, who made the enquiry from Canada, also states that her Great Uncle Johnn Carr, had a grandaughter, Hilda Rimmer, who married a Richard Todd. Hilda was born in 1909, so the marriage would have taken place approximately circa 1930. As Hilda was a cousin to the late Simms Mitchell, one time Mayor of Southport, this would make Brenda Pearson his cousin once removed.

Stir this pot a little more, and you find that John Todd married a Jane Halsall on the 31st March, 1725. John died in 1754 and Jane in 1751. Their only son John, married Margery Rimmer on the 19th January, 1752. This Margery died in 1775, and John in 1808. They had five daughters and four sons. Their daughter Jennet, born in 1754 married a William Carr on the 3rd April, 1775. Jennet's brother Robert, born 1759, married Martha Rimmer, on the 1st April, 1782, an appropriate day, as family reseach can make a right fool of anybody! Jennet's sister Ann (born 1764) married James Aughton on October 23rd, 1783, making William Carr and James Aughton brothers-in-law.

While all this was going on I had another enquiry locally, also from the Woodland's photo, of another student, who was connected with the Todd-Carr branch, and also to the Barton family, as another of Jennet's sisters Jane, born 1770, married John Barton in 1791, who seemed to be a relative of ours through my Auntie who married into the Barton family. I have passed the British Columbian enquiry over to the Carr families, who still live in Guildford Road. I live a stones throw from Carr Lane, where the Carr family had two farms, and many other places and connections, Carr Moss, and Carr Moss Lane, Carr House Bretherton, Carrhouses near Lunt, comprising over 100 relatives locally, and twice as many in surrounding areas, including the Fylde. This should surely prove that you cannot research any family 'Betwixt Ribbel and Moerse' without encountering a Rimmer.

Finally in alphabetical order the Watkinson family appears to commence unobtrusively enough in North Meols Parish records with Richard Watkinson, died 1775, married to Elizabeth Bond in September, 1732. Elizabeth died in 1786. They had two boys and two girls, plus a boy, Peter, who died in infancy. The eldest surviving son Peter (born 1744) married Elizabeth Rimmer, same age as herself, in the same year that her first child, Cicely, was born in 1768. Peter's sister, Elizabeth, born 1747, married John Sutton (1747-1818) on 25th February, 1771. Their children do not appear in the Watkinson family tree, but in the Sutton family tree, they are listed as having six children, bringing marriage contacts with Wrights, Warings, Blundells, Croppers, and Bakers. One of the Watkinsons, Ann (1868-1963) married Robert Sutton (1869-1952). Ann was one of eight children. Their children do not appear in the Watkinson's tree, but in the Sutton tree, they had three sons, one of whom, Richard (1906-83) was the author of the book on Marshside dialect. Kate Rimmer (1881-1970) was a relative, who had contact with my mother for many years. She was the only child, or grandchild of Thomas Sutton (1849-81) and Martha Watkinson (1849-68) as it was their only son, Richard Peter Sutton (1880-1930) who married Kate Rimmer. There is no record of any children.

A little anecdote interposed here, concerning one branch of the Watkinsons, will illustrate that the more you learn, and the longer you live, the less you know, especially in the field of geneology.

All Watkinsons were known, by the abbreviation of their surname, into the nickname 'Wokky'. There was a family of Watkinsons who lived round the corner to us in Thornton Road, High Park. There is only one surviving member of the family still living there in the family residence. She is Mrs.

Winnie Treadwell, now a widow, but still known, and referred to by us, and the local paper Southport Star, as 'Winnie Wok'. We still have an association going back to our childhood days, and I can still recall, when very young, we trailed off to perhaps Hesketh Park. Very often also we went down Hesketh Road, to the Aerodrome Hangar, which housed ex World War One Pilot, Giroux's flight of pleasure-ride aircraft, and played around the sea bank, which is now the coast road, and also the Golf Links, and on the sea shore, which acted as landing area and slipway for the planes.

Returning, very often tired, dusty and thirsty, we always called at a cottage in the sandhills occupied by Watkinson's relatives, where we were always sure of a drink, and a 'jam butty', from 'Auntie' Watkinson. This cottage was totally isolated, in an area of sandhills stretching from behind Cambridge Road, covering the whole corner of Hesketh Road, to where Brocklebank Road was built, later on. The cottage was reached by just a foot trodden pathway through the sandhills, which were covered by the low growing bushes of dewberries, or loganberries, a species of winberries, as we used to call them, purple in colour, and very succulent, especially to small huyngry children. I can still savour the flavour of them today. Just a small childhood reminiscence similar to many hundred of experiences of countless numbers of people still alive today.

There is however a sequel to this charming little childhood experience, which I had in June, 1990, when on my way to do further research on 'Little Ireland' at the Hesketh Golf Club. From information received from my brother Albert, who had recently rediscovered it, I stopped in Hesketh Road on the corner of Brocklebank Road. Between the corner house on Brocklebank Road, and the next house, from the Cambridge Road entrance, between No. 17 and 19 Hesketh Road, is an overgrown pathway, which now leads nowhere, as it is sealed in by the back gardens of Cambridge Road and Hesketh Road and Brocklebank Road. This is the original path to the cottage, through the sandhills, which covered the whole area to Park Crescent, before this part of Hesketh Road was built, or any part of Brocklebank Road. The only building in this whole area was the Watkinson's cottage, nestling in the folds of the sandhills. It was, for me, a real waft of nostalgia, from 75 years or so ago.

The twist in this little tale lies in the fact that, after all these years, I have just found out that the 'Auntie' Watkinson, from the cottage, was, before her marriage, a Rimmer, and from Marshside. I have not yet worked out the implications of this information, concerning geneology, but it illustrates, once again, the impossibility of confining the ubiquitous Rimmers into any form of complete geneological sequence.

CHAPTER 8

THE RIMMERS AND SOUTHPORT

When we move into the 19th century, the full impact of the Rimmer's infuence on local community affairs, particularly in respect of the development of Southport, becomes more apparent, from both historical, and municipal records and press reports.

Prior to the establishment of an official Lifeboat Service in 1840, many of the Southport fishermen were employed in operating a private enterprise for a rescue service, as well as fishing trips. It was on record that fishing boats, around the turn of the 19th century, up to 1808, would go out at high water, and trawl until the next tide. At that time, many deep sea fish were among the catches, which included Flukes, Gurnett, Soles, Turbot, Cod, and Ray. Many boats were recorded as being unfit, as they were blown off course, to places as far away as Ireland, Isle of Man, and Walney Island.

My grandad sailed on much safer craft in later years, to the Isle of Man, and Walney Island, where they were formerly engaged in the transporation of wool, in co-operation with the Monks, as the Rimmers were engaged in the wool trade connected with Little London, for many years, from about the 15th century.

In 1816, a fund was raised to provide a lifeboat, but it was so unseaworthy, that boatmen refused to put to sea in it.

The first official Lifeboat was put into service in 1840. This was the Rescue, and the Coxwain was Richard Rimmer. The boat did service until 1861, and Richard Rimmer was Coxswain until 1846.

Even before the decline of such enterprises as fishing trips, and the ferrying of passengers across the Ribble by fishermen was replaced by paddle steamers, the Rimmers were exploring new avenues of enterprise, consistent with the expansion of Southport.

On the 4th May, 1844, the first issue of The Southport Visiter appeared, to replace the town's first newspaper named the Southport Pleasure Boat, which was withdrawn after only thirteen issues, in 1842. The Visiter comprised only eight pages, the first and last of which consisted solely of advertisements, one of which referred to Richard Rimmer, a linen and woollen draper whose statement that, "he was grateful for favours conferred," indicated that he was already then well established in business, and further informed his customers that he had in stock, "a large variety of goods, recommended for durability, and cheapness." "They may be equalled by some, but unsurpassed by none."

I am not certain if this was the same Rimmer who appeared in later advertisements of Boothroyd, Sons, and Rimmer, of 293-309 Lord Street, about the middle of the 19th century, but according to the logos on the side of the horse drawn van, and mechanized vehicle, depicted in the advertisement, they were also cabinet makers, with removal and storage facilities at the factory in West Street.

This business had been opened by William Jolley in 1825, when he was at Richmond Hill, where the Atkinson Library is now situated. When he moved across the road to new premises, which are still there, he was joined by Samuel Boothroyd. There was a report in the Liverpool Mercury of 25th September, 1835 that the, "house and shop of Messrs Jolley and Boothroyd, had been broken into by two young men, who took £40-£50 worth of silks, and £150 of broadcloths," which they hid in the sandhills. They were caught, after being spotted, at 'Birchedale', where they had first asked for directions to Southport. The last sentence of the report reads, "This is the second house breaking this year in this hitherto peaceable and harmless village."

The many other varied enterprises and business concerns of the Rimmers, connected with Southport, are too numerous to list. It is interesting to note however, that a contemporary concern, such as the Rimmer hairdressing establishment, which operated in London Street, was, in similar fashion to John Rimmer's Boot and Shoe Shop, on the corner of Shellfield Road and Marshside Road, operated by whole families, and successive generations, of Rimmers, for many consecutive periods in time. A retention perhaps, of reticence exercised by them, in former tribal activities?

Consistent with the continuous fight against the vagaries of wind and sea, tragedies were constantly occurring. In 1851 Richard Alty and Peter Rimmer, were drowned when their boat Joseph and Mary was wrecked.

Also in 1869, seven cart shanking shrimpers from Marshside, most of them close relatives of the two Rimmers who were included, were drowned by the incoming tide, when caught in a sudden dense fog. "They that go down to the sea in carts" a near biblical quotation, was coined on this sad occurrence.

Although there were no Rimmers by name, listed when the worst lifeboat disaster in maritime history took place in December 1886, most of the crew of the ill-fated Eliza Fernley, were close relatives of the Rimmers. John Robinson, who was only 18, the youngest member of the crew, was found on the shore, only a short distance from the wreck, in the early hours of the following day. He died in the arms of his in-law, Thomas Rimmer, in the star grass on the sandhills, where he had been laid.

The entire crew of the St. Annes lifeboat, Laura Janet, which was found capsized on Ainsdale Beach, were drowned. The bodies of the lifeboat crews were laid out in the Palace Hotel outbuildings where, ironically enough, my

Uncle Bob, aged 22, was taken, in March 1927, after his fishing boat had capsized in a sudden squall, on the corner of the same Spencer's sandbank, that caused the loss of the Eliza Fernley lifeboat.

The tragic parallel between these two incidents, also occurs in the fact that, Henry Robinson, a relative, and one of the two survivors of the 1886 disaster, to my knowledge was still asserting, 50 years later, that many more lives could have been saved. In my case, I was, 60 years after our own personal tragedy, still campaigning for the restoring of a life-saving craft at Southport, as the coroner at the inquest deplored the fact that there had been no boat kept at the Pier, after the Lifeboat Station had been closed, only a few months earlier, in 1926.

In an article entitled 'Lifeboat for Robert' in the Southport Star in July 1989, I had appealed for the newly inaugurated inshore type of rescue craft, to be named 'Robert Rimmer', as the first lifeboat coxswain was a Rimmer, and the last custodian of the Lifeboat House was 'Grandfather Rigby'! He was from my grandmother's side. She was married to my grandfather, Robert Rimmer.

The final irony in these events, is the fact that the final appeal by relatives of those who had suffered a similar drowning tragedy, had led to the success of the inauguration, at long last, of a light draughted, inshore rescue craft. Also one victim of the fishing boat tragedy, lived only two streets away from where my Uncle Bob lived, and where his ill-fated boat was built in the back garden. At least the lifeboat did have the word 'Rescue' printed on the side, the connection therefore being made with the first Southport Lifeboat named 'The Rescue' in 1840.

Although grief, occasioned by loss of life at sea, was regarded as private, and generally accepted as an occupational hazard, any financial assistance afforded by the townspeople who raised funds for the relief of dependent relatives was accepted, and applied, with dignity. The number of local catastrophies was very high, and never properly recorded, except for many instances of the adoption of fishermen's and lifeboatmen's orphaned children, being taken in by relatives, and even in one instance, by a clergyman.

In its total lifeboat history, Southport had only six coxswains, serving seven lifeboats, in a span of 86 years. The first lifeboat, 'The Rescue' saved 176 lives out of a total of close on four hundred. It has to be said therefore, that the Rimmer clan, together with their in-laws, certainly justified their participation in all aspects of community life. The last surviving member, and the youngest crew member of the last Southport Lifeboat, the John Harling, Mr. Harry ('Pen') Wright, died in November 1990 as I was 'penning' these notes. He was 87, one of our contemporaries, and best known characters of Marshside. He was in the crew as the youngest member, when the John Harling went out for the last time, to rescue the crew of the Delorain, in rough seas, off Freshfield Point in 1921. The John Harling was in service from 1904, and rescued over 63 lives. Richard Wright was coxswain from 1920-25. Thus ended the most notable era of tragedy, disaster, and rescue, associated with the raging seas off, and the soft yellow sands on, the beaches of 'Sunny Southport'.

So unobtrusive was the Rimmer's attitude to the whole spectrum of their occupation of the area, that, over the years I have found it extremely difficult to ascertain the complete geneology of my connection with them. One of the hardest tasks ever allocated to a professional historian or amateur scribbler such as myself, is to get a fisherman to talk, and even then, to get the full information from him.

Although civic records are easily obtainable for the last two centuries, the full story cannot be told. Lifeboat records are well accounted for, and you can follow my steps, for instance, to the Fog Bell, at the top of Marshside Road, erected under the auspices of the Fernley Observatory. The inscription on the plaque states that, "This Fog Bell was erected in 1869 with the object of preventing a similar disaster to that which occurred when the seven fishermen named below were drowned off the coast whilst fishing Wm. Hesketh, P. Aughton, I. Rimmer, P. Rimmer, R. Wright, J. Wright, P. Wright. Rebuilt by John Geddes 1896." The impact of such occurrences, on such a small fishing community as Marshside was then, can only be imagined. A tragedy so profound, as to be press reported nationally, and articled in the 'London Times'.

On the civic front, Southport continued to expand and prosper. Improvement Commissions, and similar bodies were concerned with local administration and affairs, and the levying of rates until 1867, when the town was granted a charter giving it County Borough status identical to the Improvement Act of 1865.

In the municipal elections, held in 1867, there were four Wards, West, Craven, Talbot and East, each with six councillors and two aldermen. Although it was a non-political election, it was not without incident, as the returning officers for West Ward declared that many voting papers were invalid, owing to the ommission of the word 'Southport', on nomination documents for West Ward. Subsequently however, Seth Rimmer, and Sam Boothroyd, were elected as councillors for West Ward. This was probably the first incursion of the Rimmers into civic affairs, which has continued until the present. In my early days in the 1920s in High Park, there was another Rimmer Councillor. He was Enoch Rimmer, who was a councillor in 1923, and, in similar fashion to my grandad, preached at Old Park Lane Methodist Church. He was also proprietor of The Southport Weekly Herald, which was published from 1915 to 1945, at printing works at the rear of No. 13 High Park Road, near the Methodist Church, now replaced by Church Close, at the junction with Old Park Lane. The paper was delivered, once weekly, on Thursday, the price varying from $\frac{1}{2}$d. to 1d., some were also delivered free of charge. You also got a running commentary on local affairs from the little old fellow who delivered ours. He used to constitute the highlight of the week for my grannie, always throwing in some cryptic remark, or joke, such as on one bonfire night, his parting shot was, "Mischief night last night, seventeen doormats on our front doorstep!"

Enoch Rimmer's daughter, Margaret Barton, who lives in Churchtown, confirmed these details in 1990. She attended the Old Park Lane Church from the age of 5. The printing business, although now a single-handed venture, is still being run by Mr. Hodge, who comes from out of town farming stock.

Without a doubt, the 'Jewel in the Crown' of our family in particular, and in general of all the Rimmers, and the history of Southport, was William Rimmer (1861-1936), Bandmaster and Composer. He was two years older than my grandad, who was his cousin. They both died in the same year, 1936. I have described previously, the only occasion on which I met him. As far as I can ascertain, my grandad was a native of Little London, and married my granny who was Lucy Rigby, presumably of the same area, at Zion Independent Methodist Church, St. Lukes Road.

William Rimmer, Bandmaster and Composer, was listed as being born in Birkdale in 1861, and later living near, or in, 'Little London', at 28 Forest Road about 1892-1896-7. He was at 43 Arbour Street about 1899, and then at Field House, 56 Belmont Street, from 1900-1908. From around 1910-11, until at least 1934, he lived at Beech Cottage, 70 Belmont Street. It is self evident therefore, that despite his work, which took him to all parts of the country, and abroad, for considerable periods, he maintained contact with the town of Southport, which he did so much to publicize, a real 'Sandgrounder'.

He began piano lessons at the age of 9, and at 15 years of age he became side drummer of the Southport Rifle Band in 1877. He subsequently played cornet solo with many well-known northern brass bands. He was joint conductor with A. E. Bartle, of Southport's first Town Band, which, together with the Southport Municipal Band, 40 strong, with two double basses, and the Southport Pier Orchestra, he conducted for several years. He was also conductor for Southport Orchestral Society, and executive member of Southport Musical Festival, and conducted for the Sunday afternoon Brotherhood meeting at Southport Tabernacle.

From the age of 30, when he was appointed conductor of Southport Artillery Volunteer, and Skelmersdale Old Bands, he was trainer to many well known bands, for many years, at least a decade, Black Dyke Mills, Besses o' the Barn, Kingston Mills, Radcliffe Old, Rishton, Crooks, Wingates Temperance, Hebden Bridge, Irwell Springs, Shaw. He formed several bands, including the Foden Motor Works Band, which he formed in 1908.

As a composer, not only of brass band music, his output was truly phenomenal. Apart from composing scores for all the bands he trained, he also composed music of a different type, for various occasions, nationally, and internationally, using five different pseudonyms to retain his chief concern for music for his own bands. When the Southport Town Band came under his direction, he recorded his own compositions, amongst others, for Columbia Records, which became collectors items.

From 1898-1909 his bands won over 90 prizes, including 20 firsts, at major contests, where he was known to conduct several bands, in each contest, at Belle Vue and Crystal Palace. His record at Crystal Palace and Belle Vue, for consecutive annual wins with Wingates Temperance, has never been equalled, or beaten. For the years 1910-1911-1912, he was composer, and arranger, for Test pieces for Crystal Palace Championships.

It was because of his ability to build up an unknown band to championship standard, that he became a legend in the brass band world, and was subsequently known as "The Doctor of the Brass Band World", in the many references in brass band journals, to his career.

William Rimmer died in Southport, on Sunday, 9th February, 1936. On the 21st March, 1936, the BBC presented a hour's radio tribute "Homage to Rimmer", featuring his compositions and arrangements, played by Foden's Motor Works and three other bands. My grandad died in the same week as William Rimmer.

As far as I can ascertain, our family had maintained contact with Rimmers in the Belmont Street area, including one auntie of ours, Lucy, in particular, who had married, and gone to live in Preston, where they had a chemist shop, Spencers, a business which had been first established on the corner of Oak Street and Hart Street. They maintained this contact at least up to the commencement of World War Two. When my mother had been married a couple of years prior to World War One, she lodged with my father for a short time in Rimmer's Avenue, in the Belmont Street area, presumably with relatives. In the absence of any information to the contrary, I have always assumed that Rimmer's Avenue was so named, as a tribute to William Rimmer.

Only a short distance away from these Rimmer connections, is the home of Arthur Rimmer, at No. 18 The Walk, whose researches into the Rimmer family led to the publication, in 1983, of a book 'What's in a Name', (the family of Rimmer and its origins).

Arthur Rimmer, who was born in 1899, had a grandfather nicknamed 'Tommy Tuff', a fisherman, and lifeboatman.

One of my grandfather's brothers was Tom, 'Tuffy' Rimmer, who lived with his sister Esther, in Old Park Lane, at the other end of the town. He was also a lifeboatman, and fisherman, perhaps only a coincidence that can occur in a closely related community.

There was also another Tommy Rimmer in Old Park Lane, an accomplished organist and composer, who combined musical activities with William Rimmer. I am led to believe that quite a number of unpublished musical scores, written by both musicians, separate, and together, were still in existence in recent years.

It would be as well, I think, to conclude this Rimmer chapter, by recounting a sequence of remarkable events, concerning my mothers association with the world of film making, with which Southport has quite long lasting links, from the turn of the 19th century.

We all thought she was fantasising, when, over a period of many years, she recounted many stories, such as a Jesson connection with a British diplomat in Russia, and a certain 'Count Chicago', as we made it out to be. It was however, one story that she persisted in telling, of how all the fishing people of Southport, and district, had taken part, in filming, as extras. They had no costumes, she said, the women appearing in ordinary attire, and the men turning their coats inside out for effect! With the introduction of television in the 1950s, the stories increased. When she spotted a film star named John

Gregson, in a series called 'Gideon of the Yard', she said he was a relative of ours. Also, at the same time, she said that an old time Western actor, named Wallace Ford, was born on the 'Isle of Wight' Farm, in a caravan!

Subsquently, however when John Gregson appeared on a visit to Southport, it was to trace his roots with the Sutton founders of early Southport. When he did not have much early success with this, my mother said that if he had gone to see her, she would have sorted this out in no time at all, a statement which is substantiated in the next chapter of this book.

That was one up to 'Little Nell', as we called her, but closely following these events, I happened to mention this incident to a resident of Kew Road, who was the charlady at work. I also referred to the assertion that my mother had made, concerning Wallace Ford. To my surprise, she said that the statement was true, and also, that a neighbour of hers had Wallace Ford staying at her house, when he came over from Manchester, prior to setting out for Hollywood, when he had come to Southport to visit his birthplace.

That was another truth, sorted from the welter of 'fantasy', but later on, when a series called 'Wagon Train' appeared on television, we said she couldn't possibly be right in asserting that this was made on the sand near the Palace Hotel, with the fisherfolk, and all the local horses and wagons. We told her that there had been a film called 'Blue Peter', or some such title, that we had seen in the making, but that was at Ainsdale, and included an African village.

She was adamant however, that it was the 'Mormons', and definitely at Birkdale, and stuck to this story for the rest of her life. We lost out on the 'fantasy' concerning the Russian 'Count Chicago', also, as my brother, when attending an exhibition in Birmingham contacted relatives there, as my mother had been married to Walter Jesson who was a master tailor, who had come to Southport, via relatives in Warrington. Apart from working in a self employed capacity, in Bispham Road, he also did work for Ellidges, in Eastbank Street, and also E. R. Guest, in Zetland Street. We visited these relatives in Birmingham, and also relatives in Wales, with some quite astonishing sequels.

One thing we found out from an auntie and cousins, we went to stay with for many subsequent years, was the truth concerning my mother's 'fantasy' of the Russian Count. We were shown many documents, and records in a family bible. The Russian diplomat was indeed, an actual person, a relative stationed in a Russian city, not named, as so many had their names changed after the Revolution in 1917. We were however, shown a photograph of twin girls, probably in their teens, when it was taken. They were the diplomats daughters, who accompanied their parents to Russia. One of them became enamoured of a Russian Count, attached to their Embassy Staff. He however, fell in love with the other twin, whom he subsequently married. The other girl pined away, and so the story goes, died of unrequited love. When I enquired how we had obtained such an absurd story of a 'Count Chicago' from my mother, I was informed that, phonetically speaking, and making allowances for Rimmer pronunciation, it was not far off the mark, as the Count's name was Zhivago!

The final sequence to the film episodes, came in a series called 'Southport — Then and Now', on local history, published in the Southport Star.

The first article was in the issue dated 18th May, 1979. My mother would have been 93, on that day, had she not died two months earlier, due to the after effects of being knocked down by a car in Bispham Road, two years previously.

The article concerned the story of film producer, G. B. Samuelson, who was born on July 6th, 1888, at the small tobacconists shop which is still there, on the corner of West Street, and Neville Street, at the rear of the former Victoria Hotel, now the Maritime Flats complex.

George Berthold Samuelson was the third son of a young Jewish couple, of whom little is known, except that they were immigrants, possibly of Germanic origin. He was destined to become a pioneer, firstly of the British, then the Hollywood film industry, during the silent movie era.

His schooldays, in Southport, cannot be traced accurately, but he was thought to have been a school mate of two well known theatre ladies, Phyllis and Zena Dare. When he left school, he was known to have worked in Adler and Sutton's Concert Party, and then, as general assistant manager, to the concert party at the Pier Pavilion. In 1909, he opened the New Electric Theatre at Victoria Hall, London Street, the exact location of which I was never able to define. I did locate, and list, the cinemas already operating though. About 1910, Samuelson became a film renter, and established the Royal Film Agency, in Tulketh Street. He left Southport with his parents in 1911 to live in Birmingham, a link I was able to confirm through relatives there.

He had done experimental filming, mainly on Southport sands, and in 1914, he returned to complete, or recreate, the filming of the Mormon's desert trek, from Sir Arthur Conan Doyle's story, "A Study in Scarlet".

The focal point of all this research concerning which, I had been requested to cooperate with by Harold Dunham, a Middlesex man, who was doing research for a book on the Samuelson family, lies in the photo of the film making depicted elsewhere in this book. It was supplied to me, direct from the National Film Archive Stills Library, in London.

Before I obtained the photograph, it had been published in the 18th May edition of the Southport Weekly, on what would have been my mothers 93rd birthday. Coincidentally, it was also the last edition, as the paper became the Southport Star, in its next issue, on the 1st June, 1979.

Even in its reduced size, and in newspaper print, I was struck by the resemblance of one of the extras, amongst all the film props of covered wagons and horses, who bore a startling resemblance to my mother.

My brother Bernard, and his wife Florence, as reported in the next issue of the Southport Star on June 1st, were now interested in this development. It was Florence, who called in to the Star office, then in London Street, to identify my mother on their original photo.

When I received the photograph from the National Film Archive, enlarged, and with much more detail, I found that, not only was my mother on the photo, but also my Granny. They are on the right of the picture. My grandmother is at the front, with a white shawl draped across her knees, and my mother is immediately behind, in a tall hat, typical of that period.

Samuelson is the man wearing the straw hat, in the dark suit. The man on the left of him, in shirt-sleeves, and Trilby hat, is the Director, George Pearson. I don't know if any other family members were involved, as my Uncle Bob would only be 9 years of age. The man in the middle of the picture in the 'gansey', and peaked hat, is small enough to have been my grandad, but the inscription on the gansey probably indicates that the man is a lifeboatman. This is possible, as this photo was taken only a short distance away from the Lifeboat House, on the Birkdale Sands, in front of the Palace Hotel.

The subsequent research I carried out for, and with, Harold Dunham, involved quite a number of people, not only from the Rimmers and the fishing fraternity, but also from some old acquaintances. Remembrance of an old 'gang' acquaintance, Jim 'Barney' Oldfield, who had died some little time previously, reminded me that we had used their premises in Stanley Street, for gang meetings, and promotion of a club, 'The Southport Cosmopolitans', who also met at the Floral Hall on Sunday afternoons in the Winter, at Arthur 'Snakey' Jacobson's, musical 'tea parties'. 'Oldfield's Cabs', were well known, now perpetuated as Oldfield's Motors. We very quickly found, from family records, and recollections, that Oldfield's had been involved in the supply of horses, and equipment, for the film making. As for the bulk of the 'Covered Wagons', and horses, I approached the Draper family of Cemetery Road, whose wagons and horse drawn coaches, have been notable, for many years, conveying people in the old fashioned style, to the Waterloo Coursing at Altcar. Unfortunately, Harry Draper, an old friend of long standing, a real mine of information on many local history happenings, had also passed away. Amazingly enough, however, it was his mother, a familiar figure to us, for many years, in riding habit, and long whip, a real old style character, to whom I turned for the bulk of information. Although then well over ninety, and bedridden, she supplied a complete account of the film making, and all their equipment, together with names and addresses of people involved, much to the delight of Harold Dunham.

The Samuelson's were subsequently to achieve world wide notability, with their connections, with their Panavision, Panaflex, and Panasonic companies. Lenses by Panavision, still flash across the film credits, as they have done for years. Samuelson Lighting, is also a newly formed company, all developed from their original Cricklewood Works.

To me however, interesting though as it may well be, all these progressions pale into insignificance against the fact that as reported in the article entitled 'The Saga of Little Nell', written by me in June 1979, in the Southport Star, all the so called fantasies, except one, of 'Little Nell', had proved to be the truth. The one last 'fantasy', that of the Rimmers belonging to a "LOST TRIBE OF ISRAEL', follows in the last chapter of this book.

CHAPTER 9

THE LLOYD—PEET—GREEN DYNASTY

In the recounting of the geneological connections with the local community, I have left the Lloyde, or Lloyd, dynasty until the last, not simply because of its historical content, but also as a reversal from the perhaps dull and tedious repetition of the endless dates etc. attendent upon any such project. We can look at this one from our own present surroundings, and inhabitants, and work backwards into time, from the present day.

We observe the Lloyd geneology in one branch, by starting at the Natterjack Toby Grill in Ainsdale where, many of us remember, as being built on the site of the old Plaza cinema, and there the single track railway ran across the present car park, from the Old Mill, in Mill Road, to the railway sidings, past the new Millhouse residential complex, after crossing over Liverpool Road, and running behind the Ainsdale laundry site, and the rear of Burnley Road, to join the mainline at Ainsdale.

Inside the front entrance, on the wall of the restaurant is a plaque, stating that the Natterjack Toby Grill was opened by J. R. Lloyd, CBE, on Wednesday, 20th April, 1988.

James Lloyd, who performed this ceremony in his capacity as chairman of the Bass Brewery Group, was the son of Richard, 'Dick' Lloyd, who was the Mayor of Southport 1952/53. Many people will remember Dick Lloyd, from his association with the White Hudson factory in Shakespeare Street.

Dick Lloyd was one of at least a dozen children (two dying in infancy) born to James (1863-1907) and Mary Jane Peet (1863-1934), who farmed Peets Farm in Peets Lane. They had inherited the farm from their parents, Paul Lloyd 1838-74, and his wife Mary Peet, who is listed as dying in 1876. Historians say that Peets Lane, was named through this 'Granny Peet'. People have also thought mistakenly, the site of Peets Farm, as being at the Botanic Road End, where there is still a cluster of cottages named Peets Lane.

For the purposes of this account of the Lloyds, and their connection with the Peets—Greens—Gregsons, Rimmers and other offshoots, it would be as well to define the true location of Peets Farm, and the Lane it gave its name to.

In the previous reference to Peets Farm in the details in the account of the location of the 'Steeles', I have given the correct location of the farm as being in approximately the middle of the 'Steeles', on the lane referred to as Peets Lane, which took its name from the farm.

I have confirmed all the details of the 'Steeles', and the farm and the lane, which ran from Botanic Road, then past the farm and through Bibby's Wood, now Henley Drive, to Hesketh Park railway station.

All these locations are detailed in the memoirs of Paul Lloyd, brother of Dick, which I have studied at length this year 1990, at the Atkinson Library, where the memoirs lie, still unpublished.

I have also, with the aid of my brother Albert, and his wife Dorothy, a member of the Peet—Green branch of the family, located the true site of Peets Farm, which is easily identified by reference to any street map of Southport.

When the 'Steeles' were starting to be built on, from 1927 onwards, Peets Farm survived, after the new Churchgate was built, for several years, until it was demolished to make way for King's Hey Drive, and the northern end of Carisbrooke Drive. Towering above the houses at the rear of No. 58 Churchgate, No. 10 King's Hey Drive, and No. 66 Carisbrooke Drive, is a huge Willow tree, clearly visible in this three cornered section, from the roadway. This tree, according to my brother Albert, could be one of the trees still growing there long after we played in the pool and ditch, beside the lane which passed the farm. We can also recall that, from the late nineteen twenties, until its demolition, apple trees, also from the original orchard mentioned in Paul Lloyd's memoirs, were still flourishing in these back gardens. As Paul Lloyd, who was born in 1886, (the same year as my mother), was only 20 when he was already in Canada in 1906, it is not beyond the bounds of possibility, that the Willow tree is an original one from the farm. Some of the apple trees also contained in these gardens, could be original ones, from at least our childhood days.

When Paul Lloyd visited Churchtown, after his retirement on his 65th birthday, on 28th July 1951, from the Alberta Civil Service, it was for the purpose of taking a holiday, as his brother Dick was being inaugurated as Mayor of Southport in 1952-3. In his memoirs referring to this visit, he stated that, "the old farmhouse and buildings still stood, and the orchard was laden with fruit, What memories." My sister-in-law Dorothy, can also remember visiting the farm in 1955, which was under various ownerships, until its demolition. It is possible therefore, that Paul Lloyd was able to see the farm building, which was then almost surrounded by houses, although there would only be the present short length of the lane, containing the cottages at the Botanic Road end, still remaining.

He also refers to meeting his "old schoolmaster, G. J. Vine, after an absence of 45 years, who knew me as if it was yesterday, as did my dear friend and teacher John Austin Lloyd, who was not related to me." The G. J. Vine referred to, was made headmaster when Paul Lloyd was in Standard 2. G. J. Vine was a Cornishman, who succeeded Mr Goosen. Mr. Vine could speak the so-called 'Marshside' dialect, as could the Rector, the Rev. Charles

Hesketh Knowlys. This was not the dialect that the Rimmers brought with them from Norway, and injected into the local dialect of North Meols, but was a mixture of Anglo-Saxon, and North Mercian speech patter, which could be counted as the norm, for counties as far apart as Lancashire to Shropshire, and the Midlands. The influx of workers into North Meols had also its effect. The John Austin Lloyd referred to, was our old headmaster at All Saints School, Wennington Road from the 1920s onwards. I believe he had also been at Norwood Road School as well, but I do not know the exact date. Leonard Rimmer was headmaster at Norwood Road Junior School in the 1930s. Austin Lloyd was Paul Lloyd's teacher, when Paul Lloyd recalls that he took six boys from Churchtown School to Chester, for an outing, a great event in those days, but typical of John Austin Lloyd, who will never be forgotten by us, while we are still alive. Austin Lloyd was also still teaching Paul, when he reached the school leaving age of 13. He had reached the top Standard, then Standard Seven, and then an extra category termed X7. This method was continued by Austin Lloyd at Wennington Road All Saints, when he had to introduce a still further class of Double X7, to cope with the increasingly proficient academic qualities of some brilliant scholars of our generation, of which I am proud to say my elder brother Bernard, (nicknamed 'Bernardo Del Carpio' by Austin), was included, and was the recipient of a book prize for topping the class of 1927.

Before proceeding with Paul Lloyd's adventures, after being persuaded to stay on at school as a Pupil Teacher, it would be as well to examine his life in North Meols, in his earlier days. The recounting of his local experiences up to the age of eighteen, is not only pertinent to the Lloyd—Peet—Green dynasty, but also to the lives, and the locations of our childhood, and includes the present recollections of many of us, even today, allowing of course, for discrepancies of childhood memories, and even fantasies. His earlier recollection he says, was that, about the age of $2\frac{1}{2}$, he used to join the children of about 3 years of age, coming from Churchtown, then crossing over the ditch into John Waring's field, to pick buttercups and make daisy chains.

His next memory is one of his most poignant ones, when just before the age of 4, he recalls a near tragedy, when his older brother Dick, was pushing their baby brother William, down in the lane, in a four wheeled pram. Dick, seeing a water rat, told Paul to wheel the pram on, while he chased the rat. Unfortunately, Paul lost control of the pram, which also contained their cousin, Hugh Gregson. The pram toppled over, and ended upside down in the ditch. Paul ran home to his mother, who was working in the shippen, with his Aunt Rachel, who was milking. They ran quickly to the spot, but there was no sign of the babies, only the pram upside down, with the wheels still spinning. Paul remembers them extracting the children, and knee deep in the ditch, hooking mud out of the children's mouths and noses. Paul recalls this scene with horror, and has referred to it, on his visits home to England, on several occasions. The Aunt Rachel referred to here, was Rachel Peet (1869-1943), who was married to Peter Lloyd, who was born in 1867. They had eight children, four girls, Ada Ellen, (1901-03), Margaret,

Rose Hannah, and Jane. They had four sons, John, William and Harold. It was their eldest son, Hugh Gregson (1891-1917), who was the infant in the pram with William. The sad sequel to this event is, that both babies subsequently died tragic deaths in young manhood, as Paul recalls. Hugh Gregson was killed in Flanders in 1917, at the age of 26. Paul has recorded that his brother William, who died in 1931, had served with Allenby in the near East, was 24 when he died. William apparently left two children, Peggy and Michael, but I have no details of his family. Paul Lloyd also mentions another Rachel, but she was Rachel Gertrude, his sister, of whom there is also no information, other than the fact that she died at the age of 26.

The lane and ditch, and Bibby's Wood, were the haunts of our childhood, together with the rest of our beloved 'Steeles', which covered approximately a square mile. There was room for several football pitches, and many people will still remember the tennis courts on the Rookery side of Hesketh Drive. We had our early school matches on the 'Steeles', and our contingent of scruffy ruffians, also had an annual football match, against the Southport College, who also used the 'Steeles' for sports. We invariably walloped them by a considerable margin, in spite of lending them a couple of our lads to bolster up their side. It was a luxury for us to play with real goal posts, which they used to take away after their games. We generally had to make do with jackets or a couple of sticks for goal posts. We also had matches with the St. Simon's Boy's Brigade, who had their pitch, and the luxury of a dressing hut, in the corner, behind Roe Lane, where there was a set of iron railings, and swing gate, across the opening, to what is now Derwent Avenue. The Scouts, and the Children's Sanatorium, from Hawkshead Street Hospital for Children, had an area in the corner behind Rectory Road, and Bibby Road, now covered by Maybank Close, on which, in later years, in the early thirties, we built a cricket pitch, and erected a cricket pavilion, when I was at Whiteside's Garages of Roe Lane.

One part of the 'Steeles', across the ditch from Peets Farm, was unplayable for ball sports, as it was still ridged from ploughing in previous years. Although the farm was completely isolated, I don't ever remember anyone going into the orchard scrumping apples, and I don't remember ever seeing the well in the orchard, that Paul Lloyd refers to. The only other building, Sycamore Cottage, along this section of Peet's Lane, was at the junction of the lane with the footpath which led to the railway crossing at Hesketh Drive, now the 'White Bridge'. Sycamore Cottage is shown as being at the west side, of what is now Henley Drive, and its present junction with Hilbre Drive.

The railway line ran alongside what is now Hilbre Close, to Hesketh Park station, which was opened with the West Lancashire Railway in 1878, when the first stretch of the railway line was established, from Windsor Road to Hesketh Bank. Paul Lloyd does not mention Sycamore Cottage, and it certainly was not there in our time. The railway, from Southport to Preston, was completed in September 1882, in time for Preston Guild Week, so it is quite likely that the cottage was demolished to make way for the White Bridge.

One incident, which took place on Paul Lloyd's 4th birthday needs clarifying, as it has taken exactly 100 years from 1890 to 1990, when I discovered the true facts about Paul Lloyd's 'christening' ceremony. There are discrepancies concerning this event, in subsequent historian accounts, and even in the family recollections, and assumptions.

In his account, Paul states that on this particular day, he was cleaned up, and attired in a new white shirt. His cousin, Hugh Gregson aged two, who was also to be christened at the farm, was attired in a girls frock and apron.

The family were all peering through the front windows, to look for the Minister, who was coming from the Rectory, to perform the ceremony. Paul describes how he looked through the thorn hedge alongside the lane, and saw a large man in black clothes, carrying a white thing on his arm, crossing the plank laid across the ditch. He took fright at this, and hid in a brick dog kennel in the orchard. He was spotted by his 'granny', and hauled out, and although somewhat dishevelled, and dirty, the Minister, having now donned his surplice, conducted the service, in a dialect that Paul did not understand. The reason for this, was that the Rector, Rev. Charles Hesketh Knowlys, although he could speak the local dialect, spoke in his normal educated tones. Paul remembers the Minister's baleful stare, and the struggle he made, being lifted up, and his head being held and'wetted, and the subsequent banning, upstairs, in disgrace.

It is at this point that offical and family accounts differ. The Rectory, at that time, was only a short distance away in Roe Lane, where the site is now covered by Bamber Gardens, and even in our time, only a short distance, about just over 200 yards away, from where we played, in the same ditch, in front of the farm.

It is quite possible that this event therefore, constituted a private christening ceremony, and indeed it is not entered in North Meols records at St. Cuthbert's. It differs from the present family contention, that, as they were non-conformists, attending Churchtown Congregational Church, there would be no possibility of there being an Established Church of England baptism. On the other hand, there is no record of Paul Lloyd being christened at the Congregational Church.

Being connected with the family, with Lloyd—Peet—Green connections, through my brother Albert's marriage, when I set out to do the Rimmer connections with all the aforesaid geneological family tree, I considered it the appropriate time to set the records straight, after the lapse of over a century.

With the assistance of various individuals, official and unofficial, I found that, in North Meols Parish Records, there is a marginal, unofficial, entry of the baptism of Paul Lloyd, alongside the recording of the Baptism of Richard Lloyd, on September 12th, 1883, son of Mary Jane and James Lloyd, labourer, of Peets Lane Farm. So it appears that Paul's brother Dick, was officially baptised at St. Cuthbert's, but Paul Lloyd's Baptism was a private affair, and added later, as an unofficial entry, probably around 1890.

I am sure that these two baptisms were only undertaken by the family to enable them both to attend the Parish School that Dick attended, and paid for, in pence, for his attendance. Paul, who went to the Parish School at 5 years of age, only paid for 2-3 months before it was stopped. Dick had paid by then, for two years longer than Paul. Historians have made great play on Paul's attendance at the first Sunday School lesson, by the Rev. Charles Hesketh Knowlys, before Paul was five years of age, but the simple truth is, that this was the one and only time, that both Dick and Paul attended the Sunday School at the Church together, and Paul's only appearance at Sunday School. The school was the National School, which had taken the place of the ancient grammar school of North Meols in 1826, but by 1859, the school had been moved to a new building, and was then known as St. Cuthbert's Church of England School. This was the school that Dick and Paul attended. In 1911, it was purchased by Southport Corporation, and rebuilt as Churchtown Council School. Astounding as it may seem, Paul Lloyd mentions 'Owd Dobbins', the same truant master that we had. Paul was in the infants kindergarten, then in the infants class of Miss Blanche Barker, moving into Standard One at the age of six. He also mentions Miss Catherine Gregson, a former pupil teacher, who was born in the village, and was probably a relation of his.

The Lloyd family's connection with the Congregational Chapel in Botanic Road was very staunch, as it was in other parts of Southport. The 1840 Ordnance Survey Map shows the Independent Chapel, and the Independent Sunday School, together in Botanic Road. The Independents had been founded by an ex-Anglican clergyman named Hall, who established his own independent chapel at Hawes Side. Hall's Chapel was situated in what is now Hall Street, named after the Chapel. The building of Hall's Church was under the sponsorship of a prosperous Liverpool builder from Liverpool, Bartin Haigh (who died in 1848) who had settled in Brunswick Villa, on the corner of Lord Street and Manchester Road. Haigh rebuilt the Independent Chapel at Churchtown, to his own architectural design in 1830, which was in turn, rebuilt in 1901. Contrary to the success of the various other sectarian developments adhering to the principle of free worship, the Independents did not develop, and consequently became reformed as Congregationalists, who were well established in Churchtown by the time Paul and Dick Lloyd became members of the Congregational Church. Subsequently in later years, Dick Lloyds daughter Beryl, married Fergus Johnson, son of the minister of Churchtown Congregational Church. Beryl is in her 80s, and lives in Aberystwith. The family background, and associations with the Congregational Church, also supplements the adamant assertion, that if there had been baptismal associations with the established church, it was only obligatory in respect of school attendance. In later memoirs, Paul records that he "never knew what church his father was brought up in, and his father never mentioned the subject, but he was, withall, ever kind and considerate, and very good living."

When Paul Lloyd left school, he states that the whole family, including his father, started to attend Churchtown Congregational Chapel, where his father rented a pew. Paul considered the service to be less formal than the Church of England, "permeated with love and awe of God, and the congregation more rational, and mundane, more like a Social Club, or Friendly Society." Both Dick and Paul were members of the Christian Endeavour, which was held once a week, in a large room, alongside the Chapel. The darkest side of this church connection occurred later on, when Paul was called upon to give a lecture, as was the practice of all the 40 or so members, in turn. Paul chose for his subject "The Evils of Alcohol". He was praised for this, in glowing terms, by the leader, who referred to the "terrible handicaps that Paul had suffered, owing to the manner in which his grandfather had died." Brother Dick arose without a word, and walked out of the room, and Paul followed. On the way home, Paul asked what the leader had referred to, and Dick said that Grandfather "liked his ale." This was the last time they attended Christian Endeavour Meetings. Their father and mother were disgusted, and offended. I only include this private family reference to illustrate the damage that could be occasioned by just one derogatory remark, particularly in the strictly moral atmosphere which prevailed in those early days. It appears also that the implication of over-addiction to the 'demon drink', was, in this case, totally unfounded. In a letter to his sister Alice, who died in 1978, Paul, writing in 1970, gives an indication of their close family attachments, when he refers to his Grandfather "meeting 'The Reaper' with a smile, and asking at the last moment for his pipe." Also in the same letter, Paul says "as time goes on, our tribe dwindles as nature dictates. It is a law we all must try, it is as all mankind must face."

Paul's grandfather, also Paul, can hardly present the figure of a venerable old gentleman, as according to Parish Records, he was born in 1830, and died in 1874, at the age of 36. His wife, the original "Granny Peet" died two years later, in 1876, so she could not have been the "Granny" who pulled Paul Lloyd out of the dog kennel at his christening, at the farm in 1890, nor could the stories of "Granny Peet", and Paul, at the farm be correct. I have spent some time perusing Paul Lloyd's memoirs, and he states that his "granny" pulled him out of the kennel, but he does not name her as "Granny Peet". There is however another 'granny' mentioned in his memoirs, "Owd Harry Douses wife, Granny Rimmer, who gave me my first 'leg up' in the world, she was the village midwife. May their souls rest in peace." His words seem to imply more than just a professional connection, as Granny Rimmer could have been present at Paul's baptism, also as a relation, as there had, by now, been several Rimmers intermarried with the Lloyds. I have since been informed by Gladys Harrison (nee Lloyd) that a great deal of confusion arose from the fact that both her grandparents were called Lloyd. Her father's "breed" as she terms it, came from Marshside and Churchtown, and are related to the Wrights, Rimmers, and Gregsons, and Bartons. It was her mother's family who came from Ainsdale and Waterloo. Her paternal grandfather, M. Lloyd, was involved with Canning Road Chapel. I mentioned him as having a founder member's stone plaque on the Chapel, when I did the accounts of Canning Road and Chapel Street

Congregational Churches. The Jenny Comstive I also mentioned as having a "founder's stone plaque" on Canning Road, is I presume, the Comstive related to my grandmother. I remember also, that when the film star, John Gregson, came to trace his roots, both Auntie Jane, and my mother, could show him connections with both our families. As cousin Hugh Gregson, was christened at the same time as Paul, it seems reasonable to assume that the "Granny" and Grandfather in question, were from the Gregson side of the family, from Marshside.

Gladys Lloyd also recalls, that when her Gran lived in Peets Lane, she also used to visit her husband's grandmother, who lived across the Steeles at the corner of Roe Lane. She was a Tomlinson, a cousin of Amos Tomlinson, whom many will remember, as Amos and 'Polly', were well associated with the Rechabite movement in Churchtown. They were former Mayor and Mayoress of Southport. The Rechabite office, if memory serves me well, was situated above the former Co-op shop in Botanic Road, opposite the Churchtown Police Station premises, and Porters Saddlery shop. The Harrison's, one of whom Bill's brother, Ron, lives in Birkdale, always carried the Tomlinson name incorporated into their family name. Paul Lloyd's memory, even in later years was very sharp. He remembers that he saw an old, tin type, photo of his father holding 'Owd Doll', the farm horse. His father as he states, was always known as 'Jem'. This is a parallel reminiscence with the 'daisy chain' recollection, when Paul was only about 2½.3 years of age. He recalls also, that his father's father, Paul Lloyd, had been a builder, and had built 3 houses in Scarisbrick, on land belonging to the Count de Casteja, a French Count who had bought the land from the Scarisbricks. There was a curious system of insurance connected with property in those days, as the houses were built, and insured on the life of Grandfather Paul's oldest son William, born 1860, then an infant. On William's death, the Count would possess the whole property. However, as William lived on to the age of 80, having only died in 1940, the property remained in the Lloyd's possession by William, who had the farm in Southport Road, at Pool Hey. It is only a few years ago, that the surviving son of the Count died. There are still quite a few houses in Scarisbrick which have puzzled people with the De Casteja name, and date plaque, being still quite visible. One of the most outstanding of these is the land agent's house at Jackson's Common, near Diglake, Scarisbrick, which was built when the De Casteja's occupied Scarisbrick Hall in the 19th century. If the demon drink did contribute to the early demise of Paul's other grandfather, at 36, he was certainly a very busy lad up till then. We are obviously confusing two sets of grandparents here.

Concerning the various farm activities, it appears that the children were always included, both at home, and elsewhere. They seem to have been included very often, in events at their Great Grandparent, Gregson's Farm in Marshside, where they bred shire mares, from stallions owned by Shaw of Winmarlee, and Parbold. Akbar, Hector and Nimrod, were mentioned in this respect. I have only recently checked this breeding of horses, in the Winmarlee or Winmarleigh area, as it is now known, which is still carried on today. This was on a bright summer day in June 1990, when, also nearby, was a convoy of brightly coloured gypsy caravans with their piebald ponies, having travelled there from the Appleby Horse Fair. This was in the River Cocker estuary, near Pilling, on the Fylde. The caravans, similar to the ones that visited Foul Lane, have lodged here annually for centuries. The Pilling area was the worst hit area in the Great Flood that covered North Meols, and Martin Mere, in the sea innundation of 1720. The number of lives lost in this district was so great as to never have been fully recorded. It is also evident from further research, that many of the Rimmers, and other seafaring families from North Meols, and Crossens, went to the assistance, by boats, of the people in the Pilling area. I recalled also that many years ago, I researched, and found, the old chapter house of the nearby Cockersands Abbey, on a windswept open site near the sea. This is the Abbey that has played so great a part in the recording of our own, local history, records. A most moving, and emotionally connected series of incidents, forward and backward in time. Many of the reminiscences of Paul Lloyd are recalled, not only from his memoirs, but also from personal contacts with his family, on visits he made home in 1958 and 1962. My own personal contact with him was probably on both occasions, once when he was visiting his sister Jane, at Poulton Road, and the other occasion, when he visited my sister-in-law Dorothy, and her husband, Albert, at Hunts Cottages. My brother, Albert, was working at Meols Hall at the time, so my recollections are an amalgam of past, and present events of the time, from several sources. Paul Lloyd's recollections of Churchtown, Marshside, and the farm and the 'Steeles', made a fascinating comparison with our own experiences, and also with the people, past and present, who lived there. Conversation could progress into the small hours, so it is only possible to list a few reminiscences, some are too intimate, and unprintable, in any case.

There are no idle hands in the routine around a farm, and both Dick and Paul, were involved in this, from an early age. Milking was done mostly by mother, and Aunt Rachel. His father 'Jem' was involved mostly with activities involving 'Owd Doll', the shire mare, in the dialect "Aar 'Owd Doll can poo' three tuṅ on't cart up't hill." Lapses into dialect, occur all through these early reminscences, "Thas's broken Fork steyl" (handle) — "Hast bin down 't Peets Loòan to't lung hey?" (long field) "Is thi fayther 'ad hoo-um?", were all quite understandable in the local dialect. In this context, I well remember a phrase which stuck in my mind from early childhood, when I heard my Auntie Hester say to my mother, "Art gooin' t' morn at neet, t' churchyéard, t' buryin?" In local dialect this would be interpreted as "Are you going tomorrow, at night, to the funeral at the churchyard?" This was incomprehensible, as how could anyone go to a funeral at night. It was only just recently, when I was researching variations in the six Nordic languages, I discovered that, in the West Norse language used by the Rimmers, before leaving West Norway, the phonetic and literal translation of the phrase "Morgan-Neet" in West Norse, is "tomorrow", so "t' morn at neet", in the local dialect is "tomorrow night", but in pure West Norse, it simply means "tomorrow". Small wonder, that when the Rimmers spoke in a mixture of local dialect, interspersed with Nordic, and Biblical language, even members of our own family, raised only on the local dialect, could not understand them.

There are many contemporary reminiscences from Paul Lloyd memoirs and conversations, concerning mainly North Meols and Churchtown in particular. Many of us still equate with references to Churchtown locations. Paul states that there were no footpaths, side walks or 'parapets' in his early days. Three hundred yards from the farmhouse, towards the village, was the timber yard of John Henry Threlfall, and one of Paul's friends, Young Tommy Threlfall, was 18 months older than Paul. Paul also states that his mother's cousin was owner of the Bold Hotel. He mentions buying a shirt for half a crown at Tom Watkinson's Tailor's Shop, but not paying for it, as mother would pay later. 'Owd Billy' gets a mention, as he peddled cottons etc. in a sheet tied at the corners. Rowbottom's shop was the venue where a tin of Irish Black Twist was available for $\frac{1}{2}$d. and 1d., possibly for his father. The utilization of a clean pillowslip for collecting flour from Thwaite's Mill continued on to our days. Everyone had a nickname, even an inebriate gentleman named 'Cossin Joe', who also turned up in High Park 'Cossin' being idiomatic for cursing and swearing. In later years Paul writes of meeting a Churchtown carpenter, Jack 'Tal' Saul, in Moose Creek, in Canada. I have mentioned the 'fun loving' derivation of 'Tal' from our school playground days. Many of Dick and Paul's early adventures concerned a donkey named, inevitably, "Neddy", who had been given to them by Aunty Betty Robinson. Neddy had previously been employed taking children for rides along the edge of the sea. Neddy quickly settled down to a life of adventure on the farm. On occasion he would head for the shore, as he did one day, when a cow bolted. Neddy went as well, and had to be headed off at the railway crossing then called 'Twig Mollies', a quarter of a mile away, down the lane leading to Carrier's Lane. This was the railway crossing, by the White Lodge, at the top of King's Hey Drive, which, in our day, had been converted into the "Red Bridge", as the line had then been electrified. Neddy was pastured with the cows, in a field next to 'Home Field', one side of which was fenced with a cop, in Chase Hey's, which ran on from my aunties row of cottages, back to Peets Lane. Paul mentions riding Neddy along the loose sandy road, through Hesketh's "Bibby's Wood", where we also played in the callow days of our youth, then taking a short cut home from Myrtle Cottage, which I never found. I presume it was somewhere near Hesketh Park station, as they took the lane which ran alongside the railway, on the opposite side to the Henley Drive section of Peet's Lane. This would be what is now Rawlinson Grove, where the lane ran through a small hamlet called 'The Willows'. The lane here turned towards home, along Carriers Lane, over the White Lodge Farm railway crossing, 'Twig Mollies', turning right into Chase Heys, and past 'owd Li Jas' to Peet's Lane. I never found out who or what, was 'Li Jas', but I think she lived in a cottage which was in the Churchtown Fair field, at the junction of old Churchgate and Peet's Lane. I remember that a near relative of ours, 'Old Paul' Cadwell, lived there, until his wife died, and he went to live in a one roomed cottage, at the Botanic Road end, of the row of cottages which face Mill Lane. It had no bedroom, just a curtained off alcove. 'Old Paul' was a large, black bearded, fearsome figure of a man, who struck terror into us when we had to call. All this row of cottages have been converted into one dwelling now. In picture postcards, and photos, it can be identified, as it is taller than the other buildings, and bears the street nameplate 'Botanic Road', but this row of cottages has always been regarded as being in Peet's Lane.

The small hamlet named on the 19th century map which shows the railway, and was called 'The Willows', can be identified by Willow Cottage, in Rawlinson Grove, behind the house on the corner of Rawlinson Grove, and Coudray Road. This cottage is in a remarkable state of preservation, but I do not know the exact date, as the cottages were built at varying dates around 1700. I do remember the building of the 'new house', called 'Willow Lodge', on the corner, in the early 1920s, and as I explained to the present owner in the summer of 1990, I can recall jumping off the top of the bay window, onto a pile of sand, during its construction. I also told him of the 'Topping Out' ceremony of a new building which took place there. This consisted of the placing of a Union Jack on the chimney, when the roof was completed. He was rather surprised when I told him that my brother Bernard, found a harp in the attic, when we later made our unofficial inspection of the nearly completed house. The mystery of the harp discovery was never solved, but I think it could have come from one of the cottages, demolished to make way for the new house.

There is a row of cottages, probably part of the same hamlet, across the road, on the corner of Coudray Road and Hesketh Drive. Number 39 is now also comprised of No. 41, which does not now exist as a number. Attached to this cottage is Thorn Tree Cottage, No. 43 Coudray Road, on the corner of Hesketh Drive. This would previously be the corner of Carriers Lane, which continued along the part of Coudray Road across Hesketh Drive, through what is now Silverthorne Drive, and across the railway at White Lodge, to Chase Heys. The footpath from Beresford Drive, past Silverthorne Drive, and Coudray Road, to Cambridge Road, is still there. It was formerly the footpath which led from Peets Lane Farm, to Cambridge Road.

Thorn Tree Cottage is the one referred to earlier, where we used to call in for drinks of water, also in the early 1920s. I've never been able to establish what relationship, if any, the old lady bore to our family.

The cottage was also the subject of enquiries I carried out in conjunction with the Willow Tree Cottage, and hamlet. The present occupiers, Pam and John Halsall, were most cooperative, and took the trouble to provide me with, not only a photograph of the cottage, but also the location of the Willow Cottages hamlet, on a photostat. Also supplied, was a six page copy of the conveyance, made on the 21st day of May 1928, between Hesketh Estates, and John Jackson, for the purchase of the cottage for £400. The cottage and outbuildings, comprised ten and a half poles. The plan which accompanied the conveyance, also details the necessity of maintaining a 3ft. 6in. passageway to other property, from Hesketh Drive, to presumably the rear of the adjoining cottages in Coudray Road.

Thorn Tree Cottage, probably circa 1700, according to one historian, has an upstairs bedroom, similar to the one in Chase Heys built in 1722, and the other one in Botanic Road. These were sometimes constructed for the working of cotton and silk weaving, and in some cases, as in Birkdale, also as an 'upper room' for the conducting of non-conformist meetings. The beams of the bedroom in Thorn Tree Cottage, are old ships masts, and the floor is constructed from old oak 18" wide boards. The actual age of the cottage is not known, but a stone with an incised cross dated May 25th, 1740, was found in the garden. A large stone trough, although originally in the cottage, now used for garden plants, could have been a pig trough. An unusual feature, not usually found in cottages, is a window at the side, arch shaped and gothic in appearance. This might not have any ecclesiastical connection, nor the incised stone, which might have, at one time, been a boundary marking. It is reputed that the thorn tree, after which this cottage was named, was a silver thorn, which, if true, could have been of some significance in the naming of nearby Silverthorne Drive. Most of the cottages in the area were dated from the 18th century, and all sorts of ship's timbers were used in their construction.

The climax of the two boys' connection with Neddy the donkey, came shortly afterwards, before Paul went to school. Neddy had acquired the knack of nosing open the latch of the gate of the railway crossing, 'Twig Mollies', which allowed the gate to swing open of its own accord. Neddy would then amble alongside the railway track, hotly pursued by the boys, when the alarm was raised. On this occasion, he had nearly reached Hesketh Park station, before being headed off. This was the most southerly limit from the farm, that the boys had been on their own. They decided to carry on, and have a look at Southport. It is not clear what route they took, but they remember passing the junction of Manchester Road, by Trinity Church, and entering Lord Street at its north end. Dick was facing front, steering Neddy, while Paul sat with his back to Dick, facing backwards. Paul's description of the wonders of Southport's tree-lined boulevards, its glittering shops, the general all pervading, panoramic scene, of the elegant horse drawn, and donkey carriages, the top hats and crinolines of the occupants, and pedestrians, the terraces, gardens, the hotels and municipal buildings, constituted an evocative scene, which remained forever in Paul's memory. Neddy, well used to crowds and bustle, conveyed the boys the full length of Lord Street, as far as the ornamental lamp marking the site of Old Duke Sutton's 'Folly'. They rounded this, and traversed the full length of Lord Street again, and back home to the farm, full of wonderment at their adventurous feat. Little did the many people who acknowledged their progress, could possibly conjecture, that the driver of the donkey would, around half a century later, traverse the same tree lined boulevard, many times, in one of the world's best known luxury limousines, in his capacity as Mayor of Southport, including one Civic Ceremony, retracing most of the journey of the little donkey, and its burden on that memorable day. This was on the occasion of the Inaugural Church Service, of Richard Lloyd, as Mayor of Southport 1951/52, which took place at Churchtown

Congregational Church, the ceremony being witnessed by Paul Lloyd, who had travelled from his home in Canada to be present. Neddy was not at the farm just for amusement only, as the Lloyds pastured cows in a meadow, a mile and a half away, across the railway line. He was also saddled up to take cows to pasturage, thorugh the village, and past the Botanic Gardens, and also over Crossens railway bridge, onto Marshside and Crossens Marshes.

The boys would also linger, when time permitted, along the way, as Paul mentions, "Th 'owd Poo' which flows into Botanic Gardens", as a draining canal, from the Rimmer's ancient 'Snoterpool'. Although the talk was of hooks and lines, he comments on the snigs, and eels, in a more sentimental tone, when he ruminates on the eels going to Bermuda to breed and die, and returning, floating across the Atlantic, as he describes it, "like darning needles". Then growing into elvers, and then fully grown eels.

A remark I do remember, was about a connection, between Peets Farm, and the Pinfold, where stray cattle were 'pounded'. Not on the scale of a 'Calgary' cattle round up, with only one donkey available. It was quite a puzzle, until I found a reference relating to the Pinfold at Churchtown, being under the control of Peets Farm. Paul Lloyd also mentions that Jack Franklin was at some time the official Pound Pinfold Keeper. These facts remained a puzzle to me for a long time, and were only reconciled with the assistance of John Scholes, then curator of the Botanic Museum. The main entrance to the Botanic Gardens was, prior to 1874, the site of the village prison, and the Pinfold. The prison, known locally as the 'Round House', was a small building, with circular walls of brick, a flagged floor, and a domed roof. When the Botanic Gardens were formed in 1874, the Round House, and the pound were demolished, and the cattle pound was re-erected in Peets Lane, on Peets farmland, close to Churchgate. This had probably also been demolished in later years, when the farmland became Bibby Road, and the new Churchgate. The residents therefore, of the recently erected Chase Heys complex, might be interested to know that they are sitting on 'Neddy's Patch'. Perhaps, one moonlight night, they might observe the phantom shade of one small donkey, still rounding up invisible cattle into Peet's Lane 'Pound'. I had also been curious about a small square building, which still stands next to the Bankfield Lane Bridge, but this however turned out to be not some preserved, listed, historic structure, but the ticket office entrance to the Gardens, made redundant by the present ornamental entrance gates, erected in 1937, as a memorial the late King George V.

Paul Lloyd does describe another visit to Southport, which would be around 1895, when the annual May Pageant was held. The assembly was made in Churchtown, and taken by horse drawn tram, along to the Rectory residence, of Mrs. Anna Maria Alice Hesketh, who was then over 80 years old. Her husband was the Rev. Charles Hesketh, rector of North Meols from 1835, who died in 1876. The Rookery, as the Rectory was then known, was in Roe Lane, not to be confused with the later Trinity 'Rookery' Sports Ground, which was constructed alongside the south side of Bibby's Wood, and had a rookery in the tall trees. There were many rooks in the trees all along Roe Lane. They all made daily excursions to the feeding grounds on Blowick Mosses, hence the description of 'Crowlands', and Crowland Street, where the gasworks were constructed and so named in the 19th century. Paul Lloyd also mentions a 'school of rooks', from the Rectory rookery, on one of their grain fields, between the Peets Lane Farm, and the Rectory.

A small display was held in the grounds of the Rectory for the old lady's benefit, then the children remounted the tram floats, and progressed to Southport for the big parade, where the main feature was the appearance of a lifeboat, with the 'crew' in full rig, which was lent for the occasion by the Lifeboat Institution. The lifeboat was the Edith and Annie, commissioned in 1888, its launching carriage drawn by a groomed team of powerful shire horses. It was responsible for the saving of 12 lives before it went out of service, in 1902. The 'crew' on this occasion, was composed of the sons of the lifeboatmen, albeit somewhat dwarfed by the sou'westers, ganseys, and cork jackets, provided for the parade.

At the age of ten, Paul Lloyd recalls that they went weeding down mangels, and 'tornups' (turnips), and general thinning out of vegetables, with sacking tied round their knees, helping their Uncle James, who was ploughing the edge of the field, marked by three drainage canals, which emptied into the sea, a mile away. This was evidently not at Peets Lane, and could have been at their Uncle James Gregson's farm at Marshside. The three drainage canals are no doubt the Three Pools at Crossens, emptying into the sluice. Paul also mentions the many Irishmen, carrying scythes, coming from Liverpool, to work in the fields at Harvest time, and digging potatoes (chats), in the Autumn. The "exiles from Erin" as he calls them, "enjoyed their work, and had many jolly nights with the locals. There was no Irish question, or troubles in Churchtown." He calls them "level headed, wholesome and well behaved." They came for several years, each autumn, until Paul left school.

The school leaving age, at that time, was about 13, but Paul was asked by Mr. George Vine, to stay on, as a pupil teacher. Paul did this, and combined teaching with studying. He took a first class certificate in Scientific Knowledge, combined with Temperance, Biblical Knowledge, and Shorthand. His research was done in the village library, in connection with which, he recalls the Librarian's daughter, "a beautiful girl, descendant of 'Old Duke Sutton', who founded the town of Southport, a native of Churchtown, which was called the Mother of Southport." He had previously done research at the library for the lecture the "Evils of Alcohol", which he presented at the Christian Endeavour meeting at the Congregational Chapel, some time previously.

After six months of teaching 'Reading, Writing, and Arithmetic', Paul asked to be released, and took a job as office boy to James Jump, at the princely wage of 2/6 per week, rising to 5/- per week, plus 6d per night, of five hours overtime, for auditing, plus a light meal. He took all his money home to his mother, being rewarded by 6d per week spending money. He could do 100 words per minute in shorthand, but this was not required from an office boy. His employer was the Head of the Guardian Society for the Protection of Trade. The Jump family was well known in North Meols historical records, when as far back as 1692, Laurence Jump made up the sum of £20 for the benefaction, forfeited by Richard Ball, in connection with the old Grammar School. The tablet, still in the Church, does not however record Lawrence's gift. This was another mystery solved in the process of research, hitherto not known. Robert Jump, one of the house holders in the Hearth Tax returns in Birkdale, had two hearths, indicating that the Jump family were people of substance, and benefaction, unobtrusively.

A few months later, Paul applied for, and obtained a position as Assistant Secretary to the Education Committee of the Victoria Science and Art School, at the Cambridge Hall, a job which also included the duties of Assistant Curator of the Atkinson Art Gallery. During the $3\frac{1}{2}$ years in this occupation Paul also studied, and obtained extensive knowledge in Advanced Physiology, Building Construction Drawing, Magnetism, Electricity, and Joinery, a mixed bag indeed, but which proved to be of immense benefit to him through life.

He was subsequently offered a job as Assistant Cashier at the Borough Tramways Office, with an increase in salary, from 8/- to 10/- per week. This job was not only taken for salary increase, but because he had been fascinated by trams, since the days of horse drawn vehicles in Churchtown.

During this two year period at the Tram Office, he also took training in the Southport Company of Mersey Division, Royal Naval Volunteer Reserve, after spending the time in the Tram Office, which consisted of maintaining records of mileages, costing, and electricty consumption, until 10 p.m. each evening when the cashing up of receipts was completed. Whilst at the Tram Office, Paul had obtained a Provisional Patent for his invention of a semi-automatic seat, to provide a dry surface for tram drivers, who were at that time exposed to the elements, with only heavy clothing for protection. This invention was considered to be a highly efficient and valuable addition, to tram cars.

In between jobs, and in any spare time, Paul had been going to sea on steam trawlers, sailing from Fleetwood, where he learned steamship and navigation, and describes one trip, when in a storm, the ship piled up on rocks off Rathlin Island. This is a spot I know very well, visible from the Antrim Coast Road, well frequented by holidaymakers. As a matter of interest, it is notable as the place where Robert the Bruce had his encounter with the spider which encouraged his successful return to Scotland.

Paul had frequently expressed his difficulty in orienting to urban activities, and staying out late at night, until the early hours of morning, with only the prospect of any advancement in career lying in 'dead men's shoe's. His expressed preferment of emigration to Canada, as many of his contemporaries were doing, eventually led to fruition, and a passage to Winnipeg, Manitoba, was booked for him for the 27th February, 1906, by Canadian Pacific Railways. Paul's ultimate destination was Edmonton, Alberta.

Before he left England, Paul sent the plans and specification of his patented seat device, to a firm in Cardiff. There has never, to my knowledge, been any development taken place, in respect of this.

Paul Lloyd, age 20, was seen off at Princes Landing Stage, Liverpool, to board the SS Lake Erie, by his father, mother, and a few friends. As Paul said many years later, "It was the only time I saw my father show any emotion."

Paul Lloyd led a pioneer life, at first, in Canada. His experiences with the Indians in Moose Jaw Creek, and subsequent adventures, read like a 'Boys Own Paper' serial. Ironically, after a happy marriage in 1913, with Canada having no navy, he served in World War I, enlisting in the 66th Battalion of the Canadian C.E.F. army, where he initially put his mechanical skills to good effect, training recruits. He was already an accomplished marksman, from his pioneer days, so he soon became proficient in the uses of the Lewis Machine Gun, then the Maxim Machine Gun, Rifle, Revolver, and field guns, together with his expertise in seamanship. Although promoted quickly to the rank of Sergeant, he refused commissioned rank. He had no desire to command. He was given leave to harvest crops, and had to leave the army to look after his farming interests. He however, had service in Normandy and Flanders. By a strange string of coincidence, the ships carrying him to Europe, took on the Mersey pilot at Liverpool, and docked at the very same landing stage from which he had departed as a youth. He left for Europe, his ship being the SS Olympic, sister ship of the Titanic, with a destroyer escort circling around them, passed, as Paul says "in a dream," the Irish Coast, and Rathlin Island, the scene of his earlier shipwreck.

After the war, in 1919-20 his farm had a bad time, in a poor harvest. By now, his wife Mary was ill in hospital. They had three children by then. His first born, a son, James William, had been born before Paul left for the army. They had another son Dick, and a daughter Helen. All the family were quite happy on the farm, where they also attended the Church and Sunday School, at Gideon Lake, where Paul was preacher.

After his wife's death in 1940, Paul subsequently married again, and it was a daughter from this marriage, Barbara, who accompanied him on his visit in 1962. Another coincidence occurred on another visit in 1964, when he came over on the SS Lock Gowan. The captain of the ship Capt. Arison, turned out to be living then, in a house near Hesketh Park, on land that was at the edge of the former Peet's Farm, cow pasture. Paul Lloyd closed his memoirs in March 1865, after presenting a Royal Commission on Government Organisation in 1960. He had however by then, been retired, which he had done so on his 65th birthday, on the 28th July 1951.

He maintained a stream of correspondence, mainly with his sisters Alice, Mrs. A. Thompson and Jane, who was married to George Curzon Green ('Kruger'), also Ellen, who was married to William Pearson. This correspondence lasted at least until the January of 1970, the year before Paul Lloyd died, in 1971, at the age of 85. All through the years of correspondence, Paul Lloyd expressed an unending stream of nostalgia, from the time he felt, as he said, terribly homesick, at "Just the age of 20 years old, and far from dear old Lancashire," expressing, "high regard, and affection, for the good old Sandgrounders." At various times he related his experiences, particularly of the early years in Canada he had spent in unpopulated areas, assessing land, often camping out. "Only rarely have I shot deer or bear, for food, I would much rather let them live. I have covered many thousand miles by land, water and air, met many dangers, but managed to side-step them, some with a rifle, but mostly by good judgement." He recalls that on one occasion, on a visit to Churchtown, "I met many village friends, and fishermen, with whom I had sailed on both schooners and steam trawlers, from whom I had learned much of the sea and ships."

Paul's last letter, written to his sister Alice, in which he refers to his Grandfather "meeting the Reaper" and referring to the "dwindling of our tribe as nature dictates. It is a law we all must try, it is as all mankind must face," seems to indicate some presentiment of his own demise, as he concludes, "For myself, I can say, I have run a race that kept me alert to God's dictates."

The memoirs of Paul Lloyd cover 43 chapters. I am sure you will agree with me, that the quotation of these few incidents from his long life, are well worth recording.

Alice, who died in 1978, and Ellen who died in 1979, left alive one other sister and a brother. The sister, Jane, born in 1897, was regarded as 'Auntie Jane' to all of our family, when her niece Dorothy, married my brother Albert, in June 1943. Auntie Jane's husband was George Curzon Green. The George Curzon in his name, was probably after George Curzon, who was MP for Southport from 1886 until 1898, when he was appointed Viceroy of India. The fashion has always been in vogue, of 'dubbing' the newly born, after notabilities of the day. His nickname 'Kruger', is evocative of the Boer War. The nickname 'Kruger' no doubt originated when he formed his own 'boyhood army', known locally as 'Kruger's Army', which stuck to him all his life. In later years when compiling a family tree, a relative described 'Kruger' as "a real rough diamond, but most of the Lloyd family have reason to be grateful to him." He was always ready, and able, to disperse sound commonsense advice, to anyone who required it. We had known 'Kruger' from childhood, a very popular local character, especially as when he was employed at the local gasworks, dispensing coke from the container shute, into our sacks and trucks, we got a very generous measure indeed, with coke spilling out of sacks, and trucks, in all directions. The trucks, which we could hire from 'Owd Briscoe', in Bispham Road, were fitted with old, cast iron, mangle wheels, but some of our home made outfits, utilizing old pram wheels, very often couldn't take the strain, especially in the early days before the Canning Road estate was built, when there was only a muddy cinder track, from the tramsheds to Milton Street, which invariably resembled a Flanders, shell pitted, battlefield.

After 'Kruger' died, and also his other son Billy, 'Auntie Jane' went to live with her son Harry, and his wife Dorothy. Eventually they came to live around the corner to us in Heathfield Road, where 'Auntie Jane' died in

1987, aged 89 years. Harry subsequently became quite a celebrity operating 'Harry's Wine Bar', where he dispensed home made wines to all his friends. The wine bar was formerly constructed in an outhouse, where Harry has been interviewed, on several occasions by press, radio and television.

This 'wine bar' is only a stones throw away from the Natterjack Toby Grill, the starting point of this rambling excursion into just one branch of a family tree, where Harry's cousin, James Lloyd, CBE, son of Dick Lloyd, and nephew of Paul, and 'Auntie Jane', performed the opening ceremony only two years previously. This journey, back into time, of over a century in duration, and covering thousands of miles, is only one small facet, of one family tree, converting names, dates, and places, from the printed record pages, into living entities, with their attendant stories of triumphs, tragedies, love, hate, births and deaths. A full circle indeed, but not the full story, as it is impossible, once you start an investigation into any family tree, to draw it to a successful conclusion. I had, for instance not been able to connect another brother of Dick and Paul Lloyd, until I found that he was listed in the family tree as Harold. He eventually turned out to be Harry Peet Lloyd (1891-1965). He started his working life, after studying very hard, with the old Lancashire and Yorkshire Railway, became an express driver in the days of steam trains, and then the electric and diesel trains, just at the introduction of the latter. His later years were spent in his office at Euston Station, where he was accredited as being the best informed person on British Rail. He was so dedicated to the railways, that he introduced Improvement Classes, at his Southport home, for the purpose of guiding young men, by detailed diagrams, through the complexities of steam engine workings. He always worked, voluntarily, for the Southport Infirmary, where, in those days, you were not admitted without payment, before the Welfare State came into being. He became a member of the Board of Management, and a Vice President, and his name was on the Honours Board, in the Board Room. He will be remembered, mostly by local people, as being the inaugurator of the 'Penny in the Pound' subscription scheme. He was also connected with the founding of the Railway Club, in Southport. His son Ronald lives in Ainsdale, and seems to have inherited his father's love of railways. Ronald, (christened Harry Ronald), and his wife Joan, have one son, Paul.

The Lloyd Dynasty can be traced back as far, at least, to 1700 in local records, but there were Peets in the Snowdonia area, long before then. Harry is an old Welsh name, given to many ancient Welsh Kings, still perpetuated in the Lloyd—Peet—Green family. Harry Green from Heathfield Road, was named after Harry Peet Lloyd. My grandmother was connected as a Rigby, with the Comstives, one of whom, was the wife of Harry Peet Lloyd. She was a 'foreigner' from Waterloo, but there are other Comstives, dotted around Southport and Ainsdale. A great deal of confusion is engendered by the fact that Harry Peet Lloyd's son, Ronnie and Gladys, his sister, therefore had two grandparents named Lloyd, and this probably accounts for the 'Grannie' who appears at the christening of Paul Lloyd, and the 'Grandad' mentioned in his memoirs. The Lloyds were also connected with Bartons, Wrights, and Gregsons, from Marshside and the Penwortham Gregsons, intermarried with Duke Sutton. Most of these people can eventually be classified, through relatives and intermarriages, as 'Sandgrounders'.

There is one person with whom I have been contacted with for many years, in the Lloyd family, and to whom I have turned to for help on compiling their family tree, the most difficult task of all, and still full of anomalies. She is the daughter of Harry Lloyd, Gladys, now widowed with two sons, one a journalist and living in Bristol. I contacted her only recently, when I was writing a serial in the 'Southport Star' concerning the history of two Congregational Churches, Chapel Street and Canning Road. Gladys's husband, Bill Harrison, had been responsible for the inauguration of a Church newspaper in the 1920s, concerning the two churches, 'The Sunday School Observer'. I was a correspondent for this, and had sent all my copies to Bristol, where Bill had gone to work for the Bristol Aero Company. Gladys returned all these newspaper copies to me for reference, and by a strange coincidence, they arrived on the same day that I discovered the gravestone of the Rev. George Greatbatch, which had been placed in the Birkdale Cemetery, alongside an obelisk marking the re-burial place of remains from the graveyard of Chapel Street Congregational Churchyard, when it was demolished in 1963 to make way for Littlewood's store. The connections are endless, because my old Church, Canning Road Congregational, still thriving after revival as Canning Road Chapel, still bears an 'M. Lloyd' founder's nameplate, and also one for 'Jenny Comstive'. Auntie Jane's daughter, Margaret—Peet—Green, formerly a nurse at the Paraplegic Ward of the Promenade Hospital, was married there.

Initially I am supposed to be recounting the connection between only the Rimmers, and the various local families, and in this respect, they, even apart from personal present relationships, creep into the Lloyd—Peet—Green dynasty. The Lloyd family tree, seems to have only officially started locally, in 1734, with the marriage of Peter Lloyd to Mary Charnley. The Charnley family can also be traced to a Rimmer connection. In the Lloyd connection, there is a record of the marriage of Robert Rimmer, to Ann Lloyd, in February 1837. Her brother John, married a Ruth Rimmer in 1835. This marriage produced 4 boys and 4 girls, and started the Green's connection with the Lloyds, because two of their daughters, Margaret, (born 1841), had four or more children by Henry Green, whilst Ellen (1848-1929), had 14 children by Jabez Green.

It was the marriage of Peter Lloyd (1800-1889) to Ellen Barton in November 1824, which produced six boys and one girl. One of the sons, Paul (1838-1874), married Mary, who is supposed to be the original 'Granny Peet', whose birth is not listed, but died in 1876, who gave her name to Peet's Lane, and presumably Peet's Farm, unless the farm was already there, belonging to the Peet family. As I have quoted previously, if she died in 1876 as stated, she could not have been the 'Granny' who pulled Paul Lloyd out of the dog kennel, at his christening, in 1890. They are definitely recorded as being the parents of James Lloyd (1863-1907), married to Mary Jane Peet

(1863-1934), who were the father and mother of Dick and Paul Lloyd. The Peet family seemed to have had extensive farm holdings in the area, as they had another farm in Pool Hey, also in New Cut Lane. One of the other Lloyds at least, was in the farming business. He was Paul, in our younger days, referred to as 'Owd Pop Lloyd', who kept a herd of cows in Heysham Road, and pastured them on the field in Canning Road, near to Mark Halsall's Farm. This was opposite Mr. Blenkinsop's field. He kept his herd at the back of his dairy, in Bispham Road. When Billy Clay was driving livestock, mostly pigs, from his farm in High Park Road, along Bispham Road, to the railway sidings at Meols Cop, it was more evocative of a wild western cattle stampede, if they were being driven at the same time as the cows were returning from pasture, along Canning Road.

One story, which seems to have been told by historians in various versions, concerns the youngest son of the Peter Lloyd, and Mary Charnley, who head the Lloyd family tree. This was George, born in 1747. At the age of 29, George was already married to Sussannah Rainford of Halsall, and working as a labourer in Birkdale. In 1776, before his 30th birthday, he was wrongfully convicted of arson, and chose the option of enlisting in the Manchester Militia, as an alternative to serving a prison sentence. His wife was so convinced of his innocence, that it subsequently caused her death. George served in Gibraltar for sixteen years, before his discharge. He is supposed to have married again, but there is no official record of this. He was treated as a pariah by the local 'hoi polloi', practically destitute, on a pension of about £7 per year. He was however, befriended by the parish curate John Mawdsley, to whom he became devotedly attached, until John Mawdsley died in 1814, after George had nursed him through many years of sickness. In the meantime, George's reputation had been restored, when, about the year 1796, a woman made a death-bed confession to John Mawdsley, that she had committed the offence that George had been convicted of. George died in 1819 at the age of 71. There had been several distorted storied, versions of "The Birkdale Pensioner", as one historian told it, but the true facts were obtained for me from Parish Records, when Mr. Roger Fleetwood Hesketh was Mayor of Southport 1951-52, the year before Dick Lloyd himself was the Mayor in 1952-53. I have indeed been fortunate, over the years to have access to so many various sources of information to confirm the accuracy of historical fact.

These few instances of geneology, scanty as they are, and tracing mostly Rimmer and relative family connections, have nevertheless encouraged many researches into family trees. I must however instill a word of caution to anyone who attempts such an excursion into the past, having been bitten by the ancestral research bug. There can be surprises, not always pleasant ones, in store. For instance, a friend and colleague, Jean Hillier, who over the years has painstakingly deciphered, and typed my handwritten scribblings, finally succumbed to the bug herself, and set off in search of family connections, mainly Ainscoughs, in the Parbold area. To date, the most significant discovery has been the establishment of links even through the Rimmers, and the inevitable Sutton—Linaker—Gregson chain back to the

'Old Duke'. There are also Ainscough—Gregson horse breeding links around Parbold, referred to in Paul Lloyd's memoirs. Other offshoots, such as Bartons, crop up, and there appear to be a couple of dubious 'skeleton in the cupboard' connections, with earlier members of the Todd family.

I had an experience myself, of this "keep it dark, skeleton in the cupbaord" reticent approach to unactuated events, which occur in family lives of any generation, in the instance of 'Auntie Betty' of Bank Nook. Apart from the fact that I was too young to have known about her, even in later years, nobody told me very much about her, apart from the impression I had, that she was a very good living person. It was only in 1989, when I was informed, after newspaper articles I had written, concerning my Grandad Rimmer, and my Uncle Bob's fishing experiences, that a relative through my grandad's side, informed me that 'Auntie Betty' was married to 'Fleetwood Robin' of Bank Nook. I was told that she was deeply religious, and a member of the 'Plymouth Brethren' who met in 'The Room', the small church in Old Park Lane I have previously mentioned. Although, as I have recounted, many local people quite respectable, and well connected, were members, apparently 'Fleetwood Robin' took exception to 'Auntie Betty's' connection with this church, or any other religious order. He was wont to abuse her cruelly, and frequently tore up, and burnt her Bibles. On the day I have spoken about, when she was knocked down in Manor Road, it has never been established whether she was finally leaving her husband, to return to relatives in High Park, or if she deliberately flung herself under the horses hooves. The fact that she requested a Grace Rimmer, no relative, not to take her back to Bank Nook, would suggest that she had left there in a distracted, and confused state of mind. She died, next day, without disclosing any further details, so there the matter rested, unsolved even now, a justly defined 'family secret' would you not agree?

CHAPTER 10

THE ORIGIN OF SPECIES —
KING ARTHUR — ROBIN HOOD

Reverting once again to the many youthful, apparently unanswered and unsolved questions, concerning the Rimmer's initial origins, some of the rather cryptic replies of my grandad, would stand a lot more examination than is apparent on the surface. The remark about looking for northern lights in the sky as indication of their Nordic origin, were not as I thought then, a reference to the Blackpool illuminations.

Some twenty years later the quite literal illumination of the 'Leets' referred to by my grandad, flashed across my mind in World War Two, when I was on Home Guard duty, on Southport Promenade, at a corner house at the top of Leyland Road. The sergeant in charge was about to alert the Dawn Patrol, as there appeared to be an air raid, quite a frequent occurrence, taking place at the Vickers shipyards, at Barrow. He was puzzled at the absence of any alarm having been given, and the lack of anti-aircraft gunfire, and the accompanying shrapnel from them, which usually caused us to duck for cover, behind the sea wall. It indeed, appeared to be a particularly heavy raid, but there was no noise, and suddenly I realized, that what we were witnessing, was no air raid but a display of the Aurora Borealis, the Arctic 'Northern Lights'. 'Aurora', Goddess of the Dawn, 'Borealis' meaning northern, relating to the Northern Arctic Circle winds, was putting on a display, the like of which I have only seen once again, in my lifetime. The leaping, twisting, tortured forms, the conflagration of shimmering light, and the heavens ablaze with celestial storm arcs, tumbling and trembling in the Northern sky, ablaze with electrical, explosive, but silent, discharges. Although such displays are still to be seen, I realized then, that modern, urban town dwellers, dazzled by street lights etc., have lost the starry heavens. Such a display could only be seen in a war time blackout, or perhaps by the fishermen at sea or a lone shrimper, such as my grandad, at dawn, on Southport sands. One could well understand, that such a spectacle, viewed in the cold Arctic heavens, would be evocative of the Norse Gods and Warriors, still fighting their battles in 'Valhalla'.

As is the norm with all fishermen, my grandad could forecast weather with uncanny accuracy, utilizing natural elements of wind, sky and sea, and also the movements and activities of birds, and even the opening and closing of plants at various times, and in certain variable conditions. With regard to our youthful expeditions to sea shore, park or countryside, he could not only predict the weather, but also the precise time of our necessary departures, and arrivals, dictated by weather conditions. We soon learnt to ignore these at our peril.

He was always observant of the wild birds of the region on marsh, mere or estuary. He maintained that the Great Bay, where the Rimmers landed, a thousand years ago, although he did not know this by name, was still the largest estuary in the country.

He knew the origin of many species of birds, and their times of arrival, and departure. He knew that the pink footed geese came from the icy tundras of Greenland, and Iceland, together with whooper swans. Also that the Bewick swan, as we now know it, 'came wi't wind', straight from Siberia, and had been coming for untold years before the Rimmers arrived, for in its day, Martin Mere, probably at one time the largest lake in England, was known and used by the Roman, Vikings, and even King Arthur, and all throughout the middle ages by monastic establishments, until its use was curtailed by drainage for arable land, in the 17th century.

A transformation which my grandad would surely approve of, was in 1972, when the Wildfowl Trust acquired 363 acres of marshland, to create a now internationally known, Wildlife Centre. It now has hundreds of resident arctic swans, and other, antipodean natives, teals and ducks. The autumn of 1989, saw the country's largest ever influx of majestic Bewick swans from Siberia, accompanied by a couple of Black Swans. The black swans, after an absence of several years, come mainly from the Washington, Tyne and Wear Centre, which is their first landfall, coming on the latitude from Siberia. In the autumn of 1990, a sighting has been made of a male, pinkfoot goose on Martin Mere, which was ringed in the 1988 Wildfowl expedition to a National Park in North East Greenland. The latest sighting of a rare species was in July 1991, when a Temmincks Stint, a tiny, high Arctic wader was seen at the Martin Mere Reserve. It appears therefore, that the future of Martin Mere will be assured for posterity in the respect of wildlife, especially with the additional estimated, seventeen thousand geese, on the Bank's marshes, constituting a third of the world's population in all, on a prolific area of feeding ground, along the sheltered shoreline, and the Mere. There are more birds now at Martin Mere, Red Wagtails, Lapland Buntings, Winnets, Reed Buntings, Skylarks, Curlews etc. The mudflats abound with Dunlins, Red Shanks, and Oyster Catchers. Sir Peter Scott echoed the words of my grandad when he said Southport was the only town in Britain, that the geese fly over regularly, and that the Ribble Estuary is the longest Estuary in Britain, containing some of the world's rarest birds. I have seen such rare and exotic birds at Ainsdale, as the Golden Oriole, and the Bee Eater, the latter on a garden fence, at the last house in Shore Road, in pre-war days, before the new estate was built. The Bee Eater, a brightly coloured bird, a native of the Nile Delta, was thought to have come over on a ship into Liverpool. It was eventually scared away, by too many officially organised sightseers, but these are only transitory happenings. It is to be hoped however that, for as long in the future, as in the past, the geese will continue to embark from their icy habitats, to cross thousands of miles of ocean and land, heralding their arrival, and sojourn in Britain, by filling the air with the familiar 'Wink-Wink' and 'Honk Honk', we have come to know so well, both in the autumn and winter skies, from September to March.

One final ornithological item, concerns a feathered species very common now to our urban surroundings. It is the Collared Dove, Streptopelia Decaoto, to give its official title, described as "having a narrow, half black collar at the back of its neck." It breeds in Asia, from Turkey to Japan. It is indigenous to the Caucasus mountains, and originated in the Mount Ararat area. It is now widespread, in counties in Britain, arriving there, via the Hebrides and Shetland Islands and across Europe. How long this dove has been in our area is not known, nor how it arrived, perhaps 'wi't wind', but a legend attached to it could very well be in the 'Comfrey (Knit Bone)', source of classification. It appears, that as we all know, that Noah and the Ark, after the flood, were safely lodged on Mount Ararat. Noah had sent forth the raven which, "went to and fro until the waters were dried up off the earth", and did not return. He then sent a dove, which however, "found no rest for her foot", and returned to the Ark. Noah waited another seven days, and then "sent the dove out upon the waters." In the meantime however Noah, to make sure it would be recognisable as the dove he had sent, if it returned, marked the back of its neck with some of the pitch used in the original construction of the Ark, and kept for the caulking of any leaks which might occur, while the Ark was afloat upon the waters. The dove duly returned, with the olive branch, so that Noah knew "the waters were abated." He waited another seven days then "sent forth the dove which returned not again to him any more." However, the mark made by the black pitch on the dove's neck, remains there to this day as a symbol, like the Rainbow in the cloud, of the "everlasting covenant between God and every living creature," and Noah, "that neither shall there any more be a flood to destroy the earth." A delightful, but improbable little tale no doubt. I have noticed however, that from a colony of these 'collared' doves, which inhabit nearby trees, that, when I put out scattered, wild bird seeds, which contains maize, there is always just one bird from the colony, which makes a quick foray, and a peck or two, before returning for other members of the flock. Is this 'lone ranger', which appears alone, every morning, at the same time, reverting to primeval instinct, inherited from its forebears, who was sent out as a scout from the Ark, "alone upon the waters." More likely perhaps to be just another made-up fairy tale? I cannot include mention of 'The Birkdale Nightingale' into this ornithological, sequence, for the simple fact that 'The Birkdale Nightingale' is not a feathered species at all, but the name given by locals, to the 'Natterjack Toad', now a protected species, dwelling in the 'slacks' of the Ainsdale Reserve. When in full song it can be heard as far as a mile away. Apart from the Birkdale Sandhills, from which it has been driven further south over the years, it had a 'run' from the 'slacks' parallel, with the 'Fisherman's Path', to and from the lake at Ainsdale, where they used to cross near Toad Hall, even when the roads had been established. Foxes, from the pine woods at Formby Hall still use this route, but the Natterjack is now confined by property development etc. to the area where it can be monitored and protected, at one of the few locations in the country where it still survives.

So far, all the historic data concerning our ancestors, long before the Rimmers arrived, lies in geological, rather than the geneological records discussed so far. Martin Mere undoubtedly, is the key to unlock the door of knowledge in this respect. We have discussed many of these aspects in the geological survey in Chapter One of 'Betwixt Ribbel and Moerse', and the discovery on the Mere, of relics of a bygone age, skeletons of elk, deer, antelope and even whales and other extinct species, many of them 5000 years or more in age. Tangible evidence of man's early presence is still with us, in such an object as the single, most important archeological discovery of the dugout canoe, discussed earlier.

Since "Betwixt Ribbel and Moerse" was first published, condensed in size as it was, at least four archeological surveys have been made, based on information in the book, and carried out to a successful conclusion. There are other projects pending, but there is one other sphere of activity, hitherto only partly examined, which is contained, not in the skies above, or on the surface, but underneath Martin Mere.

From notes I had discarded, written well over half a century ago, it appeared that, with the discovery, over along period of time, probably after the Mere was drained, of ancient spear heads and flints, that something more than peat lay on the bottom of the Mere. Indeed, the very peat of which the mosses are largely composed, tends to preserve, even human bodies, in a remarkable state of preservation, but isolated discoveries do not give sufficient indication of a definite location. If therefore, people had fished the mere all those years ago, they must have had a lakeland village, or camp, but where?

As most of the relics recovered from the Mere, were made at the Crossens side, when the Sewage works were constructed, it was logical to assume that the high ground, or the 'Kross Ness' as it was later referred to, was an ideal sheltered location. However, even here, it was shown that, as well as two others found nearby, a boulder was discovered during excavations which were made for the new pumping station in 1959. This boulder, brought by glacial flow from Dumfriesshire, during the Ice Age, was an indication that this area had been subjected to considerable disturbances for a long time, and unsuitable for lakeside habitation (see photos, 1, 2 and 4).

Where then to build this lake village, or neolithic stone age camp, to gain shelter from the cold east wind, 'fra' Siberia'? Only one spot was suitable, and that on the eastern side of the Mere, but sheltered from the east wind by a 'Brow', in similar fashion to the manner in which the fishermen on the coast, thousands of years later, built their cottages in the 'Brow' of the Sea Cops. Quite simply, the 'Brow' I am referring to, on the Mere, is of course Mere Brow, near Holmeswood. Mere brow is a natural stone eminence, an extension of the Parbold foothills of the Pennines, a shelter, not only from the east wind, but also providing the stone, from which Neolithic man would fashion his Stone Age implements. An archeological discovery in this area would prove whether it is indeed fact, not fiction, that the earliest inhabitants dwelt on the 'Rim of the Mere'. The final answer to this little enigma is in my opinion, two fold. Firstly, there is definite evidence that there was a 'Kranug', or in the modern translation 'Crannog', which was an ancient Celtic lake dwelling, somewhere near the Mere Brow, or Parbold end, of Martin Mere which could have been associated with the Rimmer's ancestors, and ultimately with King Arthur, and Joseph of Arimathea.

Secondly, I still believe that the discovery on the Mere, of older artefacts, have definitely indicated that there was also, a much older dwelling place, that could date back at least to the Stone Age, and that Mere Brow is the most likely location for excavations to be made, for both Stone Age, and the later lake dwellings. I also hold the contention that, as there was plenty of room on the Mere, for more than one lake dwelling, that there could have been a 'Crannog' on the west side, built by 'Rimmer' ancestors, probably near the 'Snoterpool'. Many relics have been found in the Crossens area, as evidenced by Bulpit's photograph, circa 1899, in the Botanic Museum, taken with the canoe on a cart, which has recently been identified, as being taken near Crossens Church. One other personal clue I can add, is that, when I first started my schoolboy scribblings, and the collection of local artefacts, I came into possession (I will not disclose the source), of a sliver of blackened wood, which was said by my grandad to be from a 'batter on't Mere, thousands of years 'sen." Years later, I was allowed to examine the canoe at the Botanic Museum, and fit the piece of wood into the place from which it had 'accidentally' fallen. I found, many years later, that the "batter" referred to, was "Batr", which was Nordic for boat, and "sen", was still in common use locally, meaning "ago". Perhaps some day soon, excavations on the Mere will reveal more discoveries. There can be no doubt however, that Martin Mere, was the catalyst that welded together all the segments of our history from the prehistoric, with a geological record stretching back to over 200 million years, down to the Post Glacial, Recent Period, of about half a million years. After its first inhabitants, at least the neolithic stone age dwellers, there is the evidence of ancient British occupation, around its perimeter, in the presence, still defined by the Earthworks in the Scarisbrick Hall Park, and Rufford, the partly excavated Boar's Head Den Tumulus at Parbold, (photo No. 18) and the 'Moat' on Ormskirk Golf Links, where excavations have recently taken place. The excavations recently carried out at Altcar, also come within its sphere of influence, as does the moat referred to as 'King Arthur's Ring' or 'Court', near Sefton Church, now decimated, or should I say desecrated, by a new by-pass road (see photo No. 38). There is another ancient 'Moat', listed at Manor House, Maghull. As an update to these details it was announced, on my 76th birthday in March 1991, that Sefton Council has also stated, that a designated conservation area concerning Lunt Village, Homer Green, and Carr Houses on the Ince Blundell estate is to be preserved. The medieval settlement of Lunt is documented from 1260, and the medieval settlement of

Homer Green, has surviving buildings, dating from the 16th century. The most interesting item, however, lies in the fact that Homer Green Farm, which I have always considered to be of more ancient origin, is now to be preserved as a 'moated site', much older than the dwelling of the former Molyneaux family of 1402. Many of these moated areas are of prehistoric origin, linking up in a great arc around Martin Mere.

In the Parbold area, overlooking Martin Mere, the most identifiable prehistoric site in the area is the Boar's Head Den, Tumulus, on top of Parbold Hill (see photo No. 18). It has been partly excavated many years ago, and a burial urn, and some artefacts removed. At nearby Ashurst Hall, is another ancient 'Moat', and another one at Spa Roughs, Lathom, is listed as an 'Earthwork'. On the west side of Parbold Hill was 'Brandreth Delph' quarry, now identified by Brandreth Close. This was the former Delph Tea Gardens, where we had Sunday School outings in the 1920s. The caves, then still remaining in the quarry, sealed off by metal grilles as being unsafe, are undoubtedly of prehistoric origin, and reputed to have been occupied partly by Sir Lancelot, of Arthurian fame, (see Chapter Two). At the top of the quarry, was a boating lake, used by picnickers, and Sunday School Parties. Across the top of the hill which was called Hunters Hill, was another quarry, now completely demolished. The caves, the hill, and the burial tumulus, all have pre-historic connections, and doubtless connected with hunting, and the fishing on the Mere down below. A personal connection with the area, lies in the presence of Hilldale Mission, another Sunday School outing area, which stands on the main road, on the corner of the lane, which led up to Hunter's Hill Quarry. As I write, in December, 1990, my Grandad's niece, Anna Jane, Mrs. Turner, passed away in her 86th year after being caretaker, with her husband, of Hilldale Mission, since the 1920s.

There are many other prehistoric moats, and sites, dotted around Martin Mere, at Ingrave Farm, and Bradley Hall at Eccleston and underneath the site of Croston Castle. The most interesting, and important, of all the places, and events, concerning the Ancient British, Roman, Viking, and King Arthur influence, are depicted in the sketch, on page 15 of Chapter Two, of 'Betwixt Ribbel and Moerse'. They are connected with the Roman Road from Coccium (Wigan) which runs to the confluence of the Rivers Darwen and Ribble, at Walton Le Dale. They are all but a short distance to the north east of Martin Mere. On the east of this road, and to the east of Euxton, there are two prehistoric sites, at Rotherham Top, and Pickering Castle. The road, which was the only metalled road in the area, was built by the Romans, over an ancient British trackway. It ran northwards through the grounds of Worden Hall, Leyland, where Roman coins and rings were found. I have myself found a stretch of this road running through a field near a hawthorn hedge near Worden Hall. The main wing of Worden Hall was demolished by fire, which occurred during World War II. In 1960 Mr. Roger Fleetwood Hesketh bought, and erected the Obelisk which now stands in the wooded triangle in front of St. Cuthbert's Church, and the Hesketh Arms, opposite Meols Hall entrance.

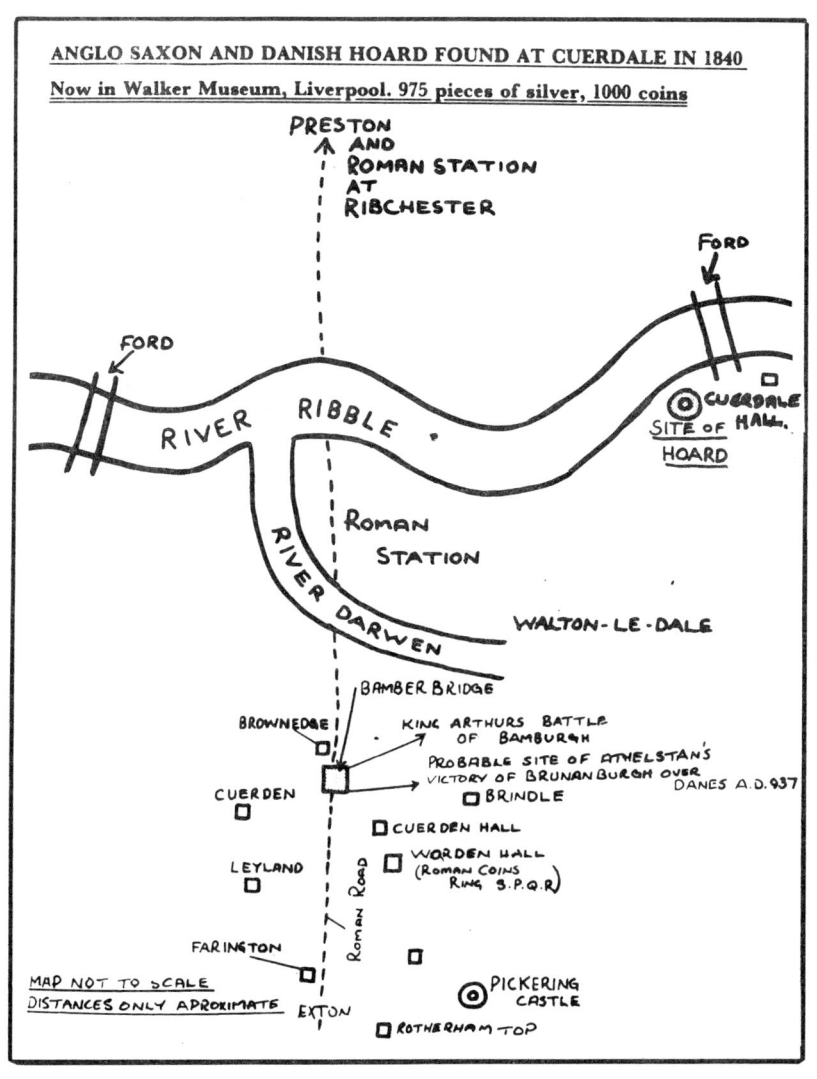

```
ANGLO SAXON AND DANISH HOARD FOUND AT CUERDALE IN 1840
Now in Walker Museum, Liverpool. 975 pieces of silver, 1000 coins
                    PRESTON
                    AND
                    ROMAN STATION
                    AT
                    RIBCHESTER
                                                    FORD
     FORD
                                              ○ CUERDALE
                                              SITE OF HALL
        RIVER  RIBBLE           •             HOARD

              R            ROMAN
              I            STATION
              V
              E
              R
                D
                 A
                  R
                   W                     WALTON-LE-DALE
                    E
                     N
                          BAMBER BRIDGE
            BROWNEDGE    KING ARTHURS BATTLE
                  □    → OF BAMBURGH
                         PROBABLE SITE OF ATHELSTAN'S
          CUERDEN      → VICTORY OF BRUNANBURGH OVER
              □         □ BRINDLE         DANES A.D. 937
                        □ CUERDEN HALL
            LEYLAND   R □ WORDEN HALL
              □       o  (ROMAN COINS
                      m   RING S.P.Q.R)
                      a
            FARINGTON n
                  □ □  R
MAP NOT TO SCALE       o    □   ○ PICKERING
DISTANCES ONLY APROXIMATE  a        CASTLE
                       d EXTON
                         □ ROTHERHAM TOP
```

Worden Hall has been restored, and is now an arts and crafts centre, with a nature trail. It was the ancestral home of the Farington family. I well remember, when I used to visit the Lancashire County Council vehicle repair depot at Riverside, near Worden Hall on business, the stores manager, a keen local history enthusiast, was astonished, and delighted when I told him that the office we were in, was situated exactly over the Roman Road, and all its attendant history.

A short distance to the east of the Roman Road, at Bamber Bridge, is what is thought to be the probable site of Brunanburgh, where King Alfred's grandson, Athelstan, defeated the Danes in 937 AD. Nearby also, is the reputed site of King Arthur's last battle of Bamburgh. Both these site names were later changed to Bamber Bridge. The Romans had a factory at Walton Le Dale, and a Roman Station, Rigodanum, lay between the two rivers. A short distance away, at a bend in the River Ribble near Cuerdale Hall, was found what has since transpired to be the largest, and most important treasure hoard ever made, of Anglo Saxon, and Viking artefacts, coins, brooches and jewellery. This find was presumed to be a war chest, which was thought to have been lost when the defeated armies fled northwards, across one of the two wooden fords crossing the river. Part of the treasure had slid down into the river, and never 'officially' recovered. After this discovery in 1840, 975 pieces of silver and 1000 coins were lodged in the Walker Museum in Liverpool. In this year, 1990, one hundred and fifty years later, after many representations from interested bodies, and individuals like myself, and Granada ITV, an exhibition, combining these artefacts, coins and brooches, with a Viking Craft display, was held at the Liverpool Museum in William Brown Street, from May to September. Independent sources have assessed however, that the total items to date, of this treasure hoard, number 8500 pieces of silver alone, so it is to be hoped that we have not seen the last of this treasure trove.

Our own locality too, is not devoid of treasure trove connections. I have pointed out to many enquirers, that there are many areas still unexplored in the area. Roman coins have been found all along the 'Churchgate' track, and on Birkdale Common. Only recently has a discovery been made of one such coin, at the Nixon's Lane approach to Anderson's Farm, which might afford some clue as to the passage of the 'Roman' trackway through the area.

Not very far away from this spot, at Penwortham (Roman — Peneverdentum) is another historic site, near the site of the Benedictine Priory, founded by King Stephen. The present church of St. Mary the Virgin (see photos 55 and 56) dates to the 14th century. At the Domeday Survey, there is mention of King Edward holding the Castle, and refers to the "fishing, and woods, and eyries of hawks." Behind the church is an ancient earthwork known as Castle Hill, which I have climbed. Standing above the river, it must have been 100ft. or more in height at one time. The deep fosse, which separates the hill from the church, probably makes it seem higher than it really is.. As far as I can tell it represents a Norman Fortress, on the site of a Romano-British encampment. About $\frac{3}{4}$ of a mile from here, probably buried under the electricity works, was Hangman's Bank Wood, where there was Hangman's Bank Cross, covered over when the river was diverted. There were also two wells here, St. Annes, near Penwortham church, and St. Mary's, which I can remember, had a spring running into a stone trough by the roadside (see page 29). It was only with a 'tongue in cheek approach' that I originally included the Arthurian legend into 'Betwixt Ribbel and Moerse'. I found, sadly, in the course of research, that many previous poets, and historians, had distored Arthurian legends, owing to the lack of contradiction by contemporary people, unable to check details or stories, by virtue of the fact that most of them were unable to read, let alone write. This enabled chroniclers to angle myth, legend, and fact, to support any theory they wished to promote. Modern scientific investigation however has proved, for instance, that the great circular shield, formed supposedly by the Knights of the Round Table placing their shields together when meeting, and still on display at Winchester, is nothing but a hoax, as it was proved that this 'Round Table' could have only been made several hundred years later, owing to the age of the wood, as shown by the 'ring per year' method. Other historical records, such as Tintagel Castle being the centre of occupation by King Arthur, was proved to be false, as the castle was only constructed after his death.

Consequent documented events have however, now proved that Arthur was a real historical figure, and that his activities, particularly in the north, have been established beyond doubt. Although the locations, and events, concerning King Arthur in the Bamber Bridge area might be considered conjectural, it has been definitely established that, concerning Arthur's Welsh connection, it was considered that the Welsh had a valid claim. It was, that the country, occupied by the Celtic tribes in the North Solway estuary, and the Lowlands of Scotland in an area around Dumfries, known as the Kingdom of the Rheged, which included also the Caledonii and Selgviae Celtic tribes and the whole of the Caledonian Forest, was part of the Welsh Celtic ancestral homeland.

It was for this reason that King Arthur mounted an expedition against Gwennolus, King of Scotia (Scotland), and the '13 kingdoms', which comprised the whole of the region north of Hadrians Wall, known to the Welsh as Guaul, ('the wall'). The whole of the north, in the ancient Welsh book Y'Gogledd, refers to the decline and setting of the 'Heroic Age', in the 6th and 7th centuries. Cross references of historical records show that Arthur successfully defeated "The Thirteen Princes of the North", and believing that history needs a bit of a giggle now and then, I introduced into a recent historical article, the perfectly true story, that one of the defeated "Princes", was a certain King Coel, corrupted into a nursery rhyme as 'Old King Cole'. He certainly had nothing to be merry about, but he had 'three fiddlers', and his 'pipe' was his private 'piper'. It is not confirmed whether his bowl held porridge.

Although the Roman Road at Bamber Bridge might be assumed to have been a minor one, the facts prove it to be otherwise, as it linked up with Coccium (Wigan), and Manchester, to the south, and to the north, crossing the Ribble, onto Ribchester (Bremetennacum) by another link road. The Roman Road to the north is identified in Preston itself by Watling Street Road, and it can be identified by the A6 road and railway line, as it runs parallel, and in some places, lies under the railway line, which runs to Carlisle (Luguvalium) and onto Glasgow, thus completing a great highway, from the Channel to the Clyde. On the approaches to Carlisle incidentally, is a perfectly preserved mound and ditch, called 'King Arthur's Court' which gives some idea what the one at Sefton looked like.

Although Roman Roads in this region are not readily identifiable, they can be found still at Jeffrey Hill, in the Ribchester area. If you wish to establish say for instance Watling Street, find the little village of Affetside, near Bolton, stand by the ancient stone cross, and you are then on the great Roman Road of Watling Street, which runs clean through the village. This spot, one of the main stations the Romans established, is exactly halfway between London and Edinburgh.

King Arthur's activities around Martin Mere, and in the Douglas Vale, listed in Chapter 2 of 'Betwixt Ribbel and Moerse' and the story of the Douglas Chapel 'The Chapel in the Valley', aroused much interest in historical circles, and also in the press, and finally a television interview took place, with a view to the production of a documentary film on the Arthurian Legend, concerning the Douglas, and the Mere.

At least half a dozen Lancashire newspapers and magazines produced reviews, and as it happened, projects were mooted as to the reconstruction of the site at Castlefield, connected with Sir Lancelot's journey from Parbold. Interest was heightened, especially as I could supply information, confirmed by Balliol College, and the Arthurian Society at Oxford, that these events were well authenticated by modern historical research. The Roman road leading to Castlefield, was confirmed to have been built over by Manchester's first railway terminus, which has now been coverted into one complex, which includes the ITV Granada studios. I am however, unable to confirm the assertion that the portion of cobbled road, depicted as Coronation Street, is actually on top of the Roman road.

The area of approximately five square miles around Parbold, had provided all the ingredients required, for inclusion into the myth, legend and history, of King Arthur. Ancient earthworks, fairy glens, Delphs, site of castle, caves, lake, ancient chapel, and battle sites.

From the time of the Garden of Eden, as recorded in the second Chapter of Genesis, the fruit of the tree of the knowledge of good and evil was regarded as the apple. The Latin Bible interpretation for evil, is 'Malam' which means apple, credited with imparting such knowledge. This fruit has mystical significance associated with divination, and 'other world' connections, and was supposed to possess healing properties, especially so in the legend of King Arthur. In respect of the healing property, this is why King Arthur was said to have been taken, after his death, to the Celtic paradisical 'Island of Apples'.

Quoting again from Chapter Two, Martin Mere was described as "Mair Tain Moir", a wide, insular water near the coast." Sir Lancelot of the Lake, was supposed to have been given rule over this part of Lancashire, and the derivation of Lancashire implies that it was composed of the Celtic 'Lanc', and 'lod, or lot', implying a people, hence Lancelot's shire, or Lancashire. King Arthur, selected by Ambrosia to command his army, is reputed to have defeated the Saxons in twelve pitched battles, four of which took place in the region of Douglas Vale, and Linius, or lake of Martin Mere. Another battle, which cannot be authenticated, is supposed to have taken place in one of three towns near Southport, buried by a tidal wave. This was in a great estuary, named by Ptolemy, the 2nd century Roman map maker, as Belisama, which shows no existence then, of the Ribble or Mersey. 'Bel' is Celtic for 'mouth', used in many Irish and Isle of Man locations. In Ireland,

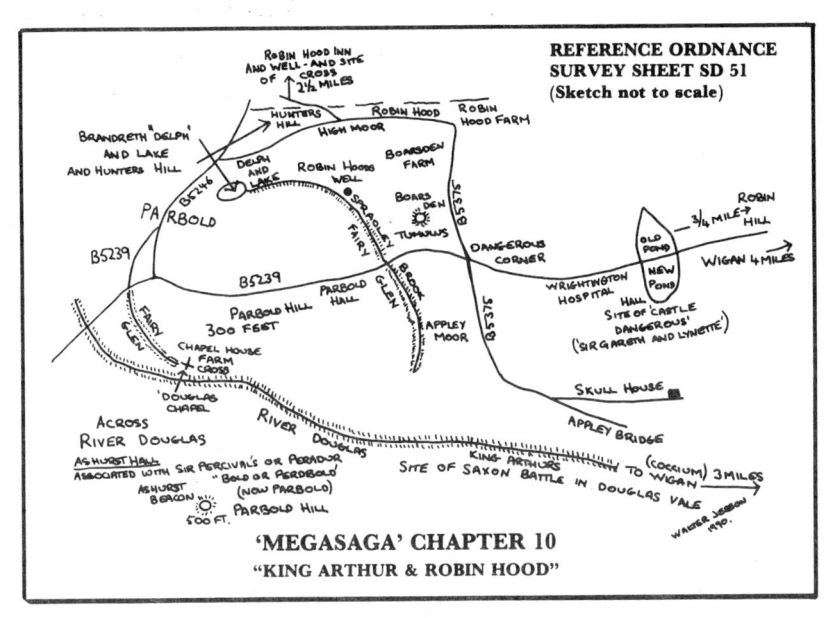

Belisama was pronounced 'Violish aune', and corrupted to Ballyshannon, and literally means that 'the rivers are navigable'. Therefore, in the demarcation of the coastline by Ptolemy in the second century, there is no River Mersey, Alt, Ribble and of course no River Douglas. Only one other water course is shown, and that is the delta of the Great Bay or Belisama, up which the Snoterpool flowed to connect up with the great inland lake of Martin Mere.

In later centuries great earthquakes, and subsequent floods, movements of the ocean bed, such as the Great Drift, now being traced by oceanographers, which stretches right through the Atlantic Ocean to Iceland, caused the Ribble to finally break through into the Great Bay, and formed also, a new entrance in the Ribble estuary. This was the Douglas, so named and used by King Arthur. Earlier Vikings, sailing into the Ribble, and up the Douglas, had named it the Askyr, after the Ash Tree, described in the Norse Cosmology. The whole area therefore was regarded by both the Vikings and King Arthur, as sacred territory. I have traced the course of the Douglas or Astland, from the Hesketh Bank, and Tarleton Mosses, from Ribble Bank Farm, occupied by the Slinger family, which is off the Guide Road leading to the crossing over the Ribble to Freckleton. This is probably the nearest point to the confluence of the Astland, or Douglas, with the Ribble. Where the river runs through the Longton Marsh and onto the Little Hoole Marsh then Much Hoole Marsh, past Becconsall Hall, built in 1667, occupied by the Melling family, it actually becomes two rivers. The old river loops at Tarleton Lock, where King Arthur's 'port' was situated. It is joined by the canal, which runs side by side with the River. The old course of the river can be traced through Sollom Lock, where the new river course is strengthened by its confluence with the Rivers Yarrow, and Lostock, which have their source in the hills above Chorley. The Douglas, or Astland, twists and turns through Hoscar Mosses, and Rufford, Burscough, and Parbold, where its progress, and events connected with it, have been well recorded. In conjunction with canals, tunnels, and viaducts, through, and underneath Wigan, it reduces in strength, and width, past the vicinity of Haigh and Blackrod, across or under the A6, on to Lever Park, near Horwich, climbing up to Rivington Pike. Then on to its source, which is a convergence of springs on the boggy moorland on Winter Hill, near the TV Transmitter Station, the mast of which, is visible from its entry into the Ribble, approximately 30 miles away, and all along its course. It has been, and still is, walkable, along its entire length.

King Arthur built, or made use of, an existing port on the River Douglas, which is a welsh derivation, 'Duglis', 'Dubo' — Black 'glais' — stream, the "Black Stream", emptying into the Belisama. Utilising the Roman trackway, running through Churchgate from Warrington to Penwortham, he could link up with the road to the north, also with land and sea links from Wales, to complete the conquest of Scotland, and with his activities and links with Ireland, forge the gigantic English-Welsh-Irish, Celtic triangle.

King Arthur's battle at Blackrod, took place on a Roman station fortified by Saxons. The subsequent castle built on the site, was officially investigated in 1846, and 1952. Artefacts, such as a crown, and key, found in the first search were however, lost. The battle site, at East Drummersdale Farm, close to New Lane, is still marked on Ordnance Maps as 'Batloom'. Formerly the site was known as 'Battle Holme', but the site had hitherto only been referred to as being legendary. There have been a few artefacts, mostly coins, dating from the Roman era found in the New Lane area, which has not been fully researched, in respect of its connection with the Batloom battle site, or with the lake village possibility, in connection with the source of the 'Snoterpool'. I did remark to a near relative, who was working on a farm on the Mere several years ago who was interested, to keep an eye open for 'Excalibur'. He subsequently turned up with a sword that had been found in the vicinity. Alas, it was not ancient enough to be the legendary weapon, as the sword and scabbard being of different periods were difficult to identify, but as they appear to be perhaps of the civil war, trooper or dragoon, cavalry period, the find is interesting enough. It is still in the Botanic Museum, but not catalogued, or identified. Not perhaps such an exciting discovery as one would wish, but still nevertheless indicative of the potential that this region offers, even today, in the field of local research.

However, in the autumn of 1988, whilst I was carrying out research concerning the Rimmer's presence in the area as fishermen and farmers, associated with Martin Mere, I had occasion to confirm their connections with Pinfold, Scarisbrick, and had been informed that a cottage, at the crossroads, previously covered with ivy for many years, had now been cleared. It was reputed to be a chapel, belonging to the Derby and Lathom family, who had established the nearby Augustinian Priory at Burscough, in the 12th century.

When I examined the cottage, it appeared to have been reconstructed in Georgian Style, identified by the fan shaped, shell mounting over the doorway. An incised stone cross, above the doorway, indicated an ecclesiastical connection. However the general disalignment and disproportion of doorways, windows, and fireplaces, the thickness of the walls, and part of a very ancient stairway, indicated the existence of much older stonework, above and below ground. Examination of the photos, and general aspect of the Douglas Chapel at Parbold (see photos No. 25 and 26 and reconstructed sketch on page 122), indicated that the two buildings were of the same proportions and ages.

Assuming the acceptance of the information, that the Douglas Chantry Chapel was raised by King Arthur, to commemorate his victory over the Saxons, then the Pinfold Chapel could have been erected for the same purpose. In both cases, the distances between the two battle sites, and their respective chapels are approximately the same, thus perpetuating the custom that King Arthur had, of constructing a commemorative edifice at the scene of every successful battle.

There are many names, and places, locally, to connect the Arthurian legend with the Cult of the Apple, and its obvious connection with the Garden of Eden. Apples were originally the fruit of the Ash tree. Some apples are still grown on Ash trees in the Wye Valley, near the church dedicated to St. Dubricius, in an area with strong Roman, and King Arthur connections. Apples were a running theme in Celtic literature, associated with Druids and mistletoe, magic and invisibility. Probably, in connection with the town lost off the coast of Southport associated with King Arthur, we can see how the Ash connects to the apple, by quoting a few instances in the area, around the Mere in the Southport area. Thomas Rimmer built the Ash Tree Inn in 1790, which was replaced by the Portland Hotel around 1910. Ash Tree Farm, was on the opposite corner. Ash Tree Lane was Bedford Road, from its junction with Wham Lane (Stamford Road), and led to Ash Tree Hills (Bedford Park). Haig Avenue was previously known as Ash Lane, Ash Street, is still there. There was an Ash Tree Inn in Halsall. Spradley Brook runs through a grove of trees, from the top of Parbold Hill, through the 'Fairy Glen' to Appleby Moor, and Appley Bridge. Across the valley is Ashurst Hall, and Ashurst Beacon, 500 ft. high, used as a signalling post to the Roman Fort at Coccium (Wigan). Druids and Wizards could always raise mists or fog, at the scene of battles, by use of mystic apples, or in any time of danger. The question might be asked, facetiously of course, why is the M6 motorway at Shevington, where it crosses the River Douglas, more frequently fogged up than any other section. I have run through patches of fog there, when the road has been clear on both sides. Has the mist of King Arthur's battle with the Saxons, which took place immediately below, been forgotten to be lifted by the wizards?

The same thing happens at the Isle of Man, where the legend still persists, that 'Mannin' put a protective mist over the island when there was danger. Many Viking expeditions reported they couldn't find the island, for the fogs in the area. I have seen, on a clear summer's day, flying into Ronaldsway, a blanket of fog over the island, when there was no fog anywhere else in the Irish Sea.

Sheer bunkum of course, like the legend of King Arthur's white steed, appearing, always in a mist of course, on Martin Mere. For many years I wrote a succession of ghost stories every Christmas, and in 1976, I was assisted by our former resident cartoonist, Bill Tidy, when I included an item concerning the fact that, at least two seperate hunting parties, had seen a white horse in the mist and fog, early in the year. I then poised the question, could it have been a manifestation of, perhaps the ghostly steed of King Arthur? Subsequently I was approached by a gamekeeper from the Mere, one day, when I was at Bill Leatherbarrow's garage, at Carr Cross. He told me that there had been more incidents the next year, and that there was no animal reported missing. He had mentioned these incidents to his father, who was a gamekeeper before him, known to us, as he had chased us off Scarisbrick Estate property many times, but was now retired. He informed his son that, early one foggy morning, he was aroused by the dog barking furiously at the door, with his neck hairs standing on end, obviously very agitated. The dog would not go outside, but looking out, he had seen a white horse on the front lawn. The vision was quickly shrouded in mist, and a subsequent search of the area revealed no trace of horse, or even hoof prints, nor any disturbance in the soft ground on the border of the grass. All there was across the lawn, were his own two sets of footprints, going and coming, in the dew on the grass. When asked why he hadn't mentioned the incident, the gamekeeper's father said that quite probably people would have thought he was 'barmy', and would have had him put away. Although I have 'debunked' many of these ghostly manifestations in the past, I must admit there are some incidents which have been quite inexplicable, and I find that at least one in four people believe in ghosts, past and present.

The Norsemen or Vikings, as we know them, had no doubts about the region of Martin Mere being of great importance. They named the river now known to us as the Douglas, 'Askr', which comes from Norse cosmography, meaning Ash Tree, on which the Sacred apples, associated with Adam grew. Adam in Norse cosmography, also means 'root', or 'man'. The Vikings always carried 'sacred apples' in their longboats, and to them the 'Askr' was a sacred river, as was the Mere also regarded as a sacred lake. The proximity, and coincidental connection, between the conjectured site of King Arthur's last battle, and the victory of Athelstan at the two sites, a few miles away from the Mere, point to a definite connection between the Norsemen, and King Arthur, and Martin Mere. So too, there can be some credence in the legend of King Arthur being taken to the Celtic paradisial 'Island of Apples', one of three islands, reputed to be Whassum Island, on Martin Mere. Also there is an accompanying legend that, after Excalibur was tossed into the Mere, and assuming that magic apples did not revive the dead King, the funeral barge bore the King up the River Askyr, or Douglas, westwards to Avalon for burial in Ireland. All these legends, and locations, fit quite easily into local topography. Many of the subsequent accounts by historians, and poets distorted these facts by introducing romanticism in favour of historical conjecture. It is possible to equate legend with fact, in many myths, and legends, in various periods of time. For instance, Norse Cosmology describes 'Yggdrasil' as the "Ash Tree, upon which the structure of the universe is based." The Gjallarhorn the 'horn of Alarm is kept under the 'great Ash", to be blown when the "hostilities of the evil powers are afoot." This legend equates exactly with the legend of the Arthurian period, where King Arthur, and his Knights, lie sleeping in the cave beneath the sacred ash tree, awaiting a blast from the 'horn of alarm', when evil threatens.

All these facts and fantasies, myths and legends, have prevailed down the centuries. They can be angled to suit anyone's pet theory. From the 6th century, works of the English historian Gildas, who incidentally, never left the south coast, can be added to Geoffrey of Monmouth's Historia Regum Brittanica, written in the 12th century, purporting to be a History of Kings of Britain, from 1136 BC, to the death of King Cadwaller, in Rome in 689 AD. It is however, only the translation of a very ancient book in the Welsh language.

Sir Thomas Malory wrote Morte D'Arthur in 1485, a real hotch potch of chivalrous nonsense. It was he who coined the romantic phrase, "Which would be found inscribed on Arthur's Grave HIC JACET ARTHURUS REX QUONDAM REXQUE FUTURUS — "Here lies Arthur, the Once and Future King."

The poets Sir Walter Scott, and Tennyson, however, did promote the north as the location of many of King Arthur's activities. In Tennyson's 'Idylls of the King', I quoted him (page 12) in one passage, as saying "Lancelot spoke, and answered him in full, as having been with Arthur, in the fight which all day long, rang by the mouth of the violent glen, and in the four wild battles by the shore of Douglas."

Myths and legends apart however, there is no doubt that there was a 6th century Celtic Warrior Leader, promoted later to 'King' Arthur, whose name was a derivation of the Roman 'Artorius'. He was introduced by the Romano-British prince, Ambrosius Aurelianus, whom he succeeded as King Arthur. He held back the marauding forces of invaders, principally Saxons, in twelve major battles, ranging as far north as Linius, described as a "wide insular water, near the sea coast, called "Mair Tain Moir", now known as Martin Mere. Four of his battles were fought along the Douglas, before his expedition against the 'Thirteen Princes of Scotland'. He was a champion of Christendom, and was identified with the Quest for the Holy Grail, brought to Britain by Joseph of Arimathea, for safe keeping. The legend that Joseph visited the region of Martin Mere has persisted for centuries, and will be commented upon later.

The most authentic accounts of King Arthur's exploits are Celtic. In Wales there were 'Tales from the Red Book of Hergest' — 'The Black Book of Carmarthen', and the works of Taliesin, and 'Tales of the Mabinogi'. In Scotland is 'The White Book of Rydderch', and the oldest Scottish Poem 'Goddodin', and to complete the Celtic triangle, in Ireland "Echtra Connla', and O'Rahilly. There are many individual accounts also, of great antiquity, penned by the monks of various regions.

Historical, mythical, or conjectural, all these facts added together, do constitute support for the claims, made by many professional historians, over a long period of time, that West Lancashire can compare favourably with many other countless British localities, in its claim to be the home of some of the Arthurian legends.

One sequel of the publication in Chapter Two of 'Betwixt Ribbel and Moerse' perpetuating the Arthurian legend locally, was an interview with a television executive, based in Manchester, who was proposing to make a documentary of King Arthur's exploits in the River Douglas, and Martin Mere area. The accounts contained here, are additional notes, and new research, culminating in the discovery of the cottage at Pinfold, Scarisbrick. The television executive, Mr. Nicholas Wilding, who has strong Southport family connections, has formed his own television company, called 'Excalibur'. He has already had a documentary on the Rochdale Rushbearing ceremony, shown on BBC television, and it is to be anticipated that the enormous amount of work and effort necessary to transpose written words into moving pictures, will eventually be completed, and 'Excalibur' will arouse King Arthur, and his exploits to 'view', in Douglas Vale and Martin Mere. Before leaving the Parbold area, so closely related to King Arthur's exploits, I would like to draw attention to another British folk hero, a most unlikely character you might have considered to have been in any way associated with this part of the country. I refer to Robin Hood, and quoting from page 126 of 'Betwixt Ribbel and Moerse', in the last chapter, dealing with ancient crosses and holy wells, I have referred to the Robin Hood Cross, and Well, being near to the Robin Hood Inn, 1¾ miles south east of Croston. The Ordnance survey of the area, which took place in 1858, states that Robin Hood was born in Yorkshire, in the 13th century, and travelled the Pennine Hills extensively, giving his name to many such places.

Three miles to the south east of here, on the B5375 road which crosses Parbold Hill from Appley Bridge, is an area named Robin Hood. Close by is Robin Hood Farm. Less than half a mile away, on the top of Parbold Hill, near to Boars Den Tumulus, and fed by Spradley Brook, is Robin Hood's Well. All three locations are within a compass of half a square mile. Approximately two miles away, to the east, is Robin Hill. There are other locations in the area, such as Robin Hood's Lane, and probably many more, all in the proximity of sites associated, but divided by many hundreds of years in time, with King Arthur, in the district. There appeared to be no connection however between these events, and places, until a couple of years ago, when gas board workmen, working in the Oxenholme district of Kendal, uncovered a vast system of caverns extending for many miles underground. Although these were quickly sealed off, it was estimated that they could be connected with a similar system, as at Ingleton, of natural caverns in Yorkshire. There were some apparently wild conjectures bandied about, that as Robin Hood, who for most of his life, led a guerilla, semi-fugitive existence, much of it hiding in caves and caverns, could have used this route, and others, as he was known to have an affinity with the 'Bowmen in Kendal Green', and also the 'Bowmen' from Bowland Forest, in the Trough of Bowland, well known for their successes at the battles of Crecy, and Agincourt, with their longbows. All very fanciful and conjectural, but where does the Parbold connection between King Arthur and Robin Hood come in, hundreds of years apart? Nowhere, except for tha fact that, if Robin Hood did come to the Parbold area, and holed up in some handy caves, what about the ones at Brandreth Delph, reputed to have been occupied by Sir Lancelot and Guinevere? He could have ranged the whole terrain from here, indeed places such as Hunter's Hill, and Hunger Hill, and Boars Den, are more evocative of Robin Hood's proclivity of living off the land, than any other characters. In his day, the great forest, which stretched from Rufford and Burscough to Crossens, would be still in existence as would the great forest, later submerged by earthquake (Page 7-8). Tarlesco Wood, the location of a great number of eagle eyries, was only a couple of miles away from Lathom Park, and the Parbold district (Chapter Eleven). He was the scourge of such places as the Barony of Penwortham, where the castle was held in the time of King Edward, Robin's implacable foe. He was definitely of North Country, or Midland stock, said to have been born at Lockesly, in Yorkshire. In later years, it was said that he was associated with Barnsdale Forest in Yorkshire, and of course, the Sherwood Forest of Nottingham. His father held lands in Loxley in Staffordshire, where he was known as Robin of Loxley. His medieval outlaw existence took him to many places, Parbold could have been amongst them. One small affinity he did share with former occupiers on this area, King Arthur and the Vikings. When danger threatened, he too sounded the 'Horn of Alarm', but in a practical manner, carried on his person, rather than in the mythical sense as in Arthurian Legend, or Viking Cosmology. Over the centuries the stories concerning brave Knights, and fair damsels have been fantasised, and romanticised beyond measure, I rather like the down to earth English translation, in one of the Nordic Heroic Sagas I came across in research, where the saga narrative in general, is more plain, and restrained. For instance, it tells of two Vikings in Greenland, with the small man attacking a big man on a cliff, by the sea, and in the struggle, they fell over the edge. The smaller man, who was a better swimmer, undid the big man's belt, pulled his trousers around his feet, and drowned him. The big man was Rag'narr Loóbrók ('Shaggy-Breeches'!). The translation says, "in an artificial world, as among Arthurian Knights, heroes would not have fought like this, but in the real world men fight with desperation, and not always with dignity." The whole scenario of history is therefore distorted, even today, with inaccuracies, in time, and events. We are fortunate therefore that the constant discovery of true locations and events does much to counter exaggerations that are incredible, or even absurd.

CHAPTER 11

RIMMERS AND DAN —
GENESIS — EXODUS — NUMBERS — REVELATIONS

There is therefore one other final factor that is predominant in the conclusion of this 'Saga', or 'Story'. It is mystery, which clouds the main theme that runs through this narrative, and poses the question, who and what, are the Rimmers, and where did they really come from?

It is true that we have traced their arrival here, to their 'promised land', from Nordic regions, and established themselves in peaceful occupations which have lasted a thousand years. In some small measure, we have examined their relationships with the many other families who have come into the district over the years, but still constituting the larger proportion of the population, even today. Unlike other families, it has been impossible to maintain any degree of geneological progression by official 'family tree' methods, because of the large numbers, and the original, closely knit, almost tribal attitude, adopted by the early Rimmer settlers.

No professional historian, to my knowledge, has ever attempted to define the mystery of their true origin, and it has been left to a few members of the Rimmer clan, over the years, to trace their own roots. The early part of this 'saga' shows that these roots are documented in the Nordic Sagas, as constituting a dynasty, connected with the tribe of Dan. There it stops, and for over half a century, I have attempted to unravel the mystery.

After my grandad's few cryptic remarks concerning my enquiries as to the Rimmer's origin, the only other answer I could elicitate was "It's 'aw in't Bible" so what does approximately sixty years study of the Bible tell us. I remember now, my mother taking an interest, in the account of a sect which called themselves, the British Israelites, who claimed they were the remnants of one of the tribes of Israel, who were descendants of the tribe of Benjamin. All the tribes of Israel, were scattered, after the sacking and destruction of Jerusalem, by the Romans, in 70 AD, as foretold by the prophets, and Jesus, (Matthew, Chapter 24 V2). My mother said when she mentioned this account that, "we are the remnants of a lost tribe of Israel." In later years, researching the territory of the tribes of Israel, I found that Benjamin was a tribe adjoining the territory of the tribe of Dan. The tribe of Dan however, lived on the shores of the 'Great Sea' as the Mediteranean was called in those days. As my Grandad said, "They have allus lived on't watter." when referring to the Rimmers as 'living on the rim', of such places as Martin Mere, and the Black Sea. This was only a very tenuous, conjectural clue, but it led me to a long trail through many lands, to track down the tribe of Dan, always presuming of course, that they were the forefathers of the Rimmer 'tribe'.

The tribe of Dan, in the time of Genesis, was on the shore of the 'Great Sea'. Less than 50 miles from where the tribe of Dan built the city of Dan, opposite the ancient Port of Tyre, was the Port of Byblos, the oldest known city in the world. Byblos was the centre of ancient book production, for which they imported papyrus from Egypt, in the time when the Pyramid of Cheops was built, 4600 years ago. Byblos gave its name to the Bible, or Book, on which these notes are based. The earliest form of writing was done by the Sumerians in Mesopotamia, in 3400 BC, on clay tablets.

The first five books of the Bible, the Pentateuch, the five books of the Torah Law, were written by Moses, covering the years 1900-1250 B.C.

Moses, whose name means 'saved out of water', was born of course in Egypt, of the house of Levi, probably in the years between 1520 and 1550 BC. Noah was supposedly born 1056 years after the creation of Adam, who conjecturally, was 'created' in 4058 BC, his name was taken from 'earth'. Therefore Moses was only recording pre-history of his own time, and of times long ago, before even the written word could be used. The Bible therefore, is the truest record of all time, but dates, and lengths of years are misleading. There are for instance, at least 1500 errors, in the King James' version of the Bible, owing to mis-translations through the centuries. There are also many books called the Apocrypha, not included in the Bible, some because they are not in Hebrew. Genesis Chapter 5 mentions Enoch, "who walked with God, and he was not, for God took him." Enoch, whose name has been perpetuated throughout time, through the forefathers, and the tribe of Dan, down to the Rimmer tribe today, was seventh in line from Adam. The 'Book of Enoch', believed by some to be the oldest in the world, covers a period, before Adam, of 9560 years BC, to the flood in 2438 BC. It was said to be "fictional" and "given to the earth by celestials." No real credence can therefore be accorded to dates. As for the ages given at that time, Adam 930 years, Enoch 365, Methuseleh 969, it has been suggested that 'years' at that time, were only lunar months, a quite feasible supposition. In the days of Genesis, the forefathers of the tribe of Dan, lived on the shore of the Mediterranean, in the time when the Hittites were in control of the area. The Hittites, an extinct, long forgotten civilization, once occupied the whole area between the Upper Mesopotamia, and the Mediterranean. They inherited crafts, and arts, from the Sumerians of Mesopotamia. The Hittites built the first Pyramids in Mesopotamia, and elsewhere, and it has been recently discovered that they were the predecessors of the Phoenecians, who, in later years, were neighbours of the tribe of Dan. In later years, as recorded in Chapter 23 of Genesis, when Sarah died, Abraham was given the cave of Machpelah, by the Hittites, also the field, and the land and trees near Mamre. Abraham however, in honour bound paid a token of 400 Shekels of silver. This was, at that time, in the land of Hebron. It seems that the forefathers of the Dan Tribe moved around with the times, but in the main they were seafarers. Historians have made play on the deathbed statement of the Rimmer tribe woman, previously quoted, that she was leaving more descendants than accompanied the Patriarch Jacob into Egypt." This would be after Jacob decided, by God's instruction, to go to dwell in Egypt, after Joseph was made governor. This is mentioned in Genesis, Chapters 46-49 which contains probably the first mention of Dan as a 'Tribe'. The settlement, in Egypt, was made around about 1870 BC, and lasted until 1440 BC. Jacob made a phophecy, after his name had been changed to Israel, to his sons. This was in the year 1715 BC, and of the tribe of Dan he said, "Dan shall judge his people, as one of the tribes of Israel." In this context, all the 12 tribes of Israel were equated to the signs of the Zodiac, starting with Reuben as Aquarius, on to Dan as Libra etc. Jacob's last request was to be buried with Abraham, and his wife Sarah, and also Jacob's wife Leah, in the cave of Machpelah, in the land of Canaan.

The second Book of Moses, Exodus, lists the Tribe of Dan in Chapter 1 Verse 4, but no details of population are given, until the departure of the Children of Israel. Then it states in Exodus Chapter 12, that the whole multitude, after 430 years in Egypt, numbered "Six hundred thousand on foot that were men, but there were also children, and a mixed multitude also with them, and flocks and herds, and cattle (V 37-38)" under the leadership of Moses and Aaron.

In Chapter 1 of Numbers, which was written by Moses on the plains of Moab from 1512 to 1473 BC, we see that in the wilderness of Sinai on the 1st day of the second month, in the second year after leaving Egypt, the Lord commanded Moses to take a census. or recording, which lasted 38 years and 9 months, of all males aged 20 years and upwards, who were able to go forward to war in Israel.

The total population then, would be 2-3 million, out of which was forged a military force of 60,355. Even as it says in Verse 39, "of the tribe of Dan, were three score, and two thousand and seven hundred," which shows the advance in numbers of the tribe, in spite of their wanderings. They had also acquired the Standard Banner of the Eagle, which is still in use today in religious and masonic chapter rituals, to represent the Tribe of Dan. This census however, is only recorded here to show the increase in the numbers of the tribe of Dan, before the move into Canaan, after forty years in the wilderness. The Bible is a wonderful, and accurate book, in the respect that it invariably presents two, or more aspects of the same events, by different observers, to obtain a dimensional view. I can only record the participation of the tribe of Dan in the journey from Canaan to Egypt under the Patriarch Jacob, the sojourn in Egypt, then the Exodus, the wanderings in the desert for forty years, and the resettlement of the tribe of Dan, as a tribe of Israel, on the shores of the Great Sea.

The references I give, are not in chronological order, but only to show the varying fortunes of the tribe in connection with other people and places, in mostly Biblical locations. Incidents can be conjectural in the extreme, in fact, and fantasy, linked together in 'saga' or 'story' form, rather than in historical context. The fact is indisputable that, wherever they went, the tribe of Dan, or the Rimmers, if you wish, always lived on, or near the seas, rivers or lakes, for various reasons, from 'messing about in boats' to chipping runic stones, and inscriptions, on any handy stone slab. Wherever they went, they always utilized pitch or tar, mostly in the natural state, from any source available, also willow or reeds, or papyrus, in the old days. Consider, if you will, two of the widest, and wildest examples of this. Even as late as the 19th century, many of the Rimmer fishermen had emigrated to Vanouver, and naturally had taken to operating fishing boats for their livelihood. It is well recorded that they could not obtain willow, which was not grown in British Columbia at that time. They sent word back to Marshside for a quantity of a particular willow, grown in that area. The purpose of this, believe it or not, was to make their clog soles from this willow, combining it with the pitch they used for caulking their boats. It was a method they had used, from time immemorial, for waterproofing purposes. Willow Farm in Marshside Road, is still quoted as one source. Now cast your mind back some 3500 years, when the tribe of Dan was living in exile, along the banks of the Nile. A woman of the nearby tribe of Levi, had given birth to a male child. Pharoah had decreed that every newborn son had to be thrown into the Nile, to keep the Hebrew population down. So an ark, or basket, of papryus reeds was made, and waterproofed with pitch, and bitumen, and laid, containing the child, in the reeds by the river. So was Moses 'saved from the water', but who do you think made the unsinkable reed basket? No prize for guessing the correct answer to this one. The tribe of Dan is also known to have used pitch, and bitumen, from the Red, or 'Reed' Sea, as it was then known, to fashion reed, or papyrus boats, for fishing. It has been suggested too, that to implement the crossing of the Red Sea, in the flight from Egypt, Moses received good advice, when, and where, to cross in the shallow marshes, as the Sea was tidal, and many Israelites were helped by the utilization of light reed craft, which could be easily carried. Archeologists recently carrying out investigation in the area, have discovered quantities of artefacts, and warlike equipment, to date the time, and place of the crossing, which was probably in the time of Rameses II, although no Bible account names which Pharoah, perished with his host of pursuing warriors, 600 chariots and men, captains and cavalry. The land of Goshen, occupied by the Israelites, given to them by Joseph, in the Nile Delta, was of course in parts very marshy, and shallow, and it is known that the larger reed boats, and rafts could carry massive quantities of goods, and cattle and people, in quantities up to 40 tons in weight. To transport about six hundred thousand Israelites by this method would have been a prodigious task, so sceptics are perforce to accept this 'passover' as a miracle, just as the Isrealites in the land of Goshen, were not subjected to the other plagues, laid upon the Egyptians. The exact location of the crossing, as described in the Bible, has just been confirmed by recent archeological discoveries, as being at Quatara, 30 miles south of Port Said.

Wherever the tribe of Dan went, in Biblical lands, they utilized the natural sources of pitch and bitumen, invariably found in marshy lakes, and they were never far away from any of these places, also containing papyrus or reeds. The reed boats were all made to the same design, high at the prow and stern, to enable them to ride, even across oceans, on long journeys. In the Bible, Isaiah 18 V2 reports that his homeland was visited by messengers, who came across the sea in reed boats. Papyrus ships, of the same construction as those on the Nile, sailed as far as Ceylon and the Ganges in India, averaging 75 nautical miles in 24 hours, roughly a speed of three knots. Curiously enough, the high prow and stern design of vessel, was adopted later by the builders of the Viking ships.

The Danites return to Caanan, was not altogether a peaceful one, neither are the accounts by some historians very favourable. They had been associated with the rest of the Israelites, with the setting up of the Golden Calf, whilst Moses was on the mountain receiving the Ten Commandments. I remember that from my very early days, and almost until she died, my mother, quite seriously, and in a somewhat scathing tone, when any mention of her 'tribe' or intermarried relations, showed any signs of undue enthusiasm in the accumulation of wealth, was wont to remark, "They are still worshipping the Golden Calf." I know this sounds quite absurd, but it was the expression "still", that has impressed me, and over the years of research has led me to find out if there was any connection between the Rimmers, and the Danites. I can only quote a few salient details, from the mass of text that has accumulated over the years, but I can mention a few. From the years of the 13th century, to the 11th century BC, there are many factors, relative to Danite activity, quoted in the Bible. Judges, Chapter 1-2 relates to the activities of the Philistines, who at the time when the Iron Age came into being, and having chariots of iron, dominated the area, which later became Palestine, until the days of David. The Hittite empire was demolished, and many of the tribes scattered. This was because the Lord was angry, owing to the Israelites turning once again, to the worship of Baal and Ashtaroth — male and female fertility gods. Chapter 1 V34 of Judges tells of the Amorites "forcing the children of Dan into the mountains, and would not suffer them to come into the valley."

The whole of the 18th chapter of Judges, relates how the Danites set up an expedition, and established a northern kingdom. They built the city of Dan, after destroying the city of Laish. They also set up a Golden Calf, using the Ephod and Teraphim, from the house of Micah, in Mount Ephraim, they had taken previously, and used these for the purpose of divination, forbidden by the Lord.

These events all took place in the northern portion of the Jordan Valley. The southern part of the valley was well known for familiar Bible scenes, Israelites crossing its drained bed near Jericho, and later, Naaman bathing seven times in the waters of Jordan, to be cured of leprosy. Most notable of all, Jesus coming to be baptised by John. The low region in the centre, is part of the Great Rift Valley, a geological fault, extending from Syria to Africa, mentioned many times in the Bible as the 'Route of Kings' or 'Kings Highway'. This was also a trade route, which was used by the Children of Israel in their various journeys to Egypt. It runs even now, from the Sea of Galilee to Aquaba, on the Gulf of Aquaba, which empties into the Red Sea, east of the Sinai Peninsular. Isaiah, in his amazing prophecies called it, before it was constructed, a "Way of Holiness', a highway to Assyria, out of Egypt, prophesying the flight from Egypt, "a highway for God, every valley to be raised up, every mountain and hill laid low. No lion will prove to be there, no ravenous beast, the ransomed of the Lord will return on it, and come to Zion with song, and everlasting joy upon their heads." As the lady on her deathbed in North Meols, eleven centuries later cried, "Reach for your Bibles". When referring to her "descendants, being greater than those who accompanied the Patriarch into Egypt," she was echoing the exhortation of Isaiah to "Seek ye out the book of the Lord, and read." Just as valid today, if you want to trace the tracks of the Danites, and the Rimmer tribes. Today also, you can visit the Jordan Valley, and see the mound where the city of Dan was built. One of the streams of the Jordan runs from here, one of the three main sources of the Jordan, coming from the snows of Mount Hermon. In this area also was Caesarea Philippi, where Jesus was a visitor, just before he was transfigured on a "lofty mountain". The Jordan River falls a thousand feet in about three miles. The valley flattens out into another area associated with the Danites. This is the Hula Basin, which in earlier days was a shallow, broad, marshy area, known as Lake Hula, or Huleh. A map of ancient times will show this lake, which was north of the Sea of Galilee. This shallow, marshy, area was used by the Danites, because of the abundance of papyrus reeds, and natural pitch, for their reed boats. Fishing the waters, with an abundance of wild life, herons, Storks, Pelicans and many birds, including the 'turtle dove' with the strange marking on its neck, from the Kingdom of Ararat, some 500 miles to the north east. The bird sanctuary now forms part of a nature reserve, but the marsh and lake, was from time immemorial, and still is, on the birds migratory route from Europe to Africa.

When the children of Dan made a subsequent settlement as a tribe of Israel, it was typically on the coast of the Great Sea, about a hundred miles from the city of Dan. Whilst they were in the north, they had become associated with the Phoenicians, and absorbed their method of using dovetailed wooden planking, from the cedars of Lebanon, for their ship construction. They sailed to all quarters of the then known world, trading as far as the British Isles. When the Pharoah's tomb, at the foot of the pyramid of Cheops, was excavated, a ship, not a funeral boat, was uncovered. Thick planking sections of cedarwood, sewn together, were on each side, in air tight containers, piled in stacks, as fresh as when buried, 4600 years ago — 2700 years before Christ, and built on the same architectonic methods, as the reed boats. The Danites therefore, had by now, absorbed shipbuilding methods from several ancient civilizations and places they had been in. When they arrived in the Nordic regions, it may be only coincidence, but the Viking longship design, albeit more practical, and not so elegant as the Egyptian Royal barges, and Phoenician vessels, was eventually constructed on the same lines as the reed boats, with the crescent shaped bow and stern, designed to bear the brunt of heavy seas. The clinker built method of overlapping planks, was also used in precisely the same construction as that used by seamen of this area, even on the racing skiffs used on the Marine Lake, in Sunday School Rowing circles. A recent discovery on the Sea of Galilee, of the remains of a craft, dating from the time of Jesus, also appears at first investigation, to be of similar construction. At the time of the ministry of Jesus, the Tribe of Dan had been well settled in, as a legitimate, appointed member, of the Tribes of Israel. However in AD 66, there occurred the Jewish revolt against the Romans.

As prophesised by Jesus, just prior to his Crucifixion, that Jerusalem would be "encompassed by the armies of the Gentiles, and there shall be not one stone left upon another," Luke Chapter 21 gives the full story. The siege of Jerusalem began in the full moon, in the spring of AD 70, by the Roman Emperor Titus, and by August AD 70, the city was razed to the ground. Israel's existence in Palestine was over. The tribes were scattered, and "led away captive into all nations". Of the tribe of Dan, there appears to be no indication as to their movements. It is quite likely that they escaped by sea, in preference to a hazardous journey by mountain routes, but they, or a remnant of the tribe, ended up on the shores of the Black Sea, in the region of the Caucasus mountains, almost under the shadow of Mount Ararat. As my grandad said "Ay, we were round about thee'r", when questioned about Noah's Ark.

There is one other factor that is a puzzle in connection with this exodus. In 'Betwixt Ribbel and Moerse' on page 14, I referred to the legend of Joseph of Arimathea visiting this area, carrying with him the Chalice, or Holy Grail, said to be used at the Last Supper. He was then, a fugitive also, from the Holy Land, a rich merchant, who had traded with the Phoenicians who invented the Alphabet, and had been to Britain previously with them, to negotiate the purchase of tin from Cornwall. If Joseph was seeking a hiding place for such a holy relic, what was he doing with it in this wild region. What connection had he, with anyone locally, that he knew. Where then did he hide it — in some northern cavern system, such as Parbold? Did King Arthur and his Knights, come to this region searching for it? Was there any truth in the legend that a youthful Jesus, had been to Britain with Joseph previously, or that he was related by later descent to King Arthur in any way?

If these conjectures seem to plumb the depths of absurdity, as I considered them to be in my early attempts to extract even a mythical, and legendary story, of such a remote, apparently uninteresting region, in which we dwell, then we must also examine a few facts that have emerged in subsequent research.

For instance, this man Joseph of Arimathea, a rich man from a sect of people bitterly opposed to Jesus (who was his nephew) and all his works, a Pharisee, and a prominent member of the Sanhedrin Counsel. John describes him as a disciple of Jesus who, although he was in fear of the Jews, besought Pilate to allow him to take away the body of Jesus. Luke describes him as a counsellor, a good man and just, who did not agree with the counsel, and their deeds. Luke described how Joseph took down the body of Jesus, wrapped it in linen, laid it in a new, unused, sepulchre which indicates the wealth and standing of Joseph, as only very rich people could afford a stone tomb in those days. Matthew also describes the same scene as Luke, and John, in the same details, stating that Joseph rolled, probably with hired assistance under the direction of Nicodemus, also a member of the Sanhedrin, a great stone to the door of the sepulchre. At the time of the scattering of the tribes, Joseph of Arimathea, whilst dwelling there in Samaria, was only about 10 miles inland from the Port of Joppa, on the coast of the Great Sea, a principal port of the tribe of Dan. They were therefore, both in concordance with the Phoenicians, in trade, and shipping, so it is not beyond the bounds of possibility, that some members of the tribe of Dan, had been by sea, to Britain. So in later years, when Joseph was a fugitive, where better to go, than a far off place, where he could contact friends. Had not Jesus also exhorted his disciples to spread the word, to the "outermost islands", and have not many people since then, believed that the "outermost islands" were the "Blessed Islands", now known as Great Britain. Is it not possible also, that quite a number of the tribe of Dan, had already gone by sea, to Britain, fore-runners of the later arrival of the Nordic seafaring 'Rimmers', one thousand years ago? It is well known that Joseph, as a merchant, sponsored the Phoenicians in the transportation of tin from the mines of Cornwall, and had visited Britain many times. His presence in the Glastonbury area is also well authenticated.

King Arthur's kinship with Jesus appears to be a real fanciful conjecture, but there again, research has proved that Arthur was a real person, but not born in Britain. His origin is not certain, but when he was brought here by Ambrosia, his name was said to be Arturius, which could be of Middle Eastern ancestry.

If some, or all, of these conjectures, are so improbable, why did the composers of such hymns as Blakes 'Jerusalem', and all the lusty voices, mostly female, who have subsequently performed them, by so doing, perpetuated the myth of "those feet in ancient times", and the "Holy Lamb of God", walking upon this "green and pleasant land"?

Although it might be assumed that the tribe of Dan had shaken the dust of the desert from their shoes, and finally settled in the North, it was not to be conclusive. We know the stonemasons of the Danites, had set up a runic stone for the Swedes, on the shore of the Black Sea, and it was thought that this was a Nordic based expedition of the Swedes. Research however, proves the contrary, and shows that the Danites, or Rimmers, had set up an expedition in reverse, and taken the Swedish Vikings across Europe, then through the Black Sea, and the Bosporus Straits into the Great Sea, or

Mediterranean, then on to their former homeland of their ancestors, in the Holy Land. The runic stone at Berezanji on the Black Sea, dates from the 11th century, during the Viking expansion, which started in the 8th century, and therefore supports the contention that it was set up on the return journey to Palestine. The Vikings established a base further north than the tribe's own original territory. They called the town Arksborg, because it was situated in a bay, which later, in the time of the Crusades, became Acre, in the Bay of Acre, opposite the Sea of Galilee, which was about 30 miles inland. This would be an agreeable siting for the Danites to visit their ancestors old territory, about 75 miles down the coast. There is a later account that King Sigurd Jorsalafari who landed at Arksborg, on his crusade to Palestine in 1107, afterwards said, "the farthest point I reached on this journey was the Jordan, and I swam over the river." A sequel tot his expedition was the discovery of a Runic stone at Maeshowe, in Orkney, about 1152, which states, in reference to the King, that the crusaders to Jerusalem, "broke open the Orkney grave mound." There is no indication that the Rimmers were involved in the cutting of this stone, or the account, as their main body of settlers, had by then, already landed in England.

Once again, even during the editing of these notes, further information comes to hand, to implement the chain of coincidence, that occurs whenever I commence to collate text, on a current subject. In December 1990, it was announced that archeologists had unearthed a 5 inch long figurine of a calf, made of bronze, copper, lead and silver, burnished apparently, to shine like gold. It is believed that the calf dates back to 1550 BC, before the Israelites conquered Caanan, and was used in worship of the pagan god El, or his son Baal, and that it may be a prototype of the Golden Calves mentioned in the Bible. The calf dates from before the Israelite Exodus, and was found in the ruins of the ancient Port of Ashkelon, sister port to Joppa, of the tribe of Dan. It is curious also that the 'Ash' derivation, occurs right through all historical records, as here in Ashkelon. Ashtaroth is also an alternative name for the fertility god Baal, where once again the Ash reference occurs.

It is a very tenuous thread of fact and conjecture, that leads us from the banned 'fictional' book of Enoch, which records pre-human events from 9560 BC, to the flood in 4000 BC, to Councillor Enoch Rimmer, who recorded events of Southport in his weekly Heralds, in the 20th century AD. The only topographical feature we have left to contemplate, is the Botanic Gardens Lake, and the 'Old Pool', the 'Snoterpool' of the Rimmers, which still runs to, and from, the sea. Standing on its bank, is the Bishop Shepherd Primary School, in Devonshire Road, High Park, the successor to my old school, All Saints, Wennington Road, which was the inspiration for the penning of these notes, mostly comprising material too lengthy to be included in 'Betwixt Ribbel and Moerse'.

I have, since the establishing of the new Bishop Shepherd school, forwarded books, maps and memorabilia, including a home-made recording of some of the poems and the schoolsong, and history of the old All Saints School ('College'), for their collection. The northern corner of the school is actually abutting onto the 'Snoterpool' stream, and coupled with the site of the nearby former Excelsior Firework factory, an account of which has been published in a British Museum Archivist Magazine, the whole aspect affords just one little corner of our ancestral heritage, for further generations of pupils to study. Reviews, and press reports, have stated quite correctly, that I started to gather information at an early age, at All Saints school, mostly on local history, because of the lack of adequate information in history books, of this region. I still possess the red exercise book in which, several million words ago, I started to write, utilizing one end of the large table used for shrimp picking, the other end when not in use, occupied by my Grandad, who not only braided his own shrimp nets, but also made all the tackle, such as the wooden braiding needles, by hand. Of course there was also, notes to be made for his sermons, subjects to be discussed, and then the cryptic remarks on the origin of the Rimmers, which form the basis of this book. I have pondered long on this project, and only when studying the Nordic literature, did I find how I could present it.

In 'Betwixt Ribbel and Moerse', which is only a condensed version of the whole text, every historical fact was checked, and double checked for accuracy. All the locations named were visited, all the sketches were executed by me, and all the photographs were taken on an ancient box camera (circa 1912).

So it is, that whilst most of the historical text, and geneological details, will stand a great deal of critical scrutiny, the only method I can employ, to present the main theme of this book, which deals with the largely conjectural origins of the Rimmer ancestry, is to present it as a 'Saga', as I have explained at the beginning. Furthermore, there is one other aspect I can present, which may alleviate some of the acrimonious criticism, which I am sure to be subjected to, by daring to tread upon the hallowed ground of the 'Reticent Rimmers' origins.

Recall, if you will, an explanation I gave, of the derivation of the word 'Ligger', meaning 'Liar', which we used in our schooldays, and explaining that this came from the West Norse, 'Lygi', (lie or falsehood), brought to thse shores by the Rimmers, and introduced into the local dialect, together with many other expressions of Nordic origin.

Well it so happens that, in Old Norse literature, there is a language terminological subject, referred to as 'Lygi-Saga' or 'Lying Saga'. In this context it illustrates that historical, and unhistorical, 'sagas', were carefully distinguished. 'Lygisqgur' was a technical term for those known to be unhistorical. As far as my researches show, all the 'saga' stories, and poems related by Rimmer skalds are historically, and poetically accurate, and, as I have stated earlier, have been preserved and accepted, by the appropriate establishments, in many countries, as truly authentic records.

You will have to decide for yourself, whether other parts of this 'saga', apart from Nordic records, are credible, or whether I am presenting you with a 'Lygisqgur', or a large complement of 'poetic licence' in connection with the myths and legends, and Biblical accounts.

As is the case with "Halfdan the Black", I am only a "Half Rimmer", but in this respect I can take a somewhat objective view of the Danite, and

Rimmer tribal progression. I have had a veritable mass of correspondence, and enquiry, from all parts of the world concerning Rimmers, and their integration with other families. Never at any time, has any Rimmer, or relative, expressed any pretensions of aggrandizement, to anything other than enquiries relating to family matters, and connections. I have stressed their pre-Christian, idolatrous links, within the early tribe of Dan, but also I have tried to illustrate, and record, their progression from the Holy Land, as a truly Christian one, spreading the 'word' along their journeys into idolatrous regions, gathering the respect of, and conversions to, their Biblical beliefs. They were granted lands and kingdoms, many of them integrating, and intermarrying with the Scandinavian peoples, and also those of Iceland and Greenland, and then into America, and Canada, with many of them remaining in these places as permanent settlers. Even today, in places as far apart from North Meols, as British Columbia, there are archeological researches, and excavations, still taking place. By the time, shortly after the remnants of the Tribe of Dan we now call Rimmers, left West Norway for these shores one thousand years ago, the whole of the Scandinavian, and associated Arctic areas, had been converted to Christianity. Locally, the Rimmer's general civic activities, and their church and chapel, and commercial and fishing proclivities, have been, although obtrusive, very progressive, and thorough, in the development of North Meols into Churchtown village, and subsequently of our (once fair) town, of 'Sunny Southport'.

Even if you accept some of the historical text of this narrative, but reject its main theme, of the attempt to discover the origin of the Rimmers, there a few final observations to consider.

The Bible abounds with references to 'horns' or 'trumpets', used on various occasions from Moses' 'Horn of Jubilee', to the 'seven angels, with seven trumpets of Revelation'. In later mythology, and legend, we read of King Arthur's 'Horn of Alarm', and the Norse Gjallarhorn 'Horn of Alarum', to be sounded when evil threatens. Even in my days, my mother constantly quoted a typical Rimmer biblical reference, to the time when Gabriel will blow the 'horn of resurrection'. Daniel was a Judean exile in Babylon, in the years 618 BC — 536 ('circa', which means 'about'). We are surely all aware of his prophecies, and interpretation of dreams, but also especially of the feast of a thousand grandees, utilizing the golden vessels brought from the Temple at Jerusalem, held by Belshazzar, on October 5th, 539 BC, at which the writing on the Wall "Mene, Mene, Tekel, Upharsin," was written. Daniel, who was not at the feast, he was a vegetarian anyway, was sent for, and he interpreted the writing — "God has numbered your days, you are weighed in the balance and found wanting. Your kingdom is to be divided between the Medes and Persians." This is nothing to do with our story, but it was a favourite one of my grandad in our younger days.

Once again, as in many other instances, just before this book goes into print, I have to include further evidence concerning Daniel, and the interpretation of Nebuchadnezzar's dreams.

The Dead Sea Scrolls found in 1947, have since been held by a clannish group of scholars who refuse to publish much of the material in their possession. Small parts of the manuscripts are now exhibited in a museum called 'The Shrine of the Book', which is ironically, situated underground, in Jerusalem.

As well as the discovery of the Scrolls at the foot of Wadi Qumran, other caves, now eleven in number, from the year 1952 have been uncovered in some nearby ruins, thought to be the remains of a Roman fort. Over 400 manuscripts covering all the books of the Hebrew Scriptures, have yielded up over 40,000 fragments of scrolls.

Although the whole area of Qumran, and to the north around Jericho and south near Masada, have revealed caves and scrolls, another discovery was made in the first cave to be found, which contained the 25ft. long scroll of Isaiah's prophecy, on seventeen sheets of carefully prepared animal skin. This scroll is a thousand years older than any other surviving copy. With the release of more information, due to world wide public demand, by the year 1956, more finds were made of leather fragments from the Book of Daniel which were with the Isaiah Scroll. This showed that the Book of Daniel, written by him in Babylon in 536 BC was in Aramaic, which was also spoken by Daniel in the interpretation of Nebuchadnezzar's dreams, and the writing on the Wall. Therefore the inference is that Daniel was not of Hebrew extraction but of some other un-named, Judean tribe, involved in the Babylonian exile. It cannot be proved that Daniel, was from the tribe of Dan, but his powers of divination and prophecy certainly came from some tribe with similar traits and attributes.

It is not however the interpretation of dreams, writings on walls, or prophecies, that I want to draw attention to, but a vision that Daniel had, possibly about 551 BC, in the third year of the Kingship of Belshazzar, when Daniel was at the palace of Shushan, in the jurisdiction district of Ellam, in the eastern region of Babylon. He was beside the river of Ulai, when he began to see visions of saints, who made various prophecies. Then there appeared to him a figure in the form of a man, and then a voice was heard which called out to the man, "Gabriel, make this man to understand the vision he has seen." Daniel fell upon his face in fright, but Gabriel said to Daniel, "Understand, O son of man, that the vision is for the time of the end" meaning the winding up of history and God's final judgement. This is the first time that Gabriel, God's 'messenger' Angel, is mentioned in the Bible. Gabriel is also the one who will blow the last trumpet at "the time of the end", as told to Daniel. St. Paul, in his Epistles to the Corinthians in the year 55 AD, refers to Gabriel's message to Daniel. When Handel wrote the "Messiah", he included this prophecy of Daniel's, as written by St. Paul in the first book of Corinthians, Chapter 15 V51. Then he concluded the messianic oratorio with the bass solo, which starts with the words "behold I show you a mystery." The 'Messiah' was a favourite work for the musical Rimmers of our household, and their relatives, all the soloists, choristers and organists, who would foregather round the pedal operated harmonium, for many practices, prior to the Christmas rendering of their favourite oratorio, in the many churches and chapels in the town. It was not however a favourite with such of us, who at that time, had to perform, in relays, to maintain the pressure on the wooden handled air bellows of the wind organ, in our local church.

It is a curious coincidental factor, that these final words of the 'Messiah' were actually written, only less than a score of miles away from where, in later years, the Rimmer 'Rymers' and others, so vociferously, and enthusiastically, rendered the full score of the oratorio. George Frederick Handel (1685-1759), only completed the final part of the 'Messiah', the night before he departed from the small port of Parkgate, on the Wirral, for his voyage to Dublin, where the first rendering of the 'Messiah' was given on April 13th, 1742. The Messiah, from the Hebrew 'Masiah', which means 'anointed', was based on Old Testament prophecies concerning Jesus, 'The Deliverer'. It was written after Handel became court composer, and settled in England in 1712. I have often pondered whether the Rimmers, who took part in the rendering of the 'Messiah', ever realized that they were relating the history of their own tribe in the musical prophecies. It seems more than coincidence also, that many of the works of Handel such as 'Saul and Israel in Egypt', 'Samson', 'Joseph and his Brethren', Belshazzar' and 'Jeptha', are concerned with, and connected to, the tribe of Dan's biblical actitivites.

I have endeavoured in these last few paragraphs, to reach some successful conclusion in this narrative concerning its central theme, of connection with the origin of the Rimmers, through the Biblical Tribe of Dan. I thought I could perhaps discover, in the corresponding last chapter of the Bible, some final message. However the Revelation of St. John the Divine, written in 96 AD, apart from many allegoric, and prophetic quotations, which are irrelevant, the one historical reference I did discover was, that when the 'book of seals' was opened, the tribe of Dan was not listed in the 12 Tribes of Israel, bearing the "seal of God". Indeed, the tribe of Dan is not mentioned here at all, as the tribe of Joseph, founded in Egypt, makes up the number to 12. Furthermore, as in previous references to the 12 Tribes, the tribe of Dan is invariably listed last. So the inference, that the tribe was not a true Israelite tribe, or that they had already disappeared, or scattered, seems to be acceptable. Furthermore, when Gabriel made an appearance with the "books of seals", he was ordered to "close it at the end, as the mystery of God should now be finished."

Therefore to bring this narrative to a close, unfortunately without any definite proof, but only supposition and conjecture, of the Rimmer's origin with the Tribe of Dan in Biblical times, I can only transpose the words of God, given to Daniel, by the messenger Angel Gabriel, quoted by St. Paul to the Corinthians, and included at the ending of the 'Messiah' by Handel — "Behold, I leave with you a mystery."

MEOLS HALL (See Chapter 2)

Meols Hall in the North and Formby Hall in the South denote the approximate extent of Rimmer influence in the area.

FORMBY HALL (See Chapter 6)

FORMBY MILL

A FORMBY COTTAGE

CHURCHTOWN MILL (See Chapter 3)

This was a peg and post mill, similar to Birkdale and Ainsdale Mills. It replaced the ancient water mill, situated on an island in the Snoterpool, in the 16th Century. We collected flour, from the steam mill which replaced it, in pillow cases. This mill was still in operation in the middle of the 19th Century.

ASH TREE INN 1790 (See Chapter 6)

Built by Thomas Rimmer 200 years ago. It was fashionable in the reign of William IV for donkey rides from Southport. 'Fiddler' Harry Rimmer played here and other places. The hill and flag were an indicator, and scenic point. Two more extensions were made, and a bowling green added, and the flag placed on the roof by 1910, when the Inn was replaced by the Portland Hotel. Part of the cobbled front can still be seen. Part of the site of the Bowling Green is on Bedford Park Recreation Ground, the only surviving part of Birkdale Common.

LITTLE IRELAND (See Chapter 5)

This photograph of 'Little Ireland' was probably taken towards the end of the 19th Century, about 1890, after the boundary extensions were made in the 1865 Southport Improvement Act, incorporating 'Little Ireland'.

The Southport Directory of 1876, states that 'Little Ireland' consisted of 47 households, and a school." It was generally supposed that the inhabitants were descendants of families driven out of Ireland by the potato famine in Ireland, in the 1840s, but in fact they were also the descendants of Scandinavian ancestors, who had conquered Ireland, before settling on the Lancashire coast, as early as the 8th Century.

The enlargement of this photograph, kindly provided by the Botanic Gardens Museum, shows the buildings to be mainly of brick construction. The appearance of the existing school building, described in Chapter Five, indicates more than just a cottage village complex. The appearance and general aspect of the inhabitants, also indicates something better than the, 'low squalid looking place, devoid of all sanitation arrangements' appellation, afforded it by some quarters, probably more interested in entrepreneurial potentiality, than in ethnic, or environmental considerations. The woman isolated on the left of the photo, is carrying a 'leup' or shrimping basket, obviously not part of a posed group, but even in working clothes, hardly 'squalid' in appearance.

In the distance, the outlines of 'Fleetwood Arms' or 'New Inn' situated in Bank Nook, built about 1840, can be seen, but not the Homeopathic Cottage Hospital, built next to it in 1906. The sandhills on the right ran on to 'Cockle Dicks' farm. Although the site is generally agreed to have been cleared round about 1904, Francis Bailey's 'A History of Southport' states that it was cleared for the new Municipal Golf Links, and also states that the Municipal Golf Links were constructed at the North End of the Promenade from 1913 onwards, from land reclaimed from the foreshore. He also states, in the same paragraph, that the Hesketh Golf Club was founded in 1885, so perhaps there was another Municipal Course, or the project was Council orientated. The favourable description that Paul Lloyd's memoirs give (in Chapter 9) of the Irish community in general, conflicts with officialdom's assertion that they were "unable to integrate with other local people".

(Photo, Botanic Gardens Museum).

BIRKDALE WINDMILL (See Chapter 6)

This was a post and peg, corn grinding mill. The main body of the mill, together with the wooden sails, were turned to catch the wind from any direction. It stood on a brick base, the whole structure standing on an embankment near the boundary of North Meols and Birkdale. It was not a new mill, but was bought at Kirkham in the Fylde in 1750. It stood on the site of Globe House at No. 18 Mosley Street. There is a name and number plaque over the door of the entrance to the Kentucky Derby, Elton Fabrications concern which was formerly the Birkdale Electric Cinema, standing on the corner of Mosley Street and Grove Street, near Upper Aughton Road opposite the Blundell Hotel.

The outbuildings on the left of the sketch, identified by the chimney at the rear, were probably the lime kiln, known to be in existence in Grove Street for many years, used for the compulsory, yearly decoration, of leased farms and outbuildings in the area.

The Millers Cottage, built in 1790, shown on the right, stood across the road to the Mill. Mosley Street and Everton Road, were then known as Mill Lane. At No. 89 Upper Aughton Road, standing behind the main road, and to the side of the former St. Peter's School, now used by the Air Training Corps, is Eden House, built in 1886. When the present owner of this house took up occupation of it in the late 1950s, Mr. Stewart Sykes, he built a brick bungalow in the grounds at the front of Eden House, on the site of an older building, reconstructed from old timber, and bricks, including an original back wall. Judging from the general alignment of the original structure, and the proximity to the site of the mill, it is now thought that this site is that of the Old Millers Cottage, and now being over 200 years old, qualifies as a listed building. It is visible from the corner of Grove Street and Mosley Street.

Before the Rimmers, coming from Little London along the old Churchgate track, naming it 'Snuttering Lane' (Cemetery Road), made a road from there into Birkdale North End, Mill Lane was the only connection between North Meols and Birkdale by a recognised route. Rimmers and their relations had then been established in Birkdale since the early Viking days.

Considerably altered over the years, Birkdale Mill survived until the 19th Century. Peter Travis was the miller in 1845, but in the late 1860's the mill was vandalised, and burnt, and finally destroyed. Next to the entrance of the door to the Kentucky Derby building, the original lower step and portico, of the original Globe House can still be seen. The outer fabric of this building has to be maintained as a preserved edifice, which the present owners, Elton Fabrications, have done in first class tasteful style.

'THE COTTAGE', BIRKDALE (See Chapter 6)

'The Cottage', 74 Liverpool Road is the oldest building remaining in Southport and is a 15th Century farmhouse of the cruck type construction clam stap and daub, built by the Rimmers and incorporating many of the features of the primeval lodges that the first Rimmer settlers built one thousands years ago. Whese were similar to dwelling places they had built in their long sojourn for many centuries in Nordic regions. In the 13th Century, Birkdale was so named from 'Birch', a dale of Birches, and 'Dalr' meaning Dale. It was formed by Rimmers moving from the Snoterpool area along the 'Kirk Gate' track. The Rimmers, double in number to other inhabitants, intermarried not only with Norsemen, but also local people including Irish and Wirral women. Together they levelled the dale and established an enclosure of farmhouses known as Birkdale North End. North End House or Farm was probably the original farm settlement, traces of which can still be seen behind Cookson's Nursery across North Side Lane now Liverpool Road. The Carr's, relatives of the Rimmers had a farm to the North on Crosby Road. There are traces of outbuildings at the rear of 34 Crosby Road. 'The Cottage' was a public house by the year 1600 operated by 'Host' Rimmer. The Carrs also had a half share in the present cottage. It has stood throughout the Stuarts, the Hanoverians, the Victorians, Edwardians and Windsors. It has seen the Civil War of Cromwell, the Restoration of Charles II, the founding of the American Colonies, the dissolution of the British Empire, and two great wars, and assorted minor ones.

Two years after standing empty after the death of the last occupant, James Rimmer, cab and taxi proprietor, who was photographed at the cottage in 1971, at the age of 77, planning permission was granted for outline development of the area for dwellings. The ensuing cries of protest from all quarters resulted in the Ministry of the Environment intervening to declare the cottage a scheduled ancient monument, and it is to be hoped that it will remain as such for many years to come.

THE MARSHSIDE RIMMERS — BOOT AND SHOE HOUSE (See Chapter 6)

This is the Rimmer residence, and Boot and Shoe shop, still situated on the corner of Marshside Road, and Shellfield Road. It can be dated by the fact that Martha Rimmer, is not on the photo, as she had just been born, in 1900. Peter Rimmer is on the left. John, father of Hannah and Vera Wignall, who have kindly lent me the photographs, is in the middle. The gentleman on the right, wearing clogs, is Grandfather John Rimmer, who together with my grandfather, were cousins of William Rimmer, the Brass Band exponent. The two little girls are Peggy and May. To the left of the photograph, the square bay window, was the workshop, indicated by the sign on the wall. The figure, apparently looking out of the window on the right, is actually a reflection of a lady leaning on the wall, not a ghost! The whole of this house and shop complex, was continuously occupied for many years. I am convinced that it was the shop I went to, for my grandad's 'gansey' wool. Hannah Wignall, nee Rimmer, was not on this photo, as being now 87 years of age, she had left the premises when she was around 4 years old.

RIMMER FAMILY GROUP CIRCA 1904 (See Chapter 6)
Back Row Left to Right: Jane; William; Ann; Betty; John; Robert
Middle Row: Grandmother Hannah; May; Peggy; Grandfather John
Little Martha is sat at the front.

AINSDALE MILL (See Chapter 6)

This sketch, by the Author, was copied from a photograph, which was taken on the day his mother was born, on the 18th May, 1886. She was then Ellen Rimmer, daughter of Robert Rimmer, fisherman cum-Methodist Minister from Little London, who was a descendant of one of the former millers, John Rymer, of the late 17th Century. The mill built in the early part of the century, was a post and peg wooden mill, but was rebuilt, as depicted, as a brick tower mill, around the end of the 18th century. Also another relative, William Rymer, stated in 1664, that the Ainsdale boundary with Halsall, and later Birkdale, ran through the mill house. In the sketch, water is being drawn from a pump, which I believe was connected to the 'Springwale', mentioned in 1556 (page 42 of 'Betwixt Ribbel and Moerse'). This spring was struck by roadworkers in the 1960's, in Segars Lane (Old Smithy Lane), near the site of Thomas Rimmer's Blacksmith Forge. The efforts to control the flow of water and reference to the 'Springwale', occasioned a great deal of interest, and press coverage. There is a full account of the Mill, and its fate, in Chapter Six of this book. In 1809, John Rimmer, when he was the Ainsdale miller was awarded a silver cup, value five guineas, for draining on the Ainsdale Mere and Mosses. He died in 1821 a man of substance leaving land in Halsall and as far as Leyland and Liverpool, also he left legacies of £600 in livestock and dairy effects. The 1841 census mentions Blacksmith Thomas Rimmer, living with the miller, but separate from the mill and the Smithy probably in the Millhouse Lodge flats area of today.

DUKE'S FOLLY (See Chapter 7)

This engraving dates from the 19th Century and shows the completed Hotel, known at various stages as 'The South Port Hotel' and the 'Royal Hotel'. When it was originally built in 1792, it was a wooden structure used mainly for bathing, mainly on the occasion of the Churchtown Fair, held on the Sunday following August 16th and Birkdale Rushbearing Fair a fortnight later. When Southport held its official Centenary celebrations in 1892, it was accepted that Sutton's bathing enterprise marked the foundation of the town. The original bathing hut, is the house, shown on the right. It had been enlarged at various stages, as it was used as a hunting lodge, by the Duke of York, when staying at Ince Blundell. It was generally used as a hostel, but never habited, as it was erected without a licence, drinks and refreshments were conveyed for special occasions. It was originally constructed of driftwood from the beach, but there are records of timber laden carts, making incredible journeys across the Moss, with wood for the enlargement of the 'Folly', in 1798.

OLD STOCKS, CHURCHTOWN (See Chapter 7)

This is the oldest record of the old stocks, with the posts, and bottom wooden rails complete. The posts are inscribed on the side "John Linaker 1741" when he was Steward of the Manor. Only the posts, now railed in, are still standing. There is some doubt as to their original position, as the Market Cross was listed as being near the 'Griffin Inn', or Bold Arms as it is now known, with the stocks presumably nearby.

As stated on page 99 of 'Betwixt Ribbel and Moerse' I have quoted correspondence from the Rev. W. E. Bulpit in 1903, and the late Lieut. Col. Fleetwood Hesketh from Meols Hall in 1960, which does not define the original situation of the Cross or stocks.

When Colonel Hesketh however purchased the obelisk to replace the Cross he had it placed in the triangular plantation in the front of the Church and the 'Black Bull', or Hesketh Arms, as it is now called.

One thing is certain however, is the fact that the last occupant of the stocks used in 1861, was a Rimmer, for a case of drunkenness!

'THEY THAT GO DOWN TO THE SEA' (See Chapter 8)

This 'shanking' cart is similar to the ones referred to in Chapter 8, when seven fishermen were drowned, when caught in the fog, whilst shrimping, in 1869. This lead to the installation, of the Fog Bell, erected under the auspices of the Fernley Observatory, which still stands at the top of Marshside Road. Three members of the Wright family, two Rimmers, and an Aughton, and Hesketh were the victims, all inter-related.

WILLIAM RIMMER AND SOUTHPORT CORPORATION BAND 1913
(See Chapter 8)

WILLIAM RIMMER (See Chapter 8)

William Rimmer — born 1861, died 1936. Conductor of the Southport Corporation band for many years. Quite apart from conducting the Southport Corporation Band, he achieved fame as a composer/arranger and as a brass band teacher. He even produced test pieces for the 1910, 1911 and 1912 Crystal Palace World Championships. And talking of competition, perhaps his most outstanding feat was to win both major brass band contests — at Belle Vue and at Crystal Palace — for two consecutive years with the same band. (Photograph reprinted with kind permission of G. A. and A. G. Burgess of Gesbur Studios, Southport).

"A STUDY IN SCARLET" — FROM SIR ARTHUR CONAN DOYLE'S STORY OF THE MORMONS DESERT TREK — 1914 Location on Birkdale Sands by the former Palace Hote. My mother is on the right of this picture. She is sitting behind my grandmother who is at the front holding a white shawl on her knees. G. B. Samuelson is the man in the black suit wearing a straw hat. The man in shirt sleeves and Trilby hat is George Pearson, the Producer.

'THE STEELES' (See Chapter 9)

Thes three cottages, which are detailed in Chapter Three — standing on the corner of Hesketh Drive, and Roe Lane, mark the southern boundary of the 'Steeles'. The much used cinder track, running diagonally from the old Churchgate, which ran from the Smithy in Botanic Road, ended at the Swing Gate, which was there in our days. Hesketh Drive was then only a sandy cart track. These cottages date from the early 1700's, there were cottages in the area, with field holdings, before this date. Richard Rimmer was one of several families of this name. In North Meols 1640 Parish Records, he is listed as the Pinder Assistant, to the Law Man, or Burleyman, responsible for the upkeep of field boundaries, and water courses, in an area called "The Wite Hill', later perpetuated in the name of the "White Bridge" over the railway, near the 'Willow Cottage' hamlet in Hesketh Drive.

THORN TREE COTTAGE — 43 COUDRAY ROAD (See Chapter 9)

Situated at the corner of Coudray Road and Hesketh Drive, built in 1720. The beams in the roof of the bedroom are old ships masts, and the floor boards upstairs consist of old oak, 18" wide.

An incised stone, found in the garden, bears the date, underneath a cross, of May 25th, 1740. It is not known whether this was a boundary marking, or the burial stone of some human or animal. The cottage is thought to have been named formerly Silverthorne Cottage, as both red and white flowering hawthorne trees grew there. This has also lead to the assumption that the nearby Silverthorne Drive housing estate was so named because of this. Two cottages next door have been made into one dwelling which is listed as No. 39. Across the road in Rawlinson Grove is Willow Cottage probably built around the same time. Another cottage was pulled down to make way for a modern house on the corner of Rawlinson Grove and Coudray Road. This was named Willow Lodge and the whole area was listed on 19th Century Hesketh Estate deeds as Willow Cottages.

OLD COTTAGES — CAMBRIDGE ROAD (See Chapter 9)

These two cottages standing opposite Cambridge Court and Emmanuel Road were replaced by the two bungalows No. 70 and 70a.
They were near the path, still in existence, between No. 78 and Tower Dene Prep. School No. 76, which runs through to Beresford Drive, crossing the old Carriers Lane at 'Twig Mollies' railway crossing which was replaced by the 'Red Bridge'. This path, running on to Bank Nook was used by the Taylor family 'Twig Harry's', whose farm premises on Carriers Lane were used for basket and lace making. Similarly another path used to run along Cambridge Avenue to Clengers Brow, Bakers Lane, and Marshside. Both well used in our time from Peets Lane Farm and Chase Heys.

THATCHED ROOF OF OLD SOUTHPORT (See Chapter 9)

This sketch shows my brother Albert, behind hedge, in post-Second World War army beret, worker for, and ex-gunner, and batman to the Fleetwood Hesketh brothers of Meols Hall, in the 'Doyles', 'Duke of Lancasters Own Yeomanry'. On the ladder is John (Jack) Howard, ex Great War Navy veteran. He lived in Cockle Dicks Lane, and coincidentally was deformed by an attack of the same rheumatic type of fever that crippled 'Cockle Dick' himself in his later years.

Mr. BAKER'S HOUSE, ROE LANE. (opp. Park Road) 1932 (Demolished)

"EVICTION OF THE IRISH INHABITANTS OF LITTLE IRELAND"

This postcard, one of Auntie Hester's 'stack', caused quite a furore when it was first issued, erroneously, as depicting "Eviction of the Irish inhabitants of 'Little Ireland'.
Even when re-issued as being located in Churchtown, there were objections, as the cottages belonging the the Lord of the Manor, were always, as now, kept in good repair.
Being sold principally in the Town Centre, the cards were regarded as being in bad taste and a poor advertisement for the area in general. They were published locally, by E. Kay of High Park Road. Lack of sales however, lead them to become so scarce as to become a 'Collectors Item'!
I myself am of the opinion that they were part of the row of cottages demolished to make way for the building of the Jubilee Hall, now Church Close, in High Park Place.

THE OLD DUNGEON AND PENFOLD

The Dungeon with the Penfold in the rear, stood near the entrance to the Botanic Gardens. They would most likely have stood on the Bankfield Lane side, of Fine Janes Brook. The Dungeon was removed in the middle of the 19th Century but the Penfold survived until it was transferred to Peets Lane Farm in the late 19th Century.

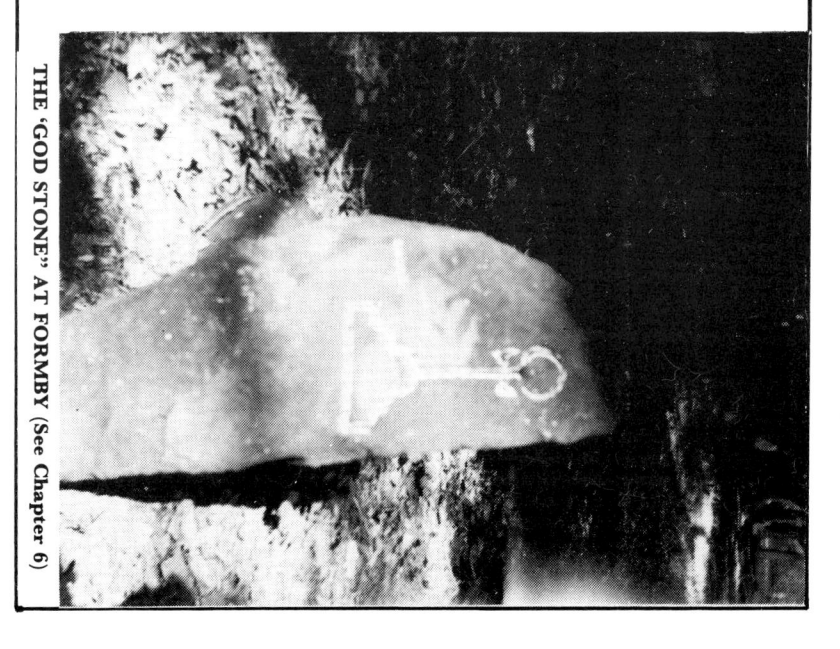

THE 'GOD STONE" AT FORMBY (See Chapter 6)

DEMOCRACY AND THE WELFARE STATE

DEMOCRACY
and the
WELFARE STATE

The Two Wests in the Age of Austerity

EDITED BY
Alice Kessler-Harris
and Maurizio Vaudagna

Columbia University Press
New York

Columbia University Press
Publishers Since 1893
New York   Chichester, West Sussex
cup.columbia.edu
Copyright © 2018 Columbia University Press
All rights reserved

Library of Congress Cataloging-in-Publication Data
Names: Kessler-Harris, Alice, editor. | Vaudagna, Maurizio, editor.
Title: Democracy and the welfare state : the two wests in the age of austerity / edited by Alice Kessler-Harris and Maurizio Vaudagna.
Description: New York : Columbia University Press, [2017] | Includes bibliographical references and index.
Identifiers: LCCN 2017007541 (print) | LCCN 2017031018 (ebook) | ISBN 9780231542654 (e-book) | ISBN 9780231180344 (cloth : alk. paper) | ISBN 9780231180351 (pbk. : alk. paper)
Subjects: LCSH: Welfare state—European Union countries. | Welfare state—United States. | Capitalism—Political aspects—European Union countries. | Capitalism—Political aspects—United States. | Democracy—Social aspects—European Union countries. | Democracy—Social aspects—United States.
Classification: LCC HD7164 (ebook) | LCC HD7164 .D45 2017 (print) | DDC 330.12/6—dc23
LC record available at https://lccn.loc.gov/2017007541

Columbia University Press books are printed on permanent and durable acid-free paper.

Printed in the United States of America

Cover design: Jordan Wannemacher
Cover image: Photograph of women marching to demand better housing (DAMS 9370), Leonard Covello photographs [PG107], Historical Society of Pennsylvania

To all of our students
in the hope that they will continue to explore the past
in order to shape the future

Contents

Acknowledgments xi

INTRODUCTION
The Uneasy Promise of the Welfare State
Alice Kessler-Harris
1

ONE
Historians Interpret the Welfare State, 1975–1995
Maurizio Vaudagna
27

PART I
**Democracy and the Welfare State
in Europe and the United States** 59

TWO
Reconciling European Integration and the National Welfare State:
A Neo-Weberian Perspective
Maurizio Ferrera
61

THREE
Democracy After the Welfare State: An Interview
Ira Katznelson
82

PART II
Varieties of Retrenchment 105

FOUR
Privatization and Self-Responsibility: Patterns of Welfare-State Development in Europe and the United States Since the 1990s
Christian Lammert
107

FIVE
Paradise Lost? Social Citizenship in Norway and Sweden
Gro Hagemann
128

SIX
Social Citizenship in the U.S. Affordable Care Act
Beatrix Hoffman
148

SEVEN
In the Shadow of Employment Precarity: Informal Protection and Risk Transfers in Low-End Temporary Staffing
Sébastien Chauvin
176

EIGHT
From the Welfare State to the Carceral State: Whither Social Reproduction?
Mimi Abramovitz
195

PART III
Gender, the Family, and Social Provision 227

NINE
Family Matters: Social Policy, an Overlooked Constraint on the Development of European Citizenship
Chiara Saraceno
229

TEN
Transforming Gendered Labor Policies in Sweden
and the United States, 1960s–2000s
Ann Shola Orloff
249

ELEVEN
Breadwinner Liberalism and Its Discontents
in the American Welfare State
Robert O. Self
273

PART IV
Possibilities of Resistance 295

TWELVE
Nationalism's Challenge to European Citizenship,
Democracy, and Equality: Potential for Resistance
from Transnational Civil Society
Birte Siim
297

THIRTEEN
Poor-People Power: The State, Social Provision,
and American Experiments in Democratic Engagement
Marisa Chappell
319

FOURTEEN
Grassroots Challenges to Capitalism: An Interview
Frances Fox Piven
342

Selected Bibliography 361
Contributors 373
Index 379

Acknowledgments

THIS BOOK is the product of many years of fruitful institutional and personal cooperation. Our transatlantic conversation on the past, present, and future of social rights would not have taken place without the involvement of many scholars and friends who contributed their insights, advanced suggestions and criticisms, and extended their support. As a result of our collaboration and our individual work, we have accumulated an impressive array of debts of gratitude to institutions, scholars, and friends. We are happy to acknowledge them here.

Our warmest thanks go to the Italian Academy at Columbia, headed by David Freedberg, which helped us mount a conference. Columbia University's Global Center, located at Reid Hall in Paris, housed a provocative workshop out of which many of the papers in this book come. We especially thank Paul LeClerc for initial support and Brunhilde Biebuyck and her staff for the splendid hospitality extended to our 2013 workshop. Their friendliness and efficiency, along with the welcoming site of the Global Center, contributed enormously to the success of our endeavor. Not all participants in the Paris conference are represented in this book, but many of their questions and comments, advanced in particular by Paul-André Rosental, Yohann Aucante, Elodie Richard, Laura Lee Downs, Mario Del Pero, Nicolas Barreyre, Bert Silverman, and Ulla Wikander, have found their way into these essays. Special thanks to Neil Gilbert for his many excellent challenges.

Our gratitude goes as well to the Department of Human Studies of the University of Eastern Piedmont and, for their support and friendship, to the Americanist colleagues of CISPEA (Interuniversity Center for American History and Politics), especially its director, Raffaella Baritono. At Columbia University we had initial help from the Women Creating Change project of the Center for the Study of Social Difference. We thank the Department of History at Columbia and Columbia University's Alliance Program, which funded the participation of four graduate students in Paris. The presence of George Aumoithe, Lindsey Dayton, Nick Juravich, and Suzanne Kahn proved to be a stimulating addition. Sciences Po provided warm cooperation. Lindsey Dayton fielded the logistics with efficiency and verve.

A particular thank you goes to our partners, Bert Silverman and Milena Montecchio, who were both full participants in this endeavor.

Our biggest debt is to our students. We have dealt with issues of welfare-state history in our courses and seminars. In both the United States and Italy our students, graduate and undergraduate, have greatly helped us mature deeper interpretations and have fed our commitment with their enthusiasm and their new ways of seeing. At a time when, almost simultaneously, both of us have retired from teaching, we dedicate this book to the students who will continue to challenge us as they create the scholarship of the future.

DEMOCRACY AND THE WELFARE STATE

Introduction

The Uneasy Promise of the Welfare State

ALICE KESSLER-HARRIS

IN THE DECADE between 2005 and 2014, more than two-thirds of households in twenty-five high-income economies experienced stagnant or declining real incomes. In Italy, more than 90 percent of households fell into this category; in the United States, 80 percent of households did so. Declining real wages, the economic pundit Martin Wolf tells us, along with immigration and cultural changes threaten those in middle-income groups.[1] They account for political discontent everywhere, for the rise of what Wolf and others call populist rage. Much of this rage has come from workers who feel their livelihoods threatened and their middle-class lifestyles under siege. It is directed not at the wealthy, whose incomes have grown exponentially, but at the governments that have failed to sustain and expand economic opportunity. And it emerges in demands that governments reduce or eliminate spending on programs that have, for nearly a century, mitigated the effects of inequality by providing economic security for the poor and the vulnerable. In short, increasing numbers of people in the "Two Wests"—Europe and the United States—have come to question the welfare state.

Challenges to redistributional government spending came home to roost in the early years of the twenty-first century. Spurred by neoliberal ideas that promised prosperity if only the heavy hand of government were removed, nations turned away from earlier commitments to aid the less fortunate. Europeans reduced their long-standing commitments to decent living for all. Americans abandoned the notion that governments could be relied on to level the playing field to ensure a fair race for success. Global competition and the decline of good jobs spurred discontent. High unemployment and an uncertain job market provoked a climate of despair among young people convinced that their lives could not duplicate the economic successes of their parents. Trade-union membership and influence declined; governments failed to meet promises of expanding prosperity. Rising immigration and a surge of refugees seeking to escape violence and intimidation in their home countries galvanized hostility to foreigners and provoked fear for the future.

Faced with these stresses, the populations of many high-income countries (including France, Austria, Hungary, and the United States) experienced sharp expressions of discomfort that came from both the Left and the Right. A new populist Right promoted neonationalist, antiliberal, anti-immigrant, and antipluralist parties in France, Austria, Germany, Italy, Scandinavia, and the former socialist countries of Central and Eastern Europe. Some of the nationalist parties appealed to traditions of authoritarian statism that had characterized European conservatism in the early part of the century. Others revived principles of authoritarian social support familiar to twentieth-century Europe and to Latin American countries like Argentina, which had used widespread social benefits to create consensus and stifle opposition.

Political and social conflict provoked new cleavages and repressive reactions. Demands for fiscal austerity limited aid to the poor and stimulated efforts to privatize public benefits like old-age pensions and schools. Britain and the United States shifted more and more of the costs of public education onto individuals and families. Fear of global competition and critiques of global economic cooperation provoked nationalist fervor. Donald Trump won the U.S. presidency by vowing to "Make America Great Again." His platform included promises to impose high tariffs on goods made outside the country and to build a wall between the United States and Mexico. Overwhelmed Europeans questioned the European Union's generous policy of admitting refugees. Britain voted to leave the European Union largely because it feared an influx of migrants.

What, then, of the promise of the welfare state? Would it disintegrate under the stress of globalization? What were the implications of the apparent end of the twentieth-century accommodation between capital and labor? Would the state abandon its promise of decent and dignified lives for all? And, crucially, what would happen to democracy, to the expanding voice promised to workers, the poor, and the disadvantaged? Would that voice seek refuge in strong leadership, or would it find a new vision of cooperation and justice?

We did not begin this book with a pessimistic outlook, nor did we intend to explore the events of the day. Rather, alerted to the apparent failure of optimism and the concurrent diminution of belief in cooperation and compassion that had underlain much of twentieth-century thought, we sought to explore the implications of major challenges to the twentieth-century welfare state. We—an interdisciplinary group of historians and social scientists—assembled in Paris in June 2014 to discuss what seemed to us to be an emerging crisis for democracy and democratic participation. Some of us had met before as part of an ongoing series of transnational conferences on the development and institutionalization of social rights. In previous encounters, we had explored the ways in which social rights (to pensions, housing, unemployment insurance, health care, education, leisure, and so on) had been adopted and institutionalized by various states.

This time, we flagged a more ambitious agenda. Aware of the myriad challenges to state intervention to protect the well-being of working people, we wanted to understand more about the effect of neoliberal ideas and "free-market fundamentalism" on state priorities. Concerned with the rise of a right-wing politics that emphasized the liberty of individuals over the welfare of the community, we noted that in an age of global capitalism, welfare retrenchment, and economic austerity, democracy seemed no longer to be partnered with a restrained capitalism. In that spirit, our workshop set out to examine the effect of the widespread decline of the welfare state on long-standing claims to social citizenship. We wondered how increasing inequality would affect democratic participation in Europe and the United States. This, after all, was the critical issue.

Almost all discussions of the twentieth-century expansion of the welfare state in relationship to democracy begin with the British social theorist T. H. Marshall. In a 1949 lecture, Marshall famously argued that citizenship had expanded over the course of two centuries from guarantees of civil rights to political representation and that an expansion of social rights had become the last requisite for democratic participation.[2] Political rights, he noted, could not be fully exercised by a population that lacked basic social and economic amenities. A malnourished, uneducated, hopeless people could not be trusted to vote, nor could they participate effectively in their own governance. Adequate sustenance, affordable health care, decent housing, a reasonable education, and regular employment were all, he thought, fundamental components of democratic practice. Marshall described, and to some extent rationalized, what seemed already to have become the consensus in Western industrial societies by the end of World War II.

The Western industrial nations had already begun to work toward creating a working relationship between democracy and capital by the late-nineteenth century, when workers everywhere expressed a profound discontent with their working conditions and standards of living. Unionizing, striking, and other tactics often disrupted production and produced violent retaliation. Labor parties spread, and socialist ideas threatened capitalism itself.

Needing a stable environment in which to build factories and a reliable and skilled workforce, corporations sought to provide them in various ways. Germany famously experimented with the process of ameliorating the lives of working people and their families under Bismarck. The process escalated in the years around World War I as the idea of social insurance emerged and as states took on the task of administering insurance against workplace accidents and unemployment. By the 1920s, large corporations (most notably the Ford Motor Company) experimented with what became known as welfare capitalism. In those years, too, many countries increased their investments in public schooling, housing, and public transportation and began to offer help to widowed mothers. France, eager to draw women into its workforce, developed a crèche system. With the dramatic exception of public education, the United States was slow to develop a national program of social benefits. Instead, beginning in the 1920s, it encouraged a few well-intentioned employers to experiment with loyalty programs such as sports teams, paid vacations, and old-age pensions for long-standing (largely white, male) employees.[3]

In the prosperous 1920s, these private efforts seemed promising, but the Great Depression of the 1930s rendered them everywhere unworkable and challenged the efficacy of the free market. The rising appeal, or threat, of socialism (enhanced by a seemingly successful Soviet communism) provoked a reexamination of social planning. Responses varied. At one end of the scale, Sweden developed the concept of a *"folkhem,"* out of which would come solidaristic social policies that involved ensuring jobs at good wages for all. Germany and Italy adopted a right-wing fascism that promoted government partnership with large corporations. In return for political loyalty, these programs provided jobs and security to the favored. Support for economic planning grew in most Western industrial countries.

The economic crisis hit poor people hard in the United States, producing marches of the unemployed and protest movements that everywhere blamed the ravages of capitalism for creating misery. To forestall social unrest, the U.S. government provided relief in the form of job creation, wage and hour regulation, and production targets in key industries. Not without opposition from states that believed the federal government had no business intervening in the lives of individuals, the United States passed the Social Security Act of 1935. The act provided cash relief for the children of single mothers and the aged poor as well as old-age pensions and unemployment insurance for many industrial workers. Perhaps most crucially, the United States for the first time acknowledged the role of trade unions as the collective voice of working people. Corporations sometimes reluctantly cooperated with these measures in order to achieve the stability they needed.

Arguably, World War II turned the tide with regard to capital-labor cooperation, demonstrating that regulation and planning could effectively organize the economy. The British economist William Beveridge's 1942 report sketched out the benefits and rights that would be necessary in order to establish a reunified citizenry in the wake of World War II.[4] His 1944 follow-up made the case for full employment. These widely influential reports heralded the dawn of a general postwar consensus: that a stable prosperity required secure, more equal, and fairer economic arrangements. To attain this standard required a reciprocal relationship between democracy and capital. It would require sustained increases in productivity, agreements to share the gains of productivity more equally between capital and labor via taxation and transfer payments, and full employment policies. To achieve these, governments would be called on to promote the general welfare; corporations would be asked to pay their fair share of the costs.

The resulting systems had different names and different emphases in Europe and America. The sociologist Ralph Dahrendorf labeled the Northern European pattern a "social democratic consensus." His colleague Gøsta Esping-Andersen called it "welfare capitalism." Some scholars referred to the U.S. experience as the development of "the New Deal Order." Others in the United States referred to it simply as "liberalism." But as benefits spread and a sense of entitlement to state services and state protection grew, the notion of a "welfare state" took hold.

Whatever the label, leaders in Western Europe and the United States agreed, as Roosevelt proclaimed in his "Four Freedoms" address and in the Atlantic Charter, that the future would rely on a "mixed system," where market, private enterprise, and public action joined together to safeguard widespread, balanced prosperity.[5] The mixed system provided that democratic government would regulate business to prevent cutthroat competition, extreme labor exploitation, and unlimited profits. At the same time, regulation would reduce risks for capitalists and incentivize investment, thereby ensuring the creation of jobs. An increasingly productive, satisfied, and stable workforce would increase profits so that there would be plenty to go around. Generous social (and, in the United States, increased military) spending would enhance economic growth. Government spending in education, health, public transport, housing, old-age pensions, and family support would expand market demand and corporate profits. As the historian Gary Gerstle summed up the happy compromise: "Government could be an effective tool for managing, even democratizing capital."[6]

To achieve the necessary social and economic stability, corporations conceded collective bargaining to trade unions: it was more efficient for them to negotiate with a collective voice. And besides, trade unions policed their members, reducing turnover and disciplining workers where necessary. Similarly, corporations could rely on government agencies to compensate the losers by providing unemployment insurance, a dole, and other payouts to ensure that the very poor did not rise up. More generous Western European countries provided job retraining and family-support systems as well. Just as families in trouble could rely on government intervention, so could private corporations that ran into trouble expect government rescue via tax expenditures with the support of tax money. The mixed system would thus generate public-private agreement and sustain the welfare-state order.

None of this would have been possible without the unacknowledged aid of poorer countries, many of them former colonies of the industrial world. Colonial territories had historically been sources of raw materials and markets for low-quality consumer items, while metropolitan areas dominated different sorts of industrial capacity. The rapid end of European colonial empires in the thirty years following World War II did not end these relationships. The cheap raw materials from former colonies at once subsidized welfare-state provisions and provoked consternation within nations about how to distribute benefits. If generous "Third World" programs sometimes provided aid to former colonial nations, the basic function of present and past colonies was to provide cheap labor to the metropolis, thus subsidizing the costs of rising living standards and welfare programs.

The balance between the prerogatives of capital and the demands of governments rested on the underlying logic of the industrial order. Framed within national borders and the ethnic communities that dominated them, industrial prosperity relied on a disciplined labor force and the social cohesion promoted by a more equal distribution of income. Early welfare states promoted these ends, aiming for social stability and cooperation, even though they could not always achieve it. In the United States, for example, racial and ethnic tensions limited pensions and unemployment insurance to those holding particular jobs, which excluded the vast majority of African American workers, male and female. A rhetoric of fairness in the United States disguised these prejudices. But, as historians have now demonstrated, it was no accident that policies tied to specific kinds of wage work excluded agricultural and domestic labor, sectors dominated by men and women of color.[7] It now seems clear that the initial welfare regime of the 1930s was primarily designed to benefit workers and families in industrial employment.

Gender-based policies were especially useful in fostering national purpose. Nations that required high levels of female employment tended to offer family benefits such as paid maternity leaves and subsidized childcare that released women from the home to enter the workplace.

Others, such as Austria and Spain, where popular consensus balked at female wage earning, tilted benefits in the interests of working males. In the United States, gendered biases ensured the adoption of policies that provided differential benefits to those who participated in wage work (men) and those who did not (in the 1930s, mostly women).

Egalitarian and solidaristic policies found their most complete expression in countries with strong trade unions and effective labor parties.[8] Famously, the Scandinavian countries imposed high taxes on individuals and corporations to produce some of the fairest and most equitable wages and benefits in the world.[9] There and elsewhere, a commitment to universal benefits such as adequate housing, national health care, and mothers' pensions promoted solidarity among citizens and loyalty to the state.

In contrast, cultures of individualism inhibited the development of universal benefits, turning "welfare" into a subsidy for the poor rather than an entitlement of citizenship. That culture manifested itself in the market-related welfare state that characterized the United States and distinguished it from most "social" European counterparts (with the possible exception of Britain). In the 1970s, scholars began to talk about the United States as manifesting "internal colonialism"—that is, a system that maintained a large group of unemployed or underemployed workers in order to assure the availability of a surplus labor pool. Such individuals and their families lived on the margins, supported by black-market jobs, illicit activities such as drug running, occasional minimum-wage or seasonal jobs, and a welfare system that provided women and their children with sufficient support to fend off starvation and keep a roof over their heads but not to live decently. Some estimated that by the 1980s, this pool of largely impoverished individuals and their families amounted to a quarter of the American population and up to half of African American families. Except under unusual circumstances, their voices did not find their way into the electoral system, undermining democracy.

Ideologically, the mixed system provided an important counter to the Soviet Union's claim to protect the well-being of its citizens as well as the expansion of the Soviet Union into satellite nations. Responding fearfully to these events, Western European nations and the United States promoted inclusionary ideologies of democracy and liberty that relied on wide public participation and economic opportunity based on merit. The welfare state offered an inclusionary model and an egalitarian spirit. It would allow fair participation and representation in a democracy, nurturing national loyalty in return for benefits. It would constitute the glue that held nations together.

Fueled by cheap raw materials and a commitment to industrial success, the new welfare states remained market economies where most people derived their incomes from gainful employment in private business. Private enterprise, people on both sides of the Atlantic agreed, fostered dynamism in producing new goods, developing technology, and ensuring the relative prosperity of increasingly larger social groups. Prosperity underlined the capacity of the state to provide the resources that ensured rising standards of living and expanding social rights for all. It assured the willingness of the state to rein in the abuses of capital while tolerating the demands of trade unions. And it sustained continuing faith in democratic governance that held social welfare and the needs of capital in balance. Encouraging both economic growth and social security, the welfare state would become a powerful tool to constrain capitalism and promote democracy, producing a happy blend of satisfied labor in a context of social and political citizenship.

From the mid-1940s to the mid-1970s, the "mixed system" enjoyed a high level of popular confidence. For three glorious decades (called *les trente glorieuses* by the French) national governments, sometimes prodded by the European Union, assured continued prosperity, guaranteed high levels of employment, levied graduated taxes needed to finance social and economic security, and coordinated economic growth in such a way that welfare beneficiaries would not be so numerous as to push the national budget out of control. The mixed system allowed a market economy to flourish and encouraged government intervention in pursuit of the public interest. Governments created fiscal and monetary policies that stabilized economic cycles, ensured full employment, and regulated big business. At the same time, and to different degrees, they protected the victims of disease, old age, invalidity, and unemployment from poverty. They reduced infant mortality, increased longevity, provided workers and their families with decent housing conditions, and offered educational options adequate to sustain a dignified lifestyle for everybody. Through progressive taxation, the rich provided resources to help the poor. Inequality due to merit or inherited wealth persisted, but, overall, standards of living rose, and, as the economist Thomas Piketty has now demonstrated, the level of inequality declined.[10] In the glorious years, welfare states, in their different incarnations, performed the miracle of making capitalism generally more productive and more equitable.

But—in the 1970s, that began, visibly, to change as institutional and technological developments began to unravel the industrial system. Productivity declined, inflation spiraled, production escalated its move into cheaper markets, and corporations began to abandon commitments to stable and well-educated labor markets. They balked at supporting a welfare state they no longer needed. Confidence in the government's capacity to balance the democratic desire to tame capitalism against corporate desires for ever-expanding profit shares broke down. Conflict over the division of the economic pie in a stagnant economy increased. Business blamed heavy taxation; the Left targeted insufficient public spending on the poor and the absence of funds for housing, schools, and job training. Politically, the welfare state suddenly seemed an unacceptable burden, its restraints on capital onerous. Efforts to achieve social justice gave way to concerns with economic growth.[11]

Changing technology played a key role, facilitating the movement of capital, destroying old jobs, turning new ones over to robots, and allowing the transfer of design and development among countries at the touch of a computer key. The new information technology helped make manufacturing portable; it deprived the home country of jobs, purchasing power, and tax revenue, all of which were essential to support their welfare programs. Increasingly, corporations abandoned former commitments to community and national well-being to serve the interests of their own bottom lines. Crucially, as labor-force demands changed, employers no longer needed stability so much as they wanted flexibility. Trade-union practices, they now argued, stood in the way of economic growth. Taxation made their products uncompetitive.

In the popular imagination, globalization seemed to blame. Previously colonized nations took advantage of the new technologies to draw capital their way. They attracted increasing portions of their populations to industrial jobs whose relatively low wages at once made their products competitive with those of the developed world and provided significant rises in living standards for the world's poor. These populations sought jobs wherever they could find them, often relied on the labor of children to sustain families, and undermined their own traditional family systems by utilizing women to make ends meet and exporting female labor to send currency home. The resulting stream of migratory labor to Western industrialized nations created marginalized populations within them, increasing claims to state services and forcing states to come to terms with how they served citizens as opposed to foreign residents or transient workers.

Arguably, too, globalization reduced the number of good jobs available to working people, creating an equality gap greater than at any time since the early twentieth century within nations and between them. It undermined national loyalty, especially that of corporations eager to shed the responsibilities and high taxation embedded in their commitments to community and nation and to reap the profits of international trade. Together, globalization and technology dramatically expanded consumer society, providing access to individual material comforts in Western democracies that transcended the imaginations of previous social-policy makers. To critics on the Left, the politics of collective well-being receded in the public search for bigger and better cars, houses, boats, and refrigerators.

Marshall had argued that effective democratic participation required an extension of social rights; he had not anticipated the consequences of technological transformation. In an era of new technology, prosperity "at home"—and the ability to continue to pay for the benefits provided by the state—rested on the capacity to send jobs to former colonies and sometimes to entice their residents to emigrate to the former industrial heartland. Were these new residents to be counted among the included, or were they to be positioned in excluded categories? Were they guest workers, *braceros*, and contingent laborers? Or were they entitled to fair treatment, to economic security, to public education, to health care, to old-age pensions, to the protection of the state? Were they, in short, to be treated as citizens, and if so, could they effectively be included in the polity and entitled to the privileges of democratic voice?

These questions resonated as the European Economic Community consolidated its borders and took over the policing of migration and trade. Since its beginning, the European Union had stressed the primacy of a free-market policy, in contrast to the modest social planning that underlined the welfare state. As long as pan-European economic growth kept everybody happy, the tension between the two directions remained hidden. But as economic pressure built, national efforts to sustain robust welfare states came into conflict with the EU commitment to build markets through the free movement of capital and labor within the European Union. Any nation that admitted foreigners provided a route to all the other nations within it. As large cities throughout the European Union developed enclaves of foreign-born families whose living conditions and cultures seemed to undermine those of citizens, xenophobia spiraled upward, approaching the levels of racism that had long characterized the United States.

As the European Union grew from its original six members in 1958 to twenty-eight members in 2016, issues of national-versus-European identity honed the sharp divisions that emerged between EU "bureaucrats" and advocates of nationally based social rights. The European Union never successfully built a network of social rights—its failure inhibiting the creation of a "European" identity and encouraging the separate nation-states within the union to resist the regulations emerging from Brussels. The conflict would continue into the twenty-first century, affecting the capacity of every state to determine its own national welfare policies and underlying the resistance to increasing numbers of migrants and refugees.

Nor was the United States immune to the tensions of immigration. Long experience with the "melting pot" had produced a rhetoric of assimilation and accommodation to immigrants. But as a sturdy underclass of black and Hispanic workers began to demand access to civil and political rights and to protest the discriminations built into the existent welfare systems, the doors opened to unskilled workers from Asia, South Asia, South and Central America, and Africa.[12] New immigrants challenged the well-being of the poor. Some economists argue that they made it possible to hold down wages and especially to restrict attempts to increase the minimum wage along with the rising cost of living.

On the right, critics of the welfare state grew vociferous as the 1970s drew to a close. To resolve the financial and economic crises of that decade, they demanded a lifting of the regulatory order. But this required persuading a skeptical public. The success of welfare states, especially in Western Europe, had lifted many people from poverty and uncertainty.[13] Government commitments to at least a modicum of social justice had encouraged different groups to articulate demands for their piece of the pie. A politics of identity emerged as women, racial and ethnic minorities, and sexually diverse groups sought the shelter of the welfare state's protective umbrella. The growing sense of citizen entitlement fueled the fury of a right-wing political establishment that continued to believe the poor lacked the will to succeed; that government aid nourished dependency instead of independence; that bearing children outside of marriage was irresponsible and required punishment, not support; and that minorities and women did not need "affirmative action" so much as they needed ambition and motivation to work.

In this economic environment, a long tradition of economic thought found a receptive audience. Inspired by Frederick Hayek and his colleagues in Chicago, Virginia, Austria, and London, a newly inspired group of neoliberals on both sides of the Atlantic demanded that nations abandon the regulatory order that had been the linchpin of the mixed system. Government intervention in the economy, they argued, was the problem. In their view, social spending was counterproductive. Aid to the poor encouraged dependence on government largesse and stifled individual initiative. Public schools failed, said Milton Friedman, because students had no investment in the product.[14] Trade unions interfered with the free flow of capital and with individual choice. An unregulated free market in money and goods would, they argued, produce a fair and prosperous economy. Stimulated by these arguments, the British, in 1979, elevated Margaret Thatcher to prime minister; the Americans followed a year later, electing Ronald Reagan to the presidency. Ascendant neoliberal ideas now governed policy in these two nations and would soon spearhead antigovernment sentiment in politics and social life.

How would voters be convinced that unfettered free-market capitalism was in their self-interest? How would they be persuaded to let go of the lifeline that had stretched from the state into family life for several generations? There are many answers to this question, but the late-twentieth-century climate of austerity and the fear of debt surely contributed its piece. As unemployment remained at a relatively high rate and as government revenues fell, the Reagan and Thatcher administrations offered "supply-side" economic theories as solutions to stagnation. Reduce taxes on the rich and on corporations, they argued, and the benefits would trickle down to the rest of the economy. In fact, reduced taxes produced less revenue. In the absence of reductions in military spending, that left less money for social programs, leaving them underfunded and less capable of satisfying clients. Neoliberals dug deeper. They blamed government, which, in their view, could not do anything efficiently. They advocated the deregulation of banking systems and financial markets that restricted or taxed the flow of capital. They promoted the privatization of such formerly public ventures as hospitals, schools, prisons, and the military; tarnished the reputations of and sometimes destroyed the trade unions that spoke up for redistribution of wealth; and questioned the concept of "welfare" as a misspent resource.

As the call for free markets took hold everywhere, the traditional gap between European social responsibility and the market-oriented United States narrowed. Many European states conceded to the mantra of privatization and reduced, albeit less than in the United States, formerly generous transfer programs. Corporate executives, especially in the United States, no longer acknowledged trade unions as legitimate partners in creating a shared prosperity. Their resistance led to declining union power almost everywhere, but nowhere as much as in the United States. On both sides of the Atlantic, a growing gap between the social goals of liberal democracy and the demand for free markets produced a rush toward the center. Labor parties adopted elements of free-market goals, embracing privatization and sometimes austerity in an effort to remain politically viable.

Instead of finding compromise with willing partners, democratic voices encountered stern resistance to fostering the social good. In the end, successfully confronting new ideologies of market fundamentalism would depend on the electorate. But by the start of the new millennium, large numbers of the old working class, disillusioned by job losses and the costs of the welfare state and lacking the alternative solutions that trade unionism, socialism, and social democracy had once provided, turned to the free market for solutions. Capitalism had won an ideological battle. It had parted company from liberal democracy.

The United States provides a dramatic case in point. For many years, the separate states of the United States, which each set their own rules for administering federal elections, shaped the electorate through the imposition of poll taxes, literacy tests, and voter intimidation. To discourage "undesirable" voters and those with contrary views, political-party functionaries resorted to a series of antidemocratic strategies. They redrew voting-district lines to confine the poor and people of color to a few carefully drawn districts whose representatives could then easily be overwhelmed or marginalized. These gerrymandered areas guaranteed majority-white representation in the remaining areas. In the 1960s and 1970s, a resonant civil-rights movement, aided by a liberal Supreme Court, challenged efforts to silence the voices of people of color. Together, court orders and federal-government supervision dramatically increased the numbers of African American voters, especially in southern states.

But, as neoliberal ideologies inspired skepticism about federal-government intervention of all kinds, resistance to its mandates grew. Several American states engaged in ongoing campaigns to deprive racial minorities of the vote. Sometimes, especially in the South, this took the form of outright violence and intimidation. More subtle efforts involved such methods as requiring prior registration at inconvenient times or in places inaccessible to those without cars, demanding government-issued identification (like drivers' licenses) from the elderly and the poor who did not drive, depriving those convicted of criminal felonies from voting for the rest of their lives, stationing police officers with guns in voting places, and so on. But the coup de grace occurred in the fall of 2013, when the Supreme Court lifted a long-standing ban on pouring money into political campaigns. The court's decision in *Citizens United v. FEC* allowed a well-funded and rising new Right to find its way into the heart of politics and Congress. With money no object, attacks against government action of all sorts increased geometrically. The need to raise money colored election campaigning. In the 2016 presidential campaign, Bernie Sanders declared that his campaign funds came mostly from small, two-figure donations; Donald Trump claimed—falsely, it turned out—that he would fund his own campaign; pundits excoriated other candidates for accepting corporate contributions that would ensure their indebtedness to donors.

Electoral politics constituted only one mechanism for silencing the poor. Other more subtle strategies persisted. Famously, the United States has brutally silenced many of those who depend on state support with a strategy of tying benefits to wage work. Unlike many European benefits, which are distributed to all citizens, the United States has traditionally imposed demeaning conditions on the receipt of benefits by the poor. The most onerous of these is the demand for compensatory wage work at minimal wages and without equitable childcare. The result in the United States is to deprive some women and their children of the time to participate in political activities.[15] Lacking adequate voice, the poor have paid a large price: inadequate health care, the absence of subsidized childcare except for the very poor, and decreased support for public schools in favor of charter schools and vouchers to pay for private-school tuition. In 1996, the end to a sixty-year-old welfare system that entitled the poor to decent standards of living produced a dramatic increase in child poverty and homelessness—and perhaps in domestic violence as well. Instead of an entitlement to economic security, the poor got income-tax credits available only to those with jobs, housing vouchers inadequate to pay prevailing rents, and a more generous allocation of food stamps meant to ensure that they did not starve. The general absence of concern for the social welfare of the poor was visible in the early twenty-first century in rising malnutrition among children, high infant-mortality rates, and lower life expectancies especially for men and women of the lower middle classes.[16]

Confusion in ideology and expectation has affected European and American publics alike. All over Western Europe, and particularly in the United States, the growing gap between rich and poor has become a lively political issue, leading to public demonstrations and political tensions. Workers and scholars frequently disagree as to whether the fundamental task of government is to preserve the well-being of all or whether it is to help corporations take the initiative. As we narrow the sphere of compassion, we have grown accustomed to new words like "time limits," "benefit caps," the "hidden welfare state," "asset building," and "personal responsibility." Some of these expressions clearly reflect policies that have pushed social policy backward to the restrictive arena of safety nets, shifting the quality and quantity of benefits from adequate to minimum and pathologizing recipients incapable of taking care of themselves physically and morally. But the process of welfare reform that had its beginning in the late 1970s has been open to a variety of directions; a range of political, intellectual, and ideological perspectives; and wide potential for framing new policy programs. For example, in the United States the recipients of government aid have been effectively silenced by coercive measures that include poor educations, forced labor for single-parent families, and incarceration for "quality-of-life" offenses. These measures have deprived millions of mostly black and Hispanic individuals of their voting rights. In Europe, xenophobia characterizes the domestic politics of many nations and limits the social mobility of naturalized citizens and their children. How, then, do we begin to think about democracy in an age of exclusion?

If scholarly and political concerns about the effects of declining social rights on democratic participation are now widespread, their effects have been uneven. In Europe, the retreat of the welfare state has been slower and more complicated; the residual power of labor unions and left-wing political parties continues to promote the interest of the poor, and it remains possible to imagine a society in which some basic social services would be available to any human being, independent of his or her citizenship status or territorial location. Yet the tensions of labor migration have fostered challenges to a shared social citizenship that may signal more widespread but far weaker economic security for citizens of the world. In the United States, tensions over border control with Central and South American states have given rise to rampant discrimination with regard to education, health care, and employment, threatening the human rights of the excluded. Those who lack political power, including children, many women, and members of racial and ethnic minorities, have little or no economic security.

In the United States, the shift to a new information technology has produced a growing resentment among working people and a palpable fear for their future independence. As the presidential election of 2016 revealed, increasing numbers of men and women have accepted the mantra of individual responsibility, demanding that government do something for *them*, rather than for the poorest among them. The election and its aftermath witnessed the emergence of long-suppressed elements of radical nationalism, overt racial violence, and exclusionary policies. Their concerns feed into those of the very rich, who question whether majoritarian rule serves the purposes of free-market capitalism.

In Europe, efforts to hold the European Community together have been threatened by the same rising nationalist impulses. While democratic majorities have managed to retain many of the benefits of the welfare state, including maternity and paternity leave, reasonable paid vacations, and old-age care, powerful right-wing nationalist parties have emerged everywhere. The Right has invoked a populist rhetoric to convince uneasy voters to consider narrow self-interest at the cost of other groups. It challenges the legitimacy of government action to serve the interests of any (including women, minorities, and sometimes the disabled) who cannot help themselves. This divisive rhetoric has promoted nationalist calls to oppose additional immigration and promote the privileges of their own citizens. Public sentiment in France, Austria, Hungary, and Italy has warmed to these calls. Britain responded to them by voting to leave the common market in an effort to protect the country from an influx of foreigners.

Still, many Europeans continue to embrace an active Left. The Spanish Podemos and the original Greek Syriza have bravely proposed notions of cooperation, compassion, equality, and justice, even at the cost of financial sacrifice. Expounding on the benefits of Europeans' willingness to subject themselves to significantly higher taxes than residents of the United States typically will tolerate, the *New York Times* columnist Eduardo Porter notes that for their sacrifice of income, Europeans got "free time." Additionally, he suggests, their continuing commitment to social well-being provided Europeans with "lower poverty rates, lower income inequality, longer life spans, lower infant mortality rates, lower teenage pregnancy rates, and lower rates of preventable death."[17]

The United States demonstrates no such commitment. To be sure, the lively Occupy movement challenged inequality. Black Lives Matter drew attention to rising incarceration rates and police violence against black youth. And the self-proclaimed socialist Bernie Sanders's 2016 campaign for the presidency, which drew huge and admiring crowds, suggests that a sentiment to restrain capitalism still exists. The centrist Hillary Clinton won the popular vote by nearly three million votes. But in the end, appeals to conscience lost the day to the divisive and fear-mongering rhetoric of Donald Trump, who, in the course of his campaign, attacked Muslims, immigrants, women, and African Americans. The rise of radical nationalism is raising fears once thought to be a closed chapter in the history of Western civilization.

The consequences of current changes in welfare-state practices and assumptions about social rights are rarely examined in comparative frames. Their impact is therefore poorly understood, especially with regard to democratic activism. The essays in this book take new directions in social rights and the meaning of social welfare as their starting point and ask how the changes now underway are affecting democratic participation on both sides of the Atlantic. If the foundations on which the old welfare states were built are breaking down and, as a result, the social compact that protected the poor and expanded democratic participation no longer thrives, how do we imagine the process of political, social, and economic integration? What changes are necessary in the welfare state? How will democratic participation be sustained? Or will it be?

Many of the ideas presented here were developed in the course of an extended conversation on transatlantic social rights that has taken place over a decade in workshops in New York, Paris, and Turin, Italy. Separate workshops have focused on the historical development and dissemination of social rights during the twentieth century and on the relationship of those rights to the expansion of social citizenship and democratic participation. Beginning with an exploration of the concept of social rights in relationship to the welfare state, the project moved to examine the emergence of new rights-based social policies between World War I and II. A third meeting spread its purview to the period in and after World War II. In 2009, Kessler-Harris and Vaudagna edited *Democracy and Social Rights in the "Two Wests"* (Torino, Italy: Otto, 2009), a book, published in paper and online, that reproduced some of the key papers from those meetings. For this volume, we drew on the products of a workshop held at Columbia University's Reid Hall in Paris and cosponsored by CISPEA (Interuniversity Center for European-American History and Politics), a consortium of transatlantic-studies institutes connecting five leading Italian universities. We also invited participation from members of an ongoing New York City workshop now called "Social Justice After the Welfare State" and sponsored by Columbia University's project on Women Creating Change, an offshoot of the Center for the Study of Social Difference (CSSD).

We asked the participants in our June 2014 workshop to think about the impact of changing notions of the welfare state in light of their own work. To encourage different and differing voices, we drew on contributors from Denmark, France, Germany, Italy, the Netherlands, Norway, and the United States. Our authors include young as well as experienced scholars who have grappled with these questions from interdisciplinary perspectives. They are political scientists, sociologists, policy theorists, and contemporary historians, a mix that reflects the insights as well as the skills that different disciplines bring to the subject. The mix enables explorations of the meaning of the current contraction of some social rights even as, in other respects (incarceration, job training), some states have expanded their remit. It also enables a larger question as to how the effort to diminish national boundaries in the European Union affects labor mobility and the construction of a new citizenship. For example, Maurizio Ferrara opens the issue of whether a "European social-welfare model" will be able to surmount the boundaries posed by national cultures and states. Christian Lammert calls attention to how redistributive policies across the Atlantic shape political participation. Chiara Saraceno notes that different approaches to family account for how social benefits are restrained and facilitated by national borders.

The chapters in this book reflect the eclectic approaches of their authors. They adhere to no common definition of the welfare state: indeed, consensus around such a definition might have been impossible to reach. Rather, we shared a notion that such a state was one that provided for the well-being of its citizens so that they might more effectively participate in the polity. To achieve this end, as scholars have frequently pointed out, states have taken dramatically different paths.[18] Some, as the chapters by Abramowitz, Hoffman, and Saraceno illustrate, have had less interest in promoting effective participation than in silencing protest.

The chapters are comparative in two senses: some provide examples among European countries (Ferrera, Hagemann, Siim); others (Hoffman, Katznelson, Lammert, Orloff, Vaudagna) suggest transatlantic exchanges. A third group draws comparative inferences from material drawn from within one country (Chappell, Chauvin, Self) or rethinks the vital issues faced in different places (Piven). We note that the essays are rooted in different conceptual frameworks: some within the state (Katznelson, Saraceno, Orloff), others in institutions fostered by the state (Abramowitz in prisons, Saraceno in the family, Chauvin in the workplace).

Yet the chapters speak to one another as well as to larger issues. Gender permeates many of them—acting as a comparative thread to test out the policies and purposes of states with regard to such issues as equality and the value of care giving. Orloff's comparative exploration of Swedish and U.S. policies, for example, reveals how employment-related support systems affect the participatory potential of women (mostly mothers) in the employment and political arenas. Everywhere (and especially in the United States) the contributors note a shift away from state support for public goods to an insistence on "personal responsibility."

European states, though less aggressively, followed this pattern as they experienced dramatic changes in the heterogeneity of their labor forces. Sweden partially privatized pensions and reduced its commitment to housing for all; Britain enfeebled its celebrated National Health Service. Everywhere an antigovernment rhetoric expounded on the viability of continuing government services in the face of declining economic growth. Complaints about government inefficiency, corruption, and excessive regulation abounded. In the face of this data, none of the essayists took for granted the continuation of social-democratic options. Instead, implicitly and explicitly, they pose questions about whether democracy (which relies on a modicum of equality) is not in jeopardy. And they question the influence of demographic and population shifts that give voice to women and racial minorities.

All the chapters in this volume have adopted the rubric of the "Two Wests," a concept within which we have worked for several years now. The Two Wests acknowledges that the United States and Europe share a common history of social rights designed to enhance national loyalty and democratic participation among their citizens. We do not see the welfare state as an exclusively European affair that contrasts with a United States depicted as the land of individualism and the market. Yet, even as it recognizes commonalities, the idea of the Two Wests accommodates crucial distinctions between Europe and America and among European nation-states. Against the idea, mostly held by European scholars, that the two sides of the ocean are more distinctive than similar, it holds steady the common goals of Enlightenment philosophy with regard to notions of individual liberty and social responsibility. At the same time the demarcation of Two Wests enables us to distinguish an American focus on individual liberty and freedom from the European emphasis on achieving the collective good.[19] As well, the Two Wests takes into account scholarly and political conversations around the emergence of a "widening Atlantic" that see the United States and Europe moving in different directions after the end of communism.

Each author approaches the subject through a particular national and empirical lens. Placed against one another, these various perspectives allow a comparative view that encourages us to think simultaneously about the common elements in Western values and to situate the evolution of those values against a complex and expanding global environment. For example, Ira Katznelson notes that governments dramatically expanded their social-policy initiatives in the period following World

War II in the context of a painful victory against fascism and a continuing Cold War with communism. These conditions, he argues, laid the groundwork for a "golden age" of welfare benefits that rested on the acquiescence of a public that accepted much greater coercion than they had been wont to do. Birte Siim sees these benefits eroding in the face of the "conflict between attachment to national identity on the one hand and the inability of nations on the other to secure the social, civil, and political rights of their people." She asks what might happen if the identities of citizens could be channeled from nation-states to a wider European domain. Chiara Saraceno offers us a view from the family. In her view, social policies might better be pegged to the functions of family members: as breadwinners, caretakers, or parents rather than to national citizenship or residence.

These perspectives juxtapose differing points of views in ways that not only enrich transnational studies but also shed light on how and under what circumstances an expansion of social rights seems to have led some citizens and groups of citizens to greater or lesser degrees of democratic participation. Marissa Chappell's essay is illuminating in this respect: the poor people's movements that she studies directly link demands for greater generosity in the distribution of public benefits to the creation of grassroots organizations that seek representation in the political sphere. Miriam Abramovitz shows how the state undermines this demand for greater voice by imposing coercive measures that remove even the vote from those who do not play by the rules. The cumulative impact of these measures and the increased incarceration they produce is to undermine the families of the poor, to reduce their capacity to speak, and sometimes to move the tasks of social reproduction from women and their families to the state. Frances Fox Piven focuses on the power of disruptive social movements to influence the democratic process when electoral politics fails or is masked by money. For the marginalized, social movements exert pressure to move the welfare state in directions of fairness.

Strategies for change, and particularly ways of exerting voice, are deeply dependent on the institutional structures created in the golden years, and they are struggling to resituate themselves in a postindustrial environment. As Beatrix Hoffman notes in her exploration of the Affordable Care Act in the United States, "the structure and nature of social programs shape possibilities for citizen action and participation."[20] Gro Hagemann explains that the desire of Norwegian housewives to participate in the labor force and the state's need to maintain a relatively high birth rate together account for the generous social policies offered to households in the postwar period. Sébastian Chauvin's fine-grained examination of temporary workers shows how the distinctions among them explain differences in workforce commitment and the lack of political solidarity among people who seem similarly situated. In his provocative essay, Robert Self turns to the conflict within a racially divided America. He interrogates the interests of late-twentieth-century capitalism to explain the withdrawal of political support for the welfare state. A focus on particular institutions, these authors help us understand, is essential to understanding how ordinary people approach issues of exclusion and inclusion.

Together, the essays in this book explore the interaction between democracy and the social rights and benefits that have characterized much of twentieth-century Europe and the United States. This collection asks what these changes have meant and will continue to mean for social and political cohesion. Separately and together, the essays address the question of how changes in the distribution of wealth and well-being speak to the meaning of citizenship in a post-welfare-state era. They provoke us to ask: Can we imagine the perpetuation of democratic citizenship in this new era of information technology? How will the transformation and reconceptualization of state provision affect present and future conceptions of citizenship and political participation? Will the changing nature of capitalism generate new social and political pressures that forever destroy a commitment to collective responsibility?

NOTES

1. Martin Wolf, "Global Elites Must Heed the Warning of Populist Rage," *Financial Times*, July 19, 2016.
2. Thomas H. Marshall and Tom Bottomore, *Citizenship and Social Class* (London: Pluto, 1987).
3. Sanford Jacoby, *Modern Manors: Welfare Capitalism Since the New Deal* (Princeton, N.J.: Princeton University Press, 1999).
4. Karl de Schweinitz, *England's Road to Social Security: From the Statute of Laborers in 1349 to the Beveridge Report of 1949* (London: Barnes, 1972).
5. Franklin D. Roosevelt, "The Annual Message to the Congress, January 6, 1941," in *The Public Papers and Addresses of Franklin D. Roosevelt*

(New York: Macmillan, 1941), 663–672; Maurizio Vaudagna, "The United States and Social Rights at Home and Abroad: The Rise and Decline of 'Freedom from Want,'" in *The New Deal and the American Welfare State: Essays from a Transatlantic Perspective (1933–1945)* (Torino: Otto, 2014), 317–319; Steve Fraser and Gary Gerstle, *The Rise and Fall of the New Deal Order, 1930–1980* (Princeton, N.J.: Princeton University Press, 1989).

6. Gary Gerstle, *Liberty and Coercion: The Paradox of American Government* (Princeton, N.J.: Princeton University Press, 2016), 275.
7. Ira Katznelson, *Fear Itself: The New Deal and the Origins of Our Time* (New York: Norton, 2013); Mary Poole, *The Segregated Origins of Social Security: African Americans and the Welfare State* (Chapel Hill: University of North Carolina Press, 2006); Alice Kessler-Harris, *In Pursuit of Equity: Women, Men, and the Quest for Economic Citizenship in Twentieth-Century America* (New York: Oxford University Press, 2001).
8. John Kenneth Galbraith, *American Capitalism: The Concept of Countervailing Power* (Boston: Houghton Mifflin, 1952); John Kenneth Galbraith, *The New Industrial State* (Boston: Houghton Mifflin, 1967).
9. Diane Sainsbury, *Gender Equality and Welfare States* (Cambridge: Cambridge University Press, 1996).
10. Thomas Piketty, *Capital in the Twenty-First Century* (Cambridge, Mass.: Belknap Press of Harvard University Press, 2014).
11. Judith Stein, *Pivotal Decade: How the U.S. Traded Factories for Finance in the Seventies* (New Haven, Conn.: Yale University Press, 2011); Jefferson R. Cowie, *Stayin' Alive: The 1970s and the Last Days of the Working Class* (New York: New Press, 2012).
12. Pyong Gap Min, ed., *Mass Migration to the United States: Classical and Contemporary Periods* (Altamira Press, 2002); Mae Ngai, *Impossible Subjects: Illegal Aliens and the Making of Modern America* (Princeton, N.J.: Princeton University Press, 2004).
13. Eduardo Porter, "A Bigger Pie, but Uneven Slices," *New York Times*, December 7, 2016.
14. Milton Friedman, *Capitalism and Freedom* (Chicago: University of Chicago Press, 1962).
15. See Kessler-Harris, *In Pursuit of Equity*, 272–273, for an example of congressional disdain for women who tried to make time to participate under such circumstances.
16. Patricia Cohen, "Research Shows Slim Gains for the Bottom 50 Percent," *New York Times*, December 7, 2016.
17. Eduardo Porter, "The Case for More Government and Higher Taxes," *New York Times*, August 3, 2016.

18. See, for example, the essays in Neil Gilbert and Rebecca A. Van Voorhis, eds., *Changing Patterns of Social Protection* (New Brunswick, N.J.: Transaction, 2006).
19. Along with Gary Gerstle, *Liberty and Coercion*, we do not buy into the strong state/weak state distinction often made between Europe and America. Rather, we see the American struggle to reconcile liberty with the role of the federal government to even the playing field for individuals as central to the American story.
20. Beatrix Hoffman, "Social Citizenship in the U.S. Affordable Care Act," this volume, chap. 6; and see Colin Gordon, *Dead on Arrival: The Politics of Health Care in Twentieth-Century America* (Princeton, N.J.: Princeton University Press, 2003).

CHAPTER ONE

Historians Interpret the Welfare State, 1975–1995

MAURIZIO VAUDAGNA

SOCIAL SCIENTISTS AND HISTORIANS WRITE THE HISTORY OF THE WELFARE STATE

After more than a half-century of modern social policies, World War II ushered in an era that witnessed the marriage of Keynesian economics and social security.[1] The notion of the "welfare state" emerged as a political, social, and economic order where the state played a key role in protecting and promoting the economic and social well-being of its citizens. Its definition fell within two clusters of meaning: on the one hand, the welfare state was a "mixed system" of public/private economic cooperation that fostered a policy of growth and full employment and, on the other, it promised a protective policy of socioeconomic security. As a result, the idea of justice expanded to include new meanings: "social justice" and "social rights" became qualities of democratic citizenship as essential to the individual as civil, personal, and political rights.

After World War II, historicist social scientists initiated and went on to dominate the field of social policy and welfare-state history. For the most part, they interpreted that history with a pronounced presentist vision of the past. Founded by the British public intellectual Richard Titmuss, the social-science approach aimed to explain the links connecting "modernization," liberal democracy, and social provision.[2] The egalitarian wartime social services, Titmuss argued, reflected the sense of solidarity held by families and communities, fed the principle of equal citizenship, and powerfully contributed to the victory of freedom.

Titmuss inaugurated a trend in social scientists' historical explorations of the welfare state that has continued to this day. Endless examples could be cited. For example, since the 1960s the Swedish sociologist Walter Korpi has embraced a neo-Marxist interpretation of the democratic class struggle as the core of the social-democratic welfare state.[3] In 1971, the American economist Gaston Rimlinger published a comprehensive study of the historical traditions that had originated different transatlantic "paths" to social security.[4] Equally comparative was the book published in 1981 by the joint U.S.-German research group led by the sociologists Peter Flora and Arnold J. Heidenheimer.[5] Their interpretation joined the substantial ranks of publications by scholars who thought of the welfare state as a functional necessity of modern liberal capitalism. In particular, Flora and Heidenheimer focused on the social state as "an answer to increasing demands for socioeconomic equality in the context of the evolution of mass democracies."[6]

Until the late 1970s and early 1980s, professional historians of welfare-state development were almost nonexistent. "It takes a yardstick," the American historian Peter Baldwin held in 1992, "to measure the thickness of the glaze that commonly descends over historians' eyes when the topic of the welfare state is broached."[7] Their noninvolvement came to an end as the welfare state became a problem area in the late 1970s and as observers noted that the decades of economic growth and welfare expansion that had followed World War II, along with the "magic" of a growing market economy supported by government spending at a viable rate of inflation, were decisively a thing of the past.

Why had the welfare state morphed from an ever-growing wunderkind in the first three-quarters of the twentieth century, but especially in the postwar *trente glorieuses*, into the alleged source of economic stagnation, as the revitalized free-market neoconservatives were claiming in the 1980s? Baldwin argued that the late interest of historians in the welfare state's past stemmed "from the inevitable delay with which historians respond to topics."[8] Empirical, subjectivist, humanistic—

historians were hardly at ease with comparisons and model-based interpretations. Moreover, since the late 1940s the welfare state, a term that originated in 1930s Britain to distinguish democratic social protection from its totalitarian counterpart, has appeared a given of the European "century of the state." Yet the 1970s and 1980s witnessed the crisis of Keynesianism, the rise of stagflation, the rethinking of economic growth, and a demography that expanded the ranks of the needy while producers shrank in number and influence. The language of welfare expansion was replaced by that of "retrenchment," curtailment, and reform. In the late 1970s, the first signs of welfare decline put social provision at the center of the policy agenda, media reports, and public awareness. As well, European postwar historical scholarship, which had hitherto been permeated by idealistic philosophy and had kept the social sciences at arm's length, was now calling for cooperation and cross-fertilization.[9] At this point, noted historians entered the field of social policy and welfare-state history in both continental Europe and the United States.[10]

British and Scandinavian scholars led the field because of their countries' leadership in European social-security building.[11] The United States lagged behind despite having a long tradition of training specialized historians of welfare and social work. The most prominent of them, Robert Bremner, Roy Lubove, Walter I. Trattner, and Clarke E. Chambers, had started out as historians of poverty, child reform, and urban renovation and had then expanded their interests to include social policies and institutions.[12] All of them shared a strong sense of civic commitment, but the profession saw their field as marginal and distant from the central agenda of the national U.S. history.

HISTORIANS REVISIT THE WELFARE STATE'S PAST: METHODS AND INTERPRETATIONS

The turning point in welfare-state history was one element of the historiographical watershed that took place during the 1980s. It was a paradigm shift that led to an important revival in the study of the American government and the idea of the "century of the state,"[13] leading to interpretations of the United States as a part of international history. The end result was a revolution in terminology and the move away from "welfare before the welfare state," as the British historian David Gladstone has titled his book.[14] American social-policy historians adopted the concept of the "welfare state," which had been conspicuously absent not only from U.S. public conversation but also from its scholarly language. Though apparently a minor verbal shift, moving from "welfare" to "welfare state" in fact signified a major conceptual turning point. The pre-1980s welfare and social-work historiography had identified welfare with social assistance to the needy and social work with the "professional altruist," as the historian Roy Lubove had titled his 1965 study of social work as a career.[15] The American notion of "welfare" looked like the British idea of the "social-service state," which provided, as the Italian sociologist Chiara Saraceno argues, "a limited series of services to a small, circumscribed sector of the citizenry that is the poorest."[16] But the "Keynesian full-employment welfare state" was radically different: it indicated a social and political formation, a "mixed system," one that since the late-nineteenth century had increasingly characterized, if to different degrees, all industrialized countries. Its core meaning was that the state assumed the responsibility of "decommodifying" at least some areas of the supposedly "natural" working of the market to provide many of its (male) citizens with an appropriate degree of economic and social dignity. Governments were to protect workers against the main economic risks of modern urban-industrial life, like old age, invalidity, illness, and unemployment, while at the same time engaging in a "politics of growth" that through public spending and business incentives would guarantee high levels of employment opportunities. In a nutshell, the welfare state did not refer mainly to "the poor" but to the "rights of citizenship," and it was not concerned with "minimums" but with "adequate" public performances in terms of relative equality, redistribution, and quality of life. The new understanding of the welfare state allowed a new generation of U.S. welfare historians to frame fresh interpretations of the American social provision.[17]

In Europe, historians' new commitment derived primarily from events that "propelled the complex labeled 'the welfare state,'" as Flora and Heidenheimer put it, "away from the role of an auxiliary mechanism, into the institutional core of western societies."[18] Generalist historians came finally to consider the social provision's past as an essential component of national and international histories, instead of as only a peripheral question that pertained to industrial relations, the socialist challenge, and the problem of poverty. As a consequence, the Europeanist historian Tony Judt, who never wrote a welfare-state history proper, is considered one of the main interpreters of its pivotal role in modern European history.[19]

The new historians innovated both the methods and interpretations of social-welfare history and depicted anew the historical interactions of liberal democracy and the social provision.

Historians critiqued social-science history for sacrificing particularity, contextualization, and agency on the altar of regularity. James T. Patterson, for example, has faulted social scientists for "letting overarching interpretations take the place of historical research into the particular circumstances and ideas that have decidedly affected the development of social welfare."[20] Social scientists retorted in a similar mode: In 1984, the culturalist John Baxendale criticized the British feminist historian Pat Thane's *The Foundations of the Welfare State* because "pragmatist history . . . only gives the visible part of the story," while "the author had adopted no theoretical position or analytical strategy."[21] While most social-science historicists have now abandoned single-factor theories, a different analytical style persists nonetheless: social scientists look for the theoretical and the model-oriented, while historians are more interested in the empirical, in case studies, and in the multiplicities of human and intellectual agencies. The welfare historian Michael D. Katz has argued: "I . . . aim for middle-level generalizations rather than the more embracing theoretical explanations that influence many of the new histories of welfare."[22] It goes without saying that historical narratives rely on conceptual frameworks as well as the cherry-picking of events, but their interest in the specifics of past occurrences and in the contradictions of human agents make those narrations more flexible, comprehensive, and in the end more convincing as "precedent," "lesson," or "laboratory," even when historians write them with deliberate presentist aims.

Historians have rejected the notion of the welfare state's functional necessity to twentieth-century modern capitalism because, in Parsonsian terms, it would have "augmented, usurped, and made consonant with modernity many functions previously performed by the family, the church, the guild, and the local community."[23] A number of national studies have weakened the idea of a more or less cohesive "European social model" and emphasized instead different "national paths."[24] Historians have stressed that different goals and forces have given rise to modern social protection. They cite the desire of different actors to contain class struggle, stabilize the labor force, help "weak" workers, or provide for the multitudes of the industrial poor. Differences in origins have also encouraged these historians to examine varieties in welfare-state generosity, coverage, and redistributive potential. In most European cases, as in the pathbreaking social-insurance program in 1880s Bismarckian Germany, the original client of the initial social provision was the male, industrial laborer; most agricultural, domestic, or white-collar workers were only included after World War I, often at the cost of abandoning other redistributive goals. Women were either excluded or treated as "dependents" of their husbands and fathers. Other exclusions were due to ethnic and racial discrimination: notably, U.S. African Americans were mostly left out of America's "incomplete" social protection until after World War II.[25]

Historians have placed modern democracy, with its alleged qualities of freedom, equality, and justice, at the center of their investigations and have downplayed the celebratory depictions that social scientists had developed in the 1970s. Historical interpretations have expanded the social scientists' periodization, which held that the dawn of the modern welfare state coincided with World War II and the victory of democracy. Historians have instead situated social policy "laws and practices," Peter Baldwin has argued, "in the context of a much more extensive *long durée*, showing the way in which the welfare state represents a fundamental reorientation of social relations."[26] Moreover, situating the welfare state's origins in the 1880s allows for a more nuanced view of the long competition in social measures among liberal democracy, the authoritarian monarchy, fascism, and communism.[27]

The relationship between individual liberty and social protection has been ambiguous since the Middle Ages. The liberty of the individual has often been a precondition for the enjoyment of social protection, but, even more often, benefits have been conditioned on the imposition of severe limitations on personal freedom. The "welfare client" of the more distant past was not really a citizen and often lost his or her individual liberty and franchise in exchange for a modicum of protection. This tension has also been true of the twentieth century. The fear of government's inroads into personal liberty has generated, the historian Linda Gordon has argued, "the contrasting tradition of suspicion of the controlling power the state gains in the very act of assuming that responsibility [for people's welfare]."[28] According to the antistatist, conservative opinion of the welfare-state scholar Stephen Pimpare, controls became more intrusive as social protection was increasingly publicized and federalized, and "an applicant had little power indeed, and was made a supplicant, forced by the state into a subordinate passive role."[29]

In the case of the "Old World," if the welfare state has often been considered a "crowning originality" of twentieth-century Europe, then its expansion has been inextricably entwined with the "tragedy" of war, racism, and dictatorship that characterized Europe in the first half of the century. Until World War II, liberal democracies often lagged behind dictatorships in their willingness to provide social protection, and many New Deal reformers feared that welfare expansion required a degree of public coercion. Concern was not out of place: many international observers believed that increasing social protection was the order of the day, while political and civil rights remained secondary national variables. Not only Italian but also American commentators admiringly drew close parallels between fascist corporatism and the "first" New Deal. In reaction, Depression-era Britain coined the term "welfare state" to distinguish the democratic social provision from its totalitarian counterparts. In 1941, Franklin D. Roosevelt rationalized the worldwide problem of want in the language of freedom, and in his noted 1942 *Report* the British advocate William H. Beveridge went out of his way to show that universalist social rights were coherent with democratic liberties. In liberal countries, the expansion of social provision ignited a passionate transatlantic debate on the concepts of "negative" and "positive" freedom, the former excluding government from individual discretion, the latter stressing active state support for an individual's life projects. Only under the aegis of positive freedom could the interventionist state be fully inserted into the tradition of liberal constitutionalism.[30]

Throughout modernity, the growth of public social protection has been inextricably tied to periods and concepts of "emergency." Alleged exceptional conditions of life-threatening danger, unrest, or destitution often persuaded governments to suspend democratic liberties and call for exceptional national cohesion, and these exceptions and emergencies allowed them an unprecedented amount of hands-on interventionism, which would have been unacceptable in "normal" times.[31]

The gravest emergency has been war, especially the shock of World War II. As the historian Ike Burson notes of the United States, "over the course of U.S. history, significant new welfare policies and programs have been created during periods of major armed conflicts."[32] His comment might be extended to the whole of the industrialized world. In 1998, the Danish-American historian Jytte Klausen emphasized this link in her "from warfare to welfare" interpretation, arguing that "the expansion of the state that accompanied war mobilization and economic shortages between 1939 and 1945 was critical to the creation of the postwar welfare state."[33] In turn, the German historian Martin H. Geyer retraced the wartime ideological battle between Nazi and Allied social-protection plans. In mid-1940, the Reich's economic minister, Walther Funk, made public his *Grosswirtschaftsraum* (Greater Economic Sphere) plan. German war aims were to be seen as not "imperialistic but social," and a few months later Deutsche Arbeitsfront (DAF), the Nazi workers' front, publicized the universalist blueprint of "the social provision for the German people." Its benefits depended on people performing their "duties and obligations" to the national community, as opposed to the liberal notion of social rights. John Maynard Keynes said ironically of it that "about three-quarters of the passage quoted from the German broadcast would be quite excellent if the name Great Britain were substituted for Germany or the Axis,"[34] a sign of how deeply intertwined liberal and authoritarian social policy projects still were at the time.[35]

But war and its deadly technology were also a tragic equalizer. Shared dangers reduced class differences, linked people in joint solidarities, and allowed for formerly unthinkable equalities. The most notable statement of the modern "universalist social-security state," the Allied answer to Nazi social promises, and the origin of the late 1940s British welfare state—that is, the *Beveridge Report*—was published in late 1942 in the wake of the Luftwaffe's mass bombing campaign, and it promised postwar Britons extensive, egalitarian social rights. War leaders ceased to promise their peoples national aggrandizement and instead offered postwar social and personal security and prosperity. Anglo-American New Dealers and Lib-Labbers in occupied Germany and Italy helped form the new cadres of a "democratic welfare" based on the notion of citizenship and social rights outlined by the United Nations. It made up no small part of the reeducation of formerly fascist nations in their transition to liberal democracy.

"Emergency" as a cause of welfare expansion could also mean social and economic disruption, as was the case of the German Weimar Republic, the French Popular Front, and the American New Deal. In the case of the Depression-era United States, the link between emergency, welfare building, and democratic liberties was very tight. New Deal legal reformers frequently made use of the notion of an "emergency" to justify legislation that otherwise rested on shaky constitutional ground. Even in Sweden a fundamental motivating force in building its comprehensive welfare state originated not only in the "emergency" of the Depression but also in the outbreak of radicalized industrial conflict that had followed World War I, at the time the most intense in Europe.

HISTORICAL SOCIAL SCIENTISTS AND NEW INTERPRETATIONS OF THE WELFARE STATE

In the 1970s, the political scientist Frances Fox Piven and the public intellectual Richard A. Cloward published an enormously influential pair of books that revisited the U.S. experience of the welfare state.[36] Emphasizing that "policies make people," Piven and Cloward held that social control and "capitalists' insurance" were welfare's main purpose and that social benefits would "regulate the poor" and feed their submission. Only if their social cohorts launched protest movements of their own would welfare change its meaning. As Gordon has argued, Piven and Cloward "virtually defined the way that radicals thought about welfare policy and welfare rights movements since the 1960s."[37]

In 1990, the Danish sociologist Gøsta Esping-Andersen articulated a new, pivotal interpretation of the main "paths" of the modern welfare state.[38] Merging historical and structural factors, Esping-Andersen argued that there were three regimes of transatlantic welfare capitalism: a liberal one, mainly embodied by the United States and Australia, where the market principle remained prevalent and social benefits minimal; a statist-corporatist version, mainly represented by Germany, Austria, and Italy, where the government's hands-on attitude went together with professional, trade, and craft identities to define who was entitled; and finally a universalist, social-democratic path, which was particularly Swedish and was informed by an egalitarian, redistributive ethos, drawing needed welfare funds from general tax revenues.

These books stressed the relevance of the U.S.-European comparison in social-state history studies. In the American case, the historians generally often discussed whether the United States was a welfare "latecomer" vis-à-vis the allegedly more advanced "European social model." The historian Daniel Levine argued that between 1880 and 1920 many European countries had already adopted unemployment insurance and universal assistance programs, while in America, because of the fragmentation of America's political institutions, it fell to the states to approve mothers' pensions and workmen's compensation laws.[39] The progressive historian Michael B. Katz held that, in contrast to the European "mature" social-security regime, the United States had instead developed a "semi welfare state" because of the divisions separating public assistance and social insurance, local variation, public projects being entrusted to private agents, and the lack of a national health-care service.[40]

In 1998, the transatlantic historian Daniel Rodgers published a prominent example of *"histoire croisée,"* which confirmed the "latecomer" interpretation.[41] Rodgers recognized the validity of "European primacy" as he reconstructed the endless flow of American thinkers, decision makers, journalists, and policy planners who, from the Progressive Era through the New Deal, visited, studied, and learned from Europe at a time when the provision of welfare was at the core of the U.S. reform agenda. Europe, Americans of the time believed, was the place where new measures of welfare-state expansion were first tried.

The most important exception to this argument was the period between the 1930s and the early 1950s. The sociologists Margaret Weir and Theda Skocpol have argued that "among the countries that avoided the breakdown of democratic institutions, Sweden and the United States were the sites of the boldest answers to the crisis by reformist political leaderships."[42] The New Deal and social-democratic Scandinavia framed the liberal answer to fascist and communist social policies and to their criticism that a liberal hands-off policy in welfare protection was a cruel class legacy of the "stupid nineteenth century." For some years, the United States took the lead in conceiving and expanding the democratic welfare state, from the New Deal's "radical moment" season of 1935–1936, Roosevelt's "Four Freedoms Address" of January 1941, and the Atlantic Charter in August of the same year to the United Nations Declaration of Human Rights of 1948 proclaimed by Eleanor Roosevelt.[43]

FEMINIST HISTORIANS, GENDER, AND WELFARE-STATE HISTORY

In the 1980s and early 1990s, European and American welfare-state history registered another, even more radical reinterpretation, this time developed by feminist historians exploring women's history. A transatlantic group of female historians started writing on women's wage labor, women's poverty, women in the family, and women and children and contributed to both the expanding field of women's history and to the history of the welfare state.[44]

Feminist scholars shared the goal of recovering women's lives from the obscurity to which androcentric history had committed them, and they acknowledged women's agency in their quest for self-realization. Widespread "gendered imaginations," to borrow Alice Kessler-Harris's phrase, that is, the deep-rooted belief of the appropriate place of men and women in society, portrayed women as "dependents" and justified those in authority in denying women the full privileges of citizenship.[45] In spite of these historians' different research backgrounds and interests, whether it was about women's jobholding, children, families, poverty, participation, or the "work-family dilemma," all of these scholars explored public and private social services, government regulation, and cash transfers. All considered the measures and institutions that fall under the rubric of "social provision." Their scholarly agendas were therefore bound to focus on welfare-state history.

By the early 1990s, other relevant contexts encouraged these historians to study the welfare state. Sexist social provisioning reinforced the public and private power structure of the patriarchal order. Feminists criticized progressive historians of social security for failing to consider women as autonomous actors and continuing instead to treat them as dependents on the "family wage" their fathers and husbands supposedly earned. At the same time, feminist-historicist social scientists were crucial in helping dismantle the conceptual framework of traditional interpretations of the welfare state. In her early historical books, the British sociologist Jane Lewis dealt with androcentric definitions of motherly and child welfare, which complicated the relationship between women's caring regimes and outside paid work in England. Moreover, the rise of social and medical professionalism delegitimized feminine discretion in planning family life to the point that women in specialized jobs often helped strengthen the patriarchal regime whose premises they had deeply internalized.[46]

More fundamentally, the adoption of the concept of "gender," first launched in the 1970s by Gayle Rubin and popularized after 1986 by Joan Scott, transformed the feminist historians' conceptual toolbox. Gender, in the historian Eileen Boris's definition, is "an identity experienced by individuals . . . a discursive system that expresses relations of power through definitions of sexual identity and practice. . . . It permeates society, modes of thought, economic life, and political praxis."[47]

Far from diluting women's history, gender became the guiding framework within which to comprehend how men and women functioned in relation to one another. It enabled historians to revisit the welfare state and ask how it had structured and internalized notions of masculinity and femininity. The gender lens went beyond the critique of women's dependency to explore the structural foundations of the social state.

Feminist historians' reassessment of social provision moved in different directions. In the first place, "the feminist consideration of the welfare state," as Gordon emphasized in 1990, stood "in a complex dialogue with the older scholarship: bewildered and critical because of its inexcusable neglect of women and gender, sharing the general perspective of support for state responsibility for the public welfare."[48] As the political philosopher Nancy Fraser argued, "early second-wave feminists sought less to dismantle the welfare state than to transform it into a force that could help to overcome male domination."[49] For example, the "Age of Roosevelt," which earlier interpretations had reduced to a "halfway revolution," became in the hands of these historians a radical moment in U.S. history. Gordon stressed that the New Deal and the Social Security Act in particular constituted "the central legislation of the U.S. welfare state" and called the New Deal expansion of the federal government the "third American revolution."[50] As a consequence, Berkowitz concluded, "historians working on women's history and American state development have converged on the question of the welfare state."[51]

For the most part, however, feminist historians advanced an array of critiques of modern social provision. Some of them might be placed under the rubric of "compensatory history," through which "the majority finds its past," as Gerda Lerner titled her influential 1979 book against the identification of humanity with masculinity.[52] Traditional welfare historians mainly considered women as beneficiaries of public services and transfers, either as "dependents" or as the mothers and widows of citizens. They saw women as belonging "naturally" to a domestic sphere of house chores and child rearing. Since social scientists grounded traditional definitions of citizenship in the "independence" made possible by property, or military service, or wage work, woman's "dependence" amounted to denying her citizenship.[53] For example, historians linked early-twentieth-century transatlantic social-welfare concerns with "maternalism." That concept reserved benefits to women who conformed to the Victorian model of the "'social,' 'spiritual,' or the 'domestic American' motherhood."[54] A maternalist benefit structure excluded many women from entitlements based on marital status, race, ethnicity, and even profession or trade. Far from creating "independent" citizens, women were treated as dependent non-citizens. In the end, the emerging welfare state had "enforced traditional gender roles in an often intrusive and impersonal way."[55]

Feminist welfare historians also focused on agency and contestation, showing how women had proven themselves influential framers of the ideas and politics of international social provision. Their place in and their attitude toward the state became all-important. In the United Kingdom, said the historian Pat Thane, "welfare provision has . . . to a great extent been administered, and welfare policies to some degree made, by women, voluntary and paid, trained and untrained, though they have been most prominent at the lower level."[56] In the same vein, in the U.S. women's settlement houses, religious associations, social clubs, and public leagues there developed a feminine political culture that preceded the franchise, emphasized social reform, and framed a vision of social fairness. When in the late-nineteenth century "social-justice reformers" lost confidence in private, local means and entered the national arena, they envisioned a "mother state" different from the patriarchal "Minotaur state" pursued by contemporary male reformers. As the feminist historian Sara M. Evans has emphasized, while female "social-justice reformers" could not on their own bring about the welfare state, they laid "the groundwork for what was to be called in the 1930s the 'welfare state,'" which in many ways resulted in what could be called a "women's New Deal."[57] Women were "key players" in debates over social and labor legislation. "They may have played a greater role in the United States than elsewhere," Alice Kessler-Harris argues, "because in the early twentieth century a relatively weak American state encouraged the growth of powerful women's organizations with important political clout."[58] In a comparative vein, the historian Katherine Kish Sklar has observed, on the one hand, a link between centralized states and weak women's movements and, on the other, the presence of strong movements and decentralized governments. The end result, however, was nevertheless paradoxical, considering that women and children were often better protected in countries with developed statist social provisions, even if women's movements in those societies were rather marginal.[59] That was the case in Britain, which, since the 1840s, had enacted gender-neutral, government-sponsored, protective legislation. Even more paradoxical was the case of France, where both unions and women's movements were very weak, and an alliance of conservatives, social Catholics, paternalist employers, and nationalist pronatalists enacted in the interwar years a network of family allowances that, in Susan Pedersen's opinion, "has proven much more effective in safeguarding a decent standard of living than has the British pursuit of the elusive family wage."[60] Miriam Cohen and Michael Hanagan argued that "in the case of all reforms, the United States put the greatest emphasis on welfare politics as gender politics, because of a lack of a tradition of universal entitlement and because of constitutional limitations on the power of the state to interfere with the rights of families and of individuals."[61] In contrast to the British sociologist Thomas Marshall's famous tripartite distinction of democratic citizens' rights, women had made a claim to social rights before the vote, or, as Bock and Thane argued, "women were ... struggling not only for political rights, but also for social rights." It was often the experience of women's voluntary work among the poor that convinced them to demand the vote. Only the state had enough resources to deal with poverty, and accessing those resources required political rights.[62]

Linda Gordon concluded that for most of the history of the welfare state, "men as well as women [have] conceived of the welfare state as female."[63] The consequences of this gendering were in some ways counterproductive to the fight against inequality: "feminist social reformers" often internalized the patriarchal order and contributed to a social policy that "modernized gender inequality by politicizing and codifying social roles and relations."[64] The political scientist Mimi Abramovitz has held that the welfare state "replaced patriarchal control of women in the home with a more diffuse control of women in the male-dominated state."[65]

In feminist-historical thought, "the critique of discrimination quickly developed into a structural critique of welfare."[66] The object of this criticism was not only women's exclusion from the welfare state but the very core features of the social provision, which were deeply embedded within a set of androcentric concepts. The aim of this line of critical inquiry was, therefore, to reformulate the very foundations of the social state.

In Europe, issues of war and peace, as well as demographic decline and child mortality, loomed large among the women social reformers, who made more progress under liberal regimes during a period when dictatorships reinvigorated masculinist principles and hierarchies. In the United States, the "bifurcated, two-streams" nature of American welfare was a pivotal structural problem thematized by feminist criticism. Liberal and radical historians had already emphasized the unfairness of "two-tier" social provision: on the one hand, a more generous set of contributory insurance programs and, on the other, stingy, biased, intrusive assistance for the poor.[67] The introduction of gender as a conceptual lens has offered new insights into the bifurcated system of social provision, which was originally partitioned into a "male stream" and a less generous "female stream" of welfare assistance. The male stream was conceived as an entitlement and government obligation, while the female stream was subject to means testing, moral prescriptions, and discretionary eligibility. Eligibility for the Aid to Dependent Children program subjected mothers to a proof of moral fitness and provided allowances not for them but only for their children. In the end, according to the sociologist Gwendolyn Mink, the New Deal emerged as the main modernizer and publicizer of the patriarchal hierarchy.[68]

The feminist critique of "progressive" social provision was bound to innovate radically what Fraser has called "the social-democratic imaginary" along the lines of "national cross-class solidarity," "more or less extensive welfare states," and "class redistribution." But "this historic class compromise," Fraser has added, "rested on a series of gender and racial-ethnic exclusions."[69] The link of class and gender in welfare-state history became more complex when issues of race and ethnicity also came to the fore. Discrimination was a defining feature of so-called American racially structured patriarchal capitalism. Some feminist scholars emphasized shared cross-racial goals: "women reformers—middle and working class, white and black . . . contributed to the development of the welfare state," argued Abramovitz: "middle class women of both races fought for protective labor laws, mothers' pensions, maternal and child health programs, and against child labor and low living standards."[70]

But the racialized structure of American life prevented an easy solidarity. The historian of black women's work Jacqueline Jones denounced white feminist historians' lack of attention to agricultural and domestic labor, the only work available to most black women throughout much of American history. Jones criticized the tendency of many white feminist historians to apply to African Americans conceptual categories that failed to take racism into account.[71] The historical narration of women's dependence on a male "family wage" did not work for black Americans. For a long time, racist policy makers saw to it that if any public programs for African American families existed, they were segregated. Black men were often excluded from social benefits because they lacked the stabilized, union jobs the New Deal social legislation was most committed to supporting. In contrast to the bourgeois single-earner family ideal, poverty and discrimination pushed many black and minority women into menial, underpaid jobs, which meant that the nature of their needs for support services differed from those of white "maternalists." Black mothers insisted on childcare facilities and other work-facilitating measures, while white women's welfare proposals were often racist, and their associations often barred black women. Excluded from state welfare, black women often had to rely on private institutions like churches, clubs, and leagues. As Gordon put it, "the white women's welfarist activity played a role in maintaining, even reinforcing, class and race exclusions." Maternalists made aid to minority women highly conditional, demanding they avoid paid jobs and insisting they drop their cultural traits to conform to a white, universal, maternal ideal.[72] In the end, however, this utterly marginalized condition activated a number of black women welfare activists. Their action is an early example of the kind of recipients' mobilization where social and civil-rights reform largely coincided.

The British social historian Sheila Blackburn summed up the achievement of historians of gender when she wrote that "in the past twenty years, feminists have accomplished a much needed re-appraisal of the development of social policy."[73] With the feminist contribution, the interpretation of the historical welfare state will never be the same, and the limitations and biases of the welfare state are now much more clearly visible than before. Historians of gender and feminists have reinvented the concept of social justice, which the social-democratic imagination had interpreted in terms of economic fairness, growth, relative egalitarianism, and national solidarity via cross-class cooperation. Henceforth, the welfare state would need to address issues of gender and racial justice.[74]

Thanks to the very close cooperation between feminist historians and social scientists, the distance that had characterized earlier schools of welfare history rapidly diminished. Two important collections of essays published in the United States in 1990 and in Europe in 1991, both including feminist historians and historicist social scientists among their authors, signified the transatlantic coming of age of women's history and the welfare state as a mature historiographical issue. Differences persisted, with historians stressing empirical case studies and social scientists arguing over conceptual frameworks. Nevertheless, shared emancipationist ideals, the feminist social scientists' interest in the past as laboratory, and the historians' attention to the social scientists' conceptual networks engendered an intense cross-fertilization, along with numerous joint research undertakings.[75]

How could historical interpretations contribute to women's emancipation and the transgressive potential of second-wave feminism? "Some thought," Kessler-Harris has argued, "that capitalist patriarchy could be changed through changes in the family.... Others thought that the only way to fight for equality, and for women's liberation ... was by granting women access to wage work that would yield both dignity and independence to women, neither of which they could find in a family still largely governed by male incomes and male structures."[76]

On the one hand, family-centered "maternalism" stressed women's difference as mothers, while on the other hand, activists for women's rights argued that liberation was to come via economic fairness, which meant women winning their independence through access to dignified wage work. Both visions encompassed "historical movement, historiographical or analytical approaches, or contemporary political strategy."[77]

In many countries, the legitimation of nascent social provision began with protections for "special" workers subjected to harsh labor conditions, such as miners or sailors, or for "weak" subjects, such as war widows, mothers, and children. All these categories of people "deserved" labor protection. Mothers had other merits as well: they had traditionally acted as domestic "social workers" for children, the aged, and the sick, and so emerging social security could be interpreted as the publicizing of women's familial care work. Furthermore, "mother-citizens"[78] were worthy of the general gratitude of the nation because, as the Norwegian historian Gro Hagemann put it, "women manage . . . the human material which is decisive for the future of our country."[79] Motherhood merited, therefore, an exception to the individualist principle of self-help, and "mothers' aid" emerged as a defining feature of fledgling American social provision. According to the historian Sonya Michel, "maternalism" was a set of "ideologies that exalted women's capacity to mother and extended to society as a whole the values they attached to that role: care, nurturance and morality."[80] The distinguished sociologist Theda Skocpol has placed issues of defense, nation, and family at the center of her analysis and has argued that maternalism empowered women.[81] Her interpretation also contributed to the "latecomer" debate. Skocpol held that soldiers' and widows' pensions together with mothers' aid represented the defining, early maternalist U.S. policies that addressed social security and income support. As the reviewer Nancy Folbre has argued: "She uses these examples to argue that the United States, far from laggard, was actually a pioneer in the development of social-welfare policies for mothers and the elderly."[82]

While many welfare historians accepted maternalism at the turn of the twentieth century as a pivotal moment in women's history and the history of social services, some of them, including Judith Sklar and Sonya Michel, argued that the relevance of maternal virtues could be considered as avenues of women's liberation and social reform to be "recognized" by present-day American society as a whole. Their opinion ignited an intense controversy.[83] "The economic barrier," Hagemann has argued, "has been among the most difficult for women to surmount."[84] In Europe, women affiliated to socialist parties rarely privileged their motherly difference. In Britain, Labour Party housewives thought of themselves as "workers in the home," and the women's section of the party was nicknamed "the housewives' trade union." Often their hope was that women and men would converge in the search for social justice, and they tried to frame concepts that would stress equality but avoid sameness, for example, "equality in difference." References to paid industrial work were uninterrupted: in 1908 Sweden, an article stressing that childbearing, childcare, and upbringing were to be considered work as much as paid factory employment created a national fury, and three years earlier, in 1905, the Swedish social-democratic women's leaders Emma Danielsson and Anna Sterky stressed that "a man who abandoned a woman carrying his child could be compared to a strike-breaker who had turned on his mates."[85] A number of present-day transatlantic feminists objected to such maternalist rhetoric, which conflated women with motherhood and equalized women and children in the labor market. John Stuart Mill had already said as much in his 1869 survey of the feminine condition.[86] Maternalists, stressed Eileen Boris, "tended to ignore the special needs mothers might have as workers."[87] Protective labor legislation, which defined women as "weak workers," on the one hand sheltered them from extreme exploitation and long hours and, on the other hand, legitimized wage differentials, barriers to skilled jobs, and career ceilings. American maternalists had supported mothers' pensions and pure milk stations but opposed programs that facilitated women's access to wage work, public childcare, or equal treatment on the job.

Alice Kessler-Harris has given the subject in-depth attention. She argues that women's public participation depends on their achieving economic independence and "full economic citizenship." Since her pathbreaking 1982 book on women wage workers, Kessler-Harris has pointed out that throughout U.S. history the notions of work and of holding a paid job have been the leading principles of full citizenship and political participation. Only the dismantling of the "gendered imagination" that ties men to wage labor and women to domesticity will allow women to achieve the full rights of citizenship. "The idea that some people (generally women)," Kessler-Harris has argued, "would gain benefits by virtue of their family positions and that others (mainly men) would do so by virtue of their paid employment marks the commitment of the United States to its version of the welfare state."[88] In the United States, the "right to work" has been the outstanding prerogative of socioeconomic citizenship and the precondition to full political equality.

Vis-à-vis this goal, social protection has played the ambiguous role of sometimes fostering and sometimes slowing down the cause of economic independence and women's liberation:

> Because it is predicated on the economic independence of every individual, economic citizenship can be restricted as well as enhanced by social citizenship. Indeed the two are often at odds. For example, policies that enhance motherhood may offer social rights while closing paths to economic citizenship. This happened in the United

States when mothers' allowances, pension rights for widowed housewives, and stipends from the program of Aid to Dependent Children required female parents to restrict their access to the labor market or suffer a loss of benefits. . . . At the same time economic citizenship requires a range of gender-encompassing social rights, including most especially a fully integrated labor market that permits, but does not assume, domesticity for either sex.[89]

Feminist historians have embraced the healthy dialectic between past and present. The early Norwegian feminist historian Ida Blom, whose University of Bergen opened the first European center of women's studies in the humanities in 1985, recalled that the 1972 fight to prevent Norway from entering the European Union, where no women occupied a decision-making position, sparked her interest in women's issues.[90] As a consequence, feminist historians have looked at the welfare state through the lens of women's emancipation. To understand best the scope of their innovation, one need only compare their interpretation to that of traditional progressive welfare scholars. One could describe it as a "battle on the left." In 1996, the left-liberal Michael Katz argued that, if he were to rewrite his noted 1986 *In the Shadow of the Poorhouse*, he "would pay a great deal more attention to the role of gender."[91] The maturing of this interpretative divide was famously revealed when in 1988 Gordon criticized the by-then classic analysis of the American social provision by the socialist scholars Piven and Cloward and argued that "the nature and functions of the welfare state cannot be adequately explained without an analysis of the sexual division of labor, and the dynamics of relations between the sexes."[92]

The writing of the history of the welfare state has come a long way since historians' interest in the subject came of age in the early 1980s. In the United States, the publication in 2005 of the *Encyclopedia of Social Welfare History in North America* signaled the maturity and significance of these studies.[93]

Issues of justice, democracy, and participation have frequently inspired historical innovation. New debates about the meaning of these issues in the past revealed both nuances and limits of the twentieth-century social state that had earlier gone undetected. The end result is that the rather triumphant assessment of the welfare state that historical-social scientists framed in the 1970s has been critically revisited in terms of universality and generosity, inclusions and exclusions, and redistribution, as well as the possibility of personal liberty, independence, and participation and their connection to justice and liberal democracy.

In recent years, new issues have been developing in the writing of welfare-state history. For example, the present-day astounding global migrations have led to a renewed interest in the history of social provision and human rights. In response to the dramatic movements of people across the borders of nation-states, researchers have begun to take more seriously the criticism of the implications of social and economic benefits based on citizenship in a nation-state. While recent demographic trends have made this a pressing concern, it is nonetheless an old issue. Recent research on the Free City of Trieste in northeastern Italy at the end of World War II—when the city became a major crossroads for refugees and migrants—has revealed that a state of emergency in meeting the bare essentials of human necessity may make the concept of citizenship useless. As the historian Gloria Nemec has argued, "the endless proliferation of needs might become the precondition for an endless proliferation of rights."[94] The great population transfers in the wake of World War II in Europe and elsewhere, and the vital needs these "new poor" cried out for, helped formulate the social rights included in the 1948 UN Universal Declaration of Human Rights in a non-national, humanitarian language.

There is, however, a core of meaning around which the entire history of the democratic welfare state has revolved, the one that Franklin D. Roosevelt summarized in his "Four Freedoms Address": all the liberties Roosevelt named were in fact interdependent, indivisible, and necessary to ensure a dignified material existence for all, a comprehensive participatory citizenship, and a vibrant democracy. Many contesting movements, groups, and individuals have tried in the last half-century to expand the welfare state to include hitherto excluded subjects and to count on the welfare state as a force of democratization and participation. It is a goal that, together with redistribution, has become more and more important in the making of present-day social policy. The core criterion by which to assess the success or failure of the welfare state remains the same: its impact on democracy, citizenship, and justice. The political scientist Christian Lammert has shown in this book that welfare retrenchment and social provision are in danger of being reduced to a minimalist "safety net," a result that would stifle participatory democracy.

Today, the public and scholarly debate as to what comes next revolves around a "postwelfare society," or a "new welfarism."[95] How can historians and social scientists continue to develop their questions in a way that can help clarify the social requisites of a just, vital democracy and a universal citizenship based on human rights? In the past, the welfare state often proved intrusive, illiberal, and exclusionary. Nevertheless, the ideal of human freedom also made up a part of the original inspiration of the democratic welfare state. Chiara Saraceno has summarized the issue in the following terms:

> Institutions, cultural models, established interests, and forms of legitimization, which have been framed by specific historical arrangements, are the foundations upon which present-day welfare regimes meet the problems that arise from the changes occurring in the three foundational areas of explicit or implicit cross-gender, cross-generational, and cross-category compromises, that is, the demographic balance, the family and marriage stability, and its solidaristic bases through time.[96]

In particular, the historians' predilection for context may prove of immense value in connecting welfare-state studies with the larger picture, especially at a time when scholarly analysis often concentrates only on the inner workings of the welfare state. Reinterpretations of the history of the welfare state show that scholarly debate remains crucial if we are to solve the difficult problems that today endanger ideals of distributional justice and universal democratic participation.

NOTES

1. Edward D. Berkowitz, "How to Think About the Welfare State," *Labor History* 32, no. 4 (Fall 1991): 497.
2. Richard M. Titmuss, *Problems of Social Policy*, in *History of the Second World War*, United Kingdom Civil Series, ed. W. K. Hancock (London: His Majesty's Stationary Office, 1950). This was his main historical work and was part of the huge official British history of World War II.

3. Walter Korpi, *The Working Class in Welfare Capitalism: Work, Unions, and Politics in Sweden* (London: Routledge, 1963).
4. Gaston V. Rimlinger, *Welfare Policy and Industrialization in Europe, America, and Russia* (New York: Wiley, 1971).
5. Peter Flora and Arnold J. Heidenheimer, *Developments of Welfare States in Europe and America* (New Brunswick, N.J.: Transaction, 1981).
6. Ibid., 8. For an equally comprehensive history of the welfare state published in 1982 by a distinguished German sociologist, see Jens Alber, *Vom Armenhaus zum Wohlfahrtsstaat: Analysen zur Entwicklung der Sozialversicherung in Westeuropa* (Frankfurt: Campus, 1982).
7. Peter Baldwin, "The Welfare State for Historians: A Review Article," *Comparative Studies in Society and History* 34, no. 4 (October 1992): 695.
8. Ibid., 696.
9. On the uses of history in social-science studies of public welfare, see Bruce S. Jansson, *The Reluctant Welfare State: Engaging History to Advance Social Work: Practice in Contemporary Society* (Belmont, Calif.: Bruce/Cole Cengage Learning, 2009).
10. Asa Briggs, *The Social History of England* (New York: Viking, 1983); Henri Hatzfeld, *Du pauperisme à la securité sociale. Essai sur le origines de la securité sociale en France, 1850–1940* (Paris: Armand Colin, 1971); Arnaldo Cherubini, *Storia della previdenza sociale in Italia, 1860–1960* (Roma: Editori Riuniti, 1977); Jose Harris, *Unemployment Politics: A Study in English Social Policy, 1886–1914* (Oxford: Clarendon, 1972); Pat Thane, ed., *The Origins of British Social Policy* (London: Croom Helm, 1978); Pat Thane, *The Foundations of the Welfare State: Social Policy in Modern Britain* (London: Longmans, 1982); Michael B. Katz, *In the Shadow of the Poorhouse: A Social History of Welfare in America* (New York: Basic Books, 1986); James T. Patterson, *America's Struggle Against Poverty* (Cambridge, Mass.: Harvard University Press, 1981); Daniel Levine, *Poverty and Society: The Growth of the American Welfare State in International Comparison* (New Brunswick, N.J.: Rutgers University Press, 1988); Peter Baldwin, *The Politics of Social Solidarity: Class Bases of the European Welfare State, 1875–1975* (Cambridge: Cambridge University Press, 1990); Wolfgang J. Mommsen in collaboration with Wolgang Mock, *The Emergence of the Welfare State in Britain and Germany, 1850–1950* (London: Croom Helm, 1981); Gerhard Albert Ritter, *Von Wohlfahrtausschutz zum Wohlfahrtstaat: Der Staat in der Modernen Industriegesellschaft* (Köln: Markus, 1973).
11. Asa Briggs, "The Welfare State in Historical Perspective," *European Journal of Sociology* 2, no. 2 (1961): 228; Asa Briggs, *The Age of Improvement, 1783–1867* (London: Longmans, 1959); Bentley B. Gilbert, *The Evolution of National Insurance in Great Britain: The Origins of the Welfare State* (London: Joseph, 1966); Elisabeth Wilson, *Women and*

the Welfare State (London: Tavistock, 1977); Ida Blom, *Nasjonal reisning: pressgruppepolitikk i Grønlandsspørsmålet, 1921–1931* (Bergen: Universitet i Bergen, 1972); Staffan Marklund, *Paradise Lost: The Nordic Welfare States in the Recession, 1975–1985* (Lund: Arkiv, 1988). For an overview of the history and historiography of the Scandinavian welfare states, see Siri Ingvaldsen, *Democracy and the Welfare State: The Nordic Nations Since 1800* (Aarhus: Turbine, 2009).

12. Clarke A. Chambers, "Toward a Redefinition of Welfare History," *Journal of American History* 73, no. 2 (September 1986): 407–433. See also Robert H. Bremner, *From the Depth: The Discovery of Poverty in the United States* (New York: New York University Press, 1956); Walter I. Trattner, *From Poor Law to Welfare State: A History of Social Welfare in America* (New York: Free Press, 1974); Clarke E. Chambers, *Seedtime for Reform: American Social Service and Social Action* (Minneapolis: University of Minnesota Press, 1963); Roy Lubove, *Poverty and Social Welfare in the United States* (New York: Holt, 1971); Roy Lubove, *The Struggle for Social Security, 1900–1935* (Cambridge, Mass.: Harvard University Press, 1968).

13. See, for example, Stephen Skowronek, *Building a New American State* (Cambridge, Mass.: Harvard University Press, 1982); Barry Karl, *The Uneasy State: The United States from 1915 to 1945* (Chicago: University of Chicago Press, 1983).

14. David Gladstone, ed., *Before Beveridge: Welfare Before the Welfare State* (London: Institute of Economic Affairs, 1999).

15. Roy Lubove, *The Professional Altruist: The Emergence of Social Work as a Career, 1880–1930* (Cambridge, Mass.: Harvard University Press, 1965).

16. Chiara Saraceno, "Azione operaia e politica sociale: lo sviluppo del welfare state in Inghilterra, Francia e Stati Uniti," *Prospettiva sindacale*, no. 4 (1977): 94. Author's translation.

17. Katz, *In the Shadow of the Poorhouse*; Patterson, *America's Struggle Against Poverty*; Edward Berkowitz, *America's Welfare State: From Roosevelt to Reagan* (Baltimore, Md.: Johns Hopkins University Press, 1991); Levine, *Poverty and Society*; Baldwin, *The Politics of Social Solidarity*; Edward Berkowitz and Kim McQuaid, *Creating the Welfare State: The Political Economy of Twentieth-Century Reform* (New York: Praeger, 1980). Not all historians accepted the notion of the "welfare state." According to the neo-institutionalist Edward D. Berkowitz ("How to Think About the Welfare State," 490–491), historians borrowed the term from sociologists, who see it as the "inevitable result of the modernization process," but "inevitability . . . is the enemy of history."

18. Flora and Heidenheimer, *The Development of Welfare States in Europe and America*, 6.

19. Tony Judt, *Postwar: A History of Europe Since 1945* (London: Penguin, 2005).
20. James T. Patterson, "Comparative Welfare History: Britain and the United States, 1930–1945," in *The Roosevelt New Deal: A Program Assessment Fifty Years After*, ed. Wilbur J. Cohen (Austin: University of Texas Press, 1986), 137.
21. John Baxendale, review of Pat Thane, *The Foundations of the Welfare State* (London: Longman, 1982), *Critical Social Policy* 4, no. 10 (June 1984): 144.
22. Katz, *In the Shadow of the Poorhouse*, xv.
23. Flora and Heidenheimer, *The Development of Welfare States in Europe and America*, 6.
24. Jens Alber, "The 'European Social Model' and the USA," *European Union Politics* 7, no. 3 (2006): 393–419.
25. Michael D. Katz coined the term to stress the lack of a system of public health care in the United States. Katz, *In the Shadow of the Poorhouse*, x, 333–334.
26. Baldwin, "The Welfare State for Historians," 707.
27. Timothy W. Mason, *Sozial Politik im Dritten Reich: Arbeiterklasse und Volksgemeinschaft* (Opladen: Westdeutscher Verlag, 1977); English ed.: *Social Policy in the Third Reich: The Working Class and the "National Community,"* trans. John Broadwin (Providence, R.I.: Berg, 1993); Marie-Louise Recker, *National-Sozialistische SozialPolitik im zweiten Weltkrieg* (Munich: Oldenburg, 1985); Karl Otto Albrecht, *Wie Sozial Waren die Nationalsozialisten?: Der vermeintliche nationalsozialistische Wohlfahrtstaat* (Frankfurt: Fischer, 1997); Geoffrey Campbell Cocks, *State of Health: Illness in Nazi Germany* (Oxford: Oxford University Press, 2012). See also Ernest Peter Hennock, *British Social Reform and German Precedents: The Case of Social Insurance* (Oxford: Clarendon, 1987).
28. Linda Gordon, "The New Feminist Scholarship of the Welfare State," in *Women, the State, and Welfare*, ed. Linda Gordon (Madison: University of Wisconsin Press, 1990), 10.
29. Stephen Pimpare, "Toward a New Welfare History," *Journal of Policy History* 19, no. 2 (2007): 240.
30. See William Henry Beveridge, *Social Insurance and Allied Services* (1942; repr. London: Her Majesty's Stationery Office, 1968); William Henry Beveridge, *Full Employment in a Free Society* (1944; repr. New York: Norton, 1945); Jose Harris, *William Beveridge: A Biography* (Oxford: Clarendon, 1977). An early, daring article by the historian John A. Garraty first stressed parallels between the New Deal and German Nazism. John A. Garraty, "The New Deal, National Socialism, and the Great Depression," *American Historical Review* 78, no. 4 (October 1973): 907–944. On the

United States and corporatism, see Ira Katznelson, *Fear Itself: The New Deal and the Origins of Our Time* (New York: Norton, 2013), 233–238. On the circulation of welfare ideas, see Chiara Giorgi, "The Origins and Development of the Welfare State: Democracies and Totalitarianisms Compared," in *Democracy and Social Rights in the Two Wests*, ed. Alice Kessler-Harris and Maurizio Vaudagna (Turin: Otto, 2009), 329–345. These themes have been at the center of my own research. See Maurizio Vaudagna, *The New Deal and the American Welfare State: Essays from a Transatlantic Perspective, 1933–1945* (Turin: Otto, 2014).

31. See Alan Milward, *War, Economy and Society, 1939–1945* (Berkeley: University of California Press, 1977).
32. Ike Burson, "War and Social Welfare (United States)," in *Encyclopedia of Social Welfare History in North America*, ed. John M. Herrick and Paul H. Stuart (Thousand Oaks, Calif.: Sage, 2005), 427. See also Patterson, "Comparative Welfare History," 127.
33. Jytte Klausen, *War and Welfare: Europe and the United States, 1945 to the Present* (London: Palgrave, 1998), 1.
34. Martin H. Geyer, "Social Rights and Citizenship During World War Two," in *Two Cultures of Rights: The Quest for Inclusion and Participation in Modern America and Germany*, ed. Manfred Berg and Martin H. Geyer (Cambridge: Cambridge University Press, 2002), 144, 149.
35. Important parallels between the German pre-Nazi and Nazi corporate-welfare measures and their U.S. counterparts have been detected by the Germanist historian Tilla Siegel. See Tilla Siegel, "Welfare Capitalism, Nazi Style: A Reevaluation of the German Labor Front," *International Journal of Political Economy* 18, no. 1 (1988): 82–116.
36. Frances Fox Piven and Richard Cloward, *Regulating the Poor: The Functions of Public Welfare* (New York: Pantheon, 1971); Frances Fox Piven and Richard Cloward, *Poor People's Movements: Why They Succeed, How They Fail* (New York: Viking, 1979).
37. Linda Gordon, "What Does the Welfare State Regulate?" *Social Research* 55, no. 4 (Winter 1988): 609.
38. Gøsta Esping-Andersen, *The Three Worlds of Welfare Capitalism* (Cambridge: Polity, 1990).
39. Levine, *Poverty and Society*.
40. Katz, *In the Shadow of the Poorhouse*, ix–x. See also James T. Patterson, "Comparative Welfare History," 139.
41. Daniel T. Rodgers, *Atlantic Crossings: Social Politics in a Progressive Age* (Cambridge, Mass.: Harvard University Press, 1998).
42. Margaret Weir and Theda Skocpol, "State Structures and the Possibilities for 'Keynesian' Responses to the Great Depression in Sweden, Britain, and the United States," in *Bringing the State Back In*, ed. Peter B. Evans,

Dietrich Rueschemeyer, and Theda Skocpol (Cambridge: Cambridge University Press, 1985), 107.
43. The term "the radical moment" is drawn from Katznelson, *Fear Itself*, 227–275. On the New Deal as a deviation from the main trends of U.S. twentieth-century history, see Jefferson Cowie, *The Great Exception: The New Deal and the Limits of American Politics* (Princeton, N.J.: Princeton University Press, 2016); on the innovations of the social-policy debate in the wartime United States, see Martin H. Geyer, "Social Rights and Citizenship During World War Two," 149–157.
44. Pat Thane, *The Foundations of the Welfare State*; Gisela Bock, *Zwangsterilization im Nationalsozialismus: Studien zur Rassenpolitik und Frauenpolitik* (Opladen: Westdeutscher Verlag, 1986); Ida Blom, *Synd eller sund fornunft?Barnebegrensning I Norge c. 1890–c. 1930* (Oslo: Universitetsforl, 1980); Ann-Sophie Kalvermark (Ohlander), *More Children of Better Quality? Aspects of Swedish Population Policy in the 1930s* (Stockholm: Almquist and Wiksell, 1980); Susan G. Pedersen, *Family, Dependence, and the Origins of the Welfare State: Britain and France, 1914–1945* (New York: Cambridge University Press, 1993); Victoria De Grazia, *How Fascism Ruled Women: Italy, 1922–1945* (Berkeley: University of California Press, 1992); Laura Frader, "Social Citizens Without Citizenship: Working-Class Women and Social Policy in Interwar France," *Social Politics* 4 (Summer/Fall 1996): 111–135.
45. Alice Kessler-Harris, *In Pursuit of Equity: Women, Men, and the Quest for Economic Citizenship in Twentieth-Century America* (New York: Oxford University Press, 2001), 5–6, 205–206. See also Alice Kessler-Harris, *Out to Work: A History of Wage-Earning Women in the United States* (New York: Oxford University Press, 1982); Linda Gordon, *Woman's Body, Woman's Right: A History of Birth Control in America* (New York: Viking Penguin, 1976); Linda Gordon, *Heroes of Their Own Lives: The History and Politics of Family Violence* (New York: Viking Penguin, 1988); Rosalyn Fraad Baxandall and Susan Reverby, *America's Working Women* (New York: Norton, 1976); Jacqueline Jones, *Labor of Love, Labor of Sorrow: Black Women, Work, and the Family from Slavery to the Present* (New York: Basic Books, 1985); Lois Scharf, *To Work and to Wed: Female Employment, Feminism, and the Great Depression* (Westport, Conn.: Greenwood, 1980); Susan Strasser, *Never Done: A History of American Housework* (New York: Pantheon, 1982); Mary Jo Buhle, *Women and American Socialism, 1830–1930* (Urbana: University of Illinois Press, 1981).
46. Jane Lewis, *The Politics of Motherhood: Child and Maternal Welfare in England, 1900–1939* (London: Croom Helm, 1980); Jane Lewis, *Women in England: Sexual Divisions and Social Change* (London: Prentice Hall, 1984). See also the Scandinavian sociologist Arnlaugh Leira, *Welfare States*

and Working Mothers: The Scandinavian Experience (Cambridge: Cambridge University Press, 1992).

47. Boris, *Home to Work*, 4. See Joan Scott, "Gender: A Useful Category for Historical Analysis," *American Historical Review* 91, no. 5 (December 1986): 1053–1075; and also Gisela Bock, "Women's History and Gender History: Aspects of an International Debate," *Gender and History*, no. 1 (1989): 7–30.
48. Gordon, "The New Feminist Scholarship on the Welfare State," 10. This essay can be considered the birth certificate of the new feminist welfare-state focus.
49. Nancy Fraser, "Feminism, Capitalism, and the Cunning of History. An Introduction" (Paris: Fondation Maison des Sciences de l'Homme, 2012), 5; Berkowitz, *America's Welfare State*. On the New Deal historiography, see Alonzo L. Hamby, "Introduction: Historians and the Challenge of the New Deal," in *The New Deal: Analysis and Interpretation*, ed. Alonzo L. Hamby (1969; repr. New York: Longman, 1981), 1–8.
50. Linda Gordon, *Pitied but Not Entitled: Single Mothers and the History of Welfare* (Cambridge, Mass.: Harvard University Press, 1994), 4. The sentence is from Carl Degler, *Out of Our Past: The Forces That Shaped Modern America* (1959; repr. New York: Harper and Row,1970), 379. However, Gordon also noted that "in 1935 Social Security excluded the most needy groups from all its programs, even the inferior ones. These exclusions were deliberate and mainly racially motivated" (5, 291).
51. Berkowitz, "How to Think About the Welfare State," 489.
52. Gerda Lerner, *The Majority Finds Its Past: Placing Women in History* (New York: Oxford University Press, 1979).
53. In the early twentieth century, the French feminist Léonie Rouzade said, "if one gets rights for killing men, one should get more rights for having created humanity." In Gisela Bock and Pat Thane, eds., *Maternity and Gender Policies: Women and the Rise of the European Welfare States, 1880s–1950s* (London: Routledge, 1991), 8.
54. Bock and Thane, eds., *Maternity and Gender Policies*, 8–9; Gwendolyn Mink, *The Wages of Motherhood: Inequality in the Welfare State, 1917–1942* (Ithaca, N.Y.: Cornell University Press, 1958).
55. Sara M. Evans, *Born for Liberty: A History of Women in America* (1989; repr. New York: Free Press, 1997), 5.
56. Pat Thane, "Visions of Gender in the Making of the British Welfare State: The Case of Women in the British Labour Party and Social Policy, 1906–1945," in Bock and Thane, eds., *Maternity and Gender Policies*, 93.
57. Evans, *Born for Liberty*, 196, 205. The formula "Minotaur state" appears in Gisela Bock and Pat Thane, "Editors' Introduction," in Bock and Thane, eds., *Maternity and Gender Policies*, 7.

58. Kessler-Harris, *In Pursuit of Equity*, 15.
59. Katherine Kish Sklar, "A Call for Comparison," *American Historical Review* 95, no. 4 (October 1990): 1109–1114.
60. Pedersen, *Family, Dependence, and the Origins of the Welfare State*, 420.
61. Miriam Cohen and Michael Hanagan, "The Politics of Gender and the Making of the Welfare State, 1900–1940: A Comparative Perspective," *Journal of Social History* 24, no. 3 (1991): 470.
62. Bock and Thane, "Editors' Introduction," 6.
63. Gordon, "Social Insurance and Public Assistance," 26.
64. Mink, *The Wages of Motherhood*, 8.
65. Mimi Abramovitz, "Women and Social Welfare (United States)," in *Encyclopedia of Social Welfare History in North America*, ed. John M. Herrick and Paul H. Stuart (Thousand Oaks, Calif.: Sage, 2005), 447.
66. Gordon, "The New Feminist Scholarship on the Welfare State," 19.
67. See, for example, Katz's notion of a limited "semi-welfare state"; Katz, *In the Shadow of the Poorhouse*, 215.
68. Mink, *The Wages of Motherhood*, 8–9.
69. Fraser, "Feminism, Capitalism, and the Cunning of History," 8.
70. Abramovitz, "Women and Social Welfare (United States)," 449.
71. Jones, *Labor of Love, Labor of Sorrow*, 6–7.
72. Gordon, "The New Feminist Scholarship on the Welfare State," 25; Mink, *The Wages of Motherhood*, 13.
73. Sheila Blackburn, "How Useful Are Feminist Theories of the Welfare State?" *Women's History Review* 4, no. 3 (1995): 369–370.
74. Fraser, "Feminism, Capitalism, and the Cunning of History," 10–12.
75. See Gordon, ed., *Women, the State, and Welfare*; and Bock and Thane, eds., *Maternity and Gender Policies*. For an even closer cooperation, see Sara M. Evans and Barbara J. Nelson, *Wage Justice: Comparable Worth and the Paradox of Technocratic Reform* (Chicago: University of Chicago Press, 1989); Nancy Fraser and Linda Gordon, "Contract Versus Charity: Why Is There No Social Citizenship in the United States?" *Socialist Review* 22, no. 3 (July–September 1992): 45–67; Nancy Fraser and Linda Gordon, "A Genealogy of Dependency: Tracing a Keyword in the U.S. Welfare State," *Signs* 19, no. 2 (1994): 309–336.
76. Alice Kessler-Harris, "What Happened to Second-Wave Feminism," presentation given on January 4, 2015, at the roundtable on *America and the Left: Past and Present*, at the annual meeting of the American Historical Association; https://www.youtube.com/watch?v=cCLktyNq18.
77. Sonya Michel, "Maternalism and Beyond," in *Maternalism Reconsidered: Motherhood, Welfare, and Social Policy in the Twentieth Century*, ed. Marian van der Klein, Rebecca Jo Plant, Nicole Sanders, and Lori R. Weintrob (New York: Berghahn, 2012), 22.

78. See Kessler-Harris, *In Pursuit of Equity*, 15. The theme is drawn from Ruth Lister, *Citizenship, Feminist Perspectives* (1997; repr. London: Palgrave, 2003), and is also discussed in Kessler-Harris, *Out to Work*, chap. 7.
79. Gro Hagemann, "Citizenship and Social Order: Gender Politics in Twentieth-Century Norway and Sweden," *Women's History Review* 11, no. 3 (2002): 422.
80. Michel, "Maternalism and Beyond," 23.
81. Theda Skocpol, *Protecting Soldiers and Mothers: The Political Origins of Social Policy in the United States* (Cambridge, Mass.: Harvard University Press, 1992).
82. Nancy Folbre, "Review of *Protecting Soldiers and Mothers*," *Theory and Society* 26, no. 4 (December 1995): 869.
83. For the maternalist position, see Sonya Michel and Seth Koven, *Mothers of a New World: Maternalist Politics and the Origins of Welfare States* (New York: Routledge, 1993).
84. Hagemann, "Citizenship and Social Order," 418.
85. Anne-Sofie Ohlander, "The Invisible Child? The Struggle for a Social Democratic Family Policy in Sweden, 1900–1960," in *Maternity and Gender Policies*, ed. Bock and Thane, 64–66.
86. John Stuart Mill, "The Subjection of Women (1869)," in John Stuart Mill and Harriet Taylor Mill, *Essays on Sex Equality* (Chicago: University of Chicago Press, 1970).
87. Cited in Michel, "Maternalism and Beyond," 24.
88. Kessler-Harris, *In Pursuit of Equity*, 4.
89. Ibid., 13.
90. Alice Kessler-Harris, "A Conversation with Ida Blom," *Perspectives on History* (December 2006), https://www.historians.org/publications-and-directories/perspectives-on-history/december-2006/a-conversation. Early Scandinavian scholars led the way in focusing women's history. Ellen Fries was the first woman to get a Ph.D. in Sweden in 1883; she became a historian, participated in the founding of the Swedish feminist movement, and wrote short women's historical biographies.
91. Katz, *In the Shadow of the Poorhouse*, xiv–xv. Katz examined recent gender-based welfare history books in his essay "Segmented Visions: Recent Writing on the History of Welfare in America," *Journal of Urban History* 24 (January 1998): 244–255, but stuck to his former interpretation.
92. Linda Gordon, "What Does the Welfare State Regulate?" *Social Research* 55, no. 4 (Winter 1988): 628. In the same issue, Piven and Cloward wrote a reply to Linda Gordon, stressing that "family concerns and family politics have not determined the shape of the main welfare state programs. To the contrary, in the clash with market interests, family interests have consistently given way; and in the clash with market actors, women acting out

of family interests have consistently been defeated." Frances Fox Piven and Richard A. Cloward, "Welfare Doesn't Shore Up Traditional Family Roles: A Reply to Linda Gordon," *Social Research* 55, no. 4 (Winter 1988): 644–645.
93. *Encyclopedia of Social Welfare History in North America*, ed. John M. Herrick and Paul H. Stuart (Thousand Oaks, Calif.: Sage, 2005).
94. Gloria Nemec, "Carità pubblica, assistenza sociale e politiche di welfare: il caso di Trieste," in *Donne e famiglie nei sistemi di welfare: Esperienze nazionali e regionali a confronto*, ed. Roberta Nunin and Elisabetta Vezzosi (Florence: Carocci, 2007), 83.
95. Christian Lammert, "Privatization and Self-Responsibility: Patterns of Welfare State Development in Europe and the United States Since the 1990s," and Maurizio Ferrera, "Reconciling European Integration with the National Welfare State: A Neo-Weberian Perspective," both essays in this volume.
96. Chiara Saraceno, "Non solo genere," in "Modelli di welfare state e interpretazioni di genere," ed. Elisabetta Vezzosi, *Contemporanea* 3, no. 1 (January 2000): 134. Author's translation.

PART I

Democracy and the Welfare State in Europe and the United States

CHALLENGES TO the welfare state have increased dramatically in the new millennium. Originally designed to promote economic security and political harmony in a world where capitalism had run rampant, early welfare states relied on widespread public support to maintain a balance between social fairness and the profit drive. But the apparent success of capitalism against the communist world and the increasing focus on austerity in the wake of globalization and financial crises have led to calls for greater market autonomy and less state intervention. In an age of retrenchment, democracy and social justice command less interest.

Europe and the United States illustrate the retreat from democracy. Maurizio Ferrera focuses on the post-1970s conflict between the European Union and the welfare state, wondering whether reconciliation is possible, and in what terms. His conclusion sounds an optimistic note on the possibility of a reformed "neowelfarism" engendered by a new, committed European leadership that may reconcile people with the old dream of the European Union. In turn, Ira Katznelson has illustrated in historical and contemporary terms the participatory potential of postwelfare America. In our heterogeneous societies, he argues, democratic activation is engaged not by pretending to erase differences but thanks to the shared confidence in common rules of the game, rules that give each opinion a chance.

These cautiously optimistic forecasts have come into question in light of political events in 2016. These include the challenges of ever-increasing refugee populations, Britain's vote to exit the European Union, and the rise of a populist right in the United States. We may now want to ask if the efforts of almost every welfare state to acknowledge the claims to inclusion of diverse marginalized groups—an effort that seemed so successful in the late twentieth century—may not have come at the cost of the welfare state itself.

CHAPTER TWO

Reconciling European Integration and the National Welfare State

A Neo-Weberian Perspective

MAURIZIO FERRERA

THE NATIONAL WELFARE STATE and the European Union are two precious legacies of the twentieth century. However, their coexistence is fraught by unresolved tensions, even a potential clash, which the recent crisis has markedly exacerbated. When, how, and why did the original "elective affinity" between the national welfare state and the EU begin to weaken? Is "reconciliation" possible? If so, how? These questions lie at the center of current academic and public debates. The aim of this chapter is to cast new light on these questions by drawing on Weber's theory, in particular his insights about the relationship connecting values, ideas, and politics. The chapter is organized as follows: the first section presents the topic and summarizes the debate. The second and third sections will illustrate the intellectual and political logics that have guided the development of the welfare state at the national level. They will then discuss the process of supranational economic integration, highlighting the responsibility of these intellectual and political logics in generating the clash. The fourth section will offer a reinterpretation of the current crisis in neo-Weberian terms and will hint at some possible scenarios.

WELFARE AND INTEGRATION: THE ROOTS OF "DECONCILIATION"

As has been shown in a wealth of historical, legal, and political studies, tensions between the national welfare state and European integration have been intensifying since the 1970s. An increasingly stronger "economic space" has come partly to encapsulate national welfare institutions, imposing exogenous constraints on their functioning, including the processes by which they internally adapt to changing social needs and demography. National governments are still largely free to determine the internal structure of social programs and spending, but through the principle of free movement, competition rules, and the rules of coordination of national social-security systems, the EU has raised two basic challenges to the national welfare state. The first is a challenge to the national welfare state's territorial boundaries, through the explicit prohibition of most cross-border restrictions regarding access to and consumption of social benefits and, to some extent, the provision of services. Within the EU, those who cross national borders share domestic spaces and carry at least some core social rights (such as pensions) across the territory of the whole EU. The second challenge has addressed the "right to bound," that is, the right of each national welfare state to determine autonomously who can or must share what with whom and then to enforce compliance through specific organizational structures backed by coercive power, like, for example, setting up a compulsory public-insurance scheme for a given occupational category.

Since the mid-1990s, the literature discussed the destabilizing consequences for domestic social protection of economic integration and its delicate readaptation efforts, necessitating the notion of "semisovereign" welfare states.[1] Two strands of the debate demand special attention. The first concerns legal frameworks and decision-making rules, suggesting that the tension is essentially a contest between "market-making" and "market-correcting" logics. Market-making provisions can be adopted by striking down domestic barriers through simple regulations or court rulings that do not require complex bargaining processes ("negative integration"). Market-correcting measures require instead the formation of political majorities within the Council and the support of the Commission. In other words, decision rules make "positive integration" much more demanding—and thus less successful—than negative integration.[2] A second and more recent strand of this debate has tried to bring the process of European integration under the umbrella of the classic "state-building" school, aimed at analyzing the historical formation of nation-states.[3] According to this perspective, EU integration is a new phase in the long-term development of the European state system, characterized by a gradual weakening of spatial boundaries and an overall restructuring of sociopolitical and institutional configurations. The welfare state was, and still is, a key component of the nation-state. But, to reiterate, by imposing increasing challenges to its institutional foundations, integration has brought about a "sovereignty contest" over the bounding rules that govern social sharing practices.

The post-2007 crisis has exacerbated existing tensions and created new ones. The clash between nation-based social-protection needs and Economic and Monetary Union (EMU)–induced austerity and spending cuts has rapidly escalated and entered the electoral arena, where it is generating a new, turbulent cleavage between pro- and anti-EU actor coalitions.[4] The crisis has also revealed a more or less latent distributive cleavage between richer "paying" member states and poorer "receiving" member states. The problem of a "Transfer Union" has gained increasing political salience[5]—even if only as a matter of financial aid to countries under fiscal stress, without any consideration of the web of "invisible" gains and losses linked to the EMU. The general strain between solidarity and economic integration has broken down into four distinct tensions: (1) market making versus market correcting at the EU level, (2) national social sovereignty and discretion versus EU law and conditionality, (3) intra-EU "system competition" between high-wage/high-welfare member states and low-wage/low-welfare member states ("old versus new" member states or "West versus East"), and (4) payers versus beneficiaries of cross-national transfers and financial assistance ("core versus peripheral" member states or "North versus South").

These four lines of tension intersect, creating complex policy dilemmas, political turbulence, and a further erosion of popular legitimacy for the EU. While the scholarly literature largely agrees on the nature and intensity of the current predicament, prognoses tend to diverge. At one extreme we find a position of dead-end pessimism: tensions and conflicts cannot be solved at the EU level, and thus the only solution is to "bust" the status quo (including the euro), repatriate competences, and fence off supranational intrusions from domestic arrangements and policy agendas.[6] At the other extreme, we find the federalist position: the EU should swiftly turn into a fully-fledged federal superstate equipped with an adequate central budget and with the powers to tax and approve social spending.[7] In the middle we find a variety of "realist" positions, including "supranational incrementalism,"[8] where a reconciliation between Europe's economy and European society would prove difficult but not impossible. To some extent, the process has been underway for some time. A recognizable "social space" has been emerging within the EU architecture, especially since the treaty revisions of Amsterdam and Lisbon and the launch of employment and social "processes" based on Open Method of Coordination (OMC). As emblematic examples we can mention the Charter on Fundamental Rights; common labor and social-security standards; soft laws on employment, social inclusion, and pensions, as well as on health care and long-term care; and, more recently, the so-called social provisions of the Lisbon Treaty and the social targets of the Europe 2020 strategy.[9]

Although rich and insightful, the scholarly debate on "Social Europe" has two weak points: specifically, its poor conceptualization of both the *political* and the *intellectual* logics that underpin institutional and policy developments. By "political dimension," I mean the sphere where at various levels elected leaders and state officials make choices regarding both welfare-state building and EU building. This understanding of politics combines different types of rationalities: epistemic-instrumental ("puzzling" for problem solving), consensus seeking ("powering" through the democratic process), and axiological ("valuing," i.e., opting for a specific cause to serve, some ultimate objective that gives "meaning" to political change and persuades those affected by such change). Likewise, by "intellectual dimension," I mean the sphere where ideas and broad normative symbolic visions are generated, justified, and weighted against their ends, instrumental implications, and substantive consequences. These two dimensions—political and intellectual—are practically intertwined but should be kept analytically distinct in order to sort out their intrinsic logics and their causal significance.

The loose articulation of these two dimensions is especially lamentable for the "supranational incrementalist" approach, which has ambitions both to explain the tension between the national welfare state and European integration while also maintaining normative commitments to institutional reconciliation. During the 2000s, incrementalist scholars tended to suggest that the social space was the outcome of some form of gradual, evolutionary adaptation essentially linked to problem pressures. From this point of view, the post-2007 crisis appears as the effect of a powerful exogenous shock, but the implicit expectation is that sooner or later an institutional "bounce" is going to take place. This perspective is not adequate to explain the logic of how these changes occur, since it remains ultimately anchored to quasi-functionalist assumptions at the macro level as well as to theories of reactive policy learning and "political voluntarism" at the micro level. How can we enhance the theoretical understanding of institutional frictions, the margins of maneuver that are available to purposive political actors, their strategies of response, and thus dynamics of persistence versus change?

Often, "grand thinking" requires that we stand on the shoulders of great thinkers. I suggest we take a step back and revisit the theory of Max Weber. Why Weber? Because his legacy (as further developed by neo-Weberian theory) is precious and salient for capturing the role of both the intellectual and political spheres in the processes of institution building and change. Weber's thought is especially useful for this task by virtue of his general theory of "value spheres" as well as his analysis of the nexus between "(social) science" and "(democratic) politics." The general theory of "value spheres" casts light on the way in which ideas, values, and power typically interact in molding the strategies of political leaders, allowing under certain conditions for creative change. Which, incidentally, is exactly what is needed in the EU today.

THE WELFARE STATE AND EUROPEAN INTEGRATION AS AN INTELLECTUAL PROJECT

For Weber, the emergence and consolidation of a number of new life orders, or value spheres, was a prominent feature of European modernity. These orders slowly gained independence from religion and began to operate according to an autonomous inner logic (*Eigengesetzlichkeit*). Weber listed these spheres as the economic, political, intellectual, erotic, and aesthetic.[10] "Ideal interests in particular characterize the intellectual sphere," that is, by the search for rationalized meanings, interpretations, and explanations of the natural and social world (which thus became increasingly "disenchanted"), through the exercise of theoretical reason. Weber did not use the concept of ideology in any systematic sense. Recent Weberian theory, however, has suggested that the grand twentieth-century ideologies (socialism, liberalism, and Christian democracy) have affirmed themselves as secular "theodicies":[11] like religion, they have provided symbolic visions of "salvation" (though they are "this-worldly" rather than "other-worldly"), or, in other words, they have provided rationalized justifications of the problems of "suffering" and "injustice" as well as prescriptive agendas on how to combat them through practical action.[12]

Although value spheres are sometimes treated in quasi-ontological terms, they ultimately exist in individual agents. Thus *intellectuals* are typically producers of ideas for the sake of ideas—whether they serve as scientists, philosophers, or ideologues. As long as the meanings of their actions remain "ideational" rather than linked to material interests, however, intellectuals can specify their mission along a continuum between pure epistemic devotion and socially engaged thinking. But in recent years, Weberian theory has elaborated a more neutral and articulated sociology of intellectuals, one centered not only on the contrast between "seekers of pure knowledge" and "committed thinkers" but also between intellectuals proper and members of the *intelligentsia*.[13] Intellectuals are highly creative and typically individualistic thinkers, busy with the task of imparting meaning to the world and incessantly perfecting such meaning. The intelligentsia is a much wider group of educated people who belong to various social strata and possess varying degrees of status consciousness but who are still able to act on ideal interests per se. Rather than producing original and innovative knowledge, the intelligentsia is engaged in developing, reinterpreting, preserving, popularizing, and, as it were, carrying ideas to the threshold that separates the intellectual from the other practical spheres, especially the sphere of politics.

Weber dedicated little attention to the welfare state—which had emerged in Germany during the 1880s—and much of what he said was critical. He did not understand or foresee that the welfare state would become the key institution of the European state during the twentieth century. Nevertheless, there is little need to emphasize that one can fruitfully read the welfare state and its rapid rise through a Weberian lens. From the intellectual standpoint, one can make at least three observations. First, prior to the development of a concrete institution that served economic, social, and political purposes, the welfare state was (and remains) above all an intellectual project, the child of those novel secular doctrines that sought to address the problem of injustice and suffering.[14] During the twentieth century, "social protection" against unpredictable risks and needs in a market society became a dominant *Wertidee* that—through the mediation of politics—prompted a gradual but thoroughgoing cultural and institutional reconfiguration of European societies. Second, the welfare state took center stage in the "critical" debates of all salient epistemic arenas: debates about the normative implications, instrumental rationality, and external consequences of social-protection programs.[15] Third, the welfare state became a privileged locus of encounter between expert (nomological) knowledge and practical politics. Especially after World War II, social policies became the main preoccupation and target of domestic political agendas, and the competence and advice of social scientists (in particular, the "clarifications" of lawyers and economists) turned into valuable resources for leaders and bureaucrats at all levels.[16] To a large extent, welfare-state building changed the very nature of politics as a value sphere. In addition to the choice of ultimate values and the exercise of power, another task gained salience within this sphere as Weber defined it: "puzzling" about how to resolve the substantive issues now under the remit of the state.[17]

We can say that in Europe during the second half of last century the welfare state became the normatively charged image of a national, democratic, political community. Intellectually, this community was held together by the rational administration of a widely supported secular theodicy whose core commitment was to a general doctrine of distributive justice throughout society. A small number of key intellectuals and a vast intelligentsia located along the boundary between the intellectual and the political spheres maintained and transformed this image of the welfare state. Of course, turbulent ideological conflicts over the meaning of social justice were a persistent feature of the twentieth century. At times, the goals of compensatory redress and secular "salvation" squarely challenged the logic of the market sphere, or, conversely, the promotion of individualistic and meritocratic principles clashed with established redistributive practices and their underlying justifications. But the need for a minimum of "overlapping consensus" as to who was entitled to what was never questioned, nor did anyone doubt the desirability of the basic foundations of the modern welfare-state project, such as compulsory social insurance. One must note that the programmatic ideas that addressed social justice and how to achieve it remained markedly national in their character. As a matter of fact, the precondition for the mere possibility of these shared frameworks was the existence of deep-seated beliefs in commonality (Weber's *Gemeinsamkeitsglauben*) or the feeling of belonging to a community (*Gemeinsamkeitsfühle*) that anchored expectations of reciprocity and asymmetrical solidarity with those who were especially vulnerable.[18]

The intellectual roots of the European integration project were distinct but not wholly unrelated to those of the welfare state.[19] The founding members of the European project hoped to bring about peace and promote economic growth in the wake of the destruction wrought by World War II. Some of them (including prominent intellectuals like Altiero Spinelli) were ambitious federalists who genuinely believed in the viability of a United States of Europe. While they were certainly idealists, they were not naïve. In the context of the late 1940s and early 1950s, a rapid move toward supranationalization was a plausible intellectual scenario, especially after the establishment of the European Defence Community and the concrete commitment of its member states to merge it with the European Coal and Steel Community, giving rise to a European Political Community.[20] The withdrawal of France in 1954 blocked that process, but early supranationalization was nevertheless an "objective possibility" (in Weber's terms) during that critical juncture. After this possibility fell flat, realist positions prevailed at forging integration, which was downgraded to an essentially economic process. The European Economic Community was to take care of market integration and make sure that France and Germany would irreversibly befriend each other through increasing trade flows and interdependence.[21] This arrangement initially worked exactly as expected, giving rise to a positive-sum game. Far from being jeopardized, the key institution of the member states, specifically the welfare state, was actually supported by economic integration. Intellectually, the challenge was essentially that of applying expert knowledge in order to maximize the benefits of a rational administration of integrating markets. There were few incentives for critical discussions of ultimate values, as the predominant stake was instrumental efficiency. And the same held true for the development of ideologies, with the exception of rather general federative ideas. Since the European Economic Community was to be programmatically uninterested in national social contracts and only aimed at feeding them with the dividends of growth, there was little need to raise issues of common identity, fairness, redistribution, or social justice at the supranational level. Certainly there was no push to raise the issue of interpersonal transfers, nor much incentive to discuss cross-national transfers as well.

In hindsight, we can see that this ambiguity at the heart of the intellectual framing of the development of the EU was a sort of "original sin," one that bears a significant responsibility for subsequent derangements in the EU's mission and practice. The division of political work between the Economic Community and member states led naturally to a division of intellectual work. Brussels became the champion of market liberalism, while issues regarding "suffering" and "injustice" remained the prerogative of the symbolic and discursive arenas of nation-states. As legal scholars have shown, the process of integration relied on the rule of law to produce, implement, and adjudicate its public policies. But it is not entirely correct to say that the Economic Community only dealt with markets, even during the 1960s and 1970s.[22] Right from the beginning, European integration was about more than just making markets based solely on the principles of undistorted competition and economic freedom.[23] It was also about "nondiscrimination" and, later, "equal opportunities" and efforts to "civilize" social spheres, for example, introducing fairness into gender relations.[24] But these effects made themselves felt in a slow, incremental fashion, often through the work of a politically less visible body, like the Court of Justice. And, more importantly, they were not accompanied by an explicit theodicy, that is, a wider, symbolically meaningful framework capable of counterbalancing the weight of liberal market ideas while also reaching the various European publics.

A second factor contributing to the intellectual hegemony of market liberalism and its increasingly closer identification with the project of European integration is related to the make-up of the intelligentsia who sit in the driver's seat of this project. It is no secret that in this seat (naturally starting with the European Commission) key officers with economic training, as well as professional economists acting as external advisers, played a dominant role that was even more influential than that of the founders. It could hardly have gone differently, given the content of the original compromise mentioned above and the essentially economic nature of the treaties. But the economists' monopolization of the intellectual sphere prompted a gradual symbolic drift that has transformed the instrumental benefits of economic integration (greater openness, more competition, larger markets) into "final" goals: goals worth being pursued and defended as ends in themselves and not as instruments to bring about, support, or improve a "good society" (ostensibly one that is prosperous, free, and just). As a result and since the 1990s especially, many have increasingly perceived the EU as the "friend" of the market and the "enemy" of solidarity.[25] It was no coincidence that the French debate on the "pillars" of the EU, which developed following the Maastricht Treaty, should have led to a religious metaphor: the European Union as a "temple of competition" fiercely guarded by the priests of economic orthodoxy.[26]

In his discussion of politics, Weber pointed to "irresponsibility" as the worst sin that can be committed by a politician, which he defined as the failure to consider the consequences of one's actions.[27] Science can help politics to be responsible by sensitizing it to this problem. However, intellectuals can in their turn become irresponsible when they indulge in dogmatism, treating their symbolic constructions as "real," univocal, and uncontroversial depictions of reality, refusing to revise them in the face of contradicting evidence and persevering in drawing prescriptive implications from stylized analytical constructs. The intelligentsia is especially prone to fall victim to this type of irresponsible dogmatism, especially when its members come to occupy policy-relevant administrative positions. When scientific or moral dogmatism combines with a bureaucratic ethos, there is a high risk of "organized irresponsibility," which can have pernicious consequences for neighboring value spheres.[28]

Are these terms appropriate to describe the epistemic technocracy that has formed in Brussels and Frankfurt around the Economic and Monetary Union (or in Washington, for that matter)? Even within the economic profession there is today an intense debate over the intellectual flaws—cognitive, theoretical, and empirical—of those mainstream economic "nomologists" who have elaborated and prescribed the austerity paradigm.[29] It may well be the case that the logic of national welfare is inherently antithetical to the logic of supranational economic integration and that the reconciliation scenario lies outside the range of objective possibilities—at least in the present historical constellation. Before arriving at such a gloomy conclusion, however, we should at least place the issue of the reconciliation front and center in Europe's intellectual agenda, removing the obstacles built by the organized irresponsibility of monetarist "economism" and encouraging a more wide-ranging and forward-looking analysis.

THE WELFARE STATE AND EUROPEAN INTEGRATION AS POLITICAL CONSTRUCTIONS

Weber's political theory rests on two fundamental concepts: (1) the political community (*Politische Gemeinschaft*), a territorial social group ultimately held together by the monopoly of legitimate violence and under the control of specialized institutions; and (2) the political value sphere (*Politische Wertsphäre*), a life order, an agency orientation whose overarching purpose is that of forming, keeping together, and promoting the political community regardless of other purposes. While there is by definition no politics without political communities, the political value sphere is the historical product of modern rationalization, the liberation of political agency from extrinsic systems of value—most notably religion. Political modernization led to the rise of the bureaucratic *Rechtsstaat*, resting on legal-rational legitimation, and eventually to its subsequent constitutionalization and democratization (the liberal-democratic *Rechtsstaat*). Its adoption of liberal democracy was not, however, the last stage of development of the modern state as an autonomous "enterprise" (*Betrieb*). Weber was well aware of the functional expansion of the state between the end of the nineteenth and the beginning of the twentieth century—an expansion guided not only by the logic of formal rationalization but also by a new logic of substantial rationalization or, in other words, the standardized provisioning of groups with certain material goods and services.

The welfare state has created a new type of citizenship rights, specifically, entitlements to social protection that have spread throughout the social structure and have crystallized new status and interest groups defined by their position vis-à-vis tax-welfare schemes. Lepsius and Flora were among the first to note that the expansion of entitlements has become a novel, structurally significant dimension for life opportunities and group formation: in addition to the Weberian *Besitzklassen* and *Erwerbungsklassen*, a new *Versorgungsklass* has emerged, made up of persons drawing their income mainly from the state by virtue of guaranteed access to public transfers and services.[30] Interacting with democracy, the welfare state gradually changed the substance of the

Staatsräson, that is, the ultimate value in politics. The *salus populi* remained the *suprema lex* of all political leaders "by vocation," but it was redefined from meaning mere physical security to denoting social and economic well-being. The basis of legitimation shifted from inputs to outcomes, on the state's capacity to manage the economy, create wealth, and tax and spend to honor entitlements. Retrospective and instrumental (*do ut des*) voting (voting based on performance) became more important than prospective voting (voting based on ideological affiliation or at least contingent to partisan proposals). Formal *Staatsräson* shifted into substantial *Wohlfahrtsstaatsräson*.[31] The preservation of the state as such became increasingly dependent on the availability and control not only of coercive but also material resources; legitimacy and durable compliance in their turn came increasingly to depend on the capacity of leaders to satisfy the welfare demands of a multitude of groups.

Safeguarding the "conditions of possibility" for a welfare state is an enormous challenge requiring historically unprecedented competences and qualities on the part of responsible political leaders. While still resting on the maintenance of external security, internal order, and the cultivation of "commonality" among citizens, the pursuit of *Wohlfahrtsstaatsräsons* calls for the deployment of a wide array of instruments and capacities. The picture is further complicated by a second factor. Performance-based legitimation rests on a web of political exchanges between service bureaucracies and social clienteles. With the institutionalization of entitlements, these exchanges become increasingly rigid. Once conceded as a matter of right, *Versorgung* is taken for granted and tends to run dry as a source of partisan loyalty and overall political legitimation. Honoring voters' entitlements does not bring enough electoral credit, while their modification (let alone withdrawal) may become the cause of withering blame and punishment. Substantial rationalization through the welfare state squeezes from below the margins of maneuver of the circuits of both electoral and corporate representation. According to the literature on the changing dynamics of representative democracy at the domestic level,[32] the crisis of the welfare state is one of the major challenges faced by political leaders and parties seeking simultaneously to respond to voters' material and ideal demands and effectively to solve collective problems in a complex and interdependent world. The logic of *Versorgung* tends moreover to provoke negative externalities in other value spheres, most notably the economy. The inexorable tendency of a monolithic understanding of rationality to elbow out alternative ways of perceiving the world is a well-known tenet of neo-Weberian theory.[33] Although early attacks by mainstream economics on social protection were often inaccurate and exaggerated, it is also documented that the specific institutional structure of certain entitlement programs in certain countries has indeed had negative effects on efficiency and competitiveness.

Let us now turn to the EU. The state-building school considers European integration a new phase in the long-term development of the system of European states: the sixth juncture after state building, capitalist development, nation building, democratization, and the formation of welfare states. While the earlier phases (with the partial exception of capitalist development) essentially involved the creation of coterminous territorial and membership boundaries around national political communities, the new phase prompted by the Treaty of Rome works in the opposite direction, toward a gradual weakening, redefinition, and even removal of traditional boundaries, a process that is increasingly challenging the nation-state as a coherent and largely self-contained territorial "system." The EU pursues the loosening of these boundaries for an overarching objective: market integration. It is not entirely correct, however, to define the EU's mission since the late 1950s exclusively in terms of stateless market building. Over time, the EU has in fact endowed itself with an increasing number of "state" features and instruments, most notably a bureaucratic apparatus, an independent judiciary, and a quasi-constitution demarcating its sovereign competences and powers. As shown by Bartolini, there is no doubt that, politically, European integration constitutes a clear attempt at center formation—typically the first necessary step toward the creation of any territorial political community.[34] And around this process a number of collective actors (like the Commission and the Court of Justice) as well as a series of individual leaders have appeared on the scene, moved by clear political motives: self-aggrandizement and power seeking at the service of the European "cause." This should not surprise us. Markets are the most impersonal form of social relation, but they do provide a minimal community-building (*gemeinschaftend*) component by virtue of the commonality of interests shared between actual and potential market actors. Functioning markets require territorial peace, ethical norms, and enforceable rules. What is blatantly missing in European integration qua political process is the logic of *Staatsräson*, or, to put it another way, explicit incentives for engaging in that conduct whose absolute objective is to maximize the monopoly of *legitimate* power over all those affected by EU decisions and policies.

For a brief moment in the early 1950s, with the establishment of a European Defence Community and later a European Political Community, the objective possibility for the emergence of a distinctively supranational *Staatsräson* seemed within reach. The negative vote of the French Parliament (which was, ironically, a solemn act of democratic legitimation) foreclosed that scenario and pushed the integration process along the market-building track. A second opportunity presented itself in the early 1990s when three *Berufpolitiker* (Mitterrand, Kohl, and Delors) developed a common interest in promoting a political quantum leap in the integration process. A leap occurred with the Maastricht Treaty and the establishment of the Economic and Monetary Union. But it was not a quantum one: the common currency was born with a fault in its original design, devoid as it was of an accompanying framework of economic and institutional governance. In the subsequent decade, the 2000s, a turbulent political process led to the adoption of the Lisbon Treaty in 2009. As has been rightly emphasized, this treaty was an important step in building a democratic polity.[35] The coming of the financial crisis, however, has encouraged a rapid return to intergovernmentalism, led by France and Germany, and centered on the European Council.[36]

But the incomplete and weak second-order monopolization of coercive power was and is not the prime obstacle to the emergence of an EU *Staatsräson*. Instead, the main problem is the almost total absence of incentives (let alone duties) for supranational authorities to seek legitimation or to engage seriously with the representation nexus, which has remained more or less confined within national political arenas. It is certainly true that as long as the pursuit of *Marktsräson* produced growth, economic integration could count on output legitimacy and thus on a tacit permissive consensus among national voters. And it is also true that supranational authorities (most notably the Commission) have indeed adopted consensus-seeking strategies, especially vis-à-vis the interest groups affected by its policies, a strategy that Vivien Schmidt has dubbed "governing *with* the people."[37] But when economic integration fails to deliver (that is, fails to govern *for*), output legitimacy rapidly wanes, and interest-group involvement (governing *with*) cannot substitute for democratic legitimation: governing *from* and *by* the people, a system in which voters are the bearers of sovereignty and exercise it through electing representatives.

We must consider one last element. Formally enshrined and procedurally legitimized by the Rome Treaty, the unbridled pursuit of *Marktsräson* has resulted in an overstretched expansion of the criteria of market rationality within other value spheres, challenging their institutional foundations. The national welfare state has been a notable victim of this overstretch. The victim was not without sin, as was shown above: the institutionalization of social-protection entitlements has often pushed their *Versorgung* rationality well beyond its "natural" scope of validity. But there is no doubt that since the 1990s—and especially after the onset of the financial crisis—welfare schemes have suffered at the hands of the hegemonic pretences of a supranational *Marktsräson* unwilling to compromise with *Wohlfahrtsstaatsräson* or come to terms with the demands of European voters, even at the price of turning the EU into an all-purpose scapegoat, thus further undermining its legitimacy.

RECONCILIATION: THE NEED FOR RESPONSIBLE LEADERSHIP

Writing at the beginning of last century, Weber envisioned a future of political and social ossification within the vise of bureaucracy and capitalism.[38] The inevitable consequence would be a number of restrictions: of the rights to individual liberty, the horizons of possibility to direct historical change, and the latitude to make ethically engaged political choices. Fortunately, that prophecy has not materialized. Albeit after a slow and tormented takeoff, society and politics in the second half of the twentieth century have been able to tame bureaucracy and capitalism significantly by means of liberal democracy and the welfare state, while developing innovative value frames capable of providing meaning to the world and collective life. With the demise of the *les trentes glorieuses*, however, it must be acknowledged that new dynamics of ossification have been gradually emerging. The welfare state has become the key factor in political and social stability, but the interplay connecting electoral competition, social provisions, and entitlement legalization has tended to generate irresponsible distributive spirals as well as a fiscal crisis that has come to undermine the sustainability of the welfare state itself. The great twentieth-century secular theodicies have lost their symbolic traction as well as their capacity to mobilize people socially and politically.

A history of equally contradictory trends seems to have characterized the other novel developmental path opened after World War II: European integration. Founded as a strategy of market unification, this process initially acted as a multiplier of growth and wealth at the service of distribution between elite and social clienteles in domestic arenas. In the last three decades, the EU has also played an important role in containing the political-economic degeneration related to the logic of *Versorgung*, specifically, by fighting monopolistic closures, encouraging nondiscrimination and gender equality, and controlling inflation and unsustainable public deficits. But the Union has itself fallen prey to an endogenous sclerosis, hugely amplified during the financial crisis, resulting from the excesses of *Marktträson* and the unwillingness or incapacity of leaders to define and defend a normative mission of community building for Europe.

At this point, one might wonder whether Weber's pessimistic scenario as to the fate of late modernity has not returned again in a new form. At the national level, politics appears under siege by old interests and new passions, which are difficult to manage under tight fiscal constraints. At the supranational level, the capitalism/bureaucracy vise seems to be reconstituting itself under a technocratic machine largely inspired by "organized irresponsibility." The alarms against a possible loss of rights seem exaggerated now, but the risk of a gradual erosion of the principles of limited government, separation of powers, and democratic accountability is a real one, as is—more generally—the risk of a restriction of the "horizons of change" and of the margins for ethically engaged political decisions. Is this a resurrection of the ghosts of the "iron cage" (guarded by bureaucrats) and a "new slavery" under neocapitalist domination? Perhaps there is indeed an objective possibility for that spectral scenario to become reality. Compared to the early twentieth century, however, we can count on a good half-century of liberal-democratic institutions and strongly institutionalized democratic practices: all the "demonic" alternatives experienced in Europe have fortunately been scratched off the list of objective possibilities (or so it seems plausible to hypothesize). If it takes place within a tamed and objectified liberal-democratic arena, conflict itself may acquire politically generative functions. As argued by Habermas, for example, the rise of euroskepticism may force pro-EU parties and leaders to make political and symbolic investments at the service of the EU cause unambiguously.[39]

European politics, in its double dimension as a community and as a value sphere, is now faced with enormous challenges. But there are possibilities for a reinvention of its mission on a continental scale, specifically, politics and its "productive" function for the other value spheres of society and their interactions. The intellectual debate has already explored various possible options. At one gloomy extreme we find the idea of a *European Bundesrepublik*, a form of EU building under German hegemony.[40] At the other extreme lies the scenario of a "neomedieval" reconfiguration of powers, borders, and sovereignties along new territorial and functional lines in the direction of a novel system of domination characterized by polycentrism and polyphony but still manageable in terms of both responsiveness and responsibility.[41] In the middle ground there are many other less drastic options, summarized by various metaphors, often (and not coincidentally) couched in the form of oxymorons such as "community of states,"[42] "federal association,"[43] "democracy,"[44] and others still.

The critical juncture in which Europe currently finds itself is far from reaching resolution. We are still sailing in a Weberian open sea of possibilities. The history of European integration shows that the EU is able to give its best in times of crisis. In other words, there is at least some reason for optimism. And even if the substantive agenda is definitely post-Weberian, the point of reference remains the one so masterfully illustrated in Weber's Munich conference: the emergence of a responsible and far-sighted form of *Berufpolitik* capable of creatively using political power to balance social demands and systemic imperatives without an excess of compromise to reality and its limits, that is, without giving up on one's commitment to values. Discussions about rules and institutional devices are undoubtedly necessary. But fine-tuning the machinery of government is today less important than reforging a sense of shared political destiny among European peoples, a preference for being united, and a preparedness to be committed to common political action. In other words: what is needed—especially in the eurozone—is leadership capable of "aiming for the impossible" (Weber's passionate exhortation). Necessary now are leaders willing to govern in the spirit of *EUräson*, with a view to defending and further promoting a larger cultural project in the service of peace, freedom, and the expansion of those life chances—which are essentially political values—born in the 1950s and effectively summarized in the first part of the Lisbon Treaty.

NOTES

1. Stephan Leibfried and Paul Pierson, eds., *European Social Policy Between Fragmentation and Integration* (Washington D.C.: Brookings Institution, 1995); James A. Caporaso and Sidney Tarrow, "Polanyi in Brussels: Supranational Institutions and the Transnational Embedding of Markets," *International Organization* 63 (2009): 593–620; Martin Höpner and Armin Schäfer, "Polanyi in Brussels? Embeddedness and the Three Dimensions of European Economic Integration," MPIfG Discussion Paper 10/8 (Cologne, Max Planck Institute for the Study of Societies, 2010).
2. Fritz W. Scharpf, "The Asymmetry of European Integration, or Why the EU Cannot Be a 'Social Market Economy,'" *Socio-Economic Review* 8, no. 2 (2010): 211–250.
3. Stefano Bartolini, *Restructuring Europe* (Oxford: Oxford University Press, 2005); Maurizio Ferrera, *The Boundaries of Welfare* (Oxford: Oxford University Press, 2005); Peter Flora, "Externe Grenzbildung und Interne Strukturierung. Europa und Seine Nationen," *Berliner Journal für Soziologie* 10 (2000): 157–166.
4. Hand Peter Kriesi, "Restructuring of Partisan Politics and the Emergence of a New Cleavage Based on Values," *West European Politics* 33, no. 3 (2010): 673–685.
5. Philipp Bagus, *The Tragedy of the Euro* (Auburn, Ala.: Mises Institute, 2010).
6. Wolfgang Streeck, *Gekaufte Zeit. Die vertagte Krise des demokratischen Kapitalismus* (Frankfurt: Suhrkamp, 2013).
7. Daniel Cohn Bendit and Guy Verhofstadt, *For Europe* (London: Penguin, 2012).
8. Ferrera, *The Boundaries of Welfare*; Anton Hemerijck, "The Self-Transformation of the European Social Model(s)," *International Politics and Society/ Internationale Politik und Gesellschaft* 4 (2002): 39–66; Anton Hemerijck, *Changing Welfare States* (Oxford: Oxford University Press, 2013); Jonathan Zeitlin and Martin Heidenreich, eds., *Changing European Employment and Welfare Regimes: The Influence of the Open Method of Coordination on National Reforms* (London: Routledge, 2009).

9. Eric Marlier and David Natali, eds., *Europe 2020: Towards a More Social Europe?* (Brussels: P. I. E. Lang, 2010).
10. Max Weber, *The Essential Weber: A Reader*, ed. Sam Whimster (London: Routledge, 2004).
11. Stephen Kalberg, "Should the Dynamic Autonomy of Ideas Matter to Sociologists?" *Journal of Classical Sociology* 1, no. 3 (2001): 291–327.
12. In the language of modern philosophy, a theodicy is a doctrine that tries to reconcile the historical evidence of evil with the existence of God. For Weber, the elaboration of theodicies throughout history must be seen as a response to the "problem of meaning" inherent in the human condition, i.e., making sense of the fact that the good can suffer and the evil can prosper (theodicy of suffering), or, more simply, that some people achieve greater results than others (theodicy of good fortune). See Max Weber, *From Max Weber: Essays in Sociology*, ed. by Hans H. Gerth and C. Wright Mills (New York: Oxford University Press, 1946).
13. Ahmad Sadri, *Max Weber's Sociology of Intellectuals* (Oxford: Oxford University Press, 1992).
14. Michael Freeden, *Ideologies and Political Theory* (Oxford: Oxford University Press, 1996).
15. Douglas E. Ashford, *The Emergence of the Welfare States* (Oxford: Basil Blackwell, 1986).
16. Peter Flora and Arnold J. Heidenheimer, "What Is the Welfare State?" in *The Development of Welfare States in Europe and North America*, ed. Peter Flora and Arnold J. Heidenheimer (New Brunswick, N.J.: Transaction, 1981); Peter Flora, ed., *Growth to Limits: The Western European Welfare States Since World War II* (Berlin: De Gruyter, 1986–1987).
17. Hugh Heclo, *Modern Social Politics in Sweden and Britain* (New Haven, Conn.: Yale University Press, 1974).
18. Claus Offe, *The Democratic Welfare State: A European Regime Under the Strain of European Integration* (2002), http://www.eurozine.com/articles/2002-02-08-offe-en.html.
19. Mark Hewitson and Matthew D'Auria, eds., *Europe in Crisis: Intellectuals and the European Idea, 1917–1957* (Oxford: Berghahn, 2012); Richard Swedberg, "The Idea of 'Europe' and the Origin of the European Union—a Sociological Approach," *Zeitschrift für Soziologie* 23, no. 5 (October 1994): 378–387.
20. Ernst Haas, *The Uniting of Europe: Political, Social, and Economic Forces* (Stanford, Calif.: Stanford University Press, 1958).
21. Alan Milward, *The European Rescue of the Nation State* (Berkeley: University of California Press, 1992).
22. Ferrera, *The Boundaries of Welfare*.

23. Lisa Conant, *Justice Contained: Law and Politics in the European Union* (Ithaca, N.Y.: Cornell University Press, 2004).
24. Paul Magnette, "The Fragility of Liberal Europe," *European Political Science* 8 (2009): 190–200.
25. Maurizio Ferrera, "Friends or Foes? European Integration and National Welfare States," in *Global Europe, Social Europe*, ed. Anthony Giddens, Patrick Diamond, and Roger Liddle (Oxford: Polity, 2006), 257–278.
26. Pascal Lamy and Jean Pisani-Ferry, *L'Europe de nos volontés* (Paris: Plon, 2003).
27. Weber, *From Max Weber*.
28. Sadri, *Max Weber's Sociology of Intellectuals*.
29. J. Kay, "The Map Is Not the Territory: An Essay on the State of Economics," *Institute for New Economic Thinking*, 2008, http://ineteconomics.org/blog/inet/john-kay-map-not-territory-essay-state-economics.
30. Reiner M. Lepsius, "Soziale Ungleichkeit und Klassenstrukturen in der Bundesrepublik Deutschland," in *Klassen in der Europaeische Sozialgeschichte*, ed. Hans Ulrich Wehler (Göttingen: Vandenhoeck & Ruprecht, 1979); Flora and Heidenheimer, "What Is the Welfare State?"
31. Sheldon S. Wolin, "Democracy and the Welfare State: The Political and Theoretical Connection Between Staatsräson und Wohlfahrtstaatsräson," *Political Theory* 15, no. 4 (1987): 467–500.
32. Peter Mair, *Representative Versus Responsible Government* (Cologne: Max Planck Institute for the Study of Societies, 2009).
33. Reiner M. Lepsius, *Ideen, Interessen, Institutionen* (Opladen: Westdeutscher Verlag, 1990).
34. Bartolini, *Restructuring Europe*.
35. Armin von Bogdandy, *Democratic Legitimacy of Public Authority Beyond the State* (2011), http://papers.ssrn.com/sol3/papers.cfm?abstract_id=1826326; Jürgen Habermas, *Zur Verfassung Europas. Ein Essay* (Berlin: Suhrkamp, 2011).
36. Sergio Fabbrini, "Intergovernmentalism and Its Critics," *Comparative Political Studies* 46, no. 9 (2013): 1003–1029.
37. Vivien Schmidt, "The European Union: Democratic Legitimacy in a Regional State?" *Journal of Common Market Studies* 42, no. 4 (2004): 975–999.
38. Max Weber, *The Protestant Ethic and the Spirit of Capitalism*, trans. Stephen Kalberg (Los Angeles: Roxbury, 2001). Originally published in German in 1905–1906.
39. Jürgen Habermas, "Demokratie oder Kapitalismus? Vom Elend der nationalstaatlichen Fragmentierung in einer kapitalistisch integrierten Weltgesellschaft," *Blätter für Deutsche und Internationale Politik* 5 (2013): 59–70.

40. Ulrich Beck and Edgar Grande, *Cosmopolitan Europe*, trans. Ciaran Cronin (Cambridge: Polity, 2007). Originally published in German in 2004.
41. Jan Zielonka, *Is the EU Doomed?* (Cambridge: Polity, 2014).
42. Jürgen Habermas, "Democracy, Solidarity, and the European Crisis," *Eurozine*, May 7, 2013.
43. Frank Fischer, Gerald J. Miller, and S. Sidney Mara, *Handbook of Public Policy Analysis: Theory, Methods, and Politics* (New York: Marcel Dekker, 2006).
44. Kalypso Nicolaidis, "Democracy and Its Critics," *Journal of Common Market Studies* 51, no. 2 (2013): 351–369.

CHAPTER THREE

Democracy After the Welfare State

An Interview

IRA KATZNELSON

Conducted by Nick Juravich and Maurizio Vaudagna

NICK JURAVICH: Let's begin with the big historical, definitional questions: the relationship of the welfare state at its moment of origin to the "-isms" of the nineteenth and twentieth centuries: capitalism, socialism, liberalism. And, as a consequence, the relationship of the welfare state to democracy, which is not an "-ism" but is related to and entangled with those others I mentioned. And that leads to questions you've raised at other times, about how the "golden age" emerges, and whether there was a golden age, and what kinds of democracy and participation characterize it.

These fundamental historical narratives are all-important to understand the challenges to solidarity that emerge in the era of neoliberalism and the opportunities and limits that characterize the globalized world we live in today.

IRA KATZNELSON: Why don't we start with what I take to be a pretty standard picture about which I have questions, the idea of the "golden age," which often is represented, perhaps differently in each of your views, as a post–World War II phenomenon that later runs into trouble, in a big way, during the 1973 oil crisis. What characterizes that historical moment is a confluence of trends that produced support for an enlarged social-policy role for central governments. This characterization begins with an empirical claim. Compared to earlier periods, there was a stepwise change, a significant increase, a new equilibrium level of participation by government in providing resources, whether by insurance or transfers, to citizens through instruments that are buttressed by elements of coercion—namely, taxation—and distribution through largely democratic, legalized decision. So this is a story, across the democratic political spectrum, from center-right to center-left, of a significant enough degree of consensus that the state should be used as an element both of stabilization and redistribution. Typically, welfare states in this period are understood, with good reason, to have been backed by multiple sources of overlapping support that, together, made it possible to put this equilibrium in place, irrespective of whether a center-left or center-right government was elected. In this country, you could move from Truman to Eisenhower, you could move from Christian Democrat to Social Democrat in Germany, or vice versa, and you broadly would have the structure remain intact.

One other important feature of this period was the understanding that these various, typically relatively wealthy Western countries had succeeded in defining what might be called a social minimum. Sometimes called a "right"—we can argue about T. H. Marshall—because a right is something that never can be taken away, and in democracies, very few things can never be taken away, as we have learned. But if not a right, a kind of normative minimum below which old people would not be without pensions, below which poor people would not be without some kind of income support, etc. And at this moment, this age, golden or not, these minima were made possible by a constellation of supporters who were not necessarily otherwise all in one camp or in one location. There were large elements of dominant economic forces in market-capitalist societies that backed newly robust welfare states for reasons of stability, or accumulation, or justice, or some mix of these goals, or fear of the other—the communist other, particularly—or who wished not to return to circumstances in which fascists might regain appeal. Thus they supported higher taxes and more distribution through public means. Further, this was a peak period for new forms of bottom-up association, especially trade unions. It also was an era in which traditional institutions, especially the church in Catholic countries, also subscribed to statist social policies. Of course, churches, unions, capitalist firms, and so on do not ordinarily compose one team. And they did not have, as Gøsta Esping-Andersen, among others, has pointed out, the same vision or goals for a welfare state. But for their own singular reasons and for shared, overlapping reasons, including broad normative support for liberal democracy, they backed, within limits, a modern welfare state.

However, it is worth observing that even at this "golden" moment—"golden" in inverted commas—each source of support was characterized by internal tension. It was not just within the capitalist class that many people possessed views like Hayek's, or of others like Hayek's, about freedom, the state, and the market versus state, with deep suspicions about what they viewed as inherently predatory features of the modern state. But for a time, these were subordinate voices. There were many in the trade-union movement who also were deeply suspicious of the state as an instrument, whether or not it was acting as a "committee of the bourgeoisie." Among more conservative unionists, traditions of voluntarism were much valued. Better, on this view, if the working classes would self-organize insurance societies than have them be organized through the state. Likewise, many within traditional institutions like the church thought that the welfare state was an inimical instrument of secularization and that any separation of church and state advanced by secular social policy could threaten such core values as traditional family structures. Thus it is not as if the period's consensus, even at the peak, ever was one-dimensional or uniform. And the broad agreement that did exist was dependent on commitments forged during the wars first against fascism and Nazism, then against Stalinist Bolshevism, and on the sharp increase in resources by virtue of postwar capitalism's economic successes. It was this distinctive situated context that shaped the experiences, dispositions, and behavior that underpinned support for welfare states.

ALICE KESSLER-HARRIS: So what breaks down?

IRA KATZNELSON: Let's first go back. Even for the "golden age," from 1945 to 1973, we had better be aware that there was no single welfare-state mode or a common proportion of gross domestic product (GDP) that went through the state. There were many bases of variation, not just spending levels or the mix of insurance and transfers, but the social bases of welfare states, certainly in gender terms, as the female participation rate in the workforce varied quite a lot. Germany being very low, for example. There were huge qualitative differences even within and between countries thought to be arrayed in different places in the hierarchy. Both the United States and Britain, to take that close comparison, fit into what Esping-Andersen calls the "liberal" version of the welfare state. But their mix of policy generosity was very different: state pensions have been significantly deeper and better in the United States; health care significantly deeper and better from a welfare-state perspective in Britain. Looking at these policy arenas, it is not possible to say that one or the other country had the more advanced welfare state. For old people, especially after Richard Nixon indexed Social Security and advanced a 25 percent increase in a single year, thus lifting many elderly people out of poverty, the U.S. looms strong and normatively attractive. Reciprocally, had one only looked at pensions in Britain, it would have appeared as a very weak welfare state. But if, instead, one considers health. . . . There also was a great heterogeneity of unit scale. National welfare states were fashioned in countries that were very different in size, demography, heterogeneity, age distribution, workforce participation rates, and degrees of federalism. In all, the "golden age" appellation tends to flatten a complex social reality and promote an overly simple nostalgia for what we have lost. The bases for what has been lost have to be located both in what was shared despite these differences but also by attending to which aspects of the loss were particular to specific differences.

To back up, how did we get to this "golden age"? When I first read Karl Polanyi's *The Great Transformation* as an undergraduate, my fellow students and I were pressed to consider where welfare states came from. Most of us found Polanyi's analytical story to be very powerful, especially under quasi-democratic conditions, then under more democratic conditions. At its core was the profound manner in which he identified "society defending itself" against the risks of the market, especially risks having to do with the labor market. If the nineteenth and early twentieth century composed the moment when modern labor markets burst on the scene with industrialization, proletarianization, and so on, then there was this forceful pushback. We sometimes forget the ironic aspects inside Polanyi's analysis, his critique of social democracy in the 1920s for having succeeded to impede the market just enough to make it not work very well but not enough to provide social justice. In consequence, that social-democratic impulse opened the door for fascists who were able to claim that representative, constitutional democracies are incapable of solving the dilemmas thrown up by market capitalism, but that we, with a strong-S State—as Mussolini would have said, "the State is everything,"—we who are proud totalitarians can solve these problems in a way that liberal democrats cannot. So one long-haul force for the modern welfare state came from pressure by citizens who feared, rightly, the risks attendant to capitalist industrialization, proletarianization, and working-class formation.

A second long-term cause can be found in the growth, in the late nineteenth and early twentieth century, not only of a capitalist class of a new kind but of the sectorial organizations of capitalists who sought in different ways to reduce the risks of the marketplace for themselves, not on behalf of workers but on behalf of their firms and their sectors. So you get people who run steel mills talking to one another and organizing, not quite creating monopolies, as they did want to defeat one another in the marketplace, but creating all kinds of common institutions and practices. And for some significant part of the manufacturing new world, there was a growing sense that a priority requirement was a public framework to guarantee a floor underneath the labor market in order to gain a stable workforce, a stable investment climate, and a sufficient degree of public legitimacy for modern capitalism. This also was a period, especially in Catholic countries, when the church came to understand that it could not secure the allegiance of mass publics if it was seen to be simply against the secular state by holding on to its hegemony in education and to its welfare hegemony. It would do better to try to influence the character of welfare states than to oppose them in every way and see them as competitors.

MAURIZIO VAUDAGNA: Let me pick up the point you made about the welfare state as an avenue of participation. Not only did it take a long time before the opinion prevailed that the welfare state was coherent with liberty, after a protracted period when it was thought that coercion accompanied social protection, but it took an even longer period of time before scholars determined that social protection might be necessary for effective participation. Now we are at a more difficult time of welfare-state retrenchment, and still there is a lot of talk about the making of a new welfarism that would empower citizens and create participation. So, how do you see the issue of the relationships between social policy and participation? On the one hand, progressives talk of expanding democratic citizenry as a way to mold responsible citizens, while, on the other, responsibility is the banner of the conservatives, who hold that up to now the polity has only recognized entitlements and that it is time for the citizen to become "responsible" in the meaning conservatives attach to it.

IRA KATZNELSON: Let me, if I may, come to the participation issue in just a second. But as you were asking your questions I realized there were two things I should have said earlier. First is a point about the United States and Europe. The postwar welfare state throughout Europe—leaving Scandinavia slightly to the side, but the rest of Europe—was a "New Deal" welfare state, the product not only of the forces already discussed but also the result of an American hegemony that sent to Europe models drawn from the left side of the American New Deal, whether in the Marshall Plan or other forms of institutional arrangements. Despite enduring differences across the ocean, European social democracy after the war was more like the left part, what in America is called the liberal part, of the New Deal, than like 1920s social democracy of the type criticized by Polanyi.

MAURIZIO VAUDAGNA: You're saying the opposite of Daniel Rodgers's *Atlantic Crossings*, which showed influence moving westward.

IRA KATZNELSON: *Atlantic Crossings* is persuasive for the earlier Progressive period. At minimum, let's just say there was a very powerful Atlantic crossing during the "golden age" in the other direction. Why? Because the United States was a successful democracy that never suspended elections—even Britain suspended its democracy during the war—and never had to pass an enabling act while pioneering forms of social policy that created a modern welfare state, especially the Social Security Act of 1935. This American model was received well, even worshipped, by people who had very different political priors.

To return to your point about fascism and communism, look at the very earliest days of the New Deal, its more radical days, when it tackled not only issues of distribution and security but issues of political economy in a more fundamental way, as in the National Industrial Recovery Act. The first Roosevelt administration used the state to interject itself into the marketplace in a way that went well beyond the dreams of a democratic Left before the New Deal by drawing on elements of corporatism, primarily from Italy, and planning, primarily from the Soviet Union. Then, there were articles by Rexford Tugwell and others about democratic corporatism, democratic planning, and how it is that democracy and policies that might seem so antithetical can go together. It was this impulse, to the extent that it created a framework, that entered into postwar European discourse and surrounded the welfare state: It was possible not just to have social insurance and redistribution, but imagine a political-economy role for the state that borrowed from, yet democratized, instruments of intervention in capitalism that otherwise would have been unthinkable under democratic conditions and that were thought to require Bolshevism or fascism. In these ways, the New Deal was important as a model and as a catalyst. Curiously, just as the left part of the New Deal was losing out in the United States, it was winning on its own terms within the Labour Party in Britain and within social-democratic parties on the continent.

ALICE KESSLER-HARRIS: So, just, a challenge. I don't disagree with the last part of your argument. But I do with the first part, that is, with the notion that the European welfare state was based on an American model, a New Deal model. The benefits of the American welfare state in those early years are generally employment related: employment determines not only standing but the level of benefits. In Europe, that's rarely the case.

IRA KATZNELSON: Actually, I agree in part with your objection. That is to say, as I stressed earlier, there was a great deal of heterogeneity, even greater than you've just said. There was nothing in the United States like the decommodification of the health system that took place in Britain: that was wholly outside the employment system, but it was a general right of citizens, who became eligible for health care funded through the general tax system. Still, Britain was full of employment-connected social policy, though child allowances were not: a mother with one or more children received benefits. But the same was the case in the more targeted policies of ADC and AFDC. In the United States, they were placed outside an employment infrastructure, at least until President Clinton's welfare reform. So yes, there are these differences, but all these countries have had social-insurance systems funded by job holders and job-related taxes and that provide accrued benefits.

I think what is most distinctive about the American welfare system is its federalism, or key aspects of it, especially regarding poverty policy, which is decentralized. And of course, these policies were decentralized largely because of southern worries, Jim Crow worries. If you ask why Aid to Dependent Children in the 1935 Social Security Act produced an outcome in which benefits in Mississippi were a fraction of those available in New York, it was because each state regulated the size of the benefit. To be sure, employment issues mattered, for there was an effort not to exceed the given wage structure of the state, not to go above the wage structure of dirty agricultural work and maids' work, except when they were kept outside the system altogether, as with old-age pensions. It was mostly because of the unwillingness of southern elites to have black people secure certain levels of benefits.

ALICE KESSLER-HARRIS: But talk a little bit about the effect on participation of the differentials in how the benefits are provided.

IRA KATZNELSON: So here's an irony. Let's come to the participation issue, because it is extremely important. Countries identified with more robust welfare states tend to be more centralized and more state-centered, more governed by central bureaucracies. In relationship to that, there exists a complicated set of questions about the nature and meaning of participation. So what do I mean? In Sweden, an exemplary country for so many of us, at least for the golden period, so much is decided in peak-association bargaining between the state, trade unions, and capital. Everything from how much inflation and how much unemployment to the scale of various kinds of welfare-state arrangements. These are negotiated by peak association, not settled by mass participation.

ALICE KESSLER-HARRIS: But the ILO represents, or historically represented, more than 90 percent of the working population, and therefore you could say that it reflected the voice of the many.

IRA KATZNELSON: I am going to make exactly that point. But what does this mean for patterns of participation? This is an elite-driven negotiated system that proved to distribute resources in a much more egalitarian manner than in Britain or the United States. But is it more participatory? From one angle, yes, for just the reason you said: the citizens are represented through their union. The workers are represented through their union. But, of course, people have multiple identities, and there is a flattening of interests. Not every worker has identical concerns. And with strong corporatism there is a version of Robert Michel's "Iron Law of Oligarchy." Party and trade-union leaders essentially run a private negotiation system, which, like it or not, produces an authoritative outcome. And we know—think of Austria as well as Sweden—that strong corporatist systems like this, systems that seem incredibly representative and participatory in some critical ways, have generated a huge recoil not just from the top down but from the bottom up, as it seems as if democratic politics does not matter at all because a tiny elite controls and makes decisions about everything. This is not an argument against the Swedish model, but I am cautioning against saying, "Sweden: high on participation; United States: low on participation." And there are substantive issues. Compare being an automobile worker, not today, but in 1962, in the United States and Sweden. Pension benefits and key aspects of health-care benefits not only were at least as good in the United States, but the people who had negotiated them for you were people you might even know face to face. They were not from every industry; they were from *your* industry, your union leaders, your shop leaders. If you don't like them, or if you don't like the deal, you can vote it down, you can vote them out. So your Blue Shield/Blue Cross benefits, or your pension benefits, were the product of a very robust process. Now, we also know that this proved to be a vulnerable process. So participation comparisons have to be handled with care.

Among the poor, however, there was much lower participation in the United States. That is why the so-called War on Poverty created new models for participation. The poor, especially the poor of color, had been left out of the game of social rights and citizenship in a way that was not the case in the most advanced corporatist countries. So we have to be careful in talking comparatively about participation and the welfare state to get underneath broad-brush descriptions to specify temporalities, mechanisms, and diversity of fact and meaning.

MAURIZIO VAUDAGNA: Your historical interpretation is very important to connect the past of the welfare state with its present and foreseeable future, which is one of the main goals of this book. The participation you are talking about was taking place under conditions that nowadays seem very far back in time. Unions are declining, the ability of parties to represent is not what it used to be, avenues of participation are much more complicated than under the bygone conditions you were talking about. The social provision as an avenue of public participation has become much more of a problem, independent of whether we look at services afforded by the public or private sector, by centralization or localism. So: how do you see the possibilities and avenues of participation in the age of welfare retrenchment? How participatory are the postwelfare regimes that we are living in? And what could be a definition of participating citizenship in a postwelfare liberal democracy?

IRA KATZNELSON: Of course, this is not a simple question. I am prepared to have opinions about things that I have no reason to have opinions about! Yes, I am willing to speculate. But let me come back to something you said at the very beginning, which had to do with the word solidarity. It seems to me that one of the most positive features of successful social-policy regimes is that they build a sense of common fate, common responsibility, common citizenship. But I would resist the idea that social rights ever were rights in the same sense as civil and political rights. Distinctions, like those of the philosopher Ronald Dworkin, have to be made. He reminds us that a right is like a trump card that can never be taken away. Social policy, by contrast, is part of normal democratic politics, and ordinary democratic politics is always provisional. Sometimes, health care is organized—as the Swiss do, not just the Americans—through private insurance companies, or it can be organized through public insurance companies. These are matters for democratic contest and debate, thus not quite rights. What is a right is a sense of some minimum below which no citizen should fall. Even in the United States, it is almost impossible to find even the most conservative politician who would say, "let 'em starve, let the baby die of hunger, let the child be illiterate." So there is a social minimum, but how far above that social minimum policy should go is a matter of democratic debate. For that reason, though it may have appeared that we were on a trajectory to instantiate "welfare rights" as rights, they have never achieved that status.

MAURIZIO VAUDAGNA: Since the UN Universal Declaration of Human Rights in 1948, the notion of social rights has never been established as solidly as have political and civil rights. They have been further weakened by being caught in the Cold War conflict between East and West, when liberal democracies waved the banner of civil and political liberties and the communist countries that of the social state.

IRA KATZNELSON: I agree with you. But the issues of solidarity, and of common citizenship, inevitably bump up against two kinds of distributional conflicts. One of which is: given that ultimately, even in a rich country, resources are limited, how will they be divided? Will we privilege ending poverty among old people or children? You can say, "well, we should end it among both," but in the United States there has been a demonstrated priority in the last half-century to reduce poverty radically among the aged but not among children. No one will say, "we wish to have more poor children," but the distribution of resources has been such that one group has been privileged over the other. That is not just a normative or a practical matter but a matter that plays on the politics or nonpolitics of solidarity. Imagine that a president of the United States, a candidate, would campaign and say: "we're going to reduce social security benefits by 25 percent, and take all that money—which is quite a lot—and address the fact that we have a crisis of child poverty. We will not lower taxes, we will keep the money in the state system, but we'll spend it very differently." I promise you this will be a source of conflict.

So that's one source of tension. Another distributive source of tension has to do with the inevitable conflict over not just how *much* to tax but *how* to tax, and who to tax. Assuming a welfare system of any kind, whether funded through insurance payments or through general tax transfers, someone is paying. It is inevitable that some will pay more than they gain. If everybody gains more than they pay, the system will be bankrupt. Even in the "golden age," even under the best conditions, conditions of significant economic growth when the pie is growing, even then there were distributional decisions and conflicts. Once you enter a world in which not only is there much lower growth but, for a large part of the population, wage stagnation, then the question arises of whether they would prefer to have their taxes cut, even if the great majority of benefits go to the top tier, or if they would prefer to have a more robust social-welfare state. Under even Habermasian undistorted communications—which we don't have, but if you had it—it is not obvious that a stronger welfare state would be the popular choice.

MAURIZIO VAUDAGNA: And as a consequence they prefer to buy certain services on the private market, and therefore the whole balance of public and private in the traditional social provision is changing exactly because of what you say. On this matter I have done some reading on Sweden, where at some point the middle class accepted high taxes and universal welfare rights because the government was able to show that the public social provision was efficient and supported the middle class too. Elsewhere, for example in my country, Italy, if one gets a nonlethal disease and has got to wait four months before being treated, it is very likely that, if he or she has got a decent income, he or she will utilize a private health provider because the public health service is so slow. The result is that low-income people are at a disadvantage with respect to the provision of health service. To move on, after touching the fundamental issue of taxes as a foundation of solidarity and as the precondition of a comprehensive welfare state, there is another area that elicits a huge amount of discussion on how solidarity is to be forged, and which kind of solidarity—that is, immigration and multiculturalism. Think, for example, of Will Kymlicka's work on Canada: the idea that the welfare state was based on a certain cohesion of ideas and ethnicity and that therefore a society that becomes more pluralistic, more ethnically varied, that receives a lot of new immigrants, is bound to cut resources, social services, and transfers for both the old-stock citizenry and for the newcomers.

IRA KATZNELSON: I think this, arguably, is a logical tendency, but I think empirically it is actually not exactly right. Why do I say that? I'll start here, in this country. Do we constitute a common community? Now, in the United States, there's an interesting historical lesson. From 1880–1881 until the mid-1920s, many millions of strangers came. Catholics, primarily, Jews—who came in all their own heterogeneity—Italians, Poles, Swedes, Germans, Russians, and so on. They didn't speak the same language, some were heavily rural, some were heavily urban, and they were different than the predominantly Protestant and more agrarian America. And somehow, the degree of communal trust and the set of networks each subgroup had got translated, in the history, say, of the growth of union movements like the CIO, into shared trust across ethnic lines. Now, I am not saying that this proved automatic or easy, this moving across ethnic and religious lines. This mass immigration and absorption was the largest such experiment of its kind anywhere in the West. Now, of course, we know that the door was shut in 1924 and that it did not reopen until 1965, so you could argue it was under conditions of the creation of a second generation that this integration occurred. And I understand the countertrends. Nonetheless, it is true that not just the Democratic Party but also the Republican Party became remarkably more heterogeneous as they incorporated the children of immigrants. Unions also played a key role. The union movement was the product of subgroup collaboration, at times even across racial lines, and thus helped provide a solidaristic if heterogeneous social basis for the U.S. welfare state. Now, the really interesting question is: under what contextual traditions could that have happened? Perhaps under two contextual conditions that do not exist today. One was the dire emergency having to do with the utter collapse of capitalism in the 1930s, and the other was the remarkable success of capitalism in the postwar growth period.

MAURIZIO VAUDAGNA: *Les trente glorieuses.*
IRA KATZNELSON: Today we are in between. We have not repeated, even after 2008, except perhaps in Spain or Greece, the persistent unemployment rates and deprivation levels of the 1930s. But we have also not produced a climate of optimism and growth. So in today's situation in the political economy more pluralism may be especially stressful. Under 1930s conditions, everyone was driven down together by the emergency, and in the subsequent growth period, everyone could imagine gains together. In this middle zone, the competitive dimensions of subgroup citizenship become potentially more urgent and more pressing.

MAURIZIO VAUDAGNA: Can I ask you to develop further the opinion you just gave? You seem to say that even nowadays, in spite of their decline, in spite of their troubles, traditional avenues of representation and participation like unions and parties are still viable ways for socializing and solidarizing that do not have to be given up in our hopes for the future. It seems to me that in this country, and in different European countries too, this is controversial terrain. Even at Columbia University graduate students' seminars the opinion has often been voiced that these traditional channels of representation and participation have lost most of their potential.

IRA KATZNELSON: Yes, it is controversial. Let's start with the zone less of the welfare state as such but of democracy, its core institutions of parties, mobilizing civic associations including, but not only, unions, elections, parliaments, that are at the heart of constitutional democracy. When they grow very weak—and they have grown weaker—when they grow excessively weak, there is nothing that can replace them. That is, in the absence of the robustness of these institutions, other forms of participation run the risk of opening doors to demagogy and to the kind of spectator politics represented in your country by Berlusconi. But the point I am making is that certain forms of more direct populism, certain forms of antisystem politics, which have robust support in parts of the Left, also have robust support at other parts of the spectrum. These open up to new kinds of Peronism, mass, not-quite-democratic mobilizations that often promise social-welfare benefits, but at the cost of meaningful democracy.

MAURIZIO VAUDAGNA: It would be interesting to discuss the use and meaning of the word "populism" in this country and in Europe in both history writing and public life. It is a very controversial concept. For Europeans, "populism" is a political attitude that easily leans toward violating the very foundations of liberal democracy.

IRA KATZNELSON: And in parts of Latin America. But in the United States, the word is often associated, especially by the Left, with robust democratic participation. On the right, the Tea Party is a deeply participatory institution, with a mass base rooted in many institutions, including evangelical churches. Its members work through democratic procedures, elections, primary elections and the like, and they are deeply suspicious of welfare states, except social insurance for the elderly. But this surely is an antistatist impulse and, they would say, a democratic impulse and a popular mass impulse. It is far more successful today in this country than any left-wing mobilization. The closest we came to it was the first Obama election, which had a certain kind of mass-mobilizing character, but that was particular to a moment and candidate.

So if we ask about the welfare state as an instrument of participation, we really have to ask questions to which I do not know the answer. One set concerns institutional design. How do we design social programs to elicit identification, interest, mobilization, solidarity, trust, all these values, which then have a recursive element, so that participation leads to a virtuous circle of more trust, more solidarity, more active mobilization in favor of normatively attractive values, which then, if they work actually to improve people's lives, can generate further support? A critical element is exactly what the Tea Party in America says is not possible—I believe it could be possible—which is effective, successful governance characterized by a situation in which money is deployed by state institutions to create appealing public goods in health and other key arenas of social life. There is a project that you may know well that Bo Rothstein has been running at Gothenburg. Their central finding is that, among other things, support for social policy comes in settings where government not only is thought to be efficient and effective and not corrupt but where it *is* so—actually, objectively, is so—and that this is a very uneven phenomenon in much of the world. Where government does not deliver the goods, where there is a lot of rent seeking, where there is corruption, there is little support for a robust state. Here in New York State, the leader of the Democratic Party in the legislature has just been convicted of corruption, and the leader of the Republican Party is on trial for corruption.

MAURIZIO VAUDAGNA: Even in the Vatican now, we have this whole series of wonderful scandals.

IRA KATZNELSON: But this produces not just demobilization but, much more, a profound skepticism about the state, about its capacities and its justice. So what would we mean by a participatory welfare state? We have to look at institutional design and performance. And we need successful models, and we need them under conditions that are not terribly hospitable, because capitalism is not generating a bounty, yet there is no desirable alternative on offer, broadly, to market capitalism. Very few people in the West are mobilizing to be like China, which itself is a market-capitalist system, but authoritarian. Under these conditions, it becomes very difficult to generate significant majorities in favor of participatory welfare-state experiments, as opposed to hunkering down to protect what you have.

MAURIZIO VAUDAGNA: This line of conversation reminds me of the idea that Nick was stressing on participation and localism, local government and local experiments, that is, the whole issue of the centralized/decentralized welfare state. Nick, would you like to pick up this point?

NICK JURAVICH: I would, and there are many directions we could go in. I pick up this phrase "the patterning of class" from one of your own books, *City Trenches*, and think about, particularly in my own work but also just in this larger context, how both services are distributed, delivered at the local level, but also how problems for the welfare state, whether they are problems of changing demographics or problems of available resources, emerge often at the local level, and what that means in different settings and different kinds of contexts. Another early book of yours I think of is *Black Men, White Cities*, which is again about a kind of set of conditions that are particular, if comparable, and how those generate certain kinds of tensions and certain kinds of political, and participatory, and deliverance problems.

IRA KATZNELSON: Let's start with a subject that, as you noted, I spent time with. One of the highly distinctive features of the American scene, which had implications for social policy, was a kind of practical and normative segmentation, dividing the world of work, where many people thought of themselves as workers, as labor, from the world of home, where people thought of themselves as ethnics, or as members of this or that religious community, or neighborhood communities. And American social policy was, has been, divided between responsibilities that are primarily local, but in which the competition and politics has been about services and ethnicity and neighborhood, versus other forms of social policy—like that of social insurance, Social Security—in which being a worker and being a citizen in general has meant more than being a local. And some issues, like, Nick, the one you care and write about, education—as compared to France—is profoundly a local matter in the United States. Under some spatial conditions, that produces a sense of solidarity and "us." So if you have a common school system in a city of six hundred thousand people, under conditions especially before mass suburbanization, people of different backgrounds are sharing in the same system. Therefore, parents are a pressure group for expenditure, for decent education, for mobility possibilities for their children, and so on. Once you have localism under conditions of the exit from urban public schools by middle- and upper-middle-class families to new spatial suburbs, where each local unit is its own school district and where schooling is tied very heavily to distinctive real-estate markets, and therefore to particular class niches, then the game of education and of potential solidarity under local conditions becomes very different.

As Nick also knows, because he writes about it, there have been episodes in the last half-century or more where institutions of local participation have been created—school-board elections, for example—that tend to elicit extremely low participation rates, about which most citizens are profoundly skeptical. There also is a very long-standing tradition of critical analysis, as in Grant McConnell's *Private Power and American Democracy*, a book from the mid-1960s. McConnell, who was writing a critique of many things, including localism, said the more local you get in terms of public policy the more likely you are to have policies dominated by local elites, and those elites tend to be a consortium of business leaders, political leaders, and so on. Paradoxically, there is less meaningful participation locally than in Washington, where there is a fuller, more genuinely pluralist form of political representation. I am not arguing that he was right in all respects, but he identified important countercurrents. We cannot assume, automatically, that the local generates more robust and meaningful participation. We should ask about the conditions that determine whether central or local participation is more likely to generate practical and normative solutions that are highly desirable, including enhanced patterns of participation. Presently, we do not have good enough answers.

MAURIZIO VAUDAGNA: Direct democracy has always been experimented with, but it has always been complicated and ambiguous in many ways. For example, in Italy we have condominium meetings that are supposed to be participatory moments at the local level, which, however, display all the troubles you were mentioning. That is, that they create small inner groups of attendants that end up monopolizing the selective interests that are actually represented.

IRA KATZNELSON: I want to add one footnote, which is the following. There is a wonderful book, *Beyond Adversary Democracy*, written some years ago by Jane Mansbridge. She argues—and I think this bears on how we design a welfare state and how we get participation—that there are two models of democracy. One she calls a "friendship" model, the other an "adversary" model. What is a friendship model? We are all in this together. We are one community of fate. And therefore, ultimately, despite whatever differences we have, we are friends. We share interests in common. In that model, deliberative democracy seems very appealing. If only we could get citizens who are all friends to deliberate together, either behind a veil of ignorance, or without a veil of ignorance, we would get normatively desirable and legitimate solutions. Model number two: in a complicated, pluralistic, heterogeneous world, a world that is capitalist, ethnically diverse, geographically spread out, with different cultural values—for abortion, against abortion—democratic politics is adversarial. It is not a discussion among friends but a contest among citizens who hold a great variety of preferences, values, and interests, some of which are very hard to compromise on. The hard question is how to build a robust welfare state under those conditions. To do so, there has to be enough overlapping agreement about common rules of the game that people are willing to play: because they trust that the game is not rigged, that it's not the same winner all the time. And second, this has to be a game of provisional outcomes, where results can change by way of participation. If you believe that child poverty is more important than old-age poverty, you might affect that by participating. If you believe that traditional family values, even patriarchal values, are better than gender-equal values—I'm not arguing for that position—if you participate in political life you can argue why that outcome is desirable. This adversarial model asks citizens and their representatives to make collective decisions despite their differences. For those of us who come out of social-democratic traditions, our traditional models are not good enough because they have been models about capitalism and workers, or about various kinds of us-them, elite-people models, which do not quite give enough attention to the institutions and conditions under which they can work, under conditions of great adversarial heterogeneity. If we really believe in the value of robust participation, then the question is participation within an institutional frame that can allow for the possibility of recurrent and not always identical, collective decisions being made, within which outcomes are provisional within limits of a social minimum and within limits of democratic rights. Liberal democracy, yes; a social minimum, yes; and with both, robust forms of adversarial participation.

MAURIZIO VAUDAGNA: Together with some hope of a successful outcome: that is to say, in the long run, if I participate, which stabilizes my democratic citizenship and voices my preference on, say, family life, and other people will do the same, I can rationally hope that at some point my participating will also impact results.

IRA KATZNELSON: That it's not a complete waste of time. There is no guarantee that "my view or no other view," and moreover, there may have to be mixed results. But with sufficient gains and benefits, active participation can be elicited. Again, a virtuous circle. Because in that way, not only may social policy be strengthened, but the support of democratic social policy can be strengthened. The value of democracy itself is renewed through use, even if democracy is messy and sometimes uncertain.

NICK JURAVICH: These are questions to pivot to, slightly, and I have three sets, but this is the first one that I think comes most directly out of what you were saying: how gender and family, and also race and ethnicity, have structured not just the welfare state but the kinds of political challenges and problems that might undermine it. And I'm not thinking here just of the argument that demographic heterogeneity or migration undermines the state, but actually questions about how, for example, the Nixon Family Assistance Plan (FAP), which elicited opposition on both the left and the right, and a kind of raising of questions about gender that led to many different levels and layers of mistrust and difficultly.

IRA KATZNELSON: I have a strong view, and I have had arguments with Frances Piven and other friends with whom I broadly share political views about this, but the Left's opposition to FAP was catastrophic. That was the single best opportunity in the American experience to create a basic minimum floor under those who were most vulnerable. The FAP would have done little at that point for the poorest people north of the Mason-Dixon line in America, but it would have radically transformed the lives of poor people—millions of poor people—in the

South, and it would have established a principle, initiated by a Republican administration, of a funded social minimum below which nobody could fall. I saw that as a plus along every dimension: race, gender, and class.

NICK JURAVICH: Well, I'm thinking of that, but also spinning out from that more broadly. So there are many arguments that get made about the end of the New Deal era. I'm thinking of Jeff Cowie's "exception" argument. And he cites these issues not just as a sort of demographic fact but for active social movements around gender equity, around rights of families, or for social rights for African Americans.

IRA KATZNELSON: If we return to the language of a golden age, the post-1970s moment qualifies as the golden age in matters of gender, race, and sexuality. We live in a vastly fairer world now than when the welfare state was at its peak in the 1945–1973 period. We certainly live in a world of much more gender equality. We certainly live in a world—signified by gay marriage, for example—of different, validated expressions of sexuality. We have an African American president of the United States, even if that does not mean we have entered a postracial age. In fact, some features of race in America are worse than they were, but others are vastly better. The idea not just that you could have an African American president but that he could win majorities in Virginia, North Carolina, and Florida, as opposed to being lynched for having the audacity to be a candidate in those states, is a revolution. These various gains are victories for the revolutions of the 1960s. The civil-rights revolution, the gender revolution, the women's revolution, the gay revolution have transformed our world. But one of their effects has been to undercut and undermine aspects of the traditional welfare state, even regarding support among African Americans. In the 1970s and 1980s, the political scientist Vesla Weaver has shown, across the class spectrum in black America there was uniform support for a very robust welfare state. If you look at the same population today, the middle- and upper-middle-class black population offers a lower level of support than poor blacks. Class divisions within black America have grown, and that gulf has produced a much wider dispersion of support for the welfare state than existed in more solidaristic times, when blacks collectively were struggling for civil rights. You would find the same pattern among U.S. Latinos. If the Republican Party would stop bashing immigrants, they would win, as George Bush did in Texas, almost half of Latino votes, because that community's expressed preferences are quite conservative across a range of issues, certainly on abortion, but also on matters of "personal responsibility," with which you began. But the Republican Party has decided to go to war against Mexicans in general, who therefore will vote some 70 to 80 percent Democratic and thus in favor of more social spending. But this support is not stable. The point I am making is that it is not possible to reduce fairness issues to one vector, because they concern those aspects of social policy that have to do with economic distribution and those aspects of social policy that have to do with opportunity across lines of race and gender, religion and ethnicity. They do not all march in lockstep together.

MAURIZIO VAUDAGNA: On the other hand, gender criticism of the welfare state and of social-democratic citizenship, that is, the social dimension of democratic citizenship, has criticized very much the gender implications of the male worker, the patriarchal and paternalist assumptions that have accompanied the historical development of social citizenship. As a result, feminist critics have sort of reformulated the idea of social rights into that of the social dimension of human rights. Nowadays the discourse of social benefits is often formulated in terms of human rights more than in the earlier terms of social citizenship rights. This shift emerges out of a long story, because already in the UN Universal Declaration of 1948 the social provision was defined in terms of human rights.

IRA KATZNELSON: But at a time when traditional patriarchal assumptions were so common they seemed as if part of nature. But the patriarchal world and the human-rights world of social rights share in common what I was earlier calling, via Professor Mansbridge, the "friendship" assumption. That is, the traditional family model was a model of solidarity in which all were assumed to share common interests, most notably in the well-being of the family unit. Families were thought to aggregate up into a social unit, society, itself a solidaristic group of common friends. The language of the human-rights claim to social benefits likewise offers a friendship model. In spite of all our differences, we are commonly human. Both missed the adversarial. The feminist critique of the patriarchal model said exactly that, observing that women and men did not occupy the same position under conditions of patriarchy. Do not make the assumption that we are all in it together with common interests. To the contrary. Patriarchy violates our interests, holding us down, preventing us from achieving who we are, controlling everything from our minds to our bodies, and we rebel. We also see a rebellion, often but not only by conservatives, against the common human discourse by saying, "we're not exactly all the same." We have different values, different this, different that, different preferences, different interests. Unless a modern welfare state is structured by social policies that somehow take account of that pluralism, a kind of false consciousness exists, or at least a false portrait. We need to make manifest our differences and work through them, as opposed to eliding them and pretending they do not exist.

NICK JURAVICH: So I've got a pivot to the future off that. I'm thinking here, we have these questions about the "-isms" of the nineteenth and twentieth centuries, but perhaps one about the sort of the reigning "-ism," if indeed this is a fair definition of our time, which is neoliberalism.

IRA KATZNELSON: I dislike the term. Let's call it, more precisely, ultra–market capitalism.

NICK JURAVICH: Fair enough. But I think there's a response that comes from Reagan, that comes from Hayek, Margaret Thatcher, many people, that solves this problem of different social groups with different interests by saying that they are all epiphenomenal and nonexistent. The idea that there's no such thing as society. And Hayek calls "social" a "weasel word," right, that to put that in front of things is to suggest solidarities where there are not or should not be.

IRA KATZNELSON: I had a conversation this summer with the conservative philosopher Roger Scruton, who took exactly this position. "Whenever I see the word 'social,'" he says, "I know it's phony."

NICK JURAVICH: Well, and this brings us back in a way to the beginning, to Polanyi. Because it brings us back to the question: Are there still conditions, under which, as you say, we can start to think socially, but in ways that are not just about adversarial social groups but also about solidaristic social groups? And what kinds of possibilities exist?

IRA KATZNELSON: The most meaningful solidarities come from working through, not from denying, that which is adversarial. You cannot have solidaristic citizenship pretending that there is no diversity of perspectives, values, interests, and so on. On the other hand, if you just have diversity with nothing in common, that produces a disaster of a different kind. This is a field of tension that will not go away and should not be avoided. We should not search for a way to avoid the dilemma but for ways to work through it. It sounds banal when I make that point, but it seems to me to be fundamental. Now, to the critique, the conservative critique of the social, or, if you like, a neoliberal critique of the social. Again, this is a friendship-model critique arguing that ultimately we are individuals, and thus we value the human person. It is not a rightsless view; we all have a right to our individual existence, and we should not impose, or have imposed on us, a priori categories: Catholic or Protestant, black or white, men or women, rural or urban. Ultimately society is composed of the preferences and values and behaviors of persons. This is not unattractive as a view, but it represents a myth that ignores the most important feature of human relations, a feature the ancients understood, which is that humans are in relationships with one another. They are not isolated nodes, and thus there always are going to be norms and rules that govern those relations, whether it's reciprocity, or market ties, or something else. The issue is not whether there will be such connections but the form they will take. Further, network ties are mediated by identities, and those identities do not simply exist one person at a time. Scruton to the contrary, the social is not an empty or banal signifier.

Why do I dislike the term "neoliberal"? Because I think it makes "liberal" a synonym for market. Liberal is too important a word to be identified with just a single promarket position. I prefer to speak of a kind of radical market position. I would like to reserve the word for the liberal political tradition based on government by consent, rule of law, individual rights, and political representation as core values. In modern democracies, we are all political liberals. Social democrats are liberals. Conservatives, what we call in America conservatives, are liberals. What we have is debate not about whether to be liberal but about the kind of policy liberalism we wish to have. These are debates about the proper rules of transaction between the state and the market, the state and society, the state and other states. This is where the fundamental questions of democratic politics broadly and social policy in particular lie.

MAURIZIO VAUDAGNA: May I ask one little thing to finish? In the area of democratic social solidarity and human rights, one of the issues that is most difficult to be mediated in public life, and to frame a consensual decision making in both the United States and elsewhere, is what services are to be reserved to noncitizens.

IRA KATZNELSON: There are two zones about which the Western liberal tradition has little inherently to say. One, which we have not talked about, is global geopolitics. The other is the question of membership. Who gets to be a liberal citizen and enjoy advantages of this status? We do not live in a world without boundaries. The only criterion that has emerged out of the Western liberal tradition is the demand that participants must be rational actors who are capable of deliberating together on the basis of reason, not just on the basis of tradition, superstition, or magic. The most fundamental debate in the Western world in the past quarter-millennium has not been about class but about who is eligible to be a member. Women were thought not to be eligible because they were not capable of rationality. Slaves and ex-slaves were not thought to be eligible. John Stuart Mill writes, in *On Liberty*, about how backward peoples—his phrase—are not yet eligible, and he deploys the people of China as an example. From this perspective, the greatest and most successful revolutions we have experienced have been revolutions to reduce the zone of the ineligible. Today, as a result, we do not ask whether people of different ethnicities, religions, races, or genders, could be members. Rather, we inquire about the rules, norms, and conventions the newcomers must accept if they wish to be members. These are vexing matters, as we hear and see every day, but they are less holistic in character than the all-or-nothing manner in which issues of black versus white, women versus men, Catholics versus Protestants, and Europeans versus the colonized once routinely took shape.

The social-policy questions in this respect thus also have become narrower. At what point does a newcomer become eligible to collect old-age benefits or have their children not just in school but, in America, be eligible for college-tuition benefits? We thus can close by celebrating some progress.

NOTE

Nick Juravich and Maurizio Vaudagna express their gratitude to Alice Kessler-Harris for her lively participation in the first part of the interview.

PART II

Varieties of Retrenchment

NEOLIBERALISM HOLDS that economic growth, fed by an unrestrained free market in money and goods, is the essential ingredient of prosperity; decries social spending as counterproductive; and despises government interventions in market relations. Such interference—neoliberals hold—places an unbearable burden on economic growth by stifling individual initiative. After the financial crisis of 2008, demands for austerity provoked disdain for economic security, which seemed achievable only at the cost of growth. The language of "time limits," "benefit caps," the "hidden welfare state," and "asset building" cloaked welfare retrenchment in this era. It disguised policies that pushed social support backward into the restrictive arena of safety nets, pathologizing recipients and shifting the quality and quantity of benefits from adequate to minimal. This section analyses some areas where retrenchment policies loomed large.

Christian Lammert begins his comparative essay by noting that such policies, along with the trend to privatization, have increasingly transferred public responsibility for economic security to profit-driven actors. In so doing, they have limited the visibility of state intervention as well as the effectiveness of state policies in reducing inequality. This shift has, in his view, curtailed the vitality of democratic participation. The historian Gro Hagemann has argued that after the 1990s, Sweden and Norway applied their own versions of the "Third Way" but the core features of universalist welfare have mainly resisted the pressure brought about by privatization, the aging population, and the increase in immigrant noncitizens. But the challenge is not over, and it remains to be seen whether the social democrats will be able to enact a new, more active social pact. Beatrix Hoffman illustrates an important segment of this process in her examination of the American health-care system. Considered by most democratic theorists and every industrial state—save for the United States—as a perquisite for democratic participation, universal health care has run aground on the shoals of insurance-company interests. Even the passage of the Affordable Care Act in 2010 has been marred, Hoffman argues, by a refusal to consider a public alternative for the very poor. Sébastien Chauvin documents not only the increase of precarious jobs but also the ways insecurity impinges on different categories of temporary workers, effectively removing the economic certainty that would lend credence to their political participation. Finally, Mimi Abramovitz shows how repressive measures have replaced a general consensus to enable economic and social security. The carceral state, she argues, has been shaped by shifting notions of social reproduction that in turn challenge traditional modes of family life. Has carcerality, she asks, become a fundamental feature of contemporary American public life? These essays encourage us to rethink the power of social policies to regulate an engaged citizenry.

CHAPTER FOUR

Privatization and Self-Responsibility

Patterns of Welfare-State Development in Europe and the United States Since the 1990s

CHRISTIAN LAMMERT

SINCE THE 1980S, if not earlier, many have perceived the welfare state in the United States as well as in Western Europe to be under pressure and in decline. Neoliberal restructuring of major social-transfer programs has led to their retrenchment and readjustment.[1] Consequently, the relationship linking the state, welfare, and citizens has been and is still under renegotiation. This debate is most frequently framed in terms of social citizenship and the right to have or restrict access to social transfers. On both sides of the Atlantic, these shifting relationships have resulted in two major consequences. First, changes in redistributive policies affect the visibility of the welfare state. "Visibility" means that citizens identify the state as the provider of welfare.[2] The increasing privatization of social policy and the increasing popularity of the idea of self-responsibility have persuaded many to perceive nonstate actors and individuals as the producers of social benefits, instead of the state and the public. This leads to the second consequence of the current renegotiation of the welfare state: the decline of the welfare state also affects the relationship between the states and its citizens in general. Different studies have shown that the visibility of social programs produces legitimacy for the political system and at the same time encourages political participation among its citizens.[3] Using Marshall's terminology of different dimensions of citizenship rights, we might argue that changes in the dimension of social rights have consequences for political rights as well.

Marshall's conception of citizenship should be understood as an ideal type in the Weberian sense, one in which civil, political, and social rights are developed in order to allow the full participation of individuals in the community. In this sense, full membership in a community requires the political, civil, and social rights of citizenship. The exercise of the rights of citizenship in one area is dependent upon certain rights in others. Political rights, such as participation in political and social processes, are dependent upon both civil rights, in terms of individual freedoms, and social rights, in terms of a person's level of literacy and material well-being. To quote Marshall: "The right to freedom of speech has little real substance if, from lack of education, you have nothing to say that is worth saying."[4] According to Marshall, social citizenship is a universal right to real income, "which is not proportionate to the market value of the claimant."[5] One can understand social rights as reflecting the principle of status in the social sphere, so that equality of status is guaranteed by the state through the citizenship contract and not left to the market alone.

Marshall's concept of citizenship rights provides a good analytical framework to analyze recent reforms in social policy in the United States and Europe. How do North America and Europe differ in their respective trends toward privatization? What are the differences between the two in how they shift the burden of welfare production from society to the individual? What common trends in the restructuring of welfare regimes can be observed? What consequences do those shifts in redistributive policies have for the visibility of the state as the producer of welfare and social benefits? Having analyzed those trends and changes in the redistributive patterns in different welfare states, we are able to address the political outcomes of these developments. How do changes in the dimensions of social rights influence political rights in general and political participation in particular? The assumption here is that people need specific resources in order to engage actively in the political process.[6] If the welfare system is less and less able to provide those resources to specific groups in society—mainly minorities and the poor—these groups will be less likely to participate in the political process.

EMPIRICAL EVIDENCE: REDISTRIBUTION AND THE PRIVATIZATION OF SOCIAL POLICY IN THE "TWO WESTS"

There seems to be widespread agreement within the social and economic sciences that cost containment was one of the major forces shaping the rescaling or reconfiguration of social-welfare policies in Europe and North America since the 1980s.[7] Over the last three decades, social-welfare and tax-related changes in the transatlantic region have played a central role in the increase of income inequality and the rise of poverty rates. Recent studies[8] show that taxes and transfers have become far less effective at closing widening income gaps and that social-policy reforms have been at least partly responsible for the growing chasm in household income.[9]

Let us consider the major trends in inequality and redistribution in the years leading up to the financial crisis of 2008. First, if we just look at labor-market trends, we see that the dispersion of market incomes (before tax and transfers) had in fact changed considerably between the 1980s and the mid-2000s.[10] On both sides of the Atlantic, so-called middle-class households have only partially participated in the overall economic growth we have seen since 1980. Especially in the United States, but to a lesser degree in Western European countries as well, market incomes at the 10th percentile—that is, the poor—fell from 1980 until the mid-1990s and stagnated afterward. At the other end of the income spectrum, households at the 75th and 90th percentiles—the rich—have seen greater real-term increases, in both the United States and Europe.[11]

The state can correct market outcomes by means of the tax-and-transfer system. The tax-and-transfer system includes, on the one side, progressive income taxes on labor and capital and specific programs administered via the tax system, such as the Earned Income Tax Credit (EITC) in the United States. On the other side of the transfer system, we might distinguish between social-insurance programs against specific social risks like unemployment or old age and welfare programs that help people in need and that are financed primarily via tax money.

TANF, housing benefits, and food stamps are the most important ones on the U.S. side. A closer look at Europe and the United States reveals that, on average, cash benefits to households were significantly smaller than the average direct tax burden, making the average working-age household a net taxpayer, paying more money to the state than it receives from the state. Those net tax burdens were largest in the Nordic countries and the United States.[12] However, data on the average household provides no information about interpersonal redistribution via the tax-and-transfer system. Taking into account how much is paid and received by different income groups, we still can see that on both sides of the Atlantic the poorest 20 percent of households remain net benefit recipients. The United States, however, is the only country where cash benefits came to less than 40 percent of market income. In all the other countries, cash transfers added up, on average, to around two-thirds of market income.

But what about the temporal dimension? That is, what about changes in the extent of income inequality over time, and what are the reasons for those changes? According to OECD data,[13] income inequality rose in seventeen of the twenty-two OECD countries for which long-term data is available, climbing by more than four percentage points in countries such as Germany, Sweden, and the United States. We can see different patterns across OECD countries over time. Income inequality began increasing in the late 1970s and early 1980s in some English-speaking countries, notably the United Kingdom and the United States. Starting in the 1980s, this increase in income inequality became more widespread. The latest trends since the 2000s show a widening gap between the rich and the poor, not only in some already high-income-inequality countries, such as the United States, but also in traditional low-income-inequality countries such as Germany, Denmark, and Sweden, where inequality grew more than anywhere else since the 2000s.

There is a broad discussion on what drives growing earnings and income disparities. While globalization, regulatory reform, and changes in the labor market have a significant impact on these developments, we will focus on the effect of income taxes and benefits systems on the redistribution of income, since the redistribution of income is one of the main functions of a welfare system. Traditionally, cash transfers, income taxes, and social-security contributions (payroll taxes) played a major role in Europe and in the United States in reducing market-income inequality. According to OECD data,[14] these were estimated to reduce inequality among the working-age population by an average of about one-quarter. This redistributive effect was larger in most of the European countries but well below average in the United States. On both sides of the Atlantic, the extent of redistribution increased between the 1980s and the 2000s as a whole. As a result, tax-benefit policies offset some of the large increases in market-income inequality.

Since the 1990s, however, these policies have become less effective at mitigating that inequality. The OECD lists different reasons as to why the tax-benefit system has become less redistributive since the mid-1990s. Several studies have shown that, overall, the trend in redistribution was driven chiefly by benefits, or, more precisely, by changes in their receipt patterns and comprehensiveness. Changes in the number of citizens unemployed, as well as reforms to benefit-eligibility criteria, appear as particularly important factors here. Income taxes played a relatively minor role in moderating trends toward higher inequality. The effect of lower income taxes was cancelled out by more progressive taxation; they had opposing effects on redistribution. Additionally, because of their relatively flat rate structure, social-security contributions redistributed very little wealth and did not play a major role in altering redistribution directly.

Altogether, there are important differences between the United States and Europe with regard to income inequality and its impact of redistribution. That said, we can still identify similar developments in the increase in inequality on both sides of the Atlantic, as well as a trend toward a decreasingly effective tax-and-transfer system to offset inequality's rise. Nevertheless, we can identify different clusters of countries that share certain patterns of inequality[15] and that strongly remind one of Esping-Andersen's welfare typology.[16] The Nordic countries (social-democratic welfare regimes) are characterized by below-average disposable-income inequality, thanks to little dispersion in wages combined with a high employment rate. The share of part-time employment, however, is above average in those countries, contributing to inequality in labor income. Cash transfers are often universal, and household taxes tend to be largely proportional to household income, implying only moderate redistribution. In continental European countries (conservative welfare regimes), inequality originating in the labor market is slightly below the OECD average. Wages are somewhat dispersed in international comparison, and inequality is driven mainly by a low employment rate. The share of taxes and cash transfers as a part of the GDP is high, reducing household disposable-income inequality to or below the OECD average. Germany is a special case here. Inequality originating from the labor market is at or above the OECD average. Cash transfers tend to have little redistributive impact because they are largely insurance based and thus not highly progressive.[17] The United States (a liberal welfare regime) has above-average inequality that originates mainly from the labor market. Cash transfers have little redistributive impact because they are small in size and often largely insurance based.

Based on this empirical evidence, it behooves us to ask whether we can talk about any kind of convergence between the United States and Europe with regard to the extent and specific patterns of the redistribution of wealth. Conventional wisdom, supported by various empirical studies,[18] argues that in the United States direct taxes and social transfers reduce income inequalities far less than they do throughout most of Europe. In the mid-2000s, taxes and transfers combined reduced the Gini Index by 18 percent in the United States, 23 percent in the United Kingdom, approximately 30 percent in Germany, and around 40 percent in the Nordic countries. As well, more redistributive tax-and-transfer systems have the tendency effectively to limit the growth of earning gaps.

A closer comparative look at the United States (figure 4.1) reveals that inequality in market income is not particularly exceptional. Several other countries have similarly high levels of market-income inequality. When we consider inequality of disposable income, however, the United States rises to the top of the international ranking of inequality. Calculating the level of redistribution as the difference between the lengths of the two bars in figure 4.1—in effect, the number of Gini points "removed" through redistribution—the United States is ranked 19 out of 19.[19]

Immervoll and Richardson demonstrate that the Great Recession of 2008 significantly reshaped the context in which redistribution takes place.[20] They base their argument on the observation that widening income gaps as well as declining incomes among the lowest earners have created a much greater need for government support. Even several years after the onset of the recession, they observed in the data, elevated levels of benefit spending persisted.[21]

Immervoll and Richardson claim that after 2007 they have observed a substantially strengthened support system for unemployed people and low-earning families in the United States and that this strengthened support system was effected through a set of discretionary policy measures. Benefits for long-term unemployment were extended dramatically. A substantial extension of the duration of unemployment insurance meant out-of-work support has become more generous. This has contributed to a doubling of the unemployment insurance benefit-distribution rate in the United States between 2007 and 2009.[22] At the same time, benefit durations in most EU countries—although already longer than in the United States—were left largely unchanged or even shrank. Changes to the food-stamps program made it easier to access benefits, which contributed to a strong and continued rise in the number of recipients of social transfers as well. Again, eligibility criteria for minimum-income benefits in EU countries were not adjusted after the recession. The American Recovery and Reinvestment Act (ARRA) of 2009 also extended two important tax provisions in the United States: an increase in both the child tax credit and the Earned Income Tax Credit (EITC), which amounted to an extension of the largest anti-poverty program in the United States through raising benefit ceilings, especially for larger families.

Let us take a closer look at the concrete policy changes that might explain different patterns of redistribution in Europe and the United States since the 2000s. The largest number of policy changes have concerned unemployment-insurance benefits. After the onset of the Great Recession in 2008, the differences between the United States and Europe in overall generosity narrowed markedly as benefit duration was extended in the United States. Initial eligibility conditions for unemployment insurance became more demanding in several European countries during the 1980s and 1990s. But that trend toward stricter entitlement requirements tapered off in the 2000s. Since then, reforms have tended to make it somewhat easier for people with shorter employment records to qualify for unemployment insurance. In the United States, entitlement conditions have remained more or less unchanged. European countries, however, have since the early 2000s tended to reduce benefit generosity. U.S. benefit durations were extended very markedly from six months to almost two years in many U.S. states. Since the 2008 crisis, we have observed governments attempting to reduce spending and refocus support within unemployment insurance toward low-income groups. Compared with unemployment insurance, changes to unemployment assistance rules were fewer and smaller, with the major

114 Varieties of Retrenchment

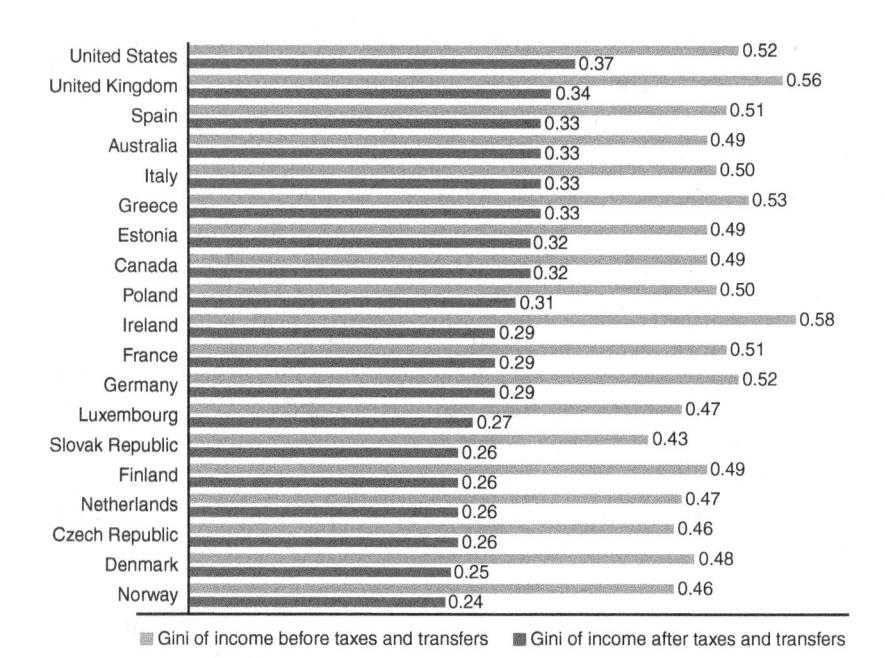

Country	Gini before taxes and transfers	Gini after taxes and transfers
United States	0.52	0.37
United Kingdom	0.56	0.34
Spain	0.51	0.33
Australia	0.49	0.33
Italy	0.50	0.33
Greece	0.53	0.33
Estonia	0.49	0.32
Canada	0.49	0.32
Poland	0.50	0.31
Ireland	0.58	0.29
France	0.51	0.29
Germany	0.52	0.29
Luxembourg	0.47	0.27
Slovak Republic	0.43	0.26
Finland	0.49	0.26
Netherlands	0.47	0.26
Czech Republic	0.46	0.26
Denmark	0.48	0.25
Norway	0.46	0.24

Figure 4.1 Contemporary crossnational portrait (LIS): redistribution through taxes and transfers.

Note: Countries ranked by inequality of disposable household income (darker bars).
Source: Calculations by Gornick and Milanovic; results based on LIS data (Wave VIII), year 2010.

exception of Germany, where in 2005 unemployment and social assistance for job seekers were merged into one single program. For long-term unemployed people who could boast relatively high previous earnings, these changes resulted in substantially lower benefit relief.[23]

Last-resort, guaranteed, minimum-income programs in the United States, as well as social assistance in most European countries, have seen relatively few explicit changes in benefit amounts. But benefit levels have frequently failed to keep up with earnings growth, and as a result recipients are likely to slip farther down the income-distribution spectrum. After 2007, benefits erosion has persisted, but less rapidly, mainly because growth in average wages was slower. The United States was an exception to this pattern, with a moderate postrecession increase relative to average wages in Supplemental Nutrition Assistance Program (SNAP) benefit levels. Although social-policy debates in the OECD countries have since the 1990s increasingly emphasized the need for "active" and "activating support," since the early 2000s observers have seen few explicit changes in basic eligibility rules.

In addition to unemployment insurance and assistance benefits, there is a third tool at the government's disposal for the purposes of transferring wealth: employment-conditional benefits. These "in-work" benefits have in some countries expanded since the 1980s. The EITC and Family Tax Credits, both targeting families with children, are prime examples of employment-conditional benefits. In the United Kingdom in the early 2000s, in-work benefits were significantly more generous than the EITC, with per-family expenditures on average about four times as high. While many other OECD countries have introduced some form of in-work benefits, their size and redistributive impact are minor.[24]

How can we evaluate the consequences of these reforms from a comparative perspective? Net Replacement Rates (NRR) are a useful way to quantify the net efforts of a range of policy changes. The OECD data indicates declining cash support for the unemployed prior to the financial crisis.[25] The largest dips are shown in countries where the generosity of more than one type of benefit was reduced. Among these countries are Finland, Poland, Germany, and France. The moderate increases in replacement rates in the United Kingdom are largely the consequence of lower in-work incomes among the relevant earners. Unlike most European countries, trends in the U.S. case are reversed, with average replacement rates falling prior to the crisis and rising afterward. This postcrisis increase was largely the consequence of the expansion of the maximum duration of benefit receipts and moderate increases in SNAP rates, which were raised by some 14 percent. Changes for unemployed families with children tended to be less damaging. Reduction in replacement rates has been smaller in the United States than in Europe, and they have even increased to some extent. Spain and the United States are the only countries where the relative income of out-of-work families with children has decreased. In the United States, this is largely explained by the failure of Temporary Assistance for Needy Families (TANF) to keep pace with inflation and earnings. Additionally, as recent studies analyzing TANF at its twentieth birthday in 2016 have shown, over time, TANF has provided basic cash benefits to fewer and fewer needy families, even when need has increased. The amount of cash assistance provided to families has eroded in almost every state, leaving families without sufficient funds to meet their most basic needs. TANF plays much less of a role in reducing poverty than AFDC did.[26] The second reason for this development is that increased income-work support, in the form of the EITC, has largely benefited families with children. The largest decline in relative incomes was generally the result of long-term unemployed jobseekers relying on unemployment assistance or social assistance for income support. For the United States, those no longer entitled to unemployment insurance have seen net replacement rates drop by two percentage points between 2002 and 2007. The SNAP increases in 2009 have to some degree compensated for a part of this loss.[27]

With regard to redistributive policies, the general trend since the 1980s indicates that states on both sides of the Atlantic—although to a different degree and from different starting points—are becoming less able to offset growing inequalities in market incomes. Changes in eligibility rules and decreasing generosity are reducing the effectiveness and efficiency of welfare states to reduce income inequality. The financial crisis of 2008 in the United States appears to have triggered a change. Efforts by the Obama administration to redistribute income and mitigate the major social and economic effects of the crisis have led to more redistribution, which has brought the United States closer to the level of most European states. But the question of whether this is a long-term trend remains to be seen.

So far we have focused mainly on trends in income inequality and the capacity of states to offset them. In order to examine major differences between redistributive systems, we must take a closer look at the differences between different welfare regimes and at two important elements of social policy that have major implications for the visibility of the welfare state: the extent of private social spending and the use of the tax system to deliver social benefits. Private social spending, although heavily subsidized by the state through the tax system, seems to be less visibly connected to the state than in previous decades. Citizens perceive private social spending as something they pay for themselves and something that is delivered by the private market. These social provisions do not connect the citizen to the state and do not produce the same amount of identification with established political institutions. They are therefore less able to produce solidarity within the political community. Another important concern is the way states use the tax system or the transfer system to redistribute income. The same argument can be made here: redistribution through the tax system is much less visible than redistribution via the transfer systems.

According to studies from the OECD, private programs can be defined as "social" when they serve a social purpose, are subject to government intervention, and contain an element of interpersonal redistribution.[28] According to OECD data, these private social programs have grown to a substantial size in many countries. Welfare-state reforms in some OECD countries have resulted in a shift from public to private social expenditures.[29] One must ask whether these shifts have a redistributive impact. How are public and private social programs able to reduce income inequality in the welfare state? If we look at the average OECD numbers, we can see that taxes and transfers reduce the Gini by, on average, 35 percent. Some European countries—especially Denmark, Finland, Sweden, and Belgium—have achieved a large redistribution of economic resources, more than 45 percent, whereas in the United States it is below 25 percent.[30] A noteworthy pattern appears if we analyze specific institutional structures and how they reduce inequality. Recent Luxemburg Income Study (LIS) data indicates that, on average, 15 percent of the redistributive impact of the welfare states can be attributed to taxes, and 85 percent to transfers.[31] Again, differences between countries are quite significant and, again, the United States is an outlier: 37 percent of redistribution comes from taxes!

One finds the same pattern of differences between European welfare states and the United States with regard to the public/private mix of social expenditures. If we are to speak of private social expenditures, it is imperative to provide a conceptual clarification of the term. One can distinguish two broad categories of private social benefits: mandatory and private social expenditures. Mandatory private social expenditures are a kind of social support stipulated by legislation but operated through the market. Voluntary private social expenditures concern benefits accruing from privately operated programs that involve the redistribution of resources across households. Comparing public and private social expenditures, the general pattern within the OECD shows that in most countries the share of public social benefits in total social expenditures exceeds 85 percent. Again, the United States is exceptional, with private funding making up nearly 40 percent of all social expenditures.[32]

118   *Varieties of Retrenchment*

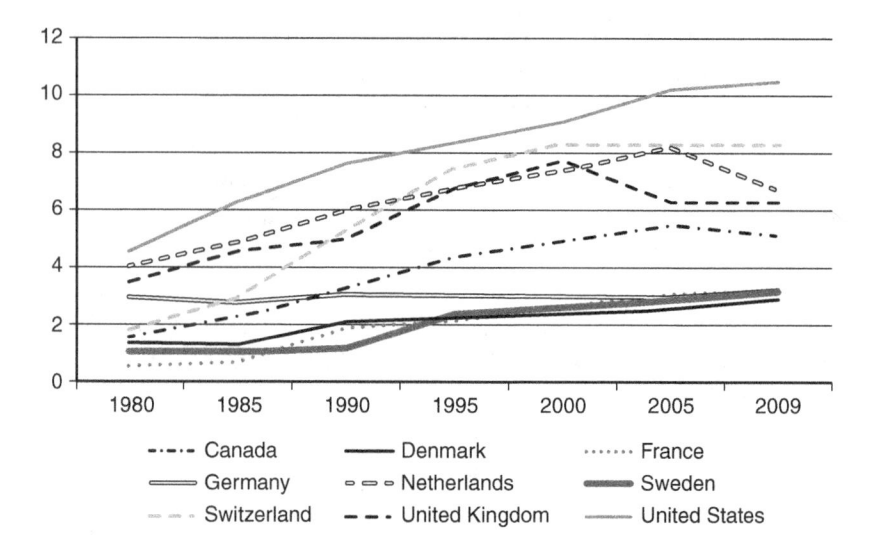

Figure 4.2 Private social expenditures as percentage of GDP, 1980 to 2009.

Source: *OECD Social Expenditures Database* (SOCX) (Paris: OECD, 2012); and own calculations.

Data from the OECD Social Expenditures database reveals that over the years private social expenditures have risen rapidly in a number of countries.[33]

As we can see in figure 4.2, private social expenditures haven risen in all countries, but to different degrees and from different starting points. The United States is exceptional again, starting from the highest level and staying above all other countries over the period. Lower public protection in some countries might encourage the rise of private social arrangements, and in other countries it might be an explicit policy objective.

One can draw two observations from this empirical picture. First, that there is a general trend toward private social expenditures on both sides of the Atlantic and, second, that the United States is exceptional in this regard. The same is true for the use of the tax system to deliver social benefits. Both of those trends are clear indicators that the state is becoming less and less visible as the producer of welfare, even if in fact the state heavily subsidizes private social expenditures and delivers major social benefits via the income-tax system. Altogether, as a consequence of neoliberal restructuring since the 1980s, the state is less effective and less visible as a producer of welfare on both sides of the Atlantic.

THE FRAMING OF SOCIAL POLICY AND THE CONNECTION BETWEEN SOCIAL POLICY AND POLITICAL PARTICIPATION

But numbers and data are just one part of the picture. Changes in social and welfare policy always require a new narrative about society's problems. This narrative framing provides reform proposals with legitimacy. To build the basis and legitimacy of a political order, this framing of a specific reform proposal must resonate with broader ideas about social policy, the role of government in providing benefits, and the relationships linking the citizen, the market, and the state. Since the 1970s, neoliberalism has been the broader frame in which issues of economic, fiscal, and social policy have been discussed in Europe as well as in the United States. The United States in the 1990s provides a good illustration of how problems of the welfare state are understood in this frame: conceptual exhaustion, delegitimation, and the necessity of dismantling "broken" social programs. In recent years, the United States' welfare system has increasingly emphasized personal responsibility, an even stronger distinction between the deserving and undeserving poor, and the exaltation of the work ethic. This system places great weight on market freedom and economic initiative while at the same time discrediting collective responsibility. In 1996, Bill Clinton signed into law the Personal Responsibility and Work Opportunity Reconciliation Act (PRWORA). The most prominent feature of the law was the termination of federal entitlements. The law replaced the most visible and at the same time stigmatizing and controversial component of the U.S. welfare system, Aid to Families with Dependent Children (AFDC), with a block-grant program to the states.

The symbolic import of the shift from social security to personal responsibility speaks volumes. It signaled the end of federal commitments to a society-wide system of security, announcing the need for individuals to take responsibility for their own fate. Responsibility is employed in a double sense: a reproductive and parental responsibility and a cost responsibility. Parents are enjoined to be responsible not simply for the well-being of their children but also for decreasing state spending. It is a notion of responsibility in which self-sufficient economic actors pursue their own well-being in the marketplace; it encodes a vision of government in which the state's role is largely minimal and negative.

In his book *Reflexive Democracy*, Kevin Olson illustrates this problem.[34] When responsibility is seen as a line drawn between the state and its citizens, the primary problem lies in deciding where the line ought to be drawn. For neoliberals, the line would presumably fall close to the state's end, allocating the lion's share of responsibility for oneself and for social spending in general to individuals. For progressives, in contrast, the line falls closer to the individual's end of the spectrum, leaving a large number of tasks in the domain of state responsibility. Justifications for drawing the line in one place or another are typically moral in character. Lawrence Mead's *The New Paternalism*, for example, is the most carefully worked-out version of the neoliberal position.[35] The progressive position, in contrast, typically focuses on the social consequences of poorly regulated markets. From this perspective, one can see Clinton's welfare reform as a functional adjunct to the economy. It helps the poor and unemployed for short periods of time but then forces them back into the labor market. The tension between the conservative and the progressive critiques of the Clinton welfare reform aptly demonstrates an important point: each of these positions is based, in different ways, on an interpretation of American political and legal culture. The progressive position rests on commitments to equality and protecting workers from exploitation. Mead's civic conservatism, similarly, is rooted in obligations of self-sufficiency and the sanctity of work, which constitute deep ideological commitments in American culture. If welfare programs are justified by a moral critique of the economy, they are subject to rejection on similar grounds. To justify welfare as a counterweight to the labor market opens it to rejection for similar reasons.

Robert Goodin provides a way out of this conceptual impasse.[36] Using Goodin's framework, the American welfare reforms go wrong because the welfare state ought to be the means to protect the vulnerable rather than a tool for enforcing work discipline upon them. Goodin makes a key methodological innovation here. He draws a justification for the welfare state out of the market itself. The welfare state, he claims, fulfills the moral presupposition of the market. We could not morally embrace the logic of the market, he argues, without also protecting people made vulnerable by it. Such an argument is important because it justifies welfare based on presuppositions of the practices in which we already engage.

This line of investigation traces deep connections between political participation and welfare that are central to understanding the relationship between social-policy reform and Marshall's concept of citizenship. This line of reasoning exploits an important but often overlooked insight: welfare is not simply a means of redistribution, nor is it a mere counterweight to the market. It is, more generally, an institutional mechanism for realizing collective goals of many different kinds. This understanding of the welfare state moves away from a focus on redistribution and class and toward a discussion of political equality; it holds that each citizen must have an equal opportunity to participate in formulating the status and privileges of citizenship itself.

Political equality seems to be one of the most deeply entrenched values in developed democracies like the United States and the nations of Europe. But the political history of these places, the United States especially, is also a story of exclusion and of restricted participation. This contradiction between values and practice poses questions of legitimacy and participatory inclusion that are widely debated in democratic theory. Presuppositions of participatory equality are in tension with the current state of affairs in U.S. society. U.S. citizens participate in politics at substantially different rates, depending on their income, education, and employment status. This might be explained by capability deficits: inequalities in people's participatory skills and, to a further extent, inequalities in structural and institutional opportunities that hinder participation. These inequalities—and this is a major point of reconceptualizing welfare—can best be ameliorated through a welfare regime that focuses on participatory capabilities. Such a regime would need to equalize the resource base of participation to some extent. More directly, it could also change the way welfare is implemented, encouraging direct participation in the creation of policy itself. In this way, policy could directly promote participatory skills while eliminating the material base of inequality.

Welfare regimes of any kind are created through politics and legislation. Most of the significant turning points in welfare policy, for instance, have been the result of organized attempts by the beneficiaries of such policies to have their needs and claims recognized. Political activism has been a crucial element in the formation of government welfare programs and distributive policies. Protest, electoral activism, and the political organization of the unemployed were instrumental in many New Deal programs in the United States. Political participation is essential for the implementation of social-policy programs, and those programs, once established, produce legitimacy for the system in general. They also enforce political participation, as can be seen in the case of Social Security and Medicare in the United States. Political participation and public policy powerfully reinforce each other.[37] In the case of Social Security, public policy activates people for political participation. This mechanism, however, can be reversed. Public policy can also deactivate people. A policy that reduces the effectiveness of the welfare state to redistribute income and that makes the state less visible for its citizens provides no incentives for political participation, as Campbell has shown with regard to senior citizens.[38] Welfare policies must be formulated through democratic political procedures in order to be legitimate. At the same time, welfare is a vital mechanism for ensuring that all citizens have the means to participate as equals. Participation, again, is vital for articulating needs and interests in the formation of welfare laws. Recent reforms in welfare and social policy pose the threat that political stability may decrease. If welfare policies fail to ensure sufficient and equal participation, then the voices of some will be amplified over the voices of others, a situation that creates a downward spiral of declining political effectiveness, decreased access to opportunities, increased political marginalization, and increased exclusion from the material resources necessary for political participation.

There is some empirical evidence in the case of the United States to confirm this argument. It is fair to speak of the United States as a trailblazer with regard to these neoliberal economic and political trends, but similar trends and discussions are taking place in Europe as well. Welfare has fared poorly in American politics over the past several decades. U.S. politicians have adeptly capitalized on the electorate's suspicion and dislike of welfare programs as a justification for dismantling them. Jennifer Hochschild's study of attitudes toward distributive justice reveals some aspects of the cultural background of these attacks on welfare programs.[39] She finds surprising consistency in distributive norms across income groups. The people interviewed by Hochschild believe that all citizens should share the same political and civil rights; they also support national health insurance, guaranteed jobs, and more progressive taxation. Rather surprisingly, this egalitarianism holds regardless of the respondent's income or occupation. Attitudes shift, however, when the topic is more purely monetary. Here we find strongly differentiating views, affirming the sanctity of private property and opposing any post hoc egalitarianism in its redistribution. The dominant pattern among respondents is a bifurcated belief in political equality and economic difference. In a more recent publication called *Class War: What Americans Really Think About Economic Inequality*, Page and Jacobs make similar claims about conflicting views in U.S. public opinion.[40] Their analysis makes a strong case that U.S. citizens are well aware of rising inequality and that they do care. But there is a deep contradiction in their understanding of the state's role in reducing inequality: U.S. citizens have deep reservations about big government in general; at the same time, a large majority of U.S. citizens support many specific redistributive programs and even are willing to pay higher taxes to finance those programs. Page and Jacobs show with their data that this support for redistributive policies transcends income levels and even partisanship. On that basis, they label the typical U.S. citizen a "conservative egalitarian" based on a mixture of conservative principles and liberal pragmatism.

Martin Gilens finds a similar ambivalent attitude toward egalitarianism and redistribution in American culture.[41] He notes a reservoir of support for most social programs, but he also observes that U.S. citizens hold strongly to market norms in their evaluation of welfare, based specifically on a clear distinction between the deserving and undeserving poor. The 1990 American Civic Participation Study has already carefully demonstrated the inseparability of politics and economy. The study finds a significant inverse relationship between people's income level and their political participation. The most affluent people are nine times more likely to give money to political campaigns, four times more likely to volunteer for one, and 50 percent more likely to vote than are the poorest people. Similar arguments can be found in the APSA Task Force on Inequality and American Democracy[42] or in Martin Gilens's recent work.[43] Differences in income are not only correlated with participation itself but more particularly with the skills people need to participate in political life. The richest people are three times more likely than the poorest to participate in a meeting in which decisions are made, organize a meeting, give a presentation, or write a letter in an average workday. This research implies that political participation has important material preconditions. Unequal resources amplify the voices of some and diminish the voices of others. Differences between rich and poor in their capacity to make their voices heard stem not solely from the ability of money to amplify what one says or from the ability of money to furnish one with the freedom to say it. Rather, wealth is correlated with people's discursive capacities in a more specific, agent-rooted sense. Occupying a position of authority and prestige gives a person a greater opportunity to develop the civic and political skills necessary to participate in both society and the political process.

A new framing of redistributive policies that emphasizes the role of the market and the individual supports the trend toward less visibility of the state in its social-policy function. Concepts of self-responsibility and private social policies thereby further weaken the legitimacy of the state. Assuming a strong relationship between social policy and political participation, those trends pose a serious threat to the principles of democracy. There is a strong and positive correlation between income and political participation. Furthermore, political participation rests on capabilities that individuals require in order to participate in the political process. As the welfare system becomes less able to help poor people by redistributing market incomes from the top to the bottom, the material base and legitimacy for political participation will crumble. An increasing number of people—especially the poor, minorities, and immigrants—will become disconnected from the political process, making the system less democratic. As Gilens and Page have observed, the majority of the American public actually has little influence over public policies.[44] Gilens and Page believe that if powerful business organizations and a small number of affluent citizens dominate policy making, then claims to democracy will be seriously threatened. The neoliberal restructuring of the welfare state, which began in the 1980s, is undermining central assumptions of a functioning democratic system. With rising income inequality as a result of changes in redistributive policies, political voices are more unevenly distributed. This is not a new phenomenon for the United States. Elmer E. Schattschneider already observed in 1960: "The flaw in pluralist heaven is that the heavenly chorus sings with a strong upper-class accent."[45] The problem in the United States today seems to be that the lower classes and parts of the middle class no longer listen to the heavenly chorus at all. The United States might be called exceptional in this regard or may just be the vanguard in developments that will also take place in Europe in the not-too-distant future. On the other hand, Occupy Wall Street and Bernie Sanders's 2016 presidential campaign might be indicators that the discourse and framing of inequality is once again changing in the United States.

NOTES

1. Paul Pierson, *Dismantling the Welfare State? Reagan, Thatcher, and the Politics of Retrenchment* (Cambridge: Cambridge University Press, 1995).
2. Christopher Howard, *The Hidden Welfare State: Tax Expenditures and Social Policy in the United States* (Princeton, N.J.: Princeton University Press, 1997); Kimberly J. Morgan and Andrea Louise Campbell, *The Delegated Welfare State: Medicare, Markets, and the Governance of Social Policy* (New York: Oxford University Press, 2011).
3. Andrea Louis Campbell, *How Policies Make Citizens: Senior Political Activism and the American Welfare State* (Princeton, N.J.: Princeton University Press, 2003).
4. Thomas H. Marshall, *Citizenship and Social Class, and Other Essays* (Cambridge: Cambridge University Press, 1950), 88.
5. Ibid., 97.
6. Amartya Sen, "Human Rights and Capabilities," *Journal of Human Development* 6, no. 2 (2005): 151–166.
7. Paul Pierson, ed., *The New Politics of the Welfare State* (Oxford: Oxford University Press, 2001).
8. Thomas Piketty, *Capital in the Twenty-First Century* (Cambridge, Mass.: Harvard University Press, 2014); Larry M. Bartels, *Unequal Democracy: The Political Economy of the New Gilded Age* (Princeton, N.J.: Princeton University Press, 2009).
9. OECD, "Divided We Stand—Why Inequality Keeps Rising" (OECD, 2011), http://www.oecd.org/berlin/publikationen/dividedwestand-whyinequalitykeepsrising.htm.
10. Herwig Immervoll and Linda Richardson, "Redistributive Policy in Europe and the United States: Is the Great Recession a 'Game Changer' for Working-Age Families?" OECD Social, Employment and Migration Papers 150 (Paris: OECD, 2013).
11. Anthony B. Atkinson, Thomas Piketty, and Emmanuel Saez, "Top Incomes in the Long Run of History," *Journal of Economic Literature* 49, no. 1 (March 2011): 3–71.

12. Immervoll and Richardson, "Redistributive Policy in Europe and the United States."
13. OECD, "Divided We Stand."
14. Ibid.
15. OECD, "Income Inequality and Growth: The Role of Taxes and Transfers," OECD Economics Department Policy Notes 9 (Paris: OECD, 2012).
16. Gøsta Esping-Andersen, *The Three Worlds of Welfare Capitalism* (Cambridge: Polity, 1990).
17. OECD, "Income Inequality and Growth," 9.
18. Andrea Brandolini and Timothy M. Smeeding, "Income Inequality in Richer and OECD Countries," in *The Oxford Handbook of Economic Inequality*, ed. Timothy Smeeding, Brian Nolan, and Wiemer Salverda (Oxford: Oxford University Press, 2009), 71–100.
19. Janet C. Gornick and Branko Milanovic, "Income Inequality in the United States in Cross-National Perspective: Redistribution Revisited," LIS Center Research Brief 1 (2015), 3.
20. Immervoll and Richardson, "Redistributive Policy in Europe and the United States."
21. Ibid., 29.
22. Austin Nicols and Sheila Zedlewski, "Is the Safety Net Catching Up Unemployed Families?" Urban Institute Brief 21 (2011), http://www.urban.org/sites/default/files/alfresco/publication-pdfs/412397-Is-the-Safety-Net-Catching-Unemployed-Families-.PDF.
23. Immervoll and Richardson, "Redistributive Policy in Europe and the United States."
24. Herwig Immervoll and Mark Pearson, "A Good Time for Making Work Pay? Taking Stock of In-Work Benefits and Related Measures Across the OECD," OECD Social, Employment, and Migration Papers 81 (Paris: OECD, 2009).
25. Immervoll and Richardson, "Redistributive Policy in Europe and the United States," 24.
26. Center on Budget and Policy Priorities, "TANF at 20: Time to Create a Program That Supports Work and Helps Families Meet Their Basic Needs" (2016), http://www.cbpp.org/sites/default/files/atoms/files/8-15-16tanf.pdf; Center for the Study of Social Policy, "Twenty Years of TANF. Opportunities to Better Support Families Facing Multiple Barriers" (2016), http://www.cssp.org/pages/body/TANF-at-20.pdf.
27. Ibid.
28. Willem Adema and Maxime Ladaique, "Net Social Expenditure [2005 ed.]," *OECD Social, Employment, and Migration Working Papers* 29 (2005).

29. Chen Wang, Koen Caminada, and Kees Goudswaard, "Income Redistribution in Twenty Countries Over Time," *International Journal of Social Welfare* 23, no. 3 (2014): 262–275.
30. Ibid., 266.
31. Ibid.
32. Wang, Goudsward, and Camalinda, "Income Redistribution in Twenty Countries Over Time," 268.
33. *OECD Social Expenditures Database* (SOCX) (Paris: OECD, 2012).
34. Kevin Olson, *Reflexive Democracy: Political Equality and the Welfare State* (Cambridge, Mass.: MIT Press, 2006).
35. Lawrence Mead, *The New Paternalism: Supervisory Approaches to Poverty* (Washington, D.C.: Brookings Institution, 1997).
36. Robert Goodin, *Protecting the Vulnerable: A Reanalysis of Social Responsibility* (Chicago: University of Chicago Press, 1985); Robert Goodin, *Reasons for Welfare: The Political Theory of the Welfare State* (Princeton, N.J.: Princeton University Press, 1988).
37. Campbell, *How Policies Make Citizens*.
38. Ibid.
39. Jennifer Hochschild, *What's Fair? American Beliefs About Distributive Justice* (Cambridge, Mass.: Harvard University Press, 1981).
40. Benjamin I. Page and Lawrence R. Jacobs, *Class War? What Americans Really Think About Economic Inequality* (Chicago: University of Chicago Press, 2009).
41. Martin Gilens, *Why Americans Hate Welfare: Race, Media, and the Politics of Antipoverty Policy* (Chicago: University of Chicago Press, 1999).
42. Lawrence Jacobs and Theda Skocpol, *Inequality and American Democracy: What We Know and What We Need to Learn* (New York: Russell Sage Foundation, 2007).
43. Martin Gilens, *Affluence and Influence: Economic Inequality and Political Power in America* (Princeton, N.J.: Princeton University Press, 2014).
44. Martin Gilens and Benjamin I. Page, "Testing Theories of American Politics: Elites, Interest Groups, and Average Citizen," *Perspectives on Politics* 12, no. 3 (2014): 564–581.
45. Elmer E. Schattschneider, *The Semisovereign People: A Realist's View of Democracy in America* (New York: Holt, Rinehart, and Winston, 1960), 35.

CHAPTER FIVE

Paradise Lost?

Social Citizenship in Norway and Sweden

GRO HAGEMANN

I often hear that Norway is privileged to have the oil. That's right.
Much more important, however, is the privilege of having
Norwegian women.
—JENS STOLTENBERG, "JENS HYLLET KVINNENE"

I TOOK this chapter's epigraph from Prime Minister Jens Stoltenberg's New Year's speech to his fellow Norwegians in 2011. Apart from the tongue-in-cheek praise he paid to those ladies present at the occasion, his words also carried a more serious message. Because women both work and raise children, he implied that evening, they constitute not only a major resource for Norway's society and economy but also a necessary premise of its welfare state. Despite Stoltenberg's assurances, however, the macroeconomic impact of women's employment may not be as important as he implied. While a greater percentage of women are employed in Norway than in much of the rest of Europe, their average working hours are, in fact, significantly lower than those of women in other European countries.[1] The proportion of part-time workers in Norway's employed population is much higher than in most European countries. Favorable part-time arrangements and generous public benefits have ensured relatively high birth rates in Norway as well as a high level of confidence in the existing system among Norwegian women.

The same state of affairs exists to a greater or lesser extent in all the Nordic countries. It is the result of a legacy going back to the 1930s and the Swedish/Nordic response to challenges following the great demographic transition. Starting with Alva and Gunnar Myrdal in 1934, free health care and childcare, as well as social support to poor families, counteracted declining birth rates. This proactive and progressive way of dealing with demographic challenges contrasted sharply with the restrictive, probirth position of more conservative circles at the time.[2] Gradually, the state's priority turned toward the employment of married women, but without abandoning its interest in high birth rates.

Other well-known features of the Nordic model took shape gradually beginning in the 1930s. Employers' and workers' organizations signed general agreements in Sweden in 1938 and Norway in 1935. During the early postwar period, all the Nordic countries established and expanded centralized pay bargaining and collective agreements. The trade unions accepted rationalization and moderation in their wage demands in return for full employment and social benefits.

The very concept of a welfare state was the legacy of a common Western heritage. Fostered by the ideas of such decisive figures as Bismarck, Keynes, and Beveridge, among many others, the postwar welfare state developed in a Western world determined to reestablish social order after a period of economic crisis, war, and totalitarianism. Despite a common basic idea of what the welfare state was and should do, its implementation varied from country to country, contingent on specificities of geography, history, and politics. On the one side, the United States has stood out with a welfare state characterized by limited public involvement, work-related rather than universal benefits, and a strong emphasis on individual responsibility. The U.S. welfare regime maintains significant confidence in the market and emphasizes private welfare projects far more than its European counterparts. At the opposite end, the Nordic countries offer comprehensive public liability, universal welfare schemes, and fairly modest private elements. But there are differences among the Nordic countries, and even between Sweden and Norway, which appear to be quite similar in history, geography, and politics; there is definitely no such thing as a joint Nordic master plan. Nevertheless, certain consistencies in political patterns, as well as Nordic cooperation over time, make it reasonable to speak of a particular Nordic approach.[3]

The Danish sociologist Gøsta Esping-Andersen led the way in distinguishing the Nordic countries from other welfare states when he categorized Western welfare regimes into three trajectories.[4] In addition to the liberal trajectory represented by the United States and the social-democratic trajectory of the Nordic states, he identifies a third, conservative trajectory, dominant in continental Europe, which is characterized by strong elements of corporatism and social rights that are often correlated to family, status, and class. A greater degree of universality and decommodification in the social-democratic Nordic regime than in the liberal and conservative trajectories implies comprehensive social rights regardless of the market and institutions based on social inequality. Esping-Andersen regarded especially the capacity for decommodification as crucial to social citizenship. "The outstanding criterion for social rights," he claims, "must be the degree to which they permit people to make their living standards independent of pure market forces."[5]

The concept of social citizenship, launched in 1949 by T. H. Marshall, includes social rights essential to making all citizens politically capable. Marshall sought to break away from the Poor Law mentality, which set self-sufficiency as a prerequisite for one's standing as a citizen. A full-fledged democracy, in his understanding, had to include a social element, if it was to incorporate the unemployed and the poor. In addition to economic redistribution, Marshall directed his attention toward education and culture. A free and accessible school system should inculcate democratic attitudes in the young generation. Similarly, the subsidized dissemination of culture would enable everyone "to live the life of a civilised being according to the standards prevailing in the society."[6] Everywhere in the West after the war, welfare states made efforts more or less in line with Marshall's principles, and the Nordic countries with more consistency than others. States carried out redistribution directly through taxation as well as by supporting education and social services. Even social housing formed a central part of social-democratic redistribution policy.

From early on, the Nordic social-democratic trajectory attracted attention and became an object both of admiration and consternation. This attention was especially true for Sweden, which from an early date emerged as the economic superpower among the Nordic countries. Outside the Nordic region as well, Sweden was considered an economic miracle, a leader in modernization, welfare, and culture. After the turning point in Western economies around 1980, interest in the "Nordic model" got a new boost. Given globalization, economic setbacks, and new economic doctrines, many states have reconsidered and even rejected the major economic rules upon which Nordic welfare was established. Compared to many Western countries, however, Nordic welfare states have fared quite well so far.[7]

The relative social and economic success of the Nordic nations seems to contradict the neoliberal economic doctrines that appeared in the wake of the Western recession, according to which the Nordic countries should have suffered because of their generous welfare systems and high public spending. Global competition, it was claimed, would force the Nordic states to follow market laws and restrict national *sonderwegs*. How can we understand the apparent survival of the Nordic countries through a period of global competition and recurrent crises? And how solid is the Nordic structure in the long run?

VARIETIES OF CAPITALISM IN SWEDEN AND NORWAY

The ongoing debate on "varieties of capitalism," which discusses the consequences of globalization and the economic paradigm shift, offers a possible starting point for understanding the enduring success of the Nordic countries. Peter Hall and David Soskice opened the debate by challenging neoliberal assumptions that the new economic order would lead to less variation among countries and make it harder to uphold national institutions and habits. In *Varieties of Capitalism*, Hall and Soskice demonstrate that, in fact, the very opposite result emerged from the turbulent decades before the turn of the twenty-first century. Countries with high costs, comprehensive welfare, and strong public governance proved more competitive in global markets. Contrary to prevailing doctrines, global markets encouraged specialization and stimulated comparative advantages in national economies. In addition, their ultimate success relied on complementary institutional forms that could balance and coordinate between nonmarket and market relations.[8]

Hall and Soskice's book stimulated a broader academic debate that contributed criticism, nuance, and new theoretical developments to our understanding of contemporary capitalism. The debate split in many directions without generating a new and authoritative theory of capitalism, but it still offers new tools for analyzing and comparing national political economies as well as the contradictions and ambiguities characterizing both modern nations and capitalism. Hall and Soskice's contribution stands out as a beginning more than an endpoint for the varieties-of-capitalism approach, but some elements of their analysis, such as the notion of complementary institutions and system coordination, remain central.[9]

In the varieties-of-capitalism approach, coordinated market economies, like those of the Nordic states, with efficient institutions to complement market and nonmarket relations, will generally fare better when adjusting to an expanding market by bracing their comparative advantages. Such intentions, in fact, were explicit in the establishment of the social-democratic welfare states in Sweden and Norway after World War II. The Nordic states never regarded social benefits as a purpose in themselves; instead, they were one part of a larger social contract. The states granted workers and mothers social security in return for their participation and cooperation in the major national aims of modernizing the economy and bringing up a new and healthy generation. They also made social collective rights, equal to or higher than those of the individual, a main pillar in the Nordic understanding of social citizenship. The Swedish term *Folkhemmet* signifies precisely this: belonging, social security, and participation for all members of society, regardless of their social status or ability—a readiness to put common interests ahead of self-interest.

Decommodification, so crucial to Esping-Andersen's understanding of social citizenship, thus became important in social-democratic ambitions of modernization and economic growth. Organized labor markets, nonprofit school systems and health care, generous social insurance, and supportive family policies bore social purposes, but they were to a large extent instrumental to economic policy as well. The concurrence between social and economic policies has been a feature of Swedish and Norwegian social democracies since 1951, embodied in the model developed by the Swedish Trade Union Confederation (LO) economists Gösta Rehn and Rudolf Meidner. The double social-economic purpose of their model, which stipulated that workers accepted the need for extensive structural rationalization, is conspicuous in its four objectives: high growth, full employment, low inflation, and income equality, implemented through centralized pay bargaining and collective agreements.

The Rehn-Meidner model worked as a key document for social democrats in both Sweden and Norway, although Sweden definitely led

Norway in implementation. Nowhere is this more evident than in labor-market policy. Labor shortage was a problem in both countries, but the Swedes were far more resolute in addressing it. During the 1950s, Sweden carried out a relocation of people to areas where labor was needed so comprehensive and efficient that it largely depopulated the Swedish countryside.

Norwegian social democrats shared the general principles of the Rehn-Meidner model, although they were far more reluctant to follow Sweden's radical structural rationalization. Instead of rural depopulation, the preservation of existing patterns of settlement became its own political purpose. Norway's more cautious implementation is sometimes misinterpreted as skepticism for modernization, but it actually reflects Norway's different variety of capitalism. Sweden had strong industrial capital in private hands and an extensive industrial sector dominated by big industry. Because of the plentiful supply of hydropower and fish, important export industries in Norway were located along the coastline, which also has the harshest weather and most barren soil. Industries in more central areas were marked by small enterprises. In addition, private financial capital was sparse in Norway, and the state had to take on a robust role in establishing and developing larger industries. Depopulation of coastal areas and a dramatic rationalization of the agricultural sector were simply contrary to the main strategy of Norway's political economy; maintaining dispersed settlement protected existing communities but also supplied necessary seasonal labor.[10]

When it came to the recruitment of female labor during the postwar decades, Swedish and Norwegian strategies likewise differed. Swedish social democrats actively facilitated female labor-market participation by offering part-time arrangements, childcare, and occupational training from an early date. They also arranged door-to-door campaigns to persuade housewives to seek employment. Norway did not undertake similar initiatives until the late 1960s. Historians and scholars of gender have debated the cause of this striking difference and have concluded that it was the result of weaker secularization and more traditional family values in Norway.[11] This is not entirely false. What these scholars fail to consider, however, are the economic and demographic differences between modern Sweden and Norway. With export industries situated along the Norwegian coast, recruiting women from the periphery to manufacturing and service work in the cities made for a doubtful economic strategy. In addition, Norway weighed the cost of a more proactive facilitation of female employment against the public expenditures required for maintaining scattered settlements and small-scale agriculture, which relied on the seasonal labor such communities supplied.

Protection of dispersed settlement, moreover, generated a stronger regional and nonurban element in Norwegian culture and politics. When first formulated in 1964, Stein Rokkan's well-known phrase "votes count, resources decide" reflected a common view of the political system in Norway.[12] From the nineteenth century on, the center-periphery dichotomy has been a major axis of conflict in national politics, expressed in popular activism and counterculture and especially in the areas of temperance, religion, and language. The founding of the Christian Democratic Party (Kristelig Folkeparti) in 1933 gave the periphery a stronger platform to advance family values and antisecularism. The social democrats also had to take into account this center-periphery conflict, given that peasants, fishermen, and other rural inhabitants made up a substantial component of the Norwegian electorate. Countercultural movements remained strong in the postwar era and demanded inclusion in investigations affecting their field of interests.

On the whole, corporative elements had a broader impact in Norway, which included interest groups and voluntary associations in the decision-making process. While there were certainly similar trends in Sweden, there they were significantly weaker. Traditional popular associations in Sweden gradually weakened as centralization and urbanization accelerated. In addition, in Sweden, organizational growth within health and social services did not take place as it did in Norway, which established social services in the municipalities.[13] The Swedish Christian Democrats were not organized until 1964 and entered parliament only in 1985. Throughout, the voluntary social sector had less legitimacy and political influence in Sweden, despite the strong role popular activism had played in the shaping of Swedish democracy in earlier phases.[14] Organized corporatism, the so-called Harpsund democracy, did not enjoy the same broad legitimacy in Sweden that it did in Norway, where it encompassed the main business, trade, and labor organizations of the labor market. The informal summit talks between the government, industry, and organizations at Harpsund resulted only in unofficial agreements, and radicalization, from the 1960s on, increasingly discredited these accords.[15]

DEALING WITH POSTINDUSTRIALISM

The 1970s were contradictory. On the one hand, they saw the end of a long and steady growth period and ushered in a decade of economic recession. On the other hand, they were radical, with growing opposition from the left initiating a wave of significant social reforms. Many of the main features now associated with Nordic welfare regimes originate in the 1970s and 1980s.

In retrospect, the recession of the 1970s marked a turning point in the social democracies of Sweden and Norway. Although the economic recession did not unleash the crisis in social democracy, it certainly aggravated it. The recession simply coincided with a shift in mentalities and more critical attitudes toward social democracy. Starting in the second half of the 1960s, public debate drew more attention to certain less favorable aspects of the social-democratic order. At the same time, new groups were entering politics: youth, women, environmentalists, and homosexuals, mostly situated to the left of the social-democratic parties, started protest movements outside of the established order. Professionals also directed more attention toward new questions that before the 1960s had barely been present on the central political agenda. These groups contested principal elements of social-democratic policy: continuous economic growth, trust in technology and science, the usefulness of regulation, and a strong state.

From the late 1960s, feminist activism also brought more women into politics and created a new focus in the debates. The Swedes took the lead, publishing findings from a major research project on women's life and work in 1962.[16] The Norwegian sociologist Harriet Holter participated in this project, and the book was published in Norwegian as well. However, it was in Sweden that the critical debate about gender roles really took off. The very term "gender role" had a huge impact in Sweden, and it started a new kind of public debate on men and women in society.[17] Only a decade later, Prime Minister Olof Palme released the social-democratic response to women's demands for equality, summarized in the new term *Jämställdhet*, a synthesis of social and gender equality.[18] A new and radical family policy followed, including a strong commitment to public kindergartens and generous parental leave. Norway, again inspired by Sweden, followed in principle but took longer to implement the most costly reforms.

Altogether, the 1970s were a period of significant social improvement, a reform period unparalleled in Swedish history and with considerable initiatives in social housing, sick pay, unemployment benefits, and medical and dental care. Taxation policy and social benefits supported married women's autonomy. The retirement age and working hours were lowered; pensions and disability benefits increased. Important workplace laws increased employment protection and encouraged the participation of workers.[19]

The Norwegian Labor Party survived the crisis of confidence that followed its defeat in the first European Community referendum in 1972. They responded with reforms aimed at the socialization of capital and the finance sector and stronger government regulation of the market. In order to convince the National Union to accept lower nominal wages, they also got directly involved in negotiations, offering tax cuts and guaranteeing moderate inflation.

For a long time, the Swedish government was reluctant to accept more radical proposals for socialization. However, it was in Sweden that the most extreme drive for socialization during this period occurred. The Swedish Trade Union Confederation (LO) formulated the Wage Earners Fund (*löntagerfonden*), which sought to give the union a share of the profits to spend toward their own collective interests. Highly skeptical of the plan, Prime Minister Olof Palme acted as moderating factor when the funds were set up in 1984. In fact, his implementation of the plan was typical of his broader response to radical opposition: he incorporated emergent radical ideas into the existent social-democratic structure.

The radicalization of the social democrats in economic policy may have, to some extent, worsened the recession or at least made the political handling of it more difficult. The expansive policies of the 1970s would soon prove beyond capacity under new economic conditions.[20] It took some time before the two social-democratic parties fully understood the new situation. In Sweden, government debt increased throughout the 1970s and 1980s and reached a dangerously high level, nearly 75 percent of GDP, in the early 1990s.[21] The policies that had been established during more prosperous times now were part of the problem. The tendency was to cling too long to instruments unsuited to the more turbulent postindustrial era. In both Sweden and Norway, the 1970s and the following decades generated hard-learned experience, economically speaking, and required a reassessment of some of the core principles of the classic social-democratic order.

Nevertheless, the radical 1970s bore positive results. Increased public spending contributed to a renewal of the social contract by, for example, including women in the workplace. Likewise, the Swedes completed a powerful structural rationalization of the steel and shipbuilding industries under the auspices of the state. In Norway, the most positive effect of radical politics was the strong public influence in the establishment of the Norwegian oil industry. Statoil was at first organized as wholly state owned, using positive discrimination to develop an oil industry of international standing. The state's firm and early grip on the oil company has continued to provide income for the Norwegian state.

Today, there is hardly a doubt that some structural adjustments were inevitable. Given their late commencement, the course of such adjustments was probably more dramatic than intended. Toward the end of the 1970s, both Nordic governments initiated some measures to reduce public spending. In both countries, the social democrats themselves initiated the corrections. In Sweden, the Social Democratic Party introduced "the third way" more than a decade ahead of British Labour. Francis Sejersted is probably right when he points to the importance of early initiatives taken by social democrats to put the brakes on excessive public consumption, beginning in the late 1970s. Although their initiatives were not immediately successful, they most certainly prevented a tough war against the labor unions while achieving the kind of social rights for which Margaret Thatcher stood.[22] Their idea was to find a new balance between macroeconomic and nonmarket purposes to replace the Rehn-Meidner model, which was about to fail. The market would be given more space without giving up basic public welfare and collective agreements. The strategists formulating the "third way" aimed hopefully at letting market forces regulate some of the problems created by excessive public control.

In social-democratic Scandinavia, influences from the American welfare model and neoliberal theory have never been as widespread as they were in the 1980s and early 1990s, when these reforms took a markedly different course. A wave of deregulation and commodification washed over all the Nordic countries, with consequences more dramatic than anyone could have foreseen. Some people enjoyed rapidly accelerating earnings, new wealth, and ostentatious consumption, but others met with uncertainty and debt. In retrospect, there seems to have been agreement on the need for some deregulation, but many argue that its implementation occurred in an unfavorable way: it was too late, too sudden, and too radical.

The deregulation of the credit market under conservative rule in Norway (1984) and social-democratic rule in Sweden (1985) immediately expanded credit and overheated the economy. When policies to cool down the swift credit expansion were finally put into action at the end of the 1980s, it was too late to avert financial collapse. In both Sweden and Norway, the state intervened in order to prevent a banking collapse, in Norway going so far as to protect even bank deposits that were legally at the risk of shareholders.[23]

In Sweden, the roaring 1980s ended in the deep economic slump of 1991, which was then followed by the most comprehensive economic crisis since the 1930s. Job loss in both competitive and more sheltered industries increased at a record pace, and unemployment rose dramatically. At its worst, unemployment shot above 10 percent, causing a painful deleveraging in many households. Falling tax revenues, along with a rapid increase in public spending, caused high budget deficits. After 1991, the state revised its policies in order to calm down the economy and halt the mounting state debts. Far-reaching reforms of the public sector were implemented, covered by "crisis packages" that the political opposition also supported. The number of public-sector employees fell by 200,000 between 1990 and 1997. In accordance with prevailing economic doctrines, many public services were also commodified, among them institutions within the education, health, and care sectors. Parts of the generous welfare transfers were tightened, sickness benefits were reduced, and levies to the unemployment funds (*a-kassan*) increased. Sweden even outsourced its system of a general additional pension (ATP), the very jewel in the crown of its social-democratic state, to financing outside of the state.[24]

Deregulation of credit markets probably triggered the deep slump of the Swedish economy in 1991. A similar process took place in Norway as well, but the landing there was softer. The oil industry contributed heavily to Norway's more fortunate outcome. The industry not only provided large revenues to the state budget, but its continuous activity also rendered unemployment nonexistent. The problem in Norway was rather a labor shortage in industries outside of the oil sector. The Swedish government, in contrast, struggled with large public debt and had to give up the last pillar in the Rehn-Meidner model, the goal of full employment.

THE STATE OF SOCIAL CITIZENSHIP

In retrospect, it seems plausible that the progressive overreaches of previous decades contributed to the breakdown of the Nordic economies and the deep recession that followed in the 1990s.[25] It is a provocative thought, however, that some of the comparative advantages of current Scandinavian policies, rooted in the progressive postwar period, would have been difficult or impossible to seed in the politics of the world of today. Strict EU and EEA rules would have prevented the positive discrimination of the government oil company in Norway and would have halted the overrunning of budgets during the extensive Swedish reform period of the 1970s. If the Nordic states had followed neoliberal doctrines, they might have endangered the very social and economic characteristics that earn them high scores in rankings of international competitiveness.

Contrary to neoliberal assumptions, however, countries with high costs, comprehensive welfare policies, and strong public governance have proven competitive in global markets. In broad outline, the Nordic countries have survived the period of recession and turbulence better than others, with more of their welfare system intact. Barring Iceland, the Nordic states emerged relatively unscathed from the 2008 finance crisis, and even Iceland recovered quite rapidly. As of 2015, Nordic countries have high scores in international rankings of competitiveness as well as in quality of life and human development.[26]

To be sure, the Nordic states have made some adjustments, many of them painful and contrary to the basic mindset of their former political economy. In addition, some fundamental changes have occurred in Swedish and Norwegian politics. Under the social-democratic hegemony, both countries institutionalized social-democratic conventions, including far-reaching governmental intervention, and corporatist negotiation. In the 1980s, Sweden broke out of this tradition but, after some time, restored negotiations and collective agreements, a move that even the conservatives fully accepted. Still, in the process, Sweden lost the social pact that had framed its previous collectivism.[27] For a while, it appeared that something similar might happen in Norway, but the national understanding between unions and employers was restored fairly quickly.[28] In both countries, there is now a common understanding that collective agreements work to resolve local conflicts and provide greater economic stability than a system centered on market-driven wage settlements. In fact, when the conservative Fredrik Reinfeldt became prime minister of Sweden in 2006, he made clear that he supported this corporatist system.

Norway emerged from turbulent times with more of its former social-democratic system intact. The deep rupture of confidence that appeared in Sweden after the 1990s crisis barely surfaced in Norway. As the Swedish sociologist Stefan Svallfors concluded from 1996 survey data, in spite of the similar levels of support for the welfare system in Sweden and Norway and similar patterns of disagreement overall, political conflict was much sharper in Sweden. In Sweden, differences of opinion more closely followed class differences and aligned with distinctions between right and left, while disagreements in Norway cut across left-right divisions. Dissimilarities between the two countries, Svallfors concludes, are "substantial when it comes to political trust and efficacy, with a much higher confidence level in Norway."[29]

Dissimilarities between the two countries should not be overstated, but there is no doubt that the Swedish debate is more polarized.[30] Large Norwegian oil revenues contribute to political differences, but oil is hardly the only reason why such differences exist. The socioeconomic structures in Norway and its strong corporative elements may also have contributed to more moderate levels of conflict. More diverse and geographically dispersed businesses, stronger communities outside the big cities, and more comprehensive means of representation extended to civil organizations in the form of public committees all may support a greater willingness to compromise within the existing political system.

Dissimilarities between Norway and Sweden are also apparent in the New Public Management drive ongoing in the two Scandinavian countries since the 1990s. The outsourcing of public services has occurred in both countries, with generally more radical implementation in Sweden. Outsourcing has affected health and social services as well as the school system, sectors financed largely by tax revenues and operated as government or municipal institutions. A recent investigation of the outsourcing of public services in each Nordic country revealed that commercial actors are growing strong in both Norway and Sweden, with noticeably stronger growth in Sweden, which also has a smaller voluntary nonprofit social sector. In Norway, social services organized by voluntary nonprofit actors have been increasing in recent decades.[31]

From the 1990s on, Sweden has transformed from a welfare state where the state took care of virtually all social services to one with growing opportunities for private commercial actors. In educational policy as well as elderly care, Sweden stands out for its extensive freedom of establishment, free user choice with a monetary follow-user principle, and even permission to transfer profits to the owners of enterprises fully financed by the state. The principles of privatization also apply to compulsory primary education, which has drawn considerable attention and concern from the Swedish public and abroad. Norwegian governments have so far been more restrictive of private schools, rejecting all proposals of for-profit private schools that would receive public funding. In Norway, growth in private schools has taken place primarily within the voluntary nonprofit sector, building on an enduring tradition of involving nonprofit actors in social services and primary education to accommodate religious beliefs or alternative pedagogy.

The nonprofit sector never established the same footing in Sweden with respect to political facilitation and cooperation. What support survived from previous popular movements was lost during the postwar expansion, when voluntary social work was mainly considered a form of degrading bourgeois philanthropy. Therefore, when the state initiated the New Public Management in the 1990s, nonprofit actors were too weak to compete with commercial operators. Even in Norway, conditions have become less favorable for nonprofit actors. Unlike in Denmark and other continental countries, the pan-European tendering conditions in Norway are practiced in a manner detrimental for nonprofit actors. This is an important matter with regard to social citizenship because nonprofits generally provide a higher degree of choice and variety than both public and commercial services. In addition, nonprofits frequently enable more individual empowerment and codetermination.[32]

The former public primary-school system, which provided everyone with roughly equal conditions, is under pressure in both countries. More freedom of choice seems to have resulted in greater social segregation. More resourceful families tend to opt out of schools in deprived neighborhoods or ones with many immigrant children. The principles of equal primary education and broad access to higher education still prevail, however. With varying success, extra measures have sought to address schools that face major problems.

The increasing social segregation of primary schools is compounded by significant changes in housing policy. As a consequence of deregulation of the housing market, real estate has attracted investment, which has brought both large profits and large losses. For urban middle-class families, the housing market has provided an extra push to move out of less affluent neighborhoods before housing values plummet. Certain remnants of social-housing policies that support the most vulnerable—recipients of social assistance, immigrant families—may even reinforce this trend. Building on initiatives from various private and municipal actors from earlier in the twentieth century, postwar social housing was a driving force in social-democratic welfare policies. In both Norway and Sweden, government housing policy included municipal and cooperative housing as well as low-interest state loans and socially acceptable rent levels. In Sweden, cooperative housing was secondary to municipal companies, offering subsidized dwellings for rent and strict regulation of the private rental market. Norway, however, generally rejected a regulated municipal rental market in favor of collective ownership through the cooperative-housing movement. Tenure was the stated goal of Norwegian social democrats.[33]

Regardless of their preferred model of postwar social housing, the actual results were similar across the two countries. The housing market faced some deregulation even as early as the 1960s, but deregulation did not gain momentum until the 1980s. Deregulation occurred only gradually, with the repeal of rent regulation, the end of privileges granted to the cooperative housing association, and the cessation of the direct and indirect subsidies offered through the state housing bank. At present, housing policy is a subject of deep concern in both countries. The downsizing of social housing has meant prohibitive costs for those entering the housing market, whether youth without significant support from home, the unemployed moving to more central areas, or immigrants trying to integrate. Social-housing policy has practically excluded all applicants apart from poor families and youth battling addiction. The entrance fee is often too high for young adults to acquire their own apartment, even if they are employed full time and earn an average salary as a teacher, librarian, or nurse.

Social integration was a key part of the *folkhem* idea, and social marginalization and exclusion remain low in both Sweden and Norway. Two years after the financial crisis in 2008, few people suffered from low income and other financial problems.[34] One trend—increasing exclusion from or marginalization within the labor market—seems alarming, even when one considers that the main reason for exclusion is the high number living on disability benefit. This group is large in both countries and is especially large in Norway. Still, in Norway the marginalized group comprised only small and falling numbers, according to Nordic statistics for the years 2006–2010, although it has seen a considerable growth in marginalization among those with poor health or no education beyond primary school. Sweden has a larger share of marginalized people in total, and that share has grown during the same period.[35]

Figures of labor-market marginalization illustrate the high standards of qualification and ability required to achieve full-time employment in the Swedish and Norwegian labor markets. In addition to growing numbers of old-age pensioners, the number of people of working age living on welfare is growing. The welfare benefits have been generous in the past, but a number of initiatives have recently sought to push unemployed and disabled people toward employment. Although social integration is part of the purpose of such employment, it may actually lead to greater marginalization. When the state increases user fees and reduces support, as Sweden has done with its unemployment insurance and sickness benefits, such initiatives can easily weaken social citizenship.

There is reason to fear that the increasing rates of marginalization observed prior to 2010 have continued in subsequent years. Disturbing incidents of growing social unrest have occurred since then. In deprived suburbs, furious rioters have demolished cars and looted shops, prevented police and ambulances from performing services, and allowed organized crime to take over local jurisdictions. In response to an increasing flow of refugees, several refugee-reception centers have been targeted with arson. Paradoxically, Sweden has the strongest underground right-wing movement among the Nordic countries.[36]

INTO THE FUTURE

The reversal of the 1990s has undoubtedly affected social citizenship in the two Scandinavian countries. Stimulated by international trends, national restructuring has undermined basic social services as well as political stability. The outsourcing of public services and deregulation of sectors under state control has been ongoing since the 1980s and 1990s, with varying results. It has increased freedom of choice and in some cases also improved the quality of services, but it has also brought about greater social inequality and moved away from the principle of universality. Nevertheless, Sweden and Norway have managed to keep their social-democratic welfare model intact. Up to the present date, the Scandinavian countries have largely maintained their system of coordinated market economies.

However, it is far from certain that the Nordic model will be able to undergo reform without letting go of some of its foundational principles. The considerable challenges Norway and Sweden face may affect the kind of social citizenship that has characterized the Nordic model. Current geopolitical events, such as falling oil prices and the escalating climate and environmental crisis, deeply influence both countries. On the national level, demographers have long pointed to the consequences of an aging population and consider it a major challenge for all future welfare states. In combination with the low employment rate among significant groups of the population, care for the elderly may challenge the sustainability of Nordic welfare universalism in the long run.[37] The continued mass immigration of refugees to Europe's welfare states deepens uncertainty and highlights the importance of successful integration. An overreaction in the restrictive direction might easily produce the opposite result, by pacifying new citizens instead of motivating them. In both countries, Sweden especially, a shaky balance exists between citizenship and human rights.[38]

The turbulent political situation has also generated uncertainty and challenges to welfare universality. The social-democratic parties have lost their political hegemony and may even be in danger of losing their moral high ground. Right-radical parties have become rather powerful in both countries. In Norway, the Progressive Party (Fremskrittspartiet) has been included in the government cabinet since 2013. In Sweden, the liberal public lost its dominance when the 2014 election made the Swedish Democratic Party (Sverigedemokraterna) the third-largest party. These parties defend Scandinavian welfare but criticize collectivism and what they perceive to be permissiveness toward immigrants and refugees.

As for the Swedish and Norwegian social democrats, they are striving to take a more proactive approach in shaping a future model by renegotiating the old social pact, which had offered a clear vision for welfare and social citizenship. The participation of social democrats since the late 1970s in welfare reform contributed to the protection of a social-democratic basis for Nordic welfare policies, more or less accepted by their conservative governments as well. But is it realistic to hope that the social democrats will regain their former power and formulate a convincing framework for a new social pact?

NOTES

1. Statistics Norway, "Velferdsstaten trenger mange i arbeid," January 25, 2010, http://www.ssb.no/offentlig-sektor/artikler-og-publikasjoner/velferd sstaten-trenger-mange-i-arbeid.
2. Ann Oakley, *Man and Wife: Richard and Kay Titmuss: My Parents' Early Years* (London: Harper Collins, 1996).
3. Niels Finn Christiansen, Klaus Petersen, Nils Edling, and Per Haave, eds., *The Nordic Model of Welfare: A Historical Reappraisal* (Copenhagen: Museum Tusculanum Press, 2006), 28–29.
4. Gösta Esping-Andersen, *The Three Worlds of Welfare Capitalism* (Cambridge: Polity, 1990).
5. Ibid., 3.
6. Thomas H. Marshall, *Citizenship and Social Class* (London: Pluto, 1950; repr. 1992), 8.
7. Comparative analyses have recently been made on a Nordic level: Jon Erik Dølvik, Tone Fløtten, Jon M. Hippe, and Bärd Jordfald, *Den nordiske modellen mot 2030: Et nytt kapittel?* (FAFO-rapport 2014), http://www.fafo.no/images/pub/2014/20393.pdf; Tor Morten Normann, Elisabeth Rønning, and Elisabeth Nørgaard, *Challenges to the Nordic Welfare State: Comparable Indicators* (Copenhagen: Nordic Social-Statistical Committee, 2014).
8. Peter A. Hall and David Soskice, *Varieties of Capitalism: The Institutional Foundations of Comparative Advantage* (New York: Oxford University Press, 2001). Many thanks to Fredrik Engelstad for bringing my attention to this book and the following debates.
9. Bob Hancké, *Debating Varieties of Capitalism: A Reader* (New York: Oxford University Press, 2009).
10. Even Lange, *Samling om felles mål 1935–1970, Aschehougs Norgeshistorie* (Oslo: Aschehoug, 1997), 11:180–194; Andreas Hompland, *To-kyrs industriarbeidarar i streik: Trælandsfos, Kvinesdal, 1925* (Oslo: Samlaget, 1984).
11. Gösta Esping-Andersen: *Social Foundations of Postindustrial Economies* (New York: Oxford University Press, 1999), 45; Diane Sainsbury, "Gender and the Making of Welfare States: Norway and Sweden," *Social Politics* 8, no. 1 (2001): 113–143; Kerstin Sörensen and Christina Bergqvist, "Gender and the Social Democratic Welfare Regime: A Comparison of Gender-Equality Friendly Policies in Sweden and Norway," in *Work Life in Transition*, vol. 5

(Oslo: Arbetslivsinstitutet—National Institute for Working Life, 2002); Klas Åmark, "Women's Labour Market Participation in the Nordic Countries During the Twentieth Century," in Christiansen et al., *The Nordic Model of Welfare*, 299–333.
12. Stein Rokkan, "Votes Count, Resources Decide," in *Makt og Motiv: Festskrift til Jens Arup Seip 1905–1975*, ed. Jens Arup Seip and Ottar Dahl (Oslo: Gyldendal, 1975), 216.
13. Per Selle, "Organisasjonssamfunnet—ein statsreiskap?" in *Ein stat? Fristillingas fire ansikt*, ed. Tore Grønlie and Per Selle (Gjøvik: Det norske samlaget 1998), 194–195; Anne Hilde Nagel, ed., *Velferdskommunen: Kommunenes rolle i utviklingen av velferdsstaten* (Stavanger: Alma Mater forlag, 1991).
14. Kjell Östberg and Jenny Andersson, *Sveriges historia 1965–2012* (Stockholm: Nordstedts 2013), 168–169.
15. Ibid., 118–119.
16. Gösta Dalström, Edmund Dahlström, Stina Thyberg, Per Olav Tiller, Harriet Holter, and Sverre Brun-Gulbrandsen, *Kvinnors liv och arbete: Svenska och norska studier av ett aktuellt samhällsproblem* (Stockholm: Studieförbundet näringsliv och samhälle, 1962).
17. Yvonne Hirdman, *Med kluven tunga* (Uddevalla: Atlas, 1998), 160.
18. Kjell Östberg, *När vinden vände: Olof Palme 1969–1986* (Stockholm: Leopard, 2010), 86–102.
19. Östberg and Andersson, *Sveriges historia*, 218.
20. Ibid., 222; Einar Lie, *Over evne: Finansdepartementet, 1965–1992* (Oslo: Pax, 2010).
21. "Statsskulden" *Ekonomifakta*, http://www.ekonomifakta.se/Fakta/Offentlig-ekonomi/Statsbudget/Statsskulden/.
22. Francis Sejersted, *Sosialdemokratiets tidsalder* (Oslo: Pax, 2013).
23. Einar Lie, *Norsk økonomisk politikk etter 1905* (Oslo: Universitetsforlaget, 2012), 164.
24. The notion "jewel in the crown" is taken from Urban Lundberg, *Juvelen i kronan: Socialdemokraterna och den allmänna pensionen* (Stockholm: Hjalmarson & Högberg, 2003).
25. Juhana Vartainen, "Nordic Collective Agreements: A Continuous Institution in a Changing Economic Environment," *Comparative Social Research* 28, no. 28 (2011): 339–340.
26. World Economic Forum, *The Global Competitiveness Report, 2011–2012* (2011), http://www3.weforum.org/docs/WEF_GCR_Report_2011-12.pdf; United Nations Development Programme, *Human Development Report, 2015: Work for Human Development* (2015), http://hdr.undp.org/sites/default/files/2015_human_development_report_1.pdf.
27. Juhana Vartainen, "Nordic Collective Agreements," 357–358.

28. Sejersted, *Sosialdemokratiet*, 455, 463.
29. Stefan Svallfors, "Political Trust and Attitudes Towards Redistribution: A Comparison of Sweden and Norway," *European Societies* 1, no. 2 (1999): 241–268.
30. Lars Trägårdh, *Den svala svenska tilliten: Förutsättningar och utmaningar* (Stockholm: SNS Förlag, 2013), 32.
31. Institute for Social Research, *Mot en ny skandinavisk velferdsmodell? Konsekvenser av ideell, kommersiell og offentlig tjenesteyting for aktivt medborgerskap*, rapport 2016:01, ed. Karl Henrik Sivesind, http://www.samfunns forskning.no/Publikasjoner/Rapporter/2016/2016-1.
32. Ibid., 82.
33. Jardar Sørvoll, "The Politics of Cooperative Housing in Norway and Sweden, 1960–1990 (1945–2013): The Swedish Deregulation of 1968 and the Norwegian Liberalization of the 1980s" (Ph.D. diss., University of Oslo, 2014).
34. Normann, Rønning, and Nørgaard, *Challenges to the Nordic Welfare State*, 69–70.
35. Ibid., 93, 99.
36. Nordic newspapers and magazines have diligently commented on this situation. For example, see Jacob Aasland Ravndal and Johannes Due Enstad, "Hvorfor så mye mer høyreekstrem vold i Sverige?" *Aftenposten*, November 3, 2015; and "Velkommen til Södertälje," *Aftenposten*, May 16, 2015.
37. Normann, Rønning, and Nørgaard, *Challenges to the Nordic Welfare State*, 22; The Norwegian Ministry of Children, Equality, and Social Inclusion, *Velferd og migrasjon: Den norske modellens Framtid*, Norwegian Official Report (NOU) 2011:7, https://www.regjeringen.no/globalassets/upload/bld/ima/velferdsutvalget/nou_velferd_og_migrasjon.pdf.
38. Lars Trägårdh, "Trenger Sverige en ny samfunnskontrakt?" *Morgenbladet*, February 12, 2016.

CHAPTER SIX

Social Citizenship in the U.S. Affordable Care Act

BEATRIX HOFFMAN

Dedicated to the memory of Quentin Young MD, 1923–2016

HEALTH CARE as a social right is fundamental to modern welfare states. Germany created the first sickness-insurance plans for workers in the 1880s, and by World War II most European nations had established some form of state-sponsored medical coverage. The Beveridge Report of 1942 defined this type of social insurance as essential to the fight against disease and poor health as well as to achieving the goal of "Freedom from Want," as it protects citizens from the interruption of wages because of sickness and from bankruptcy because of medical costs. Today, virtually all Western welfare states include systems of universal health provision. The United States remains the lone exception.

Even after the passage of the Patient Protection and Affordable Care Act in 2010, the United States still does not have universal coverage, and its hybrid public-private health system continues to reject the notion of health care as a social right. Still, the Affordable Care Act (ACA or "Obamacare") represented the most sweeping health-system reform in the nation's history. As of the end of 2016, 18 million people have received insurance under the ACA.

This chapter analyzes the Affordable Care Act and its potential for expanding or limiting social citizenship in the United States. Healthcare reform in the United States starkly reflects Andrea Campbell's formulation that "policies make citizens": the structure and nature of social programs shape possibilities for citizen action and participation.[1] Because the ACA reflects the fragmentation and limitations of the U.S. health-care system, citizen mobilization faces greater obstacles than it does under a system of universal health care. In particular, the large role of private insurance companies poses major challenges to democratic participation. Also, the ACA continues U.S. health care's tendency to divide people into separate groups with different interests, rather than unifying them as beneficiaries of a universal program.

Examining social rights in U.S. health care is crucially important because many European countries are taking steps to "Americanize" their health systems by establishing greater roles for the private sector and "markets." As this chapter will demonstrate, the American experience of a hybrid public-private health system—one dominated by private firms but heavily subsidized by government—does not bode well for democratic participation, whether through electoral politics or popular mobilization. Indeed, the system sets up great obstacles to such participation, despite the efforts of reformers.

SOCIAL RIGHTS IN THE U.S. HEALTH SYSTEM

The United States has resisted adopting universal health provision for over a century. Reformers' attempts during World War I to establish state-sponsored sickness plans for industrial workers were defeated by business interests, organized physicians, and a wave of wartime xenophobia that labeled social insurance "made in Germany." The American Medical Association (AMA) became the most prominent opponent of universal health coverage, and it successfully fought every manifestation of what it termed "socialized medicine," from federally subsidized maternity and infancy care in the 1920s to President Harry Truman's proposal for national health insurance in 1950. The AMA failed, however, to block passage of Medicare (for the elderly) and Medicaid (for the poor) in 1965. Since World War II, private, commercial health insurance grew to cover the majority of the U.S. population, mostly through workplace benefits. The main opponents of the failed Clinton health reform in 1993–1994 were not physicians but the private insurance industry, which had come to dominate both health-care financing and delivery.

The jerry-built system in place by the end of the twentieth century, leaving tens of millions without coverage, bore little resemblance to the universal health-care schemes of European welfare states. The social right to health care has never been acknowledged in the United States. The closest thing Americans have is the right to emergency care, which has existed by statute only since 1986 and is limited to stabilization in an emergency room. Retired workers have a right to Medicare if they have paid into the system, but Medicare's coverage is not comprehensive. Poor people's right to Medicaid is dependent on their state of residence, welfare recipiency, income, parental status, and other factors. Group health coverage is tied to employment, and plans in the individual health-insurance market are restrictive and (before 2010) extraordinarily expensive. Altogether, this hybrid of programs makes up the most costly health system in the world, with some of the worst health outcomes in the West, and it leaves a large portion of the population uninsured and without access to health care.[2] The U.S. health system provides neither economic security nor health protection on the scale envisioned by Beveridge and implemented by many Western nations.

Barack Obama was elected president in 2008 promising to reform, once and for all, the nation's broken health system. When he entered office, fifty million U.S. citizens and residents, about 16 percent of the population, lacked any kind of medical coverage. The remainder had health insurance through a patchwork of programs: Medicare if they were over the age of sixty-five, Medicaid if very poor, group insurance through employment, and severely restricted individual policies. Both the large numbers of uninsured and the limitations and skyrocketing expenses of private insurance led Congress finally to act. After fifteen months of conflict and compromise (discussed in more detail below), the Patient Protection and Affordable Care Act passed in March 2010.

The ACA is the largest expansion of health-care coverage in the United States since the passage of Medicare and Medicaid in 1965. Opponents of the Obama administration called it radical, even socialist. But the ACA bears virtually no resemblance to the universal health systems in most industrialized nations, and it is also a departure from earlier proposals for national insurance in the United States. Instead, "Obamacare" builds on the existing hybrid public-private health system. It imposes new regulations on insurance companies, provides subsidies to make private health plans affordable to more people, and requires everyone to have coverage or pay a fine. It expands the reach of Medicaid, the federal health-insurance program for the poor, to cover millions more low-income families, although making this compulsory on the states was forbidden by the U.S. Supreme Court in 2012. (The ACA also contains numerous measures to address health-care quality and lower costs, but this chapter will focus on the access and coverage provisions of the law.)

In some ways, the ACA enhances social citizenship and has the potential to advance it further. Thanks to the new federal subsidies, many people are now able to afford private insurance coverage for the first time, available on the new health-care exchanges or "marketplaces" set up by the states and federal government. Everyone with insurance is now guaranteed access to many preventive medical services, free of charge. The expansion of Medicaid in those states electing to do so provides greater security to poor and low-income people who were previously ineligible. Perhaps most important, by banning insurance companies from refusing applicants based on their preexisting health status and by greatly increasing federal oversight of ACA-eligible health plans, the law attempts to rebalance the power of citizens relative to the private insurance industry. This is a fundamental change to the way insurance companies do business in the United States.

However, the position of insurance companies in the ACA is a paradoxical one. At the same time that the law curtails private insurers' ability to exclude, it provides a massive subsidy to the insurance industry and guarantees large insurance companies millions of new customers. Put simply, the law requires uninsured people not eligible for Medicaid to purchase a private health-coverage product. Rather than replacing the system of private for-profit insurance that was responsible for so many disastrous aspects of the U.S. health system, the ACA consolidates and increases the industry's role and potentially its power. The central position of private insurance companies in the reformed system shapes and, I will argue, seriously limits the possibilities for citizen voice, mobilization, and participation. As the following examples demonstrate, earlier attempts by social movements to challenge the practices of insurance companies faced numerous obstacles and achieved only minor successes, and often outright failures, because of the impermeability of private business to democratic influence.

HISTORICAL EXAMPLES OF CITIZEN CHALLENGES TO THE U.S. INSURANCE INDUSTRY

The private health-insurance system in the United States expanded after World War II as employers began offering coverage as a fringe benefit. In the 1950s, the government encouraged employer health benefits by making them tax deductible. Increasingly, private commercial insurers were able to compete successfully against nonprofit carriers like Blue Cross because of their ability to "cherry-pick" healthier groups to insure. By 1970, nearly 70 percent of Americans under the age of sixty-five were covered by some form of employer-sponsored insurance.[3]

Citizen groups that have attempted to influence the massive private insurance industry have faced an uphill battle. The McCarran-Ferguson Act of 1945 ensured that insurance regulation would be left primarily to the states, without involvement from the federal government. In the 1950s and '60s, labor unions began to protest rate increases by health-insurance companies, but their campaigns had little success.[4]

In the 1970s, however, social activists began to target the insurance industry's discriminatory practices. Insurance companies had long divided policyholders by factors like age, sex, race, and occupation and set their rates according to these distinctions. Feminist and labor activists in the 1970s called attention to the ways private health insurance egregiously discriminated against women. For example, private plans charged higher premiums for women than for men. Private insurance coverage rarely included maternity care, or it required longer waiting periods for maternity than it did for other conditions. Also, exclusions for "preexisting conditions," common throughout private health insurance, included a disproportionate number of disorders exclusive to women. The campaign against gender discrimination in insurance, led by the Coalition of Labor Union Women, led to the passage of the Pregnancy Discrimination Act of 1978, which required large employers to include maternity coverage in their health plans. However, small employers and individual insurance plans were exempt. The majority of individual health-insurance plans continued to practice so-called gender rating and to exclude maternity coverage until the implementation of the Affordable Care Act, which finally banned the most blatant discriminatory practices in health insurance.[5]

Another wave of protest against the insurance industry came during the AIDS crisis. In the early 1990s, both the New York and San Francisco branches of ACT UP (AIDS Coalition to Unleash Power) established committees devoted entirely to insurance and access issues for people with HIV/AIDS. "People with life threatening diseases, especially people with AIDS, face illegal discrimination, absurd premium increases and sudden policy cancellation. *They need protection*," a San Francisco activist wrote to the California health-insurance commissioner in 1990. "Health care is a right and health insurance is a necessity, not a luxury."

ACT UP used highly visible protest tactics to bring attention to insurance discrimination. In 1990, activists staged a "phone zap" (flooding the switchboard with phone calls) against a company that had eliminated AIDS benefits unless the policyholder could prove "involuntary infection"; the company, Galaxy Carpet Mills, relented and rescinded the rule. In May 1991, one hundred ACT UP members marched from the headquarters of the Health Insurance Association of America in Washington, D.C., to the White House, carrying black coffins draped with the names of insurance companies accused of discrimination against people with AIDS.[6] However, the AIDS movement, famed for its spectacular success in changing the practices of pharmaceutical companies, was not able to achieve similar reforms in the insurance industry, at least not until the Affordable Care Act.[7]

Far from bowing to consumer and protester demands, the insurance industry continued to consolidate its economic and political power to defeat health-care reform. The Health Insurance Association of America, the umbrella lobbying group for private insurers, played a major role in the collapse of the Clinton administration's comprehensive reform plan, spending up to $30 million—more than any previous such campaign—on advertising and lobbying portraying the Clinton plan as a threat to individual health-care choice.[8]

By the mid-1990s, the majority of Americans with private health coverage were in "managed-care" plans, which attempted to cut costs by limiting access to treatments via various means including primary-care gatekeeper physicians, narrow provider networks, and preapproval requirements. Managed-care plans (also known as HMOs or PPOs) angered consumers, who felt they had lost both choice and access. Consumers pushed back against the restrictions of managed care by gravitating toward health plans with a greater choice of physicians and out-of-network services, joining class-action lawsuits against HMOs who denied care, and sharing their "HMO horror stories" with the media. However, the main consumer demand for passage of a Patients' Bill of Rights allowing greater legal recourse for HMO members did not succeed. Some states imposed stricter requirements on managed-care plans, but most only offered a cumbersome appeals process for patients alleging denial of care or payment.[9]

In the early 2000s, consumer- and health-rights groups worked to publicize insurance-company practices such as rescission (canceling policies after the policyholder becomes ill) and using the label of "preexisting condition" to deny payment for care. In the run-up to the 2008 presidential election, progressive groups formed a coalition, Health Care for All Now (HCAN), to demand national health reform. Unlike previous activist efforts, which had focused on the plight of the uninsured, HCAN decided to target the discriminatory and damaging practices of the insurance industry, emphasizing the injustices suffered by Americans *with* private health insurance. Here is HCAN's own description of its strategy, listing a myriad of insurance-company abuses:

> We began the campaign by attacking the insurance industry as the chief villain in the story of America's health insurance crisis. . . . We talked about people being denied needed care and getting dropped from private coverage because they got sick. We emphasized that medical bills were crushing small businesses, making large businesses uncompetitive and bankrupting families, including millions who had health insurance. We highlighted cancer patients who couldn't afford to live because the cost of their care exceeded a lifetime or annual limit they never knew existed in their policies. We drew attention to women whose coverage was rescinded because they were diagnosed with cancer or because the insurance company considered them at higher risk for breast cancer. We also continued to raise awareness of the health care system's unconscionable impact on the uninsured, including the thousands who die every year for lack of insurance, the inadequate access to quality care, racial and ethnic disparities in health outcomes and more.[10]

This type of rhetoric against insurance companies was used by all the Democratic presidential candidates in 2008, and especially by Barack Obama, who spoke of his own mother's struggle with insurance approvals while she was dying of cancer.

CRAFTING THE AFFORDABLE CARE ACT: POPULAR MOBILIZATION GIVES WAY TO PRIVATE POWER

Did the Affordable Care Act constitute a success for the social movements that protested the power of private insurance companies? The new curbs on insurance-company practices are a crucial victory, but they were all that progressives would win. The most powerful interest groups shaping the Obama health reform were not citizen organizations but the insurance industry itself. Insurance companies and their trade associations spent $586 million ensuring their voice would be heard in the health-reform battle.[11]

The insurance industry won a major victory when it succeeded in having the "public option" removed from the health-reform bill. Most progressives had given up on pushing for a single-payer, European- or Canadian-style system early in the debate. Instead, they and Obama took up a proposal called the "public option," which would have created a government-run insurance plan similar to Medicare, to compete with the private plans available in the new health-insurance marketplaces. During 2009, polls consistently showed that a majority of Americans supported the public option. Among physicians surveyed, 73 percent supported it, and even the formerly antireform American Medical Association agreed on the public option's importance.[12]

The insurance industry vigorously opposed the public option, even as it agreed to support guaranteed issue and the individual mandate (measures that would require private insurers to accept all customers and require all Americans to buy health insurance or pay a fine). Clearly, the option threatened private insurers' control over the market and might even lead to the insurance industry's demise. Journalists estimated that America's Health Insurance Plans (AHIP), the insurance industry's lobbying arm, spent $133 million on campaigning against the public option in the second quarter of 2009 alone—one million dollars a day.[13] Connecticut Senator Joe Lieberman, a crucial vote, refused to support the bill if the public option were included. Lieberman was closely allied with insurance companies, "accepting more than one million dollars in campaign contributions from the insurance industry and more than 600,000 dollars from pharmaceuticals and related healthcare-products companies."[14] Senator Max Baucus insisted on removing the public option before he would support the bill in his powerful Finance Committee. Baucus also had a close relationship with health insurers, receiving $1.5 million in campaign funds from the industry in 2008.[15]

Although President Obama had campaigned on including a public option in his health-reform plan, he quietly allowed the option to die, one of many compromises on the way to political victory for the ACA. One analysis notes: "The public option failed as a result of many factors, including lack of support from moderate and conservative Democrats, opposition from Republicans and health care interest groups, and ultimately an absence of strong support from the White House."[16] Apart from the Medicaid expansion and a mechanism for setting up nonprofit cooperative plans, the final bill offered no alternative to private insurance.

CITIZEN ACTION AFTER THE AFFORDABLE CARE ACT

President Obama, surrounded by cheering supporters, signed the Affordable Care Act into law on March 23, 2010. As the greatest political victory for health-care reform since 1965, the ACA was cause for celebration: "a landmark in modern U.S. social legislation," wrote the political scientists Theda Skocpol and Lawrence Jacobs, "comparable to Social Security, Medicare, and the Civil Rights Act."[17]

But the elation of reform supporters was somewhat deflated by immediate challenges from the right. Following suits brought by several conservative legal foundations, a lower court declared the law's "individual mandate," the requirement that everyone in the United States must purchase health insurance, to be unconstitutional. The Supreme Court's decision in June 2012, *National Federation of Independent Business v. Sebelius*, upheld the individual mandate under the Constitution's taxing power but struck down the requirement that all states expand their Medicaid programs to cover more people.[18]

The legal backlash against the ACA provides one example of activism spurred by the new health reform: citizen action from the right. The "Tea Party," a political movement bankrolled by corporate funders such as the Koch Brothers but enrolling numerous grassroots conservative and libertarian supporters, had gained national attention when its members disrupted "town hall" meetings throughout 2009, declaring government involvement in health care to be "tyranny" and "trampling on our constitutional rights."[19] After the law's passage, Tea Party theorists hatched the constitutional challenge to Obamacare and took it as far as the Supreme Court, supported by public rallies and marches.[20]

Right-wing anger at the Affordable Care Act continued despite the legal rulings upholding the law. Health-care reform galvanized conservatives and libertarians and is credited by Tea Party activists with invigorating their movement. Can the same be said for proreform social movements in the wake of Obamacare? This chapter next examines how the ACA may serve to mobilize progressive citizen action, both in support of the law and in protest against its limitations.

Consumer Power

The official Healthcare.gov website touts the "rights and protections" offered to consumers[21] by the Affordable Care Act. New controls on insurance companies make up much of the list: requiring insurers to cover people with preexisting health conditions and to offer free preventive care, ending lifetime and annual dollar limits on coverage of essential health benefits, requiring insurers to use 80 percent of their revenues for medical care, and banning cancellation of policies because of illness. Also listed under "rights and protections" are requirements that health plans must ensure that "you understand the coverage you're getting." The various types of coverage available to consumers on state and federal marketplaces must be explained in "plain language."[22]

In order to facilitate this understanding of health insurance, the ACA also provides funding for a new consumer-information and -assistance infrastructure. Marketplaces are required to provide "navigators and assisters" to educate communities about new health-insurance options and to help people enroll. According to one study, during the first period of open enrollment for the new marketplaces in 2014, more than 28,000 volunteers and paid workers assisted some 10.6 million people, answering questions and walking them through the application process.[23]

An army of citizens wearing T-shirts stating "Ask me how to . . . #GETCOVERED" seems to inaugurate a new type of popular participation in health reform, an "Obamacare civic activism," in the words of the distinguished labor historian Nelson Lichtenstein; navigators and assisters can act "as agents of civic engagement and citizen mobilization . . . such groups feed activism and are fed by it."[24] But some argue that helping people purchase subsidized private insurance does not constitute social citizenship. Andrew Coates of Physicians for a National Health Program, a group that advocates for a universal single-payer health-care system, writes that "peddling private health insurance policies to the working poor . . . will not strengthen democracy. . . . The present acceleration of hideous inequalities [under the ACA], long a hallmark of our unjust health system, will further erode, not restore, democracy in the United States."[25]

Insurance-Company Accountability

In addition to putting curbs on insurance companies' ability to exclude, the ACA aims to enhance democratic citizenship by "foster[ing] public participation in the health insurance sector." The law mandates that states engage with "stakeholders," including consumers, in setting up marketplaces.[26] Ratings of individual health-insurance plans will be based on an "enrollee satisfaction survey system"; such consumer input will allegedly make insurance companies more accountable to the public. Policyholders are also guaranteed certain rights to appeal health-plan decisions.[27] Plan members' rights in the ACA rest on notions of consumer appeals to private business, rather than on participatory social citizenship.[28]

Rights of individual appeal do not address the regressive aspects of private health insurance that militate against social citizenship. In order to keep their premiums within the affordability ranges required by the government, marketplace plans have adopted two highly unpopular practices: "narrow networks" and increased cost sharing. Narrow networks reduce the number of doctors and hospitals available "in network" (without extra charges) to plan recipients. Narrow networks have always been central to managed-care practices in the United States, but cost competitiveness among ACA plans is increasing the practice considerably.

Apart from limiting or even eliminating choice of doctor and hospital, narrow networks may also harm health by interrupting the patients' relationship with providers who are dropped from networks. Belatedly recognizing this problem, the government has recently instituted rules requiring limited continuity of care (ninety days) in plans with narrow networks. Also, although the ACA limits the amount of "cost sharing" (copayments and deductibles that plan members are responsible for, in addition to premiums), the amount of cost sharing in marketplace plans is significant and increasing. In 2016, "the maximum out-of-pocket costs for consumers under the Affordable Care Act will increase next year to $7,150 for an individual and $14,300 for a family," extraordinarily high costs for middle- and working-class households.[29] Numerous studies have shown that cost-sharing disproportionately hurts low-income people, larger families, and people with severe or chronic health conditions.[30] Narrow networks and high cost sharing curtail both health rights and economic security but are not subject to appeal by "consumers."

Gender Equity

The ACA addresses decades of discrimination against women in health insurance. The law forbids insurance companies from charging women higher rates than men, requires coverage of maternity care and breastfeeding equipment and support, and includes contraception among the preventive benefits that health plans must provide free of charge to policyholders. These reforms met some central demands for greater equity in health care that women's organizations had been demanding for years.[31]

However, congressional conservatives succeeded in excluding comprehensive reproductive-health services from the ACA by applying existing limitations on federal funding for abortion to the new law. State marketplace plans are allowed to ban coverage for abortions, and twenty-five states have done so. An additional six states have not banned the coverage but don't offer plans with that option. Abortion restrictions create byzantine new bureaucracies in implementing the law: "In states that do not restrict coverage of abortions on plans available through the Marketplace, insurers may offer a plan that covers abortions beyond the federal limitations, but this coverage must be paid for using private, not federal, dollars." Only one state, California, treats abortion as an aspect of maternity care and thus requires abortion coverage in all state plans.[32] Even the contraception provision has been weakened: on June 30, 2014, the U.S. Supreme Court ruled that privately held corporations could refuse to provide contraception in their employee health insurance on religious grounds (known as the "Hobby Lobby" case).

There is still some additional promise for social citizenship and gender equity in the civil-rights provision of the ACA. This provision, Section 1557, is the first federal law that bans not only race but also sex discrimination in "any health program or activity" receiving federal assistance.[33] This new protection has been utilized by gay and transgender patients to challenge various types of bias against them in the health system. Spurred by this citizen action, courts and the federal government "have interpreted the law to prohibit discrimination against people who are transgender or who fail to conform to gender stereotypes." For example, the federal Office of Civil Rights ordered hospitals to assign rooms based on patients' self-identified gender status and required a federally funded mammogram program to provide screenings for male-to-female transgender individuals.[34] Although only half of the states have passed laws specifically against discrimination on the basis of gender identity/expression, enforcement of the gender-equality provision of the Affordable Care Act applies to all health facilities receiving federal funding (virtually every such facility in the United States). As Medicare did for racial segregation five decades ago, the ACA brings federal civil-rights law to bear on long-standing health-care practices that discriminate.[35]

The civil-rights provisions of the Affordable Care Act represent a potentially important advance for social citizenship for women and LGBT people. But, so far, complaints have been brought mostly against hospitals and providers, not against insurance companies. Again, the private insurance industry, even as it accepts new, massive federal subsidies, can find ways to evade compliance. For example, HIV status is a protected category under Section 1557. But some insurance companies have used their private prerogatives to charge more for HIV drugs by placing them in the highest-cost tier of prescription benefits. Since they are no longer allowed to reject categories of people, insurers seek other ways to exclude or minimize the cost of potentially expensive policyholders.[36] Patient-advocacy groups utilized the civil-rights protections in the ACA to bring a complaint against several Florida insurance companies that charged extremely high copayments for AIDS drugs. In June 2015, state regulators agreed to require all Florida insurers to lower copayments on HIV/AIDS medications. The director of the AIDS Institute, one of the advocacy groups bringing the complaint, hailed this as a "major victory for those living with HIV,"[37] but it is a victory that highlights two limitations of social citizenship under the ACA: the continuation of profit-maximizing efforts by insurance companies and the United States' fragmented federalism, requiring state-by-state efforts by advocacy groups.

Minorities and the Poor

Despite civil-rights laws, the U.S. health-care system is still characterized by poorer health outcomes for minorities compared to whites, known in health-policy circles as "racial (or socioeconomic) disparities in health." The Affordable Care Act contains several provisions intended to ameliorate these disparities. By offering health coverage to more people of color, the insurance reforms and coverage expansions intend to reduce the large number of uninsured minorities—at the time of the law's passage, more than 50 percent of all people without insurance were members of minority groups. In addition, the ACA boosts funding for community health centers (clinics that disproportionately serve racial minority groups, particularly in inner cities), includes provisions for training more minority health practitioners, and creates an Institute for Minority Health and Health Disparities.[38]

The ACA's coverage expansions have already gone some way toward attacking racial disparities: most dramatically, within the first year of implementation (2014), inequality in health-insurance coverage between black and white children was eliminated.[39] However, several factors prevent further coverage expansion from reaching minorities and the poor in particular, including the expense of private policies (even with subsidies) and high cost sharing. Because the new health plans are only accessible via the Healthcare.gov website, rural Americans without Internet access may have no way to find out about or purchase them.[40] Because of these and other barriers to enrollment in private insurance, researchers believe that only the expansion of government insurance programs (Medicaid and Medicare) will eliminate racial disparities in rates of coverage.[41]

However, the ACA's mandatory Medicaid expansion was struck down by the U.S. Supreme Court in 2012 in *NFIB v. Sebelius* (the same ruling that confirmed the constitutionality of the individual mandate). In addition to addressing racial disparities, a Medicaid expansion may have created openings for new beneficiaries, most of whom would have been the working poor, to create new alliances and participate in health-system governance. However, less than half of the states have currently agreed to participate in the Medicaid expansion. This has serious implications for the health, insurance status, and social citizenship of minorities and the poor.

The refusal to expand Medicaid has reduced the number of people who should have been insured under the Affordable Care Act by 25 percent.[42] The result is a "shocking coverage gap" of over five million individuals with incomes too high for existing Medicaid programs but too low to afford the new marketplace plans. Those in the coverage gap "are disproportionately people of color . . . 27 percent of the uninsured are African-American and 24 percent are Latino."[43] States' refusal to expand Medicaid is also predicted to have a disproportionate, negative effect on the health status of the poor and minorities. Studies of several states that did expand their Medicaid programs (including before the ACA) are demonstrating that "the decline in mortality was greatest among nonwhites and people living in poorer counties."[44]

The truncated Medicaid expansion also has implications for citizen mobilization. In the past, poor people have utilized the Medicaid program as an organizing tool to demand health-care rights. The National Welfare Rights Organization (NWRO) in the 1970s organized Medicaid recipients in several campaigns, including a consumer-rights movement that successfully instituted consumer representation on hospital boards and review organizations, and several class-action lawsuits demanding equal treatment of Medicaid patients by hospitals. Although their victories were limited (the Patients' Bill of Rights adopted by the American Hospital Association, for example, was a greatly watered-down version of the rights demanded by the NWRO), Medicaid at least offered poverty activists a tool to bring recipients together and upon which to base rights demands.[45]

It's worth noting that Medicaid refusal itself can mobilize citizen action. When Medicaid was first created in 1965, most states adopted it within a decade, but there was one holdout: Arizona, whose conservative legislators condemned the program as federal meddling, despite the state's large uninsured population. In the early 1980s, groups within the state began to mobilize to demand a Medicaid program for Arizona. Seniors, Chicano organizations, and welfare-rights groups joined with churches to organize "Medicaid Sundays" to educate the public and obtain signatures on petitions to legislators. James Rausch, the Catholic bishop of Tucson, wrote to Arizona legislators: "As the single orphaned state in the nation's program of federal assistance for health care we have too long shuddered at the *indignity of neglect* thrust upon Arizona brothers and sisters in their destitution." He urged them "to protect the basic human right to health care. . . . This right is rooted in the innate dignity of each human person . . . the people of Arizona cannot accept . . . continued inaction" on Medicaid. Alongside fiscal considerations, citizens' mobilization helped convince Arizona finally to adopt Medicaid in 1982, seventeen years after the program was created.[46] In the twenty-first century, with dozens rather than a single state refusing Medicaid expansion, challenges to citizen mobilization are even more daunting.[47]

Immigrants

Up to one-third of the estimated thirty million people who will remain uninsured after the Affordable Care Act are undocumented immigrants, who are banned from purchasing even unsubsidized policies in the marketplaces. Such immigrants are already excluded from Medicaid, Medicare, and many state health programs. The exclusion came after bitter attacks from conservatives accusing Obama of extending health care to "illegals" in his health-reform proposal.[48]

Undocumented immigrants, excluded from literal citizenship and also from social citizenship because of their inability to benefit from government programs, may not seem like the most promising constituency for mobilization. Collective action on their part engenders threats of job loss, deportation, and family separation. Yet the undocumented and their supporters have actually been among the most active leaders and participants in social movements in the United States today. Following massive immigrant-rights protests in 2006, activists have won limited but important concessions for undocumented immigrants brought to the United States as children (known as "DREAMers"). The most significant achievement has been the DACA program (Deferred Action for Childhood Arrivals), created through Obama's executive action, allowing DREAMers temporary protection from deportation and greater access to jobs and higher education.

Similar strategies are being deployed to attack immigrants' exclusion from the Affordable Care Act. Even DACA-eligible youth are excluded from the ACA, leading the National Hispanic Leadership Agenda to petition President Obama to

> apply the fairness and equality that your Administration has shown in various other areas in the health care context and ensure that no one—regardless of their immigration status—lacks access to critical health care services. . . . For DACA recipients in need of health care, the denial of affordable care and coverage undoubtedly leads to human suffering and diminished health.[49]

At the state level, immigrant activism for health care has been strongest in California, home to one-quarter of the undocumented immigrants in the United States. Following a statewide activist campaign by immigrants and allies, including a "Health Care for All" caravan traveling the length of the state, California passed a bill in 2015 extending the full benefits of its Medicaid program (Medi-Cal) to undocumented children (but not to adults).[50] The movement is currently pressing for adoption of a state law that would allow all undocumented immigrants access to ACA health insurance.

Single-Payer Movement

Since the 1980s, a single-payer movement has attempted to change the fundamental nature of the U.S. health system by demanding comprehensive, universal health care for all. A single-payer system, like many other national health systems, would be funded by general tax revenues and would eliminate the participation of third-party insurers. The movement has fought campaigns to establish single-payer systems at the state level and to pressure policy makers to include single-payer proposals in national health reform. In both struggles, advocates have fought an uphill and often dispiriting battle. No state has adopted a single-payer system, and both the Clinton and Obama administrations dropped single-payer from consideration in their reform proposals.

The Affordable Care Act is seen as a betrayal by many in the movement. Physicians for a National Health Program (PNHP), the leading organization advocating a single-payer system, bitterly called the ACA "aspirin dispensed for the treatment of cancer. Instead of eliminating the root of the problem—the profit-driven, private health insurance industry—this costly new legislation will enrich and further entrench these firms."[51] Although some hope remained for state-level reform, the most promising single-payer proposal, in Vermont, recently collapsed because of concerns about higher taxes.[52]

But the fortunes of the single-payer movement took a surprising turn in 2016 when Vermont Senator Bernie Sanders became a viable candidate for the Democratic presidential nomination. Sanders had supported single-payer throughout his career and renamed it "Medicare for All" in his campaign platform, reminding Americans that the elderly already enjoy a successful and popular single-payer system.[53] Almost overnight, the previously obscure phrases "single-payer" and "Medicare for All" became familiar to millions who watched the presidential debates and followed the campaign on social media. Although dismissed as utopian by opposing candidates, Sanders's outspoken support of single-payer may indicate a shift in at least the rhetoric, if not the results, of health-care-reform movements in the United States. Like advocates of immigrant access, the Sanders campaign used the language of universal social rights: "Health care must be recognized as a *right*, not a *privilege*," his website reads. "Every man, woman and child in our country should be able to access the health care they need *regardless of their income*."[54]

LESSONS

All of the aspects of the Affordable Care Act discussed thus far point to the fragmented and unequal nature of the U.S. health system, even after historic reform. Under the ACA, individuals may be insured by their employer; by one of literally thousands of individual marketplace plans, which differ by state;[55] or by Medicare or Medicaid. Many also remain uninsured, whether from reluctance (individual mandate), unaffordability (the coverage gap), or exclusion (undocumented immigrants). The multitiered, complex, and partial structure of coverage works against unified citizen action, resulting instead in numerous single-issue or single-constituency movements targeting particular aspects of the system; the single-payer movement is one important exception. A limited, patchwork system ensures that there is no single target for protest or reform, and democratic energies may be exhausted by groups fighting numerous separate and different battles.

The importance of universalism in mobilizing citizen action is evident in the current attempt of several European nations to introduce elements of privatization into their health systems. The social citizenship conferred by universal health coverage extends to citizen mobilization in support of their public systems. In the United Kingdom, citizens have organized around defending the universal National Health Service (NHS) from encroaching "fragmentation and privatization." Nationwide citizen actions against NHS privatization and the austerity policies of the Conservative government are ongoing, including a London protest in June 2014 that drew fifty thousand people.[56] An announcement by the "Darlington Mums," a group of women who organized an antiprivatization march from their northern city to London, captures the social citizenship conferred by membership in a universal, public system: "The NHS is owned by us, used by us, loved by us and can only be saved by us."[57] The government has responded by denying that its reforms herald privatization—another indication of the continuing power (at least rhetorical) of commitment to universalism in the NHS.

Universalism wielded practical, not just rhetorical, power in protests against Spain's recent privatization campaign. Responding to Spain's dire economic crisis, the conservative Rajoy government in 2013 imposed new austerity measures, many targeting the country's universal health-care system. But attempts by local officials in Madrid to privatize six public hospitals were met by massive, weekly street protests. Many of the marches were led by Madrid's strong physicians' and nurses' unions and attended by many patients and ordinary citizens who declared their allegiance to universal health care. Nationwide protests also erupted against the government's new ban on nonemergency treatment for undocumented immigrants. In both the antiprivatization and immigrant-rights movements, participants used the language of universalism to condemn the government reforms, using mottos like "I Say Yes to Universal Health." Immigrant-rights protesters chanted the slogan "¿Quiénes serán las siguientes?" (Who will be next?) to argue that taking away the health-care rights of any part of the population threatened the rights of everyone.[58] These were not statements of idealism but, like the NHS defense in the United Kingdom, based on already-extensive experience with health care for all. In addition, Spanish and British protesters could unify around a single goal—protection of a single system. In Spain, at least, these systemic and rhetorical foundations for mobilization led to concrete political results. In 2014, Madrid dropped its privatization plan, and Spain's national government restored access to primary health care to undocumented immigrants the following year.[59]

European governments and policy makers exploring possibilities for (or already implementing) privatization in their health-care systems[60] should look closely at the U.S. example. Scholars are already pointing out that private health-care firms have not proven to be more efficient or inexpensive than public systems, as their supporters claim.[61] In addition, the question of democracy has received insufficient attention. This chapter has provided numerous examples of the ways in which private and privatized organizations have proven less accountable to the public and less open to change brought about by public pressure. Perhaps most important, a system dominated by private industries, as seen in the U.S. example, is vulnerable to undue political influence by these private interests. Insurance companies' track record of secrecy, heavy use of campaign donations to influence legislators, and creation and funding of front groups for advertising and lobbying does not bode well for the future of democracy or citizen participation in the healthcare system.[62] As William Beveridge declared in 1942, one desired goal of the welfare state is to redress the unequal balance of power between citizens and private interests. In many ways, privatized health systems do the opposite: they enhance private power at the expense of the people.

SOME THOUGHTS ON THE 2016 U.S. ELECTION

The limited social rights conferred by the Affordable Care Act will become a distant memory if the ACA is repealed or partially dismantled under the incoming Trump/Republican majority government. As of this writing (December 2016), the president-elect and congressional Republicans are proposing to end several key components of the ACA, including the individual mandate, federal subsidies for marketplace plans, and Medicaid expansion, while maintaining guaranteed issue and some other popular provisions. Such proposals, if implemented, will effectively eliminate the law altogether. Marketplace plans without federal subsidies will not be affordable to consumers, and insurance companies cannot profit without the individual mandate. Even partial repeal of the ACA will throw millions back into the ranks of the uninsured and will likely create even larger numbers of uninsured people than ever before (58.7 million in one study's estimate), given the inevitable disruptions in the private insurance market.[63] While elected officials use the health-care system as an ideological football, not only social rights but the health and even lives of millions are at stake.

Although major health-reform organizations are launching full-throated campaigns against ACA rollbacks,[64] the health system's fragmentation makes a unified defense challenging. Seventeen million Americans have ACA insurance, but millions more will not be as directly or quickly affected (although they will be in the long term) by the loss of subsidized marketplace plans. Activists in some states will be forced to defend Medicaid expansion; activists in other states are still fighting to implement it.

Republican threats to privatize Medicare should mobilize additional constituencies. The American Association for Retired Persons (AARP) has declared itself "on the front lines" of that battle. The AARP is one of the most powerful lobbies in the country, but its rhetoric speaks only about fighting Medicare cuts, not about preserving the ACA or extending Medicare to all.[65] The organization's lobbying efforts, limited to preserving existing benefits for its own members, reflect the narrowness of democratic voice in a system that does not recognize universal social rights.

A broader-based defense of the ACA could emerge from the civil- and human-rights movements representing those who have the most to lose under a Trump administration. Women's rights and LGBT activists can draw attention to the links between attacks on reproductive and sexual freedoms and the potential loss of the gender-equity protections of the ACA. Defenders of civil rights and the poor can demand recognition of how Medicaid cuts and the end of insurance subsidies will disproportionately hurt minority communities and exacerbate racial disparities in health. Defending health-care reform on civil- and human-rights grounds will resonate strongly with the U.S. activism tradition of the late-twentieth and early-twenty-first centuries and could lay the groundwork for a movement for universal health rights.

NOTES

1. Andrea Louise Campbell, *How Policies Make Citizens: Senior Political Activism and the American Welfare State* (Princeton, N.J.: Princeton University Press, 2005).
2. Numerous studies show that "despite spending more on health care, Americans had poor health outcomes, including shorter life expectancy and greater prevalence of chronic conditions." http://www.common wealthfund.org/publications/issue-briefs/2015/oct/us-health-care -from-a-global-perspective.
3. Jennifer Klein, *For All These Rights: Business, Labor, and the Shaping of America's Public-Private Welfare State* (Princeton, N.J.: Princeton University Press, 2003), http://www.cdc.gov/nchs/health_policy/health care_coverage_table1.htm.
4. Beatrix Hoffman, *Health Care for Some: Rights and Rationing in the United States Since 1930* (Chicago: University of Chicago, 2012), chap. 5; Klein, *For All These Rights*, chap. 6; Gerald Markowitz and David Rosner, "Seeking Common Ground: A History of Labor and Blue Cross," *Journal of Health Politics, Policy, and Law* 16, no. 4 (Winter 1991): 695–718.
5. For additional examples of consumer protest against health insurers, see Hoffman, *Health Care for Some*, chap. 5.
6. Ibid., chap. 7.
7. For important analyses of ACT UP's victories against the pharmaceutical industry, see Steven Epstein, *Impure Science: AIDS, Activism, and the Politics of Knowledge* (Berkeley: University of California Press,1996); and Jennifer Brier, *Infectious Ideas: U.S. Political Responses to the AIDS Crisis* (Chapel Hill: University of North Carolina Press, 2011). Brier notes that one reason for the pharmaceutical industry's acceptance of movement demands was that some of the demanded changes, such as quicker approval for new drugs, would benefit the industry financially. No such financial benefit would accrue to insurers from curtailing discrimination against individuals with AIDS.
8. Theda Skocpol, *Boomerang: Health Care Reform and the Turn Against Government* (New York: Norton, 1997).
9. Hoffman, *Health Care for Some*, chap. 9.
10. http://healthcareforamericanow.org/about-us/mission-history/.
11. Wendell Potter, *Deadly Spin: An Insurance Company Insider Speaks Out on How Corporate PR Is Killing Health Care and Deceiving Americans* (New York: Bloomsbury, 2010), 192.
12. Only one poll showed less than a majority (43 percent), the remainder between 50 and 77 percent support for a public option; Potter, *Deadly Spin*, 202. See also Dan Belz and Joe Cohen, "Most Support Public Option for

Health Insurance, Poll Finds," *Washington Post*, October 20, 2009; Salomeh Keyhani and Alex Federman, "Doctors on Coverage: Physicians' Views on a New Public Insurance Option and Medicare Expansion," *New England Journal of Medicine*, September 14, 2009.
13. Janet Adamy, "Despite Making Concessions, Insurers Face Renewed Attacks," *Wall Street Journal*, July 30, 2009; Glenn Thrush, "5 Things to Watch During Recess," *Politico.com*, August 3, 2010, http://www.politico.com/news/stories/0809/25709.html.
14. Scott Horton, October 28, 2009, "Lieberman Shills for the Healthcare Industry," http://harpers.org/blog/2009/10/lieberman-shills-for-the-healthcare-industry/.
15. Potter, *Deadly Spin*, 205; Chris McGreal, "Revealed: Millions Spent by Lobby Firms Fighting Obama Health Reforms," *Guardian*, October 1, 2009.
16. Helen A. Halpin and Peter Harbage, "The Origins and Demise of the Public Option," *Health Affairs* 29, no. 6 (June 2010): 1117–1124.
17. Lawrence R. Jacobs and Theda Skocpol, "Hard-Fought Legacy: Obama, Congressional Democrats, and the Struggle for Comprehensive Health Care Reform," in *Reaching for a New Deal: Ambitious Governance, Economic Meltdown, and Polarized Politics in Obama's First Two Years*, ed. Theda Skocpol and Lawrence R. Jacobs (New York: Russell Sage Foundation, 2011), 54.
18. Nathaniel Persily, Gillian E. Metzger, and Trevor W. Morrison, *The Health Care Case: The Supreme Court's Decision and Its Implications* (Oxford: Oxford University Press, 2013).
19. Martha Shanahan, "5 Memorable Moments When Town Hall Meetings Turned to Rage," National Public Radio, August 7, 2013, http://www.npr.org/sections/itsallpolitics/2013/08/07/209919206/5-memorable-moments-when-town-hall-meetings-turned-to-rage.
20. Josh Blackman, "Popular Constitutionalism and the Affordable Care Act," *Public Affairs Quarterly* 27, no. 3 (July 2013): 179–197; "Tea Party Rallies in Washington Against Obamacare," FoxNews.com, March 24, 2012, http://www.foxnews.com/politics/2012/03/24/tea-party-rallies-in-washington-against-obama-care.html.
21. The term "consumer," rather than citizen, beneficiary, or patient, is most often used to refer to participants in U.S. health care, underscoring the market-based nature of the system. See Nancy Tomes, "Patient or Health Care Consumers? Why the History of Contested Terms Matters," in *History and Health Policy: Bringing the Past Back In*, ed. Rosemary Stevens et al. (New Brunswick, N.J.: Rutgers University Press, 2006).
22. "Health Insurance Rights and Protections," Healthcare.gov, https://www.healthcare.gov/health-care-law-protections/rights-and-protections/.

23. Affordable Care Act, Title I, "New grants to states to establish or expand offices of health insurance consumer assistance to help consumers file appeals and respond to complaints" (section 1002); CMS.gov, "Consumer Assistance Program Grants: How States Are Using New Resource to Give Consumers Greater Control of Their Health Care," http://www.cms.gov/CCIIO/Resources/Grants/cap-grants-states.html; Enroll America website, https://www.enrollamerica.org.
24. Nelson Lichtenstein, "Obamacare's Other Benefit," *Los Angeles Times*, March, 12 2013, http://articles.latimes.com/2013/mar/12/opinion/la-oe-lichtenstein-obamacare-20130312.
25. Andrew D. Coates, "Selling Private Health Insurance Will Not Strengthen Democracy," *Portside News Service*, March 22, 2013, http://www.pnhp.org/news/2013/march/selling-private-health-insurance-will-not-strengthen-democracy.
26. Like "consumer," "stakeholder" is a buzzword in U.S. health care, derived from business jargon.
27. Affordable Care Act, Title I, "New national standards for internal and external appeals for consumers to challenge an insurer's coverage determinations and claims decisions" (sections 1001/2719); Nan D. Hunter, "Health Insurance Reform and Intimations of Citizenship," *University of Pennsylvania Law Review* 159, no. 6 (June 2011): 1955–1997.
28. In one definition, consumer "activation" is measured by "self-manage ment, health care encounter, shopping, and health behaviors"; Jessica N. Mittler, Grant R. Martsolf, Shannon J. Telenko, and Dennis P. Scanlon, "Making Sense of 'Consumer Engagement' Initiatives to Improve Health and Health Care: A Conceptual Framework to Guide Policy and Practice," *Milbank Quarterly* 91, no. 1 (March 2013): 37.
29. Robert Pear, "Health Law Plans to Be Rated by Network Size," *New York Times*, March 6, 2016.
30. Beatrix Hoffman, "Restraining the Health Care Consumer: The History of Deductibles and Co-payments in U.S. Health Insurance," *Social Science History* 30, no. 4 (Winter 2006): 501–528.
31. See also Sharon K. Long, Karen Stockley, and Shanna Shulman, "Have Gender Gaps in Insurance Coverage and Access to Care Narrowed Under Health Reform? Findings from Massachusetts," *American Economic Review* 101, no. 3 (May 2011): 640–644.
32. The antiabortion provisions of the ACA also generate extensive paperwork, adding to the system's inefficiency: "plans that offer abortion coverage and receive federal subsidies . . . need to collect two premium payments, so that the funds go into separate accounts. One payment is for the value of the abortion benefit and the other payment is for the value of all other services.

The plan issuer must deposit the funds in separate allocation accounts, overseen for compliance by state health insurance commissioners." Alina Salganicoff, Laurie Sobel, Nisha Kurani, and Ivette Gomez, "Coverage for Abortion Services in Medicaid, Marketplace Plans, and Private Plans," Kaiser Family Foundation Issue Brief (January 20, 2016), http://kff.org/womens-health-policy/issue-brief/coverage-for-abortion-services-in-medicaid-marketplace-plans-and-private-plans/.

33. U.S. Department of Health and Human Services, "OCR Enforcement Under Section 1557 of the Affordable Care Act Sex Discrimination Cases," http://www.hhs.gov/civil-rights/for-individuals/section-1557/ocr-enforcement-section-1557-aca-sex-discrimination/index.html.

34. "Know Your Rights-Healthcare," National Center for Transgender Equality, http://www.transequality.org/know-your-rights/healthcare; "OCR Enforcement Under Section 1557."

35. The role of Medicare in desegregating U.S. hospitals is discussed in David Barton Smith, *The Power to Heal: Civil Rights, Medicare, and the Struggle to Transform America's Health Care System* (Nashville, Tenn.: Vanderbilt University Press, 2016); Jill Quadagno, "Promoting Civil Rights Through the Welfare State: How Medicare Integrated Southern Hospitals," *Social Problems* 47 (2000): 68–89.

36. Jason Millman, "Health Insurers May Be Finding New Ways to Discriminate Against Patients," *Washington Post*, January 28, 2015, https://www.washingtonpost.com/news/wonk/wp/2015/01/28/health-insurers-may-be-finding-new-ways-to-discriminate-against-patients/; Douglas B. Jacobs and Benjamin D. Sommers, "Using Drugs to Discriminate—Adverse Selection in the Insurance Marketplace," *New England Journal of Medicine* (January 29, 2015): 372, 399–402.

37. The AIDS Institute, "Florida Requiring Insurance Plans to Limit Patient Cost-Sharing for HIV Drugs in 2016," http://www.theaidsinstitute.org/sites/default/files/attachments/TAI%20Florida%202016%20Plan%20Review%20Press%20Release.pdf.

38. Sadye Paez Errickson, Mayra Alvarez, Ralph Forquera, et al., "What Will Health-Care Reform Mean for Minority Health Disparities?" *Public Health Reports* 126, no. 2 (March–April 2011): 170–175. See also Howard K. Koh, Garth Graham, and Sherry A. Glied, "Reducing Racial and Ethnic Disparities: The Action Plan from the Department of Health and Human Services," *Health Affairs* 30, no. 10 (October 2011): 1822–1829.

39. Algernon Austin, "Obamacare Reduces Racial Disparities in Health Coverage," *Issue Brief*, Center for Global Policy Solutions, n.d., http://globalpolicysolutions.org/resources/obamacare-reduces-racial-disparities-in-health-coverage/.

40. LeeAnn Hall, "Racial Disparities in Health Care Access Magnified as More Gain Coverage," *Huffington Post*, May 8, 2015, http://www.huff ingtonpost.com/leeann-hall/racial-disparities-in-health-care-access -magnified-as-more-gain-coverage_b_7236416.html.
41. Austin, "Obamacare Reduces Racial Disparities in Health Coverage."
42. Ibid.
43. Harris Meyer, "States Refusing Medicaid Expansion Leave 5.2 Million Poor People Without Coverage, Lose $555M," *Modern Healthcare*, October 16, 2013, http://www.modernhealthcare.com/article/20131016/ BLOG/310169995; Glen Harris and LeAnn Hall, "Medicaid Refusals Create New Mason-Dixon Line," *Progressive*, July 7, 2015, http://www .progressive.org/news/2015/07/188209/medicaid-refusals-create-new -mason-dixon-line#sthash.
44. Pam Belluck, "Medicaid Expansion May Lower Death Rates, Study Says," *New York Times*, July 25, 2012.
45. Beatrix Hoffman, "Don't Scream Alone: The Health Care Activism of Poor Americans," in *Patients as Policy Actors*, ed. Beatrix Hoffman et al. (New Brunswick, N.J.: Rutgers University Press, 2011).
46. Human Rights of Arizona Collection, "Recommendations to the Arizona Catholic Conference Regarding Indigent Health Care," adopted by the Human Development Council, October 1, 1981, Human Rights of Arizona Collection, Box 64, Folder 7, Hayden Library, Arizona State University, Tempe.
47. For some examples of state-level protests against Medicaid refusal, see Josh Israel, "Missouri Protesters Arrested After Demanding Their Lawmakers Pass Medicaid Expansion," *ThinkProgress*, May 6, 2014, http://think progress.org/health/2014/05/06/3434953/missouri-medicaid-protest/; "Medicaid Advocates in Utah Stage Protest of GOP Lawmakers' Refusal to Expand the Program," *Kaiser Health News*, October 22, 2015, http:// khn.org/morning-breakout/medicaid-advocates-in-utah-stage-protest-of -gop-lawmakers-refusal-to-expand-the-program/.
48. Rep. Joe Wilson's famous shout at Obama's 2009 address, "You lie," came when the president insisted that health-care reform would not include undocumented immigrants.
49. Tony Lee, "Latino Activists to WH," Breitbart.com, October 10, 2014, http://www.breitbart.com/big-government/2014/10/10/latino -activists-to-wh-let-dreamers-exec-amnesty-recipients-get-obamacare-gov't -benefits/.
50. http://www.bloomberg.com/politics/articles/2015-06-25/california-to -foot-bill-for-health-care-of-undocumented-children. Forty-seven counties in California already provide some care to the undocumented: http://www

.latimes.com/local/california/la-me-0626-uninsured-norcal-counties-20150627-story.html. See also http://www.politico.com/story/2015/07/california-may-let-undocumented-immigrants-buy-obamacare-120249#ixzz3lNzAL4lP.

51. PNHP press release, March 22, 2010, http://www.pnhp.org/news/2010/march/pro-single-payer-doctors-health-bill-leaves-23-million-uninsured. Although many labor organizations support single-payer, some unions hold out for the preservation of existing employment benefit contracts; Steven Wishnia, "Is Single-Payer Labor's Next Step?" *LaborPress*, May 7, 2014, http://www.laborpress.org/11-municipal-government/3662-is-single-payer-health-care-labor-s-next-step.

52. Although three separate studies demonstrated that single-payer in Vermont would save money overall, the governor was unwilling to institute the required new taxes that might lead to a backlash from state residents. Disturbingly, one factor in the failure of single-payer in Vermont was the disastrous rollout of the state's Obamacare exchange, which led many residents to distrust additional reform; see John E. McDonough, "The Demise of Vermont's Single-Payer Plan," *New England Journal of Medicine* 372 (April 23, 2015): 1584–1585.

53. Single-payer advocates prefer the phrase "Improved Medicare for All" to denote the current limitations of the less-than-universal Medicare system.

54. Emphasis in the original. https://berniesanders.com/medicareforall/.

55. On how U.S. federalism limits democratic participation in the health system, see Lisa L. Miller, "The Tyranny of the Minority: American Federalism, Democratic Participation, and the Affordable Care Act," *American Constitution Society for Law and Politics*, February 24, 2011, http://www.acslaw.org/acsblog/node/18377.

56. Charlie Cooper and Serina Sandhu, "NHS 'People's March' Protests," *Independent*, September 6, 2014, http://www.independent.co.uk/life-style/health-and-families/health-news/thousands-join-new-jarrow-march-in-protest-at-nhs-cuts-9716618.html; Tanja Milevska, "UK Anti-TTIP Protests to Focus on NHS Privatisation," *EurActiv.com*, July 8, 2014, http://www.euractiv.com/section/social-europe-jobs/news/uk-anti-ttip-protests-to-focus-on-nhs-privatisation/.

57. "UK Protestors Slam 'Privatisation' of NHS," *TeleSur TV*, September 6, 2014, http://www.telesurtv.net/english/news/UK-Protesters-Slam-Privatization-of-NHS-20140906-0043.html.

58. Paul Day, "Madrid's Health Workers Strike Over Hospital Privatization," *Reuters*, May 7, 2013; "Yo Sí Sanidad Universal," http://yosisanidaduniversal.net/portada.php; Juan Luis Ruiz-Gimenez, interview with the author, Madrid, May 20, 2014; "Quiénes serán . . .": http://www.nadiedesechado.org/.

59. "Madrid da marcha atrás a la privatización sanitaria tras el último revés judicial [Madrid retreats from health privatization following the latest judicial setback]," *El País*, January 27, 2014; "Spain to Reinstate Primary Healthcare for Illegal Immigrants," *Reuters*, March 31, 2015, http://www.reuters.com/article/us-spain-health-immigrants-idUSKBN0MR20H20150331. For its ban on health care for the undocumented, Spain was also found in violation of the European Social Charter; Center for Economic and Social Rights, "Excluding Undocumented Migrants from Health Services Is a Violation of European Law," http://www.cesr.org/article.php?id=1552.
60. See, e.g., Christine André and Christoph Hermann, *Privatisation of Health Care in Europe* (Paris: CNRS, 2009 / Vienna: FORBA-Working Life Research Centre, 2009), http://www.raumplanung.tu-dortmund.de/irpud/presom/fileadmin/docs/presom/external/Publications/WP5.pdf.
61. E.g., Sergio Minué Lorenzo and José Jesús Martín Martín, "Gestión privada: ¿Mas eficiente? [Private management: more efficient?]," *Actualización en Medicina de Familia* 9, no. 1 (2013): 15–23.
62. For a detailed description of these activities, see Potter, *Deadly Spin*.
63. Linda J. Blumberg, Matthew Buettgens, and John Hollohan, "Implications of Partial Repeal of the Affordable Care Act Through Reconciliation," Urban Institute Brief, December 6, 2016, http://www.urban.org/research/publication/implications-partial-repeal-aca-through-reconciliation#.
64. "Trump's Election Puts Families USA on 'Total War Footing' in Fight to Save the Affordable Care Act," *FamiliesUSA.org*, December 6, 2016, http://familiesusa.org/press-release/2016/trump-election-puts-families-usa-total-war-footing-fight-save-affordable-care.
65. JoAnn Jenkins, "AARP on the Front Lines Defending Medicare," December 6, 2016, http://www.aarp.org/politics-society/advocacy/info-2016/defending-medicare-jj.html.

CHAPTER SEVEN

In the Shadow of Employment Precarity

Informal Protection and Risk Transfers in Low-End Temporary Staffing

SÉBASTIEN CHAUVIN

Until recently, Euro-American debates about employment precarity and the new urban "precariat" have mostly focused on the rise of short-term contracts, the narrowing of internal labor markets, and the deterioration of protected lifetime employment across the Western economies.[1] Much of the contemporary discourse surrounding the precariat still tends to rest on the presumption of an undifferentiated mass of marginalized, disposable, and eminently exchangeable employees repeatedly hired in a more or less anonymous spot market. In the past decade, however, commentators have initiated an empirical and analytical shift, substantially qualifying earlier teleologies of risk and flexibility—whether those teleologies had presented themselves as utopian or dystopian prophecies. Echoing prior scholarship critical of the myth of an unambiguously "stable" Fordist period,[2] more recent studies of employment trends in several countries—including the United States, France, and the United Kingdom—have shown (1) that overall job tenure had in fact remained quite stable in the decades preceding the Great Recession, even as neoliberal policies were being implemented; (2) that average stability in job tenure had obscured a deepening bifurcation of the labor market, where short tenures are becoming shorter and long tenures longer; and (3) that a general increase in forced-labor mobility (measured in the number of layoffs) was attended by a parallel decrease in free mobility, as approximated by a count of the number of resignations.[3]

But increases in labor-market uncertainty, along with the overall decline of social security, remains undeniable. Why, then, don't the aggregate numbers reveal the trend of intensifying precarity? What other forms of stability emerge to replace disintegrating formal welfare-state and labor-law protections? What ties the new precariat to employers? To answer these questions, we must refine our understanding of precarity. We can do this, first, by distinguishing job *insecurity* from job *instability*. It turns out that increased insecurity can in fact lead to increased stability, particularly because insecurity increases a worker's fear of unemployment, making him or her a more submissive employee. Second, we must recognize that durable employment insecurity forces ever more precarious workers to "accept work at any condition."[4] Third, it is important to take into consideration that the state is a central player in the institutional production of insecure, subordinate (un)employability, not "creating jobs for people who don't have them" but instead "creating workers for jobs that nobody wants."[5] Finally, we can sharpen the analytical focus of the study of precarity by abandoning postmodern tales of universal fragility and instead recognizing flexibility as a condition necessarily asymmetrical and power-ridden. Clearly, flexibility requires complementary inflexibility, making the issue of *who* is going to be flexible for *whom* a negotiable one. Studies of employment precarity can explore the web of institutional and social arrangements in which economic security is unequally transferred and distributed: across social, ethnic, and gender groups; between companies and workers; and among precarious workers themselves, working on both long-term and short-term contracts.[6]

Thus, one can understand precarity not only as an individual condition but also as an unequal social relation making an entire group more insecure relative to other groups.[7] But precarious workers themselves do not constitute a homogenous monolith. Many formally "contingent" employees develop long-term relationships with a limited number of employers—sometimes with one of them exclusively over the course of years. Employers cannot always easily substitute one of these workers for another. Rather than claim that external market forces now irreversibly determine precarious employment, a number of researchers have started to describe the complex informal loyalties that obtain in the shadow of formal labor protections between the new precariat and employers.[8]

In a context of increasingly complex labor-market arrangements, however, even when precarious workers do develop durable relationships of mutual loyalty with their employers the issue of *which employer to be loyal to* remains.[9] In this paper I analyze the unequal distribution of uncertainty within a precarious labor force as well as the dilemmas of loyalty faced by precarious workers with multiple employers. The analysis is based on a case study of light-industrial staffing services in the United States, sometimes called day-labor agencies. These services are typically presented as extreme incarnations of precarity. Every morning, usually as early as 4 or 5 A.M., job applicants must come and wait in the agency's offices for the possibility of work that day.[10]

This study is based on ethnographic fieldwork I conducted in and around Chicago between 2004 and 2006. It consisted of participant observation at two different day-labor agencies with racially and linguistically mixed workforces as well as in several client factories. Minute Staff was a small agency on the Southwest Side of Chicago; Bob Labor was a larger one on the Northwest Side, bordering the Polish neighborhood. I applied for job assignments in these agencies and worked as an unskilled industrial day laborer for a total of three months. Participant observation was complemented by thirty in-depth interviews with a diverse set of local actors in the light-industrial sector as well as parallel work with two Chicago community organizations that address the issue of day labor.

Spatial and ethno-racial dynamics help explain the mixed composition of the agencies I studied. In segregated Chicago even more than in other U.S. cities in the 1990s and 2000s,[11] African Americans and undocumented Latino immigrants would not often physically meet on the local labor market. The places where they lived, worked, and sought work were typically separated by space, language, and industry. When competition allegedly took place between the two groups at the bottom of the occupational ladder, they mostly experienced it at a distance, through media representations and political discourse. Chicago's day-labor industry offered a significant exception.

The immigration and criminal-justice systems have made both groups victims of state-induced unemployability.[12] The state has channeled

African American and Latino workers into the staffing industry, which functions as an intermediary employer conditionally allowing them access to light-industrial employment through a small door. Nonetheless, as low-end staffing agencies have consistently refused to locate their offices in majority black areas,[13] most African American job seekers are forced to travel to the city's immigrant port-of-entry neighborhoods early in the morning, where they commonly wait for work tickets alongside Mexican and Central American applicants.

As this chapter will show, precarity falls along different spatial and ethno-racial lines. While African American workers are less often maintained by client companies and must construct loyalty relations with agency dispatchers to ensure a maximum number of assignments, a growing number of immigrant workers are joining the ranks of "permatemps," workers who have been employed by the same factory and through the same agency for years. They owe their job security to onsite supervisors rather than to the agency dispatchers, with whom they maintain only minimal contact. Industrial permatemps, even when undocumented, do not remain in the lowest tier of the occupational ladder but may benefit from informal careers through which they gradually gain positions of authority as well as wage increases. Those informal careers are dependent on agency staff or factory supervisors, who alternately collaborate and compete for the conflicting loyalties of workers.[14]

In what follows, I describe the dispatch process in low-end staffing agencies, a process that involves a distribution of uncertainty where some workers are more equal than others. I then analyze the racialized dilemmas faced by both workers and employers over whether a worker's loyalty should lie with the agency or the final employer (the client company). Finally, I focus on the specific case of undocumented permatemps, the "informal careers" they achieve at the workplace beyond successive changes in intermediary employers, and the degraded paternalism that structures these forms of informal promotion.

DISPATCHING TICKETS, "LOYALIZING" UNCERTAINTY

Factories having recourse to staffing agencies are not merely seeking contingency; they are aiming for a *"reliably contingent labor supply."*[15]

In most of Chicago's agencies, applications stipulate that all contracts would be "at will" by default, no matter how long workers ended up working somewhere with this status, whether for four hours or ten years. Under U.S. labor law, at-will employment defines a contract that can be breached without prejudice by either party "for good cause, for no cause, or even for bad cause," to quote the famous formula employed by the Tennessee Supreme Court when it first formulated the at-will doctrine in 1884.[16] In terms of employment rights, the irony of at-will contracts is that they make workers simultaneously "permanent" (in the sense that no duration is specified) and extremely insecure,[17] as they offer no formal protection against dismissal.

With temp workers they wish to retain and make more loyal but not hire directly (especially if these workers are undocumented immigrants), client companies might offer monetary bonuses in the form of pay raises. But these monetary bonuses are rarely allocated by the agencies themselves, which overwhelmingly offer the state minimum wage as their standard rate. Theoretically, the higher a day laborer's hourly wage, the bigger in absolute terms the agency's "markup." All things being equal, agencies would benefit substantially from increasing their laborers' wages. But as Nik Theodore and Jamie Peck showed for the 1990s,[18] Chicago-area day-labor agencies adopt "quantitative" rather than "qualitative" strategies: they opt for price-based rather than product-based competition and thus prefer hiring more laborers rather than hiring them better. Moreover, given the intensive competition between agencies in the mid-2000s, the average markup on that segment of the local labor market was very low. Close margins left little leeway for day-labor services to drop their markups any lower in order to make certain laborers more loyal and "reliable." In addition to low margins, the economic dependency of agencies on their corporate clients, as well as some of the new reasons companies used temporary staffing services in the 2000s (increasingly having recourse to them for the durable externalization of a whole segment of their workforce), gave user firms a monopoly over decisions pertaining to wage levels. As a consequence, agencies for the most part do not have direct control over the compensation of their own laborers and so typically cannot retain them through monetary means.

Unable to change wage levels unilaterally, day-labor agencies instead remunerate and retain the "core" of their workforce through *certainty bonuses*, that is, guarantees of relative continuity in employment. At the center of that selective distribution of security and insecurity resides the dispatcher. Hector, the dispatcher at Minute Staff, called these workers his "regular guys." "Regular guys" knew they would have priority in being put on the "ticket." Their names would be picked up from the morning's arrival list even if their rank on it was not favorable. They could afford arriving a little later than 5 A.M.; in some cases they could even call the dispatcher the day before to find out about job opportunities or to secure a guaranteed spot on a collective ticket opening the next morning.

But these small measures of security are themselves uncertain. Failing to come, wait, and socialize regularly in the agency is incompatible with the accumulation of the internal social capital necessary for a worker to remain a part of the "core" and could lead to the dispatcher scratching him or her off the informal list of the "regulars." Indeed, there can only be a limited number of regulars. Finally, such loyalties are most often anchored not to an agency in general but to a dispatcher in particular. Uncertainty is again the rule when a different dispatcher happens to be at the counter or if a particular dispatcher is fired or quits.

The official doctrine of agencies is that workers are assigned tickets on a "first come, first served" basis, turning time into a form of capital and treating patience as a virtue.[19] Yet favoritism and informal loyalization belie the doctrine, and the dispatcher becomes the focal point of social relations within day-labor agencies. Dispatchers are objects of personal investments by day laborers, who seek to reduce the uncertainty weighing on them, if need be by having it transferred onto other workers. When in the beginning of the 2000s the sociologists Tim Bartley and Wade Roberts carried out a survey among day-labor agency workers in Tucson, Arizona, to their question, "Among the following items, what is the most important thing you have to do to get a good job assignment in an agency?" only 18 percent of the respondents chose the option "arriving early at the agency." By contrast, 35 percent opted for "having a good relationship or a good reputation with the manager or the dispatcher."[20] The gifts that workers sometimes offer dispatchers (soda, coffee, fast-food meals) essentially function as retroactive countergifts, thanking the dispatcher for the jobs they allocated them and thus revealing the nature of the allocation of work.[21]

LOYALTY TO WHOM?

But neither all levels of certainty nor all forms of loyalty are equally accessible to all types of workers. One could discern three typical conditions within the temporal hierarchy structuring the day-labor agencies I studied: that of "casual temps," who had been working for various agencies and in various factories; "regular temps," who had been employed by the same agency but sent to different client companies; and "permatemps," workers who had been employed by the same agency within the same factory for years. It would be naïve to try to classify each individual unequivocally in one or the other essentialized category. In what follows, I instead describe the system of constraints that shaped temporal positions and potential strategies. Thus, the model is not a "typology without topology." Each type is connected to the others through power relations marked by transfers of uncertainty.

The first category is that of "casual temps," working in multiple factories for multiple agencies. Within certain limits, these workers could play on the competition between agencies in order to go where the contracts are. Such a strategy makes sense when a large number of agencies happened to be in geographical proximity. It allows day laborers to play against those agencies at their own "quantitative" game—that is, by reducing uncertainty not through loyalty to one agency but through the sheer number of agencies to which they apply. As in other contexts, workers could embrace mobility, as well as the ability to leave, as strategies of resistance in the face of temporariness.[22]

The strategy, however, is not without its limits. Nomadic mobility is dependent upon two conditions: first, there needs to be a strong demand for unskilled labor at the city level; second, an individual laborer must be party to sufficiently developed information networks in order to be warned quickly enough when a big ticket becomes available at an agency. This strategy has some costs: the absence of loyalty among casual temps excludes them from the informal retribution systems that alleviate the insecurity of each agency's core workers. Consequently, casual temps are directly subjected to the "legal-rational" violence of the waiting list: they are the ones upon whom external uncertainty is transferred. These contradictions point to a major feature of precarity as a regime of workforce mobilization: it functions in such a manner that worker-initiated intermittence is simultaneously and confusingly resistance and resignation, liberation and alienation, a flight from bad jobs and a functional effect of the system of bad jobs.[23]

The second category is the one I call by the same name as that used by Minute Staff's dispatcher: "regular temps." These are laborers who, while remaining loyal to a single agency, are sent to work at multiple companies. They form the core of an agency's workforce and are the dispatcher's followers. They are the ones the agency consults at the end of a collective ticket's first day when they need to know if such and such worker in their team "worked well." In case of a labor shortage, they sometimes serve as brokers—the agency then mobilizes their relationships and networks, including friends waiting in other dispatch rooms. Rather than physically and morally performing their availability in the dispatch room, as with casual temps, regular temps only need to warn the dispatcher of their *un*availability: "please warn me if you're *not* going" was a recurring sentence dispatchers used when talking to "regulars." When a ticket came to an end or was interrupted for a few days, dispatchers would place their regulars first, regardless of where the regular temps fell on the list.

Access to this category also depends on a number of conditions. First, one must have spent a sufficient amount of time waiting at the agency. Second, one must continuously maintain an informal and friendly relationship with the dispatcher. To become or to remain a "regular," one needs to pose questions "regularly," to show oneself often, and come and talk, strategies that a worker interviewed by Bartley and Roberts called "wake-up calls" to the dispatcher.[24] In March 2005, I worked as a Minute Staff employee at a box factory I call USCartons. During the morning break, William, a black man in his thirties, explained to me what to do to be picked up by the dispatcher. "You gotta know the people. You gotta work here for a bit before you can be part of the *clique* and get the jobs. You ain't gonna get nothing if you just be sitting in the back and ain't showing yourself."

There was a certain irony to belonging to the "clique" of agency regulars. As it happened, the "regular temps" were not necessarily also the most "employable" workers. Indeed, the most prized and "reliable" laborers tended to be continuously employed more often and more durably by client factories. They spent most of their time on the latter's premises, and as a result they maintained only distant connections with the agency's staff (including the dispatcher). In contrast, people who hoped to become "regular temps" within an agency were primarily people who needed to do so, most notably because they lasted, on average, a shorter time on each ticket (at a factory). In Chicago, the workers who fell into this category were most often African American applicants.[25]

The need for in-agency clout accumulation helps explain why, as I had observed in the early stages of my fieldwork, although they tend to get fewer tickets, African American men appear to boast more freedom for themselves in dispatch rooms; why, for example, they can continuously engage the agency staff in a way that could sound aggressive and almost "dominant" at first sight. In the same way the promotion of the black female shop-floor workers analyzed in the 1940s by Everett Hughes was always seen by the management as a consequence of their "individuality" (because they had shown they were *not* like the rest of the category), the loyalization of black males in day-labor agencies tended to take on the informal character of a personal relationship with the dispatcher.[26] As with Hughes, this is not necessarily a good sign. It means they have to prove themselves more than the others. If "Mexican" day laborers are less likely to cultivate intimate discussions at the counter, if they also appear less "nervous" in dispatch rooms by comparison, it is mostly because "relational skills" are the skills mobilized by those—in this case, black laborers—who have only that strategy at their disposal.

Notably, the loyalization of a "core" of workers by an agency does not imply that the rest of the workforce is condemned to pure "contingency." Even when workers are made highly replaceable, as with casual temps, the agency still needs to maintain a stock of applicants on the premises, preferably a supply exceeding the expected labor demand. The core and the periphery of an agency are the targets of two different types of retention: personalized *loyalization* for some and impersonal and collective *stabilization* for the others.[27] To a certain extent, those two types of labor-force retention are complementary: "stabilized" workers are always needed to replace "loyalized" ones in case they are absent.

The last key category of temp workers, that of "permatemps," describes day laborers who have been kept by a single factory for years, through one or sometimes several successive agencies. These workers are the most invisible in the dispatch rooms even though, in Chicago, they probably represent the largest share of the unskilled temp workforce. The growth of this category is inextricably linked to the new function that temporary agencies began to play on the unskilled industrial-labor market in the 2000s: that of insurance companies allowing client firms to employ undocumented immigrants durably without assuming the legal and reputational risks involved in the practice.[28] Employers who resort to these "insurance" services keep their workers for years while never directly hiring them. Almost mechanically, in the context of the racially bifurcated system of workforce loyalization that obtains in Chicago between agencies and factories, light-industrial permatemps turn out to be mostly undocumented Hispanic immigrants. While final employers arguably do use temporary staffing as a way to test the reliability of "casual temps," the latter are not tested in order to become statutorily permanent employees but instead to the end of being durably recruited as "permatemps."

PERMATEMPS, IMBRICATED SEGMENTATION, AND THE RISE OF INFORMAL CAREERS

In this last section, I analyze in the factory itself the labor-segmentation consequences of these hiring processes. As it turns out, unskilled industrial permatemps do not remain in the lowest tier of the occupational ladder forever. Instead, many benefit from "informal careers," gradually assuming positions of authority, wage increases, and, for some, paid vacations beyond the eight official paid holidays granted by federal law. They also enjoy a degree of symmetry in flexibility. For example, it is easier to take a day off when one is a durable worker, even when this condition rests solely on an informal basis. The multiplication of informal careers has given rise to a peculiar type of workforce segmentation, which I call "imbricated segmentation."[29] At odds with traditional models of segregated segmentation that predict a strict containment of outsourced workers within the secondary-labor market, imbricated segmentation allows some "temp" workers into the primary market and grants them access to internal careers within factories—ironically, not in spite of but because of their additional undocumented status (which discouraged employers from hiring them directly). The limited benefits that some undocumented permatemps enjoy are not formal rights, however, but personalized, reversible, and nonportable favors that can be described as paternalistic. Moreover, in the context of mediated employment, these relationships often lead to conflicts between company and agency over the informal loyalty of "precarious" workers.

Filiberto, a Real "Fictive Temp" at a Chicago Foam Factory

Many of the ironies of informal promotion can be found in the career of Filiberto. Filiberto was an undocumented worker who was my supervisor when for three weeks in June 2006 I worked as a Bob Labor employee at USPolyst, a foam-production factory. He was born in 1978 in the state of Michoacán in Mexico. When I interviewed him, in the north of Chicago, he was twenty-eight years old. After a first unauthorized stay in the United States from 1994 to 1996, he went back to Mexico and lived for two years with his girlfriend in the city of Morelia. In 1997 he had a daughter. He returned to Chicago in 2000, where he went to work at USPolyst, loading and unloading trucks. In order to get this job, Filiberto first went to the factory, which was located a few minutes away from his home. The factory hired him as a temp laborer by sending him to a nearby agency, SuperStaff, where he filled out an application. At this agency, he provided a counterfeit Social Security card along with a counterfeit green card bought for sixty dollars on Twenty-Sixth Street. As do many undocumented migrants, he invented his own number, using the birthdates of some of his friends. Although he had changed it several times before, since 2002 he had been using the same number.

On paper, Filiberto was a highly "casual" worker. First entering the factory as an employee from SuperStaff, he was then transferred a year later to Bob Labor agency, which had made a more advantageous offer to the company. In fact, all of the factory's workforce, several dozen workers, were thus transferred in one stroke. After one more year, temps (including Filiberto) were sent back to SuperStaff. The following year, Bob Labor again became the official labor intermediary for USPolyst; one year later, SuperStaff won back the contract, only to lose it again in 2006 to Bob Labor. When I first encountered Filiberto in early June 2006, we were both employees at the same agency.

Filiberto had changed his "official" employer five times in five years. Along with the rest of the temp workers at USPolyst, he was "moved" back and forth, contingent to the intense competition waged by the two agencies, which were constantly trying to undercut the other by offering cheaper collective contracts. In reality, Filiberto never left the foam factory. Although in 2000 he had shown up to SuperStaff in person to sign his employment papers, every time the factory flipped from one labor agency to another, management sent Filiberto's application, filled out and signed, directly to the agency. Filiberto had never stepped inside Bob Labor, despite the fact that when he sat for our interview Bob Labor was the company that legally employed him and cut his paychecks.

Repeated agency changes aside, Filiberto could secure, year after year, certain advantages that other low-wage workers, legal or illegal, would envy. After two years, he asked his white manager whether he could get a week's vacation, a request that was immediately granted. The manager himself offered to make that vacation time paid time off. Filiberto visited Florida twice, and he even traveled to the Bahamas, thanks to the passport of a "legal" friend "who looked like me." Among these advantages were his good salary and the continuous raises he earned. Filiberto started work at USPolyst earning minimum wage (first $5.25, then $6.50), and he received pay raises of one dollar every year, reaching an hourly rate of $11.50 in 2006. Thanks to these pay raises, he managed to secure a monthly income of $1,700, allowing him to send regular $500 payments to his seventy-four-year-old mother in Michoacán.

In 2006, Filiberto was a shipping and receiving manager in charge of the teams loading and unloading boxes from trucks that drove in and out all day long at the back of the factory. Filiberto attributed this promotion to his excellent skills in forklift driving, which he acquired while working on the premises. He also recognized, however, that his seniority at the factory played an important role: the mere fact of his long tenure there gave him some informal authority over the other freight handlers. Nevertheless, he admitted that several of his subordinates had been in the factory for a longer time than he had: "This one was here seven years." In fact, several of them, Puerto Ricans or documented Mexicans, were permanent employees at the company. As a temp worker ("*de oficina*"), Filiberto had ended up in the position of supervising permanent freight handlers ("*de planta*.")[30] He was also responsible for the hiring (and occasional retention) of casual temps.

His direct supervisor, Julio, a Puerto Rican man in his thirties, had only been at the company for a year and a half, and his management position and title were similar to those of Filiberto's: "He's my boss, but it's the same title." With him, Filiberto had the advantage of seniority. He recognized, perhaps with excessive self-confidence, that his formal supervisor would not be in a position to fire him, even if he wanted to. Whereas Julio started at 10 dollars an hour, by the summer of 2006 he had only reached $12.25: "It depends on how he works." That is, he only earned 75 cents more than Filiberto, who commented: "I think this year it will be equal." When I asked him about possible competition between him and Julio, Filiberto answered:

"No, not competition for me!"
"And for him?"
"For him, yes, maybe for him but not for me. I know more than him. He respects me more."

As long as he remained without papers, Filiberto could not climb the internal hierarchy of the company any further. As an informal policy, the factory did not hire unauthorized workers directly and had decided, as had many other workplaces, that higher-management positions could not reasonably be outsourced to a day-labor agency. Filiberto did not challenge the ceiling he was bumping up against. He attributed it exclusively to his legal status. "If I had papers, I can be *this* position," he explained to me, pointing to a spot located midway between the "general manager" and Julio's position on the organizational chart I had asked him to draw.

USPolyst had been in contact with an immigration lawyer in the hopes of obtaining some form of legalization for Filiberto: "we talked with a lawyer and we made an application." The document, Filiberto explained, detailed how many years he had been working at—if not *for*—the company, what his role was within the company, and the reasons why management had decided to help him. Filiberto did not himself keep these papers, which remained in the factory offices: "No, not here, it's at the job. With my boss." He acknowledged the company for doing this, "they're just trying to help me," and was confident that his patience would pay off: "[The lawyer] can do it. We just have to give him time." The success of this strategy implied that Filiberto would remain loyal to his job, and to his final employer, beyond the changes of agencies to which he had been subjected. While waiting for legal papers, every Monday Filiberto would get a paycheck, at the factory, from Bob Labor.

Filiberto's case illustrates the distinctive temporality of the "careers" of undocumented permatemps: (1) on the one hand, the status of "permatemp" does not function as a path toward permanent "direct-hire" status but, on the contrary, develops to the extent that such a path does not exist; (2) on the other hand, the *status* of temporary worker—to be distinguished from its reality—defines an internal ceiling limiting upward mobility, only allowing a moderate degree of promotion into the levels of lower management. In the same way that "illegality" is for undocumented immigrants a "spatialized social condition,"[31] "temporariness" thus remains, for undocumented day laborers, a "temporalized social condition."

If, in the factories I studied, the undocumented workforce coincided quite narrowly with temp employees, then by contrast the employment status of these workers turned out to be relatively disconnected from their real position held in the places where they physically worked. These observations suggest a model of civic status–based segmentation different from traditional models of segregated segmentation. In the traditional model, one would understand undocumented day laborers as being contained within in an airtight secondary-labor market, whereas authorized workers would be on the primary market enjoying easy access to internal careers. Instead, a model of imbricated segmentation between authorized and unauthorized workers within the labor force of a workplace would better account for the existence of informal loyalization, a process that transcends civic-status inequalities as well as successive shifts in official intermediary employers.

In the segregated urban landscape of Chicago in the 2000s, light-industrial temporary staffing presented a diverse ethno-racial mix of unskilled and otherwise "unemployable" workers who were afforded a rare opportunity to experience economic competition physically. However, the hiring process functioned differently for African American men than it did for undocumented Hispanic immigrants. Whereas black applicants could boast a modicum of certainty from agency dispatchers that they would receive work, recent Hispanic migrants mostly developed loyalty relations within client factories that more readily employed them as long-term permatemps. The experience of Chicago day laborers provides arguments for rejecting teleologies of universal economic atomization and instead invites further investigation into the relations of long-term loyalty that develop in the shadow of formal employment and immigration law. Nonetheless, the triangular relation that defined the staffing industry also raised the twin questions of—for employers—which employees to loyalize and—for workers—which employer to be loyal to. The Chicago case suggests that responses given to those conundrums are often entrenched in spatial, civic, and ethno-racial inequality.

Whether dependent on agency staff or factory supervisors, informal careers and conflicting loyalties need to be taken into account by community organizations working to improve the formal day-labor sector in the United States.[32] Considering that a sizeable core of workers will develop limited careers based on informal loyalty and clientelistic relationships with "precarious" employers, mobilizing the "precariat" will require a break with the image of a homogeneously precarious workforce. Although the question of legal status is particularly central in determining the durable precarity of undocumented permatemps, the complex knot of factors that structure the contemporary precariat means that even long-awaited comprehensive immigration reform will by no means solve the problem of migrant employment precarity.[33] Indeed, that a long-term, undocumented temp could informally approach the level of benefits of a documented direct-hire in the same company says as much about the functions of temp work as it does about generalized precarity regardless of civic-status differences.

In this chapter, I provided evidence of the limits of informal promotion. In the strongly asymmetrical configuration that obtains within formal day labor, the incentives offered to some are two-sided to such an extent that one can never say if, at a broader level, they are punitive or retributive mechanisms. In the specific setting of day-labor agencies, temporal retributions (certainty, continuity, priority) tend to form a zero-sum game in which a given amount of uncertainty is distributed. Certainty for some is the cause of uncertainty for others and feeds into the latter's sense of arbitrariness. By indefinitely deflecting onto some the uncertainty that is at the basis of day labor, such a hierarchy of security does not contribute, for the most part, to reducing collective insecurity.

Finally, the present analysis of ideal-typical conditions of durable employment precarity in the United States can shed light on contemporary European debates.[34] Whereas in most countries protests against conservative counter-reforms to labor legislation have focused on limiting the number of temporary contracts (such as the *Contrat à durée déterminée*, or CDD, in France), the U.S. case of the "at-will" contract might help shift our focus toward a more threatening project. As we saw, the "at-will" contracts under which day laborers work in most Chicago agencies are in substance *permanent* contracts—which, ironically, could be broken at any time. Permanent contracts (such as the *Contrat à durée indéterminée*, or CDI) are not protective for being permanent but because of an architecture of proworker features that were attached to them as a result of decades of labor struggle and progressive social legislation. As it happens, the bulk of counter-reforms in Europe today are not taking the form of a heightened promotion of temporary contracts but aim instead at depriving permanent contracts of most of their protections. By bringing employment relations closer to the indeterminate precarity of the "at-will" regime, these conservative reforms will no doubt bring with them many elements of the degraded paternalism described in this chapter, informally linking the precariat to its employers, within and beyond intermediation.

NOTES

1. Ulrich Beck, *Risk Society: Towards a New Modernity* (London: Sage, 1992); Richard Sennett, *The Corrosion of Character* (New York: Norton, 1998); Paul Osterman, *Securing Prosperity: The American Labor Market: How It Has Changed and What to Do About It* (Princeton, N.J.: Princeton University Press, 1999); Serge Paugam, *Le salarié de la précarité. Les nouvelles formes de l'intégration professionnelle* (Paris: PUF, 2000); Francoise Carré, Marianne Ferber, Lonnie Golden, and Stephen Herzenberg, *Nonstandard Work: The Nature and Challenges of Changing Employment Arrangements* (Madison, Wis.: Industrial Relationships Research Association, 2000); Patrick Cingolani, *La précarité* (Paris: PUF, 2006); Arne Kalleberg, "Precarious Work, Insecure Workers," *American Sociological Review* 74, no. 1 (2009): 1–22.
2. David M. Gordon, Richard Edwards, and Michael Reich, *Segmented Work, Divided Workers: The Historical Transformation of Labor in the United States* (Cambridge: Cambridge University Press, 1982).
3. Damien Sauze, "La stabilité de l'emploi en France: conquête sociale ou résultat de politiques patronales?" *Travail et Emploi* 103 (2005):113–122; Christophe Ramaux, *Emploi: éloge de la stabilité* (Paris: Mille et une nuits, 2006); Ann Huff Stevens, *The More Things Change, the More They Stay the*

Same: Trends in Long-Term Employment in the United States, 1969–2002, NBER working paper W11878 (December 2005); Kevin Doogan, "Long-Term Employment and the Restructuring of the Labour Market in Europe," *Time and Society* 14, no. 1 (2005): 65–87; Francis Green, *Demanding Work: The Paradox of Job Quality in an Affluent Economy* (Princeton, N.J.: Princeton University Press, 2006); Ralph Fevre, "Employment Insecurity and Social Theory: The Power of Nightmares," *Work, Employment, and Society* 21, no. 3 (2008): 517–535.

4. Robert Castel, "Au-delà du salariat ou en deçà de l'emploi? L'institutionnalisation du précariat," in *Repenser la solidarité: l'apport des sciences sociales*, ed. Serge Paugam (Paris: PUF, 2007), 415–433.

5. Jamie Peck, *Workfare States* (New York: Guilford, 2001), 6; see also John Krinsky, *Free Labor: Workfare and the Contested Language of Neoliberalism* (Chicago: University of Chicago Press, 2007); Guy Standing, "The Precariat: From Denizens to Citizens" *Polity* 44, no. 4 (2012): 588–608.

6. Leah F. Vosko, *Temporary work: The Gendered Rise of a Precarious Employment Relationship* (Toronto: University of Toronto Press, 2000); Jamie Peck and Nik Theodore, "Contingent Chicago: Restructuring the Spaces of Temporary Labor," *International Journal of Urban and Regional Research* 25, no. 3 (2001): 471–496; Nicolas Jounin, *Chantier interdit au public: enquête parmi les travailleurs du bâtiment* (Paris: La Découverte, 2008); Erin Hatton, *The Temp Economy: From Kelly Girls to Permatemps in Postwar America* (Philadelphia: Temple University Press, 2011); Gretchen Purser, "'Still Doin' Time:' Clamoring for Work in the Day Labor Industry," *WorkingUSA* 15, no. 3 (2012): 397–415.

7. Sébastien Chauvin, *Les agences de la précarité. Journaliers à Chicago* (Paris: Le Seuil, 2010).

8. Alain Morice, *Recherches sur le paternalisme et le clientélisme contemporains: méthodes et interprétations*, Mémoire pour l'habilitation à diriger des recherches (Paris: EHESS, 1999); Jounin, *Chantier interdit au public*; Sébastien Chauvin and Nicolas Jounin, "L'externalisation des illégalités. Ethnographies des usages du travail 'temporaire' à Paris et à Chicago," in *Les paradoxes de l'économie informelle. À qui profitent les règles?* ed. Laurence Fontaine and Florence Weber (Paris: Karthala, 2011), 113–138; Vicki Smith and Esteher B. Neuwirth, *The Good Temp* (Ithaca, N.Y.: Cornell University Press, 2008); Emine Fidan Elcioglu, "Producing Precarity: The Temporary Staffing Agency in the Labor Market," *Qualitative Sociology* 33 (2010): 117–136.

9. Heidi Gottfried, "Mechanisms of Control in the Temporary Help Service Industry," *Sociological Forum* 6, no.4 (1991): 699–713; Esther Neuwirth, "Blurring Corporate Boundaries: Staffing Agencies, Human Resource

Practices, and Unions in the New Employment Relationship" (Ph.D diss., University of California–Davis, 2004).
10. Robert E. Parker, *Flesh Peddlers and Warm Bodies: The Temporary Help Industry and Its Workers* (New Brunswick, N.J.: Rutgers University Press, 1994); Peck and Theodore, "Contingent Chicago"; Tim Bartley and Wade T. Roberts, "Relational Exploitation: The Informal Organization of Day-Labor Agencies," *WorkingUSA* 9 (2006): 41–58; Purser, "Waiting for Work"; David Van Arsdale, "The Recasualization of Blue-Collar Workers: Industrial Temporary Help Work's Impact on the Working Class," *Labor* 5, no. 1 (2008): 75–99; Elcioglu, "Producing Precarity."
11. William J. Wilson, *When Work Disappears: The World of the New Urban Poor* (New York: Knopf, 1996); Roger Waldinger, *Still the Promised City? African Americans and New Immigrants in Postindustrial New York* (Cambridge, Mass.: Harvard University Press, 1996); Nelson Lim, "On the Back of Blacks? Immigrants and the Fortunes of African Americans," in *Strangers at the Gate: New Immigrants in Urban America*, ed. Roger Waldinger (Berkeley: University of California Press, 2001), 186–226; Jennifer Gordon and Robin A. Lenhardt, "Rethinking Work and Citizenship," *UCLA Law Review* 55 (2008): esp. 1179–1180.
12. Jamie Peck and Nik Theodore, "Carceral Chicago," *International Journal of Urban and Regional Research* 32, no. 2 (2008): 251–281; Chauvin, *Les agences de la précarité*; Purser, "'Still Doin' Time.'"
13. Peck and Theodore, "Contingent Chicago," 490.
14. Chauvin, *Les agences de la précarité*.
15. Peck and Theodore, "Contingent Chicago," 486.
16. *Payne v. Western & Atlantic Railroad*, Tennessee 1884.
17. Chauvin, *Les agences de la précarité*.
18. Peck and Theodore, "Contingent Chicago."
19. Purser, "Waiting for Work"; Van Arsdale, "The Recasualization of Blue-Collar Worker"; Chauvin, *Les agences de la précarité*.
20. Bartley and Roberts, "Relational Exploitation," 47.
21. On similar examples of gift giving in analogous employment situations, see Dennis Brooks and Karamjit Singh, "Pivots and Presents: Asian Brokers in British Foundries," in *Ethnicity at Work*, ed. Sandra Wallman (London: Macmillan, 1979), 85–111; and Gretchen Purser, "Waiting for Work: An Ethnography of a Day Labor Agency," Institute for the Study of Social Change, ISSC Fellows Working Paper (2006).
22. Gabriella Alberti, "Mobility Strategies, 'Mobility Differentials,' and 'Transnational Exit': The Experiences of Precarious Migrants in London's Hospitality Jobs," *Work, Employment, and Society* 28, no. 6 (2014): 865–881.
23. Jean-François Germe, "Instabilité, précarité et transformations de l'emploi," *Critiques de l'économie politique* 15–16 (1981): 53–91.

24. Bartley and Roberts, "Relational Exploitation."
25. Peck and Theodore, "Carceral Chicago."
26. Everett Hughes summarizes the injunctions weighing on black workers in the polishing room with the following words: "You are on trial. I doubt whether you can make it, but if you do I will give you credit. Most people of your kind can't make it. I shall be astonished if you do." Everett Hughes, *The Sociological Eye* (New Brunswick, N.J.: Transaction, 1971).
27. Chauvin, *Les agences de la précarité*.
28. Chauvin and Jounin, "L'externalisation des illégalités."
29. Chauvin, *Les agences de la précarité*.
30. Spanish terms express more frankly that tenure or contract duration has nothing to do with the division between "temps" and "perms."
31. Nicholas De Genova, *Working the Boundaries: Race, Space, and "Illegality" in Mexican Chicago* (Durham, N.C.: Duke University Press, 2005), 8.
32. Sébastien Chauvin, "Bounded Mobilizations: Informal Unionism and Secondary Shaming Amongst Immigrant Temp Workers in Chicago," in *Neoliberal Capitalism and Precarious Work: Ethnographies of Accommodation and Resistance*, ed. Rob Lambert and Andy Herod (Northampton, Mass.: Edward Elgar, 2016), 72–95.
33. Shannon Gleeson, *Precarious Claims: The Promise and Failure of Workplace Protection in the United States* (Berkeley: University of California Press, 2016).
34. Chauvin and Jounin, "L'externalisation des illégalités."

CHAPTER EIGHT

From the Welfare State to the Carceral State

Whither Social Reproduction?

MIMI ABRAMOVITZ

FEMINIST SCHOLARSHIP has demonstrated that the welfare state underwrote the work of social reproduction; that is, it enabled activities that furthered procreation, socialization, sexuality, nurturance, and family maintenance. Carried out by families as well as other public and private social institutions, social reproduction includes making food, clothing, and shelter available for immediate consumption; ensuring the health and productivity of the current and future labor force; providing for people too old, too young, or too sick to care for themselves; and socializing family members into the wider social order. Historically, social reproduction includes women's unpaid labor (even when they work outside the home) as well as women's low-paid labor in the market. Social-reproductive labor converts the wages of paid workers into the means of subsistence for the entire household.[1]

State support for social reproduction has varied with each of the two major economic crises of the twentieth century: the collapse of the economy in the 1930s, which gave rise to the U.S. welfare state, and the financial crisis of the mid-1970s, which gave rise to the neoliberal backlash against the welfare state. According to the Social Structures of Accumulation (SSA) theory, such crises occur over several decades as major institutional arrangements, policies, and ideological paradigms assembled to address a prior crisis fail to sustain profits, economic growth, and social stability. The deterioration of existing arrangements undermines the social, economic, and political structures—including the institutions of social reproduction—that supported growth in the first place. The developing crisis further exposes fundamental contradictions built into the market economy, which regular fiscal- and monetary-policy tools cannot readily resolve. Instead, their resolution requires a major restructuring of the system, or a new SSA, which emerges only after protracted political struggle. For example, the economic crisis of 1930s yielded a new SSA, marked by the New Deal and Keynesian economic policy. Its call for expanding the welfare state sought to correct problems associated with laissez-faire capitalism and consequently provided support for social reproduction. The economic crisis of the mid-1970s, however, yielded a neoliberal politics that sought to undo the redistributive elements of the New Deal and the Great Society. It called for a smaller state, greater reliance on market forces, and reduced expenditure on family maintenance.[2]

This chapter explores the crisis in social reproduction in the United States that surfaced as the decline of the postwar Keynesian SSA exposed three contradictions in the welfare state, giving rise to neoliberalism and the "carceral state."

CONTRADICTIONS OF THE NEW DEAL WELFARE STATE

Successful social reproduction requires adequate wages, sufficient income support, and low unemployment. In contrast, successful capital accumulation depends on low wages, low benefits, and high unemployment. When the requirements of capital accumulation cause the standard of living to fall too low, the lack of income can undercut the capacity of families to carry out the socially assigned caretaking and reproductive tasks on which both businesses and families depend. Under these circumstances, a crisis ensues: the requirements for profitable economic production undercut the conditions necessary to carry out critical family maintenance.

Crises in social reproduction accompanied both the collapse of the economy in the 1930s and the financial crisis in the mid-1970s, but the response of the state to each differed dramatically. The collapse of the economy in the 1930s led to the first major crisis in social reproduction in the twentieth century. Hidden beneath rapid economic growth, booming profits, and the giddy consumerism of the "roaring twenties," the working classes suffered a falling standard of living, mounting social problems, and a breakdown in social reproduction. This failure of social reproduction, combined with demands for intervention from both business leaders and popular movements, made it clear that the federal government had to play a larger role in the economy to ensure both successful social reproduction and profitable economic production.[3] Born from political struggle, the new welfare-state programs effectively, if not equally, redistributed income downward, expanded the role of the state, and otherwise assumed some responsibility for social reproduction. From the New Deal to the Great Society, the U.S. welfare state (inadequate as it was) generated conditions for both high profits and family maintenance. A growing number of redistributive social-welfare programs, supported by high tax rates and deficit spending, shifted the costs of carework from the household to the state and to some extent deprivatized social reproduction. This benefitted many white women and some women of color, who are the majority of the nation's care workers inside the home and out, especially in the public sector. While carrying out new social functions, the expanded welfare state did not neglect the accumulation interests of business. Its cash-assistance programs created conditions for profitable economic activity by increasing private purchasing power, channeling low-wage women workers onto the bottom rungs of the labor market, and stabilizing the economy during recurrent downturns.[4]

Between 1945 and the mid-1970s—years of relative prosperity for many households—the economy grew, the middle class swelled, productivity and wages increased, the average standard of living improved, the gap between the rich and poor narrowed, and the overall poverty rate fell by half. The expanded welfare state provided the working class with a modicum of economic security, socialized more of the costs of social reproduction, and helped quiet unrest. In distributing income downward, the welfare state reduced chronic poverty but also obscured deep-seated inequality and legitimized the state as an institution that treated all groups fairly, if not equally.[5]

The postwar welfare state contained a second contradiction, one grounded in its twin regulatory and liberatory powers. The regulatory welfare state controlled the lives of women, rewarding them for their compliance with prescribed work and gender roles and subjecting them to moralistic behavior rules that reinforced race, class, and gender hierarchies. The regulatory welfare state also promoted the political stability prerequisite for profitable capital accumulation by containing political conflicts over poverty and inequality. Simultaneously, the welfare state, as it emerged in practice, contained an unexpected liberatory potential that fostered political struggle. When welfare-state benefits operate as an alternative to the market wage, they have the potential to decommodify labor, increase the bargaining power of marginalized groups, and promote political activism. Access to benefits encourages collective struggle to the extent that it shifts the balance of power between the individual and the state, labor and capital, women and men, and persons of color and white persons. Welfare creates conditions amenable to political struggle and democratic participation.[6]

From 1935 to 1975, the expanding welfare state, combined with active and often militant popular movements, altered the balance of power in ways that benefitted many women. Social unrest in the 1930s fueled support for the New Deal, and the victories of the social movements of the 1960s further bolstered the liberatory potential of the welfare state. Gains made by the labor, civil rights, and women's liberation movements reduced economic insecurity, fears of unemployment, and discrimination, challenging white hegemony and patriarchal controls. The largely female welfare-rights movement shifted the balance of power further and won more respectful treatment and higher benefits from welfare departments around the country. The labor, civil rights, and gender "accords" the state negotiated in response to movement pressures improved standards of living, built solidarity, advanced democratic participation, expanded the state's capacity to support social reproduction, legitimized the system as fair to all, and otherwise created amenable conditions for resistance.[7]

Finally, reproducing capitalism requires the state to establish appropriate conditions for accumulation while legitimating its actions to voters. But these two functions can, as James O'Connor has argued, contradict each other. For one, the state promotes capital accumulation by investing in projects and services that enhance labor productivity, lower the reproduction costs of labor, and increase profit. However, because market economies tend to reproduce inequality and introduce considerable instability into the lives of ordinary people, a capitalist class that helps itself at the expense of others appears unfair and loses legitimacy. Welfare programs limit political disruption among the most marginalized or dispossessed groups. If and when the state can no longer support the cost of both accumulation and legitimization, something has to give.[8]

Between 1945 and 1975, the expanding welfare state contributed to both accumulation and legitimation. Welfare programs fueled accumulation by supplying business with a steady stream of consumers; ensuring a healthy, educated, and properly socialized workforce; easing the impact of economic downturns; and appeasing social movements. Modestly redistributing income, wealth, and power downward, the expanded welfare state also contained social despair, reduced distrust of the government, and legitimized state authority. In the mid-1970s, faced with a major economic crisis that undercut profits and growth, national leaders concluded that the economic and political costs of legitimation had become too high and called for dismantling the welfare state. In their view, rising welfare expenditures had created undue pressure to increase taxes and interest rates. Consequently, soaring interest rates discouraged the borrowing necessary for profitable investment. At the same time, deindustrialization and the export of jobs abroad reduced the reliance of business and industry on U.S. workers and consumers and weakened the power of the labor movement. Politically, elites concluded that welfare-state benefits and social movements had shifted the balance of power too far in favor of the working class, raising the cost of maintaining social peace (legitimization) beyond what they were willing to pay: the excessive democracy created by the postwar welfare state had to be reined in.[9]

In response to the second major economic crisis of the twentieth century, the nation's leaders targeted the expanded welfare state, which they now saw as a threat to the economic and political status quo. In contrast to the 1930s, when national elites begrudgingly called upon the government to bail them out, neoliberals in the 1970s blamed the crisis on "big government," the gains of social movements, and the costs of the welfare state. Partnered with the religious Right, neoliberals also blamed the crisis on what they called the absence of "personal responsibility" among the poor. They condemned "deviant" sexual behavior and economic expenditures that violated mainstream family norms. To enforce compliance, they favored punitive behavior-modification policies and anticrime measures.

Proponents of neoliberalism in business and government called for a U-turn in public policy that would remake the nexus of the market, the state, and citizenship from above. Seeking to restore the primacy of the market, lower labor costs, and weaken the influence of social movements, they sought to undo the New Deal and the Great Society by redistributing income upward and downsizing government. Their well-known tactics included tax cuts, reduced social spending, privatization (shifting social-welfare responsibility from the public to the private sector), devolution (shifting social-welfare responsibility from federal to state government), and mounting an assault on the social movements best positioned to resist austerity. The neoliberal shift in public policy emphasized economic production over social reproduction and accumulation over legitimization. It reinvigorated the regulatory and punitive functions of the welfare state while constraining a liberatory potential that had briefly altered the balance of power between the haves and the have-nots. The retrenched and reprivatized welfare state fueled a new crisis in social reproduction. Given the gendered division of labor, women picked up the slack at home and at work.[10]

THE CURRENT CRISIS IN SOCIAL REPRODUCTION

The current crisis in social reproduction arose from the neoliberal framework that reallocated social-welfare resources among the family, the market, and the state. A combination of social and market trends weakened each of these institutions, which over the prior fifty years had operated (albeit imperfectly) as the three pillars of support for social reproduction. Since the 1970s, heterosexual marriage, which mainstream observers hailed as central to successful social reproduction, became a less reliable site for carework among working-class women of all races. Fewer and later marriages and reduced (male) breadwinner support (due to job loss and stagnating wages) made it difficult for married, cohabitating, and otherwise partnered individuals to earn enough to maintain their households. Faced with economic insecurity, more white middle-class women followed women of color into the workforce:

some by choice, some as resistance to homemaking, but most just to make ends meet.[11]

However, the labor market often failed women as well as men. Sex-segregated occupations channeled many women into low-paid jobs, where they also suffered persistent gender and race wage gaps, sexual harassment, and other forms of discrimination that undercut their earnings, morale, and capacity for carework. The increased employment of women outside the home also exacerbated the mounting care void within households, a burden that the state might have reduced with paid family leave, helping women balance work and family responsibilities.

Neoliberalism also weakened the third pillar of economic security, the welfare state, to which some women turned when family and market support faltered. Unlike the postwar welfare state, which socialized some of the costs of social reproduction, the neoliberal welfare state fueled the carework crisis by simultaneously gutting and "reprivatizing" state health, education, and welfare programs and shifting the cost of social reproduction back to women in their homes, a process that Maria Mies calls "re-housewifization."[12]

Though less often noted, the hollowing out of the welfare state also affected the social-reproductive work of large numbers of women employed in public and nonprofit human-service jobs. The retrenchment of welfare-state programs cost many women workers their hard-won and union-protected jobs in both sectors and required remaining welfare-state workers to perform more public carework with fewer resources, less staff, reduced organizational capacity, and weaker unions. The diminished welfare state, combined with the ongoing attack on public-sector unions, deprived women of higher wages, better fringe benefits, and other important protections. This "war on the poor" has also been called a "war on women": as the guardians of social reproduction, women faced triple jeopardy as the majority of welfare clients, workers, and public-sector union members.[13]

Forty years after the U-turn in public policy, reams of evidence show that the end of the Fordist-Keynesian social compact—combined with deindustrialization and the exportation of production abroad—exacerbated the contradictions embedded in the welfare state. Proponents of neoliberalism promised that their promarket, antistate strategy would generate economic growth and that the benefits would trickle down to the average person. However, the data show that while the upward redistribution of income and wealth benefited large corporations and already wealthy individuals (women among them), the promised prosperity failed to materialize among the working class. Instead, neoliberalism promoted profitable capital accumulation for those at the top but job loss, poverty, inequality, and punishment for those at the bottom, especially for women over the age of eighteen, who comprise 60 percent of all poor persons in the United States.[14]

Many ask how "the people" were convinced to accept a U-turn in public policy that undermined their well-being, self-interest, and political power. Neoliberals built support for policies that harmed the lives of the average household by resorting to what Naomi Klein calls the "shock doctrine," or the creation or exploitation of a crisis and the manipulation of resulting fears to impose policies that people would not otherwise support. In this case, welfare-state opponents played to five prevailing panics that blinded people to their own self-interest: economic panic among an anxious middle class suffering falling wages and disappearing jobs; racial panic among white people as persons of color and immigrants institutionalized their hard-won gains; moral panic induced by changes in women's roles, family structure, and the advance of women's and gay rights; political panic among elites who feared the dispossessed would blame them for the nation's mounting social and economic problems; and crime panic created by officials seeking more authority, who stoked fears of rising crime rates and the incapacity of the state to control uprisings and social movements, in the hope that a worried public would accept more policing, social control, and punishment instead of mediation as the way to manage the poor and working classes.[15]

THE CARCERAL STATE

Instead of supporting the welfare state, neoliberalism exacerbated its contradictions. It supplemented the diminished welfare state with punitive programs that favored economic production over social reproduction, accumulation over legitimization, and regulation over liberation, fueling an attack on women. By the mid-1970s, an abandoned commitment to the Keynesian welfare state had weakened both social reproduction and the authority of the state. The state sought new arrangements to manage widespread economic insecurity as it spread from the poor and working classes to the middle class and from people of color to the white population; the state's deficit of legitimacy; and potential political resistance in the legislature, the voting booth, and the streets. Drawing on the shock doctrine and public fears of crime and disorder, the state adopted a more punitive mindset and redirected vast fiscal and administrative resources toward the criminal-justice system. The result, often called the "carceral state," compromised the conditions necessary for successful social reproduction.[16]

The extended reach of the carceral state marks a major milestone in American political development, rivaling in significance the expansion and contraction of the welfare state in the postwar period. Carceral-state policies tightened the traditional tough-on-crime pathway to prison. They also created and/or enlarged noncriminal pathways to punishment and jail, known variously as the double regulation of the poor, governing through crime, the shadow carceral state, and carceral debt. These policies targeted the same populations devastated by the evisceration of public resources, ensnared millions of people in the penal system, exacerbated the crisis of social reproduction in ways that affected women in particular, and threatened the nation's democratic institutions.

THE TRADITIONAL PATHWAY TO PUNISHMENT: TOUGH ON CRIME

The staggering growth in the state's capacity to police, punish, and imprison—what Michelle Alexander has termed the "New Jim Crow" because of its racial disparities—began in the late 1960s and early 1970s, as the increasingly neoliberal state got "tough on crime" and enacted mandatory minimum sentences, stiffer drug laws, and "three strikes and you're out" and other harsh policies that encouraged quick court decisions and prolonged sentences in place of the prior emphases on services, rehabilitation, and prevention.[17]

Despite falling crime rates, more than 2.2 million individuals are currently behind bars, a 500 percent increase over the past thirty years. In the United States more than any other country, the number reflects a deliberate increase in the number and type of offenders sent to prison and the deliberate imposition of longer sentences. African Americans are disproportionately represented in the incarcerated population, and since 1980 women have comprised its fastest growing group, their rate of incarceration increasing at nearly double the rate of men. With more than one million women behind bars or under the control of the criminal-justice system, the female prison population is eight times larger now than it was in 1980. In 2014, prisons held twice as many African American and 1.2 times as many Latino women as white women. In addition, the number of adults sentenced to probation has ballooned from 816,525 in 1977 to 3,826,209 in 2000 and to more than four million in 2010. In 2014, women comprised about 25 percent of all probationers and 12 percent of all parolees, statuses that regulate where they live, with whom they associate, and whether they can own a car. Probationers also face random drug tests and warrantless searches and are forced to pay excessive court fees at risk of imprisonment.[18]

Tough-on-crime policies play havoc with the work of social reproduction, given the family responsibilities of both women in prison and women with an incarcerated family member. Some 25 percent of women, and 44 percent of all black women, in the United States have a family member in prison. More than 60 percent of women in state prisons have a child under the age of eighteen, and the parent(s) of more than three million children are imprisoned or on probation. The economic consequences of incarceration compromise family stability, the foundation of social reproduction. Nearly half of incarcerated parents contributed financial support prior to incarceration. If incarceration rates had not increased during a twenty-four-year period, the U.S. poverty rate would have fallen by 20 percent rather than remaining relatively steady. When fathers are incarcerated, family income drops by an average of 22 percent. When no parent remains to care for a child, extended family members frequently step in, often without proper support. An estimated 65 percent of families with an incarcerated member cannot meet basic needs. In addition to poverty's well-known outcomes, children with an imprisoned parent suffer stigma, the loss of family ties, traumatic separation, and mental-health issues, and they often live in communities disrupted by the high concentration of adults in prison. The economic hardship women and men released from prison face further undercuts social reproduction, making it difficult, if not impossible, for them to get back on their feet, develop enduring adult relationships, and care for their children properly.[19]

NONCRIMINAL PATHWAYS TO PUNISHMENT

The carceral state supplemented traditional tough-on-crime policies with a growing reliance on noncriminal pathways to punishment. The latter expanded the reach of the carceral state beyond the estimated 2.2 million imprisoned persons to include more than eight million people (one in twenty-three adults) under some form of state control (jail, prison, probation, parole, community sanctions, drug courts, immigrant detention); nearly 12 million people jailed annually; and the estimated 7.5 percent of all adults who are felons or ex-felons. The noncriminal pathways to punishment include the double regulation of the poor (punishing single motherhood), governing through crime (criminalizing single motherhood), and the shadow carceral state (criminalizing noncriminal behavior). All have major consequences for women and the work of social reproduction on which individuals, families, and the wider society depend.[20]

The Double Regulation of the Poor

During the past thirty to forty years, the neoliberal state gradually integrated social welfare and penal polices into a combined poverty policy, punishing welfare-state recipients, most of them women, who did not comply with prescribed work and gender roles. Wacquant argues that downsizing the welfare state and upsizing the penal state represent two sides of the same coin, which together effect the "double regulation" of poverty in an age of deepening economic inequality and diffusing social insecurity. The same moral behaviorism guides both the welfare state and the penal state, both of which employ similar techniques of control (stigma, surveillance, punitive restrictions, and graduated sanctions) to "correct" client conduct. Among other outcomes, this double regulation undermines public support for the welfare state, limits its capacity to underwrite the costs of social reproduction, and opens the door to criminalizing poor women and especially single mothers.[21]

The double regulation of the poor is not altogether new. The welfare and carceral states share a long and intertwined history and similar logics about the causes and appropriate remedies for social problems. Since at least the 1950s, the two systems have worked together to punish the poor. Southern conservatives regularly opposed major civil-rights legislation in criminological terms, arguing, for example, that "integration breeds crime." Dixiecrats also inserted into civil-rights bills policies such as stiff mandatory minimums, a denial of federal benefits to convicted felons, and sentencing enhancements for vaguely defined violations, which served as policy models for major crime bills in the 1980s and 1990s. President Johnson framed the urban crisis as a breakdown of law and order, criminalized the period's rebellions and civil disobedience, and spent War on Poverty funds on his War on Crime, targeting black youth to prevent "future crimes." In 1994, Clinton signed a historic criminal-justice bill that mandated harsher sentences, provided states with financial incentives to adopt tougher crime laws, and eliminated federal funding for inmate education. By accelerating incarceration and spending on prisons, the now controversial legislation spawned the era of mass incarceration. At the same time, some local urban police forces began to militarize.[22]

The double regulation of the poor grew as welfare-state policies became more punitive, if not immediately carceral. Postwar public assistance and child-welfare programs subsidized the cost of social reproduction, however begrudgingly. At the same time, they embraced a deep distrust of the caretaking capacity of single mothers, especially those who were women of color. Like other welfare-state policies, the programs rewarded women who complied with prescribed gender roles but penalized those who could not or chose not to, defining them as "irresponsible" and "undeserving." In the 1960s, as more women of color joined the rolls, these views hardened, making the always-harsh welfare state even more punitive. The rules hardened again in the 1980s and 1990s to build public support for the ongoing effort to dismantle the welfare state. Playing to racial tensions, Clinton's 1996 Personal Responsibility and Work Opportunity Reconciliation Act added new measures that directly punished single motherhood by lowering benefits, stiffening work requirements, intensifying surveillance, and denying aid to children born to a mother "on welfare." If the 1996 welfare reform penalized single mothers by rescinding benefits, the 1997 Adoption and Safe Families Act penalized single mothers by taking away their children. The 1997 child-welfare law shifted the program's goals from "family preservation," or helping children remain at home, to "child protection," which placed children in foster care or adoptive homes after a mere fifteen months in state custody to protect them from "abusive" mothers. Some children genuinely benefitted from protection, but state officials unnecessarily removed others from the care of their mothers, especially single mothers of color, confusing poverty with neglect. The state justified these welfare penalties by labeling all recipients "welfare queens," unfit mothers who had kids for money, lived high on the hog, and cheated the system. The child-welfare system justified child removal by stigmatizing women in the child-welfare system as "bad mothers."[23]

GOVERNING THROUGH CRIME

As social-welfare policy increasingly operated in tandem with law enforcement, "governing through crime" became more common. According to Simon, governing through crime makes crime and the fear of crime the rationale for inserting penal policies into noncriminal domains.[24] Incorporating penal policies into social programs, public schools, public housing, and other venues accelerated mass incarceration. Manipulating the fear of crime helped justify practices previously deemed unacceptable, such as bringing the police into welfare investigations, denying public benefits to convicted drug felons, imposing zero-tolerance disciplinary rules in public schools, and otherwise criminalizing women responsible for the work of social reproduction at home. From punishing single mothers, the state began to criminalize their behavior.

"Welfare queens" and welfare fraud became national obsessions during the early 1970s. While the original welfare queen was criminally sentenced for large-scale and sophisticated welfare fraud, her story sparked sweeping antifraud campaigns that painted many innocent women as lazy, sexually promiscuous welfare cheats. Welfare departments enlisted law-enforcement agencies to conduct antifraud campaigns that relied on random home visits to recheck eligibility, imposed criminal penalties, and required fingerprinting of all recipients. Relentless media attention to welfare-fraud convictions subjected many women to surveillance and the risk of arrest and jail. Police officers began to accompany child-welfare workers on home investigations, ostensibly to protect them from possible harm. The highly visible presence of law enforcement helped criminalize single mothers in the eyes of family, friends, and neighbors, undercutting community ties. Anonymous tip lines turned neighbors into informants who reported recipient "welfare cheats" for earning wages, sexual impropriety, or owning "inappropriate" consumer goods, often just to settle petty disputes.[25]

Welfare policy also continues to punish convicted drug felons after their release from prison. The 1996 welfare reform imposed a lifetime ban on welfare and food stamps, used mostly by women, for this population. Between 1996 to 2011, 180,100 women in the twelve states that implemented a full ban lost benefits (the count is greater when it includes partial state bans). Public-housing policy banned drug felons and allowed evictions for drug use by a visiting child or grandchild. These restrictions heavily burdened women (25.1 percent), who in 2011 were more likely than men (16.2 percent) to be incarcerated for minor drug offenses. Indeed, 31.5 percent of all female offenders in 2013 were arrested for drug trafficking. Upon release from prison or in the absence of incarcerated family members, women pick up most of the work of social reproduction with diminished resources, which increases the risk of recidivism and reduces their capacity for family care. Perhaps this is why women are more likely than men to be arrested for minor property crimes. Since the mid-1970s, some 30 to 40 percent of women have been arrested for shoplifting, "bad checks," and welfare and credit fraud. Reflecting women's economic inequality and vulnerability, poverty-driven crimes aim to support the work of social reproduction.[26]

Like the family, the church, and the welfare state, schools are also institutions of social reproduction, enforcing norms and reproducing social hierarchies, including those of race and gender. With the rise of violence in urban schools, elites manipulated reasonable fears in ways that criminalized and marginalized black youth. After high-profile school shootings in the early 1990s, schools joined forces with the police to monitor student conduct, which led to record rates of arrest, expulsion, and even jail for minor offenses such as smoking, talking back, and having a cell phone in the classroom. The zero-tolerance policies schools adopted relied heavily on surveillance cameras, security guards, and metal detectors, causing schools to resemble prisons and transforming them from sites of democratic education to sites of social control. Between 1974 and 2010, the number of suspended students doubled annually, from 1.7 million to 3.7 million.[27]

Zero-tolerance policies facilitated the school-to-prison pipeline for black boys, viewed as violent, as well as black girls, perceived as promiscuous, loud, profane, and unruly. Girls of color, especially African American girls, face harsher and more frequent discipline than their white peers and are six times more likely to be suspended than white girls (even for defending themselves against sexual harassment, bullying, or other threats). In contrast, black boys are only three times more likely to be suspended than their white counterparts. Pushed-out students are three times more likely than their peers to drop out by the tenth grade and to get into trouble with the law. For girls, such outcomes ensure psychological distress but also low-wage work, economic insecurity, and other hardships that diminish their chances to develop the relationships and secure the resources necessary to support the work of social reproduction as adult women and mothers.[28]

The Shadow Carceral State

Beckett and Murakawa define the "shadow" carceral state as the often-invisible expansion of the state's traditional punitive laws to a wide range of low-profile criminal and noncriminal procedures that punish and detain people who have not violated the law. These civil, administrative, and legally hybrid pathways to punishment mimic traditional ones but exist outside the official criminal-justice system. Without officially recognizing these mechanisms as penal, the state uses them to criminalize ordinary behavior, detain immigrants without due process, create new crimes, and generally presume rather than prove the guilt of persons involved. Examples include civility codes, minor misdemeanors, and the compulsory detention of immigrants. In these and other ways, the shadow carceral state places an ever-larger share of the population on a broad but invisible noncriminal pathway to punishment that compromises their economic status, well-being, and capacity for effective social reproduction.[29]

Faced with a sagging economy and retrenched welfare state, the poorest often turn to panhandling, selling drugs, or other nonmarket activities to make ends meet. Women arrested for disorderly conduct, vagrancy, prostitution, drug trafficking, and other minor offences typically engage in this behavior to compensate for economic hardship and, in many cases, to provide for their children. In the 1990s the Supreme Court outlawed general vagrancy and loitering laws, forcing cities to devise other ways to prohibit these behaviors. Influenced by the broken-windows theory, officials criminalized such noncriminal acts and banished people from contested urban spaces in order to prevent more serious future crimes and restore "order" and "civility." These practices did little to address the underlying causes of homelessness, prostitution, or poverty. However, they broadened the range of behaviors subjected to police monitoring and increased law enforcement's power to charge, arrest, and jail those viewed as disorderly.[30]

Since the mid-2000s, local governments have also criminalized minor misdemeanors. They have subjected a greater number of behaviors to fees, fines, and arrest, including driving with an expired license, putting one's feet up on a subway seat, jaywalking, and driving with a broken taillight. A focus on truancy is especially important to mothers, who are responsible for social reproduction. In many urban schools, truancy now incurs criminal sanctions, including fines, shackling students, and sending both child and parent to jail. In Jacksonville, Florida, for example, antitruancy police arrested parents and charged them with a first-degree misdemeanor for contributing to the delinquency of a minor and a second-degree offense for failing to require school attendance. In Berks County, Pennsylvania, more than 1,600 parents—most of them mothers—have been jailed since 2000 for the failure to pay truancy fines of $300 per each unexcused absence after three. As will be noted below, such minor offenses and the resulting fines often pull people into the criminal-justice system for years at a time.[31]

The policing and punishment of noncriminal behavior also involves immigration control. The United States has a long history of criminalizing, denying entry, and deporting immigrants. However, since the 1990s, the federal government increased deportations, built numerous immigration prisons, and imprisoned immigrants never convicted of a crime. Today, the federal government routinely applies compulsory detention—a criminal penalty—in cases involving noncriminal immigrants and asylum seekers awaiting adjudication. More than half of the detained were never convicted of a crime, and existing convictions often involved immigration-specific behavior, such as illegal entry. Ten percent of the 32,000 detained every day by the U.S. Immigration and Customs Enforcement (ICE) are women who become permanently separated from their children. ICE often transfers the women to facilities hundreds or thousands of miles from their communities and then denies them access to telephones and the legal materials necessary to locate their children, coordinate childcare, and liaison with family courts to preserve parental rights.[32]

Despite decades-old Supreme Court rulings that incarceration for nonpayment of debt is unconstitutional, in many states "carceral debt" (also known as "criminal-justice debt") has become another pathway to punishment and prison. In thirty-six states the prison population more than tripled as a share of population since 1978, in spite of falling crime rates in the 1990s. Overall, criminal-justice costs have increased over 650 percent, from $35 billion in 1982 to more than $265 billion in 2012. Faced with ballooning costs and budget deficits and politically unable to raise taxes, cities and states around the country have created new revenue sources to cover the cost of the carceral state's policing, jails, prisons, and courts. States increasingly transfer costs to defendants, offenders, and prisoners, imposing fees at every step of the way, from the courtroom to prison to probation. In effect, the state charges defendants simply for being in the criminal-justice system.[33]

Unlike fines designed to punish or to provide restitution to crime victims, these new fines and fees cover state correctional-system costs and even supplement general revenues unrelated to the administration of criminal law. In Ferguson, Missouri, the poster child for such practices, a 95 percent white police force raised 20 percent of its budget by imposing exorbitant fees, fines, and court costs on a 70 percent black population. However, Ferguson is not alone. The percentage of inmates nationwide reporting such court-imposed costs rose from 25 percent in 1991 to 66 percent in 2004 and to 80.8 percent today. Police departments also fund themselves with civic asset forfeiture, seizing private property such as a car or a home without a warrant when law enforcement suspects the property was implicated in the commission of a crime. Civic asset forfeiture creates powerful incentives to police for profit instead of justice. Paige and Soss refer to carceral debt as the "financialization" of government functions. They described the trend as a new version of a long-standing "predatory system of government," in which the normal workings of the welfare state, the criminal-justice system, and other public institutions generate new fields of profitable economic activity. Following neoliberal principles, carceral debt benefits the affluent by expropriating and exploiting subordinate groups. Developed alongside the privatization of prisons and probation services, carceral debt disproportionately burdens female prisoners and women who support incarcerated family members. As noted above, about one in four U.S. women, and 44 percent of black women, have a family member in prison, and women frequently assume responsibility for at least part of a relative's legal and prison costs. In one study, women made up 83 percent of family members paying incarceration-related costs, on average more than $13,000 a year. The resulting financial hardship, combined with emotional wear and tear, disrupts the social-reproductive work women perform, including raising children and earning an income to support other family members.[34]

Courts across the country require people charged with minor misdemeanors to pay a wide range of fees and fines at numerous points in the criminal-justice system. Court charges include: bail fees of usually 10 percent of the total bail amount (more if the fee goes unpaid); preconviction fees, including for submitting a public-defender application, pretrial incarceration, and electronic monitoring devices; sentencing fees, including for restitution orders, administrative costs, and reimbursement of the public defender and prosecution; and other court fees, including jury fees, warrants for failing to appear, and crime-lab analyses. In Rhode Island, the most common reason for imprisonment is court debt, which comprises 17 percent of all jailings and almost 2,500 incidents a year. In Michigan, after Frederick Cunningham pleaded guilty to forging a prescription for pain medication, he paid $1,000 in court costs. One Ohio town of sixty residents collected more than $400,000 in one year in fines assessed in its "mayor's court."[35]

Offender funding also targets probationers who cannot afford their entire court debt and pay for the "privilege" of being put on probation instead of being imprisoned for nonpayment. In other words, the court sentences people to probation simply because they need time to pay down their fines and court costs. Under this "pay-only" probation, the longer it takes offenders to pay their debts, the longer they remain on probation and the greater their supervisory fees. Over one thousand courts nationwide place several hundred thousand adults under probation every year by for-profit companies that require payment for their services or risk fines, arrest, or imprisonment. Increasingly privatized probation programs have effectively repurposed probation into a muscular debt-collection tool, with all costs billed to the debtor. While most courts do not track how much probation companies collect, Human Rights Watch estimates that for-profit probation companies in Georgia alone earn at least $40 million in revenues from such fees.[36]

Mass incarceration is extraordinarily expensive. The fiscal costs of corrections alone amount to more than $80 billion annually, a budget approximately the size of the federal Department of Education. Corrections costs represent the third-largest category of spending in most states, after education and health care.[37] To cover costs, many states and cities charge inmates "pay-to-stay" fees. Justifications include decreasing the cost to taxpayers, teaching inmates a lesson for their criminal acts, and reducing frivolous requests for services by inmates. One official stated, "You do the crime, you will serve the time, and now you will also pay the dime."[38]

Michigan passed the first correctional-fee law in 1846 (authorizing counties to charge inmates for medical care), but the growth of this practice has a more recent vintage in the War on Crime in the 1970s and the War on Drugs in the 1980s. By 2004, approximately one-third of county jails and more than 50 percent of state correctional systems had instituted pay-to-stay fees. Today, all fifty states defray prison costs in this manner, often by docking the inmate's commissary account (which a female family member, who is also poor, typically funds). Fees include per-diem charges (often higher than those of local hotels); charges for specific items like toilet paper and clothing; and charges for health and social services such as medical copayments, dental visits, DNA tests, work release, physicals, medication, prescriptions, nurse sick calls, and hospital medical treatment. For-profit companies such as Corrections Corporation of America (CCA) and the GEO Group provide most of the services; they also manage prisons, detention, and deportation facilities. For these private corporations, higher prison censuses yield higher profits. In 2015, the CCA, the country's largest for-profit prison operator, made a profit of $3,356 per prisoner, at the taxpayers' expense. Prisoners rely on family members, often women, to pay "criminal-justice fees." Family members absorb the cost despite the loss of income that the imprisoned family member previously provided; nearly half of prisoners had contributed 50 percent or more to their family's total household income prior to incarceration. Tasked with the work of social reproduction, women also struggle to sustain family contact despite the odds. Along the way, they incur debt to pay for the exorbitant cost of phone calls operated by the for-profit prison communications industry, travel to distant prisons, and background-check fees prisons require of many visitors. Although staying in touch is critical for family stability and reentry, an inability to pay bills limits contact and causes families to fall apart.[39]

Last but not least, large numbers of the poor end up behind bars because they cannot afford to pay household debts. Just as neoliberal economic policies send the poorest of the poor into the informal labor market to make ends meet, so austerity policies have forced 80 percent of all U.S. households to finance privately the cost of social reproduction by incurring debt. The growing use of credit (mortgages, car loans, credit cards, and student loans) to cover basic needs represents one of the biggest shifts in the balance sheets of U.S. families over the past thirty years. Many households use second mortgages not to buy a house or build home equity but to meet daily needs. The privatization of household debt is particularly problematic for working-class households trying to build a normal life. Debt among these households comprised half of their income in 2013, up from one-fifth in 2007. High debt can encourage the use of shaky financial products like payday loans, car-title loans, and predatory or subprime mortgage loans. Fringe banks that charge high fees and interest rates target low-income women, especially women of color, who are trying to keep their families together, and they incur major debts that put them at high risk for jail time for nonpayment.[40]

Growing incarceration for nonpayment of court, prison, or household debts has led to the resurgence of "debtors' prison," trapping borrowers in a web of fines and multiyear prison sentences. Although U.S. courts outlawed prison terms for nonpayment of debt, officials sidestep these legal constraints by charging people with civil contempt of court or failure to comply with a court order to pay their debt instead of nonpayment. Authorities typically enlist for-profit companies who use aggressive tactics such as threatening jail and flouting procedural safeguards to collect court-imposed fines and fees.[41]

The consequences are severe. In one state, the average felony debt added up to $2,500. Interest on the debt continues to accrue, so that even after four years of faithful payments, a debt of $2,500 would grow to $3,000. The American Civil Liberties Union found former inmates with debts ranging from several hundred dollars up to $35,000. Estimates suggest that carceral debt represents 60 percent of the income of former inmates and that more than ten million people owe more than $50 billion in debt. Carceral debt operates as a regressive tax that falls heaviest on the poor and people of color, who are overrepresented among those arrested and less able than affluent offenders to pay court costs. Unlike European "day-fines," U.S. fees and fines do not consider ability to pay.[42]

Once again, women pick up the slack. The wife of an inmate at Florida's Marin County Correctional Institute told a reporter, "It's like [families] are a private ATM for the corrections department and they know there's nothing we can do about it." The chief justice of the Washington State Supreme Court shed light on this dynamic, observing of usage fees, "the spouses, who are mostly women, must then dig deep again if they are to offset the State's cut. In doing so they undoubtedly deprive themselves of funds that could be devoted to the purchase of necessities for them and their children. Such a scheme strikes me as not only unwise but unfair."[43]

WEAKENING DEMOCRATIC INSTITUTIONS

The decline of the U.S. welfare state and the simultaneous political, economic, and social disenfranchisement associated with the carceral state has weakened the nation's democratic institutions. Laws banning convicted felons from voting have politically disenfranchised an estimated 5.85 million, or 2.5 percent, of all voting-age Americans and disproportionately influenced election outcomes in communities of color. Ex-felons often must satisfy the payment of all criminal-justice debts in order to resume voting privileges. Debts assessed to recoup the operating costs of the justice system act as a modern-day poll tax and pose an insurmountable obstacle to the resumption of voting rights and broader civic participation. Only those who pay their debts regain voting rights after a criminal conviction, and those who cannot become permanently disenfranchised. The United States not only disenfranchises most of its prisoners; it is also the only democracy that routinely rescinds the vote of large numbers of people on parole or probation, as well as of ex-offenders who have completed their sentences but remain subject to carceral debt.[44]

U.S. policies also subject felons to economic disenfranchisement by erecting substantial barriers to an individual's postprison economic advancement. Former felons, as well as those with unpaid carceral debts, are generally restricted from employment, public housing, and student loans and denied access to pension, food-stamp, welfare, disability, and veteran benefits. States often prohibit former offenders from working in certain professions, including plumbing, catering, and even haircutting. Low-income communities further suffer community disenfranchisement. When tallying the population for congressional reapportionment and for local redistricting, the U.S. Census counts disenfranchised prisoners where they are imprisoned instead of at their prior residence. Many former felons must also forfeit their right to serve on a jury. Finally, mass incarceration generates fear and silences dissent.[45]

The enlarged carceral state described in this chapter has transformed the democratic promise of equal social, economic, and political opportunity for all by shifting authority toward law enforcement and corrections at the local, state, and federal levels. The expansion of the carceral state poses a threat to democracy among not only the marginalized but also within the wider society. Its policies legitimate separate political and legal universes for whole categories of people, routinely denying them a range of rights and access to state resources. Threats to fair elections, accurate and representative censuses, and core civil liberties and social benefits have condemned millions to civil death, creating a large and permanent group of social outcasts.[46]

Strengthened state capacity to control the lives of millions has further reshaped the distribution of power in ways that affect everyone, not just the marginalized.[47] As the carceral state reaches ever-greater sectors of society, if we do not find ways to challenge the trends that gave rise to the carceral state in the first place, the current reconfiguration of citizenship more broadly will continue. A weakened sense of community, combined with economic and political malaise, could be politically explosive. As Tocqueville and Beaumont warned, "While society in the United States gives the example of the most extended liberty, the prisons of the same country offer the spectacle of the most complete despotism."[48]

A DEEPER CRISIS IN SOCIAL REPRODUCTION

The standard argument for a penal system is the need to achieve retribution, deter crime, and ensure public safety. However, Dollovitch argues that the primary function of the U.S. penal system is not public safety but instead the exclusion and control of persons officially labeled as criminal. Gilmore adds an economic rationale: faced with a crisis of profit in the mid-1970s, capital turned to prison construction as a private-investment opportunity. Prisons also warehouse those pushed out of the market economy. By excluding prisoners from the jobless count, mass incarceration lowers the nation's official unemployment rate. Other scholars highlight political factors. The criminalization of poverty was not a response to rising crime rates, which actually dropped during the late-twentieth century. Nor was the carceral state simply an attempt to shrink "big government." Rather, the criminalization of the poor rationalized a renewed emphasis on the accumulative function of the welfare state and its traditional regulatory role and attempted to rein in its liberatory potential. That is, the neoliberal state needed new mechanisms to manage marginalized populations and reassert its authority and legitimacy, given the reduced support for social reproduction. Piven and Cloward argue that the postwar welfare state expanded and contracted public relief to regulate marginal labor and maintain social order. Wacquant suggests that the state has replaced this central regulatory mechanism with a more vigorous deployment of the police, courts, and prisons.[49]

Few scholars mention the deepening crisis in social reproduction generated by the expanded carceral state. More than 77 million Americans have a criminal record. Almost one in three adults is or has been involved with the criminal-justice system. Indeed, the rise of the carceral state has exacerbated the already deep crisis in social reproduction created by slow economic growth, stagnant wages, the gender wage gap, and a forty-year attack on the U.S. welfare state. Eleven states spend more on prison than education. The costs of mass incarceration, the third-largest item in the federal budget behind health and education, compete with social-welfare programs that underwrite the cost of social reproduction.[50]

To the extent that incarceration tears families and communities apart, it disrupts social reproduction. Most directly, the large-scale imprisonment of mothers and fathers undermines family stability, the foundation of social reproduction. It deprives children of a known caretaker, increases the likelihood of divorce and child removal, and breaks family and community ties. Incarcerated parents increase the risk that their children will become homeless, drop out of school, suffer health and psychological problems, and become incarcerated themselves. Incarceration intensifies a family's economic hardship with joblessness; loss of access to public assistance, housing, food stamps and other government benefits; and seemingly endless carceral debt. Former prisoners find that their prison records pose significant and at times insurmountable barriers to reentry as productive individuals, reliable providers, and integrated family members. The many fees and fines former prisoners incur force their households to forgo basic necessities to avoid arrest and jail for nonpayment of debt.[51]

In brief, incarceration disrupts the lives of low-income families, depletes their communities, and weighs heavily on family members who manage social-reproductive tasks in the face of emotional pain and diminished resources. Given the gendered division of labor, women typically take the lead in struggles to sustain family relationships, access housing and jobs, address health challenges, and maintain contact with incarcerated family members. Yet there is virtually no public discussion about the human toll of a carceral state that deprives thousands of families of resources needed to carry out the work of social reproduction. This structural violence, in turn, reduces resistance among the oppressed.[52]

What is to be done when the demise of the welfare state and the rise of the carceral state have undercut democratic institutions as well as social reproduction? If incarceration continues to break up families, if the carceral poll tax continues to bridge public budget deficits, and if the state no longer adequately supports social reproduction and continues to block civic engagement, what social institution will support the critical work that underpins capital accumulation, family well-being, and social solidarity? Much of the academic literature is silent on this question, despite the fact that the carceral state undermines democratic institutions and abandons marginalized persons to a frighteningly uncertain fate.

Rather sudden and recent changes in prison policies, initiated at the end of the Obama presidency, had the potential, if developed further, to restore some of the state's lost legitimacy. Overcrowded prisons and rising prison costs have sparked a bipartisan movement to lessen charges for drug possession and release minor offenders from prison, despite protests by the for-profit-prison industry. The spread of opioid and heroin use to predominantly white suburbs has also encouraged a reconsideration of rehabilitation in place of incarceration for addicts.[53]

These few prison reforms under discussion prior to the Trump administration might have made some small difference. However, they did not address the underlying factors that led to the rise of the carceral state in the first place. A more powerful answer may lie in new social movements. The good news is that the most recent attacks on basic human and legal rights, welfare-state programs, and democratic institutions have sparked a new and massive outpouring of resistance among people from all walks of life, not seen since the 1960s. Led initially by Occupy Wall Street, Black Lives Matter, the Fight for Fifteen, and immigrant-rights organizations, more recently the newly reconfigured women's movement and the local town meetings where people are rising up angry to let Donald Trump know his policies cannot stand, have both expanded and intensified the fight back. If unified and sustained, these collective demands for a more just and democratic social order hold out hope for change. Mass action worked in the past to secure basic rights and right basic wrongs. For now, the resistance may only contain the worst of the wars on welfare, women, persons of color, immigrants, and the poor. For the future, it suggests the promise of the well-known Chilean song and widespread protest chant, which declares: "The People United Will Never Be Defeated!"

NOTES

1. Mimi Abramovitz, "Women, Social Reproduction, and the Neoliberal Assault on the U.S. Welfare State," in *The Legal Tender of Gender: Law, Welfare, and the Regulation of Women's Poverty*, ed. Shelley A. M. Gavigan and Dorothy E. Chunn (Oxford: Hart, 2010), 15–46.
2. David Kotz, *The Rise and Fall of Neoliberal Capitalism* (Cambridge, Mass.: Harvard University Press, 2014); Mimi Abramovitz, "Economic Crises, Neoliberalism, and the U.S. Welfare State: Trends, Outcomes, and Political Struggle," in *Global Social Work: Crossing Borders and Blurring Boundaries*, ed. Carolyn Noble, Helle Strauss, and Brian Littlechild (Sydney: Sydney University Press, 2014), 225–241.
3. Maurizio Vaudagna, "The United States and Social Rights at Home and Abroad," in *The New Deal and the American Welfare State: Essays from a Transatlantic Perspective, 1933–1945* (Torino: Otto, 2014).
4. Mimi Abramovitz, "Saving Capitalism from Itself: Whither the Welfare State?" *New England Journal of Public Policy* 20, no. 1 (2004): 21–32; Mimi Abramovitz, "The Welfare State: A Battleground for Human Rights," in *Human Rights in the United States: Beyond Exceptionalism*, ed. Shareen Hertel and Kathryn Libal (Cambridge: Cambridge University Press, 2011), 46–67.
5. Abramovitz, "Women, Social Reproduction, and the Neoliberal Assault"; James O'Connor, *The Fiscal Crisis of the State* (New York: St Martin's, 1973).
6. Mimi Abramovitz, *The Lives of Women: Social Welfare Policy from Colonial Times to the Present* (Boston: South End, 1996); Frances Fox Piven and

Richard A. Cloward, *The New Class War: Reagan's Attack on the Welfare State and Its Consequences* (New York: Pantheon, 1982).
7. Frances Fox Piven and Richard A. Cloward, *Poor People's Movements: Why They Succeed and How They Fail* (New York: Vintage, 1977); Mimi Abramovitz, "The Reagan Legacy: Undoing the Class, Race, and Gender Accords," *Journal of Sociology and Social Welfare* 19, no. 1 (March 1992): 91–110.
8. O'Connor, *The Fiscal Crisis of the State*, 1–11.
9. Theresa Amott, *Caught in the Crisis: Women and the U.S. Economy Today* (New York: Monthly Review, 2003); Steven Greenhouse, "The Corporate Assault on Wages," *New York Times*, October 9, 1983; Samuel P. Huntington, "The United States," in *The Crisis of Democracy: Report on the Governability of Democracies to the Trilateral Commission*, ed. Michel J. Crozier, Samuel P. Huntington, and Joji Watanuki (New York: NYU Press, 1975), 114–115.
10. Abramovitz, "Saving Capitalism from Itself," 21–32.
11. Sandra Ezquerra, "Spain, Economic Crisis, and the New Enclosure of the Reproductive Commons," *Monthly Review* 65, no. 11 (April 2014): 22–35.
12. Maria Mies, *Patriarchy and Accumulation on a World Scale: Women in the International Division of Labour* (London: Zed, 1986), 16.
13. Mimi Abramovitz and Jennifer Zelnick, "Privatization in the Human Services: Implications for Direct Practice," *Clinical Social Work Journal* 43, no. 3 (September 2015): 283–293; Mimi Abramovitz, "The Feminization of Austerity," *New Labor Forum*, 21, no. 1 (Winter 2012): 30–39.
14. Abramovitz, "Economic Crises, Neoliberalism, and the U.S. Welfare State"; U.S. Census Bureau and U.S. Bureau of Labor Statistics, "Age and Sex of All People, Family Members, and Unrelated Individuals Iterated by Income-to-Poverty Ratio and Race: 2014," *Current Population Survey (CPS) Annual Social and Economic (ASEC) Supplement*, POV01, https://www.census.gov/hhes/www/cpstables/032015/pov/pov01_100.htm.
15. Naomi Klein, *The Shock Doctrine: The Rise of Disaster Capitalism* (New York: Henry Holt, 2007); Abramovitz, "Economic Crises, Neoliberalism, and the U.S. Welfare State."
16. Loïc Wacquant, *Punishing the Poor: The Neoliberal Government of Social Insecurity* (Durham, N.C.: Duke University Press, 2009).
17. Michelle Alexander, *The New Jim Crow: Mass Incarceration in the Age of Colorblindness* (New York: New Press, 2012).
18. The Sentencing Project, "Fact Sheet: Trends in U.S. Corrections," 2016, http://sentencingproject.org/wp-content/uploads/2016/01/Trends-in-U.S.-Corrections.pdf; Center on Budget and Policy Priorities, "Changing Priorities: State Criminal Justice Reforms and Investments in Education," by Michael Mitchell and Michael Leachman, October 28, 2014,

http://www.cbpp.org/research/changing-priorities-state-criminal-justice-reforms-and-investments-in-education; The Sentencing Project, "Fact Sheet: Incarcerated Women and Girls," November 2015, http://www.sentencingproject.org/doc/publications/Incarcerated-Women-and-Girls.pdf; Institute for Policy Studies, "The Poor Get Prison: The Alarming Spread of the Criminalization of Poverty," by Karen Dolan with Jodi L. Carr (Washington, D.C.: Institute for Policy Studies, 2015), http://www.ips-dc.org/wp-content/uploads/2015/03/IPS-The-Poor-Get-Prison-Final.pdf, 17; U.S. Department of Justice, Office of Justice Programs, Bureau of Justice Statistics, *Probation and Parole in the United States, 2014*, by Danielle Kaeble, Laura M. Maruschak, and Thomas P. Bonczar, Bulletin November 2015 NCJ 249057, http://www.bjs.gov/content/pub/pdf/ppus14.pdf.

19. Hedwig Lee, Tyler McCormick, Margaret T. Hicken, and Christopher Wildeman, "Racial Inequalities in Connectedness to Imprisoned Individuals in the United States," *Du Bois Review: Social Science Research on Race* 12, no. 2 (Fall 2015): 269–282; The Sentencing Project, "Women in the Criminal Justice System: Mothers In Prison," Briefing Sheet, May 1, 2007, http://www.sentencingproject.org/wp-content/uploads/2016/01/Women-in-the-Criminal-Justice-System-Briefing-Sheets.pdf; U.S. Department of Justice, Office of Justice Programs, Bureau of Justice Statistics, *Parents in Prison and Their Minor Children*, by Lauren E. Glaze and Laura M. Maruschak, Special Report NCJ 222984, August 2008 (revised March 30, 2010), http://www.bjs.gov/content/pub/pdf/pptmc.pdf; The Annie E. Casey Foundation, "A Shared Sentence: The Devastating Toll of Parental Incarceration on Kids, Families, and Communities," April 2016, http://www.aecf.org/sharedsentence.

20. Marie Gottschalk, "Bring It On: The Future of Penal Reform, the Carceral State, and American Politics," *Ohio State Journal of Criminal Law* 12, no. 2 (Spring 2015): 559–604; Julilly Kohler-Hausmann, "Guns and Butter: The Welfare State, the Carceral State, and the Politics of Exclusion in the Postwar United States," *Journal of American History* 102, no. 1 (2015): 87–99; Loïc Wacquant, "Crafting the Neoliberal State: Workfare, Prisonfare, and Social Insecurity," *Sociological Forum* 25, no. 2 (June 2010): 197–220; Katherine Beckett and Naomi Murakawa, "Mapping the Shadow Carceral State: Toward an Institutionally Capacious Approach to Punishment," *Theoretical Criminology* 16, no. 2 (May 2002): 221–244.

21. Wacquant, "Crafting the Neoliberal State," 197–220; Kohler-Hausmann, "Guns and Butter," 87–99.

22. Wacquant, "Crafting the Neoliberal State," 197–220; Marie Gottschalk, "The Carceral State and the Politics of Punishment," in *The SAGE Handbook of Punishment and Society*, ed. Jonathan Simon and Richard Sparks

(Los Angeles: SAGE, 2013), 205–241; Elizabeth Hinton, "'A War Within Our Own Boundaries': Lyndon Johnson's Great Society and the Rise of the Carceral State," *Journal of American History* 102, no. 1 (June 2015): 100–112; "Justice in Focus: Crime Bill @ 20," *Vera Institute of Justice*, http://crimebill20.vera.org/justiceinfocus#chapter-119969; Peter Beinart, "Hillary Clinton and the Tragic Politics of Crime," *The Atlantic* online, May 1, 2015, http://www.theatlantic.com/politics/archive/2015/05/the-tragic-politics-of-crime/392114/.

23. Abramovitz, *Regulating The Lives of Women*; Karen Swift, "'Risky Women': The Role of 'Risk' in the Construction of the Single Mother," in *The Legal Tender of Gender: Law, Welfare, and the Regulation of Women's Poverty*, ed. Dorothy E. Chunn and Shelley A. M. Gavigan (Oxford: Hart, 2010), 143–164.

24. Jonathan Simon, *Governing Through Crime: How the War on Crime Transformed American Democracy and Created a Culture of Fear* (New York: Oxford University Press, 2006), 330.

25. Julilly Kohler-Hausmann, "'The Crime of Survival': Fraud Prosecutions, Community Surveillance, and the Original 'Welfare Queen,'" *Journal of Social History*, 41, no. 2 (Winter 2007): 329–354; Julilly Kohler-Hausmann, "Welfare Crises, Penal Solutions, and the Origins of the 'Welfare Queen,'" *Journal of Urban History* 41, no. 5 (September 2015): 756–771; Dorothy Roberts, "The Racial Geography of Child Welfare: Toward a New Research Paradigm," *Child Welfare* 87, no. 2 (2008): 125–150.

26. The Sentencing Project, "A Lifetime of Punishment: The Impact of the Felony Drug Ban on Welfare Benefits," by Mark Mauer and Virginia McCalmont, November 2013 (updated September 2015), http://sentencingproject.org/doc/publications/cc_A%20Lifetime%20of%20Punishment.pdf; Todd Clear and Natasha Frost, *The Punishment Imperative: The Rise and Failure of Mass Incarceration in America* (New York: NYU Press, 2013); U.S. Sentencing Commission, *Overview of Federal Crimes Cases, Fiscal Year 2013*, by Glenn R. Schmitt and Elizabeth Jones, Research Publication, August 2014, http://www.ussc.gov/sites/default/files/pdf/research-and-publications/research-publications/2014/FY13_Overview_Federal_Criminal_Cases.pdf; Darrell Steffensmeier and Emilie Allan, "Gender and Crime," *Encyclopedia of Crime and Justice*, http://www.encyclopedia.com/doc/1G2-3403000129.html.

27. Schott Foundation for Public Education, African American Policy Forum, "Race, Gender, and the School-to-Prison Pipeline: Expanding Our Discussion to Include Black Girls," by Monique W. Morris, September 2012, http://schottfoundation.org/resources/race-gender-and-school-prison-pipeline-expanding-our-discussion-include-black-girls; Marianne Kaba

and Erica R. Meiners, "Arresting the Carceral State," *Jacobin* 2 (2014), https://www.jacobinmag.com/2014/02/arresting-the-carceral-state/.
28. Schott Foundation, "Race, Gender, and the School-to-Prison Pipeline"; Marie Gottschalk, "The Long Reach of the Carceral State: The Politics of Crime, Mass Imprisonment, and Penal Reform in the United States and Abroad," *Law & Social Inquiry* 34, no. 2 (Spring 2009): 439–472; Karen G. Bates, "Study: Black Girls Are Being Pushed out of School," *NPR Code Switch: Race and Identity, Remixed* (blog), February 13, 2015, http://www.npr.org/sections/codeswitch/2015/02/13/384005652/study-black-girls-are-being-pushed-out-of-school; Michael B. Katz and Mike Rose, *Public Education Under Siege* (Philadelphia: University of Pennsylvania Press, 2013).
29. Beckett and Murakawa, "Mapping the Shadow Carceral State," 221–244.
30. Ibid.; Jennifer Schwartz and Darrell Steensmeier, "The Nature of Female Offending: Patterns and Explanation," in *Female Offenders: Critical Perspectives and Effective Interventions*, ed. Ruth T. Zaplin (Sudbury, Mass.: Jones and Bartlett, 2008), 43–75; Dennis Baker, *The Right Not to Be Criminalized: Demarcating Criminal Law's Authority* (Burlington, Vt.: Ashgate, 2011); Katherine Beckett and Steve Herbert, *Banished: The New Social Control in Urban America* (Oxford: Oxford University Press, 2010).
31. Katz and Rose, *Public Education Under Siege*; Michele Norris, "City Arrests Parents to Fight Truancy," *ABC News*, February 28, 2016, http://abcnews.go.com/WNT/story?id=130460&page=1; Dana Goldstein, "Inexcusable Absences," *New Republic* 246, no. 3 (March–April 2015): 32–37.
32. Gottschalk, "The Long Reach of the Carceral State," 439–472; Beckett and Murakawa, "Mapping the Shadow Carceral State," 221–244; "Migrant Rights & Justice: Impact of Detention on Women Revealed at Congressional Briefing," *Women's Refugee Commission*, June 24, 2009, https://www.womensrefugeecommission.org/rights/55-detention/803-congressional-briefing-on-june-24-to-reveal-impact-of-immigration-enforcement-on-women-and-families.
33. Center on Budget and Policy Priorities, "Changing Priorities: State Criminal Justice Reforms and Investments in Education," by Michael Mitchell and Michael Leachman, October 28, 2014, http://www.cbpp.org/sites/default/files/atoms/files/10-28-14sfp.pdf; Brennan Center for Justice at New York University School of Law, "Charging Inmates Perpetuates Mass Incarceration," by Lauren-Brooke Eisen, 2015, https://www.brennancenter.org/sites/default/files/blog/Charging_Inmates_Mass_Incarceration.pdf; Brennan Center for Justice at New York University School of Law, "Criminal Justice Debt: A Tool Kit for Action," by Roopal Patel and Meghna Philip, 2012, https://www.brennancenter.org/sites/default/files

/legacy/publications/Criminal%20Justice%20Debt%20Background%20 for%20web.pdf.
34. Joshua Paige and Joe Soss, "The Predator State: Race, Class, and the New Era of Indentured Citizenship," unpublished paper presented at the Seminar on Neoliberalism, Roosevelt House, Hunter College, New York, April 1, 2015; Ella Baker Center for Human Rights, Forward Together, and Research Action Design, "Who Pays? The True Cost of Incarceration on Families," by Saneta deVuono-Powell, Chris Schweidler, Alicia Walters, and Azadeh Zohrabi, September 2015, http://whopaysreport.org/wp-content/uploads/2015/09/Who-Pays-FINAL.pdf.
35. "Is Charging Inmates to Stay in Prison Smart Policy?" Brennan Center for Justice at New York University School of Law, n.d., https://www.brennancenter.org/states-pay-stay-charges; "Jailing the Poor: Court Debt and Incarceration in Rhode Island," Family Life Center Policy Brief, 2008, *Open Doors*, http://opendoorsri.org/sites/default/files/brief_debt.pdf; Joseph Shapiro, "As Court Fees Rise, the Poor Are Paying the Price," *NPR All Things Considered*, May 19, 2014, http://www.npr.org/2014/05/19/312158516/increasing-court-fees-punish-the-poor; American Civil Liberties Union Radical Justice Program, "Hearing on Municipal Policing and Courts: A Search for Justice or a Quest for Revenue; Written Statement of the American Civil Liberties Union Before the United States Commission on Civil Rights," March 18, 2016, https://www.aclu.org/sites/default/files/field_document/aclu_statement_usccr_03182016_municipal_courts_and_police_choudhury.pdf.
36. Human Rights Watch, "Profiting from Probation: America's Offender-Funded Probation Industry," by Chris Albin-Lackey, February 2014, https://www.hrw.org/sites/default/files/reports/us0214_ForUpload_0.pdf.
37. Brennan Center for Justice, "Charging Inmates Perpetuates Mass Incarceration."
38. Brennan Center for Justice, "Is Charging Inmates to Stay in Prison Smart Policy?"
39. Ella Baker Center for Human Rights, "Who Pays?" 1–61; Chandra Bozelko, "The Prison-Commercial Complex," *New York Times*, March 21, 2016.
40. The Pew Charitable Trust, "The Complex Story of American Debt: Liabilities in Family Balance Sheets," July 2015, http://www.pewtrusts.org/~/media/assets/2015/07/reach-of-debt-report_artfinal.pdf?la=en; Genevieve LeBaron and Adrienne Roberts, "Toward a Feminist Political Economy of Capitalism and Carcerality," *Signs: A Journal of Women in Culture and Society* 36, no. 1 (Autumn 2010): 19–44; Larry Checco, "From the Great Society to the Debt Trap," *Inquality.org*, June 2, 2015, http://inequality.org/great-society-debt-trap/.

41. Institute for Policy Studies, "The Poor Get Prison," 5–35; American Civil Liberties Union of Ohio, "The Outskirts of Hope: How Ohio's Debtors' Prisons Are Ruining Lives and Costing Communities," April 2013, https://csgjusticecenter.org/wp-content/uploads/2013/07/2013-ACLU-of-OH-report.pdf; Brennan Center for Justice, "Criminal Justice Debt"; Beckett and Murakawa, "Mapping the Shadow Carceral State"; American Civil Liberties Union, "Hearing on Municipal Policing and Courts."
42. Shapiro, "As Court Fees Rise"; Jessica Lussenhop, "U.S. Inmates Charged Per Night in Jail," *BBC News Magazine*, November 9, 2015, http://www.bbc.com/news/magazine-34705968; Alexes Harris, "The Cruel Poverty of Monetary Sanctions," *Society Pages*, March 4, 2014, http://thesocietypages.org/papers/monetary-sanctions/; American Civil Liberties Union, "In for a Penny: The Rises of America's New Debtors' Prisons," October 2010, https://www.aclu.org/files/assets/InForAPenny_web.pdf.
43. Brennan Center for Justice, "Criminal Justice Debt," 1–47.
44. The Sentencing Project, "Felony Disenfranchisement: A Primer," by Jean Chung, May 2016, http://www.sentencingproject.org/wp-content/uploads/2015/08/Felony-Disenfranchisement-Primer.pdf; Alicia Bannon, Mitali Nagrecha, and Rebekah Diller, "Criminal Justice Debt: A Barrier to Reentry," Brennan Center for Justice (blog), October 4, 2010, https://www.brennancenter.org/publication/criminal-justice-debt-barrier-reentry; Ann Cammett, "Shadow Citizens: Felony Disenfranchisement and the Criminalization of Debt," *Penn State Law Review* 117, no. 2 (2012–2013): 349–405; Gottschalk, "The Long Reach of the Carceral State."
45. Legal Action Center, "After Prison: Roadblocks to Reentry: Report on State Legal Barriers Facing People with Criminal Records," 2004, http://lac.org/roadblocks-to-reentry/upload/lacreport/LAC_PrintReport.pdf.
46. Ibid.
47. Marie Gottschalk, "Hiding in Plain Sight: American Politics and the Carceral State," *Annual Review of Political Science* 11 (2008): 235–260.
48. Gustave de Beaumont and Alexis de Tocqueville, *On the Penitentiary System in the United States and Its Application in France* [1833] (Carbondale: Southern Illinois University Press, 1979), 79; cited in Gottschalk, "Hiding in Plain Sight," 236.
49. Sharon Dolovitzh, "Exclusion and Control in the Carceral State," *Berkeley Journal of Criminal Law* 16, no. 2 (2011): 259–339; Ruthie Gilmore, "Globalisation and U.S. Prison Growth: From Military Keynesian to Post-Keynesian Militarism," *Race and Class* 40, no. 2/3 (1998–1999): 171–188; Frances Fox Piven and Richard A. Cloward, *Regulating the Poor: The Functions of Public Welfare* (New York: Vintage, 1971); Wacquant, *Punishing the Poor*.

50. Brennan Center for Justice, "Charging Inmates Perpetuates Mass Incarceration."
51. Eric Eckholm, "In Prisoners' Wake, a Tide of Troubled Kids," *New York Times*, July 4, 2009; Ella Baker Center for Human Rights, "Who Pays?"
52. American Civil Liberties Union, "In for a Penny"; David G. Gil, *Unraveling Social Policy: Theory, Analysis, and Political Action Toward Social Equality* [1973] (Rochester, Vt.: Schenkman, 1992).
53. Robert T. Chase, "We Are Not Slaves: Rethinking the Carceral State Through the Lens of Prisoners Rights," *Journal of American History*, 102, no. 1 (June 2015): 73–86.

PART III

Gender, the Family, and Social Provision

THE CONNECTION between social provision and the family is one of the defining features of the history of the welfare state. Even when economic depressions and feminist politics have eroded the social and ideological foundations of the traditional family, welfare planners have both assumed and encouraged patriarchal family arrangements and, especially, a so-called nuclear family composed of a breadwinner husband/father and a homemaking wife/mother.

The rise and decline of "breadwinner liberalism" in the United States is the subject of the historian Robert O. Self's chapter. The limited welfare state based on the breadwinner-wage model that liberals built between the 1930s and the 1950s was challenged in the 1960s and after by movements for gender and racial justice that demanded redistributive policies based on justice for the neglected. Liberal political leadership proved unable to reform welfare to meet the new demands that emerged in these years; nor could it satisfy newly emerging needs of the post-1960s pluralist family. The tension subsequently paved the way to the revival of free-market neoconservatism. The sociologist Chiara Saraceno illustrates the link between changing definitions of the family and the implementation of new social policies. She concludes that in Europe, family-related social rights encouraged previously untried family arrangements across gender and intergenerational lines. But these changes were also infused with a pan-European sense that some kind of government-family cooperation would be necessary to support children. If differently enacted in various countries, this sense has provided a source of coherence within Europe. Such a consensus, as the sociologist Anna Shola Orloff deftly reveals, is encapsulated in the Scandinavian experience. There generous childcare arrangements have supported the close tie between expanding maternal employment and equality in wages and family arrangements. We also have some preliminary evidence that such arrangements enhance the political voice and the political representation of women.

CHAPTER NINE

Family Matters

Social Policy, an Overlooked Constraint on the Development of European Citizenship

CHIARA SARACENO

ACROSS EUROPE'S WELFARE STATES, the legal definition of the family is crucial to the exercise of social rights. A significant relationship exists between social policy and civil-law definitions of who or what constitutes a family, especially when applied to family-based rights and duties (for example, survivor pensions or fiscal benefits). Thus, the more states center social rights and duties on the basis of family relationships, the greater the likelihood that official institutions will resist enlarging the legal definition of the family not only on account of moral values but also because of matters of public finance. It is no coincidence that in recent years it has been easier to enlarge the definition of the family to include nonmarried heterosexual couples and same-sex couples specifically in those countries where rights and obligations attached to the family are narrower. In countries where social rights are more intimately connected to the family, governments have been much slower to redefine the legal definition of the family or open its boundaries. There are exceptions to this general trend, the most notable being Spain, where legal family obligations and social policies were once as familialistic as those in Italy but where since the early 2000s family law has changed radically to include same-sex marriage, adoption by homosexuals, and to open assisted-reproductive technology (including recourse to a donor) both to two- and same-sex couples as well as to singles. In turn, changes in the legal understanding of which relationships may be defined as "family" has prompted a trend toward a greater degree of individualization and defamilialization in Spain's social policies.[1]

In recent decades, a number of issues have brought increased attention to the role of the state in shaping the context in which families are formed and operate. Women's demands for equal rights, the increase in the extent of married women's—particularly married mothers'—participation in the labor force, and the concomitant decline of the male-breadwinner model have weakened many assumptions on which the family, the workplace, and the gender division of paid and unpaid work are based. Declining fertility and an aging population have at many levels tipped the balance between generations not only within societies but also within families.[2] Marital instability and the return of job-market insecurity together have caused an increase in the risk of poverty in particular for children and for women. These changes have affected the structure and composition of so-called social risks.[3] Together with the growing complexity and differentiation in patterns of family formation and in family arrangements and practices,[4] these changes lead one to question the efficacy of existing policies that are based on previous assumptions of the meaning of family and gender.

What happens in families has become a matter of considerable debate and public interest in many countries. In some cases, policy makers have become more proactive in their approaches to family matters, and supranational bodies have also showed an inclination to modify and support specific family and gender arrangements. For example, the European Union's Employment Strategy (EES) has drawn a model of motherhood and wifehood that includes working for pay and, to a much lesser extent, a model of fatherhood and "husbandhood" that includes unpaid family work. The ideal family model that the EES proposes is based on the assumption of a dual-earner household—the universal-breadwinner model, to use Nancy Fraser's (1994) terminology—but not so much a combined universal-breadwinner and universal-*carer* model.[5]

The Organization for Economic Co-Operation and Development (OECD) also promotes a dual-earner model, although OECD countries in the European Union have implemented their visions of the family unevenly with regard both to women and men's behavior as well as to the practical support offered them by national policies. It might be pointed out that it is somewhat paradoxical that the dual-earner (and partly dual-carer) family model is promoted at a time of high couple's instability, which at best fragments earning and caring across households. At worst, it leaves single parents, mostly mothers at that, playing the role of both single earner and single carer.

THE STRUCTURING AND DESTRUCTURING OF FAMILY OBLIGATIONS THROUGH SOCIAL POLICIES

Three dimensions of social policy appear particularly relevant in shaping the institutional context in which specific patterns of family arrangements, gender, and intergenerational interdependencies take shape. We can call these three dimensions familialism by default, supported familialism, and defamilialization.[6] Each of these three aspects intersects with a divide that has been described as the commodification/decommodification faultline.[7]

First, commodification/decommodification. Here, commodification refers to a person's reliance on the market for insurance against risks and for the provision of health and care services. Decommodification, on the other hand, indicates a person's independence from the market for the satisfaction of his or her needs. This decommodification of health and care services may occur through access to public resources, or one might achieve it by means of resources provided by the family; there are different consequences for inequalities of gender and class depending on how health and care are decommodified. Furthermore, in order to gain access to decommodification via the welfare state, individuals often need to be able to enter and remain in the labor market, that is, to be commodified.[8] This is a crucial issue for women with family responsibilities, and, for different reasons, it has become increasingly important for the young.

Let's now turn to the expectations concerning family arrangements inscribed in social policies. First, we may speak of familialism by default, or unsupported familialism, when there are neither publicly provided alternatives to family care nor financial support for it. This dimension of familialism by default can be either implicit or explicit. An explicit example of familialism by default would be financial obligations within the generational chain, or kinship networks, that are in fact prescribed by law. In the latter case, we should more precisely speak of *prescribed* familialism.

Second, supported familialism. Supported familialism occurs when policies support specific family members in keeping up their financial or care responsibilities, usually through direct or indirect financial transfers, patterns of taxation, and paid leaves.

Last, defamilialization. Defamilialization refers to the individualization of social rights. For example, minimum-income provisions, entitlement to higher education, and the right to receive care are often individually held rights that are not pegged to a person's status as a family member. Defamilialization reduces family responsibilities and dependencies. Particularly in the areas of health, care, and education, defamilialization may occur through both state (or state-financed) and market provisions.[9] With regard to social justice and the role of the family in it, however, these two paths to defamilialization—through the state and by means of the market—do not have the same conceptual status. Inevitably, the ability to have recourse to the services market is mediated by family resources, and this access both strengthens and is dependent on social inequalities. Defamilialization may also occur through volunteer and third-sector intervention. In many countries, these are an important part of the overall welfare mix. If they are formally integrated into public policies, as is the case of care services provided through long-term care insurance in Germany, we may include them in the system of public provision. Otherwise, as in the case of defamilialization via the market, they may be conceived of as intervening in the area left to familialism by default.

The way social policies are located within the familialization-defamilialization divide has an impact on the shape and duration of gender- and generation-specific family interdependencies. It also affects the degree to which policies acknowledge different family arrangements (e.g., cohabitation without marriage or same-sex couples) and take for granted gender-specific behaviors with regard to these same responsibilities. It is fair to say that the higher the degree of both prescribed familialism and familialism by default by governing institutions, the more restrictive will be their acknowledgment of alternative family forms. As well, the more social rights are dependent on strict definitions of the family, the more will intergenerational family responsibilities pose a burden to individual family members, and the more that burden will fall along gendered lines, with women being primarily responsible for care and men for financial support. To a lesser degree, the gendering of carework may also occur in the case of supported familialism.[10] Given prevalent gender scripts and the division of labor, women are more likely than men to take advantage of leave and other care allowances. Supported familialism, however, may also be a way of acknowledging the value of care giving within families, of allowing time to care,[11] and therefore supported familialism might encourage the acknowledgment that work for pay is not the only meaningful and socially valuable activity in life. Furthermore, supported familialism may also offer incentives for rebalancing gender responsibilities in childcare. This is the case for policies that specifically reserve a quota of leave time for fathers, encouraging them to take time off paid work to care for their child.

From the perspective of gender relations, the complex interplay of familialization and defamilialization produces several different effects. Some policies allow women with family responsibilities to remain in the labor market and independent of another person's income, regardless of their care responsibilities. The degree to which care policies allow women to be both "commodified" and "defamilialized" influences their ability to provide for themselves through, for example, the provision of services (by purchasing defamilialized carework or by taking advantage of decommodified carework) and paid-leave entitlements.

Other policies acknowledge caring for dependent family members (children, dependent adults, frail elderly relatives) as an activity deserving of financial support in its own right (decommodified supported familialism). This can occur through, for example, care leaves and allowances as well as through care-linked contributions toward old-age pensions.

Still other policies support men's shouldering of care responsibilities. For example, entitling fathers to paternity and/or parental leave, with or without a reserved quota for them (decommodified supported familialism for men).

With regard to intergenerational interdependencies and obligations, the important effects differ according to a different set of dimensions: First, the degree to which the state takes up part of the responsibility of the cost of children as consumers of goods, through child-related direct and/or indirect income transfers (decommodified supported familialism).

Second, the degree to which the state in its various articulations takes up the cost of children as consumers of time, either in the form of decommodified supported familialism (paid leave) or in the form of decommodified defamilialization (services) that may shape the lives of parents. Especially important is the age at which children are no longer considered their parents' responsibility with regard to income maintenance and so become fully entitled to their own benefits.

Defamilialization in old age rests on the degree to which the old are entitled to their own income, irrespective of their work and contributory history (decommodified defamilialization), for example, through some kind of minimum guaranteed pension, and, by contrast, the degree to which their financial support, in case of need, is implicitly or explicitly their children's responsibility (familialism by default). It is also affected by the degree to which the (nonhealth) care needs of older people are met by public support either through decommodified supported familialism or through the direct or indirect provision of nonfamily care.

Another dimension, one that cuts across these concerns, should be added, although comparative data for it are lacking. Namely, this dimension is whether and in what circumstances members of "nonstandard" families are entitled to the same benefits as the members of "standard" families. For instance, one must consider whether the nonbiological parent in a same-sex couple is entitled to parental leave, or whether heterosexual or homosexual civil unions are treated as married couples in survivor pension benefits or in the tax system (for instance, in France, within the *pacte civil de solidarité* [PACS], they are not, nor until 2014 were they in Germany). It is fair to say that most social policies are based on the assumption that families are always organized around a stable heterosexual couple and that intergenerational ties and obligations are not complicated by divorce and remarriage (or, in any case, repartnering).

In the case of children, financial and care responsibilities may cross household boundaries when parents are divorced or do not live together. In real life, although not always in social policies and in civil law, these responsibilities may also cross parental statuses, with stepparents providing as much, and sometimes more, care and financial support as a noncohabitant legal and biological parent. In the case of same-sex parents, the nonbiological parent may sometimes be the main financial or care provider of a child, even if, as happens in some countries (like, for example, in Italy), his or her status as a parent is not legally acknowledged. These restrictions on the legal definition of the family can have a material impact on the well-being of a child; the lack of recognition of these alternative relationships may result in a child's heightened exposure to vulnerability when either parent dies or if the relationship between parental partners breaks up.

The interplay between legal definitions of the family on the one hand and social policies on the other has been at the core of many analyses of the welfare state. Yet the different dimensions that make up the complex institutional and normative framework in which gender and intergenerational relationships are regulated are mostly addressed by literatures and research fields that rarely speak to one another. For instance, responsibilities toward infants and toddlers are objects of a different literature than that concerning responsibilities toward grown children. Responsibilities toward elderly kin are part of a still different field of research. Only recently, and mostly only within the research on social care that deploys a critical lens on gender, have scholars begun to address jointly the family, the state, and the community when considering issues concerning the allocation of responsibilities for the care of children and the elderly.[12] Integrating the existing research is made even more difficult by the fact that in most analyses only a very few policies are considered, sometimes even only one, rather than the overall scope of the policy package. Looking at maternity and parental leaves without also looking at childcare-services coverage, for instance, provides only a very partial view of the available options.[13] As well, the specific function of income transfers and of taxation deserve closer attention, especially as crucial features of the institutional context within which dependencies and interdependencies across gender and generational lines are constituted.

In what follows, I will summarize the results of a comparative study that focused on how social policies frame gender and intergenerational arrangements in families within EU countries.[14]

WHAT INTERGENERATIONAL AND GENDER-SPECIFIC BEHAVIORS ARE EXPECTED BY SOCIAL POLICIES IN EU COUNTRIES?

Our 2010 study compared different sets of policies concerning both gender and intergenerational obligations, particularly in matters of care and financial maintenance. These include maternity and parental leave (duration and level of compensation), childcare coverage through publicly funded services, care leave for workers caring for a nonchild family member, care-related notional contributions toward pension benefits, survivor pensions, forms of couple's taxation, and payments for care. The countries studied were twenty-three EU countries plus Norway.[15]

Not surprisingly, given the complex set of policies taken into consideration, no clear-cut clustering of countries emerged. Three broadly distinct approaches did, however, stand out with regard to the balance struck between, on the one hand, familialism by default, supported familialism, and defamilialization and, on the other, commodification and decommodification. Within each group, countries tend to differ in one or more policy, and some countries lie on the boundary between two different approaches. Furthermore, a substantial number of countries appear to be so internally heterogeneous that assigning them to one or the other approach would be highly misleading. This is partly because, in most countries, approaches differ with regard to upward and downward obligations as well as with regard to obligations of finance and care. Without erasing their differences, table 9.1 summarizes the main policy dimensions across which groups of countries appear to be more similar.[16]

The first policy approach that emerges with a fair degree of clarity is the mix between supported familialism (relatively long and well-paid parental leaves), decommodified defamilialization in the case of childcare (comparatively high childcare coverage), and decommodified defamilialization (comparative high service coverage) in the case of care for the elderly. This approach is present in Denmark, Norway, and Sweden. It clearly supports a dual-breadwinner model as well as the principle of individual financial autonomy for both sexes. It also supports autonomy (defamilialization) between adult generations, both financially and with regard to care. This expectation is even inscribed in law, in so far as legal obligations to provide support are restricted to

Country-specific policy approaches at the crossroads of familialism/defamilialization and commodification/decommodification

Prevalent policy approach	Decommodification of care through supported familialism		Decommodified defamilization of care		Rebalancing gender responsibilities in childcare[5]	Acknowledgment of unpaid family care in contributions		Fiscal support for male-breadwinner household[6]
	Child[1]	Old[2]	Child[3]	Old[4]		Child	Old	
Strong DF/weak SF								
Denmark	+	-	++	++	=	-	-	+
Norway	+	=	+	++	+	+	-	-
Sweden	+	-	++	+	+	+	-	-
Strong SF/weak DF								
Austria	=	+	+	+	-	++	++	+
Czech Republic	++	+	—	+	-	+	+	++
Germany	=	+	-	+	+	+	+	++
Estonia	+	+	=	+	=	+	-	+
Hungary	++	+	—	-	=	+	-	-
Lithuania	++	+	—	-	=	+	+	-
Luxembourg	=	=	-	=	++	++	++	++
Slovakia	-	+	-	-	-	++	++	+
Weak SP and SF								
Greece	=	-	—	-	+	+	-	-
Italy	-	+	-	-	=	++	-	+
Latvia	=	=	=	-	=	+	-	-
Poland	-	+	—	-	-	++	++	++
Portugal	-	+	-	+	=	+	-	++

(continued)

TABLE 9.1 (*continued*)

	Decommodification of care through supported familialism	Decommodified defamilization of care	Rebalancing gender responsibilities in childcare[5]	Acknowledgment of unpaid family care in contributions	Fiscal support for male-breadwinner household[6]
Spain	-	-	-	+	+
Internally divergent					
Belgium	+	++	=	++	++
Finland	+	=	=	missing	-
France	=	++	-	+	++
Ireland	——	-	=	+	++
Netherlands	=	++	+	-	+
Slovenia	+	=	=	missing	-
United Kingdom	+	=	=	+	+

NOTE: DF = defamilialization; SF = supported familialism

[1] The value ++ is assigned when the effective leave is 72 weeks or over, + when it is between 52 and 71 weeks, = when it is between 26 and 51 weeks, - when it is between 15 and 25 weeks, and —— when it is below 15 weeks.

[2] The value + is assigned when there is a caring allowance either of free use or specifically aimed at compensating a family member.

[3] The value ++ is assigned when coverage is 61% and over, + when it is between 40 and 60%, = when it is between 30% and 39%, - when it is between 15% and 29%, and —— when it is below 15%. Reference is to children 0–3.

[4] The value ++ is assigned when coverage through services (directly or through allowances enabling one to buy services) is 20% or above, the value + when coverage reaches 10% but is below 20%, and the value - when coverage is below 10%.

[5] The value ++ is assigned when the reserved quota for fathers is up to six months and is paid at 60% or over of lost wages; the value + when the paid quota is up to two months; the value = when the leave is well paid but there is no reserved quota (or very short, as in the case of Finland) or when the reserved quota is substantial but the parental leave is compensated at a low rate. The value - is assigned when there is neither a reserved quota nor a good compensation of the parental leave.

[6] The value ++ is assigned in case of income splitting and + when there are tax deductions for the financially dependent spouse. The value - is assigned when there is individual taxation with no allowance for a financially dependent spouse.

parents of underage children. Explicit support for a rebalancing of the gender responsibilities in care giving, through a take-it-or-leave-it fathers' quota in parental leave, is also present in this approach, except in Denmark, where no such quota exists. In all these countries, however, there is little acknowledgment of unpaid family work through notional contributions toward a pension, survivor pensions, leave for elderly care, or cash-for-care allowances.

The second comparatively clear approach is more ambivalent concerning intergenerational and gender-specific expectations, given its strong orientation toward supported familialism and a comparatively weak decommodified defamilialization through services in childcare. In the case of care for the frail elderly, this model is characterized by default familialism, with weak supported familialism through cash-for-care payments and care-leave entitlements. This approach emerges most clearly in Austria, the Czech Republic, Germany, and Luxembourg. In Estonia, Hungary, Lithuania, and Slovakia, the policy framework is similar, although with a somewhat different balance. In particular, Hungary and the Czech Republic, followed by Estonia, have the highest degree of supported familialism through both leave and transfers in the case of children. But in the case of the elderly, they are nearer to the familialism-by-default approach, since they have very little both in the way of services and cash allowances. The supported-familialism approach in childcare seems to encourage mothers to remain formally attached to the labor market by granting lengthy job protection through long—and in some cases, very long—paid parental leave, but with reduced childcare coverage after that leave expires. This combination makes it difficult for mothers to return to work. Incentives for fathers to share a portion of parental leave are usually absent or weak in this group of countries, with the exception of Luxembourg and, since 2008, Germany. Finally, the negative tradeoff between earning and care giving for women is partly compensated in old age by survivor pensions and by noncontributory equivalents for periods spent caring for both children and the frail elderly.

The third approach is found in countries that leave a large amount of room for familialism by default (and therefore also through defamilialization via the market for those who can afford it), since decommodification in these countries is weak, whether through supported familialism or publicly supported defamilialization. This approach does not actively support women's financial autonomy and only offers limited protection from the financial costs of the gender division of labor. Greece, Latvia, Italy, and Poland—albeit in varying combinations—display this pattern most clearly. Poland has both one of the shortest effective leaves and one of the lowest levels of childcare and elderly-care coverage through social services in the European Union. It also offers no incentives for a rebalancing of gender roles in childcare. Within this group of countries, Greece (at least until 2010) stands out in offering a comparatively strong incentive for fathers to take a portion of parental leave, since the first three months are compensated at around 60 percent of lost wages. But in Greece, even before the financial crisis, there were few other measures supporting the care needs both of young children and the frail elderly, either in the form of supported familialism or of decommodified defamilialization.

As well, in Greece and Latvia the acknowledgment of caring time through noncontributory equivalents is low and restricted only to the care of children. Survivors' pensions are also low. Italy has a less generous parental-leave policy and weaker incentives for fathers than both Greece and Latvia, while also having a low rate of decommodified defamilialization for both children under three and the elderly. Although the taxation and child-benefit systems in Poland consistently disadvantage women's earnings at the lower end of the income scale, in Italy and Spain there is a contradiction between individualization at the level of taxation and, at the same time, the household-income test for qualification for child benefits. Portugal, notwithstanding its comparatively high women's employment rate, offers a short effective leave, coupled with a low provision for childcare services and a fiscal system that supports financially asymmetrical couples. Within this group of countries, Spain and Portugal are the most dynamic, since in recent (precrisis) years they have attempted to raise the degree of defamilialization in the case of the frail elderly through payments for purchasing care services. Portugal is actually an outlier in this group, given its higher level of decommodified defamilialization for the old. All of these countries also have cash-for-care measures for the elderly, with no limitation on its use (a form of implicit supported familialism).

While the boundaries between the second and third approach are largely a matter of degree, it is difficult to assign many of the countries under consideration to any of the three approaches, since they appear to be internally divided between supporting a dual-earner model through decommodified defamilialization (even if at the cost of not fully acknowledging unpaid family care) and a modified form of the male-breadwinner/female-carer model. France, for example, offers a degree of decommodified defamilialization of childcare that is very similar to that of the Nordic countries, and it also comes close to these countries in its elderly-care policies. It likewise recognizes care-giving periods in the pension scheme (restricted to the care of children, as in Sweden), but only as an alternative to work-related contributions, which is, indirectly, a way of defining caring as an alternative to paid work. At the same time, in contrast to the Nordic countries, the French fiscal system supports asymmetrical couples, although to a lesser extent than the German system. It also includes long intergenerational financial obligations in its civil code. In the Netherlands, financial support and public long-term care provisions for the frail elderly belong to the first approach, while childcare measures (parental leave and care services for children under the age of three) are more closely linked to the second approach. Belgium appears even more defamilialized than the Nordic countries with regard to childcare coverage but not in parental leave, which compared to other EU countries is of rather short duration. In taxation, acknowledgment of care giving in pension schemes, survivor pensions, and elderly care, Belgium is similar to Germany and thus also to the second approach. Finland, Ireland, Slovenia, and the United Kingdom occupy an intermediate position on all or most policy measures.

Overall, the Nordic countries seem to offer the most consistent framework for both supporting autonomy between adult generations and promoting gender equality within families. They offer, however, little recognition of unpaid carework when the care recipients are not young children. No leave provisions for the caring needs of a seriously disabled family member are available in these countries, except in the case of a medical prognosis of death. Given the acknowledgment of civil unions and same-sex marriages in these countries, social policies in principle do not discriminate among married, unmarried, heterosexual, or same-sex partners and parents.

The second approach offers a much higher degree of acknowledgment of unpaid family care (and possibly of the wish to provide it), but within a framework that, with a fairly high degree of consistency, presumes and supports both intergenerational interdependencies and a gendered division of labor, along with its attendant costs for women's labor-market participation and women's financial autonomy. The countries belonging to this group include both those where same-sex couples may have a legal status and countries (Lithuania and Slovakia) where they do not, and therefore where they are denied access to the same family-linked social rights as heterosexual couples and parents.

The third approach, with its low degree of both decommodified defamilialization and decommodified supported familialism, is clearly the least favorable model, both from a gender-equality perspective and with a view toward intergenerational autonomy, as evidenced by not only the great dependence of the frail adults on their children's support but also by the longer dependency of the young on their parents. By default, extended familialism strengthens social inequalities among households and among women. The scarcity of services, in fact, strengthens the economic differences between those who can afford commodified defamilialization through recourse to the market and those who cannot. The large recourse to the migrant care-labor market, which not by chance has developed particularly in the Mediterranean countries characterized by weak decommodified defamilialization, is not equally available to all households.[17] This particular group of countries also includes the highest number of those not providing any legal status for same-sex couples or the nongenetic parents within them: Italy (where same-sex couples, but not same-sex parents, have been acknowledged a legal status since May 2016), Latvia, and Poland.[18] In these three countries, therefore, the two actual parents cannot share parental leave; the nongenetic parent has no legal obligation to support his or her children; and, now with the exception of Italy, the surviving partner is not entitled to a survivor's pension.

The first conclusion to draw from the consolidated picture outlined here is that national policies continue to promote different family arrangements across the European Union, along both intergenerational and gender lines, which constrain the transferability of social rights across borders. The so-called European social model, which should underpin European citizenship, is actually fragmented in the area of those social rights most closely associated with family relationships. This differentiation appears particularly resilient in the face of decades of EU interventions in the area of gender equality, women's employment, and childcare. This resilience suggests that perhaps national policy frameworks are not easily changed by directives and recommendations, at least not without substantial changes at other levels: in the broader culture, the labor market, and in the minds of major policy players.

A second lesson we can draw from this integrated analysis is that, despite the wide differentiation of policy approaches across the European Union, a measure of convergence is currently emerging. We can observe this convergence in social policies directed toward the care of young children. With varying degrees of enthusiasm and at different levels of consistency, all the countries under consideration here seem to agree on a shared family-state responsibility for the care of the very young through a mixture of supported familialism (leave and child benefits) and partial defamilialization. Distinctions persist concerning the duration and compensation of parental leave as well as concerning the incentives for fathers to take a share of it. That is, there are significant differences in the duration and gender specificity of policies that lend themselves toward supported familialism in the area of childcare as well as the degree of (partial) defamilialization for very young children. The notion of the care needs of the old as a public responsibility seems to be less universally acknowledged across the European Union. Actually, even in the most generous countries, those boasting a longer tradition of intervention in this field, budget constraints in the face of an aging population have motivated cuts in the services offered, thus inducing a partial recommodification and/or refamilialization of the care needs of the elderly.[19] At the same time and contrary to developments in childcare, in most countries the income security of the old has been weakened for new cohorts entering pension age because of pension reforms that have changed criteria for entitlements.

While families are shrinking because of a demographic shift toward an older population, they might nevertheless be expected to take up a larger portion of the responsibility for caring for elderly family members, as in many cases they are already doing for those young people caught in the midst of a long economic crisis that has complicated their transition to autonomy. In many countries, there is no specific financial support for family carers. The leave instrument, which is the cornerstone of supported familialism in the case of children, exists in only a few countries for the care of an old relative—Austria, Belgium, Germany, and Italy—and with the exception of Italy, it is mostly unpaid. But the increase in women's labor-force participation, as well as the rise in the statutory retirement age in most EU countries, will render this instrument increasingly necessary, particularly if the availability of services is reduced.

These differences in policies concerning family arrangements complicate those that already exist in civil law. As a result, in a geographical and political area premised on the principle of internal mobility, family arrangements are not always transferable, both at the legal level and with regard to the social rights attached to them. A Swedish father working in Italy might discover that if he wants to take parental leave he must do it without compensation, even though in his native country he would be entitled to two fully compensated months. Reconciling having a job and a preschool child are widely different matters for a Danish mother and a Polish one. Having a large family does not pose the same economic burden for low-wage workers in France, Spain, or Italy, given the great differences in child-linked income transfers in those countries. All things being equal, growing old presents quite distinct risks for individuals and families depending on where one lives in the European Union. A Dutch same-sex partner of an Italian man or woman may discover that he or she can neither adopt the child of his or her partner nor ask for parental leave in Italy, even if the couple was married in the Netherlands and both are acknowledged as parents in that country. An employee working for a Belgian firm in Italy and living in a same-sex partnership may not be entitled to paternity leave if she or he is the nongenetic parent of a child belonging to that person's partner, although this hypothetical worker would certainly be entitled to it in Belgium, where same-sex marriage exists. Examples abound of this kind of nontransferability of social rights.

The differences in civil and social rights across the European Union, and what is at times the impossibility of applying them across borders, weakens the idea of a common European citizenship, at least in the crucial sphere of individual life. From this perspective, the European Union is similar to the United States, which also displays interstate differences at the level of legal and social policy. But while the welfare state is a far more robust entity in the European Union than in the United States, there is an increasing imbalance across Europe in the strictness with which the European Union enforces its rules on member countries regarding social-policy targets, particularly when it comes to family arrangements. Except for the directive on maternity and parental leave, all other targets in this field, if they are brought up at all, are consigned to the level of recommendations. This failure to establish universal social rights across the European Union is an even greater problem in the field of civil law. The only exceptions to this failure are matters of fundamental rights or nondiscrimination, in which case the European Court is called upon to adjudicate the matter.

This is not to say that nothing changes or that there are no trends toward convergence within the geographical and political space of the European Union. Discussion within the European Union, as well as the complex web of directives and recommendations issuing from the EU government itself, have helped delineate an ideal model of family arrangements, particularly when it comes to the care of young children. Both the European Court and the European Court for Human Rights are playing an important role in pushing for changes in national laws concerning family arrangements, particularly with regard to same-sex couples. Yet each country is moving at its own pace and finding different solutions. Not all families or all family relationships have the same acknowledged status across the European Union; they constitute a vulnerable and only partially acknowledged dimension of EU citizenship.

NOTES

1. Margarita León and Mauro Migliavacca, "Italy and Spain: Still the Case of Familistic Welfare Models?" *Population Review* 52, no. 1 (2013): 25–42.
2. Manuela Naldini and Chiara Saraceno, *Conciliare famiglia e lavoro. Nuovi patti tra i sessi e le generazioni* (Bologna: Mulino, 2011).
3. Mary Daly, "Changing Family Life in Europe: Significance for State and Society," *European Societies* 7, no. 3 (2005): 379–398; Giuliano Bonoli, "Time Matters: Postindustrialization, New Social Risks, and Welfare-State Adaptation in Advanced Industrial Democracies," *Comparative Political Studies*, 40, no. 5 (2007): 495–520; Margitta Mätzke and Ilona Ostner, "Introduction: Change and Continuity in Recent Family Policies," special issue of *Journal of European Social Policy* 20, no. 5 (2010).
4. Göran Therborn, *Between Sex and Power: Family in the World, 1900–2000* (New York: Routledge, 2004).
5. Daly, "Changing Family Life in Europe"; Ann Orloff, "From Maternalism to 'Employment for All': State Policies to Promote Women's Employment Across the Affluent Democracies," in *The State After Statism*, ed. Jonah Levy (Cambridge, Mass.: Harvard University Press, 2006), 230–271.
6. For the conceptual development of these dimensions, see Sigrid Leitner, "Varieties of Familialism: The Caring Function of the Family in Compara-

tive Perspective," *European Societies* 5, no. 4 (2003): 353–375; Chiara Saraceno, "Gendered Policies: Family Obligations and Social Policies in Europe," in *Gender, Welfare State, and the Market*, ed. Thomas P. Boje and Arnlaug Leira (London: Routledge, 2000), 135–156; Chiara Saraceno, "Family Change, Family Policies, and the Restructuring of Welfare," in *Family, Market, and Community: Equity and Efficiency in Social Policy* [1997], ed. OECD, Social Policy Studies 21 (Paris: OECD, 2000), 81–100; Chiara Saraceno, "Social Inequalities in Facing Old-Age Dependency: A Bigenerational Perspective," *Journal of European Social Policy* 20, no. 1 (2010): 32–44; Chiara Saraceno and Wolfgang Keck, "Can We Identify Intergenerational Policy Regimes in Europe?" *European Societies* 12, no. 5 (June 2010): 675–696; Chiara Saraceno and Wolfgang Keck, "Towards an Integrated Approach for the Analysis of Gender Equity in Policies Supporting Paid Work and Care Responsibilities," *Demographic Research* 25, no. 11 (2011): 371–406.

7. The concept of commodification/decommodification was first introduced by Gøsta Esping-Andersen, *The Three Worlds of Welfare Capitalism* (Oxford: Polity, 1990); Gøsta Esping-Andersen, *Social Foundations of Postindustrial Economies* (New York: Oxford University Press, 1999). The intersection of this divide with the familialization/defamilialization one has been first suggested by Ann S. Orloff, "Gender and the Social Rights of Citizenship: The Comparative Analysis of Gender Relations and Welfare States," *American Sociological Review* 58, no. 3 (1993): 308–328.

8. As Orloff and others have pointed out. See Orloff, "Gender and the Social Rights of Citizenship."

9. See Rosemary Crompton, *Employment and the Family: The Reconfiguration of Work and Family Life in Contemporary Societies* (Cambridge: Cambridge University Press, 2006).

10. Walter Korpi, "Faces of Inequality: Gender, Class, and Pattern of Inequalities in Different Types of Welfare States," *Social Politics* 7, no. 2 (2000): 127–191.

11. Arnlaug Leira, "Childcare in Scandinavia: Parental Responsibility and Social Right," *L'Homme Z.F.G.* 19, no. 1 (2008): 81–103; Arnlaug Leira and Chiara Saraceno, "Care: Actors, Relationships, and Contexts," in *Contested Concepts in Gender and Social Politics*, ed. Barbara Hobson et al. (Cheltenham: Edward Elgar, 2002), 55–83.

12. The pioneering comparative works in this perspective have been those by Jane Millar and Andrea Warman, *Family Obligations in Europe* (London: Family Policies Study Centre, 1996); Anneli Anttonnen and Jorma Sipilä, "European Social Care Services: Is It Possible to Identify Models?" *Journal of European Social Policy* no. 2 (1996): 87–100; Anneli Anttonnen, John

Baldock, and Jorma Sipilä, *The Young, the Old, and the State: Social-Care Systems in Five Industrial Nations* (Cheltenham: Edward Elgar, 2003).
13. As demonstrated in the pioneering analyses of Janneke Plantenga, Chantal Remery, Melissa Siegel, and Loredana Sementini, "Childcare Services in 25 European Union Member States: The Barcelona Targets Revisited," in *Childhood: Changing Contexts*, ed. Leira Arnaugh and Chiara Saraceno (Bingley: Jay Press/Emerald, 2007).
14. The study was part of a larger, EU-funded project on intergenerational relationships coordinated by Pearl Dykstra—the Multilinks Project. Within it, a database on what have been identified as policies dealing with intergenerational obligations within families has been constructed; it can be found at http://multilinks-database.wzb.eu/info/project-info. The detailed results of this particular study have been published in various publications, namely, Saraceno, "Social Inequalities in Facing Old-Age Dependency"; Saraceno and Keck, "Can We Identify Intergenerational Policy Regimes in Europe?"; Saraceno and Keck, "Towards an Integrated Approach for the Analysis of Gender Equity in Policies Supporting Paid Work and Care Responsibilities"; and Wolfgang Keck and Chiara Saraceno, "The Impact of Different Social-Policy Frameworks on Social Inequalities Among Women in the European Union: The Labour-Market Participation of Mothers," *Social Politics: International Studies in Gender, State & Society* 20, no. 3 (2013): 297–328.
15. Because of insufficient data, Bulgaria, Cyprus, Malta, and Romania had to be excluded from the analysis. The data on which the analysis is based may be found at the Multilinks database.
16. Childcare coverage (column 3) refers only to services for children under three, since this is the age group where there are the largest cross-country differences; see Saraceno and Keck, "Can We Identify Intergenerational Policy Regimes in Europe?"
17. Francesca Bettio, Annamaria Simonazzi, and Paola Villa, "Change in Care Regimes and Female Migration: The 'Care Drain' in the Mediterranean," *Journal of European Social Policy* 16, no. 3 (2006): 271–285; Manuela Naldini and Chiara Saraceno, "Social and Family Policies in Italy: Not Totally Frozen but Far from Structural Reforms," *Social Policy & Administration* 42, no. 7 (2008): 733–748; Franca Van Hooren, "Varieties of Migrant Care Work: Comparing Patterns of Migrant Labour in Social Care", in *Journal of European Social Policy* 22, no. 2 (2010): 133–147.
18. Bulgaria, Cyprus, and Romania, not included in this analysis, also do not acknowledge same-sex couples.
19. Clare Ungerson, "Whose Empowerment and Independence? A Cross-National Perspective on 'Cash for Care' Schemes," *Ageing & Society* 24

(2004): 189–212; Emmanuele Pavolini and Costanzo Ranci, "Restructuring the Welfare State: Reforms in Long-Term Care in Western European Countries," *Journal of European Social Policy* 18, no. 3 (2008): 246–259; Saraceno, "Social Inequalities in Facing Old-Age Dependency"; Patricia Frericks, Per H. Jensen, and Birgit Pfau-Effinger, "Social Rights and Employment Rights Related to Family Care: Family Care Regimes in Europe," *Journal of Aging Studies* 29 (2014): 66–77.

CHAPTER TEN

Transforming Gendered Labor Policies in Sweden and the United States, 1960s–2000s

ANN SHOLA ORLOFF

ACROSS THE WEST—or the "Two Wests," to adopt the language of this volume—systems of social provision and regulation (my preferred term for what are often called "welfare states") increasingly promote maternal employment. This is a striking change in both social policy and the gendered division of labor: gone is the legal and political framework—a mix of positive supports and discriminatory provisions—undergirding men's breadwinning and women's housewifery, primary care giving, and sometimes paid employment of the last century. This is one of the most significant political transformations of our time. It is a good time to think anew about how to attain gender equality and women's liberation in the shadow of rising economic inequalities but also, with reinvigorated feminist activism, about the possibility of new opportunities for emancipatory feminist projects. How might these be affected by social-policy shifts toward mandating, and sometimes supporting, maternal employment? What are the prospects for feminist redesigns of work and care?

To investigate these processes of transformation and better understand the prospects for feminist initiatives, I examine gendered policy formation and change over the last half-century in the United States and Sweden. I focus on *gendered labor policies*, conceptualized as those that affect the levels and quality of mothers' and fathers' employment and unpaid care giving; the division of domestic and care-giving labor between men and women within and across households, regions, and countries; and the links between patterns of labor and men's and women's access to power and valued resources and their capacities for autonomy. This set of policies overlaps with "family policy," including parental leave, social assistance for solo mothers, or family allowances but also includes the regulation of discrimination in employment.

The United States and Sweden are two countries to which scholars return again and again as ideal types of different approaches to both social provision and gender equality: the United States as a paragon of liberal-feminist interventions focusing on equal opportunities in the labor market, with very little public support to care giving or work-family "reconciliation," and Sweden as the exemplar of social-democratic policies promoting maternal employment and offering extensive public supports to women's care giving, alongside encouragement to fathers' care. These policy differences reflect other long-standing dissimilarities in the two countries' partisan complexion, state structure, legal systems, place in the international system of states, religious legacies, and perceived ethnic and racial composition, as well as more specific orientations to matters of gender, family, and reproduction. Yet one can point to some intriguing similarities, including their convergence around logics of maternal employment and in the break, among the majority of feminists, from the maternalist views of their first-wave predecessors. In contrast, in other rich democracies in continental Europe (save France), policies in support of maternal employment have emerged more recently and are still troubled by secular-religious conflicts and the recalcitrance of Catholic political forces.[1] Both have strong and globally influential feminist movements, formal commitments to gender equality, and political elites who see themselves as global leaders in gender equality. Analysts often compare different states' policies to see which is "better" for women or for gender equality, but I prefer to use the comparison as an occasion for considering divergent political constraints and opportunities. Those dedicated to greater social justice and to women's equality and freedom, too, share an interest in competing models, even if they are not fully transposable.

Many think of the transformation of gendered labor policies as a single process of progressive change.[2] Yet I argue that shifts in the dominant logic of gendered labor policies are best thought of as encompassing two sets of changes, powered by distinctive forces.[3] The first set dismantled explicitly gender-differentiated welfare states by eliminating supports to men's breadwinning and (some) women's full-time, lifelong care giving, along with the discriminatory legal apparatuses that kept women from full economic citizenship. The second set has expanded women's economic opportunities and the supports for maternal employment in varying ways and may be coupled with the encouragement of men's care giving. It is important to note that these processes have not necessarily been sequential.

In this essay, I provide an overview of developments in the United States and Sweden with respect to several key policy areas: parental leave and childcare, regulation of employment to eliminate gender discrimination, social assistance, and taxation. The historical narratives are relatively well known; my purpose is not to unearth new facts about the events. Rather, examining both countries' policy trajectories in terms of two distinctive processes will give greater clarity about what has happened, will allow for more precise explanations of *why* these distinctive sets of changes have occurred, and may also contribute to thinking about what new changes would be desirable and possible.

CHALLENGING THE BREADWINNER-HOUSEWIFE LOGIC IN GENDERED LABOR POLICIES IN THE 1960S AND 1970S

Policies supporting women's lifelong and full-time care giving and housewifery and men's breadwinning were fatally weakened in both the United States and Sweden in the 1960s and 1970s. This was an era in which second-wave feminists and their allies articulated visionary gender-egalitarian projects, imagining a set of state social policies that would support women's equal citizenship, with many common elements: expanded access for women to better employment opportunities, childcare, parental leave, encouragement of men's care, and changing workplace organization to accommodate "encumbered workers." But, as we know all too well, the patterns of successes and setbacks varied considerably. Yet in both polities, policy shifted toward supporting maternal employment, albeit more unevenly in the United States than in Sweden.

In Sweden in these decades, governments were controlled largely by the Sveriges socialdemokratiska arbetareparti (Social Democratic Workers' Party of Sweden), or SAP, while U.S. Democrats shared power with Republicans. Democrats were more favorable to legal changes promoting gender equality than was the GOP, but the Democratic Party did not resemble the SAP as a relatively united actor dedicated to gender equality and able to access significant state capacities for the formulation and implementation of gendered labor policies promoting maternal employment. U.S. feminists organized across a range of organizations and operated as a "sophisticated interest group," agitating for a range of policies quite similar to those supported by Swedish feminists, most of whom worked inside the SAP.[4]

Let's start with the processes that eroded and, in some cases, eliminated support for policies organized around logics of gender difference and inequality, such as those that sustained breadwinner-housewife/caregiver households. In both the United States and Sweden, feminists, political and economic elites, union members, and judges came to see gender-differentiated policies as discriminatory rather than protective. This era saw the overturning of "protective" labor legislation, which had been premised on the priority of women's marital and reproductive functions and supported by early-twentieth-century labor and social-justice feminists concerned about harsh industrial conditions.[5] By the 1960s, many saw such laws as "discrimination": they prevented women from accessing all occupations, including those with better remuneration and opportunities for upward mobility.[6] Explicitly gender-based provisions in social-insurance programs were also overturned, and programs were made "gender-neutral," although the structural advantages enjoyed by programs for wage earners as compared with those for caregivers remained.[7] Of particular significance in both countries in the early 1960s were government commissions on women's status, which examined women's situations, helped initiate far-reaching political changes that overturned discriminatory provisions in both social-insurance and workplace regulations, and unraveled supports for women's full-time and lifelong care giving and men's breadwinning privileges.[8]

In the United States, a Democrat-controlled Congress, supported by the courts, passed relatively strong forms of action against discrimination, such as the Equal Pay Act of 1963 (an amendment to the Fair Labor Standards Act), which forbade explicit wage disparity based on sex; the 1964 Civil Rights Act (combining action against racial and sex discrimination), which established the Equal Employment Opportunities Commission (EEOC), a federal agency to enforce laws against workplace discrimination; and the 1978 Pregnancy Discrimination Act, which outlawed discrimination on the basis of pregnancy and required that it be treated as are temporary disabilities. The EEOC, with pressure from women's and civil-rights movements, became for a time an important actor in promoting equality in employment, and the courts emerged as significant regulators of gendered employment practices.[9] Discrimination in education was targeted in Title IX of the 1972 Education Amendments (to the Higher Education Act of 1965); as women gained credentials, they were able to enter formerly masculine professional positions in much greater numbers. These efforts, assisted by government affirmative-action programs, paved the way for well-situated women to enter the upper ranks of corporations and to gain entrance to the armed forces, police and firefighting units, and, sometimes, the skilled crafts. Feminists, spurred by the feminist legal theorist Catharine MacKinnon, named sexual harassment as an element of sex discrimination and succeeded in gaining regulations that effectively outlawed many of these practices.[10]

Swedish feminists also targeted employment discrimination but made use of different modalities than did Americans, and they had less success in establishing a strong antidiscrimination framework in the labor market. The social partners, rather than the courts, eliminated gender-discriminatory wage classifications. "In the early 1960s, LO (the Landsorganisationen i Sverige, the blue-collar trade-union confederation) and the Swedish Employers' Association (SAF) negotiated an end to a separate women's wage classification" and coupled this with the LO's solidarity-wage policies to improve the wages of the lowest-paid workers, disproportionately women.[11] More direct efforts to regulate the workplace to promote gender equality (including efforts against sexual harassment) were rebuffed, leaving these concerns in the hands of labor-market partners.[12]

Feminists first proposed the elimination of joint taxation in the late 1960s as part of an expansive menu of policy changes to bring greater gender equality. Although it provoked negative reactions from many housewives who wanted to keep the family as an economic unit, the

Social Democratic Women's Federation split on the question. Alva Myrdal and others argued for individual taxation as a liberating force for working-class women and ultimately prevailed in 1970.[13] U.S. tax policy, however, was not targeted for similar changes until the 1980s, and joint taxation has been retained even as contradictory provisions such as dependent-care tax credits have been enacted.[14]

In Sweden, one of the key pillars of maternalism—employment-linked maternity insurance—was eliminated simultaneously with the construction of the much-heralded gender-neutral, paid parental leave, a key element of support for maternal employment and work-family reconciliation. But in the United States, there was no policy legacy of support to maternal employment, nor any health-insurance program in which maternity coverage might have been extended to include income support for new mothers or new parents.[15] In the 1960s and 1970s, political struggles around ending policies that supported (some) women's full-time and lifelong care giving to support maternal employment converged on proposals to reform the one social-assistance program offering support to (very poor, single, and disproportionately racial and ethnic minority) parents of young children: Aid to Families with Dependent Children (AFDC, or "welfare"). AFDC was the "maternalist" policy that in practice came closest to Sweden's employment-linked maternity insurance, but, critically, it was both targeted (on very low-income and unpartnered mothers) and not formally linked to employment. The original model for AFDC had been support for full-time care giving until children reached adulthood. As the program expanded, it became, de facto, a form of maternity leave and unemployment insurance for unpartnered poor women. Yet the program's stigma and work disincentives discouraged any thought of expanding it to create parental leave for all mothers or parents.

Hesitation about destroying support for full-time care giving in a racially divisive and highly unequal context undercut policy proposals making AFDC into a program to mandate and support maternal employment. Indeed, nonfeminist reformers on the center and left had not given up on the "traditional" gender division of labor, and there were continuing concerns about breadwinner families among poor African Americans.[16] The Aid to Dependent Children–Unemployed Parent (ADC-UP) program—an extension of "welfare" that was supposed to help more two-parent families with unemployed fathers, understood as largely black and poor—remained extremely marginal after it was enacted in 1961.[17] Advisors to President Richard Nixon proposed a program for the "working poor," based on the Negative Income Tax, the Family Assistance Plan (FAP).[18] The FAP would have helped many poor two-parent families, bolstering the position of poor employed men, who were disproportionately men of color. However, southern conservatives in Congress opposed it because of its projected effect on low-wage local labor markets.[19] The defeat of FAP fatally weakened the idea of using family policies to support breadwinning men; certainly, some American men have sustained breadwinning, but with little explicit policy support.[20]

Sweden did not provide large amounts of social assistance designed to allow poor single mothers to care for their children full time, because its policies operated on the assumption that single mothers would receive help as working parents.[21] The policy path to a care allowance for single mothers, that is, a policy similar to AFDC and one supported at various times by right-wing parties in Sweden, was not the "default" option, given the long-standing presumption that single mothers should be employed. And by 1981, the rationalization of general assistance decisively foreclosed the path, making it clear that care allowance was for last-resort cases, not to allow full-time care giving, although this occurred in a context of much greater support for all families.[22]

Let us now turn to the processes that brought in policies to support maternal employment, starting with paid parental leave. At its 1969 congress, the SAP endorsed innovative policy proposals aimed at encouraging a more equal sharing of care giving and supporting mothers' employment. By 1974, all parties supported the transformation of existing employment-linked maternity insurance into parental insurance with a very high replacement rate, thought necessary to encourage men to take up leaves. The Social Democratic Women's Federation argued for a shorter workday for all employed persons, as a way to enable care giving and to normalize the "encumbered" work life.[23] But this proposal was sidelined by SAP leaders, and eventually the bourgeois coalition government of the late 1970s "instituted a right for parents of young children to work part-time at part-time wages, firmly entrenching the work life that was normative for partnered parents—but inadequate for solo mothers."[24] In the United States, paid-leave legislation, though discussed among feminists, was not even introduced in Congress until

1984, when the Women's Legal Defense Fund first began to campaign for the program. It took ten years to get it passed, as Republicans and small-business organizations opposed the law.

Fierce debates accompanied the shift in the gender logic of U.S. social-assistance programs away from the formal support of full-time care giving to supporting and mandating (single) mothers' employment.[25] In the 1960s, only AFDC offered any kind of assistance to single parents with care-giving responsibilities that interfered with employment; most mothers faced the risks of income interruption due to childbirth and care giving on their own. Moreover, AFDC was administered in a racially discriminatory way, categorizing women of color as "employable mothers" who should work for pay; this helped reinforce views of full-time care giving as a privilege unjustly denied to people of color.[26] While AFDC's racial discrimination was successfully challenged in the 1960s, the program was politically embattled. Some argued for the employability of all mothers on welfare; others sought to support mothers' full-time care giving (or at least the option for women to stay out of employment to attend to their youngest children, something like parental leave). But this "pro–maternal employment" position came in conservative, "casework" or rehabilitative, and feminist variants, and disagreements among them stymied reform efforts.[27] Organized welfare mothers, predominantly African American, in the National Welfare Rights Organization opposed work requirements, but the concerns of the mainly employed women who made up most feminist organizations were not particularly congruent with the advocacy of "rights" to full-time care giving support.

The political quandaries posed by reforming AFDC blocked new policies designed to support employed mothers. After the election of President Richard Nixon in 1968, liberals lost control of the welfare debate. The outcome was a steadily increasing stream of work incentives, poorly enforced requirements for certain mothers to enter employment, and poorly resourced support services for working mothers—but never an expansion of social provision to help the employed poor and most two-parent families.[28]

Expansive, affordable, quality public childcare services were central elements of the Swedish gender-equality model, enabling maternal employment. The National Preschool Act of 1975 obligated public authorities to provide care services, and successive governments in this period expanded childcare.[29] Here, we see a clear contrast to the United

States, where the mixed orientations to mothers' employment undermined the expansion of childcare services. In 1971, at the height of feminist mobilizing in the United States, the Comprehensive Child Development Act was passed; it "declared that comprehensive child development programs should be available as a matter of right to all children regardless of economic, social, and family background, although priority would be given to those with the greatest economic and social need . . . [It] included federal standards for quality and money for training and the purchase of facilities."[30] But Nixon vetoed the bill, citing it as a "communistic" measure and unacceptable in the midst of the Cold War. After this, *public* childcare services were limited to a minority among the very poor, namely, welfare clients or those transitioning off welfare. In the following years, private services expanded greatly, drawing on the low-wage labor of the large flows of immigrants to the United States and fueled as well by dependent-care tax credits enacted in the 1980s.[31] One could see these private services as functionally analogous to Sweden's expanding public childcare in terms of supporting maternal employment, though with quite different implications for service quality and social inequalities.

DEVELOPING LOGICS OF MATERNAL EMPLOYMENT IN GENDERED LABOR POLICIES IN THE 1980S AND 1990S

Across the global North in the 1980s and beyond, neoliberal politics and the distancing of center-left parties from workers' organizations created a harsher climate for social provision, but gendered labor policies were a notable, if partial, exception, suffering less retrenchment and seeing some significant expansion of support for maternal employment. The policy developments of the 1960s and 1970s decisively shaped these later trajectories.

In the United States, political energy directed at reforming welfare, with its formal model of the full-time care-giving mother—and the ensuing racial bitterness—made the politics of supporting maternal employment divisive, including for feminists. Mounting pressure to institutionalize a model of maternal employment in social policy took the shape of bringing employment mandates to AFDC (and other welfare policies) and far less successful attempts to institutionalize supports for the paid work of all mothers and parents. Such expansion as did occur tended to work via tax credits. The United States had seen the expansion of antidiscrimination frameworks to encompass affirmative action, which encouraged women's employment but without family policies to help employed mothers in dealing with their care needs. The contradictory elements of U.S. gendered labor policies both reflected and sustained deep political, social, and cultural conflicts over ideals of motherhood, gender, race, and masculinity. The political parties became increasingly polarized over gender issues, sometimes coded as "culture wars."[32] These splits showed up in political struggles over the Equal Rights Amendment, abortion, reproductive technologies and rights, affirmative action, welfare, and tax policy; culturally, the notion of "mommy wars" pitted "stay-at-home moms" against "working" (i.e., employed) mothers.

In Sweden, as it became clear that simply opening generous parental leave to men was insufficient to unseat deeply entrenched gendered divisions of labor, government commissions and the wider society increasingly concluded that policies should be aimed at changing men by encouraging their care giving. In the ensuing two decades, Swedes pursued "daddy politics" and initiated innovative policies directed at encouraging men's care giving but not the strengthening of labor-market regulation. The politics of Swedish gendered labor policies were perhaps less fractious than their U.S. counterparts, but daddy politics did get some pushback from forces dedicated to modifying rather than eliminating the gendered division of carework. To the extent that center-right parties gained influence, they tried to introduce "choice" as an element of policy, driven by a different orientation to maternal employment: one more congruent with a "modified" gender division of labor in which women do more care than men but are still expected to be employed and not as an attack on the basic assumption that women would be employed.

In the United States, "welfare reform," that is, the retrenchment or elimination of women's entitlements accessed on the basis of carework and the restructuring of entitlements around employment mandates, dominated the policy landscape from 1980 until the 1996 fulfillment of President Bill Clinton's promise to "end welfare as we know it" with the passage of the Personal Responsibility and Work Opportunity Reconciliation Act (PRWORA) and the elimination of AFDC. Both presidents Ronald Reagan and George H. W. Bush garnered support from their constituencies with welfare cuts and tough talk but left in place a formal model of motherhood based on full-time care giving for at least some welfare recipients. In 1988, the Family Support Act (FSA) was passed, requiring all AFDC parents—mothers as well as fathers—with children three years of age and above to work or undergo training; states had the option of imposing the work requirement on parents of children as young as one year. Thus, poor women, disproportionately women of color, were expected to combine parenting and paid work. But the FSA looked more radical than it was; having incorporated what expert opinion said was needed to reduce "dependency" and to promote the employment of single mothers on welfare, it did not fulfill its goals, for actually enabling poor single mothers with often difficult caring needs and barriers to employment would have been extremely expensive, and few states were willing to pay. The picture of an essentially unreformed welfare system influenced public and elite opinion, and the FSA thus helped usher in more far-reaching reforms.

The "Third Way"–oriented Democratic Leadership Council and then-candidate Bill Clinton responded to Republicans' political successes in using welfare as a "wedge issue" with an "inoculation" strategy on welfare, which meant the abandonment of the Democrats' traditional defense of AFDC. Clinton entered office promising thoroughgoing changes to AFDC, such as a requirement for mothers to engage in paid employment, initially on a part-time basis and with government jobs offered if private employment was not available.[33] The PRWORA of 1996 eliminated AFDC, replacing it with Temporary Assistance to Needy Families (TANF), and it ended the entitlement, only firmly established in the 1960s and 1970s, of poor single parents, overwhelmingly mothers, to social assistance that allowed full-time care giving.[34] In addition to lifetime limits on welfare receipt, TANF required its beneficiaries, whatever the age of their children, to engage in some form of employment or community service (better known as "workfare") almost immediately and to be fully employed after two years. This act was a turning point in U.S. social policy that might be characterized as the demise of the maternalist strand of provision, bringing welfare in line with the regulation of employment in assuming that women, including mothers, would be employed.[35] The new work requirements were initially accompanied by increased funding for and the relaxed regulation of childcare, but "enabling" elements of the law, in contrast to often punitive regulation, have rarely been fully implemented.[36] Yet Clinton and policy advisors like David Ellwood were also committed to "making work pay," for mothers as well as fathers, through the expansion of the Earned Income Tax Credit (EITC).[37] The EITC was expanded several times during the 1980s and 1990s, raising both single mothers' employment rates and the incomes of poor employed parents, especially single mothers.[38]

In Sweden, social democrats' gender-equality rhetoric starkly contrasted with the reality of women taking the vast majority of parental leave.[39] It became clear to many that parental leave was far from sufficient to bring men to a full sharing of care giving and domestic work. Indeed, government commissions reporting in 1979, 1982, and 1990 pinpointed men as the primary source of inequality in families because they left responsibilities for children and household to women and thereby weakened women's position in the labor market. Governmental working groups developed proposals to encourage men to take up more care, paving the way for the "daddy politics" of the 1990s.[40]

Although the SAP was responsible for the extension of maternity into parental leave, Liberals initiated earmarked "daddy leaves," those distinctive elements of Nordic gender-equality policy. In 1990, the SAP government lost, and a center-right government—diverse in terms of family and gender politics—came to power; the Liberal Party, one of the coalition partners, was culturally quite radical. The government established a "Daddy Group" (officially, the Working Group on Fathers, Children, and Working Life), which in its 1993 report proposed a "daddy guarantee" of three months of parental leave to encourage men to assume more responsibility for care and to allow women to devote more time to the labor market. The rhetoric around the proposals drew from feminist analyses of the "gender system": for example, that part-time work and parental insurance allow women to give birth and to "reconcile" paid work and family work, but at the price of economic dependency and reproducing men's advantages.[41] Bengt Westerberg, the minister for social affairs and chairman of the Liberal Party, championed the introduction of the daddy month, a provision coming into force in 1994, whereby the parent who did not take the majority of the parental-leave entitlement (almost always the father) had a month earmarked for him/her, which would be lost if it was not taken ("use it or lose it").[42] The "daddy month" was supported across the political spectrum, with few exceptions.[43]

Parties of the center-right advocated care allowances for the majority of mothers as an alternative to the ideal of equally shared leave. This should be seen as reflecting a different orientation to mothers' employment than that of the Social Democrats but not as a return to the old breadwinner-housewife model. In the 1990s, Christian Democrats, who had initially opposed daddy leaves (an earmarked month or parental-leave "quotas"), demanded and won a payoff from their bourgeois coalition partners: a "cash-for-care" scheme, established in 1994. The care allowance was vehemently opposed by the SAP and feminists as antithetical to gender equality by undermining women's position in the labor market. Given politically imposed fiscal constraints, it could not be generous enough for men or single mothers to use it, and it only made sense within a two-parent family in which the father remained employed while the mother used the allowance.[44] The "cash-for-care" scheme was abolished after six months, when SAP returned to power, yet it was to return in the 2000s, again at the behest of an ideologically diverse center-right coalition government.[45]

Feminist policy activists introduced parental-leave legislation in the United States in the early 1980s, but progress in constructing support for maternal employment—or any workers' care-giving needs—had no political traction with Republican administrations. Parental leave was simply off the table until the 1990s, when Democrats returned to power. The Family and Medical Leave Act was the first bill signed into law by President Clinton, in 1993. Reflecting the fiscal and political constraints of the time (small-business interests in particular were resistant), the leave was (and still is) unpaid and limited to the employees of organizations employing more than fifty people. Income differences are critical for whether and how people can take leaves. Some argue that this de facto reinforces *women's* responsibility for carework, given their lower average incomes, but given the increasingly uneven distribution of income among women and men, husbands do not always earn more than their wives, and women who want to invest in their careers will sometimes resist this economic logic. The measure, despite its shortcomings, is notable in that it is an individual and gender-neutral entitlement rather than being tied to a family unit, as is the case with Sweden's parental leave. It leaves open the option for a fully individualized and paid leave to be enacted in the future, although for this to happen, some deep political changes will be needed.

The political difficulties of Bill Clinton's second term undermined momentum for progressive policy changes, and these were effectively stopped after the (contested) election of Republican President George Bush in 2000. National security was the dominant concern, but to the extent that the Bush administration dealt with gendered labor or welfare policies at all, it was to promote faith-based provision and private contracting. Reproductive rights suffered, and the enforcement of antidiscrimination law was lax at best. With social policy languishing nationally, some progressives worked at the state level, with limited success. In contrast, the declining fortunes of the SAP in the 2000s did not lead to the same blockage of gender-equality measures. This reflects a strong contrast in the character of right-wing parties and coalitions in the two countries. "Neoliberals"—economic liberals in Swedish terminology, fiscal conservatives in U.S. lingo—are very powerful in both. But in the United States, religiously oriented social conservatives were and are far more powerful within the Republican Party than such forces on the right side of the political spectrum in Sweden; in the United States, these forces have been significant in opposing supports for maternal employment, men's care giving, and women's reproductive rights. The Right in Sweden champions "choice" within family policies but does not position itself in opposition to gender-equality policies, as do some elements within the Republican Party. Explicit commitment to feminism characterizes the Left in Sweden, as the SAP followed the Left Party in declaring itself a feminist party in 2001; more recently, even center-right politicians have declared themselves feminists.[46]

The SAP-led government of the early 2000s, competing for women's votes, offered improvements to the existing policy framework of support to maternal employment and encouragement of men's care giving.[47] The persistent unequal sharing of leave between men and women continued to be a source of concern for feminists and social democrats but is more acceptable on the right. This fuels political debates about whether and how to promote fathers' care giving or greater "choice" around leaves. The bourgeois government, which succeeded the SAP in the mid-2000s, has broken from earlier gendered labor policies in one extremely important respect: they have introduced tax cuts for household services, which give extremely generous incentives to households to hire domestic workers. Vociferously opposed by the SAP, this policy has encouraged the expansion of migrant domestic labor and, according to some observers, could be a turning point in Swedish welfare provision, leading toward a less egalitarian approach to care.[48] Sweden moved a bit closer to the U.S. model of supporting the private provision of services through tax policies, and the policy appears to be opening up income differences in the type and quality of services parents can access.

With the election of Democrat Barack Obama as president in 2008, many antifeminist policies pursued by the GOP were reversed, and gender-equality concerns returned to the national agenda. Democrats' plans to promote gender equality have almost all been along the lines of improved labor-market regulation and enforcement of pay equity, however. The first law signed by President Obama was the Lily Ledbetter Act, which allowed women greater access to judicial remedies for discrimination but did little to address other concerns around gendered labor patterns, including severe care deficits and difficulties in balancing paid work and care. In a recent political initiative, "The White House Summit on Working Families," the Obama administration calls for a wide-ranging discussion of the needs of working families, but links are all to resources about pay equity.[49] Had a Democrat succeeded Obama, the increasing interest in paid leave might finally have yielded policy fruit, which would have marked an extremely important shift in U.S. gendered labor policies, finally complementing regulatory action in the labor market with some source of positive support for maternal employment through public support for care.

Those who would implement *feminist* gendered labor policies face divergent political challenges across different polities, including those created by past policy legacies and the distinctive trajectories by which they have been changed. Swedish feminists, especially in the SAP, had the advantage of earlier policy legacies supportive of women's employment as they sought to expand these policies to enable all women and men to earn and to care. Generous parental leaves were built on the basis of employment-related maternity allowances that had been developed as part of sickness funds for the employed population and later extended in the direction of offering universal maternity coverage (albeit at a basic level). The United States had no maternalist employment-enabling legacy on which to build, and it had to break with women's nonemployment as an ideal and race- and class-bound privilege. Sweden's policy legacy—in the context of a unified state structure and strong social-democratic party—was more available for gradual, expert-led reform in the direction of supporting mothers' employment than was the U.S. policy legacy, especially given the context of fragmented state structure and a weaker center-left party. Still, neither U.S. nor Swedish feminists can be satisfied with the current state of affairs.

Feminists and women reformers helped build a gendered system of social provision and regulation, although they were far from being the principal architects and worked from a position of relative political weakness. That system supported some women when the family wage system failed (when their husbands or fathers of their children could no longer be counted on due to death, desertion, or divorce), but it simultaneously created institutional barriers to women as they increasingly entered the paid labor force and sought advancement. As such, feminists bidding farewell to maternalism, under conditions of far greater political strength, has been a key part of the politics that have led to the destruction of many explicitly gender-differentiated programs and provisions. The risk of politics that destroy old institutional orders is that we do not always know that there will be a good, reliable replacement for what has been eliminated. This was clearly the case with U.S. welfare reform, when support for full-time care giving on the part of the most vulnerable populations was dismantled but supports for employed motherhood and parenthood were never guaranteed. Today, it is those guarantees we still seek. Sweden did not so fully dispense with maternalism as rework it in an attempt to make men as well as women "encumbered workers," that is, employees also engaged in care giving. But Swedish feminists face difficulties in transforming the workplace to allow workers who are also caregivers to advance; with women disproportionately taking leaves and reduced workdays, women continue as "junior partners" in terms of wage earning in coupled households or, when single, suffer from lower living standards. Work, although transformed, has not been regendered in a gender-egalitarian direction nor rendered entirely compatible with care . . . yet.

Whether new policies supporting maternal employment might develop in a more egalitarian direction remains an open question. On a political field characterized by "complex inequalities," including a global care chain that supplies care workers to deal with the outsourced responsibilities once performed by both Swedish and U.S. housewives, those who aspire to social justice will have to navigate policy reforms carefully. Many feminists support a dual-earner/dual-caregiver ideal, sometimes configured as "symmetrical parenthood," the notion underlying at least some proposals for restructured parental leave; others support fully individualized leave entitlements, which are being debated in Sweden and the other Nordic countries at the moment. Here, the idea is to find new levers for encouraging men's care and a gender-equal balancing of work and care. Yet some women resist the idea of giving up care-giving leaves as "women's rights," while others worry about "parental symmetry" being invoked as a component of national identity that may exclude some population groups, particularly migrants.[50]

A number of U.S. feminists would like nothing better than to bring the Swedish model of dual earner/dual caregiver to American shores.[51] But if achieving such a model is hard in Sweden, it is more so in the United States, for many reasons: the political gridlock characterizing our current politics, the lack of policies on which to build, and the greater diversity of gendered projects and practices. And given the poverty of supports available for maternity and care more generally, it is perhaps not surprising that for other U.S. feminists, maternalism remains a potent source of imagined capacities to deal better with intense paid work and under-resourced care responsibilities. They still long for the classed and racial privilege of work-life "balance," figured diversely: the baby nursery next to the CEO's office, the perfect nanny, or being supported financially by a partner who does not demand subservience in return for allowing a mother time to care.

I suggest that we work toward not an impossible gender symmetry nor a nostalgic maternalism but a *gender-open* approach, one that would dislodge stubborn gender hierarchies in a pluralist fashion, allowing for differences in how gender-egalitarian arrangements are imagined and lived. There are a number of normative considerations—having to do with diversity and inequality, democratic politics, and the depth of gender—upon which I can touch only briefly here.[52] Populations are becoming more diverse in terms of lifestyle and ideology and in terms of class, racial or ethnic, and religious forms of difference, inequality, and power. Moreover, people demand more "choice" over the arrangement of their life courses, with different visions of desirable gender relations. There are class, racial, ethnic, and religious differences in parents' capacities and desires to take parental leave or to make use of other policies geared to work-family reconciliation or women's employment advancement, and thus we should ask if democratic majorities want to remake gender to achieve "parental symmetry" or if they prefer some other vision of greater equality, perhaps one that is still gender differentiated.

Nancy Fraser has persuasively argued against a "universal-breadwinner" model, famously contending that women should not be "made into men."[53] Arguing instead for "a universal-caregiver" model that approximates the Swedish dual-earner/dual-caregiver ideal, she insisted that men should be "made into women," that is, what most women are now: encumbered workers. But if women cannot be made into "men" (wage earners only), why should we assume men can be made into "women" (worker/caregivers)? This argument ignores the cognitive, psychic, and cultural investments of both men and women in gender difference, even if we accept, as I do, that gender is constructed. Care and domestic labor are deeply gendered; even when men care, it is not usually seen as equivalent to women's care: it is "fathering" rather than "mothering."[54] This is not necessarily at odds with demands for gender equality, but it is quite possibly at odds with demands premised on parental symmetry. Of course, there are also differences among women and among men in inclinations and capacities around care, employment, and partnering. Investments in gender difference do not indicate all men or all women desire the same thing: partnered reproductive families in which each partner does equal caring and employment. This is all the more reason to pause before prescribing a "single norm of the socially useful person."[55] People want to "do" and "redo" gender differently: why not "gender openness" rather than gender symmetry or maternalism?

Gender openness is a pluralist and egalitarian vision of gender, care, and employment that respects diversity and democratic accountability, signaling the acceptance of a variety of life practices and choices among women and men in how they want to care, work, and partner. But such a vision will require public support to facilitate those practices and choices: policies such as individual sabbaticals or leaves for multiple purposes (care, training, vocation), with incentives to encourage men's care giving; better regulation and subsidy for care services; and opening supports to care giving to people in all kinds of care-giving relationships, wherever they occur.[56] It will depend on reversing many of the economic and employment practices that characterize our age, allowing people to substitute time for money, providing people with time to care and to work for pay, giving people options for job sharing and diverse career paths, and reversing ecologically unsustainable consumption and production patterns.[57] Gender openness would lead to improved social and ecological outcomes, but most significantly, it would allow us to pursue gender equality on a terrain of social complexity and diversity.

NOTES

1. See, for example, Kimberly J. Morgan, *Working Mothers and the Welfare State: Religion and Politics of Work-Family Policies in Western Europe and the United States* (Stanford, Calif.: Stanford University Press, 2006); Timo Fleckenstein, "The Politics of Ideas in Welfare-State Transformations: Christian Democracy and the Reform of Family Policy in Germany," *Social Politics* 18, no. 4 (2011): 543–571.
2. For germinal analyses of shifts from "male-breadwinner" to "adult-worker" models, see, for example, Emanuele Ferragina and Martin Seeleib-Kaiser, "Determinants of a Silent (R)evolution: Understanding the Expansion of Family Policy in Rich OECD Countries," *Social Politics* 22, no. 1 (2014): 1–37; Jane Lewis, "Gender and the Development of Welfare Regimes," *Journal of European Social Policy* 2, no. 3 (1992): 159–173; and Jane Lewis, "Gender and Welfare Regimes: Further Thoughts," *Social Politics* 4, no. 2 (1997): 160–177.
3. I develop the analysis of these two aspects of policy change as "destructive" and "constructive" processes, linked to recent developments in historical institutionalism and the theorizing of states and gender, in Ann Shola Orloff, "Gendered States Made and Remade," in *The Many Hands of the State*, ed. Kimberly J. Morgan and Ann Orloff (New York: Cambridge University Press, forthcoming).
4. Julia O'Connor, Ann Shola Orloff, and Sheila Shaver, eds., *States, Markets, Families: Gender, Liberalism, and Social Policy in Australia, Canada, Great Britain, and the United States* (New York: Cambridge University Press, 1999), chap. 6; Åsa Lundqvist, *Family Policy Paradoxes: Gender Equality and Labour Market Regulation in Sweden, 1930–2010* (Bristol: Policy, 2011), 1–2, 9.
5. Ulla Wikander, Alice Kessler-Harris, and Jane E. Lewis, *Protecting Women: Labor Legislation in Europe, the United States, and Australia, 1880–1920* (Champaign: University of Illinois Press, 1995).
6. Dorothy Sue Cobble, *The Other Women's Movement: Workplace Justice and Social Rights in Modern America* (Princeton, N.J.: Princeton University Press, 2005); Alice Kessler-Harris, *In Pursuit of Equity: Women, Men, and*

the *Quest for Economic Citizenship in Twentieth-Century America* (Oxford: Oxford University Press, 2003).
7. On the United States, see, for example, Richard V. Burkhauser and Karen C. Holden, *A Challenge to Social Security: The Changing Roles of Women and Men in American Society* (New York: Academic Press, 1982), 7. In Sweden, housewives' insurance (a part of sickness insurance) was made gender neutral by being extended to men, as "home husband insurance" (*hemmamake föräkring*), before being criticized and phased out entirely in the 1970s. Åsa Lundqvist, personal communication, April 24, 2012.
8. Lundqvist, *Family Policy Paradoxes*, 58; Cynthia Harrison, *On Account of Sex: The Politics of Women's Issues, 1945–1968* (Berkeley: University of California Press, 1989).
9. Nicholas Pedriana and Robin Stryker, "The Strength of a Weak Agency: Enforcement of Title VII of the 1964 Civil Rights Act and the Expansion of State Capacity, 1965–19711," *American Journal of Sociology* 110, no. 3 (2004): 709–760; Nicholas Pedriana, "Help Wanted NOW: Legal Resources, the Women's Movement, and the Battle Over Sex-Segregated Job Advertisements," *Social Problems* 51, no. 2 (2004): 182–201.
10. Catharine MacKinnon, *Sexual Harassment of Working Women: A Case of Sex Discrimination* (New Haven, Conn.: Yale University Press, 1979); Kathrin S. Zippel, *The Politics of Sexual Harassment: A Comparative Study of the United States, the European Union, and Germany* (New York: Cambridge University Press, 2006).
11. Jane Jenson and Rianne Mahon, "Representing Solidarity: Class, Gender, and the Crisis in Social-Democratic Sweden," *New Left Review* 1, no. 201 (September–October 1993): 76–100.
12. Lundqvist, *Family Policy Paradoxes*, 80; Laura Carlson, *Searching for Equality: Sex Discrimination, Parental Leave, and the Swedish Model, with Comparisons to EU, UK, and U.S. Law* (Philadelphia: Coronet, 2007), chap. 3; R. Amy Elman, *Sexual Subordination and State Intervention: Comparing Sweden and the United States* (Providence, R.I.: Berghahn, 1996).
13. Lundqvist, *Family Policy Paradoxes*, 67.
14. Edward J. McCaffery, *Taxing Women: How the Marriage Penalty Affects Your Taxes* (Chicago: University of Chicago Press, 1999).
15. In the United States, the lapsing of the innovative Sheppard-Towner maternal-health provisions in 1929 and subsequent failures to enact public health insurance foreclosed the possibility of constructing supports for maternal employment out of sickness insurance that included maternity provision. See Theda Skocpol, *Protecting Soldiers and Mothers* (Cambridge, Mass.: Harvard University Press, 1992).

16. The United States has had little to offer mothers who were not extremely poor, nor to married parents. Comprehensive income support for all poor people, which could have assisted a more diverse array of families, had been blocked in the late 1940s. See Margaret Weir, *Politics and Jobs: The Boundaries of Employment Policy in the United States* (Princeton, N.J.: Princeton University Press, 1992).
17. Jennifer Mittelstadt, *From Welfare to Workfare: The Unintended Consequences of Liberal Reform, 1945–1965* (Chapel Hill: University of North Carolina Press, 2005).
18. Jill Quadagno, *The Color of Welfare: How Racism Undermined the War on Poverty* (New York: Oxford University Press, 1994).
19. Some northern liberals joined them in opposition because it would have meant lower payments to those of their constituencies who received welfare. See John Myles and Paul Pierson, "Friedman's Revenge: The Reform of 'Liberal' Welfare States in Canada and the United States," *Politics & Society* 25, no. 4 (1997): 443–472; Christopher Howard, *The Hidden Welfare State: Tax Expenditures and Social Policy in the United States* (Princeton, N.J.: Princeton University Press, 1997), 65–69.
20. Suzanne Mettler writes of the "submerged [U.S.] welfare state" and how it offers tax breaks and subsidies especially to better-off Americans, but in ways that disguise its public character. See Suzanne Mettler, *Soldiers to Citizens: The GI Bill and the Making of the Greatest Generation* (New York: Oxford University Press, 2005); see also Ann Shola Orloff, "Markets Not States?: The Weakness of State Social Provision for Breadwinning Men in the United States," in *Families of a New World*, ed. Lynne Haney and Lisa Pollard (New York: Routledge, 2003), 217–244.
21. Celia Winkler, *Single Mothers and the State: The Politics of Care in Sweden and the United States* (Lanham, Md.: Rowman & Littlefield, 2002).
22. Ibid., 222–226; Walter Korpi, "Faces of Inequality: Gender, Class, and Patterns of Inequalities in Different Types of Welfare States," *Social Politics* 7, no. 2 (2000): 127–191.
23. Winkler, *Single Mothers and the State*, 117–8.
24. Ibid., 211–215.
25. On these policy episodes, see Marisa Chappell, *The War on Welfare: Family, Poverty, and Politics in Modern America* (Philadelphia: University of Pennsylvania Press, 2011); Jennifer Mittelstadt, *From Welfare to Workfare*; Premilla Nadasen, *Welfare Warriors: The Welfare Rights Movement in the United States* (New York: Routledge, 2005); Ann Shola Orloff, "Rethinking Power and Politics," *Social Science History* 36 (2012): 1–21.
26. Robert C. Lieberman, *Shifting the Color Line: Race and the American Welfare State* (Cambridge, Mass.: Harvard University Press, 1998); Ellen

Reese, *Backlash Against Welfare Mothers: Past and Present* (Berkeley: University of California Press, 2005).
27. First, antiwelfare conservatives, often from the South, had never signed on to the idea of supporting single mothers' full-time care giving and consistently demanded that welfare clients be forced to work (for pay or in "workfare"-like arrangements); see Chappell, *The War on Welfare*. Second, social-welfare advocates and practitioners supported the "rehabilitation" of welfare clients through employment and casework services; see Mittelstadt, *From Welfare to Workfare*. Third, feminists were in favor of offering women on welfare new training and work opportunities but were conflicted about work *requirements* in AFDC.
28. Theda Skocpol, Margaret Weir, and Ann Shola Orloff, *The Politics of Social Policy in the United States* (Princeton, N.J.: Princeton University Press, 1988).
29. Morgan, *Working Mothers and the Welfare State*, 81–82.
30. Abby J. Cohen, "A Brief History of Federal Financing for Child Care in the United States," *The Future of Children* 6, no. 2 (1996): 26–40.
31. Morgan, *Working Mothers and the Welfare State*; Sonya Michel, *Children's Interests/Mothers' Rights: The Shaping of America's Child Care Policy* (New Haven, Conn.; Yale University Press, 1999).
32. Christina Wolbrecht, *The Politics of Women's Rights: Parties, Positions, and Change* (Princeton, N.J.: Princeton University Press, 2010).
33. Kent Weaver, *Ending Welfare as We Know It* (Washington, D.C.: Brookings, 2000); David T. Ellwood, *Poor Support: Poverty in the American Family* (New York: Basic Books, 1988).
34. Unlike the debates of the 1960s and 1970s, the Congressional Black Caucus and most feminist organizations, traditional supporters of welfare support to full-time care giving on the part of poor single mothers, did not mount a defense of "welfare as we knew it" and its model of full-time mothering.
35. Ann Shola Orloff, "Ending the Entitlements of Poor Single Mothers: Changing Social Policies, Women's Employment Caregiving," in *Women and Welfare: Theory and Practice in the United States and Europe*, ed. Nancy J. Hirschmann and Ulrike Liebert (New Brunswick, N.J.: Rutgers University Press, 2001): 133–159; O'Connor, Orloff, and Shaver, ed., *States, Markets, Families*. Survivors' benefits, which assist widowed spouses of wage earners covered under Social Security, do remain, but only about 4 percent of single mothers of young children are widows (and the majority of these women are covered under Survivors' Insurance); see Irwin Garfinkel and Sara McLanahan, *Single Mothers and Their Children: A New American Dilemma* (Baltimore, Md.: Urban Institute Press, 1986).

36. Evelyn Z. Brodkin and Gregory Marston, *Work and the Welfare State: Street-Level Organizations and Workfare Politics* (Washington, D.C.: Georgetown University Press, 2013); Joe Soss, Richard C. Fording, and Sanford F. Schram, *Disciplining the Poor: Neoliberal Paternalism and the Persistent Power of Race* (Chicago: University of Chicago Press, 2011).
37. On EITC, see, for example, Myles and Pierson, "Friedman's Revenge"; David T. Ellwood, "The Impact of the Earned Income Tax Credit and Other Social Policy Changes on Work and Marriage in the United States," *Australian Social Policy* 1 (1999): 75–113.
38. Bruce D. Meyer and Dan T. Rosenbaum, "Welfare, the Earned Income Tax Credit, and the Labor Supply of Single Mothers," *Quarterly Journal of Economics* 116, no. 3 (2001): 1063–1114.
39. Lundqvist, *Family Policy Paradoxes*, 82–84.
40. Helena Bergmann and Barbara Hobson, "Compulsory Fatherhood: The Coding of Fatherhood in the Swedish Welfare State" in *Making Men Into Fathers: Men, Masculinities, and the Social Politics of Fatherhood*, ed. Barbara Hobson (Cambridge: Cambridge University Press, 2002), 92–124.
41. Lundqvist, *Family Policy Paradoxes*, 96–97.
42. Bengt Westerberg, interview by Ann Shola Orloff, August 2011.
43. The "circumscribed neoliberalism" that affected Sweden's welfare state was reflected in some relatively limited cuts to parental-leave policies, most of which were partially reversed under later administrations. For example, replacement rates were cut from 90 percent to 75 percent and then pushed back to 80 percent.
44. Winkler, *Single Mothers and the State*, 211, 228.
45. Lundqvist, *Family Policy Paradoxes*, 98.
46. Ibid., 103; Diana Mulinari, "Women Friendly? Understanding Gendered Racism in Sweden," in *Gender Equality and Welfare Politics in Scandinavia*, ed. Kari Melby, Anna-Birte Ravn, and Christina Carlsso Wetterberg (Bristol: Policy, 2008), 167–183. Some argue that gender-equality policies have become integral to the national identity of Swedes, and consider this a good thing, but worry that it may be deployed against the accommodation of some immigrants, who are seen as "backward" in terms of gender.
47. Lundqvist, *Family Policy Paradoxes*, 112–113.
48. See, for example, Anna Gavanas, "Who Cleans the Welfare State? Migration, Informalization, Social Exclusion, and Domestic Services in Stockholm," *Institute for Future Studies: Research Report* 3 (2010); Nathalie Morel, Bruno Palier, and Joakim Palme, "Social Investment: A Paradigm in Search of a New Economic Model and Political Mobilisation," in *Towards a Social Investment Welfare State? Ideas, Policies, and Challenges*, ed. Nathalie Morel, Bruno Palier, and Joakim Palme (Bristol: Policy, 2012): 353–376.

49. See, for example, "Recap from the Summit," June 23, 2014, The White House Summit on Working Families, http://workingfamiliessummit.org/about/; and U.S. Department of Labor Women's Bureau Regional Forum on Working Families, June 23, 2014, The White House Summit on Working Families, http://www.dol.gov/wb/workingfamilies.
50. Anne Lise Ellingsaeter, "The Norwegian Childcare Regime and Its Paradoxes," in *Politicising Parenthood in Scandinavia: Gender Relations in Welfare States*, ed. Anne Lise Ellingsaeter and Arnlaug Leira (Chicago: University of Chicago Press, 2011), 121–144.
51. See, for example, Janet C. Gornick and Marcia K. Meyers, "Institutions That Support Gender Egalitarianism in Parenthood and Employment," in *Gender Equality: Transforming Family Divisions of Labor*, ed. Erik Olin Wright (New York: Verso, 2009), 3–66.
52. But see Ann Shola Orloff, "Gendering the Comparative Analysis of Welfare States: An Unfinished Agenda," *Sociological Theory* 27, no. 3 (2009): 317–343.
53. Nancy Fraser, "After the Family Wage: Gender Equity and the Welfare State," *Political Theory* 22, no. 4 (1994): 591–618.
54. Andrea Doucet, *Do Men Mother? Fathering, Care, and Domestic Responsibility* (Toronto: University of Toronto Press, 2006).
55. Cynthia Willett, *The Soul of Justice: Social Bonds and Racial Hubris*. (Ithaca, N.Y.: Cornell University Press, 2001).
56. Martha Fineman, *The Autonomy Myth: A Theory of Dependency* (New York: New Press, 2004).
57. See, for example, Juliet B. Schor, *True Wealth: How and Why Millions of Americans Are Creating a Time-Rich, Ecologically Light, Small-Scale, High-Satisfaction Economy* (New York: Penguin, 2011).

CHAPTER ELEVEN

Breadwinner Liberalism and Its Discontents in the American Welfare State

ROBERT O. SELF

IN THE MIDDLE DECADES of the twentieth century, the United States established a limited, nonuniversal welfare state grounded in a male-breadwinner model of economic rights and social citizenship. Specifically, between the Social Security Act and National Labor Relations Act of 1935 and the National Housing Act of 1949, Congress erected a multitiered system of social insurance, income support, and housing organized predominantly around private employment and housing markets. Between the early 1960s and the early 1970s, that model came under assault from two interrelated forces. One was a series of economic developments that dramatically undermined the male breadwinner wage. The second was a political challenge from racial-justice advocates, feminists, and other liberal and left-wing activists and politicians who collectively claimed the welfare state was too narrow, exclusionary, and punitive. The economic crisis and political assaults from the left together destabilized the nation's fragile version of social democracy. Liberal American political culture, what I call "breadwinner liberalism," proved unable to resolve either the economic crisis or the political challenge and thereby lost both ideological legitimacy and electoral traction.

Theorizing the political coalitions that brought welfare states into being across the industrialized world and provided them with electoral support is a well-established necessity in comparative welfare-state scholarship. Peter Baldwin, summarizing and extending a good deal of that scholarship, has argued that the extent to which, and the terms on which, working-class and bourgeois sectors joined together to embrace welfare policy is one of the keys to understanding the extent of social solidarity in different nations and the political legitimacy achieved by welfare states. In an important anthology of American welfare-state history, Margaret Weir, Anna Shola Orloff, and Theda Skocpol endeavored to overcome social scientists' long-standing focus on ideology by positing an "institutional-political process" at the heart of welfare-state development. And Michael Brown, like Baldwin summarizing and extending a much wider literature, has argued that racial politics and unstable racial coalitions help explain a great deal of the relative weakness of the American welfare state in comparison to many in the West. For my purposes, the critical point is that expanding the social wage and rendering it more equitable for women and nonwhite citizens in the 1960s and afterward required legal, political, and legislative struggles that divided the liberal coalition in the United States, fracturing its already fragile solidarities for more than a generation. (It must be remembered that *liberal* in the U.S. context means something akin to a moderate social democrat.)[1]

If electoral coalitions represent a critical component of comparative welfare-state scholarship, a closely allied field of inquiry focuses on the nature of the social wage itself. Among the numerous axes along which to compare models of the social wage, two deserve attention here: male breadwinning and what Gøsta Esping-Anderson has called "decommodification." Welfare states have historically responded differently to the organization of the family economy around male production and wage earning and female reproduction under industrial capitalism. Most have valorized male breadwinning and thereby gendered social rights to one degree or another. But the attitude of welfare states to male breadwinning must be understood in conjunction with their attitude toward decommodification—toward, that is, which dimensions of male breadwinning and female reproduction are taken out of market competition and made part of the social wage. Understood along those dual axes, the U.S. model has long relied on male breadwinning and the private market to distribute the social wage. Other states (Germany, the Netherlands, the United Kingdom) have championed male breadwinning but have provided far greater public supports for it. In at least one comparative case, that of Sweden in the 1970s, the state moved decisively away from a male-breadwinner model through large-scale public support for parental leave and childcare and by deemphasizing gendered allocations of the social wage, such as widow's pensions. Understood in this comparative context, despite efforts since the 1960s to reduce the gender inequities of the social wage, the United States remains the preeminent example of a male-breadwinner welfare system heavily reliant on private-market allocations.[2]

Two decades ago, the political philosopher Nancy Fraser observed that the crisis of the industrial-era welfare state in the 1970s was "rooted in the collapse of the world of the family wage, and its central assumptions about labor markets and families." Fraser was right but underestimated the economic and social insufficiencies of the family wage itself, prior to its collapse, across the whole of the second half of the twentieth century. In economic terms, the family wage was never universal and rested on hard-won trade-union victories that proved difficult to sustain as well as on structural conditions—especially U.S. dominance in postwar global manufacturing—that were, at best, temporary. In social terms, the family wage cast women as the domestic appendages of men and cordoned nonwhites into what were effectively secondary labor markets. Any considerations of the family wage's collapse in the latter decades of the twentieth century, which was real, must therefore contend with its limited initial reach, a product of the 1930s, and the political challenges to its inclusiveness, a product of the 1960s.[3]

Under the New Deal in the 1930s, male breadwinning became the foundation of U.S. social policy and the guiding ideology of the liberal political class. The male head of household contracting his labor in the marketplace was enshrined in the New Deal welfare state, which sought to assist the breadwinner's efforts in the market. This assistance took three basic forms: (1) government support for labor unions and the right of workers to organize and bargain collectively; (2) two-tiered social insurance, in which one tier, guaranteed and near-universal, was linked to employment (unemployment insurance and old-age pensions) and the other was poor relief, or income support, linked to motherhood and disability; and (3) federal mortgage insurance, which significantly though unevenly democratized the private housing market. Inasmuch as the United States had developed a national employment and housing policy—through legislation such as the 1934 National Housing Act, the 1935 Social Security and Wagner Acts, the 1937 Fair Labor Standards Act, and the 1946 Employment Act—it was based on male-breadwinner ideology. The New Deal's "citizen worker" and the nuclear family he headed remained a mainstay of conventional liberal thinking and a cornerstone of the Keynesian consensus that guided economic policy between the 1940s and 1960s, which together can be called "breadwinner liberalism."[4]

For millions of American women, however, the breadwinner consensus belied reality. They engaged in market work for every conceivable reason—just as men did. Married women and women with children engaged in market work to lift their families out of poverty and afford basic necessities; to enable teenagers to finish school; to compensate for an unemployed or disabled spouse; to afford college tuition for children, their spouse, or themselves; to pay medical bills; or to fulfill personal goals and ambitions. Most rationales were directly related to family needs and took into account the labor still expected at home. For more and more women, "normalcy" in the mid–twentieth century meant not a blissful life cleaning the hearth and raising children but a predictable cycle of duties at work and at home—the "double day." Comparative welfare-state scholars have long held that no industrialized society has managed to accomplish social reproduction without public support—that is, female specialization in reproduction has been insufficient. The American case also demonstrates a corollary: that the market labor of men associated with male breadwinning, too, has been insufficient for social reproduction and that women's paid labor is required.[5]

The double day was more widespread in African American and Latino families, owing to the lesser job prospects for men in those families. For black women, domestic work in the homes of whites, unskilled industrial labor, and "back-of-the-house" service work constituted the narrow range of available options, outside of teaching and a handful of professional occupations for the smaller, educated middle class. However narrow the options, the paid work of black women was essential, because black men were much less likely than white men to earn a "family wage"—to say nothing of men's absence from the home altogether.

American labor markets had long been effectively "dual" markets bisected by a color line that allocated work according to a white/nonwhite hierarchy. Among Latina women, too, racialized labor markets in the Southwest and in northern cities commodified their work at poverty level and ghettoized them in agricultural and assembly-line labor and domestic work in Anglo homes. Working-class women of color rarely received anything but the worst wages at the bottom of the nation's labor market. By the late 1970s, black and Latina women represented 41 percent of women in poverty.[6]

Against the background of the double day and the dual labor market, the single most dramatic development in the U.S. labor force between 1945 and 1970 was the increasing market presence of married women and women with children. By the early 1970s, more than half of all women between the ages of eighteen and sixty-four engaged in market work, and women comprised nearly 40 percent of all paid workers. The share of the total labor force composed of men and single, childless women remained constant between 1945 and the early 1960s. But the share comprising working wives and mothers nearly doubled. By the late 1960s, one in three married women worked for wages; among African American women, it was one in two. In 1970, 30 percent of women with children under the age of six engaged in market work, a dramatic rise from 1950, when the number stood at 12 percent. By 1974, 40 percent of all women with children between the ages of three and five were engaged in market work. This gradual resort to market labor by women was part of a decades-long trend, but the acceleration of that process in the 1960s was unmistakable.[7]

Developments in the 1970s accelerated this trend, as blue-collar male wages stagnated and unemployment rose significantly, making the fragile working-class gains of 1945–1970 increasingly precarious. As the long postwar economic expansion ground to a halt after 1973, all workers, and all families, faced adjustments, but blue-collar men lost the most ground. Between 1960 and 2000, sectors they traditionally dominated—manufacturing, construction, transportation, and agriculture—went from employing nearly half of all workers in the country to employing less than 30 percent. Meanwhile, sectors that employed large numbers of both pink- and white-collar women— education, health care, retail, finance, hotel and food service, and finance and insurance—experienced the opposite trajectory, going from roughly one-third of total employment to well over half. Women were becoming more responsible for filling the jobs the economy created, but those jobs came with lower wages and fewer benefits than those the economy had once created for men.[8]

This sectoral shift was accompanied by declining rates of unionization. Together, the two made for stagnating wages. Why American unionization rates began falling in the 1970s, which became a precipitous decline in the 1980s and 1990s, is a complex story beyond the scope of this essay. Deindustrialization, automation, legacies of incomplete union saturation, political assaults from the right, and trade-union miscalculations all played a role. But union decline contributed to a clear reality: between the early 1970s and the present, the annual earnings of the median prime-aged male fell by a quarter. Underneath the numbers was an American economy more chaotic and jittery than at any time since the 1930s. Unemployment climbed steadily to just under 6 percent by 1974, which was hardly an unprecedented figure in the postwar years, but, when combined with rising inflation, it was enough to put a unique burden on ordinary wage earners. Unemployment then jumped to 8.5 percent in 1975 and spent the rest of the 1970s between 6 and 7 percent before leaping to 10 percent in the recession of the early 1980s. Many major urban areas fared terribly. In the second half of the 1970s and the first two years of the 1980s, unemployment in many American cities—including New York, San Francisco, Los Angeles, Detroit, and Buffalo—rarely dipped below 10 percent. Despite notable economic fluctuations, such a prolonged employment slump had not occurred in decades.[9]

The raw numbers paint an uncomplicated portrait. By the 1970s, more and more American families depended on women's domestic *and* paid labor. Among married opposite-sex couples—surveys of same-sex households were rarely done—wives in the labor force accounted for an average of 26 percent of family income in the decade. Among wives who worked full time and year round, their median contribution was 38 percent. Overall, 56 percent of all women under the age of fifty-five in the labor force were married, and in 1978, 70 percent of all women in the workforce had children under the age of eighteen. This surge of women into market labor allowed family income to begin to grow slightly after 1973, even as male blue-collar wages remained flat or declined in real terms. However, even as two-income families kept pace with inflation, women headed half of all families in poverty, and such households represented one-seventh of all American families by 1978.

A trend evident in the immediate postwar decades had continued through the late 1970s: the American family was not organized around male breadwinners.[10]

The foregoing economic conditions formed the crucial context in which political challenges to American liberalism took shape. Increasing market work among married women in the period 1940–1970 and the collapse of what remained of the male-breadwinner economy in subsequent decades, 1970–1990, structured the environment in which those challenges were waged. The remainder of this chapter considers three of those challenges, each of which illustrates the unraveling of key strains of the politically centrist doctrines of breadwinner liberalism: employment equality, childcare, and income support or poor relief (or what Americans have called since the 1960s simply "welfare").

More than half a century of enormous change has blurred public memory of the inequalities based on biological sex that made the 1960s so distinctly part of a different era. Women were the least remunerated, most exploited segment of the national workforce. On average, they earned roughly half of what men earned. The majority of blue- and pink-collar jobs available to women reinforced their status as servants and helpers and offered limited upward mobility: they cooked, cleaned, nursed, fetched, filed, typed, and performed rote assembly-line work. Meanwhile, professional jobs were so segregated by sex that in the mid-1960s only 3 percent of the nation's lawyers, 7 percent of its doctors, and 1 percent of its engineers and federal judges were women. A job market premised on male breadwinning and female domesticity exploited and undervalued women in both social and strictly economic terms.[11]

The most ambitious and far-reaching assault on women's second-class economic status took place in the years between the 1964 Civil Rights Act and the Supreme Court's decision in *Craig v. Boren* in 1976. The twin levers for recasting the relationship between women and market labor in these years were Title VII of the Civil Rights Act and the Fourteenth Amendment to the Constitution. When the Equal Employment Opportunity Commission (EEOC), charged with enforcing Title VII, began to consider the new law in 1965, its chairman, Franklin Roosevelt Jr., placed little emphasis on sex discrimination. Addressing racial discrimination, he believed, was of far greater import. Like most liberal Americans, the leaders of the EEOC saw racial discrimination as unnatural and harmful and sex discrimination as natural. Given the presumptions of the era and the crisis of black male unemployment, that conclusion is understandable. Nevertheless, women, including many black women, flooded the EEOC with sex-discrimination complaints, founded the National Organization for Women (NOW), and filed multiple sex-discrimination lawsuits, eventually forcing the commission to consider the marketplace's sex inequalities.[12]

Title VII litigation between 1966 and 1971 laid the groundwork for a systematic assault on the gender-based inequities of the job market. By the end of the 1960s, NOW's Legal Defense and Education Fund (LDEF)—modeled on a similar structure in the NAACP—had made Title VII suits a top priority. Another national organization, one that would in time rank among the most influential women's legal-advocacy institutions in the country, joined the LDEF: the American Civil Liberties Union (ACLU) Women's Rights Project. Led by Ruth Bader Ginsberg and a new generation of feminist attorneys, the Women's Rights Project sought to make the "right to earn a living" a reality for women and in so doing dismantle the legal architecture supporting the male-breadwinner bias of the national economy. Over the next three decades, the Women's Rights Project played an instrumental role in dismantling state-level Progressive Era protective legislation that disadvantaged women in the labor market and in securing affirmative action and equal pay in many sectors and industries.[13]

Pregnancy discrimination and what became known as sexual harassment were additional barriers to women's market equality. Women's advocates believed there were few more insidious forms of workplace discrimination than the treatment of pregnant women. The EEOC eventually concurred, issuing new regulations in 1972 under Title VII preventing many of the most flagrant practices. The Supreme Court, however, in *Geduldig v. Aiello* (1974), overruled the agency. Four years after *Geduldig*, following considerable lobbying by women's advocates, Congress passed the Pregnancy Discrimination Act, which codified in law the EEOC's early-1970s rulings. Few advances were made for fifteen years, however, until Congress passed the 1993 Family and Medical Leave Act, which authorized three months of unpaid work leave for a variety of medical and parental exigencies. Thus by the late 1990s the worst pregnancy-related abuses by employers were curtailed, but Congress stopped short of a more generous and subsidized parental-leave law, leaving the United States an increasingly isolated outlier among welfare-state nations in parental-leave provisions.[14]

The workplace was long a bastion of male sexual privilege as well. At the beginning of the 1960s, almost nothing was more common to all women than the experience of some form of sexual harassment at work. In 1976, more than 80 percent of nine thousand *Redbook* readers reported such experiences. Building on late-1960s campaigns against sexism in specific industries, in a long and demanding legal fight between 1971 and 1986 feminist activists, attorneys, and the EEOC director under President Jimmy Carter, Eleanor Holmes Norton, built American sexual-harassment law. The key, as with so much of the reconstruction of women's citizenship in these years, was Title VII. Backed by legal theory developed by feminist attorneys such as Catharine MacKinnon, Norton threw the weight of the EEOC behind a revamping of workplace-equality law. Sexual harassment, EEOC guidelines specified after 1977, was a violation of women's rights as workers under the Civil Rights Act. And though it still took a decade, to the surprise of many, the Supreme Court agreed in *Meritor Savings Bank v. Vinson* in 1986.[15]

Title VII opened one avenue for women to address workplace inequality. The Fourteenth Amendment promised another. What became known as the "Pauli Murray approach," for the civil-rights and feminist attorney Pauli Murray, proposed jurisprudence for women based on an analogy to race. If the courts interpreted the Fourteenth Amendment to require racial equality, there remained no basis on which to exclude women from analogous protections, Murray argued. Sex and race were, in the framework she proposed, equivalent in a legal sense, if not in a historical one. Sex discrimination and race discrimination were not the same, but the legal redress for each was: application of the due-process and equal-protection clauses of the Fourteenth Amendment. In the half-decade between the Supreme Court's 1971 decision in *Reed v. Reed* and its 1976 decision in *Craig v. Boren*, American women leveraged the Fourteenth Amendment to win greater market liberty, in a legal sense, than they had ever enjoyed before. In establishing the "intermediate-scrutiny" test for laws that discriminated by sex, the court in *Craig* did not adopt the same standard it employed for race ("strict scrutiny") but nonetheless laid the groundwork for the elimination of most employment and other economic laws that distinguished between women and men.[16]

That transformation remained circumscribed, however. The civil right of liberty on balance won out over the social rights of justice and equality. Women were set free to compete with men in the market, but little was done to transform that market to accommodate the unchanging necessity of women's family work. The ideal "citizen worker" remained an adult without family work, a traditional "breadwinner"—a distinct improvement over a *man* without family work but still a considerable distance from what many women's advocates believed necessary to ensure women's equality in both the labor market and the family. The double day not only did not disappear; by many accounts it became even more burdensome. And even less was done to assist working-class women from all racial backgrounds. Measured in strictly economic terms, among full-time workers, the gender wage gap closed from 57 cents (for every dollar men earned) in 1969 to 80 cents by 2009. That overall gain hid much lower figures in heavily female sectors, such as services (72 cents), and the fact that many women continued to work part time. Meanwhile, 6.5 percent of all working women remained below the poverty line (excluding the unemployed and those on welfare), a figure that was over 12 percent among African American and Latina women.[17]

In the relationship among family, state, and market, which lies at the heart of welfare states, women in the United States gained remarkable market freedom between the 1960s and 1980s. They gained new civil rights in the form of key antidiscrimination protections, and the law increasingly treated them as "citizen workers" on a par with, rather than as domestic appendages of, men. Yet in key arenas, especially women's continued centrality to family work—that is, their capacity to be mothers—they lagged far behind women in other welfare states. The Pregnancy Discrimination Act and the Family and Medical Leave Act place expensive burdens on employers rather than fully socializing the costs of those protections—they are "half" a social right. American women won epoch-defining market rights in and following the 1960s, but the essential organizing logic of both the labor market and the welfare state, that workers had no family-work responsibilities, remained unchanged.[18]

A second, related, major arena of contestation over women's social rights was childcare. In the logic of American political life, from President Johnson's Great Society through President Nixon's New Federalism and the Reagan Revolution, childcare was not conceived of as a universal social policy for all women, a new addition to the social contract. It was, rather, a limited program for poor women that aimed to reduce "dependency" by requiring the recipients of income support to earn a paycheck. Far from being a positive right of all women, government-supported childcare was imagined as a mechanism to *shrink* social rights: childcare would facilitate poor women's transition from dependents to workers.

In 1971, as part of the widespread political mobilization by women, Congress considered the most substantial attempt in the nation's history to make childcare a near-universal part of the nation's social-welfare system, part of an expanded social wage: the Comprehensive Child Development Act (CCDA). Behind the legislation stood a trio of influential feminists in Congress and an impressive coalition, including female-dominated trade unions such as clothing and garment workers and communications workers, the National Council of Negro Women, the National Welfare Rights Organization (NWRO), and NOW, among many others. The CCDA's chances looked good. Public support for state-sponsored childcare consistently registered at more than 50 percent. Fundamentally, the CCDA was an attempt among progressive political forces to counter the view of childcare as a mechanism to reduce social rights. It sought to tie together the New Deal, the black freedom and Chicano movements, the Great Society, and the women's movement. Could the social-welfare liberalism of the Roosevelt coalition be married to racial justice and the rights-based liberalism of the Great Society? And could such a fusion establish a new social right for women that reduced the discriminatory effects of motherhood by socializing a heretofore private dimension of family life?[19]

As it moved through committees, the bill became entangled in the very issues its advocates had hoped to avoid. The minimum annual income to qualify for free childcare had initially been set high in order to extend benefits to the lower middle class. Nixon's Health Education and Welfare Department (HEW) made clear that the administration would not support the high number, and it was eventually reduced by 38 percent. A second point involved control of the new program. Childcare advocates, led by the black feminists Marian Wright Edelman and Evelyn Moore of the Black Child Development Institute, believed that childcare centers should be operated at the local level. They hoped to bypass recalcitrant state officials, especially in the South. Nixon administration officials and southern politicians, on the other hand, wanted nothing that resembled the War on Poverty's focus on empowering communities, instead favoring state-run programs. Ultimately, the two sides struck a compromise: "sponsoring units" with populations of 100,000 or higher were eligible, making states and large cities the principal administrators.[20]

Anxiety over changing racial and gender norms underlay these compromises. Southern politicians knew that local control would mean racially integrated childcare centers and black-controlled institutions. Northern governors and mayors—their own political wounds from War on Poverty–inspired community coalitions still fresh—favored city-level administration, to take funding out of the hands of potentially oppositional community and neighborhood groups. Conservative religious activists and emerging antifeminists worried less about "race mixing" and community control than about what "child development" meant for the family. The bill's fiercest critics cast childcare, in the by-then-familiar antiradicalism of Cold War America, as a socialist or even "Soviet" program to replace the family with government-run childrearing. The compromises made in passing the CCDA thus revealed the prevalent fear that freeing women from some of the burdens of family work represented a dangerous threat to the social order and that community-controlled institutions undermined white dominance in the South and urban political machines in the North. Like so much of the social-wage legislation passed by the U.S. Congress in the twentieth century, the CCDA was a compromise born of American racial politics and the nation's extreme federalism and political localism.

The bill Congress sent to Nixon in December 1971, passed with narrow majorities, nevertheless promised the broadest commitment to state-sponsored childcare in the nation's history. It came closer than any previous legislation to recognizing childcare as part of women's economic citizenship. After a conspicuous delay, Nixon vetoed the bill, calling it "the most radical piece of legislation to emerge from the Ninety-Second Congress." The bill would, he said decisively, destroy "parental authority and parental involvement with children . . . when social conscience are formed and religious and moral principles are first inculcated." While women receiving income support could qualify for some subsidized childcare, on balance, women and families were left to their own devices and to the private market to care for children while parents worked.[21]

The quest to include childcare in the social rights of U.S. women never recovered from Nixon's veto. In 1976, unable to get a full bill passed, liberals in Congress compromised by agreeing to the first childcare tax credit—a small sum deducted from an individual or couple's tax bill. A renewed push for a full childcare bill in the late 1970s was defeated with Reagan's election in 1980 and the Democratic Party's loss of the Senate. The childcare tax credit was subsequently expanded in the 1990s, and in 2014 it covers up to $3,000 per child for up to two children (depending on qualifying income and other factors). Seeing this outcome as part of a broader pattern in the United States of burying social policy in the tax code, the political scientist Suzanne Mettler has called this the "submerged state."[22]

In the third and final policy arena considered in this chapter, as in the first two, developments overlapped with dramatic employment shifts alongside questions of racial and gender equity and justice. The decades-long political conflict over income support, what Americans call simply "welfare," cannot be understood outside the intense racialization of poverty in the United States. That process began with an underlying reality, a black employment crisis that dated to the 1940s and 1950s. Between 1945 and 1960, national black unemployment hovered around 10 percent, but it spiked to 15–18 percent in industrial cities such as Detroit, Oakland, and Chicago. Typically, young black men found themselves unemployed at twice the rate of their elders—as high as 30–40 percent in some cities. Automation, plant relocation, and racial discrimination closed much of the nation's industrial-labor market to young black men for nearly two decades, even as migration from southern farms to northern cities increased. In his 1964 book *To Be Equal*, the Urban League's Whitney Young estimated that "one million Negroes—one out of every four Negro workers—are unemployed," a crisis for both African Americans and the country. "Either we make these people constructive citizens, productive, and healthy," Young predicted, "or they are going to be destructive dependents."[23]

Civil-rights leaders were not oblivious to black women's fate in the labor market—where married black women at midcentury were 50 percent more likely than married white women to work for wages—but they saw the unemployment and underemployment of men as more urgent. For many civil-rights leaders, racial progress was inseparably linked to the capacity of African American families to create the male-breadwinner, female-homemaker household presumed to be enjoyed by whites. The now infamous 1965 Moynihan Report represented a scholarly version of the same idea. Theorizing that black men were "trapped in a tangle of pathology" and eschewed the breadwinner role, *The Negro*

Family: The Case for National Action argued that federal policy should reflect "a new kind of national goal: the establishment of a stable Negro family." Moynihan blamed black men's abandonment of the nuclear family on the pressures of joblessness and white racism, which, he argued, produced a "startling increase in welfare dependency," the "fundamental problem" in the contemporary black community. The report helped derail the black freedom movement at a crucial juncture, as many journalists and commentators either failed to read the entire report or distilled its complex message to the enticing and sensational "tangle of pathology."[24]

Moynihan became the public face of liberal welfare reform under President Johnson, but he was far from alone. Welfare reform since the 1950s had produced the most visible and controversial efforts to use government policy to shape the nuclear family's relationship to the market. Ironically, as Jennifer Mittelstadt has shown, it was liberals, particularly liberal officials within HEW, who had recast poor relief not as an income program for women with children but as a "rehabilitative" program designed to orient women to market work. Worried that poor relief encouraged dependency on the state, these reformers sought to return women to paid labor as quickly as possible. Like Moynihan, these reformers saw themselves as New Deal or Great Society liberals mending a broken system. President Nixon, echoing Moynihan, put it bluntly: "any system which makes it more profitable for a man not to work, or which encourages a man to desert his family rather than stay with his family, is wrong and indefensible." Welfare's supporters and critics alike by the late 1960s saw Aid to Families with Dependent Children (AFDC)—a small and until then not particularly controversial program entering its fourth decade—as encouraging male desertion.[25]

Reform efforts acquired a new urgency in the second half of the 1960s for three reasons. First, the logic of Moynihan and Watts had linked absent male breadwinners with women's welfare dependency and male urban violence. Second, the combination of black migration out of the South and the employment crisis in northern cities threw increasing numbers of African Americans onto state welfare rolls. And third, NWRO, led largely by African American women, challenged the iniquities and indignities of AFDC while encouraging women to see welfare as a right. All three developments both racialized welfare and made it fully part of the ongoing struggles over Great Society liberalism.[26]

By the late 1960s, no one liked welfare—not on the left, the right, or the center, not even the recipients themselves. Liberals in the Johnson administration and Congress hoped to raise welfare benefits and encourage the formation of male-led households, but they simultaneously pushed unwed mothers into the labor market. Welfare activists foresaw the dire consequences of this reasoning: low-wage labor at the bottom of the economy without assistance for childcare. In response, they cast welfare as a right, fought the surveillance of women's personal lives, and criticized liberals for abandoning them to degrading labor that compromised their motherhood. Conservatives, with a few exceptions, wanted to end welfare altogether. They saw it as a taxpayer drain, a travesty for the nuclear family, and a subsidy to "profligate breeders" among the black poor.[27]

To cut the Gordian knot, a few months into his presidency Nixon took a bold gamble that, he believed, would both fix and shrink the welfare system. Prodded by Moynihan, who began working for Nixon in 1969, the president endorsed the Family Assistance Plan (FAP), a proposal to provide a guaranteed minimum income to a wide range of low-income families, including both current welfare recipients as well as the so-called working poor. Its complicated formula would award greater income support for two-parent families and for families in which both parents worked. Single-parent homes and homes without an employed family member would receive less. The inclusion of working families was essential, the president explained in his first major domestic-policy speech, in August 1969: "It is morally wrong for a family that is working to try to make ends meet to receive less than the family across the street on welfare." A relatively enthusiastic House passed the bill by nearly a hundred votes, but as the bill sat in its Senate committee, its opponents on both the left and right slowly cut it to shreds. Led by George McGovern and backed by vocal NWRO activists, the liberal left charged that the FAP's formula favored working white families over impoverished black ones, that its income supports were insufficient for families and would actually *reduce* welfare benefits in a majority of states, and that it would force poor, unskilled women into the labor market with little assistance for childcare. Senate conservatives simply could not abide the idea that the federal government planned to guarantee every American family below a certain income level annual assistance—especially now that the public face of poverty was urban and black. Nixon eventually reneged on his merely politically tactical commitment to poor breadwinners, leaving the FAP to die without a Senate vote.[28]

In the decade after the FAP's collapse, conservatives linked their ascendancy in national life to vigorous critiques of "welfare." They did so in concert with renewed vilification of African American families and intensified politicizing of "welfare dependency." This vilification took many forms, such as the notorious portrait painted by Reagan in 1976 of the "welfare queen" who collected government checks and drove a Cadillac. By the late 1980s, the welfare queen had become a stock character of politics and the media. Simultaneously, black men found themselves vilified as criminals. Increasingly strict and biased drug laws at both state and federal levels overlapped with the emergence of a crack-cocaine crisis. The two produced stunningly disproportionate incarceration rates for blacks and whites. By 2000, one out of every twenty African American men over the age of eighteen was in federal or state prison (among whites, the rate was one in 180). The combination of extreme vilification of black men as criminals and black women as welfare dependent once more cast the black family itself as undeserving of national attention and as the predominant argument against a more generous social wage in the United States.[29]

Historically, American women's relationship to both the labor market and the welfare state has been conditioned by domesticity—by assumptions about women's proper relationship to marriage and motherhood. In the early 1960s, as feminists began to press their demands for economic equality on state legislatures and Congress, they confronted a difficult choice. Should they emphasize women's right to the status of the "ideal" worker, a man unencumbered by family work? Or should they emphasize women's dual responsibilities, the "double day," and reimagine the ideal worker as one who *does* have family work? And what of race? Would reformers' efforts to reimagine the ideal worker still presume a "color-blind" labor market, or should the long legacy of racial segregation be addressed as well? Each of these questions straddled the divide between civil and social rights, between freedom and justice, and hinged on the extent to which American courts would remake the marketplace and the social wage could be legislatively strengthened.

Liberal political culture, what I call "breadwinner liberalism," proved unable to resolve either the economic crisis that began to undermine what remained of the male breadwinner wage or the political challenge emerging on the left. Breadwinner liberalism was neither ideologically nor electorally powerful enough to reorient the 1930s-era American welfare state around a new kind of social wage, one that was equitable to women and nonwhites. Instead, what emerged from the resurgence of various feminisms in and after the 1960s was state support (through antidiscrimination law) for women's market competition, which privileged women whose social and human capital, especially education, was already high. Indeed, as Deborah Dinner and Katherine Turk have argued in recent work, feminist activists' attempts to leverage Title VII to end workplace discrimination evolved in tandem with neoliberal notions of the market. In the latter, invidious, intentional *individual* discrimination is proscribed, but broader, structural patterns of inequality—whether class, racial, gender, or sexual—are imagined as beyond public responsibility. In that world, individual discrimination against a worker for being pregnant might be forbidden, but the idea that support for pregnancy, childbearing, and childrearing ought to be part of a social wage, or social citizenship, is dismissed.[30]

However truncated the social wage was in the United States in comparison to more universal welfare states, the American version nevertheless embraced the premise that government ought to assist families economically. When American liberalism entered the period of political crisis recounted above, conservatives proposed and defended an alternative to the conviction that the state ought to assist families economically. In its place, they asserted a new breadwinner politics based on the notion that the state ought to protect idealized families from moral harm and crime. The shift from assistance to protection in discourses of the state can be seen across a range of political and policy arenas, from abortion and homosexuality to the War on Drugs. Gender and racial politics, in particular, facilitated the profound racialization of income support and underwrote its gradual diminishment, emblematized by the 1996 welfare-reform act. Gender and racial politics also underwrote the dramatic expansion of what scholars have come to call the "carceral state," now one of the largest and most expensive public programs in the United States: prisons.

To conclude, a brief foray into T. H. Marshall's concept of social citizenship, which has become increasingly influential in American welfare-state scholarship in the last decade, may prove useful. Marshall argued for distinctions among civil, political, and social rights. Yet in the United States, the boundary between civil and social rights has been decidedly blurry and confounding of Marshall's categorization. This is worth considering because specifying the legal points at which civil and social rights overlap, as well as the legal points at which they remain distinct, is essential to understanding the thicket of law, practice, and social outcomes in the U.S. welfare state broadly. As an example, take employment discrimination. Is the right to be protected by the state from gender and race bias in the marketplace a "civil right," that is, a procedural right of "freedom" essential to basic liberal citizenship? Or is it a substantive "social right," requiring a reconfiguring of market competition and the terms of the social wage to achieve justice? It is clearly both, but the policy implications of seeing it as a basic procedural right, the dominant interpretation, are different from the implications of seeing it as a question of substantive social justice. To interpret it as a substantive right might entail an embrace of robust affirmative action, subsidized childcare, maternity leave, educational equity, and a variety of other state-mandated provisions, while to interpret it as a procedural right requires no adjustments to the social wage. In that sense, Marshall's categories of citizenship may not be merely additive—the sum of the three greater-than-the-individual parts—but also competitive. Expansions of civil rights since the 1960s, in short, have not been inconsistent with contraction of the social wage.[31]

NOTES

1. Peter Baldwin, *The Politics of Social Solidarity: Class Bases of the European Welfare State, 1875–1975* (New York: Cambridge University Press, 1992); Margaret Weir, Anna Shola Orloff, and Theda Skocpol, eds., *The Politics of Social Policy in the United States* (Princeton, N.J.: Princeton University Press, 1988); Michael K. Brown, *Race, Money, and the American Welfare State* (Ithaca, N.Y.: Cornell University Press, 1999).
2. Gøsta Esping-Anderson, *The Three Worlds of Welfare Capitalism* (Princeton, N.J.: Princeton University Press, 1990); Lena Sommestad, "Welfare-State Attitudes to the Male Breadwinning System: The United States and Sweden in Comparative Perspective," *International Review of Social History* 42, suppl. (December 1997): 153–174.
3. Nancy Fraser, "After the Family Wage: Gender Equity and the Welfare State," *Political Theory* 22, no. 4 (November 1994): 591–618.
4. Linda Gordon, *Pitied but Not Entitled: Single Mothers and the History of Welfare, 1890–1935* (New York: Free Press, 1994); Alice Kessler-Harris and

Karen Sacks, "The Demise of Domesticity in America," in *Women, Households, and the Economy*, ed. Lourdes Benería and Catharine R. Stimpson (New Brunswick, N.J.: Rutgers University Press, 1987); Joan Williams, *Unbending Gender: Why Family and Work Conflict and What to Do About It* (Oxford: Oxford University Press, 2000); Premilla Nadasen, "Citizenship Rights, Domestic Work, and the Fair Labor Standards Act," *Journal of Policy History* 24, no. 1 (2012): 74–94; John Thomas McGuire, "The Most Unjust Piece of Legislation: Section 213 of the Economy Act of 1932 and Feminism During the New Deal," *Journal of Policy History* 20, no. 4 (2008): 516–541.
5. Sommestad, "Welfare-State Attitudes to the Male Breadwinning System."
6. Women's Bureau, U.S. Department of Labor, *Negro Women in the Population and in the Labor Force*, n.d., "To Fulfill the Rights of Negro Women in Disadvantaged Families," June 1–2, 1966, Box 129, Folder 2336, Pauli Murray Papers, Schlesinger Library, Radcliffe Institute for Advanced Study, Harvard University, Cambridge, Mass.; Jacqueline Jones, *Labor of Love, Labor of Sorrow: Black Women, Work, and the Family, from Slavery to the Present* (New York: Vintage, 1985), 301–310.
7. *Monthly Labor Review*, February 1968, 1–12; and April 1968, 14–22; U.S. Department of Labor, *1975 Handbook on Women Workers* (Washington, D.C.: Women's Bureau, 1975), 8–43; Kimberly Morgan, "A Child of the Sixties: The Great Society, the New Right, and the Politics of Federal Child Care," *Journal of Policy History* 13, no. 2 (2001): 215–250.
8. Harold Watts and Felicity Skidmore, *The Implications of Changing Family Patterns and Behavior in Labor Force and Hardship Management* (Washington, D.C.: National Commission on Employment and Unemployment Statistics, 1978), v; Brian Cashell, *Inflation and the Family Budget*, Congressional Research Service Report 79-258 E, December 19, 1979; U.S. Bureau of the Census, *U.S. Census of Population: 1960, Subject Reports. Occupation by Industry* (Washington, D.C.: Government Printing Office, 1963), table 1; "Census 2000 Summary File 3, p. 49: Sex by Industry for the Employed Civilian Population 16 Years and Over," *Census 2000*, http://factfinder.census.gov.
9. Colin Gordon, *Growing Apart: A Political History of American Inequality* (Washington, D.C.: Institute for Policy Studies, Program on Inequality and the Common Good, 2014), http://www.inequality.org; Michael Greenstone and Adam Looney, "Trends," *Milken Institute Review* (Third Quarter, 2011): 8–16; David Caplovitz, *Making Ends Meet: How Families Cope with Inflation and Recession* (Beverly Hills, Calif.: Sage, 1979), 9–10; Lawrence Mishel, Jared Bernstein, and Heidi Shierholz, *The State of Working America: 2008/2009* (Ithaca, N.Y.: Cornell University Press, 2009), 43–95, 227–261; *White House Conference on Families: Joint Hearings, U.S.*

Senate and House, February 2 and 3, 1978 (Washington, D.C., U.S. Government Printing Office, 1978), 295.
10. Ralph E. Smith, "The Movement of Women Into the Labor Force," in *The Subtle Revolution: Women at Work*, ed. Ralph E. Smith (Washington, D.C.: The Urban Institute, 1979), 1–29; Bernadette D. Proctor, Jessica L. Semega, and Melissa A. Kollar, *Income and Poverty in the United States: 2015* (Washington, D.C.: U.S. Government Printing Office, 2016).
11. Jones, *Labor of Love, Labor of Sorrow*, 232–321; Nancy MacLean, *Freedom Is Not Enough: The Opening of the American Workplace* (Cambridge, Mass.: Harvard University Press, 2006), 13–34, 117–154; Dorothy Sue Cobble, *The Other Women's Movement: Workplace, Justice, and Social Rights in Modern America* (Princeton, N.J.: Princeton University Press, 2005), 69–144.
12. *Newsletter from the Equal Employment Opportunity Commission*, July–August 1965, Box 74, Folder 1298, Pauli Murray Papers; Katherine Turk, *Equality on Trial: Gender and Rights in the Modern American Workplace* (Philadelphia: University of Pennsylvania Press, 2016).
13. Hirma Hill Kay, "Ruth Bader Ginsburg, Professor of Law," *Columbia University Law Review* 104, no. 1 (January 2004): 1–20; Elizabeth Duncan Koontz, "American Women at the Crossroads," June 12, 1970, 40/2548, Pauli Murray Papers.
14. Katharine T. Bartlett, "Pregnancy and the Constitution: The Uniqueness Trap," *California Law Review* 62, no. 5 (December 1974): 1532–1566; Deborah Dinner, "Strange Bedfellows at Work: Neomaternalism and the Making of Sex Discrimination Law," *Washington University Law Review* 91, no. 3 (2014).
15. Carrie N. Baker, *The Women's Movement Against Sexual Harassment* (New York: Cambridge University Press, 2008); Catharine A. MacKinnon, *Sexual Harassment of Working Women: A Case of Sex Discrimination* (New Haven, Conn.: Yale University Press, 1979); Francis Achampong, *Workplace Sexual Harassment Law: Principles, Landmark Developments, and Frameworks for Effective Risk Management* (Westport, Conn.: Quorum, 1999).
16. Serena Mayeri, *Reasoning from Race: Feminism, Law, and the Civil Rights Revolution* (Cambridge, Mass.: Harvard University Press, 2010), 44–63; Pauli Murray, "A Proposal to Reexamine the Applicability of the Fourteenth Amendment to State Laws and Practices Which Discriminate on the Basis of Sex Per Se," December 1962, Box 8, Folder 61, Presidential Commission on the Status of Women Papers, Schlesinger Library, Radcliffe Institute for Advanced Study, Harvard University, Cambridge, Mass.
17. U.S. Department of Labor, *Women in the Labor Force: A Databook* (Washington, D.C.: U.S. Bureau of Labor Statistics, 2010), tables 16, 27.

18. *Maternity and Paternity at Work: Law and Practice Across the World* (Geneva: International Labour Organization, 2014); Turk, *Equality on Trial*, 203–208.
19. See the speeches, memos, and letters in Box 138, Folder: Child Care, 1970–71; and Box 140, Folder: Child Care: Speeches, BA; memos and letters, Box 30, Folder 57, National Organization for Women Records, Radcliffe Institute for Advanced Study, Harvard University, Cambridge, Mass.; *Texas Report of the Governor's Commission on the Status of Women* (Washington, D.C.: Congressional Record, Government Printing Office, 1967), 34; *Report of the Commission on the Status of Women to the Governor and General Assembly of Virginia* (Washington, D.C.: Congressional Record, Government Printing Office, 1966), 45; Chisholm quoted in Congressional Record, May 18, 1971, E4526; Hearings, part 2, 536–537; National Task Force on Child Care, NOW, July 31, 1970, assorted letters, minutes, and documents, Box 42, Folder 35, National Organization for Women Records; Deborah Dinner, "The Universal Childcare Debate: Rights Mobilization, Social Policy, and the Dynamics of Feminist Activism," *Law and History Review* 28, no. 3 (August 2010): 577–628.
20. National Women's Political Caucus Day Care Alert, July 30, 1971, Box 128, Folder 2333, Pauli Murray Papers; Sonya Michel, *Children's Interests/Mothers' Rights: The Shaping of America's Child Care Policy* (New Haven, Conn.: Yale University Press, 2000), 248–251; *Comprehensive Child Development Act: Joint Hearings Before the Subcommittee on Employment, Manpower, and Poverty* (Washington, D.C.: Congressional Record, Government Printing Office, 1971), 1:165, 366.
21. *New York Times*, December 10, 1971.
22. Suzanne Mettler, *The Submerged State: How Invisible Government Policies Undermine American Democracy* (Chicago: University of Chicago Press, 2011).
23. *1960 Census Characteristics of Population*, vol. 1, table 82, U.S. Census Bureau, 1960; Herbert Hill, "Racial Discrimination in the Nation's Apprenticeship Training Programs," *Phylon* 23, no. 3 (Fall 1962): 216; Whitney Young, *To Be Equal* (New York: McGraw-Hill, 1964), 53.
24. Alice O'Connor, *Poverty Knowledge: Social Science, Social Policy, and the Poor in Twentieth-Century U.S. History* (Princeton, N.J.: Princeton University Press, 2001), 74–124; Patricia Hill Collins, *Black Feminist Thought: Knowledge, Consciousness, and the Politics of Empowerment* (Boston: Unwin Hyman, 1990), 74–78; Donna L. Franklin, *Ensuring Inequality: The Structural Transformation of the African American Family* (New York: Oxford University Press, 1997); "Reconsidering Culture and Poverty," a special issue of *Annals of the American Academy of Political and Social Science* (May 2010).

25. Melinda Chateauvert, "Framing Sexual Citizenship: Reconsidering the Discourse on African American Families," *Journal of African American History* 93, no. 2 (Spring 2008): 198–222; Marisa Chappell, *The War on Welfare: Family, Poverty, and Politics in Modern America* (Philadelphia: University of Pennsylvania Press, 2009); Jill Quadagno, "Race, Class, and Gender in the U.S. Welfare State: Nixon's Failed Family Assistance Plan," *American Sociological Review* 55, no. 1 (February 1990): 15.

26. American Civil Liberties Union, "Memorandum on the Rights of Welfare Recipients," March 1967, ACLU; Molly Michelmore, *Tax and Spend: Welfare, Taxes, and the Limits of American Liberalism* (Philadelphia: University of Pennsylvania Press, 2012).

27. Felicia Kornbluh, *The Battle for Welfare Rights: Politics and Poverty in Modern America* (Philadelphia: University of Pennsylvania Press, 2007), 92–95; National Welfare Rights Organization (NWRO), "Statement to the House Ways and Means Committee," October 27, 1969, Box 17, Folder 3, George Wiley Papers, Wisconsin Historical Society, Madison.

28. *New York Times*, August 9, 1969; "Fair Share Speech," Box 39, Welfare, John Ehrlichman Files, Richard Nixon Presidential Library, Lorba Linda, Calif.; memo to the president from Moynihan, January 20, 1970, Box 38, Welfare, John Ehrlichman Files; Mills, quoted in January 25, 1970, clipping file, Box 38, John Ehrlichman Files; Kilpatrick, quoted in *Los Angeles Times*, January 15, 1970.

39. Franklin Gilliam Jr., "The 'Welfare Queen' Experiment: How Viewers React to Images of African American Mothers on Welfare," *Nieman Reports* 53, no. 2 (Summer 1999); Franklin Gilliam Jr., "Punishment and Prejudice: Racial Disparities in the War on Drugs," *Human Rights Watch* 12, no. 2 (2000): 1–28.

30. Dinner, "Strange Bedfellows"; Turk, *Equality at Work*.

31. T. H. Marshall, "Citizenship and Social Class," in *The Welfare State Reader*, 3rd ed., ed. Christopher Pierson et al. (Malden, Mass.: Polity, 2014), 28–31.

PART IV

Possibilities of Resistance

IN THIS FINAL SECTION, contributors face the question of whether popular resistance is viable in an age of exclusion, and they explore some of the political goals and tools necessary for such opposition to develop and succeed. In the United States, recipients of government aid have been effectively silenced by coercive measures that include poor educations, forced labor for single-parent families, and incarceration for "quality-of-life" offenses. These measures have deprived millions of mostly black and poor individuals of their voting rights. In Europe, rising refugee populations fuel xenophobia and harbor increasing calls to restore national economic boundaries. Labor unions and left-wing political parties have fought unsuccessfully to resist these tendencies. Lacking a common vision of a political future, they have—as the once popular British Labour Party and the 2016 election of Donald Trump demonstrate—spectacularly failed.

The political scientist Birte Siim focuses on European issues: she demonstrates how notions of a multilayered, supranational EU citizenship have the potential to resist the nationalist comeback in European countries, which has been especially amplified by the immigration crisis.

Marisa Chappell analyzes the grassroots, multiracial movements of low-income Americans and their request and demands for redistribution and participatory citizenship. These demands, she suggests, have provoked an outcry from traditional political partisans, who have tried to stifle efforts to expand democracy. The bottom line, Francis Fox Piven suggests in a candid interview, will be a widespread popular insurgency. Only such a social movement will re-create a sense of popular solidarity and confidence in a government that advocates for social justice in the face of powerful market forces.

We are left, then, with more questions than answers. Can the welfare state survive the challenges of globalization, technological transformation, the reorganization of work, and mass migration? Can we imagine a new form of the welfare state (perhaps the universal basic income plan currently under consideration in Finland) that at once renders it functional and visible? Can we imagine a more responsive welfare state—and one less mired in bureaucracy? A 2016 British film, *I, Daniel Blake*, captures the depths to which the welfare state has sunk in the eyes of those who receive its benefits. The film dramatically reveals the cruelty inflicted on people that government was meant to serve. Welfare-state bureaucracy, the film suggests, dehumanizes those in need, making a mockery of notions of social citizenship and severing the link between government service and democratic participation. We close, then, on a note raised by Frances Fox Piven: reformers once hoped that the welfare state might empower ordinary people to become more active citizens. With Piven, we ask: is it possible that only popular uprisings will move the welfare state to its former purposes?

CHAPTER TWELVE

Nationalism's Challenge to European Citizenship, Democracy, and Equality

Potential for Resistance from Transnational Civil Society

BIRTE SIIM

THIS CHAPTER CONSIDERS the challenges to democratic citizenship posed by the growth of new forms of nationalism in post-crisis Europe, a set of challenges made even more daunting by the present refugee crisis. In light of these challenges, scholars have argued that it is necessary to reframe the meaning of citizenship. They have proposed a new, multilayered conception of what it means to be a European citizen, one that can encompass the privileges and responsibilities of an EU citizen from the local all the way up to the transnational level. Their reconsideration is rooted in skepticism about the continuing capacity of the nation-state to promote equality and social justice. In this essay, I explore the conflict between attachment to national identity, on the one hand, and the inability of nations, on the other, to secure the social, civil, and political rights of their people. I ask whether the two can be reconciled using an intersectional approach.[1]

The analytical basis for this claim is grounded in the fact that rights, political participation, and citizens' identities are no longer connected solely to the nation-state.[2] While scholars have proposed competing theories and models of equality and social justice, only a few have explicitly addressed the transnational challenge to the specific trinity of citizenship, (gender) equality, and social justice.[3] Arguably this intersectional and transnational approach may be applied to the EU context, since European integration has been studied both "from above," by focusing mainly on political institutions, or "from below," by concentrating mainly on citizens' rights, identities, and political participation.[4] Here, I hope to provide an example of what this approach might look like.

This chapter aims to make two contributions. First, to provide an overview of the theoretical debates surrounding those transnational challenges to citizenship and democracy that arise from globalization, European integration, and migration. It proposes to combine a transnational and intersectional approach to understand European citizenship, focusing on the interrelations of the EU polity and civil-society actors. Second, this chapter presents the results of empirical research to explore both the possibilities and the problems a transnational civil society faces in the attempt to create a true European public sphere capable of influencing the contemporary political agenda.[5] From this perspective, the challenges posed by nationalism to EU citizenship concern the relationship between antidiscrimination and gender-equality policies. The chapter argues that a vibrant public sphere will be necessary to promote a transnational civil society that mediates relationships between EU institutions and European citizens.[6]

THEORETICAL DEBATES: CITIZENSHIP, DEMOCRACY, AND EQUALITY IN A GLOBAL AGE

In order to assess the potentials and barriers for expanding citizenship and democracy beyond national borders, this section briefly reviews the theoretical debates surrounding citizenship, democracy, and equality in our global age. Globalization and European integration have increased migration and mobility across and within borders. This new permeability has been dogged by problems of social cohesion and the integration of immigrant and refugees within and across nation-states. The socioeconomic and political transformations linked to migration and mobility across and within nation-states have inspired postnational and transnational models of democracy and citizenship[7] challenging methodological nationalism,[8] that is, the predominant focus on the nation-state as the ruling model in mainstream social science.

With the rise of globalization have come new notions of postnational, cosmopolitan, and global citizenship. This has raised questions about what kind of a global-citizenship model is feasible and desirable. The new conditions for citizenship would seem to undermine the classical models, those based on a unity of rights, duties, participation, and identities within the nation-state. Some perceive the human-rights regime as a globalization of rights and responsibilities, which would be the essence of a globalization of citizenship.[9] One can interpret the internationalization of the human-rights norms, along with the weakening of state sovereignty, as both the end of the national-citizenship model[10] and as a new potential framework for citizenship in the global age.[11] Those who espouse "cosmopolitanism" argue that globalization could become the basis for a multilayered citizenship, one that would embrace both the notion of a global citizen and the use of international human-rights law.[12] But while this may be a desirable model, no sovereign power exists to enforce human rights at a global level. In the absence of a global authority, a viable nation-state is therefore indispensable as a guarantor of rights.[13] Some argue that the lack of a common language and culture makes true global citizenship, where individuals owe duties to the entire human race, neither feasible nor desirable.[14]

One of the premises for the cosmopolitan thesis is the fact that today citizenship and nationality have become separated; the state is no longer the exclusive reference point of sovereignty. Citizenship is now increasingly deterritorialized and fragmented into the separate discourses of rights, participation, responsibility, and identity, creating new possibilities for participation and rights both within and beyond the state.[15] One variation on the idea of cosmopolitan democracy aims to reform international organizations such as the United Nations and develop a set of binding political institutions "from above," that is, at the global level.[16] Another variation aims at forming a global civil society through which social movements and nongovernmental organizations could pursue their goals across national borders, thereby changing the dominant discourses "from below."[17] The notion of a "civic" cosmopolitanism, a citizenship model rooted in civic communities, presents a "thin" version of this same idea. It situates cosmopolitanism in actual local, regional, national, or transnational communities—with the hope of being able to mediate between nationalism and postnationalism.[18]

National rights, or citizenship, may currently be the foundation for human rights, but research indicates the presence of a trend in which struggles for redistribution and recognition are expanding beyond and across borders. Scholars make a useful differentiation between global and cosmopolitan citizenship and propose that the underlying rights of cosmopolitanism are the "rights of mobility and rights to transaction."[19] These rights are explicitly or implicitly about crossing or interacting across borders or creating new settlements. These include the rights of migrant labor; the right to hold a passport; the right to enter a country; the right of asylum; the rights of refugees and others to reside; the right to marry outside one's state; or the right to buy property, goods, and services or invest across other states.[20] These cosmopolitan rights are not, however, related to any specific duties of mobility or transaction.

THE TRANSNATIONAL CHALLENGE: DEMOCRACY, EQUALITY, AND SOCIAL JUSTICE

The political theorist Nancy Fraser has recently proposed a transnational approach that reframes the model of deliberative democracy.[21] She claims that in order to reconstruct democratic theory in the current "postnational constellation," it is necessary to problematize the national frame and reflect upon the notion of "transnational public spheres." Her main argument is that public spheres are increasingly transnational or postnational with respect to each of the constitutive elements of public opinion: The *who* of communication, the *what* of communication, the *where* of communication, the *how* of communication, and finally the *addressee* of communication, which is no longer the Westphalian state power but a mix of public and private transnational powers. This has created transnational spaces defined as spaces beyond the boundaries of the nation-state: the space where actors, actions, and institutions cross nation-state borders.[22]

Fraser's model is premised on the ideas of social justice: universal principles linking social equality (redistribution), cultural diversity (recognition), and participatory democracy (representation).[23] She holds that, in a globalizing world, the struggle for economic redistribution and social recognition necessitates the discussion of political issues at the global rather than national level. This rests on the basic claim that decisions affecting "the fate of all," for example, global warming, are increasingly taken, or not taken, at the global level. This argument has enormous implications for conceptualizing the public sphere. In deliberative democracy, the public sphere is a key concept: it enhances the legitimacy of decisions and empowers citizens vis-à-vis the state.[24] The public sphere is concerned with *who* participates and on *what* terms. Fraser has previously criticized the universal ideal of the public sphere and the potentially exclusive nature of Habermas's model. In particular, she has taken exception to his public/private divide, since the private family is an important "political" arena in reproduction and in gender roles. Her revised public-sphere model is premised upon heterogeneity and diversity, which aims to expand democracy and decenter politics from parliament to civil society.

Fraser has also discussed what sort of changes would be required to imagine a genuine critical and democratizing role for transnational public spheres under current conditions. According to her, any public-sphere theory faces a dual challenge in a postnational world: first, to create new, transnational political institutions and, second, to make them accountable to new, transnational public spheres.[25]

In what follows, we will use Fraser's approach to help reflect on the specific European context. Her take includes both a theoretical critique of the national bias of most approaches to understanding the public sphere as well as an analytical claim as to the possibility of transnational public spheres holding transnational public powers accountable. This approach to social justice is promising, since it would require a paradigm shift from "a theory of social justice" to an understanding of justice as a kind of participatory parity, one that is focused not only on the "what" of justice but also on the "who" and "how."[26]

DILEMMAS FOR EUROPEAN CITIZENSHIP AND THE INTEGRATION MODEL

Research has started to address the postnational and transnational challenges posed to citizenship by the European-integration project,[27] but the assessment of its impact on EU citizenship remains contested. The European-integration model has been interpreted as proof that a transnational democratic citizenship model is both feasible and desirable.[28] But European integration has also been understood to create a postnational citizenship based upon a deterritorialized notion of a person's rights that,[29] along with a presumption of a "Fortress Europe," contributes to an exclusionary model of citizenship.[30] Scholars point to the prevailing democratic deficit in EU institutions and the lack of popular support for the EU project overall as proof that a transnational citizenship model is neither realistic nor welcome.[31] Despite the present limitations of EU citizenship, the current definition of European citizenship, one based upon residence rather than birth, provides institutional possibilities for democratic citizenship as both a legal institution and a lived experience.[32]

Considering that the European Union has developed a multilevel structure of sovereignty, it makes sense to explore Fraser's concept of the transnational public sphere in the context of the European Union. One research question is whether these transnational powers can be made accountable to transnational European publics. This concern depends on whether a European public sphere beyond the borders of national democracy is feasible, and, if so, how such a public sphere should deal with gender and other inequalities. These research questions were addressed empirically from the perspective of diversity and gender[33] in case studies analyzing the participation of citizens in the European public sphere.

The European-integration model has expanded national citizenship to include new rights for EU citizens to move freely across national borders and to work and live legally in EU member countries. EU citizenship is defined as a supplementary form of citizenship derived from member-state citizenship, a form of "nested" citizenship based upon residence. The EU polity raises questions about how to mediate the tensions among national citizenship, EU citizenship, and the human rights of third-country nationals. European integration has created a dilemma between the national and transnational dimensions of citizenship as well as between insiders and outsiders. EU citizens have gained civic, political, and social rights linked primarily to their mobility as workers. EU public policies have addressed discrimination according to gender, race/ethnicity, sexuality, age, and handicap. Since migration policies have generally become more restrictive, it has, however, been increasingly difficult for third-country nationals to enter the European Union legally or for immigrants to obtain citizenship in a member state and be included in the European Union as equal citizens. The European Parliament has come into more power, but the political identities and belongings of citizens are still mainly tied to local/regional or national communities rather than to the EU polity.

EU citizenship and nation-state citizenship thus complement each other in a multilevel polity. The notion of nested European citizenship refers to the interrelationship between the different levels. Rights are, however, with some exceptions still equated with nationality. To enfranchise fully immigrants from outside Europe, the European Union must define citizenship in terms of residence for all people living legally in a member country.[34] At the moment, citizens of member states who are living and working legally in another EU country, as well as third-country nationals, can vote only in local elections, not in national elections. The institution of EU citizenship has facilitated the wide acceptance in member states of dual citizens, allowing individuals from other member states the right not to renounce their original citizenship upon naturalization. The global trend of increasing tolerance of dual citizenship indicates a pluralization of citizens' ties across the borders of sovereign states.[35] Migration research has shown that there is also a trend toward dual or hybrid identities,[36] especially among young people and Europeans.

The economic, political, and refugee crises can be understood as a single deep "crisis of social reproduction" that has contributed to the other challenges facing the European integration project and the free movement of workers and their families across the continent. These crises have led to the criticism of social dumping, that is, the practice of allowing employers to lower wages and reduce employees' benefits in order to attract and retain employment and investment, and "welfare tourism," helping strengthen neonationalist and euroskeptic parties and movements. Welfare cuts and austerity politics across Europe have been followed by increasing inequality, unemployment, and growing poverty. The restructuring of the welfare state has lowered standards of living while increasing despair and insecurity. This has led to a growing mutual distrust between ordinary citizens and their governments, stimulating protest, resistance, and solidarity movements. While there has been no large-scale mobilization of European citizens, the right wing has grown across the continent, as has left-wing populism and euroskepticism. Euroskeptic parties gained between one-third and one-fourth of the votes in the most recent round of European elections.[37]

Scholars have identified a gulf between the opinions of citizens, on the one hand, and the policies adopted by the European Union and European governments to solve the pressing economic and financial problems, on the other. This gap between citizens and their governments has only been exacerbated by the recent refugee crisis.[38] The nationalist positions and the euroskeptic mindset that claims that the solution to these problems is "less Europe" have only gained strength. Only a left-wing minority position proposes to strengthen the democratic influence of citizens on EU institutions and increase the EU control of banks, financial institutions, and corporations, for example, by calling for the adoption of a "Tobin tax"[39] on financial transactions. That said, it is still possible to identify a growing European-wide mobilization against austerity, a movement that demands control of the economy and the active, democratic participation of citizens.[40]

EUROPEAN INTEGRATION, THE PUBLIC SPHERE, AND TRANSNATIONAL CIVIL SOCIETY

The ideas of transnational democracy, civil society, and the public sphere imply a radical break with an understanding of democracy as an institution confined to the nation-state. Many scholars of democracy and European integration see the European public sphere as necessary if citizens are to identify with the political system and make it responsive to their needs.[41] Policy makers must be accountable within the public sphere if they are to be responsive to the concerns of their constituents. The lack of a European public sphere is therefore often understood as partly responsible for the European Union's "democratic deficit" and legitimacy gap.[42] Over the last ten years, the European Parliament (EP) has gained both power and legitimacy, and today it exercises legislative functions together with the Council of the European Union (the Council) and the European Commission. It has been directly elected every five years by universal suffrage since 1979. However, voter turnout at EP elections has fallen consecutively at each election since that date, and has been under 50 percent since 1999. Voter turnout in 2014 stood at 42.54 percent of all European voters. Compared to the nation-states it comprises, the EP has a "democratic deficit," since it does not formally possess legislative initiative.[43]

Europeanization can be defined "from above" by studying the activities of political institutions and "from below" by considering the activities of civil-society organizations. Competing methodological approaches of research and varying interpretations have led to the rise of fundamental questions concerning the public sphere in democracy. One major question raised by this debate asks how both diversity and equality can be accommodated in a democratic public sphere. Participation in the public sphere is an expression of solidarity, even if this participation does not lead to harmony,[44] and some scholars maintain that contestation is a crucial precondition for the emergence of the European Public Sphere (EPS) rather than an indication of its absence.[45]

Myra Marx Ferree's comparative and transnational approach has contributed to an understanding of the different possible meanings of equality. Ferree has called the European Union a complex hybrid, one shaped by historical conflicts and struggles. She argues that this complexity opens up the possibility for creative combinations in dealing with inequalities and differences. The hybridity of the EU model also allows for negotiation among diverse models of Europeanization. These models can incorporate competing senses of transnationalism. As Ferree writes, this flexibility makes possible "an orientation to neo-liberalism and economic competitiveness on the global level, and a specific regional claim to the distinctive success of 'Europe' as a model of modernity and social progress."[46] The particular EU framework has implications for the approach to gender equality/equity. Here, conflicts are played out mostly in relation to citizen/noncitizen differences and struggles over migration/integration as well as group differences.

Inspired by these diverse approaches to democracy, Mokre and Siim propose that the public sphere can be understood as a locus or space for conflict and struggle. These struggles might center on the inclusion or exclusion of women, migrants, and marginalized social groups in society[47] but also on the acceptance or intolerance of refugees and asylum seekers. In this approach, the European public sphere is understood as a place for political actors both to contest and negotiate policies and visions for (gender) equality and social justice. It remains an open empirical question what kinds of contestations and negotiations exist in the European public sphere. This approach makes it possible to understand contemporary conflicts concerning "social dumping" and "family benefits" as ordinary political struggles about who has the right to what kind of social and welfare benefits. These struggles are not necessarily a sign of crisis for the European integration project but could also be interpreted as a sign of democratic heartiness concerning classical issues related to redistribution, recognition, and participation, all of which concern the key questions in a welfare state: who gets what, when, and where?

RESEARCH ON GENDER AND DIVERSITY IN THE EUROPEAN PUBLIC SPHERES

Taken as a whole, the European Union's transnational institutions, history, and definition of equality are in many ways unique, and it behooves us to attempt to understand intersectionality and transnationalism from the specific European policy context.[48] The academic debate surrounding intersectionality beyond the nation-state has yet to acknowledge the European Union's particular multidimensional and transnational contexts; there are no authoritative case studies that explore the barriers and opportunities for gender diversity in the European public sphere. The research strategy of the present study is based on a dynamic approach. It is premised on identifying conflicts, struggles, and contestations and then focuses on the relationships between specific institutions and civil-society actors as well as between different groups of citizens and noncitizens.[49]

The Eurosphere project explored Europeanization "from below"—what one could call horizontal Europeanization—by focusing on how gender and ethnic diversity are discursively framed across Europe and, at the transnational level, by selected political parties and civil-society organizations.[50] The approach is an intersectional one that aims to analyze the framings of gender and diversity in the European public sphere.[51] It is an approach that homes in on intersections of gender with other kinds of differences and inequalities, and it has become prominent in recent research on the construction of gender in Europe.[52]

Siim and Mokre defined the European public sphere in the plural and further differentiated between various public arenas.[53] The methodological design encompasses multiple approaches, and the multiple sites or arenas of the public sphere can be divided into four dimensions: *the who*—i.e., the participation of citizens; *the what*, i.e., the format and issues of the public discourse; *the where of communication*; and the *outcome* of the process.[54]

The European Union consists of twenty-eight nation-states, and the motto "united in diversity" refers to the right of mobility of EU nationals within the European Union. In other words, workers and citizens may cross borders and work and live legally in any EU member country. Equal pay in the labor market and gender equality in society are fundamental principles of the European Union, together with rules against discrimination based on nationality and recognition of the rights of national minorities. European integration has gradually strengthened gender equality as a policy platform and has put on the political agenda gender-equality issues such as how to reconcile work and family, gender and violence, as well as the role of women in political and economic decision making. With the adoption of the Amsterdam Treaty and the Lisbon Treaty, combating multiple forms of discrimination became part of the EU's official understanding of fundamental rights. But while almost all political actors on the right and left have generally accepted issues of gender equality, albeit with varying interpretations, "diversity" issues remain contested, especially when connected with the challenges from migration. One thinks especially of the difficulties the EU has faced accommodating the cultural and religious diversity of new migrant groups as well as the heated antagonism between citizens and noncitizens.

Since Amsterdam (1997) and Lisbon (2009), the EU has adopted the multiple-discrimination approach as a major policy frame next to gender equality. The treaties thus provide political actors with new arenas for civil-society demands, ones beyond questions of discrimination in employment, vis-à-vis those EU institutions that concern themselves with fundamental rights.[55] With the Amsterdam Treaty, multiple discriminations became a guiding principle for addressing inequality. Article 13 mentions "sex, racial or ethnic origin and belief, disability, age and sexual orientation" as grounds of discrimination. The Charter of Fundamental Rights (2000) goes even further in the grounds it lays out for antidiscrimination as well as the rights it enumerates in relation to family protection and gender equality. With the Lisbon Treaty, the Charter became part of fundamental EU law; the Charter can be seen as a milestone in European antidiscrimination legislation, enlarging the scope of protection against discrimination and giving it the status of a fundamental right.[56]

The particular history of the EU—its political institutions and multilevel system of governance—provides an opportunity to study the inclusion and exclusion of women in democratic politics as well as the framings of gender equality and gender justice across Europe.[57] The focus in the empirical case studies was on the participation of citizens in the public sphere and the framings of gender and diversity by political elites,[58] specifically in relation to two main arenas: social-movement SMO/NGOs and political parties. Animating this study is the question of what kinds of public spheres include and exclude which groups, to what degree, and on which particular issues.[59] This approach makes it possible to identify elements of openness in various kinds of public spaces toward the idea of a European public sphere.

One of the democratic achievements of the European Parliament during the last thirty years has been the representation of women in politics. Women make up between 30 to 40 percent of the parliaments in most European countries and one-third of the European Parliament.[60] The study of women as political actors demonstrates that women also have a political presence within the European public sphere. They represent about one-third of the members of national political parties and NGO/SMOs as well as a third of the members of transnational civil organizations and the European Parliament. Research on gender and political representation has demonstrated that women's representation does not in itself change the political agenda. However, it can make a difference from the perspective of democratic politics, since it renders particular versions of state feminism possible, based upon interactions between political institutions and civil-society actors.

A diverse set of case studies has helped highlight the intersections among European social movements, for example, that between the European Women's Lobby (EWL) and the European Network Against Racism (ENAR).[61] A case study of the European Year for Combating Poverty and Social Exclusion (2010) addresses the intersections of national and transnational policy agendas and their relative concern for different inequalities as well as the interactions between civil-society organizations and the nation-state.[62] The authors find that it is important to pay attention not only to the institutional political opportunity structures but also to the influence of the discursive opportunity structures for gender diversities within the framework of the EU. The EU's unique transnational institutional framework is particularly challenging for equality policies from the perspective of gender and diversity groups. The analysis of the European Year for Combating Poverty and Social Exclusion illustrates that the EU policy framework interacts with particular national contexts in the construction of both barriers and opportunities for creating gender and diversity policy.[63]

Recent research has emphasized the importance of the discursive intersections between gender and ethnicity/race as part of the general understanding of diversity in the European public sphere.[64] It names vivid transnational debates over questions of gender that intersect with other social categories. These debates are driven mainly by civil society, for example, by the European Women's Lobby and the European Network Against Racism. On this basis, the authors argue, following Mouffe, that these debates can be understood as public spheres because they revolve around common—although contested—themes. If the public sphere is understood as a space of contestation, these findings point toward the possible emergence of a European public sphere that deals with gender and diversity issues that are of profound political importance.

This positive assessment of an emerging European public sphere as a transnational space where political actors may discuss common issues concerning gender and diversity is, however, only part of the picture. These public spheres lack crucial features of the classical understanding of that institution: specifically, *inclusiveness* and *accountability*. Inclusiveness would make it possible for everyone to take part in the public sphere. The public spheres identified in these case studies in fact exclude many of those concerned, especially noncitizens. While issues concerning Muslim women are highly contested within the national and European public spheres—take, for example, the donning of the hijab and niqab—most of the women concerned have no voice in the debate. Accountability and legitimacy are challenged because of different national and political positions on ethnicity and gender in the European public sphere. We conclude that the European public sphere we have identified is fragile and prone to failure. The common discursive patterns concerning the intersections of gender and diversity may at best be interpreted as signs of the emergence of broader European public spheres, and it remains an open question whether these debates can be generalized to fulfill the classical functions of the concept.

To sum up: the gender- and antidiscrimination-policy frame of the EU can be interpreted both as an advantage and a barrier toward promoting civil, political, and social rights. The findings indicate that actors in civil society at the national and transnational levels compete for attention in the public sphere when it comes to issues of inequality.[65] Sometimes they also collaborate toward promoting general calls for stronger antidiscrimination measures in Europe.[66] This supports the claim that conflicts, struggles, negotiations, and collaborations surrounding common issues concerning gender inequality and other species of discrimination are an essential part of European democratic debates and arguably can be interpreted as part of an emerging transnational European public sphere.

It is an open question as to whether the European refugee crisis is also a democratic crisis. One issue is whether the trends toward collaboration and negotiation among transnational NGOs organized around antidiscrimination have continued or whether the competition and struggles over resources have increased. Scholars have pointed toward contradictory political developments: on the one hand, new popular protest as well as resistance and solidarity movements have grown, especially in southern Europe and Greece, which may possibly become part of an emergent European public sphere.[67] On the other hand, right-wing populism and neonationalism has also grown, and ironically these nationalist movements have been increasingly cooperating with one another across national borders and in the EP.[68] It is not yet clear how to interpret these contradictory trends, as this depends both on our theoretical concepts and the lenses through which we read them, our normative visions as well as our empirical data.

CONCLUSION: REFRAMING EQUALITY, DIVERSITY, AND SOCIAL JUSTICE

The European Union is a multilevel polity, and gender equality has become a major policy frame, influencing claims for gender justice across Europe. With the adoption of the Amsterdam Treaty and Lisbon Treaty, the EU has arguably recognized the crucial importance of intersectional approaches to discrimination, approaches that have become a significant policy frame influencing the discourses and strategies surrounding gender, ethnic, and religious inequality as well as discrimination premised on nationality.

The vantage point of intersectionality was employed as a methodological approach to the empirical study of the articulations of gender and ethnic diversity within the European public sphere. The focus was on the participation of civil-society actors and the framing of gender and diversity issues in case studies in six EU member states, including major political parties, six national women's NGOs/SMOs, the European Women's Lobby and the European Network Against Racism as well as the FEMM Committee on Women's Rights and Gender Equality in the European Parliament. The findings illuminate the diverse articulations by major political actors across Europe of interactions between discourses of gender and ethnic diversity. They illustrate that issues of multiple inequalities and discrimination are placed on the political agenda and, from NGOs to the European Parliament, have influenced major political actors in the European public sphere.

Studies of the intersections of gender and antidiscrimination policies within the EU illustrate that the principle of full equality is a contested notion, one shaped by particular historical contingencies, institutional contexts, and situated debates. They show that multiple forms of communication around gender equality and antidiscrimination in public spheres generally, and the European public sphere specifically, are premised on deliberation and negotiations as well as on conflicts and contestation.

It is worth noting that the EU's gender-equality paradigm has led to the more or less unanimous acceptance of gender equality as a European value among political actors.[69] In contrast, we found no similar agreement as to the social value of antidiscrimination, although the Lisbon Treaty endows it with the same legal status as gender equality. Both are listed among the fundamental rights of European citizenship. The EU has accepted gender equality, but protections against other forms of discrimination remain contested among major political actors.

The transnational case studies of women's organizations have identified a plurality of voices and a diversity of interests, reflecting the heterogeneity of women as a group.[70] The EU's dual focus on gender equality and discrimination on multiple fronts has influenced the strategies of the transnational women's movements, leading them to include minority women's interests. European Parliament debates on women's representation have disclosed a surprising consensus across Europe and the left-right divide concerning proposals to adopt legally binding quotas for the representation of women on electoral lists and in corporate boardrooms. The debates reveal that the institutional framework is not structurally responsive to the plurality of women's interests.

On the basis of these empirical findings, Mokre and Siim proposed that a fragile European public sphere is emerging, one rooted in civil-society organizations concerned with questions regarding gender inequality and other forms of discrimination.[71] They also note that contradictory trends exist. On the one hand, civil activism in both fields has led to transnational networks and public spheres. On the other hand, antidiversity positions, especially anti-Muslim movements, have also moved beyond national borders. Finally, it is emphasized that the lack of *inclusiveness* and *accountability* of EU institutions remains a major democratic problem for an emerging European public sphere.

The present refugee crisis has exacerbated the EU's problems with democracy, equality and solidarity. There is a strong trend toward a renationalizing of the European public sphere, one that is especially visible in debates in the mass media and recently evidenced in both national elections as well as in elections to the European Parliament in May 2014. One question is how the present antagonism toward the project of European integration by right-wing populist leaders and mainstream leaders, like David Cameron and the recent UK vote to leave the EU, should be interpreted. It is undoubtedly a sign of a growing nationalism directed against mobility, migration, and refugees among political forces and world leaders like President Trump, dedicated to defending the exclusive rights of national citizens. The question is whether it might become a wakeup call for diverse pro-European forces, leading to new debates and strategies in support of European citizenship, democracy, and solidarity. It is also possible to find the beginnings of a transnational solidarity among migrants and among students as well as within the European left and among marginalized social groups. Can the refugee crisis inspire the kind of debates about the future of democracy and solidarity that scholars such as Fraser and Habermas have longed for? Is this the beginning or the end of the dream of the European public sphere?

NOTES

1. These scholars propose the reframing of citizenship, democracy, and equality beyond the boundaries of the nation-state: David Held, "The Transformation of the Political Community: Rethinking Democracy in the

Context of Globalization," in *Democracy's Edges*, ed. Ian Shapiro and Casiano Hacker-Cordón (New York: Cambridge University Press, 1999), 84–111; Engin Isin and Bryan Turner, "Investigating Citizenship: An Agenda for Citizenship Studies," *Citizenship Studies* 11, no. 1 (2008): 5–17; Nancy Fraser, "Transnationalizing the Public Sphere: On the Legitimacy and Efficacy of Public Opinion in a Post-Westphalian World," *Theory & Society* 24, no. 4 (2007): 7–30.

2. Isin and Turner, "Investigating Citizenship."
3. Nancy Fraser, *Fortunes of Feminism: From State-Managed Capitalism to Neoliberal Crisis* (London: Verso, 2011); Nira Yuval-Davis, *The Politics of Belonging: Intersectional Contestations* (London: Sage, 2011); Myra Marx Ferree, *Varieties of Feminism: German Gender Politics in Global Perspective* (Stanford, Calif.: Stanford University Press, 2012).
4. Birte Siim and Monika Mokre, eds., *Negotiating Gender and Diversity in the Emergent European Public Sphere* (Basingstoke: Palgrave/Macmillan, 2013); Lise Rolandsen Agustín and Birte Siim, "Gender Diversities—Practicing Intersectionality in the European Union," *Ethnicities* 14, no. 4 (2014): 539–555.
5. This discussion grows out of a number of case studies that focus on the intersections of gender and diversity in the EU polity; see Siim and Mokre, *Negotiating Gender and Diversity*; Agustín and Siim, "Gender Diversities."
6. I.e., women's, migration, and black and antiracist organizations: Agustín and Siim, "Gender Diversities"; Birte Siim, "Gender, Diversity, and Migration: Challenges to Nordic Welfare, Gender-Equality Politics, and Research," *Equality, Diversity, and Inclusion: An International Journal* 32, no. 6 (2014): 615–628.
7. Held, "The Transformation of the Political Community"; Gerard Delanty, *Citizenship in a Global Age: Society, Culture, Politics* (Buckingham: Open University Press, 2000); Saskia Sassen, "Towards Post-National and De-Nationalized Citizenship," in *Handbook for Citizenship Studies*, ed. Engin F. Isin and Bryan F. Turner (London: Sage, 2003), 277–295.
8. Andreas Wimmer and Nina Glick Schiller distinguish the different modes of methodological nationalism and show how they have influenced research on migration. They argue that the naturalization of the nation-state can be found in different disciplines and in many intellectual variations. The authors attempt to avoid the Scylla of methodological nationalism without falling into the Charybdis of methodological fluidity and the rhetoric of cosmopolitanism. Their article aims to develop a set of concepts for the study of migration that does more than reflect the preconditions

and taken-for-granted assumptions of our times. Andreas Wimmer and Nina Glick Schiller, "Methodological Nationalism and Beyond: Nation Building, Migration, and Social Sciences," *Global Networks* 2, no. 4 (2002): 301–334, esp. 327.
9. Andrew Linklater, "Cosmopolitan Citizenship," *Citizenship Studies* 2, no. 1 (1998): 23–41.
10. Yasemin N. Soysal, *Limits of Citizenship: Migrants and Postnational Membership in Europe* (Chicago: University of Chicago Press, 1994).
11. Delanty, *Citizenship in a Global Age*.
12. Derek Heater, *World Citizenship: Cosmopolitan Thinking and Its Opponents* (London: Continuum, 2002); Linklater, "Cosmopolitan Citizenship."
13. Isin and Turner, "Investigating Citizenship," 13.
14. Will Kymlicka and Wayne Norman, eds., *Citizenship in Diverse Societies* (Oxford: Oxford University Press, 1999); Christian Joppke, "Multicultural Citizenship," *Handbook of Citizenship Studies* (2003).
15. Delanty, *Citizenship in a Global Age*, 53.
16. Held, "The Transformation of the Political Community."
17. John S. Dryzek, *Deliberative Democracy and Beyond: Liberals, Critics, and Contestations* (Oxford: Oxford University Press, 2000).
18. Delanty, *Citizenship in a Global Age*, 143.
19. E.g., Isin and Turner, "Investigating Citizenship."
20. Ibid., 14.
21. Fraser, "Transnationalizing the Public Sphere"; Fraser, *Fortunes of Feminism*.
22. Agustín and Siim, "Gender Diversities."
23. Nancy Fraser, "Rethinking the Public Sphere," *Social Text* 25–26 (1990): 77.
24. Ibid.
25. See Fraser, "Transnationalizing the Public Sphere," 23.
26. Nancy Fraser, "Reframing Justice in a Globalizing World," *New Left Review* 36 (November–December 2005): 8–9.
27. Delanty, *Citizenship in a Global Age*; Thomas Faist and Peter Kivisto, eds., *Dual Citizenship in Global Perspective: From Unitary to Multiple Citizenship* (Basingstoke: Palgrave/Macmillan, 2007).
28. Jürgen Habermas, "Democracy, Solidarity, and the European Crisis," lecture delivered in Leuven, April 26, 2013.
29. Soysal, *Limits of Citizenship*.
30. Ruth Lister, *Citizenship: Feminist Perspectives* [1997] (Basingstoke: Palgrave/Macmillan, 2003), 47.
31. Shapiro and Hacker-Cordon, eds., *Democracy's Edges*.
32. Delanty, *Citizenship in a Global Age*.

33. The results from the case studies are published in Siim and Mokre, *Negotiating Gender and Diversity*; Siim, "Gender, Diversity, and Migration;" Agustín and Siim, "Gender Diversities."
34. Reiner Bauböck, "Citizenship and Migration: Concepts and Controversies," in *Migration and Citizenship: Legal Status, Rights, and Political Participation*, ed. Reiner Bauböck, IMISCOE Reports (Amsterdam: Amsterdam University Press, 2006), 15–32.
35. Thomas Faist, "Introduction: The Shifting Boundaries of the Political," in *Dual Citizenship in Global Perspective*, 1–25.
36. Wimmer and Glick Schiller, "Methodological Nationalism and Beyond."
37. At the last EP elections in May 2014, the populist parties received successful election results, but the parties broke up into different political groups after the election: Geert Wilder's Dutch Party of Freedom and Marine Le Pen's French National Front joined the Europe Freedom and Democracy group (EFD). The Danish Populist Party has become normalized. It left EFD and was accepted in Cameron's political group, the European Reformist and Conservative group (ECR). This contrasts with Hungary's far-right party, Jobbik, which is still outside all political groups, since it is perceived as too radical: http://www.europarl.europa.eu/aboutparliament/en/20150201PVL00010/Organisation.
38. Habermas, "Democracy, Solidarity, and the European Crisis," 1.
39. The "Tobin tax" was originally proposed in the early 1970s by the Nobel Prize–winning American economist James Tobin. It involves applying a small charge—of as little or less than 0.1 percent—on foreign-currency transactions to protect countries from exchange-rate volatility caused by short-term currency speculation. After the financial crisis in 2008, the Tobin tax is again on the political agenda. Eleven EU member countries have said they wish to move ahead with introducing a financial-transactions tax in order to tackle the debt crisis, including France and Germany. The tax has the backing of the European Commission. The tax is opposed by other EU countries, including the United Kingdom. The United States is also opposed to the idea. http://www.bbc.com/news/business-15552412.
40. The most well-known examples of antiausterity and democracy movements are the Spanish Podemos ("We Can") and the Greek Syriza: http://www.theguardian.com/commentisfree/2015/sep/09/the-guardian-view-on-podemos-rage-against-austerity-is-not-enough.
41. Jürgen Habermas, *The Postnational Constellation: Political Essays* (Cambridge, Mass.: MIT Press, 2001).
42. See, for example, John E. Eriksen and Erik O. Fossum, "Democracy Through Strong Publics in the European Union?" *Journal of Common Market Studies* 40, no. 3 (September 2002): 401–424.

43. Ulrike Liebert, "The European Citizenship Paradox: Renegotiating Equality and Diversity in the New Europe," *Critical Review of International Social and Political Philosophy* 10, no. 4 (2007): 277.
44. C. Calhoun, "The Democratic Integration of Europe Interests, Identity, and the Public Sphere," *EUROZINE* 7 (2004): 1–22.
45. Thomas Risse, "An Emerging European Public Sphere? Theoretical Clarifications and Empirical Indications," Working Paper 3, June 2003 (Washington, D.C.: The BMW Center for German and European Studies, Georgetown University), 5; Donatella Della Porta and Manuela Caiani, *Social Movements and Europeanisation* (Oxford: Oxford University Press, 2009).
46. Myra Marx Ferree, "Framing Equality: The Politics of Race, Class, and Gender in the U.S., Germany, and the Expanding European Union," in *Gender Politics in the Expanding European Union: Mobilization, Inclusion, Exclusion*, ed. Silke Roth (Oxford: Berghahn, 2008), 237–262.
47. Cornelia Brüll, Monika Mokre, and Birte Siim, "Inclusion and Exclusion in the European Public Sphere: Intersections of Gender and Race," *Javnost—The Public, Journal of European Institute for Communication and Culture* 19, no. 1 (2012): 35–50; Siim and Mokre, *Negotiating Gender and Diversity*.
48. This section is based on results from empirical studies of the EPS and transnational civil society presented in Siim and Mokre, *Negotiating Gender and Diversity*; Agustín and Siim, "Gender Diversities."
49. Siim and Mokre, *Negotiating Gender and Diversity*; Agustín and Siim, "Gender Diversities."
50. Siim and Mokre, *Negotiating Gender and Diversity*.
51. Birte Siim, "Political Intersectionality and Democratic Politics in the European Public Sphere," *Politics & Gender* 10, no. 1 (2013): 117–124.
52. Emanuela Lombardo, Petra Meier, and Mieke Verloo, eds., *The Discursive Politics of Gender Equality: Stretching, Bending, and Policymaking* (London: Routledge, 2009).
53. Siim and Mokre, *Negotiating Gender and Diversity*.
54. Myra Marx Ferree, William A. Gamson, Jürgen Gerhards, and Dieter Rucht, "Four Models of the Public Sphere in Modern Democracies," *Theory and Society* 31 (2002): 289–324.
55. Monika Mokre and A. Borchorst, "The EU Gender and Diversity Policies and the European Public Spheres," in *Negotiating Gender and Diversity*, 141–160.
56. Ibid., 151–153.
57. Agustín and Siim, "Gender Diversities."
58. In the Eurosphere project, the analysis of selected political parties and SMO/NGOs is based on comparisons of at least three political parties

from each country: the two most important parties, government and opposition, plus a maverick party. The analysis in this chapter focuses mainly on selected case studies of political parties in Denmark and Hungary; of right-wing populist parties in Austria, Denmark, and Norway; of six national women's organizations; of transnational activism organized in the European Women's Lobby (EWL) and the European Network Against Racism (ENAR); as well as a case study of women in the European Parliament, the FEMM Committee on Women's Rights & Gender Equality. Siim and Mokre, *Negotiating Gender and Diversity*.

59. Birte Siim, "Intersections of Gender and Diversity—A European Perspective," in *Negotiating Gender and Diversity*, 3–21.
60. Helene Pristed Nielsen and Lise Rolandsen Agustín, "Women, Participation, and the European Parliament," in *Negotiating Gender and Diversity*, 201–222.
61. Helene Pristed Nielsen, "Collaborating on Combating Discrimination? Anti-Racist and Gender Equality Organizations in Europe," in *Negotiating Gender and Diversity*, 196–197.
62. Agustín and Siim, "Gender Diversities."
63. Ibid., 539.
64. Mokre and Siim have summarized the results regarding the different ways of framing gender equality and diversity across Europe; see Siim and Mokre, *Negotiating Gender and Diversity*, 35–36.
65. Lise Rolandsen Agustín, *Gender Equality, Intersectionality, and Diversity in Europe* (New York: Palgrave/Macmillan, 2013).
66. Helene Pristed Nielsen, "Collaborating on Combating Discrimination?" 196–197.
67. The Spanish Podemos and the Greek Syriza are the most well-known examples and can be interpreted as being in between a social movement and a party. http://www.theguardian.com/commentisfree/2015/sep/09/the-guardian-view-on-podemos-rage-against-austerity-is-not-enough. The most recent initiative is Greece's Yanis Varoufakis's pan-European progressive movement, Democracy in Europe Movement 2025, or DiEM 25, launched on February 9, 2016, as an alternative to the prevailing authoritarianism and austerity: http://www.commondreams.org/news/2016/01/05/greeces-varoufakis-launch-pan-european-progressive-movement.
68. As already noted, right-wing populist parties have joined different political groups in the European Parliament, since they have quite diverse programs, discourses, and policies: http://www.europarl.europa.eu/about parliament/en/20150201PVL00010/Organisation.
69. Although the meaning of this varies considerably, see Agustín and Siim, "Gender Diversities."

70. Line Nyhagen Predelli, Beatrice Halsaa, and Cecilie Thun, "Citizenship Is Not a Word I Use," in *Remaking Citizenship in Multicultural Europe: Women's Movement, Gender, and Diversity*, ed. Beatrice Halsaa, Sasha Roseneil, and Sevil Sümer (London: Palgrave/Macmillan, 2012), 188–212.
71. Siim and Mokre, *Negotiating Gender and Diversity*.

CHAPTER THIRTEEN

Poor-People Power

The State, Social Provision, and American Experiments in Democratic Engagement

MARISA CHAPPELL

> The poor are no longer divided . . . It's not white power, and I'll give you some news, it's not black power, either. It's poor power and we're going to use it.
> —RALPH ABERNATHY, 1968

IN 2008 AND 2009, the Association of Community Organizations for Reform Now (ACORN), an organization of low- and moderate-income Americans, faced two stinging attacks from conservative activists and Republican Party operatives. In 2008, the McCain-Palin presidential campaign insisted that a handful of instances of ACORN-paid canvassers submitting false voter-registration forms added up to "massive voter fraud." They linked Democratic presidential candidate Barack Obama to the group, claiming that his interactions with ACORN in the 1980s during his stint as a Chicago community organizer amounted to "long and deep" ties. The following year, Fox News aired videos allegedly showing ACORN members advising a pimp and prostitute on how to set up a brothel, avoid paying taxes, and bring underage girls into the country for sex work. Fox interviewed the videos' creators, the conservative activists Hannah Giles and James O'Keefe, who appeared on television dressed in outrageous costumes and feigned shock that ACORN workers would collude in immoral and illegal activities.

Extensive investigations of both charges amounted to little. In the first instance, a few canvassers (whose falsified forms had been tagged as problematic by ACORN itself) pleaded guilty to providing false information, and ACORN was fined for insufficient oversight. In the second, the videos had been heavily edited; ACORN employees sought to assist the couple in finding housing and resources but did not conspire to commit illegal acts.[1] While neither charge held much weight, mainstream-media outlets took them at face value; few journalists found it difficult to believe that an organization run by, and for, the poor, mostly poor women of color, was an illegitimate political entity. For its part, the Democratic Party joined in the ACORN bashing, and only seven Senate Democrats opposed legislation revoking federal funding for ACORN Housing Corporation's mortgage-counseling and foreclosure-protection work.[2]

ACORN's fate reveals the sharp and interrelated limits on political and social citizenship faced by low-income Americans, particularly poor women of color. Opponents of antipoverty groups in the United States have long wielded charges of fraud and mismanagement to undermine organizations fighting for expanded social provision and to justify social spending cuts and invasive policing of public-assistance recipients. The components of the ACORN attacks—accusations of sexual impropriety, charges of financial and political fraud, and assumptions of political incapacity and ineptitude—echo the charges that antiwelfare conservatives in the United States have long employed against "welfare mothers" and poor minorities more generally. The accusations against ACORN raise the specter of the "welfare queen," a peculiarly American political trope that harnesses deep-rooted racialized and gendered stereotypes.[3] This is no coincidence. In the early 2000s, ACORN was the largest grassroots organization of low-income Americans, the longest lasting and most successful effort to give poor Americans a political voice, and by the twenty-first century, its 400,000 members were predominantly African American and Latino and almost entirely urban, 70 percent were women, and the organization was headed by Bertha Lewis, an African American single mother.

This chapter analyzes ACORN's thirty-year history to illuminate the relationship between social rights and political citizenship in the United States and the role of the fragmented American welfare state as an obstacle to the development of a broad-based economic-justice movement. Historians have detailed how white supremacy, male-breadwinner ideology, and the absence of broad-based working-class institutions like industrial unions and labor parties led to the development of a partial and two-tier welfare state in the twentieth-century United States. The New Deal state reserved the most generous benefits for white men with access to steady employment and relegated people of color and unwed mothers of all races to stigmatized and stigmatizing public-assistance programs. In addition, while nations throughout the "Two Wests" combined tax spending and transfer payments and rely on a mix of public and "private" social provision, scholars have long recognized the United States as an outlier in its overwhelming reliance on a "hidden welfare state": tax policies that subsidize home ownership, pension savings, and health care for the middle class. Less visibly connected to the state than transfer payments directed toward the poor, these benefits combined with the two-tiered system of direct social provision to preclude the kind of social and political solidarity that helped sustain more robust redistributive states in Scandinavia and, to a lesser extent, Western Europe.[4] White male-headed families in the United States quickly came to view such benefits as earned entitlements and to resent contributing to more visible public-assistance programs.

If the fragmented New Deal/Cold War state stemmed from unequal political power, it further deepened political inequality. It afforded white Americans access to new social rights (union membership, social insurance, home ownership) as well as an institutional voice, incorporating them into labor unions, Democratic Party politics, and suburban neighborhood associations. These institutions largely excluded men and women of color and the poorest Americans, thereby compounding their social and political marginalization. The fragmented American state, itself a result of unequal political power, thus created competing political identities and opportunities that precluded the kinds of multiracial and broad-based alliances that might have more successfully challenged neoliberal policies since the 1970s.

This chapter first explores black women's growing engagement with the state in the post–World War II decades and argues that this engagement politicized them in new ways. Well before radical citizenship theorists, low-income women articulated an integrated vision of citizenship that necessitated both social rights and participatory democratic engagement, a vision that developed alongside the growth of the postwar state and subsequently flourished in the context of assertive black activism and federal antipoverty initiatives in the 1960s. The virulent and effective resistance to these claims from policy makers and white Americans more broadly, I argue, was rooted in a forthright and explicitly racialized and gendered denial of poor women's citizenship, a denial with a long and deep history but one that had become institutionalized in new ways in the New Deal/Cold War state. The chapter then explores ACORN's effort in the 1970s to overcome poor women's marginalization and build a broad and inclusive alliance of poor and lower-middle-class Americans to demand political power and redistributive justice. This effort, I argue, faltered in the face of the deeply fragmented American state and left the American people with fewer political tools to counter neoliberalism's steady advance. This effort also offers important lessons for the future of democracy in an age of welfare-state retrenchment.

SOCIAL PROVISION AND THE POLITICIZATION OF THE POOR

In her book *A Movement Without Marches*, the historian Lisa Levenstein describes "literally a mass movement of African American women [in postwar Philadelphia] to claim the benefits and use the services of public institutions." Tracing their interactions with the city's domestic court, public schools, welfare office, public-housing administration, and public hospital, Levenstein reveals the welfare state as a site of politicization: "the collective weight of [women's] efforts," she argues, "put pressure on state authorities to respond to their demands." Turning to the state for needed assistance became a political act, as women "asserted a deeply rooted set of ideas about the responsibility of the state to provide them with basic resources and protections." The historian Rhonda Y. Williams chronicles a similar process among Baltimore public-housing tenants, particularly black women; many, she argues, "receive[d] a political education through their engagement with the welfare system." Through residents' councils and later antipoverty and welfare-rights organizations, black women claimed not only better conditions and treatment but also the right to shape policies. Although political and popular discussions portray poor women's "dependence" on public assistance as corrosive of citizenship, historians are beginning to illuminate the ways in which engagement with the state promoted robust notions of citizenship among poor women.[5]

In the 1960s, the federal War on Poverty further catalyzed political organizing among low-income women (and men). The Economic Opportunity Act of 1964 provided federal funds for local antipoverty efforts and required "maximum feasible participation" of the poor in directing those efforts. Poverty planners viewed these "community-action agencies" as a way to coordinate service delivery and combat a "culture of poverty" among the poor, but in communities across the nation, low-income Americans, working with activist organizers and poverty lawyers, used community action to demand redistributive policies and political power.[6] They found in community action a powerful acknowledgment that their voices mattered—or should matter—and that political engagement might produce substantial change. An indigenous community organizer in Durham, North Carolina, recalled that when she attended PTA meetings before becoming involved in community action, "me being low-income, they wouldn't pay me no nevermind. They counted me as a nobody," but during the 1960s, the historian Christina Greene tells us, she and other poor women in Durham built an interracial movement that confronted city officials on welfare and public-housing regulations, organized a rent strike, and started a community health clinic.[7] Susan Youngblood Ashmore explored antipoverty organizing in Selma, Alabama. She found that poor African Americans there protested the mayor's appointment of an all-middle-class (though racially integrated) antipoverty board. They demanded that there be "NO formal education requirements" for board members; it was "not necessary that a person be able to read or write," they insisted. What mattered was that the "people in the area feel that the persons they select will faithfully represent their interests and do a good job."[8] Amy Jordan found that organizing a Head Start program in Mississippi also "helped many residents begin to find their voices," particularly by empowering black women as valuable educators, policy makers, and activists.[9] Similar stories can be told about low-income Americans of all races and in all regions of the country.

These examples suggest that antiwelfare arguments deploring the "entitlement mentality" are not completely off base. Scholars have long argued that poverty itself is a danger to democracy because the difficulty of simply surviving leaves the poor with few resources to devote to politics.[10] Some studies have found that participation in public-assistance programs—as opposed to social-insurance programs—further depoliticizes the poor.[11] Yet new scholarship on the grassroots War on

Poverty demonstrates that in certain historical circumstances encounters with the welfare state have generated expectations, shaped new political identities, and mobilized poor women to demand a more robust citizenship.

But political elites—and many ordinary working- and middle-class Americans—defined poor people's activism as disorder rather than democratic engagement. Of course, sometimes that's exactly what it was. The activist academics Frances Fox Piven and Richard Cloward argued in the early 1970s that disruption was the only political lever available to the poor. Yet organized disruption is a form of democratic engagement, and even when low-income Americans weren't being explicitly "disruptive," critics denied the legitimacy of their political activities. According to Louisiana's welfare secretary in the late 1960s, for example, welfare-rights activists were simply "attempting to stir up trouble."[12] The Democratic governor of Texas shut down the state's VISTA program, which employed young people to work in antipoverty programs, insisting that "the abdication of respect for law and order, disruption of democratic processes, and provocation of disunity among our citizens will not be tolerated."[13] The critique stretched from the White House to the neighborhood bar. On one end, President Johnson deplored the politicization of the black poor, telling an aide in 1968 that "the Rap Browns and the Martin Luther Kings and the [Floyd] McKissicks and all of them are the products of community action,"[14] and the antipoverty planner and liberal Democrat Daniel Patrick Moynihan wrote an entire book condemning community action for politicizing the poor rather than simply providing the cultural tools for individual upward mobility.[15] On the other end, the white working-class men interviewed by the journalist Peter Schrag listed "welfare recipients who strike and march for better treatment" as offensive to common understandings of fair play.[16]

Critics also denied poor women's capacity to run programs or contribute to policy making. Condemning Baltimore's Self-Help Housing Program, a Democratic city-council member insisted that "people who haven't yet proved they can earn a living" could not effectively administer federal funds (though the women running the program were doing just that).[17] When three hundred Food Stamp workers (mostly low-income black women) went on strike in Louisiana, the state's welfare director declared that it had been a mistake to hire "what he called incompetent staff from the 'welfare rolls' to operate the program."[18]

And when welfare-rights activists staged a sit-in at the U.S. Capitol (to protest senators' refusal to hear their testimony on a proposed overhaul of the nation's income-support system), Georgia Senator Russell Long referred to them as "brood mares" and remarked that "if they can take the time to march in the streets and picket and sit in the hearing room, it seems to me they have enough time to get jobs."[19] In response to local officials' complaints that community action put the federal government "in the business of organizing the poor politically," Congress curtailed the program; the Nixon administration placed further limits on the use of federal funds for grassroots organizing and political empowerment.[20]

The cultural power of these negative stereotypes of the poor—with poor black women often standing in for the poor more generally—has aided opponents of social provision by denying low-income Americans a legitimate political voice, thereby compounding a lack of institutional political power. "Nonrecognition and disrespect are the typical experience of those in poverty," but in the United States women of color have experienced a peculiarly virulent form of disrespect.[21] There is a great deal of scholarship analyzing the various interlocking stereotypes that stigmatize African American women, much of it illuminating the constellation of these stereotypes into the trope of the "welfare queen."[22] For the purposes of considering political engagement, Melissa Harris Perry's discussion of the "powerful stereotype of black women . . . as shrill, loud, argumentative, irrationally angry, and verbally abusive" is particularly relevant. Perry quotes Cal Thomas of Fox News (who is discussing Michelle Obama here):

> Look at the image of angry black women on television. Politically you have Maxine Waters of California, a liberal Democrat. She's always angry every time she gets on television. Cynthia McKinney [former congresswoman from Georgia], another angry black woman. And who are the black women you see on the local news at night in cities all over the country. They're usually angry about something. They've had a son who has been shot in a drive-by shooting. They are angry at Bush. So you don't really have a profile of non-angry black women . . . except Oprah Winfrey.

In this case, Harris Perry argues, black women's anger is not acknowledged "as a legitimate reaction to unequal circumstances" but instead as "pathological"—therefore "black women's concerns can be ignored and their voices silenced in the name of maintaining calm and rational conversation." In the bigger picture, she writes, "there is no possibility of accurate, democratic recognition as citizens."[23]

In the United States in the past half-century, attacking poor women's political credibility has been a signal weapon in a movement to redistribute income upward by cutting social spending for the poor, enforcing low-wage labor-market participation, and disenfranchising hundreds of thousands of minority voters. Despite—and perhaps because of—this movement, low-income Americans, including poor women of color, have continued to organize, engage politically, and pursue public policies that reflect their vision of fairness and equity. In campaigns for "welfare rights," community control, and a living wage, among dozens of other issues, the political consciousness that some poor women developed in their interactions with various facets of the welfare state persisted. They defied widespread notions of an alienated "underclass" and challenge historians' assumptions about poor Americans' political passivity after the 1960s. The obstacles they have faced in building a broader political coalition and in winning recognition in political decision making and policy making are, in great measure, a reflection of the segmentation of the American welfare state and the political identities that it fostered.[24]

THE CHALLENGE OF SEGMENTED CITIZENSHIP

The Poor People's Campaign of 1968 reveals some of the sharp limitations to any effective assertion of poor-people's politics in the United States. The campaign was the broadest single effort to build a multiracial movement of low-income Americans—to organize the poor as a class to win a political voice and economic justice. Spearheaded by the Southern Christian Leadership Conference, the campaign brought thousands of low-income Americans to Washington, D.C., in May 1968 for four weeks of protest marches, sit-ins, and lobbying and represents an assertion of the poor as a collective political force. Its goals included expanded social provision (meaningful jobs at living wages and secure and adequate income support) as well as political recognition and authority for low-income Americans ("recognition by law of the right of people affected by government programs to play a truly significant role in how they are designed and carried out"). While the campaign's policy wins were modest, some activists viewed its very existence as hopeful. By bringing together "authentic spokesmen for poor Mexican Americans, American Indians, blacks and whites," it portended the development of a more permanent "bottom-up coalition" in American politics. The Appalachian organizer Al McSurely envisioned the campaign as the beginning of a class-conscious political mobilization of the poor. "We must not depend on anyone else but ourselves," he insisted. "To meet the needs of the poor in this country, we cannot rely on the consciences of the rich.... We can only depend on ourselves—and our organizational strength."[25]

But efforts to translate the campaign into a more permanent multiracial poor people's coalition foundered. The historian Robert Chase argues that the campaign's forthright articulation of class politics and redistributive goals were "incongruous with the continuation of white, liberal, middle-class support," which had been essential to the success of civil-rights legislation.[26] Organized labor remained ambivalent about the campaign as well; the United Auto Workers, the United Steelworkers, and a number of union locals supported the campaign, but the nation's largest labor federation, the AFL-CIO, did not. While the campaign's redistributive demands alienated the middle class, press coverage undermined its legitimacy by portraying participants as lawless rioters rather than dedicated political actors.[27] Negative portrayals of the poor—particularly the minority poor—undermined public support.

Negative reaction to the Poor People's Campaign, along with virulent backlash against "community action" and "welfare rights," suggested to many organizers on the left that the vulnerability of the poor—and poor women of color especially—to assumptions of political incapacity and illegitimacy would inevitably forestall political success. In the early 1970s, some of them sought to overcome these problems by building what they called a "new majority." "Poor and minority peoples cannot allow themselves to be isolated from the millions of other people who have similar economic interests," insisted George Wiley, or "they will continue to be the scapegoats and... bear the brunt of injustice." The "failure of the movements for social and economic change in the late 60s and early 70s," he insisted, "must lead us to ask—What is a new and viable political strategy for poor people?" His answer: "a grassroots movement that unites poor and low and moderate income people."[28] Seth Borgos and Madeleine Adamson, early ACORN staffers, described that group's mission as mobilizing "multi-racial constituencies spanning the social chasm between homeowner and public housing tenant, between skilled blue-collar worker and welfare recipient—between moderate- and low-income Americans."[29] While historians have paid a great deal of attention to the growing appeal of ethnic and racial nationalism in the 1970s, they have largely ignored this simultaneous push for multiracial economic-justice organizing.

Two veteran welfare-rights organizers, George Wiley and Wade Rathke, led the way. Both valued the democratic engagement of the poor, but both had come to view welfare rights as a political dead end. Wiley, one of the conveners of the National Welfare Rights Organization (NWRO), left that group in 1973 to start the Movement for Economic Justice (MEJ), devoted to building a "majority constituency" of the almost 80 percent of Americans earning less than $15,000 a year. Three years earlier, Wade Rathke convinced members of the Little Rock welfare-rights group he had organized to adopt the name Arkansas Community Organization for Reform Now and recruit a broader membership.[30] Neither move was uncontested. Johnnie Tillmon and other recipient leaders of the NWRO prioritized the needs of welfare mothers, as did Little Rock's Barbara Hampton, who, as Rathke remembers it, protested the group's decision by "[getting] up and pull[ing] all the shelves down in the office as she walked out forever." Despite the "bitter split," the group's organizers recalled, the break "freed ACORN to crack a moderate-income homeowning constituency."[31]

The task as Wiley conceived it was to convince "a majority of people in this country" that "[progressive] economic reforms are in their own economic self interests" and that "there is common cause between the interests of people on welfare and the lower-middle-class."[32] Organizers assumed that this majority shared economic interests but understood that the nation's racial and economic politics obscured that commonality—they must therefore "properly sensitize" lower-middle-income Americans to the benefits of allying with the poor. MEJ and ACORN sought "bridging issues" that provided "a common meeting ground for the great majority of the American people," both the "silent majority" and "the poor, oppressed, and minority people."[33]

"New-majority" campaigns that tackled specific and near-term threats, what the historian Michael Stewart Foley calls "front-porch politics," had some success.[34] Rising utility rates in the mid-1970s brought "every social element in Arkansas, from soybean farmers and small businessmen to suburban homeowners" to protest and lobby alongside low-income residents against rate increases and for rate caps. Proposed expressways in Boston and Chicago threatened both poor *and* middle-income neighborhoods, prompting successful new-majority mobilization to thwart their construction. Sometimes urban gentrifiers allied with their low-income neighbors to fight against development proposals.[35] These successes led organizers to "wax . . . optimistic," as two of them recalled, "convinced that they had found the strategic key to social change."[36]

But the segmented structure of social provision and the political identities that it nurtured made it difficult to translate individual campaigns into a longer-term political coalition. The state was a crucial arbiter of distribution—as Wiley noted, "government policies are the most likely instruments for returning a fair share of the resources to people who have been exploited in the amassing of America's wealth."[37] But state policy had shaped decidedly class-based, racially inflected, political identities. As Suzanne Mettler and Joe Soss have argued, public-policy designs "not only can affect the ways a target group is viewed in the society at large; they also can influence how group members perceive and evaluate one another," an example of policy feedback that "has major consequences for the likelihood that group members will want to join together in collective political action."[38] If interactions with the welfare state led some low-income Americans to view progressive redistribution and robust social provision as the pillars of economic justice and democracy, interactions with different facets of the welfare state promoted different ideas and identities among the "home-owning constituency" that organizers hoped to reach.

One of the "new-majority" movement's first campaigns, for progressive tax reform, illuminates the problem. Organizers in MEJ and ACORN saw tax reform as ideal for distinguishing their movements from welfare rights and for "bridging" the interests of the poor and the nonpoor. The constituency was there: by the early 1970s Americans were complaining of "pocketbook squeeze," a result of federal, state, and local policies that favored corporate interests and left residential-property owners and moderate-income wage earners to bear a growing tax burden.[39] Tax reform was also strategically significant because, as Rathke and Steve Kest argued in 1975, "center and right wing politicians, the welfare bureaucracies, and the media succeeded in convincing the broad working class majority that what the minority groups wanted was a piece of *their pie*."[40] "The victories of the 'poor' in securing increased government provision" in the 1960s, the poverty lawyer Ed Sparer lamented, "were measured in the form of increased taxes for other millions who themselves just got by," leaving "the majority coalition needed for progressive social change in this country . . . thoroughly divided, and ultimately defeated even before it had a chance to be born."[41] Speaking to a National Council of Churches Conference on Taxes in March 1973, Wiley called for a nationwide "taxpayer's revolt that is shaped and directed not against welfare mothers but . . . against the real welfare recipients who are chiseling billions and billions of dollars out of the federal treasury."[42] MEJ offered pro-bono tax preparation as a way to educate low- and middle-income Americans about the need for progressive reform, and ACORN chapters waged campaigns to eliminate sales tax on food and medicine and demand to property-value reassessments. Meanwhile, the National Committee for Tax Justice, a coalition of dozens of organizations, lobbied for progressive federal tax reform.

But the segmented welfare state had shaped middle-class—even lower-middle-class—political identities in ways that made coalition on progressive tax reform challenging. While social provision for low-income Americans in the form of public assistance, public housing, Food Stamps, and Medicaid was highly visible and stigmatized, social provision for the nonpoor was either invisible or framed as earned entitlement. "Social Security" (Old Age, Survivors, and Disability Insurance), for example, excluded many of the poorest Americans and relied on highly regressive payroll taxes, yet its framing as "social insurance" rendered it a politically protected middle-class entitlement. The mortgage-interest tax deduction allowed the middle class access to quality housing and public services as well as intergenerational wealth accumulation, yet it is rarely acknowledged as social provision or "welfare." As many historians have shown, in battles over the desegregation of housing, schools, and public services since the 1950s, white homeowners articulated a political identity that naturalized racial and class privilege by denying the role of discriminatory public policies in ensuring their own upward mobility and economic security. In battles over zoning regulations, fair-housing legislation, busing mandates, and affordable housing, middle-class white Americans have mobilized politically as "taxpayers" and "homeowners" defending their economic rights against "tax eaters" and welfare recipients.[43]

The "tax revolt" that succeeded in the 1970s, then, was not a progressive one. As progressive tax reform stalled, opponents of social provision and redistribution capitalized on widespread discontent among homeowners facing high property-tax bills.[44] Beginning with Proposition 13 in 1978, the top layer of the "new majority" in many states voted for tax reform that imposed stringent limits on property taxes. Instead of progressively redistributing the tax burden, these measures offered modest tax relief to homeowners and financial windfalls to corporate property holders. In 1975 Congress instituted a negative income tax for poor families who engaged in the labor market in 1975 (the Earned Income Tax Credit), which by the twenty-first century had become the nation's largest antipoverty program. But state caps on property taxes had a devastating impact on social provision, forcing legislatures to cut education and public-service budgets. These cuts affected middle-class as well as poor Americans, but the poor, who lack access to private recreational facilities and schools, are more reliant on public services and therefore more affected by cuts in public spending.[45]

EXPERIMENTS IN "POOR-PEOPLE POWER"

As it became clear that competing political identities made "new-majority" politics unlikely, organizers moved in two different directions. Some continued to court lower-middle- and middle-income white constituencies and strayed further from the priorities of the poor. Massachusetts Fair Share is an example. According to one of Fair Share's founders, Lee Staples, "those issues which played well for canvassing purposes in the suburbs were not unprogressive or whatever, but they weren't necessarily low-income people's issues." In "hoping to meet the middle and working class on their own ground," Fair Share and likeminded groups "restricted themselves to issues they could get majority assent to," which tended to be "mundane pocketbook issues" rather than substantive economic reforms. By the 1980s, Massachusetts Fair Share had become "almost a white, lower middle-class, upper strata of the working class, homeowners' organization." The group was still "rhetorically committed to a majoritarian strategy," one scholar has noted, but "it just so happened that the 'majority' was leaving out the concerns of low income people of color in the inner city."[46] In the 1980s, Pierre Clavel shows, some neighborhood activists found their way into policy-making positions in Chicago, Boston, and some other cities and implemented some redistribution through various sorts of "equity planning." But it was mostly white, male activists who were brought into progressive city administrations, and the victories they won had little impact on the broader structural forces that have intensified economic inequality in since the 1970s.[47]

ACORN went the opposite direction, implicitly jettisoning "new-majority" strategies and focusing on "poor-people power." In the early and mid-1970s, ACORN documents touted the group's "majority constituency"; by the 1980s, they were referring more often to "the poor and the powerless." The group's mission, one organizer insisted, was "empowerment for the poor as a class."[48] That meant fighting private corporations that exploited the poor, demanding expanded social provision for the poor, and securing an effective voice for low-income Americans in the democratic process at the very time that structural changes to the American political system were giving political elites fewer incentives to respond to low-income constituents.[49]

In the late 1970s, ACORN fought explicitly for "low and moderate income representation in political party processes."[50] The group elected some members to local office, formed alliances with a handful of state and federal legislators, and developed a national political agenda called the "People's Platform," which advocated full employment, national health insurance, and a guaranteed income, among other planks. When leaders of both political parties "politely dismissed" the platform, one organizer remembered, ACORN was particularly "angered by the Democrats" and "attributed the Party's reluctance to acknowledge the depth of their grievances to the meager representation of low- and moderate-income Democrats at the national conventions and other policy-making enclaves."[51] ACORN members invaded the Democratic National Committee's midterm convention and taped copies of the People's Platform to columns in the convention center, staged a sit-in at Carter's campaign headquarters in Philadelphia, and protested outside the DNC's Washington, D.C., office. They finally convinced party leaders to create a fifteen-member commission, headed by Mickey Leland of Texas, to develop recommendations for increasing the role of low-income Democrats in the presidential-nominating process. When leadership rejected those recommendations, ACORN members invaded precinct and district caucuses to demand implementation.[52] A decade earlier, similar protests had convinced the party to adopt an affirmative-action plan ensuring representation of women, minorities, and youth in the process. This later effort to ensure representation of the poor failed.

In the 1980s, ACORN also participated in the Movement for Economic Justice's Jobs & Justice campaign, which was designed to empower the "disproportionately minority and female . . . secondary labor force," including "welfare recipients," to shape political and economic policies.[53] The members of this constituency, ACORN insisted, "are constantly faced with the equally inadequate options of unstable and unskilled low wage work or dependence upon government income maintenance programs—both of which guarantee a life of economic hardship and struggle," and their "marginality in the economy encourages a militancy and determination that can exert significant pressure."[54] Emphasizing "direct action and worker-community linkages," the campaign was part of an effort to capitalize on high unemployment rates and the recession of the early 1970s; some organizers looked to the Unemployed Councils of the 1930s, which pressured city and federal officials to expand government job programs. Organizers assisted the unemployed in applying for federal benefits, public protests won temporary extensions in federal employment programs, and ACORN'S United Labor Unions (ULU) organized low-income service workers in hotels, fast food, and health care. By the mid-1980s, when it affiliated with the Service Employees International Union (SEIU), ULU had organized thousands of low-wage workers in five cities. One journalist referred to Jobs & Justice as the "60s poor people's campaign revived."[55] These efforts were a prelude to renewed energy within organized labor in the late-twentieth century to ally with antipoverty, faith-based, and community organizations to fight for the rights of low-wage workers, from the Jobs with Justice coalition to Justice for Janitors and metropolitan living-wage campaigns.

ACORN's homesteading campaign was another move toward militant assertions of poor-people power. In the late 1970s, "hundreds of low-income families" in Philadelphia occupied and began rehabilitating vacant homes. ACORN signed on and spread the tactic to other cities. The campaign forced concessions in many cities, and ACORN and its allies won reforms in the federal homesteading program that made it easier for low-income families to own and renovate abandoned housing.[56] The journalist John Atlas cites the squatting campaign as a turning point for ACORN; it launched the organization's involvement in urban-redevelopment efforts, which would become its primary focus in the 1990s, and shifted the organization's membership more heavily toward low-income people of color. "To the foundation officers, other community activists, and government officials," Atlas notes, "ACORN was looking more like a black, militant, poor people's association," a far cry from the "new-majority" strategy with which Rathke had begun.[57]

Neither "new majority" nor "poor-people power" has succeeded in securing a meaningful voice for low-income Americans in political decision making. The transformation of the nation's welfare system in 1990s is illustrative. Congress abolished Aid to Families with Dependent Children (AFDC) in 1996 with bipartisan support and without hearing from the women who utilized AFDC benefits; even symbolic or token efforts to include the poor in policy-making decisions that had occurred in the 1970s had been abandoned. "Reform" of the nation's social safety net for the poor, and the rhetoric surrounding it, offer to poor women only one model of citizenship: low-wage worker. In the ubiquitous welfare-reform "success story," pundits, politicians, and journalists praised individual mothers who woke well before sunrise, navigated a cumbersome public-transportation system to shuttle children to school and childcare, worked long hours for low wages, and earned a newfound dignity by becoming "independent."[58] From the halls of Congress to local welfare offices, the new regime consciously and explicitly denied the value of poor women's care-giving labor.[59] And certainly, no one asked poor women to participate in the policy-making process. If anyone had bothered, many poor women would have offered "alternative ideas" about "personal responsibility, motherhood, education and mobility, poverty and inequality, and 'deservingness'" than those articulated in mainstream welfare discourse.[60] No mechanisms existed for such political engagement, however, so these "counter-hegemonic frameworks and alternative policy prescriptions" remained marginal.[61]

Economic-justice campaigns in the twenty-first century take a variety of forms and approaches, with some activists pursuing "poor-people power" and others trying once again to assert common interests among the poor and the middle class to build a broad and interest-based coalition to win economic justice.[62] Whether built around the notion of "economic human rights" or the needs of "working parents," such efforts face formidable obstacles, given the long history of segmented social provision that has constructed clashing political identities among low- and middle-income Americans. The sources and existence of these political identities must be part of the conversation on the political left if it is to build a strong, productive, and egalitarian movement for greater economic democracy.

In the twenty-first century, some progressive organizers in the United States are once again pursuing majority strategies as the 2008 Great Recession and its aftermath continue to create hardship across a broad range of Americans. Yet in some ways the nation's political identities are even more fragmented today than they were in the 1970s and 1980s. It is true that working-class white Americans have experienced significant downward mobility and that the middle class faces rising student debt, precarious employment, and an unstable housing market. In fact, the widespread impact of welfare-state retrenchment—the gradual erosion of the social provisions that underwrote middle-class economic security in the last century—would seem to offer a propitious moment for cross-class, multiracial progressive organizing. But one need only observe the surprising political popularity of Donald Trump—a billionaire developer who promises to bring manufacturing jobs back for the white working class and rid the nation of "illegal immigrants" and Muslims—to see that the racialized and class-stratified political identities built by the New Deal/Cold War state remain stubbornly powerful and continue to shape political responses to economic crisis. An understanding of the sources and impact of these different political identities must be a central part of the conversation if the political left is to build a strong, productive, and egalitarian movement for greater economic democracy.

While ACORN's is an American story, shaped by particular class, race, and gender politics and the unique political structure of the United States, it offers broader insight. In Western Europe, working-class institutions such as strong leftist movements, industrial unions, and labor parties provided a relatively unified working-class political voice and enabled the development of more generous and less stratified welfare states. Yet in the twenty-first century welfare state, fragmentation and stratified political identities seem to be on the rise in Europe, and retrenchment itself creates new divisions. Richer nations impose crippling financial austerity on poorer members, and all EU members "have developed scales of reduced membership of the citizenry and partial access to citizenship rights," including social provision, in response to worker mobility and a refugee crisis.[63] In Europe, then, as in the United States, the physical and imagined boundaries of the nation-state itself create and sustain fragmented citizenship and sustain global economic inequalities.

NOTES

1. "ACORN Accusations," *Factcheck*, October 21, 2008, http://www.factcheck.org/2008/10/acorn-accusations/#10/18/2008; Zachary Tomanelli, "Sherrod Hoax Exposed, but Breitbart's ACORN Fraud Lives On," *Fairness and Accuracy in Reporting (FAIR)*, July 10, 2010, http://www.fair.org/blog/2010/07/23/sherrod-hoax-exposed-but-breitbarts-acorn-fraud-lives-on/; Veronica Cassidy, "Falling for the ACORN Hoax: The Strange Journalism of James O'Keefe," *FAIR*, April 10, 2010, http://www.fair.org/extra-online-articles/Falling-for-the-ACORN-Hoax; Joe Conason, "Now Reopen Breitbart's ACORN Fraud—and Get the Story Right," *Salon*, July 21, 2010, http://www.salon.com/2010/7/21/acorn_10.
2. John Bresnahan and Michael Falcone, "GOP Seizes on ACORN Funding," *Politico* (September 16, 2009), htpp://www.politico.com/news/stories/0909/27208.html.
3. Negative stereotypes of the "undeserving poor" are not unique to the United States but do take a uniquely powerful racialized and sexualized form there. Some scholars trace denigrating stereotypes of the poor elsewhere to American influence: Ruth Lister, "Towards a Citizens' Welfare State: The Three + Two 'R's of Welfare Reform," *Theory, Culture, and Society* 18, nos. 2–3 (June 2001): 92; Verity Archer, "Dole Bludgers, Tax Payers, and the New Right: Constructing Discourses of Welfare in 1970s Australia," *Labour History* 96 (May 2009): 182–184.
4. Christopher Howard, *The Hidden Welfare State: Tax Expenditures and Social Policy in the United States* (Princeton, N.J.: Princeton University Press, 1997); Adalbert Evers and Anne-Marie Guillemard, "Introduction: Marshall's Concept of Citizenship and Contemporary Welfare Reconfiguration," in *Social Policy and Citizenship: The Changing Landscape*, ed. Adalbert Evers and Anne-Marie Guillemard (Oxford: Oxford University Press, 2013), 3.

5. Lisa Levenstein, *A Movement Without Marches: African American Women and the Politics of Poverty in Postwar Philadelphia* (Chapel Hill: University of North Carolina Press, 2009), 4, 6; Rhonda Y. Williams, *The Politics of Public Housing: Black Women's Struggles Against Urban Inequality* (New York: Oxford University Press, 2004), 6.
6. Guian A. McKee, "'This Government Is with Us': Lyndon Johnson and the Grassroots War on Poverty," in *The War on Poverty: A New Grassroots History, 1964–1980*, ed. Annelise Orleck and Gayle Hazirjian (Athens: University of Georgia Press, 2011), 36.
7. Christina Greene, "'Someday . . . the Colored and White Will Stand Together': The War on Poverty, Black Power Politics, and the Southern Women's Interracial Alliance," in *The War on Poverty*, 159–183.
8. Susan Youngblood Ashmore, "Going Back to Selma: Organizing for Change in Dallas County After the March to Montgomery," in *The War on Poverty*, 314.
9. Amy Jordan, "Fighting for the CDGM: Poor People, Local Politics, and the Complicated Legacy of Head Start," in *The War on Poverty*, 280–307.
10. Ruth Lister, "In from the Margins: Citizenship, Inclusion, and Exclusion," in *Social Exclusion and Social Work: Issues of Theory, Policy, and Practice*, ed. Monica Barry and Christine Hallett (Dorset: Russell House, 1998), 29.
11. Joe Soss, "Making Clients and Citizens: Welfare Policy as a Source of Status, Belief, and Action," in *Deserving and Entitled: Social Constructions and Public Policy*, ed. Anne L. Schneider and Helen M. Ingram (Albany: SUNY Press, 2005), 291–328.
12. Kent B. Germany, *New Orleans After the Promises: Poverty, Citizenship, and the Search for the Great Society* (Athens: University of Georgia Press, 2007), 173.
13. William Clayson, "The War on Poverty and the Chicano Movement in Texas: Confronting 'Tio Tomás' and the 'Gringo Pseudoliberals,'" in *The War on Poverty*, 348.
14. McKee, "'This Government Is with Us,'" 56.
15. Daniel P. Moynihan, *Maximum Feasible Misunderstanding: Community Action in the War on Poverty* (New York: Free Press, 1969).
16. Peter Schrag, "The Forgotten American," *Harper's* 239 (August 1969): 27–34.
17. Rhonda Y. Williams, "'To Challenge the Status Quo by Any Means': Community Action and Representational Politics in the 1960s," in *The War on Poverty*, 71.
18. Germany, *New Orleans After the Promises*, 173, 177.
19. Ibid., 230.

20. McKee, "'This Government Is with Us,'" 51–52; Germany, *New Orleans After the Promises*, 100, 305.
21. Lister, "Towards a Citizens' Welfare State," 102.
22. Martin Gilens, *Why Americans Hate Welfare: Race, Media, and the Politics of Antipoverty Policy* (Chicago: University of Chicago Press, 1999); Ange-Marie Hancock, *The Politics of Disgust: The Public Identity of the Welfare Queen* (New York: NYU Press, 2004); Vicki Lens, "Public Voices and Public Policy: Changing Societal Discourses on Welfare," *Journal of Sociology and Social Work* 24, no. 1 (2002): 137–154; Kenneth J. Neubeck and Noel A. Cazenave, *Welfare Racism: Playing the Race Card Against America's Poor* (New York: Routledge, 2001); James Avery and Mark Peffley, "Racial Context, Public Attitudes, and Welfare Effort in the American States," in *Race and the Politics of Welfare Reform*, ed. Sanford F. Schram, Joe Soss, and Richard C. Fording (Ann Arbor: University of Michigan Press, 2003), 131–150; Rosalee Clawson and Rakyua Trice, "Poverty as We Know It: Media Portrayals of the Poor," *Public Opinion Quarterly* 64 (2000): 53–64; Neil deMause and Steve Randell, "The Poor Will Always Be With Us—Just Not on the TV News: A FAIR (Fairness and Accuracy in Reporting) Study," 2007, http://www.fair.org/index..php?page=3172.
23. Melissa V. Harris-Perry, *Sister Citizen: Shame, Stereotypes, and Black Women in America* (New Haven, Conn.: Yale University Press, 2011), 87, 95, 116. See also Sandra Morgen, Joan Acker, and Jill Weigt, *Stretched Thin: Poor Families, Welfare Work, and Welfare Reform* (Ithaca, N.Y.: Cornell University Press, 2010), 129.
24. This history of low-income women organizing around state policies to win greater social citizenship is not unique to the United States; see, for example, Peter Shapely, "Tenants Arise! Consumerism, Tenants, and the Challenge to Council Authority in Manchester, 1968–1992," *Social History* 31, no. 1 (February 2006): 60–78.
25. Gordon K. Mantler, *Power to the Poor: Black-Brown Coalition and the Fight for Economic Justice, 1960–1974* (Chapel Hill: University of North Carolina Press, 2013), 129, 183–184, 112, 177.
26. Chase, "Class Resurrection."
27. Gerald D. McKnight, *The Last Crusade: Martin Luther King Jr., the FBI, and the Poor People's Campaign* (Boulder, Colo.: Westview, 1998); Brenda Bretz, "The Poor People's Campaign: An Evolution of the Civil Rights Movement," *Sociological Viewpoints* (Spring 2010), http://www.virginia.edu/lifetimelearning/civilrights/articles/The%20Poor%20People's%20Campaign.pdf.
28. "A Proposal for the Establishment of a Movement for Economic Justice," May 1, 1973, Box 1, Folder 1, Movement for Economic Justice Papers (MEJ Papers), Wisconsin Historical Society, Madison, 5, 1.

29. Madeleine Adamson and Seth Borgos, "ACORN," reprinted from *This Mighty Dream: Social Protest Movements in the United States* (Boston: Routledge and Kegan Paul, 1984), Box 15, Folder "ACORN Background," Accession 2001–170, ACORN Papers, Wisconsin Historical Society, Madison.
30. ACORN changed its name to Association of Community Organizations for Reform Now when it expanded beyond Arkansas in the mid-1970s.
31. Wade Rathke, "Reflections: 20 Years with ACORN," n.d., Box 1, Folder 2, Arkansas ACORN Papers, Wisconsin Historical Society, Madison, 3; Adamson and Borgos, "ACORN."
32. George A. Wiley, "The Need for a Taxpayers' Uprising," keynote address, National Council of Churches Conference (Emergency Conference on "The Nixon Economic Agenda for the 70s"), March 5, 1973, Box 40, Folder 3, George Wiley Papers, Wisconsin Historical Society, Madison, 26–27.
33. "Why a Movement for Economic Justice," January 26 1973, Box 1, Folder 1, MEJ Papers, Wisconsin Historical Society, Madison; "A Proposal for the Establishment of a Movement for Economic Justice," 7.
34. Michael Stewart Foley, *Front Porch Politics: The Forgotten Heyday of American Activism in the 1970s and 1980s* (New York: Hill and Wang, 2013).
35. Suleiman Osman, *The Invention of Brownstone Brooklyn: Gentrification and the Search for Authenticity in Postwar New York* (Oxford: Oxford University Press, 2011).
36. Adamson and Borgos, "ACORN."
37. George A. Wiley, "Progress Report on the Planning Phase of the Movement for Economic Justice," June 20, 1973, Box 41, Folder 4, George Wiley Papers, Wisconsin Historical Society, Madison, 1.
38. Suzanne Mettler and Joe Soss, "The Consequences of Public Policy for Democratic Citizenship: Bridging Policy Studies and Mass Politics," *Perspectives on Politics* 2, no. 1 (March 2004): 61; Joe Soss and Lawrence R. Jacobs, "The Place of Inequality: Non-Participation in the American Polity," *Political Science Quarterly* 124, no. 1 (Spring 2009): 95–125.
39. Joshua Mound, "Taxpayers for Tax Justice: Grassroots Activists, the Democrats, and the Temporary Triumph of Left Tax Populism," paper presented at the Organization of American Historians Annual Meeting, Atlanta, Georgia, April 2014.
40. Steve Kest and Wade Rathke, "ACORN: An Overview of Its History, Structure, Methodology, Campaigns, and Philosophy," 1975, Box 15, Folder "ACORN: Background," Accession 2001-170, ACORN Papers, Wisconsin Historical Society, Madison, 2.
41. Ed Sparer, "Round Two: A Call to Organize the Unemployed," *Just Economics* 3, no. 2 (February 1975), MEJ Papers, Wisconsin Historical Society, Madison, 2.

42. Wiley, "The Need for a Taxpayers' Uprising," 3.
43. Matthew D. Lassiter, *The Silent Majority: Suburban Politics in the Sunbelt South* (Princeton, N.J.: Princeton University Press, 2006); Kevin M. Kruse, *White Flight: Atlanta and the Making of Modern Conservatism* (Princeton, N.J.: Princeton University Press, 2007); Robert O. Self, *American Babylon: Race and the Struggle for Postwar Oakland* (Princeton, N.J.: Princeton University Press, 2003); Daniel Martinez HoSang, *Ballot Initiatives and the Making of Postwar California* (Berkeley: University of California Press, 2010). New scholarship is beginning to explore these political tensions among whites who identified as politically liberal; see, for example, Osman, *The Invention of Brownstone Brooklyn*; Lily D. Geismer, "Don't Blame Us: Grassroots Liberalism in Massachusetts, 1960–1990" (Ph.D. diss., University of Michigan, 2010).
44. Isaac William Martin, *The Permanent Tax Revolt: How the Property Tax Transformed American Politics* (Stanford, Calif.: Stanford University Press, 2008).
45. Mound, "Taxpayers for Tax Justice."
46. Pierre Clavel, *Activists in City Hall: The Progressive Response to the Reagan Era in Boston and Chicago* (Ithaca, N.Y.: Cornell University Press, 2010), 44–47.
47. Clavel, *Activists in City Hall*; Randy Cunningham, *Democratizing Cleveland: The Rise and Fall of Community Organizing, 1975–1985* (Cleveland, Ohio: Arambala, 2007).
48. Wade Rathke, "The Association of Community Organizations for Reform Now," January 12, 1974, Box 1, Folder 5, Arkansas ACORN Papers, Wisconsin Historical Society, Madison, 6–7; Jack L. Brummel, "An Organizational Profile of ACORN, Association of Community Organizations for Reform Now," August 13, 1984, Box 15, Folder "ACORN Background," Accession 2001-170, ACORN Papers, Wisconsin Historical Society, Madison, 4.
49. Soss and Jacobs, "The Place of Inequality," 115–118.
50. Brummel, "An Organizational Profile of ACORN," 1, 3; in its early years in Arkansas, ACORN worked to get members elected to local governance. ACORN's Elena Hanggi insisted, in the mid-1970s, on the need to have "poor people in positions of power, in decision-making positions."
51. Adamson and Borgos, "ACORN."
52. Ibid.; John Atlas, *Seeds of Change: The Story of ACORN, America's Most Controversial Antipoverty Community Organizing Group* (Nashville, Tenn.: Vanderbilt University Press, 2010), 43–44.
53. Brummel, "An Organizational Profile of ACORN," 17.
54. National Center for JOBS & JUSTICE, Annual Report 1978–79, Box 14, Folder 6, MEJ Papers, Wisconsin Historical Society, Madison, 1, 17.

55. Ibid., 22; "JOBS & JUSTICE—a national campaign of the Movement for Economic Justice," n.d., Box 14, Folder 17, MEJ Papers, Wisconsin Historical Society, Madison; Atlas, *Seeds of Change*, chap. 5; Michael Kenney, "60s Poor People's Campaign Revived for Jobs Push in Boston," *Boston Globe*, July 21, 1978, Box 15, Folder 1, MEJ Papers, Wisconsin Historical Society, Madison.
56. Adamson and Borgos, "ACORN."
57. Atlas, *Seeds of Change*, 79; Kenneth J. Neubeck, *When Welfare Disappears: The Case for Economic Human Rights* (New York: Routledge, 2006), 158.
58. For criticisms of this welfare-reform success narrative, see Alejandra Marchevsky and Jeanne Theoharis, *Not Working: Latina Immigrants, Low-Wage Jobs, and the Failure of Welfare Reform* (New York: NYU Press, 2006); Morgen et al., *Stretched Thin*; Kenneth J. Neubeck, *When Welfare Disappears*, chaps. 3–4.
59. Research has demonstrated that the message of "independence" or "self-sufficiency" through wage labor suffuses TANF, from the legislation down to caseworker interactions; Morgen et al., *Stretched Thin*, chap. 4.
60. Ibid., chap. 5, quotation on 112; see also Stephanie A. Limoncelli, "'Some of Us Are Excellent at Babies': Paid Work, Mothering, and the Construction of 'Need' in a Welfare-to-Work Program," in *Work, Welfare, and Politics: Confronting Poverty in the Wake of Welfare Reform*, ed. Frances Fox Piven, Joan Aker, Margaret Hallock, and Sandra Morgen (Eugene: University of Oregon Press, 2002), 81–94.
61. Morgen et al., *Stretched Thin*, chap. 5, quotation on 131–132; John Horton and Linda Shaw, "Opportunity, Control, and Resistance: Living Welfare Reform in Los Angeles County," in *Work, Welfare, and Politics*, 207; Limoncelli, "'Some of Us Are Excellent at Babies,'" 81–94.
62. Willie Baptist and Mary Bricker-Jenkins, "A View from the Bottom: Poor People and Their Allies Respond to Welfare Reform," *Annals of the American Academy of Political and Social Science* 577 (September 2001): 145.
63. Evers and Guilemard, "Introduction," 18.

CHAPTER FOURTEEN

Grassroots Challenges to Capitalism

An Interview

FRANCES FOX PIVEN

Conducted by Alice Kessler-Harris and Lindsey Dayton

ALICE KESSLER-HARRIS: I want to begin with some general questions. Tell us first what you understand by the term "welfare state." Does something one can call the welfare state really exist in any sense?

FRANCES FOX PIVEN: Well, the welfare state is not exactly a thing. It is a conceptual map, and it is a way of delineating government policies that are not market driven (or presumably not market driven) and that produce income and services that would otherwise have to be gained through market exchanges. It is a way of categorizing the world, but the world is complicated, and there are many overlapping kinds of activities that are colored by both political-governmental and market dynamics. In this sense, defining the "welfare state" is not to unpeel the onion to find the true core. It is a rough classification, and as a rough classification, I don't have any problem with the term. Let's use it until we have a better one.

ALICE KESSLER-HARRIS: But that said, you have often been a critic, I would even say a fierce critic, of the welfare state. Are you still such a critic?

FRANCES FOX PIVEN: I am still a critic of the kinds of programs of which I was critical before. And my criticism was not directed toward broad income-support policies, adequate or inadequate. There were things that you could and should justifiably criticize about them, but my focus was always on programs that were directed specifically at the poor. In particular, and especially in the United States, income-support programs are very much colored by the poor-relief tradition. They are descendants of poor relief. In fact, Aid to Families with Dependent Children (AFDC), which was the program on which Richard Cloward and I focused when we wrote *Regulating the Poor*, was very much influenced by the state widows' pension programs it followed, and the widows' pensions programs were a species of poor relief.

ALICE KESSLER-HARRIS: Although the widows' pensions programs were also mothers' pensions programs.

FRANCES FOX PIVEN: Well, AFDC, in its later years, did also cover some men who were raising children on their own, but that was just a quirk. Basically, the people receiving AFDC, and who formed the welfare-rights movement, were women with children: they were moms. And, in fact, their role as mothers became very important as they tried to redefine their identity and give themselves a sense of dignity and a sense that they had rights that they could fight for.

ALICE KESSLER-HARRIS: When you think back upon that early 1930s, 1940s, 1950s welfare state, if we can call it that, would you say that it accomplished some good things, namely, income-support programs for poor mothers, even though it also had some adverse consequences?

FRANCES FOX PIVEN: The most important program in the American welfare state was always Social Security. And that was a program that did a lot for old people, who, without social security, often found themselves dependent on, and therefore subject to, the whims of their children (or subject to nobody's whims at all, subsisting on day-old bread). And they were, as a consequence of Social Security, much better off, and extreme poverty among the elderly fell. So Social Security, I think, was on balance a good thing, even though it is not exactly what you would call progressive policy: the revenues that support Social Security are not explicitly progressive, although the distributional formula does tend to be progressive in fact. In other words, the poorest of the old, if they are covered at all, do pretty well under that program, no matter what they paid into it. So, it is not a bad program in that sense. But most important is the automaticity: the fact that you just get your check, and you do not ever have to see a person or talk to a person.

ALICE KESSLER-HARRIS: What about unemployment insurance? Would you say that unemployment was on balance a good program?

FRANCES FOX PIVEN: Well, it was good to have some kind of income support for the unemployed, but there are features of the unemployment-insurance program that twist and contaminate it. The fact that employers have to sign off on your eligibility for unemployment insurance, for example, or the fact that very few—about 40 percent—of the unemployed are actually covered by the program. That is horrible. And the fact that you only get unemployment insurance in many states, most states, actually, now, for twenty-four weeks (it is longer during times of high unemployment). Those are all bad features. It is a very niggardly unemployment-insurance program compared to the unemployment-insurance programs of Western Europe.

ALICE KESSLER-HARRIS: Which tend to be seamless with their welfare programs.

FRANCES FOX PIVEN: So, typically, in a Western European welfare state you will get unemployment insurance for a year. And if you exhaust that benefit and are turned over to the social-assistance system, you get 90 percent or 80 percent of your benefit. So, yes, those are better systems. Despite the fact that everybody talks about the convergence of welfare states throughout the West, the European welfare states, and especially the countries that were in the lead in welfare-state development, are still much better, even though the Right has gained power in some of those countries.

ALICE KESSLER-HARRIS: Let us come to that in a minute. I just want to push you a bit. In *Regulating the Poor*, you and Richard Cloward were fundamentally critical, I would say, of the way in which the American welfare state emerged. And now you sound as though you've softened a bit.

FRANCES FOX PIVEN: No, we were talking about the program that everybody meant when they said "welfare." We were not talking about the "welfare state"; that was not a term anybody used outside of academia. Political pundits were referring to AFDC when they talked about welfare, and that was the program we were talking about.

ALICE KESSLER-HARRIS: And you would still remain just as critical of that program?

FRANCES FOX PIVEN: More critical. Because in the 1960s, in response to both the uprising of the black community as a whole and, more specifically, the uprising of "welfare moms" (supported by the legal aid that they got from the federal legal-assistance program), AFDC greatly liberalized. Court decisions struck down limitations on welfare, benefits rose, angry women in the waiting room made welfare staff much more responsive, and the rolls expanded. It was a different program after ten years of political pummeling. But when the 1996 Personal Responsibility Act was passed, it wiped out AFDC, the arena in which all of these reforms had been fashioned and fought for and won.

ALICE KESSLER-HARRIS: I want to follow up on something that you just said, which is the question of convergence between European and American welfare states. Has there been convergence? And if there has, what does that mean for the future of welfare?

FRANCES FOX PIVEN: There has been some convergence, because neoliberalism is an international development, and European governments are subject to the pressure of international economic actors (as well as European monetary institutions, which are pretty neoliberal). Nevertheless, the welfare programs that exist were forged by organized labor and labor-left political parties, which have not disappeared. There still are unions in Europe, especially in the Nordic pioneers of the welfare state, Finland, Denmark, Sweden, Norway. In fact, European states have high unionization levels, sometimes 50 to 70 percent of the workforce. So it is a different political situation. I do not see those welfare states crumbling, although I do think they are being whittled down, especially in places like Sweden and Denmark. I think there will be some convergence, but policy change does not usually occur in such dramatic spurts unless there is a period of real tumult.

There is a different development that I think is instructive for understanding and trying to predict welfare-state developments, but it is not occurring in Europe or the United States. It is occurring in the middle-income countries: Mexico, Brazil, Chile, Bolivia, Turkey, South Africa. These countries have pioneered conditional cash transfers (CCT). And although these programs started out quite small, they are expanding. They are incredible because they break entirely with the poor-relief tradition, which still influences Europe to some degree and definitely continues to influence the United States a lot. A conditional cash transfer is a program that gives cash assistance to mothers of children on condition that they take their child to the doctor, usually once a year, and send the child to school. Those are the conditions. At first, the programs were not treated as a very big historical development, but they have lasted, they have expanded, and they cover significant segments of the population in these countries.

ALICE KESSLER-HARRIS: Are they means-tested?

FRANCES FOX PIVEN: They vary in that respect. Some countries universalize the CCT, and some countries give it only to the poor, and in that sense they are means-tested. But the problem with American welfare is not just that it is means-tested. It is that getting the benefit is continually tested, tested, tested. The surveillance is continuous. And the insult is horrific. There is no insult in CCT programs.

ALICE KESSLER-HARRIS: Still, these programs sound to me very reminiscent of the old child allowances. The British, for example, still have a child allowance. It is something like £140 a month for two children.

FRANCES FOX PIVEN: And so do the Scandinavian countries. They are like that; they are much more like child allowances than they are like poor relief or welfare. And recent studies show that these programs are making a major impact both on reducing inequality and reducing poverty. And there are a couple of countries that have universalized the benefit so that everybody receives it, as everybody received children's allowances.

ALICE KESSLER-HARRIS: Do you think there is any possibility that the United States could move in that direction? For example, Nixon's Family Assistance Program might have done something like that, although it was eventually rejected by him.

FRANCE FOX PIVEN: I do not think it will move in that direction without a major upheaval, but major upheavals do occur. I think the Left in the United States has a very weak and inadequate set of ideas about income support or poverty programs. The Left always begins with full employment and raising the minimum wage. And then there is the hope that if everybody has a job, they will all become union members, and once they are union members, they will become strong, stalwart, marching members of the proletariat, I suppose. But that is not going to happen now.

ALICE KESSLER-HARRIS: I cannot help asking you the gender question here. What do we mean by full employment? Do we mean that mothers of babies or small children are going to be sent out to work?

FRANCES FOX PIVEN: Or mothers who are going to have to take care of the mother-in-law?

ALICE KESSLER-HARRIS: That's right. How, then, do we think about caring?

FRANCES FOX PIVEN: Full employment—I used to say when Reagan took office that he had a full-employment program. He was going to put everybody to work, at lower and lower wages. And he did. I think if that is the Left, the Left does not have a good set of policies for dealing with poverty and inequality in a neoliberal economy, or for dealing with the gender issues, the caring issues, that are entailed by employment, poverty, and a lousy welfare system. Or for dealing with the prospect of tens of millions of immigrants coming to Western Europe and the United States as the oceans rise.

Just think about the changes that have occurred in women's work roles in the United States over the last few decades and the new forms of exploitation that result. Women are now considered wage workers. Most of us have always worked, of course, but much of the work we did was in the home, or "caring work." Now women work at Walmarts and then come home and do the caring work as well. Or else we do without the contribution to our well-being that caring work produced.

ALICE KESSLER-HARRIS: But go back to a more fundamental question that you raised, the question of neoliberalism. Much of the historical literature on the rise of the welfare state talks about fascism, communism, and the effects of these systems on scaring people away from big or interventionist government. And neoliberal ideology picks up on those themes and has become very popular.

FRANCES FOX PIVEN: Neoliberal ideas are very loud because they are broadcasted through a very powerful propaganda machine. But it is by no means clear to me that they are very popular. True, there is talk about market freedom versus big government. But if you ask ordinary people what they mean by "freedom" (because the propagandists keep saying "freedom" as if they were another civil-rights movement), people do not mean freedom for the big financial speculators. The extraordinary success of the Bernie Sanders campaign makes that clear. Sanders's main programmatic appeals were actually taken from the New Deal handbook: higher taxes on the rich, universal health care, access to higher education, and so on. These policies imply, of course, the "big government" that is regularly invoked as the problem and the enemy by rightwing propagandists. The Sanders campaign, and his ability to attract support from the white working class, argues that popular antipathy is not to government as such but rather to the government policies dominated by crony capitalists, by predatory neoliberal policies that treat the welfare state as a terrain for profiteering.

ALICE KESSLER-HARRIS: But what about what you might call the new authoritarian working class?

FRANCES FOX PIVEN: When you look at public-opinion surveys that show popular antipathy for big government, I think you can make a good case that people are against big government because they think big government is usually crony capitalism. They think that it is the big corporate or Wall Street guys who run big government. And since that is largely correct, we have a problem. We have to try to do the ideological work that creates the possibility of a government that is not beholden to business.

ALICE KESSLER-HARRIS: So now let me turn the question in another way. Some of us have argued in the past that we need social citizenship (in the T. H. Marshall sense) in order to perpetuate democratic political citizenship. Where are you now on this question?

FRANCES FOX PIVEN: I don't disagree; it's just that I don't think talking about "social citizenship" is of much help. Welfare's rituals, investigations, and entanglements are virtually designed as a kind of public theater. And the public theater teaches everybody, including welfare recipients themselves, that welfare recipients are worthless and lazy. This is not the only problem with welfare, but it is a big part of the problem. Why do people think as they do about welfare? It has a lot to do with the way the program is structured and administered. For example, I get Social Security checks. Nobody investigates me, insults me, or asks me to take a drug test or put on an orange vest and go pick up trash in the park.

ALICE KESSLER-HARRIS: That is because you are being rewarded for having worked all your life.

FRANCES FOX PIVEN: A lot of people who get checks in the mail did not work all their lives. Big farmers, for example, receive subsidies not to grow their crops. They don't have to show that they put in forty-hour weeks to get those checks. There is no public ritual of degradation, and some of them get a lot of money. What I am trying to get at is that the way people think about the poor or programs for the poor is not writ in stone. It is writ in our institutions, to be sure, and in our propaganda. But it is not written in stone. People can change their minds about these things. And they have changed their minds about these things in the past.

ALICE KESSLER-HARRIS: Are you suggesting that democratic participation is not necessarily linked to the distribution of social benefits?

FRANCES FOX PIVEN: I think it helps to protect social programs if you have a big, dependable voting bloc. That much is true. But it is not exactly magic. T. H. Marshall makes it seem like a kind of organic connection, but I do not think it is an organic connection. After all, the welfare budget—let us take AFDC alone—expanded exponentially in the 1960s and early 1970s. Certainly during that time democratic participation, if by that you mean voting, did not expand. What expanded was riotous behavior by the poor, including welfare recipients.

ALICE KESSLER-HARRIS: Talk a little bit about what you are calling "riotous behavior," or what some of us might call "social movements," like, for example, the welfare-rights movement.

FRANCES FOX PIVEN: I think that riots are a part of social movements. Generally speaking, when people talk about democratic participation, they are not talking about welfare riots or food riots. I think it is complicated. I think that the riotous collective actions by black Americans (mainly in the northern cities, but some in the South) were significantly both encouraged and protected by the fact that there were also black voters by that time. And the numbers of black voters in the North were increasing and were important in the political careers of a lot of people in Washington, including presidents like Kennedy and Lyndon Baines Johnson. I have always thought there was a connection between electoral politics and movement politics, but in my mind there is no question that the real reform of welfare in those years occurred as a result of tumult and direct action and a lot of trouble in the cities and in the welfare offices. The Boston Riot, for example, was precipitated by the descent of police officers on a group of "welfare moms" who were demonstrating in the Roxbury welfare center. When the women called out to the street, they set the insurgency in motion.

ALICE KESSLER-HARRIS: There are two directions I want to go on this. The first direction is to note that insurgencies often have little staying power. They cannot sustain themselves without a kind of bureaucratic infrastructure, without some internal organization. And so, those social movements actually produce an internal tension, which then pulls them apart. Lacking bureaucracy, which protesters often see as inimical to spontaneity, do insurgencies really bring about any permanent changes in the long run?

FRANCES FOX PIVEN: That has been an obsession of mine. I think that the organizations that arise on the crest of social movements tend to pull the movement down. They are so preoccupied with the survival of the bureaucratic infrastructure that they have a dampening effect on the movement. That certainly is what happened in welfare rights. I think that is also a big problem in the so-called labor movement. And I think you can make a similar case for earlier movements in American history. Now, this does not mean I'm against unions. I think it is inevitable that people try to institutionalize or organize themselves in ways that sustain their gains. But that does not necessarily mean that it is the best way to push the goals of the movement forward.

ALICE KESSLER-HARRIS: Are you saying that social movements can and should continue to exist as spontaneous eruptions, one after the other?

FRANCES FOX PIVEN: As long as possible. But you cannot do it forever, because of the social forces that are pressing on the movement: repressive forces but also enticements (a budget, an office, a role on our committee to reform welfare). I was invited by the Carter administration to sit on a committee for welfare reform (which I turned down). But that's what you get when you have a movement. That is the end of the movement.

ALICE KESSLER-HARRIS: But without those things, movements end anyway.

FRANCES FOX PIVEN: Somebody else is going to have to sit in the meetings and do the work of designing the policy reforms. I knew somebody else would do it. But I am going to stay and try to do as much as I can to push the kind of leverage that is gained from insurgency, from disruption, as far as it can be pushed.

ALICE KESSLER-HARRIS: Let me play devil's advocate. A lot of people argue that that period in the late 1960s and 1970s, when the welfare-rights movement was at its most active, is the period when welfare as we know it was replaced by workfare. So one could argue that those social movements, in the end, were at least partially responsible.

FRANCES FOX PIVEN: I disagree. It has always been there. Feminism, if anything, helped puncture the efforts of moms on welfare to say that they were doing good, decent work. Because in the early days of the feminist movement, the early days of NOW, dependence on welfare was held in some contempt. And that certainly did not help. You know, it was not until 1995 that NOW became an ardent supporter of people on welfare, *women* on welfare. That took a long time. I remember Gloria Steinem telling the *New York Times* that women did not need alimony or childcare support anymore.

ALICE KESSLER-HARRIS: Right. Betty Friedan made similar arguments. You are saying that workfare was always a part of welfare. So you do not see a radical transformation in the late 1960s and 1970s?

FRANCES FOX PIVEN: The workfare programs that began in 1967, as I recall, were relatively small. And certainly the women, the "welfare-rights moms," did not take them terribly seriously. Oh, Congress huffed and they puffed. The fact of the matter is that, in the American South, for example, welfare has always been a workfare program.

ALICE KESSLER-HARRIS: For African Americans.

FRANCES FOX PIVEN: Yes. Not only in the sense that you got so little on welfare that a job picking cotton seemed reasonable. But also in the sense that people were regularly cut off welfare when there was help needed in the fields. It was a workfare program. And important in the move toward workfare, toward TANF, was the fact that being a mom no longer had the kind of legitimacy that it had earlier.

ALICE KESSLER-HARRIS: Exactly. So that while women in the welfare-rights movement were claiming that mothering was work, middle-class white women were saying that they wanted paid work outside the home.

FRANCES FOX PIVEN: It was so important to "welfare moms" to discover this justification. It was not something an organizer was doing; this was something *they* were doing. They were trying to figure out why they had a right to welfare. They would sit around—this was 1966, 1967—sit around these church basements or somebody's apartment. And what they hit on, it was so obvious, was that they were moms and that they were taking care of their kids. Mothering was their work. And when I was on the board of the Central Harlem Welfare Rights Group, even though I knew the women pretty well, they would always address me as "Mrs.": *Mrs.* Piven. And they wanted to be *Mrs.* Gillespie or *Mrs.* Jones. Everybody was a *Mrs.*

ALICE KESSLER HARRIS: Let's go back to trade unions for a minute. Most people would argue that trade unions were instrumental in creating the American welfare state—health care, Medicaid, Medicare, unemployment insurance, eventually supporting Social Security—but you are rather negative about the trade-union movement.

FRANCES FOX PIVEN: Oh no, I'm not negative about the trade-union movement, although I certainly do not think that they played a major role in constructing the welfare state. They played a major role in defending the welfare state against the attacks that began in the 1960s. Certainly, New York labor did not want to have anything to do with citywide welfare rights, but in Washington, D.C., the AFL-CIO was an ally of welfare rights, of sorts. Not marching in the streets or anything, but using their usual lobbying connections and so forth.

But I think you can make a good case that the American labor movement, with its Gompersian traditions, inhibited the development of a more European-style or Scandinavian-style welfare state. Because organized labor had, in its rather tormented history, relied on the benefits that the union could provide as an incentive for union membership. And they did not want the government to take over the provision of benefits, because they were afraid of what it would do to their membership. As a consequence, they did not offer fulsome support for Roosevelt's welfare-state initiatives.

In the heyday of the union movement, at least in terms of numbers, what did they fight for? They fought for work-related benefits. They fought for health care as a condition of employment. They fought for pensions as a condition of employment. That was their main agenda. And the strength that they wielded in creating those workforce-related benefits did undermine support for welfare-state initiatives.

ALICE KESSLER-HARRIS: But in the 1950s, when the labor movement fell in with Walter Reuther's push for work-related benefits, those benefits became the core of the American welfare state. The labor movement's push for minimum wages, for health benefits, for vacations with pay, those kinds of things, undermined what might have been a European form of the welfare state. But surely, trade unions have been supportive of the American version of the welfare state.

FRANCES FOX PIVEN: They supported a particular direction in welfare-state development. That is true. And they were not particularly interested in programs for the poor. Although, in the late 1960s, with the black movement peaking, their lobbyists did support AFDC and work-related programs. But their record is mixed. Organized labor raised the earnings of blue-collar workers; they made guys from the Okies, who worked in the steel mills, respectable. They suddenly became the middle class. This had its bad side, too: they looked down on the people who were still poor.

ALICE KESSLER-HARRIS: So, the logical consequence of what you are saying is that now, in the absence of a weak or virtually nonexistent trade-union movement, we should have a clear path to developing a more comprehensive welfare state?

FRANCES FOX PIVEN: We simply do not know. American unions helped distort the American welfare state by working to make benefits employment conditioned. The weakness or absence of unions predicts nothing. But I am inclined to begin at an easier point in the strategizing, which is to talk about what we should be against. And I think we should be radically against programs that condition the receipt of services or benefits on wage work. That was bad for the poor whether they were employed or not from the very beginning, from the first poor-relief systems, and its effects are much worse now because work is so precarious and uncertain, because we are going to have a flood of immigrants, and because of automation. So, many different developments argue against a work-conditioned welfare state. Even though it always sounds a little goofy, I think we have to go back to the idea of basic income.

Everybody knows the very rich are getting richer still. We do not have a problem of resources. We have a problem in the distribution of resources. And we have more workers than we can employ. Immigration is going to increase, and it is going to increase in ways that cannot be stopped by stupid walls. And automation is going to increase. We need some sort of universal protections against these developments. This is not a question of whether we can win those protections. This is a question of how we should think about it, and what we should fight for, the direction in which we should move. We should move toward unconditional income supports. Will we win that? I don't know.

ALICE KESSLER-HARRIS: You make two very interesting suggestions: unconditional income supports and severing welfare from work. Both, like all welfare benefits, are products of the nation-state. Yet, today, national borders seem to be everywhere much more permeable than they were before. Can any national welfare system exist in this context?

FRANCES FOX PIVEN: We also have a situation in which the nation-state, given its legal authority, its bureaucratic capacities, and its wealth, is virtually the only actor on the scene that can do anything about our big problems. Think, for example, of climate change. The antipathy to the welfare state is sort of beside the point. We cannot deal with the problems of the contemporary world without big government. The masses of people who will be on the move as their countries and their farms and villages are submerged, ruined by drought, etc.—that is one reason we will have big government. And the other reason we will have big government is that the only actor that is possibly capable of stopping the resource extraction that is producing global warming is government. Who else could do it?

ALICE KESSLER-HARRIS: Okay, but if that is the case, then how are we going to deal with the ideological anti-big-government movement?

FRANCES FOX PIVEN: Look at what happened in the United States in 1940–1941. You could even begin in 1933. It was big government that helped people during the worst years of the Depression, even though big government did not actually succeed in moving the economy out of the Depression.

ALICE KESSLER-HARRIS: In one sense you are saying that antipathy to big government, as you put it, will fade away of necessity, but, on the other hand, when it fades away, will it have destroyed or undermined any effort to sustain a welfare system of any kind? Will we simply have a big government that supports military expansion, works on issues of climate control, does not care about employment or unemployment, and uses carceral or coercive methods to deal with surplus labor?

FRANCES FOX PIVEN: I think that we have to take six steps backward. The American welfare state is not shriveling. You are assuming that it is disappearing, but it is not: it is actually growing. Even programs that are ostensibly for the poor have enormously expanded; it is just that the benefits are not really for the poor (although they are certainly called benefits for the poor). Every time the American Enterprise Institute or the Heritage Foundation adds up what we spend on poor people, they add all public programs, even those that do not benefit the poor alone. If only poor people could eat that money, but they cannot.

ALICE KESSLER-HARRIS: How do you see the American welfare state shriveling and growing? How do you see it transformed?

FRANCES FOX PIVEN: It has been transformed in the last forty or fifty years, mainly as a result of the influence of organized business interests. But there are moments when it has also been transformed by the imperative to restore order.

ALICE KESSLER-HARRIS: Much of this money is being spent on prisons, on disciplining people in various ways.

FRANCES FOX PIVEN: That's right. African Americans became rebellious in the 1950s and 1960s and 1970s, and at the same time, immigration increased (particularly Latino immigration but also some eastern European immigration). So there was a ready pool of alternate labor to do the drudgery of the American economy. They did not need African Americans anymore, and they imprisoned them, especially the rebellious young men. That is true; they did that. But is that the welfare state? When I say that the welfare state is growing, I am not including prisons, actually. We are spending more money on education, for example. We do not spend it well; that is true. But we never spent it well! You think the old welfare system was good? No, of course not!

ALICE KESSLER-HARRIS: I want to get back to refugees. Because it was the nation that set up these welfare-state systems, the welfare-state choices and incomes are limited by larger global problems, one of which is the refugee crisis. I worry that the welfare state—the good part of the welfare state that actually provides health care and education and support for poor people—that piece of the welfare state will begin to disintegrate in the face of huge claims on nations brought by these immigrant or refugee populations and by a greater priority placed on spending money in areas like climate change, policing Iran and Iraq, and so on.

FRANCES FOX PIVEN: There is plenty of money. There is plenty of money to spend. First of all, refugees have welfare needs, so they are not a separate category. They stretch the national budget to deal with needs that are welfare-state-type needs. Unless you are taking T. H. Marshall's citizenship perspective, where they do not "count" and are outside the system. In Sweden, for example, demands on housing grew, but there were other programs from which they could have taken the money. In the United States, making demands for a bigger welfare state has also been regarded as a way to exert pressure against military spending.

ALICE KESSLER-HARRIS: But that has not worked. Usually the demands for military spending have reduced the amount available for welfare.

FRANCES FOX PIVEN: But that is all a question of how much pressure. It is true that LBJ had a hard time doing guns and butter. It created a big debt and big strains inside the government apparatus, so it was not so simple. Also, the marginal tax rate at end of World War II was something like 91 percent, it was still something like 70 percent when JFK was president, and it's 38 percent now. We will not do anything for poor people unless there is political pressure. But good ideas will not make us spend it on poor people, either.

ALICE KESSLER-HARRIS: Do you think the refugees moving into Western Europe now will have any impact on welfare-state provisions?

FRANCES FOX PIVEN: I think it is going to be largely negative, actually. Merkel's momentary welcome to the refugees was a beautiful thing to watch, but I am very skeptical that she can sustain that political posture. Meanwhile, in places like Hungary, Finland, Bulgaria, the refugees are spurring the growth of right-wing parties. Greece has become an immigrant-detention camp, the whole peninsula.

I think that countries with homogeneous populations, because there is so much less internal friction and antipathy, can have a more generous welfare state. Yet I think that class differences have always been the basis of serious antipathy. Look at the history of the English welfare state. The English were relatively homogeneous. It is always said that there is much more internal conflict in the United States because of our ethnic and racial diversity, but—you must have had this experience, too—sitting in a café in a European city, say, Vienna, and watching the reactions of the Viennese to the Vietnamese who are trying to sell a few cigarettes on the street. The Viennese would spit on the Vietnamese in a minute. But Americans do not react that way. They are more tolerant, at least in the cities.

ALICE KESSLER-HARRIS: You know, even the Swedes said that when they began to see mass migration, first by Russians and then by Pakistanis, welfare-state provisions, which had been so enormously generous, began to diminish. I do not want to say that was totally a result of the increasing heterogeneity of the state, but it was perhaps partly to blame.

FRANCES FOX PIVEN: It is also a result of the growth of the Swedish Right. But the growth of the Right is not caused simply by immigration.

LINDSEY DAYTON: But there is nothing deterministic about that: that is politics. It is the same as saying that what we need is for the Left to have a better plan of opposition.

FRANCES FOX PIVEN: You might be able to say that immigration enables the Right. And certainly the Right has grown in Norway, too, but I have not seen anything to convince me that there are significant cutbacks to welfare programs pending in Norway.

ALICE KESSLER-HARRIS: Let me ask you a little bit about gender. We who are feminists think that feminism has transformed the way people think about poverty, the climate, and various other things. Yet most of the recipients of welfare benefits tend to be women or poor women or mothers. Can we think a little bit about how the push for gender equality, the push for women to be in the workforce, might itself have undermined or continue to undermine possibilities for helping the poor?

FRANCES FOX PIVEN: We talked about that a little bit before. Today I read an article by Anne Jones, who spent years in Norway. And the article was about the way in which Scandinavian feminism had transformed and improved the welfare state. She writes about paternal-leave policies, and she writes as if men and women use them equally. (I do not know if that is true—it was not true last time I looked. Nevertheless, they could use them equally.) She also writes about the childcare systems, which are much more robust than the barely existing American childcare system. And she attributes these benefits to Scandinavian feminism specifically, not to feminism in general, and I think that is fair enough. In Scandinavia, women wanted to enter into markets, economic life, political life, and a strong program for welfare-state supports accompanied that transition. Women got most of the jobs in the welfare state, and they also received a lot of the services and income supports of the welfare state. One of the aspects of welfare reform in the United States that is most scandalous, I think, is the kind of childcare arrangements that were made available, or I should say not made available, even as welfare pushed women into work. How could you push women into work without providing care for their children? And it was so confusing in a way. In 1971, there actually was legislation for childcare, but Nixon vetoed it.

ALICE KESSLER-HARRIS: Tell us what you imagine the future of the welfare state in its different dimensions is going to look like, the next twenty or thirty years.

FRANCES FOX PIVEN: I do not know what it is going to look like. It depends very much on the political dynamics, which emerge from the crisis of employment (and I think it is a crisis, given the growth of precarious labor and high unemployment levels). I just do not know. That is one of the reasons I am put off by all the people who are trouncing Bernie Sanders because he is creating a scenario that could give us a Republican, fascist president. That is the argument. But all the scenarios are pretty bad.

ALICE KESSLER-HARRIS: Given the kind of inequality that exists and the outrage at it, it seems a moment when social movements of the Occupy Wall Street sort should be sprouting from the bottom.

FRANCES FOX PIVEN: They are! This is a social-movement moment! How could we say, "nothing is happening"? An African American social movement, Black Lives Matter, has emerged and revived Black Power in a much more ecumenical form than existed in the 1970s, when it was destroyed by American cops and the FBI. It has a generous perspective and generous tactics. That is wonderful, very important. And Black Lives Matter is everywhere; anybody can start a Black Lives Matter chapter.

There is also the Fight-for-Fifteen Movement. I mean, maybe the Service Employees International Union (SEIU) intended this to be one of its smoke-and-mirrors campaigns to get more members. But whatever the union intended, it became a movement focusing on electoral politics, with incredible success.

LINDSEY DAYTON: This is how it has always been. Unions have always built on movements that people start themselves on the ground. They come in (when it is advantageous for them and when they are willing to put in the resources). And usually they pitch those resources as a means of mediating not so much between workers and employers but between workers and the state. In workers' relationship to the state, the unions are the mediating factor.

FRANCES FOX PIVEN: They all do it. But there are movements outside the unions, too. And there are movements that led to the unions. SEIU is okay; it worked out all right. The Fight for Fifteen has raised the minimum wage already, and it is not over.

LINDSEY DAYTON: The movement is also part of the broader discourse now. "$15" is like the "99 percent" of Occupy: a number that gauges whether or not something is fair. And that is as important to the movement as minimum-wage legislation. People have a sense that their work entitles them to fair pay.

FRANCES FOX PIVEN: Yes, I think it is good, and I do not think it is what SEIU intended at all.

ALICE KESSLER-HARRIS: And other kinds of social movements? Do you think environmental movements will have a good impact?

FRANCES FOX PIVEN: Yes, of course. Without an environmental movement, can you imagine what the air would be like? Look at the reaction to the Flint scandal. I mean, look at what happened in Flint. That is another kind of development in which I am very interested: the way in which debt is being used to strangle state and local government. The thievery going on is absolutely incredible, and that is what Flint reflects. The water crisis all started with an emergency manager.

Are you optimistic about the future, Lindsey?

LINDSEY DAYTON: I am optimistic that if they poison our water, someone will eventually respond with outrage.

Selected Bibliography

Democracy, Capitalism, and Inequality

Bartels, Larry M. *Unequal Democracy: The Political Economy of the New Gilded Age.* Princeton, N.J.: Princeton University Press, 2008.

Beck, Ulrich. *Risk Society: Towards a New Modernity.* London: Sage, 1992.

Delanty, Gerard. *Citizenship in a Global Age: Society, Culture, Politics.* Buckingham: Open University Press, 2000.

Dumenil, Gerard, and Dominique Levy. *Capital Resurgent: Root of the Neoliberal Revolution.* Cambridge, Mass.: Harvard University Press, 2004.

Franklin, Donna L. *Ensuring Inequality: The Structural Transformation of the African American Family.* New York: Oxford University Press, 1997.

Gerstle, Gary. *Liberty and Coercion: The Paradox of American Government from the Founding to the Present.* Princeton, N.J.: Princeton University Press, 2015.

Habermas, Jürgen. *The Postnational Constellation: Political Essays.* Cambridge, Mass.: MIT Press, 2001.

Hall, Peter A., and David Soskice. *Varieties of Capitalism: The Institutional Foundations of Comparative Advantage.* New York: Oxford University Press, 2001.

Lawrence, Jacobs, and Theda Skocpol. *Inequality and American Democracy: What We Know and What We Need to Learn.* New York: Russell Sage Foundation, 2007.

Levy, Jonah, ed. *The State After Statism: New State Activities in the Age of Liberalization.* Cambridge, Mass.: Harvard University Press, 2006.

Lichtenstein, Nelson. *American Capitalism: Social Thought and Political Economy in the Twentieth Century.* Philadelphia: University of Pennsylvania Press, 2006.

Marshall, T. H. *Citizenship and Social Class, and Other Essays*. Cambridge: Cambridge University Press, 1950.

Mettler, Suzanne. *The Submerged State: How Invisible Government Policies Undermine American Democracy*. Chicago: University of Chicago Press, 2011.

Piketty, Thomas. *Capital in the Twenty-First Century*. Cambridge, Mass.: Harvard University Press, 2014.

Skowronek, Stephen. *Building a New American State*. Cambridge, Mass.: Harvard University Press, 1982.

Transnational and Comparative Perspectives

Alber, Jens. "The 'European Social Model' and the USA." *European Union Politics* 7, no. 3 (2006): 393–419.

Anttonnen, Anneli, John Baldock, and Jorma Sipilä. *The Young, the Old, and the State: Social Care Systems in Five Industrial Nations*. Cheltenham: Edward Elgar, 2003.

Banting, Keith, and Will Kymlicka, eds. *Multiculturalism and the Welfare State: Recognition and Redistribution in Contemporary Democracies*. Oxford: Oxford University Press, 2006.

Brandolini, Andrea, and Timothy M. Smeeding. "Income Inequality in Richer and OECD Countries." In *The Oxford Handbook of Economic Inequality*, ed. W. Salverda et al., 71–100. Oxford: Oxford Handbooks Online, 2009.

Castles, Francis G. *The Future of the Welfare State: Crisis Myths and Crisis Realities*. Oxford: Oxford University Press, 2004.

Crepaz, Marcus M. L. *Trust Beyond Borders: Immigration, the Welfare State, and Identity in Modern Societies*. Ann Arbor: University of Michigan Press, 2008.

Elman, Amy R. *Sexual Subordination and State Intervention: Comparing Sweden and the United States*. New York: Berghahn, 1996.

Esping-Andersen, Gøsta. *Social Foundations of Postindustrial Economies*. New York: Oxford University Press, 1999.

——. *The Three Worlds of Welfare Capitalism*. Cambridge: Polity, 1990.

Ferrera, Maurizio. *The Boundaries of Welfare*. Oxford: Oxford University Press, 2005.

Flora, Peter, and Arnold J. Heidenheimer. *Developments of Welfare States in Europe and America*. New Brunswick, N.J.: Transaction, 1981.

Hemerijck, Anton. *Changing Welfare States*. Oxford: Oxford University Press, 2013.

Hennock, Ernest Peter. *British Social Reform and German Precedents: The Case of Social Insurance.* Oxford: Clarendon, 1987.

Katznelson, Ira. *Black Men, White Cities: Race, Politics, and Migration in the United States, 1900–1930, and Britain, 1948–1968.* Chicago: University of Chicago Press, 1978.

Korpi, Walter. *The Working Class in Welfare Capitalism: Work, Unions, and Politics in Sweden.* London: Routledge, 1963.

Mead, Lawrence. *The New Paternalism: Supervisory Approaches to Poverty.* Washington, D.C.: Brookings Institution, 1997.

Neubeck, Kenneth J. *When Welfare Disappears: The Case for Economic Human Rights.* New York: Routledge, 2006.

O'Connor, Julia, Ann Shola Orloff, and Sheila Shaver, eds. *States, Markets, Families: Gender, Liberalism, and Social Policy in Australia, Canada, Great Britain, and the United States.* New York: Cambridge University Press, 1999.

Olson, Kevin. *Reflexive Democracy: Political Equality and the Welfare State.* Cambridge, Mass.: MIT Press, 2006.

Peck, Jamie. *Workfare States.* New York: Guilford, 2001.

Rimlinger, Gaston. *Welfare Policy and Industrialization in Europe, America, and Russia.* New York: Wiley, 1971.

Rothstein, Bo. *Just Institutions Matter: The Moral and Political Logic of the Universal Welfare State.* Cambridge: Cambridge University Press, 1998.

Russell, James W. *Double Standard: Social Policy in Europe and the United States.* Lanham, Mass.: Rowman and Littlefield, 2006.

Welfare History: Europe and the United States

Berkowitz, Edward. *America's Welfare State: From Roosevelt to Reagan.* Baltimore, Md.: Johns Hopkins University Press, 1991.

Beveridge, William H. *Social Insurance and Allied Services* [1942]. London: Her Majesty's Stationery Office, 1968.

Christiansen, Niels Finn, Klaus Petersen, Nils Edling, and Per Haave, eds. *The Nordic Model of Welfare: A Historical Reappraisal.* Copenhagen: Museum Tusculanum Press, 2006.

Conant, Lisa. *Justice Contained: Law and Politics in the European Union.* Ithaca, N.Y.: Cornell University Press, 2004.

Cowie, Jefferson. *The Great Exception: The New Deal and the Limits of American Politics.* Princeton, N.J.: Princeton University Press, 2016.

Ferrera, Maurizio. "Friends or Foes? European Integration and National Welfare States." In *Global Europe, Social Europe*, ed. Anthony Giddens et al., 257–278. London: Polity, 2006.

———. *Welfare State Reform in Southern Europe: Fighting Poverty and Social Exclusion in Greece, Italy, Spain, and Portugal*. London: Routledge, 2005.

Flora, Peter, ed. *Growth to Limits: The Western European Welfare States Since World War II*. Berlin: De Gruyter, 1986–1987.

Fraser, Nancy, and Linda Gordon. "A Genealogy of Dependency: Tracing a Keyword in the U.S. Welfare State." *Signs* 19, no. 2 (1994): 309–336.

Gilens, Martin. *Affluence and Influence: Economic Inequality and Political Power in America*. Princeton, N.J.: Princeton University Press, 2014.

Gordon, Colin. *Growing Apart: A Political History of American Inequality*. Washington, D.C.: Institute for Policy Studies, Program on Inequality and the Common Good, 2014.

Habermas, Jürgen. "Democracy, Solidarity, and the European Crisis." *Eurozine*, May 7, 2013.

Hancock, Ange-Marie. *The Politics of Disgust: The Public Identity of the Welfare Queen*. New York: New York University Press, 2004.

Hatzfeld, Henri. *Du pauperisme à la securité sociale: essai sur le origines de la securité sociale en France, 1850–1940*. Paris: Armand Colin, 1971.

Herrick, John M., and Paul H. Stuart. *Encyclopedia of Social Welfare History*. Thousand Oaks, Calif.: Sage, 2005.

Hewitson, Mark, and Matthew D'Auria, eds. *Europe in Crisis: Intellectuals and the European Idea, 1917–1957*. Oxford: Berghahn, 2012.

Hochschild, Jennifer. *What's Fair? American Beliefs About Distributive Justice*. Cambridge, Mass.: Harvard University Press, 1981.

Hoffman, Beatrix. *Health Care for Some: Rights and Rationing in the United States Since 1930*. Chicago: University of Chicago Press, 2012.

———. *The Wages of Sickness: The Politics of Health Insurance in Progressive America*. Chapel Hill: University of North Carolina Press, 2001.

Howard, Christopher. *The Hidden Welfare State: Tax Expenditures and Social Policy in the United States*. Princeton, N.J.: Princeton University Press, 1997.

Ingvaldsen, Siri, et al. *Democracy and the Welfare State: The Nordic Nations Since 1800*. Aarhus: Turbine, 2009.

Jansson, Bruce S. *The Reluctant Welfare State: Engaging History to Advance Social Work: Practice in Contemporary Society*. Belmont, Calif.: Bruce/Cole Cengage Learning, 2009.

Judt, Tony. *Postwar: A History of Europe Since 1945*. London: Penguin, 2005.

Katz, Michael B. *In the Shadow of the Poorhouse: A Social History of Welfare in America*. New York: Basic Books, 1986.

Katznelson, Ira. *City Trenches: Urban Politics and the Patterning of Class in the United States.* Chicago: University of Chicago Press, 1981.

——. *Fear Itself: The New Deal and the Origins of Our Time.* New York: Norton, 2013.

Kessler-Harris, Alice. *In Pursuit of Equity: Women, Men, and the Quest for Economic Citizenship in Twentieth-Century America.* New York: Oxford University Press, 2001.

Kessler-Harris, Alice, and Maurizio Vaudagna, eds. *Democracy and Social Rights in the Two Wests.* Turin: Otto, 2009.

Klausen, Jytte. *War and Welfare: Europe and the United States, 1945 to the Present.* London: Palgrave, 1998.

Klein, Jennifer. *For All These Rights: Business, Labor, and the Shaping of America's Public-Private Welfare State.* Princeton, N.J.: Princeton University Press, 2003.

Kornbluh, Felicia. *The Battle for Welfare Rights: Politics and Poverty in Modern America.* Philadelphia: University of Pennsylvania Press, 2007.

Leibfried, Stephan, and Paul Pierson, eds. *European Social Policy Between Fragmentation and Integration.* Washington D.C.: Brookings Institution, 1995.

Martin, Isaac William. *The Permanent Tax Revolt: How the Property Tax Transformed American Politics.* Stanford, Calif.: Stanford University Press, 2008.

Michelmore, Molly. *Tax and Spend: Welfare, Taxes, and the Limits of American Liberalism.* Philadelphia: University of Pennsylvania Press, 2012.

Milward, Alan S. *The European Rescue of the Nation State.* London: Routledge, 1992.

Mittelstadt, Jennifer. *From Welfare to Workfare: The Unintended Consequences of Liberal Reform, 1945–1965.* Chapel Hill: University of North Carolina Press, 2005.

Moynihan, Daniel P. *Maximum Feasible Misunderstanding: Community Action in the War on Poverty.* New York: Free Press, 1969.

Nadasen, Premilla. *Welfare Warriors: The Welfare Rights Movement in the United States.* New York: Routledge, 2005.

O'Connor, Alice. *Poverty Knowledge: Social Science, Social Policy, and the Poor in Twentieth-Century U.S. History.* Princeton, N.J.: Princeton University Press, 2001.

Offe, Claus. *The Democratic Welfare State: A European Regime Under the Strain of European Integration.* Political Science Series 68. Vienna: Institute for Advanced Studies, 2002.

Orleck, Annelise, and Gayle Hazirjian, eds. *The War on Poverty: A New Grassroots History, 1964–1980.* Athens: University of Georgia Press, 2011.

Page, Nejamin I., and Lawrence R. Jacobs. *Class War? What Americans Really Think About Economic Inequality.* Chicago: University of Chicago Press, 2009.

Pierson, Paul. *Dismantling the Welfare State? Reagan, Thatcher, and the Politics of Retrenchment.* Cambridge: Cambridge University Press, 1995.

Piven, Frances Fox, and Richard A. Cloward. *The Breaking of the American Social Compact.* New York: New Press, 1997.

——. *The New Class War: Reagan's Attack on the Welfare State and Its Consequences.* New York: Pantheon, 1982.

——. *Regulating the Poor: The Functions of Public Welfare.* New York: Pantheon, 1971.

Piven, Frances Fox, Joan Aker, Margaret Hallock, and Sandra Morgen. *Work, Welfare, and Politics: Confronting Poverty in the Wake of Welfare Reform.* Eugene: University of Oregon Press, 2002.

Quadagno, Jill. *The Color of Welfare: How Racism Undermined the War on Poverty.* New York: Oxford University Press, 1994.

Rodgers, Daniel T. *Atlantic Crossings: Social Politics in a Progressive Age.* Cambridge, Mass.: Harvard University Press, 1998.

Schram, Sanford F., Joe Soss, and Richard C. Fording, eds. *Race and the Politics of Welfare Reform.* Ann Arbor: University of Michigan Press, 2003.

Skocpol, Theda, *Protecting Soldiers and Mothers: The Political Origins of Social Policy in the United States.* Cambridge, Mass.: Harvard University Press, 1992.

Skocpol, Theda, Margaret Weir, and Ann Shola Orloff. *The Politics of Social Policy in the United States.* Princeton, N.J.: Princeton University Press, 1988.

Silverman, Bertram. "The Rise and Fall of the Swedish Model: Interview with Rudolf Meidner." *Challenge* 41 (January–February 1998): 69–90.

Soss, Joe, Richard C. Fording, and Sanford F. Schram. *Disciplining the Poor: Neoliberal Paternalism and the Persistent Power of Race.* Chicago: University of Chicago Press, 2011.

Thane, Pat. *The Foundations of the Welfare State: Social Policy in Modern Britain.* London: Longmans, 1982.

——, ed. *The Origins of British Social Policy.* London: Croom Helm, 1978.

Titmuss, Richard M. *Problems of Social Policy,* in *History of the Second World War, United Kingdom Civil Series,* ed. W. K. Hancock. London: His Majesty's Stationary Office, 1950.

Vaudagna, Maurizio. *The New Deal and the American Welfare State: Essays from a Transatlantic Perspective (1933–1945).* Turin: Otto, 2014.

Weaver, Kent. *Ending Welfare As We Know It.* Washington D.C.: Brookings Institution, 2000.

Williams, Rhonda Y. *The Politics of Public Housing: Black Women's Struggles Against Urban Inequality.* New York: Oxford University Press, 2004.

Wilson, William J. *When Work Disappears: The World of the New Urban Poor.* New York: Knopf, 1996.
Zeitlin, Jonathan, and Martin Heidenreich, eds. *Changing European Employment and Welfare Regimes: The Influence of the Open Method of Coordination on National Reforms.* London: Routledge, 2009.

Race, Gender, and the Family

Abramovitz, Mimi. *The Lives of Women: Social Welfare Policy from Colonial Times to the Present.* Boston: South End, 1996.
Bock, Gisela. *Zwangsterilization im Nationalsozialismus: Studien zur Rassenpolitik und Frauenpolitik.* Opladen: Westdeutscher Verlag, 1986.
Brown, Michael K. *Race, Money, and the American Welfare State.* Ithaca, N.Y.: Cornell University Press, 1999.
Canaday, Margot. *The Straight State: Sexuality and Citizenship in Twentieth-Century America.* Princeton, N.J.: Princeton University Press, 2009.
Chappell, Marisa. *The War on Welfare: Family, Poverty, and Politics in Modern America.* Philadelphia: University of Pennsylvania Press, 2009.
Chunn, Dorothy E., and Shelley A. M. Gavigan, eds. *The Legal Tender of Gender: Law, Welfare, and the Regulation of Women's Poverty.* Oxford: Hart, 2010.
Cobble, Sue. *The Other Women's Movement: Workplace, Justice, and Social Rights in Modern America.* Princeton, N.J.: Princeton University Press, 2005.
Crompton, Rosemary. *Employment and the Family: The Reconfiguration of Work and Family Life in Contemporary Societies.* Cambridge: Cambridge University Press 2006.
Dinner, Deborah. "The Universal Childcare Debate: Rights Mobilization, Social Policy, and the Dynamics of Feminist Activism." *Law and History Review* 28, no. 3 (August 2010): 577–628.
Ellingsaeter, Anne Lise, and Arnlaug Leira, eds. *Politicizing Parenthood in Scandinavia: Gender Relations in Welfare States.* Chicago: University of Chicago Press, 2011.
Ellwood, David T. *Poor Support: Poverty in the American Family.* New York: Basic Books, 1988.
Fraser, Nancy. *Fortunes of Feminism: From State-Managed Capitalism to Neoliberal Crisis.* London: Verso, 2011.
Gordon, Linda. *Heroes of Their Own Lives: The History and Politics of Family Violence.* New York: Viking Penguin, 1988.
———. "The New Feminist Scholarship of the Welfare State." In *Women, the State, and Welfare,* ed. Linda Gordon. Madison: University of Wisconsin Press, 1990.

———. *Pitied but Not Entitled: Single Mothers and the History of Welfare.* Cambridge, Mass.: Harvard University Press, 1994.

Halsaa, Beatrice, Sasha Roseneil, Sevil Sümer, eds. *Remaking Citizenship in Multicultural Europe: Women's Movements, Gender, and Diversity.* London: Palgrave/Macmillan, 2012.

Hirschmann, Nancy J., and Ulrieke Liebert, eds. *Women and Welfare: Theory and Practice in the United States and Europe.* New Brunswick, N.J.: Rutgers University Press, 2001.

Hobson, Barbara, ed. *Making Men Into Fathers: Men, Masculinities, and the Social Politics of Fatherhood.* Cambridge: Cambridge University Press, 2002.

Hobson, Barbara, Jane Lewis, and Birte Siim, eds. *Contested Concepts in Gender and Social Politics.* Cheltenham: Edward Elgar, 2002.

Jones, Jacqueline. *Labor of Love, Labor of Sorrow: Black Women, Work, and the Family from Slavery to the Present.* New York: Basic Books, 1985.

Kessler-Harris, Alice. *Out to Work: A History of Wage-Earning Women in the United States.* New York: Oxford University Press, 1982.

Leira, Arnlaugh. *Welfare States and Working Mothers: The Scandinavian Experience.* Oslo: Cambridge University Press, 1992.

Lewis, Jane. *The Politics of Motherhood: Child and Maternal Welfare in England, 1900–1939.* London: Croom Helm, 1980.

———. *Women in England: Sexual Divisions and Social Change.* London: Prentice Hall, 1984.

Levenstein, Lisa. *A Movement Without Marches: African American Women and the Politics of Poverty in Postwar Philadelphia.* Chapel Hill: University of North Carolina Press, 2009.

Lieberman, Robert C. *Shifting the Color Line: Race and the American Welfare State.* Cambridge, Mass.: Harvard University Press, 1998.

Lister, Ruth. *Citizenship: Feminist Perspectives* [1997]. Basingstoke: Palgrave-Macmillan, 2003.

Lundqvist, Åsa. *Family Policy Paradoxes: Gender Equality and Labour Market Regulation in Sweden, 1930–2010.* Bristol: Policy, 2011.

Marchevsky, Alejandra, and Jeanne Theoharis. *Not Working: Latina Immigrants, Low-Wage Jobs, and the Failure of Welfare Reform.* New York: New York University Press, 2006.

Michel, Sonya. *Children's Interests/Mothers' Rights: The Shaping of America's Child-Care Policy.* New Haven, Conn.: Yale University Press, 2000.

Michel, Sonya, and Seth Koven. *Mothers of a New World: Maternalist Politics and the Origins of Welfare States.* New York: Routledge, 1993.

Millar, Jane, and Andrea Warman. *Family Obligations in Europe.* London: Family Policies Study Centre, 1996.

Mink, Gwendolyn. *The Wages of Motherhood: Inequality in the Welfare State, 1917–1942*. Ithaca, N.Y.: Cornell University Press, 1995.

Morgan, Kimberly J. *Working Mothers and the Welfare State: Religion and Politics of Work-Family Policies in Western Europe and the United States*. Stanford, Calif.: Stanford University Press, 2006.

Morgen, Sandra, Joan Acker, and Jill Weigt. *Stretched Thin: Poor Families, Welfare Work, and Welfare Reform*. Ithaca, N.Y.: Cornell University Press, 2010.

O'Connor, Julia, Ann Shola Orloff, and Sheila Shaver, eds. *States, Markets, Families: Gender, Liberalism, and Social Policy in Australia, Canada, Great Britain, and the United States*. New York: Cambridge University Press, 1999.

Neubeck, Kenneth J., and Noel A. Cazenave. *Welfare Racism: Playing the Race Card Against America's Poor*. New York: Routledge, 2001.

Pedersen, Susan G. *Family, Dependence, and the Origins of the Welfare State: Britain and France, 1914–1945*. New York: Cambridge University Press, 1993.

Rolandsen Agustin, Lise. *Gender Equality, Intersectionality, and Diversity in Europe*. New York: Palgrave Macmillan, 2013.

Saraceno, Chiara. *Families, Ageing, and Social Policy: Intergenerational Solidarity in European Welfare States*. Cheltenham: Edward Elgar, 2008.

———. "Family Change, Family Policies, and the Restructuring of Welfare." In *Family, Market, and Community: Equity and Efficiency in Social Policy*, ed. OECD, Social Policy Studies 21, 81–100. Paris: OECD, 1997.

———. "Gendered Policies: Family Obligations and Social Policies in Europe." In *Gender, Welfare State, and the Market*, ed. T. P. Boje and A. Leira, 135–156. London: Routledge, 2000.

Saraceno, Chiara, Jane Lewis, and Arnlaug Leira, eds. *Families and Family Policies*. Vol. 1. Cheltenham: Edward Elgar, 2012.

Siim, Birte, and Monika Mokre, eds. *Negotiating Gender and Diversity in the Emergent European Public Sphere*. Basingstoke: Palgrave/Macmillan, 2013.

Thane, Pat, and Gisela Bock, eds. *Maternity and Gender Policies: Women and the Rise of the European Welfare States, 1880s–1950s*. London: Routledge, 1991.

Therborn, Göran. *Between Sex and Power: Family in the World, 1900–2000*. New York: Routledge, 2004.

Wikander, Ulla, Alice Kessler-Harris, and Jane E. Lewis. *Protecting Women: Labor Legislation in Europe, the United States, and Australia, 1880–1920*. Champaign: University of Illinois Press, 1995.

Winkler, Celia. *Single Mothers and the State: The Politics of Care in Sweden and the United States*. Lanham, Md.: Rowman & Littlefield, 2002.

Social Movements and Social Policy

Alexander, Michelle, *The New Jim Crow: Mass Incarceration in the Age of Colorblindness*. New York: New Press, 2012.

André, Christine, and Christoph Hermann. *Privatisation of Health Care in Europe*. Paris: CNRS, 2008.

Atlas, John. *Seeds of Change: The Story of ACORN, America's Most Controversial Antipoverty Community Organizing Group*. Nashville, Tenn.: Vanderbilt University Press, 2010.

Beveridge, William H. *Full Employment in a Free Society* [1944]. New York: Norton, 1945.

Brodkin, Evelyn Z., and Gregory Marston. *Work and the Welfare State: Street-Level Organizations and Workfare Politics*. Washington D.C.: Georgetown University Press, 2013.

Carré, Francoise, Marianne Ferber, Lonnie Golden, and Stephen Herzenberg. *Nonstandard Work: The Nature and Challenges of Changing Employment Arrangements*. Madison, Wis.: Industrial Relationships Research Association, 2000.

Castles, Stephen, and Mark J. Miller. *The Age of Migration*. Houndsmills: Palgrave Macmillan, 2003.

Chauvin, Sébastien. *Les agences de la précarité. Journaliers à Chicago*. Paris: Seuil, 2010.

Clear, Todd, and Natasha Frost. *The Punishment Imperative: The Rise and Failure of Mass Incarceration in America*. New York: New York University Press, 2013.

Gilens, Martin. *Why Americans Hate Welfare: Race, Media, and the Politics of Antipoverty Policy*. Chicago: University of Chicago Press, 1999.

Gleeson, Shannon. *Precarious Claims: The Promise and Failure of Workplace Protection in the United States*. Berkeley: University of California Press, 2016.

Gordon, David M., Richard Edwards, and Michael Reich. *Segmented Work, Divided Workers: The Historical Transformation of Labor in the United States*. Cambridge: Cambridge University Press, 1982.

Katznelson, Ira. *City Trenches: Urban Politics and the Patterning of Class in the United States*. Chicago: University of Chicago Press, 1981.

——. *When Affirmative Action Was White: An Untold Story of Racial Inequality in Twentieth-Century America*. New York: Norton, 2005.

Krinsky, John. *Free Labor: Workfare and the Contested Language of Neoliberalism*. Chicago: University of Chicago Press, 2007.

Ireland, Patrick. *Becoming Europe: Immigration, Integration, and the Welfare State*. Pittsburgh, Penn.: University of Pittsburgh Press, 2004.

Ness, Immanuel. *Guest Workers and Resistance to U.S. Corporate Despotism.* Urbana: University of Illinois Press, 2011.

Nicolau-Smokoviti, Nitra, et al., eds. *Citizenship and Social Development: Citizen Participation and Community Involvement in Social Welfare and Social Policy.* Frankfurt: PL Academic Research, 2013.

Osterman, Paul. *Securing Prosperity: The American Labor Market: How It Has Changed and What to Do About It.* Princeton, N.J.: Princeton University Press, 1999.

Piven, Frances Fox. *Authority: How Ordinary People Change America.* New York: Rowman and Littlefield, 2006.

Piven, Frances Fox, and Richard Cloward. *Poor People's Movements: Why They Succeed, How They Fail.* New York: Viking, 1979.

Self, Robert O. *American Babylon: Race and the Struggle for Postwar Oakland.* Princeton, N.J.: Princeton University Press, 2003.

Schönwälder, Karen, Rainer Ohliger, and Triadofilos Triadofilopoulos, eds. *European Encounters: Migrants, Migration, and European Societies Since 1945.* London: Routledge/Ashgate, 2003.

Skocpol, Theda. *Boomerang: Health-Care Reform and the Turn Against Government.* New York: Norton, 1997.

Simon, Jonathan. *Governing Through Crime: How the War on Crime Transformed American Democracy and Created a Culture of Fear.* New York: Oxford University Press, 2006.

Smith, David Barton. *Health Care Divided: Race and Healing a Nation.* Ann Arbor: University of Michigan Press, 1999.

Smith, Vicki, and Esther B. Neuwirth. *The Good Temp.* Ithaca, N.Y.: Cornell University Press, 2008.

Soysal, Yasemin N. *Limits of Citizenship: Migrants and Postnational Membership in Europe.* Chicago: University of Chicago Press, 1994.

Tarrow, Sidney G., and Charles Tilly. *Contentious Politics.* Oxford: Oxford University Press, 2009.

Turk, Katherine. *Equality on Trial: Gender and Rights in the Modern American Workplace.* Philadelphia: University of Pennsylvania Press, 2016.

Vosko, Leah F. *Temporary Work: The Gendered Rise of a Precarious Employment Relationship.* Toronto: University of Toronto Press, 2000.

Wacquant, Loïc. *Punishing the Poor: The Neoliberal Government of Social Insecurity.* Durham, N.C.: Duke University Press, 2009.

Waldinger, Roger, and Michael I. Lichter. *How the Other Half Works: Immigration and the Social Organization of Labor.* Berkeley: University of California Press, 2003.

Weir, Margaret. *Politics and Jobs: The Boundaries of Employment Policy in the United States.* Princeton, N.J.: Princeton University Press, 1992.

Contributors

MIMI ABRAMOVITZ is the Bertha Capen Reynolds Professor of Social Work at the Silberman School of Social Work, Hunter College, City University of New York. She specializes in the history of the U.S. welfare state; the impact of public policy on women through the lens of race, gender, and class; the history of low-income women's activism; and the impact of neoliberalism on the U.S. welfare state, social reproduction, social services, and the human-service workforce. Her publications include *Regulating the Lives of Women: Social Welfare Policy from Colonial Times to the Present* (2nd ed., 1996), *Under Attack, Fighting Back: Women and Welfare in the U.S.* (2000), *Taxes Are a Woman's Issue: Reframing the Debate* (2006), and *The Dynamics of Social Policy* (4th ed., 2014). She is currently writing *Gendered Obligations: The History of Activism Among Poor and Working-Class Women Since 1900*.

MARISA CHAPPELL is associate professor of history at Oregon State University. She specializes in twentieth-century U.S. history, with a particular focus on politics, social policy, and the political economy of race and gender. Her publications include *The War on Welfare: Family, Poverty, and Politics in Modern America* (2009) and *Welfare in the United States: A History with Documents* (2009), coauthored with Premilla Nadasen and Jennifer Mittelstadt. Chappell's current research interest is progressive community organizing and grassroots campaigns for economic justice after the 1960s.

SÉBASTIEN CHAUVIN is a sociologist and associate professor at the Centre en Etudes Genre of the University of Lausanne, Switzerland. His research has dealt with citizenship, migration, employment, labor, gender, sexuality, and inequality, mainly in France and the United States. Following an ethnography of temporary-agency work and labor organizing in the Chicago region, he completed a collective study exploring the labor-market experience and following the union-supported mobilization of undocumented immigrant workers in France. His publications include *Les agences de la précarité* (2010) and *On bosse ici, on reste ici! La grève des sans-papiers: une aventure inédite* (2011), coauthored with Pierre Barron, Anne Bory, Nicolas Jouning, and Lucie Tourette.

LINDSEY DAYTON is a doctoral student at Columbia University and an organizer with the United Auto Workers. Her research interests include the intersection of civil rights and labor organizing, the history of racism and gender in the United States, and the role of labor and welfare policy in shaping the strategies of labor and civil-rights activists. Her dissertation, "Union House: Service-Worker Organizing in the Twentieth-Century United States," explores the ways shifting domestic ideologies, capital formations, labor and civil-rights legislation, and social-welfare policies shaped the politics of race and gender in service work and service-worker organizing.

MAURIZIO FERRERA is professor of political science at the University of Milan. He has published widely in the fields of comparative welfare states and public-policy analysis, with particular reference to the problems of European integration. His most recent English-language work, *The Boundaries of Welfare: European Integration and the New Spatial Politics of Social Protection* (2005), looks at the impact of integration on the boundaries of European welfare states. Also available in English is his *Welfare-State Reform in Southern Europe: Fighting Poverty and Social Exclusion in Greece, Italy, Spain, and Portugal* (2005). He has served on various advisory commissions at national and EU levels and has recently been awarded an ERC advanced grant for a five-year project on "Reconciling Economic and Social Europe: Ideas, Values and Consensus." He writes a column in the daily *Corriere della Sera*.

GRO HAGEMANN is professor emeritus in history at the University of Oslo. She specializes in modern Scandinavian history, gender history, feminist theory, and the history of work and welfare. Her publications in English include "*The Most Unbreakable Right of Man*": Women and Economic Citizenship (2006), "Maternalism and Gender Equality: Tracing a Norwegian Model of Welfare" (2007), and "Dutiful Wife—Disloyal Worker: Fragments of a Scholarly Ego-Histoire" (2010), all produced within the European CLIOHRES network of excellence, where she also edited the anthology *Reciprocity and Redistribution: Work and Welfare Reconsidered* (2007). She was elected a member of the Norwegian Academy of Sciences and Letters in 2007 and awarded the Gina Krog Prize in 2009.

BEATRIX HOFFMAN is professor of history at Northern Illinois University. She specializes in the history of the U.S. health-care system. Her publications include *Health Care for Some: Rights and Rationing in the United States Since 1930* (2012), *The Wages of Sickness: The Politics of Health Insurance in Progressive America* (2001), the coedited collection *Patients as Policy Actors* (2011), and "Health Care Reform and Social Movements in the United States" (*American Journal of Public Health*, 2003). Her current research focuses on undocumented immigrants and the right to health care.

NICK JURAVICH is a doctoral student in U.S. history at Columbia University, where he studies education, social movements, labor organizing, and metropolitan development in the twentieth century. His dissertation, "A Classroom Revolution: Community Educators and the Transformation of School and Work in American Cities, 1953–1981," analyzes the creation and development of programs that educators shaped and that were shaped by public schools, freedom struggles, and public-sector unions, which brought thousands of working-class women into public schools as community-based paraprofessional educators in the 1960s and 1970s.

IRA KATZNELSON is Ruggles Professor of Political Science and History at Columbia University. An Americanist, his work has straddled comparative politics and political theory as well as political and social history. He is president of the Social Science Research Council and has served as chair of the Russell Sage Foundation's board of trustees. His publications include *Fear Itself: The New Deal and the Origins of Our Time* (2014), *When Affirmative Action Was White: An Untold History of Racial Inequality in Twentieth-Century America* (2005), and *City Trenches: Urban Politics and the Patterning of Class in the United States* (1981). He is currently completing *Liberal Reason*, a collection of his essays on the character of modern social knowledge.

ALICE KESSLER-HARRIS is R. Gordon Hoxie Professor Emerita of American History at Columbia University. She specializes in the history of American labor and the comparative and interdisciplinary exploration of women and gender. Her published works include *In Pursuit of Equity: Women, Men, and the Quest for Economic Citizenship in Twentieth-Century America* (2001), *Out to Work: A History of Wage-Earning Women in the United States* (1982), *A Woman's Wage: Historical Meanings and Social Consequences* (1990), *Gendering Labor History* (2007), and *Democracy and Social Rights in the Two Wests* (2009), which she coedited with Maurizio Vaudagna.

CHRISTIAN LAMMERT is professor of North American politics and policy in the department of political science at the Free University of Berlin and a professor of North American politics at the John F. Kennedy Institute for North American Studies. His areas of interest include comparative welfare-state research and the problems of nationalism, multiculturalism, and regional integration. He publishes widely on social policy, health-care reform in the United States, and nationalism and regional integration in a transatlantic perspective. Recent publications include *Handbuch Politik USA* (2016), coedited with Markus B. Siewert and Boris Vormann; *Nationale Bewegungen in Québec and Korsika, 1960–2000* (2004); and *Revisiting the Sixties: Interdisciplinary Perspectives on America's Longest Decade* (2014), coedited with Laura Bieger.

ANN SHOLA ORLOFF is chair of the Board of Lady Managers of the Columbian Exposition and professor of sociology and political science. Orloff is the coeditor of *Remaking Modernity: Politics, History, and Sociology* (2005), with Julia Adams and Elisabeth Clemens, and the author of *States, Markets, Families: Gender, Liberalism, and Social Policy in Australia, Canada, Great Britain, and the United States* (1999), with Julia O'Connor and Sheila Shaver; *The Politics of Pensions: A Comparative Analysis of Britain, Canada, and the United States, 1880s–1940* (1993); and *The Politics of Social Policy in the United States* (1988), coedited with Margaret Weir and Theda Skocpol. Her most recent book is *Many Hands of the State: Theorizing Political Authority and Social Control* (2016), coedited with Kimberly Morgan. Her current research, *Toward a Gender-Open Future? Transformations in Gender, Global Capitalism, and Systems of Social Provision and Regulation*, explores the increasing support for mothers' paid employment over the last half-century in the United States and Sweden and the implications of those shifts for feminism.

FRANCES FOX PIVEN is an activist and professor of political science at the Graduate Center of the City University of New York. Her groundbreaking work with Richard A. Cloward, on the functions of social welfare and poor relief in *Regulating the Poor* (1971) and on the disruptive actions of the poor in *Poor People's Movements* (1979), reshaped the field of social-welfare policy. She was a cofounder of the National Welfare Rights Organization (NWRO) in the 1960s, which sought to expand and transform welfare entitlements and democratic participation, and she has received many awards for her commitment to scholarly activism. Her more recent work includes *The Breaking of the American Social Compact* (1997) and *Challenging Authority* (2006).

CHIARA SARACENO, former professor of sociology at the University of Turin and research professor at the WZB in Berlin, is presently an honorary fellow at the Collegio Carlo Alberto, Turin. Her recent publications in English include "Trends and Tensions Within the Italian Family," in *The Oxford Handbook of Italian Politics*, ed. Erik Jones and Gianfranco Pasquino (2015); and

"A Critical Look to the Social Investment Approach from a Gender Perspective," in *Social Politics* (2015). She is the editor of *Families, Ageing, and Social Policies* (2008); *Childhood: Changing Contexts*, with Arnlaug Leira, 2008; and *Handbook of Quality of Life in the Enlarged European Union*, with J. Alber and T. Fahey, 2007.

ROBERT O. SELF is Mary Ann Lippitt Professor of American History at Brown University, where he teaches and writes about urban history, the history of American politics and political culture, and American society and culture in the post–World War II era. His first book, *American Babylon: Race and the Struggle for Postwar Oakland* (2003), won four professional prizes, and his second book, *All in the Family: The Realignment of American Democracy Since the 1960s* (2012), explores gender, sexuality, and political culture from 1964 to 2004. His current project, *The Best Years of Our Lives*, is about houses, cars, and children in the twentieth-century American economy.

BIRTE SIIM is professor of gender studies at Aalborg University, Denmark. A researcher of comparative European welfare and citizenship policies, she analyzes intersections of gender, class, ethnicity, and nationality. She has led various EU research programs and presently participates in the European research project bEUcitizen: Barriers to European Citizenship, as the Danish coordinator of WP 9: Gender and Generational Citizenship (2013–2017). Her publications include *Gender and Citizenship: Politics and Agency in France, Britain, and Denmark* (2000); "Political Intersectionality and Democratic Politics in the European Public Sphere," in *Politics & Gender* (2014); and "Citizenship," in *Handbook on Gender and Politics*, ed. Karen Celis and Georgina Waylen (2013); and she has coedited *Negotiating Gender and Diversity in an Emergent European Public Sphere*, with Monika Mokre, 2013.

MAURIZIO VAUDAGNA is emeritus professor of contemporary history at the University of Eastern Piedmont, Italy, and former director of CISPEA, the Americanists' consortium of the universities of Bologna, Florence, Trieste, and Eastern Piedmont. He has given summer courses at Cornell University and at Columbia University. He is a specialist in twentieth-century American political and social history. His most recent book is *The New Deal and the American Welfare State: Essays from a Transatlantic Perspective, 1933–1945* (2014). His edited book, *Modern European-American Relations in the Transatlantic Space: Recent Trends in History Writing* (2015), won the Transatlantic Studies Association Book Prize. He is completing a history of the modern American family.

Index

AARP. *See* American Association for Retired Persons
Abernathy, Ralph, 319
abortion, 159–60, 171n32, 258, 289
Abramovitz, Mimi, 39, 43, 45
ACA. *See* Affordable Care Act
accountability: insurance-company, 158–59, 171nn26–28; in public spheres, 309, 312
ACLU. *See* American Civil Liberties Union
ACORN. *See* Association of Community Organizations for Reform Now
ACT UP, 153, 169n7
ADC. *See* Aid to Dependent Children
ADC-UP. *See* Aid to Dependent Children-Unemployed Parent
adoption, by homosexuals, 230
Adoption and Safe Families Act of 1997, 206
AFDC. *See* Aid to Families with Dependent Children
affirmative action, with maternal employment, in gendered labor policies, 258–61
Affordable Care Act (ACA), 22, 106, 148; as betrayal, 164–65; citizen action after, 156–65; citizen challenges, to insurance industry, 152–55; civil-rights provision of, 160; hybrid public-private health system, 149, 151; insurance company positions in, 151–52; lessons with, 165–67; marketplace for, 151, 155, 157–59, 162, 163, 165, 167–68; as Obamacare, 147, 151; private power of, 155–56; public option relating to, 155, 169n12; social rights, in U.S. health system, 149–52, 169n2; system of, 150–51; 2016 elections relating to, 167–68
AFL-CIO, 352
African Americans, 15, 42, 100, 282, 351; breadwinner-housewife logic with, 254, 256, 269n16; discrimination against, 7, 8, 32; employment precarity with, 178–79, 184, 189, 194n26; in prison, 288; punishment and, 203–4; rebelliousness of, 355; in school, 208–9; unemployment of, 280, 285–86; welfare dependency of, 288. *See also* Black Lives Matter

African American women, 42, 276–77, 282, 285, 286, 320; anger of, 325–26; social provision and politicization of poor of, 322–25
"Age of Roosevelt," 38
aging population, social policy for, 230
AHIP. *See* America's Health Insurance Plans
AIDS crisis, 153
Aid to Dependent Children (ADC), 41, 46, 88
Aid to Dependent Children– Unemployed Parent (ADC-UP) program, 254
Aid to Families with Dependent Children (AFDC), 88, 116, 119, 254–59, 286, 334; welfare state and, 343, 345, 349, 353
AMA. *See* American Medical Association
American Association for Retired Persons (AARP), 168
American Civil Liberties Union (ACLU), 214, 280
American Enterprise Institute, 354
American hegemony, 87
American Hospital Association, 162
American Medical Association (AMA), 149, 155
American Recovery and Reinvestment Act (ARRA), 113
America's Health Insurance Plans (AHIP), 155–56
Amsterdam Treaty, 307, 310
antifeminist policies, 263
Arkansan Community Organization for Reform Now, 328, 339n30
ARRA. *See* American Recovery and Reinvestment Act

Association of Community Organizations for Reform Now (ACORN), 335; history of, 320–21; homesteading campaign of, 333–34; investigations of, 319–20; low- and moderate- income Americans in, 319–20, 332–33; with marginalization, of poor women, 322; new majority strategies of, 332, 334; on poor-people power, 332; segmented citizenship relating to, 328, 329, 330; ULU of, 333
Atlantic Charter, 6
Atlantic Crossings (Rodgers), 87
"at will" contracts, 180
authoritarian statism, 2, 348

Baldwin, Peter, 28, 32, 274
Bartley, Tim, 181, 183
Baucus, Max, 156
Berkowitz, Edward, 38
Berufpolitiker, 74, 77
Besitzklassen, 71
Beveridge, William, 5, 33, 129, 150, 167
Beveridge Report, 34, 148
Beyond Adversary Democracy (Mansbridge), 98
big government, 199, 347–48, 354
Black Child Development Institute, 283
Black Lives Matter, 18, 219, 358
Black Men, White Cities, 96
black migration, 286
black movement, 353
Blom, Ida, 46
Boris, Eileen, 38, 45
Boston Riot, 349
breadwinner: gendered labor policies, in Sweden and U.S.

with, 249, 251–57. *See also* male breadwinner
breadwinner-housewife logic, 249, 251; discrimination relating to, 252, 253, 256; gender equality relating to, 252–53; health insurance relating to, 150, 254, 255, 268n15; joint taxation and, 253–54; legal action relating to, 252–53; maternalism with, 254–57, 270n27; with parental leave, 255; with poor African Americans, 254, 256, 269n16; sexual harassment relating to, 253, 280, 281; solidarity-wage policies and, 253
breadwinner liberalism, 227; congressional action relating to, 273; decline of, 200–201; decommodification with, 274; deindustrialization with, 278; dual markets with, 277; economic crisis of, 273–74, 278; institutional-political process and, 274; male breadwinner model, 273–75, 288–89; male sexual privilege with, 281; political challenge to, 273–74; political coalitions relating to, 274; racial discrimination with, 279, 282; racial politics with, 274; rising inflation with, 278; social wage expansion relating to, 274–75; stagnating wages, 278; unemployment with, 277–78; unionization decline with, 278; unraveling of, 279; welfare-state scholarship with, 274
breadwinner liberalism, women and: black and Latina, 276–77, 282; with children, 277; domestic work of, 276–77; double day of, 276–77, 282, 288; feminisms with, 289; increased employment of, 277–78; inequalities with, 279; reproduction with, 274; sex discrimination with, 279, 281; with two-income families, 278–79
Britain: EU exit of, 60; gender-neutral protective legislation in, 40; Labour Party in, 44; National Health Service in, 21, 166–67; public education costs in, 2; welfare state in, 356
Brown, Michael, 274

capital: democracy and, 4, 5–6; government demands and, 7; labor and, 3, 5
capitalism, 82, 96; benefits of, 10, 349; collapse of, 93; global, 3; during golden age, 86; grassroots challenges to, 342–59; ideological battle of, 14; laissez-faire, 196; modern liberal, 28; in Norway and Sweden, 131–34; ravages of, 5; success of, 59; welfare, 4, 6, 9, 31. *See also* transatlantic welfare capitalism
capitalists insurance, 35
carceral debt, 210–12, 214–15, 217
carceral state: double regulation of poor with, 205–6; extended reach of, 203, 205; neoliberalism relating to, 195–96, 199–200, 203, 205, 211, 213, 217; poverty relating to, 204, 216; punishment and crime relating to, 203, 205; rise of, 217–18; social reproduction crisis with, 217. *See also* shadow carceral state; welfare state, to carceral state

care-giving labor, of poor, 334, 341n59
cash-for-care, 261
CCA. *See* Corrections Corporation of America
CCDA. *See* Comprehensive Child Development Act
CCSD. *See* Center for the Study of Social Difference
CCT. *See* conditional cash transfers
Center for the Study of Social Difference (CSSD), 19
Central Harlem Welfare Rights Group, 351
certainty bonuses, 180–81
Charter of Fundamental Rights, 64, 307
childcare, 282; coverage for, 236, 239, 240–41, 243; decommodified defamilialism for, 236, *237–38*, 239–40; government-supported, 283; parental leave and, 251; racially integrated, 284; tax credit for, 284–85
children: breadwinner liberalism, women, and, 277; social policy for, 234–35, 236–39, *237–38*, 277
child-welfare system, 207
Christian Democratic Party, 134
citizen action, after ACA, 156; on consumer power, 157–58, 170n21, 171n23; on gender equity, 159–61; on immigrants, 163–64, 173n48; on insurance-company accountability, 158–59, 171nn26–28; on minorities and poor, 161–63; on single-payer movement, 164–65, 174nn52–53; universalism of, 166
citizens: challenges of, to insurance industry, 152–55; liberal, 104; mother-citizens, 44; participation of, 306; of Soviet Union, 8
citizenship: economic, 45; equality, social justice and, transnational challenges to, 298; Marshall on, 108, 130; rights of, 30, 71, 101; social-democratic, 101; of women, 37, 39, 54n53. *See also* social citizenship, in Norway and Sweden
Citizens United v. FEC, 15
citizen worker, 276, 282
City Trenches (Katznelson), 96
civil disobedience, punishment and, 206
civil rights, 160, 205–6; social and, 289–90; of women, 282
Civil Rights Act of 1964, 253; Title VII of, 279–80, 281
civil-rights provision, of ACA, 160
civil society, transnational, 298, 304–6, 313n5
Class War: What Americans Really Think About Economic Inequality (Page and Jacobs), 123
climate change, 354, 355
Clinton, Bill: criminal-justice bill of, 206; health reform of, 150, 153, 164; welfare reform of, 88, 119, 120, 206, 258, 259, 262
Cloward, Richard A., 35, 324, 343, 344
Coalition of Labor Union Women, 152
Cold War, 22
collective agreements, in Nordic countries, 139–40
collective bargaining, of trade unions, 6
collective good, 21, 25n19
colonial territories, 7
color, people of, 7, 320–21

commodification, 231, 236
commodification/
  decommodification, 237–38
commodified defamilialization, 242
commonality, 68
communism, 87, 347
community action, 323, 327
Comprehensive Child Development Act (CCDA), 257, 283, 284
conditional cash transfers (CCT), 345–46
congressional action, with breadwinner liberalism, 273
Congressional Black Caucus, 270n34
conservatism, in Europe, 2
consumer power, 157–58, 170n21, 171n23
contraception, 160
corporatism, 33, 130, 134
correctional-fee law, 213
Corrections Corporation of America (CCA), 213
cosmopolitanism, 299–300
cost containment, 109
costs: of marketplace, 159, 162, 167–68; of public education, 2
Council of the European Union, 304
Craig v. Boren, 279, 281
crèche system, in France, 4
credit: shadow carceral state with debt and, 214; tax, for childcare, 284–85
credit market, deregulation of, 138
crime: drug felons, 208; governing through, 207–15; penal policies relating to, 207; tough on, 203–4. *See also* carceral state; punishment; War on Crime
criminalization: of minor misdemeanors, 210, 212; of poor, 216–17

criminal justice, cost increase of, 211
criminal-justice bill, of Clinton, 206
CSSD. *See* Center for the Study of Social Difference
culture wars, 258

DACA program, 163–64
daddy politics, 258, 260–61
day-labor agencies, 178
debt: with postindustrialism, 136. *See also* carceral debt
decommodification, 231; with breadwinner liberalism, 274; commodification and, 237–38; with social citizenship, in Norway and Sweden, 130, 132
decommodified defamilialism: for childcare, 236, 237–38, 239–40; for elderly, 236, 237–38, 239–41
decommodified defamilialization, 240–42
decommodified supported familialism, 242
deconciliation, 62–65
defamilialization, 231, 232, 234, 236, 239–42, 243
deindustrialization, 278
deliberative democracy, 300
democracy: adversary model of, 98–99; capital and, 4, 5–6; crisis for, 3; deliberative, 300; free-market policies and liberal, 14; friendship model of, 98, 101; Harpsund, 134; modern, 32; participation, 3, 11; retreat from, 59; transnational challenges to, 298; welfare state and, 3, 4. *See also* European citizenship, democracy, and equality; liberal democracy

democracy, after welfare state: capitalism relating to, 82; health system relating to, 88, 91; liberalism relating to, 82; localism with, 97; mobilization relating to, 95–96; participation with, 86–87, 89–90, 94–99; representation with, 94, 97; responsibility relating to, 86–87, 96; socialism relating to, 82; social programs in, 95–97; solidarity relating to, 82, 91–93, 95, 97, 101, 102–3. *See also* golden age

Democracy and Social Rights in the "Two Wests" (Kessler-Harris and Vaudagna), 19

democratic deficit and legitimacy gap, in EU, 304

democratic institutions: of Sweden, 35, 36; weakening of, 215–16

Democratic Leadership Council, 259

democratic welfare, 28, 34

Denmark, 236, *237–38*, 239

dependent family member care, 233–35

Depression, 5, 94, 354

deregulation, of credit market, 138

desegregation, 330

devolution, 200

discrimination, 41, 302; of African Americans, 7, 8, 32; with breadwinner-housewife logic, 252, 253, 256; gender, 251; individual, 289; pregnancy, 280; racial, 279, 282; sex, 279, 281; in U.S. private health-insurance system, 152–53. *See also* multiple-discrimination approach, of EU

dispatching tickets, loyalizing uncertainty, 179; "at will" contracts, 180; certainty bonuses, 180–81; laborer wages, 180; official doctrine of, 181; regular guys, 181

domestic work, 276–77

double day, of women, 276–77, 282, 288

double regulation, of poor. *See* poor

DREAMers, 163–64

drug felons, 208

drug use, social reproduction crisis with, 218

dual-earner/dual-caregiver, 265

dual-earner household, 277–78; social policy for, 230–31

dual markets, with breadwinner liberalism, 277

Dworkin, Ronald, 91

Earned Income Tax Credit (EITC), 109, 113, 115, 116, 260, 331

Economic and Monetary Union (EMU), 63, 70, 74

economic citizenship, 45

economic collapse, in 1930s, 197

economic crisis, of breadwinner liberalism, 273–74, 278

economic environment, 13

economic integration, 69–70

economic-justice campaigns, 334–35

Economic Opportunity Act of 1964, 323

economics: barrier to, 44; growth of, 28; Keynesian, social security and, 27, 29, 30, 196, 276; postindustrialism crisis with, 138; of Sweden, 117, *118*

EEOC. *See* Equal Employment Opportunity Commission

EES. *See* European Union's Employment Strategy

egalitarianism, 123

egalitarian wartime social services, 28

EITC. *See* Earned Income Tax Credit

elderly, 236, *237–38*, 239–41, 243
electoral politics, 15
emancipation, of women, 46
employment: full program of, 347; increase, of women, 277–78. *See also* maternal employment, in gendered labor policies
Employment Act of 1946, 276
employment precarity: with African Americans, 178–79, 184, 189, 194n26; day-labor agencies relating to, 178; dispatching tickets, loyalizing uncertainty, 179–81; labor market uncertainty, 177; with Latino immigrants, 178–79; long-term relationships relating to, 177–78; loyalty relating to, 178, 182–85; permatemps, imbricated segmentation, rise of informal careers, 179, 182, 184–91; precariat, 176, 177; spatial and ethno-racial dynamics with, 178–79; study of, 177; trends of, 176–77; welfare-state and labor-law protections, 177
Encyclopedia of Social Welfare History in North America (Herrick and Stuart), 46
entitlements, 330; mentality of, 323; redistribution, privatization and, 113; for women, 258, 259, 270n35
environmental movement, 359
Equal Employment Opportunity Commission (EEOC), 253, 279–81
equality: with gender, 252–53, 301–2, 307–8, 309, 311; meanings of, 305; political, 121–25; social justice, citizenship and, 298. *See also* European citizenship, democracy, and equality;
theoretical debates, about citizenship, democracy, equality
Equal Pay Act of 1963, 253
equal rights, for women, 230
Equal Rights Amendment, 258
Erwerbungsklassen, 71
Esping-Anderson, Gøsta, 84, 85, 111, 274; on paths, of modern welfare state, 35; on social citizenship, 129–30, 132
EU. *See* European Union
EUräson, 77–78
Europe: conservatism in, 2; mobilization of, 304, 315n40; politics in, 77; populist party in, 303, 315n37; postwar welfare state throughout, 87–88; redistributional government spending in, 2; redistribution and privatization in, 109–15, 117–19; refugee crisis in, 310; socialism in, 5; unions in, 345; women social reformers in, 41. *See also* social policy, in Europe
European Bundesrepublik, 77
European "century of the state," 29
European citizenship: integration model and, 301–4; intersectional approach to, 297, 298, 306, 310, 311
European citizenship, democracy, and equality: conclusion to, 310–12; gender and diversity relating to, 305, 306–10, 316n48, 316n58, 317n64; nationalism challenge to, 297; public sphere, transnational civil society, and integration of, 304–6; reframing of, 297, 306, 308, 312n1; theoretical debates about, 298–300; transnational challenge of, 300–301

European Coal and Steel
  Community, 68
European colonial empires, 7
European Commission, 304
European Court for Human
  Rights, 245
European Defence Community,
  68, 74
European Economic Community,
  11–12, 17, 68–69, 136
European integration: dilemma of,
  301–4; gender equality
  strengthened by, 301–2, 307;
  model of, 301–2; public sphere,
  transnational civil society, and,
  304–6; after World War II, 76
European integration, national
  welfare state and: deconciliation
  relating to, 62–65; intellectual
  project of, 65–71; neo-Weberian
  perspective of, 61, 65, 73;
  political constructions of, 71–75;
  reconciliation of, 61, 65, 75–78;
  welfare, integration and, 62–65
Europeanization, 305, 306
European models, of New Deal, 87
European Network Against Racism
  (ENAR), 308, 309, 311
European Parliament (EP), 303,
  304, 308, 310, 311, 317n68
European Political Community, 74
European primacy, 36
European Public Sphere (EPS), 305,
  312; communication, 307; format
  and issues of public discourse,
  307; Greece in, 310, 317n67;
  outcome of process, 307;
  participation of citizens, 306; as
  transnational space, 309
European social-security building, 29
European social-welfare model, 20,
  31, 36

European Union (EU), 2–3, 9, 20,
  46; Britain exit from, 60;
  challenges raised by, 62;
  democratic deficit and legitimacy
  gap in, 304; free-market policy
  of, 11–12; gender equality with,
  307–8, 309, 311; growth of, 12;
  hybridity of, 305; mission and
  practice of, 69; multilevel
  structure of sovereignty of, 302,
  310; multiple-discrimination
  approach of, 307, 309; nation-
  states of, 307; right to bound
  relating to, 62; social rights
  policy of, 12, 21; state-building
  of, 73; welfare state and, 59, 344;
  welfare state national boundaries
  relating to, 62. *See also* European
  integration, national welfare
  state and
European Union's Employment
  Strategy (EES), 230
European Women's Lobby (EWL),
  308, 309, 311
European Year for Combating
  Poverty and Social Exclusion,
  308–9
euroskepticism, 77
Eurosphere project, 306
Evans, Sara, 39

Fair Labor Standards Act, 276
familialism, 231–35, 240; prescribed,
  232, 233, 234. *See also*
  defamilialization; supported
  familialism
familialism by default, 231, 232, 233,
  236; weak decommodification, 239
familialism/defamilialization,
  237–38
families, 217; definition of, 229–30,
  235; interdependencies of,

232–35; nonstandard, 234–35; policies of, 250; social provision and, 227–28; unpaid work of, 230, 241. *See also* social policy, with family obligations
Family and Medical Leave Act, 261, 280, 282
Family Assistance Plan (FAP), 99, 255, 269nn19–20, 287, 346
Family Support Act (FSA), 259
FAP. *See* Family Assistance Plan
fascism, 5, 87, 347
fascist corporatism, 33
federalism, 88–89
federal mortgage insurance, 276
female prisoners, punishment and, 204
feminism, 43, 289, 351, 357
feminist activism, 135, 137
feminist historians: on agency and contestation, 39; citizenship of women relating to, 37, 39, 54n53; on economic barrier, 44; on economic citizenship, 45; essays by, 43; gender, welfare-state history and, 37–48; gender concept of, 38; on gendered imagination, 37, 45; on middle class women, 41–42; on mother-citizens, 44; on patriarchal control, 37–38, 39, 40, 41, 43; on right to work, 45; on social reform, 39–40; on special workers, 43–44; transatlantic, 37; on welfare state, 38–41; on women's emancipation, 46; on women's New Deal, 39; on women's vote, 40
feminist-historicist social scientists, 37
FEMM Committee on Women's Rights and Gender Equality, 311
Ferree, Myra Marx, 305

fertility, decline of, 230
Fight-for-Fifteen Movement, 219, 358
Filiberto, permatemps and, 186–89, 194n30
financial crisis, in mid-1970s, 197
financial hardship, with shadow carceral state, 211–12
Flora, Peter, 20, 30
Folkhemmet, 132
Food Stamps, 330
Fordist-Keynesian social compact, 201
"Fortress Europe," 302
Foundations of the Welfare State, The (Thane), 31
Four Freedoms, 6
Fourteenth Amendment, 279, 281
France: crèche system in, 4; populist Right in, 2; social reform in, 40
Fraser, Nancy, 38, 41, 230, 266, 275, 300–302, 312
free-market policies, 3, 5; of EU, 11–12; liberal democracy relating to, 14; unregulated, 13
Friedan, Betty, 351
Friedman, Milton, 13
FSA. *See* Family Support Act
full employment program, 347

Geduldig v. Aiello, 280
gender, 101; class and, 41; discrimination elimination of, 251; diversity and, in EPS, 305, 306–10, 316n48, 316n58, 317n64; equality with, 252–53, 301–2, 307–8, 309, 311; feminist historians, welfare-state history, and, 37–48; inequality, 289; openness about, 266–67; race, sexuality, and, 100. *See also* intergenerational and gender-specific behaviors, in Europe

gender- and generation-specific family interdependencies, 232–35
gender-based policies, 7–8, 20
gendered imagination, 37, 45
gendered labor policies, in Sweden and U.S.: with breadwinner, 249, 251–57; constructive process of, 251, 267n3; destructive process of, 251, 267n3; family policies and, 250; with feminist movements, 250; gender discrimination elimination, 251; with maternal employment, 249, 250, 257–67; parental leave and childcare, 251; social assistance, 251, 255, 256; taxation, 251; transformation of, 251, 255
gender-egalitarian projects, 251
gender equity: abortion relating to, 159–60, 171n32, 258, 289; citizen action, after ACA, 159–61; contraception relating to, 160; LGBT people, 160, 168; maternity care relating to, 159–60
gender-neutral protective legislation, 40
gender-open approach, to maternal employment, in gendered labor policies, 265–66
gender representation, with EPS, 308
Germany, 34, 52n35, 110, 112, 114, 148
gerrymandering, 15
Gilens, Martin, 123, 124
global capitalism, 3
global competition, 2
global environment, 21
globalization, 10–11, 130, 131, 298–300
global warming, 354

golden age, 82; background of, 85–86; capitalism during, 86; gender, race, sexuality relating to, 100; redistribution during, 83, 91–92; rights and, 83; social base variations during, 84–85; social minimum in, 83, 91; social-policy government role in, 83; stabilization during, 83; state policies during, 85; taxation during, 83; tensions during, 84, 92; after World War II, 83
Goodin, Robert, 120–21
Gordon, Linda, 32, 35, 38, 40, 42, 46, 56n92
government: big, 199, 347–48, 354; capital and demands of, 7; intervention of, 13; postindustrialism, with debt of, 136; responsibility of, 16, 30; social-policy role of, 83. *See also* redistributional government spending
government oil company, in Norway, 139, 140
government-supported childcare, 283
grassroots challenges, to capitalism, 346–48, 358–59; AFDC relating to, 343, 345, 349, 353; welfare state relating to, 342–45, 349–57
grassroots movement, segmented citizenship, 327–28
Great Recession of 2008, 112–13, 335
Great Society, 196, 200, 282, 286
Great Transformation, The (Polanyi), 85
Greece, 310, 317n67, 356
group health insurance, 150

Habermas's model, 301, 312
Hagemann, Gro, 44

Hall, Peter A., 131
Harpsund democracy, 134
Hayek, Frederick, 13, 84, 102
Health Care for All Now (HCAN), 154–55
Health Education and Welfare Department (HEW), 283, 286
Health Insurance Association of America, 153
health reform, of Clinton, 150, 153, 164
health system, 88, 91; hybrid public-private, 149, 151; insurance with, 150, 254, 255, 268n15; social rights in, 149–52, 169n2. *See also* Affordable Care Act; private health-insurance system, in U.S.
Heidenheimer, Arnold J., 28, 30
Heritage Foundation, 354
heterosexual marriage, 200
HEW. *See* Health Education and Welfare Department
Hispanic migrants, 189
historians: new, 29–35; social-science, 31; welfare state history and, 27–29, 47; welfare state methods and interpretations of, 29–36. *See also* feminist historians
HIV/AIDS, 160–61
HMO, 153–54
Hochschild, Jennifer, 122
homosexuals, adoption by, 230
housing, in Nordic countries, 142
humanity, masculinity and, 38–39
human rights, 299–300

I, Daniel Blake (film), 296
identity politics, 12–13
ideological battle, of capitalism, 14
Immervoll, Herwig, 112
immigrants, 163–64, 173n48, 178–79, 347
immigration, 357; with carceral state, 210; increase in, 355; middle-income groups and, 1, 2; in U.S., 12, 93
inclusiveness, in public spheres, 309, 312
incomes: inequality of, 110–16; real, decline in, 1, 92. *See also* middle-income groups
income-support programs, 343
individualism: culture of, 8; of social rights, 232
industrial-era welfare state crisis, 275
industrial prosperity, 7
industrial system, unraveling of: with globalization, 10–11; with migration, 11; with productivity decline, 10; with taxation, 10, 13–14; with technological transformation, 10–11
inequality, 279; of gender, 289; of incomes, 110–16; in public spheres, 310
informal careers. *See* permatemps
information technology, 17
institutional-political process, breadwinner liberalism and, 274
insurance: capitalist, 35; federal mortgage, 276; group health, 150; with health system, 150, 254, 255, 268n15; two-tiered social, 275–76; unemployment, 344. *See also* Affordable Care Act; private health-insurance system, in U.S.
insurance-company accountability, 158–59, 171nn26–28
insurance company positions, ACA and, 151–52
insurgencies, 349–50

integration, 298; economic, 69–70; social, in Nordic countries, 142–43. *See also* European integration; European integration, national welfare state and; welfare, integration and integration model, European citizenship and, 301–4 intellectual project. *See* European integration, national welfare state and
intelligentsia, 66, 69–70
intergenerational and gender-specific behaviors, in Europe: with childcare coverage, 236, 239, 240–41, 243; convergence of, 243, 345; with frail elderly, 236, 237–38, 239–41, 243; gender division of labor, 240; legalities of, 244–45; with maternity and parental leave, 236, 239, 240, 242; with pensions, 236, 239, 240, 241, 242, 243; supported familialism, decommodified defamilialization and, 236, 237–38, 239. *See also* familialism
internal colonialism, in U.S., 8
intersectional approach, to European citizenship, 297, 298, 306, 310, 311
intersectionality, debates about, 305, 306, 309
In the Shadow of the Poorhouse (Katz), 46, 56n91
"Iron Law of Oligarchy" (Michel), 89
Italy, declining real incomes in, 1, 92

Jacobs, Lawrence R., 123
Jämställdhet, 135
Jim Crow, 88, 203
job-market instability, social policy for, 230

jobs, 2, 177
Jones, Ann, 357
Jones, Jacqueline, 42

Katz, Michael B., 31, 36, 46, 56n91
Kessler-Harris, Alice, 19, 39, 43, 45
Keynes, John Maynard, 34, 129
Keynesian economics, social security and, 27, 29, 30, 196, 276
Klaussen, Jytte, 34
Korpi, Walter, 28

labor: capital and, 3, 5; division of, 240; organized, 327
laborer wages, 180
labor force: heterogeneity of, 21; social policy for, 230
labor market: color-blind, 288; in Nordic countries, 143; uncertainty of, 177
labor movement, 350–52
Labor parties, 4
labor unions, government support for, 275
Labour Party, in Britain, 44
laissez-faire capitalism, 196
Latina women, 276–77, 282, 320
Latino immigrants, 178–79
Left, 2, 10, 18, 87, 95, 99, 346
Legal Defense and Education Fund (LDEF), 280
legislation, 40, 42, 206, 261, 263–64
Levenstein, Lisa, 322
Levine, Daniel, 36
Lewis, Jane, 37
LGBT people, 160, 168
liberal citizen, 104
liberal constitutionalism, 33
liberal democracy, 33–34, 71, 99; free-market policies and, 14;

modernization, social provision, and, 28
liberalism, 6, 82, 227
Lieberman, Joe, 155, 156
Lily Ledbetter Act, 263
Lisbon Treaty, 74, 78, 307, 310
low- and moderate-income Americans, in ACORN, 319–20, 332–33
low-income Americans, multiracial movement of, 326–27
loyalization, 184
loyalty, of temps, 178, 182–85. *See also* dispatching tickets, loyalizing uncertainty
Lubove, Roy, 29, 30

Maastricht Treaty, 70, 74
male breadwinner, 230, 241; model of, 273–75, 288–89. *See also* New Deal, male breadwinning during
male sexual privilege, 281
managed-care plans, 153–54
Mansbridge, Jane, 98, 101
marginalization: in Nordic countries, 143, 147n36; of poor women, 322
marital instability, social policy for, 230, 231
market-correcting, 62
market freedom, 347–48
market-making, 62
marketplace, 163; cost of, 159, 162, 167–68; plans on, 157, 158–59, 162, 165; restrictions with, 159; set up of, 151, 155, 158
market-related welfare state, 8, 9
Marktsräson, 74–75
Marshall, T. H., 4, 11, 40, 83; on citizenship, 108, 130; on social rights, 130, 289–90, 348, 349, 355
Marshall Plan, 87

Massachusetts Fair Share, 331
mass incarceration, 212–13, 217–18
maternal employment, in gendered labor policies, 249, 250, 257, 262, 267; affirmative action with, 258–61; cash-for-care, 261; culture wars relating to, 258; daddy politics relating to, 258, 260–61; dual-earner/dual-caregiver, 265; gender-open approach to, 265–66; parental-leave legislation, 261, 263–64; support of, 264; symmetrical parenthood relating to, 265–66
maternalism, 39, 42, 43–44, 45; with breadwinner-housewife logic, 254–57, 270n27
maternity leave, 159–60, 236, 239, 240, 242
McCarran-Ferguson Act of 1945, 152
McConnell, Grant, 97
McGovern, George, 287
Mead, Lawrence, 120
Medicaid, 352; expansion of, 151, 156, 162–63, 167; for immigrants, 164; for poor, 149–50, 151, 165, 330
Medicare, 122, 149–50, 160, 163, 165, 352
MEJ. *See* Movement for Economic Justice
Meritor Savings Bank v. Vinson, 281
methodological nationalism, 299, 313n8
Michel, Robert, 89
Michel, Sonya, 44
middle-income countries, 345–46
middle-income groups: cultural change and, 1; declining real wages for, 1; immigration and, 1, 2; populist rage of, 1

migration, 11, 47; black, 286; citizenship, democracy, equality, and, 298–300, 302; mass, 356
military spending, 355–56
Mill, John Stuart, 45, 46, 104
Mink, Gwendolyn, 41
minorities, 161–63
minor misdemeanors, criminalization of, 210, 212
"Minotaur state," 39
mixed system, 30; confidence in, 9; decline of inequality with, 10; market, private enterprise, public action as, 6, 9; prosperity with, 6–7; of public/private economic cooperation, 27; socioeconomic security with, 27
mobilization: democracy relating to, 95–96; of Europe, 304, 315n40; political, of women, 283
modern democracy, 32
modernization, liberal democracy, and social provision, 28
modern liberal capitalism, 28
modern social protection, 29, 32–33
modern welfare state, 32, 35, 67–68
Mokre, Monika, 305, 306, 312
mother-citizens, 44
Movement for Economic Justice (MEJ), 328, 329, 333
Movement Without Marches, A (Levenstein), 322
Moynihan, Daniel Patrick, 285–86, 287, 324
Moynihan Report, 285
multilevel structure, of sovereignty, 302, 310
multiple-discrimination approach, of EU, 307, 309

multiracial movement, of low-income Americans, 326–27
Murray, Pauli, 281

NAACP, 280
National Committee for Tax Justice, 330
National Council of Churches Conference on Taxes, 330
National Council of Negro Women, 283
National Federation of Independent Business v. Sebelius, 156, 162
National Health Service, in Britain, 21, 166–67
National Hispanic Leadership Agenda, 164
National Housing Act of 1934, 276
National Housing Act of 1949, 273
National Industrial Recovery Act, 87
National Labor Relations Act of 1935, 273
National Organization for Women (NOW), 280, 283, 351
National Preschool Act of 1975, 256–57
National Welfare Rights Organization (NWRO), 162, 256, 283, 286, 287, 328
nation-states, of EU, 307
Negative Income Tax, 255
negative stereotypes, of poor, 325–26, 327
Negro Family, The: The Case for National Action (Moynihan), 285–86
neoliberalism, 82, 257, 262, 271n43; carceral state relating to, 195–96, 199–200, 203, 205, 211, 213, 217; definition of, 102–3; policies of,

2–3, 13–15, 105, 119, 120, 122, 247; restructuring of, 107, 118, 124; with social citizenship, 128–29; social reproduction crisis and, 200, 201, 202
neo-Weberian perspective, of European integration, 61, 65, 73
neowelfarism, 59
Net Replacement Rates (NRR), 115
New Deal, 35, 122, 283, 286, 348; citizen worker of, 276, 282; early days of, 87–88; end of, 100; European models of, 87; fascist corporatism and, 33; patriarchal hierarchy and, 41; radical moment of, 36, 53n43; social legislation of, 42; welfare state and, 38; for white men, 321; women, 39, 198
New Deal, male breadwinning during: with federal mortgage insurance, 276; with government support for labor unions, 275; with two-tiered social insurance, 275–76
New Deal/Cold War state, 321–22, 335
New Deal Order, 6
New Deal welfare state contradictions: accumulation and legitimation, 198–99; altered balance of power, 198; big government relating to, 199; devolution relating to, 200; neoliberalism relating to, 199–200; privatization relating to, 200; social reproduction crisis, 195, 196–97, 200–202, 216–19
New Federalism, 282
new historians, 29–35
new majority campaign, 327, 328–29, 331, 332, 334

New Paternalism, The (Mead), 120
New Public Management, 141
new welfarism, 48
1930s: collapse of capitalism during, 93; depression during, 5, 94; welfare state of, 7, 29, 39
1948 Universal Declaration of Human Rights, 47
Nixon, Richard, 85, 286, 346, 357; FAP and, 99, 255, 269nn19–20, 287; New Federalism of, 282; welfare debate and, 255, 256, 257, 282, 283, 284
noncriminal behavior, punishment of, 209–10
noncriminal pathways, to punishment, 205–7
nonmarried heterosexual couples, social policy for, 229
nonstandard families, social policy for, 234–35
Nordic countries: collective agreements in, 139–40; housing in, 142; labor market in, 143; marginalization in, 143, 147n36; outsourcing in, 140; political situation in, 144; primary school system in, 141–42; privatization in, 141; recession survival of, 139; social-democratic welfare model of, 139–40, 144; social integration in, 142–43; universality of, 144
Nordic model, of social citizenship, 129, 130–31
Nordic universalist welfare state, 296
Norton, Eleanor Holmes, 281
Norway: government oil company in, 139, 140; women in, 44–45, 128, 133–34, 357. *See also* social citizenship, in Norway and Sweden

Norwegian Labor Party, 136
NOW. *See* National Organization for Women
NRR. *See* Net Replacement Rates
NWRO. *See* National Welfare Rights Organization

Obama, Barack, 150, 155, 156, 163–64, 263, 319
Obamacare, 147, 151. *See also* Affordable Care Act
Occupy Wall Street, 18, 125, 219, 358
OECD. *See* Organization for Economic Co-operation and Development
offender funding, with shadow carceral state, 212
Olson, Kevin, 120
On Liberty (Mill), 104
open assisted-reproductive technology, 230
Open Method of Coordination (OMC), 64
Organization for Economic Co-operation and Development (OECD), 110–12, 114–15, 117–18, 231
Orloff, Anna Shola, 274
outsourcing, in Nordic countries, 140

Page, Benjamin I., 123, 124
Palme, Olof, 135, 136
parental leave, 236, 239, 240, 242, 251, 255; legislation for, 261, 263–64
participation, with democracy, after welfare state, 86–87, 89–90, 94–99
Patient Protection and Affordable Act. *See* Affordable Care Act
patriarchal control, 37–38, 39, 40, 41, 43, 101

Patterson, James T., 31
pay-to-stay fees, with shadow carceral state, 213
penal policies, with crime, 207
penal system, with social reproduction crisis, 216–17
pensions, 236, 239, 240, 241, 242, 243
people, of color, 321
People's Platform, 332
permanent contracts, 191
permatemps: Filiberto relating to, 186–89, 194n30; imbricated segmentation, rise of informal careers, and, 179, 182, 184–85, 190–91
personal responsibility, 20
Personal Responsibility and Work Opportunity Reconciliation Act (PRWORA), 119, 206, 258, 259, 345
Physicians for a National Health Program (PNHP), 158, 164–65
Piketty, Thomas, 10
Piven, Frances Fox, 35, 46, 324, 343
Polanyi, Karl, 85, 102
political and social conflict, 2
political coalitions, with breadwinner liberalism, 274
political constructions, 71–75
political decision making, of poor women, 326, 338n24
political dimension, with welfare and integration, 64
political equality, 121–25
political mobilization, of women, 283
political rights, 4
politics: daddy, 258, 260–61; electoral, 15; European, 77; identity, 12–13; in Nordic countries, 144; racial, 289; Weber on, 70, 71, 75; women in, 15,

24n15. *See also* social policy, political participation and
poor: care-giving labor of, 334, 341n59; criminalization of, 216–17; double regulation of, 205–6; living standards of, 16; Medicaid for, 149–50, 151, 165, 330; minorities and, 161–63; participation of, 90; punishment of, 205–7; rich and, 16; shadow carceral state and, 213–14; undeserving, 320, 336n3; victories of, 330
poor-people power, 319; ACORN with, 332; experiments in, 331–34; segmented citizenship and, 326–31; social provision, politicization of poor, and, 322–36; undeserving poor relating to, 320, 336n3; with women of color, 320–21
Poor People's Campaign of 1968, 326–27
poor women: marginalization of, 322; political decision making of, 326, 338n24
populism, 94–95
populist party, in Europe, 303, 315n37
populist rage, of middle-income groups, 1
populist Right: in France, 2; in U.S., 60
Porter, Eduardo, 18
postindustrialism: deregulation, of credit market, 138; economic crisis relating to, 138; feminist activism and, 135, 137; government debt with, 136; radicalization of social democrats with, 136–37; recession relating to, 135

postwar welfare state, 87–88, 198, 217
postwelfare society, 48, 129
poverty, 357; carceral state and, 204, 216; culture of, 323. *See also* War on Poverty
precariat, 176, 177
pregnancy discrimination, 280
Pregnancy Discrimination Act of 1978, 152, 253, 280, 282
prescribed familialism, 232, 233, 234
primary school system, in Nordic countries, 141–42
private commercial actors, in Sweden, 141
private enterprise, 6, 9
private health-insurance system, in U.S.: AIDS crisis relating to, 153; citizen challenges to, 152–55; discrimination in, 152–53; managed-care plans in, 153–54; after World War II, 152
Private Power and American Democracy (McConnell), 97
private social benefits, 117–18, *118*
privatization, 14; New Deal welfare state contradictions and, 200; in Nordic countries, 141; in Sweden, 21. *See also* redistribution, privatization and
privatization, self-responsibility and, 107–8; redistribution and, 109–19; social policy, political participation and, 108, 119–25
productivity, decline of, 10
progressive social provision, critique of, 41
protection: modern social, 29, 32–33; social, 32, 34, 45, 65, 67; by state, 6, 11; welfare, 36; welfare-state and labor-law, 177

protective legislation, gender-neutral, 40
PRWORA. *See* Personal Responsibility and Work Opportunity Reconciliation Act
public assistance, 206
public education costs, in Britain, 2
public-private health system, hybridity of, 149, 151
public spheres, 304–6; accountability in, 309, 312; inclusiveness in, 309, 312; inequality in, 310; transnational, 300–301. *See also* European Public Sphere; value spheres theory
punishment: African Americans and, 203–4; civil disobedience and, 206; crime and, 203, 205; female prisoners and, 204; legislation on, 206; of noncriminal behavior, 209–10; noncriminal pathways to, 205–7; of poor, 205–7; public assistance relating to, 206; of single mothers, 206; traditional paths to, 203–4. *See also* carceral state; crime

race, 100, 284–87
racial and ethnic issues, in U.S., 7, 12, 15, 32
racial discrimination, with breadwinner liberalism, 279, 282
racial dynamics. *See* spatial and ethno-racial dynamics
racially integrated childcare, 284
racial politics, 274, 289
radicalization, of social democrats, 136–37
radical nationalism, 18
Rathke, Wade, 328, 329
Reagan, Ronald, 13, 102, 258, 347
Reagan Revolution, 282
real incomes, decline in, 1, 92
recession, 112–13, 135, 139
Rechtsstaat, 71
reconciliation, 61, 65, 77–78; restrictions relating to, 75, 76; social ossification relating to, 75
redistribution, 331; during golden age, 83, 91–92; with social reproduction crisis, 197
redistribution, privatization and: cost containment with, 109; crisis of 2008 relating to, 109; entitlements with, 113; in Europe, 109–15, 117–19; income inequality relating to, 110–16; OECD relating to, 110–12, 114–15, 117–18, 231; private social benefits with, 117–18, *118*; tax-and-transfer system with, 109–12, *114*, 117–19; unemployment with, 112–16; in U.S., 109–19
redistributional government spending: challenges to, 2; in Europe, 2; in United States, 2
Reed v. Reed, 281
Reflexive Democracy (Olson), 120
reform: of health system, 150, 153, 164; social, 39–40, 41; in Sweden, 139
refugees: money for, 355; population, challenges of, 60, 356; surge of, 2
Regulating the Poor (Piven and Cloward), 343
Rehn-Meidner model, 132–33, 137, 138
renegotiations, of welfare state, 107–8
representation, with democracy, after welfare state, 94, 97
reproduction: with breadwinner liberalism, 274. *See also* social reproduction crisis

resistance, 218–19, 295–96
resources, distribution of, 353
retrenchment, 105–6, 107, 201, 335
Reuther, Walter, 352
Richardson, Linda, 112
Right, 2, 3, 17, 60, 344, 356–57
rights, 62, 160; of citizenship, 30, 71, 101; golden age and, 83; national, 300; political, 4; voting, 14, 15, 16; to work, 45. *See also* civil rights; social rights; welfare rights
riots, 349
rising inflation, with breadwinner liberalism, 278
Roberts, Wade, 181, 183
Rodgers, Daniel, 36, 87
Roosevelt, Franklin D., 6, 33, 36, 47, 87, 352
Rothstein, Bo, 95

SAF. *See* Swedish Employer's Association
same-sex couples, social policy for, 229–30, 241–42
Sanders, Bernie, 15, 18, 125, 165, 348, 358
SAP. *See* Social Democratic Workers' Party of Sweden
Saraceno, Chiara, 30, 48
Schattschneider, Elmer E., 124
schools: African American students in, 208–9; in Nordic countries, 141–42; social reproduction and, 208; zero-tolerance policies in, 208
Scruton, Roger, 102, 103
second-wave feminism, 43
segmented citizenship: ACORN relating to, 328, 329, 330; challenges of, 326–31; grassroots movement with, 327–28; new majority campaign with, 327, 328–29, 331, 332, 334; public-policy designs with, 329; taxes relating to, 330–31
SEIU. *See* Service Employees International Union
Sejersted, Frances, 137
Self-Help Housing Program, 324
Service Employees International Union (SEIU), 333, 358
sex discrimination, 279, 281
sexual harassment, 253, 280, 281
shadow carceral state, 205; carceral debt relating to, 210–12, 214–15, 217; CCA and, 213; correctional-fee law, 213; credit and debt with, 214; criminal justice cost increase with, 211; definition of, 209; financial hardship with, 211–12; immigration control relating to, 210; mass incarceration relating to, 212–13, 217–18; minor misdemeanors criminalized by, 210, 212; noncriminal behavior punished with, 209–10; offender funding with, 212; pay-to-stay fees with, 213; poor impacted by, 213–14
shock doctrine, with social reproduction crisis, 202, 203
Siim, Birte, 305, 306, 312
single mothers, punishment of, 206
single parents, social policy for, 231
single-payer movement, 164–65, 174nn52–53
Sklar, Katherine Kish, 40, 44
Skocpol, Theda, 36, 44, 156, 274
SMO/NGOs, 308, 310, 311, 316n58
SNAP. *See* Supplemental Nutrition Assistance Program
social and political conflict, 2
social assistance, 251, 255, 256, 344

social benefits, 4–5, 117–18, *118*
social citizenship, 128–29, 289, 348
social citizenship, in Norway and Sweden: capitalism, 131–34; corporatism with, 130, 134; decommodification with, 130, 132; Esping-Anderson on, 129–30, 132; future of, 143–45; Marshall on, 108, 130; Nordic model of, 129, 130–31; postindustrialism, 135–38; Rehn-Meidner model of, 132–33, 137, 138; socio-democratic trajectory of, 130; state of, 139–43; universality with, 130, 144; women relating to, 128, 133–34
social compact, Fordist-Keynesian, 201
social control, 35
social-democratic citizenship, 101
social democratic consensus, 6
social-democratic welfare model, of Nordic countries, 139–40, 144
social-democratic welfare state, 28, 34
Social Democratic Women's Federation, 254, 255
Social Democratic Workers' Party of Sweden (SAP), 252, 255, 260, 262–63
social democrats, radicalization of, 136–37
social dumping, 305
social insurance, two-tiered, 275–76
social integration, in Nordic countries, 142–43
socialism, 5, 82
socialized medicine, 149
social justice, 27, 43, 298
"Social Justice After the Welfare State," 19

social legislation, of New Deal, 42
social movements, 349–50
social ossification, 75
social policy, in Europe, 108, *237–38*; for adoption by homosexuals, 230; with aging population, 230; with decline of male breadwinner, 230, 241; with declining fertility, 230; with dual-earner household, 230–31; equal rights for women, 230; family definitions with, 229–30, 235; intergenerational and gender-specific behaviors with, 236–45; with job-market instability, 230; with labor force, 230; with marital instability, 230, 231; for nonmarried heterosexual couples, 229; for open assisted-reproductive technology, 230; role of state with, 230; for same-sex couples, 229–30, 241–42; for single parents, 231; social risks with, 230; Spain, 229–30; with unpaid family work, 230, 241
social policy, political participation and: framing of, 119–25; political equality with, 121–25; responsibility with, 119–21, 124; in U.S., 108, 119–22
social policy, with family obligations: children relating to, 234–35, 236–39, *237–38*, 277; defamilialization, 231, 232, 234, 236, 240; dependent family member care, 233–35; familialism by default, 231, 232, 233, 236, 239; gender- and generation-specific family interdependencies, 232–35; for nonstandard families, 234–35; prescribed familialism,

232, 233, 234. *See also* supported familialism
social-policy government role, in golden age, 83
social programs, 95–97
social protection, 32, 34, 45, 65, 67
social provision: family and, 227–28; modernization, liberal democracy, and, 28
social provision, politicization of poor and: of African American women, 322–25; community-action agencies with, 323; disruption relating to, 324; entitlement mentality relating to, 323; with negative stereotypes, of poor, 325–26, 327; political decision making relating to, 326, 338n24
social reform, 39–40, 41
social reproduction crisis, 303; with carceral state, 217; with drug use, 218; economic collapse, in 1930s, 197; families impacted by, 217; financial crisis, in mid-1970s, 197; with heterosexual marriage, 200; neoliberalism and, 200, 201, 202; New Deal welfare state contradictions and, 195, 196–97, 200–202, 216–19; panics relating to, 202; with penal system, 216–17; in postwar welfare state, 198; prosperity and, 197; redistribution with, 197; resistance sparked by, 218–19; schools relating to, 208; shock doctrine relating to, 202, 203; with women, in workforce, 200–201
social rights, 3, 12, 21, 27; civil and, 289–90; decline of, 17; expansion of, 4, 9, 11; individualism of, 232;

Marshall on, 130, 349, 355; nontransferability of, 244; transatlantic, 19, 20; in U.S. health system, 149–52, 169n2; welfare state and, 19–20, 91
social risks, with social policies, 230
social-science historians, 31
social scientists, 27–29, 37
social security, 330; decline of, 177; Keynesian economics and, 27, 29, 30, 196, 276; transatlantic paths to, 28
Social Security Act of 1935, 5, 38, 87–89, 122, 273, 276, 343–44
social security checks, 348–49
social services, egalitarian wartime, 28
Social Structures of Accumulation (SSA) theory, 196
social wage expansion, 274–75
social-welfare model, in Europe, 20, 31, 36
socio-democratic trajectory, of social citizenship, 130
socioeconomic security, mixed system with, 27
solidarity, 82, 91–93, 95, 97, 101, 102–3
solidarity-wage policies, 253
Soskice, David, 131
Southern Christian Leadership Conference, 326
Spain, social policies in, 229–30
spatial and ethno-racial dynamics, 178–79
SSA. *See* Social Structures of Accumulation
Staatsräson, 72, 73, 74
stagnating wages, with breadwinner liberalism, 278
state-building, 63, 67, 73
state policies, during golden age, 85

Steinem, Gloria, 351
Stoltenberg, Jens, 128
Supplemental Nutrition Assistance Program (SNAP), 114, 115
supported familialism, 231, 232, 233; decommodified, 242; decommodified defamilialism for childcare with, 236, 237–38, 239–40; decommodified defamilialism for elderly with, 236, 237–38, 239–41; default familialism for elderly with, 237–38, 239; weak decommodified defamilialism for childcare with, 236, 237–38, 239–40
supranational incrementalism, 64, 69
Supreme Court. U.S., 151, 157, 160, 180, 209, 210–11, 215; cases with, 15, 156, 162, 279, 280, 281
Svalfors, Stefan, 140
Sweden, 89–90, 92, 110; democratic institution of, 35, 36; economics of, 117, *118*; *folkhem* in, 5, 142; housing in, 355; private commercial actors in, 141; privatization in, 21; reform period in, 139; women in, 44–45, 128, 133–34, 357. See also Nordic countries; social citizenship, in Norway and Sweden
Swedish Employer's Association (SAF), 253
Swedish Right, 356
Swedish Trade Union Confederation, 132, 136
symmetrical parenthood, 265–66

TANF. See Temporary Assistance for Needy Families
tax-and-transfer system, 109–12, *114*, 117–19
taxation, 10, 13–14, 83, 92, 240–41, 251, 253–54
tax credit, for childcare, 284–85
taxpayer's revolt, 330–31
Tea Party, 95, 157
technological transformation, 10–11
Temporary Assistance for Needy Families (TANF), 110, 115–16, 259, 351
temps, loyalty of, 182–85
terminology, revolution of, 29–30
Thane, Pat, 31, 39, 40
Thatcher, Margaret, 13, 102, 137
theodicies, 66, 76, 79n12
theoretical debates, about citizenship, democracy, equality: cosmopolitanism, 299–300; globalization with, 298–300; integration with, 298; methodological nationalism, 299, 313n8; migration relating to, 298–300, 302; national rights relating to, 300
Third World programs, 7
Titmuss, Richard, 28
To Be Equal (Young), 285
Tobin tax, 304, 315n39
trade unions, 5, 8, 14, 93, 352; collective bargaining of, 6; decline of, 90; negotiation system of, 89
transatlantic social rights, 19, 20
transatlantic welfare capitalism: liberal, 35; statist-corporatist, 35; universalist, social democratic, 35
transnational challenges, 298, 300–301
transnational civil society, 298, 304–6, 313n5
transnational democratic citizenship model, 302

transnational public spheres, 300–301
transnational space, EPS as, 309
transnational studies, 22, 311–12
Treaty of Rome, 73
Trump, Donald, 2, 15, 18, 295, 335
two-income families, 278–79
"Two Wests," 21, 249, 321

ULU. *See* United Labor Unions
undeserving poor, 320, 336n3
undocumented workers, 189
unemployment, 2, 13; of African Americans, 280, 285–86; with breadwinner liberalism, 277–78; insurance for, 344; redistribution, privatization and, 112–16
unions, 350, 353, 358; decline in, 278; in Europe, 345; labor, government support for, 275; membership in, 352. *See also* trade unions
United Labor Unions (ULU), 333
United Nations Declaration of Human Rights of 1948, 36, 47, 91, 101
United States: declining real incomes in, 1; democratic participation in, 3, 11; immigration in, 12, 93; internal colonialism in, 8; populist right rise in, 60; public education costs in, 2; racial and ethnic tensions in, 7; redistributional government spending in, 2; redistribution and privatization in, 109–19; social benefits in, 4–5; social policy and political participation in, 108, 119–22; social reform in, 40; as welfare latecomer, 36; welfare state and, 1, 41
universal benefits, 8

universal-caregiver model, 266
universalism, 166
universality, with social citizenship, 130, 144
unpaid family work, social policy for, 230, 241
unregulated free-market policies, 13
USPolyst, 188

value spheres theory, 65–66, 67, 71, 75
Varieties of Capitalism (Hall and Soskice), 131
Versorgung, 72–73, 75, 76
Versorgungsklass, 71
voting rights, 14, 15, 16

wage earners, women as, 347
Wage Earners Fund, 136
wages, family, 275
warfare, to welfare, 34
War on Crime, 206, 213
War on Drugs, 213, 289
War on Poverty, 90, 206, 283, 284, 323–24
Weber, Max: on intelligentsia, 66; on political power, 77; on politics, 70, 71, 75; theodicies relating to, 66, 76, 79n12; value spheres theory of, 65–66, 67, 71, 75; on welfare state, 66–67
Weir, Margaret, 36, 274
welfare: African American dependency on, 288; American notion of, 30; benefits of, 353–54; critiques of, 288; democratic, 28, 34; exclusions relating to, 32; fraud with, 207–8; Nixon and debate on, 255, 256, 257, 282, 283, 284; recipients of, 331; to welfare state, 29–30; workfare and, 351

welfare, integration and, 62, 65; intellectual dimension with, 64, 69; political dimension with, 64; post-2007 crisis relating to, 63; supranational incrementalism with, 64, 69; tensions with, 63
welfare assistance: female stream of, 41; male stream of, 41
welfare client, 32
welfare expansion: emergency cause of, 33–34, 35; language of, 29; after World War II, 21–22, 27, 28, 34, 67
welfare mothers, 320, 345, 349, 351
welfare queens, 207, 288, 320
welfare reform, of Clinton, 88, 119, 120, 206, 258, 259
welfare rights, 91, 326, 327; activists for, 325; movement for, 350–52
welfare state, 16; of 1930s, 7, 29, 39; accomplishments of, 343; AFDC and, 343, 345, 349, 353; assessment of, 46–48; as avenue of participation, 86; benefits of, 8–9, 22, 349; in Britain, 356; capitalism and, 4, 6, 9, 31; challenges to, 3, 59; changes to, 18; critic of, 343; critics of, 12–13; decline of, 3, 29, 107, 215; definition of, 342; democracy and, 3, 4; EU and, 59, 344; future of, 357–58; of Germany, 34, 52n35, 148; historian methods and interpretations of, 29–36; identity politics relating to, 12–13; industrial-era crisis of, 275; labor-law protections and, 177; liberal version of, 85; market-related, 8, 9; modern, 32, 35; national boundaries of, 62; New Deal and, 38; Nordic universalist, 296; origins of, 32; participation with democracy after, 86–87, 89–90, 94–99; postwar, 87–88, 198, 217; promise of, 3; questioning of, 1–2; renegotiations of, 107–8; social rights and, 19–20, 91; social scientists and, 27–29; transformation of, 354–55; United States and, 1; Weber on, 66–67; of western societies, 30. *See also* democracy, after welfare state; European integration, national welfare state and
welfare state, 1975–1995: feminist historians, gender and history of, 37–48; history of, 27–29, 47; new interpretations of, 35–36; past methods and interpretations of, 29–35
welfare state, to carceral state: governing through crime, 207–15; punishment, noncriminal pathways to, 205–7; punishment, traditional paths to, 203–4; social reproduction crisis, 195, 196–97, 200–202, 216–19; weakening democratic institutions, 215–16. *See also* New Deal welfare state contradictions
welfare-state scholarship, 274
welfare system: American, 88; child, 207
Wertidee, 67
Western industrial societies, 4
"White House Summit on Working Families, The," 263
white men, New Deal for, 321
widows' pensions, 343
Wiley, George, 328–30
Williams, Rhonda, 322
Wohlfahrtsstaatsräson, 72, 75

women: citizenship of, 37, 39, 54n53; civil rights of, 282; of color, 7, 320–21; emancipation of, 46; entitlements for, 258, 259, 270n35; equal rights for, 230; Latina, 276–77, 282, 320; New Deal and, 39, 198; in Norway and Sweden, 44–45, 128, 133–34, 357; in political activities, 15, 24n15; political mobilization of, 283; as reformers, 41; support of, 12, 87; as wage earners, 347; in workforce, 4, 7–8, 13, 200–201. *See also* African American women; breadwinner liberalism, women and; female prisoners, punishment and; feminist historians; poor women

Women's Legal Defense Fund, 256
Women's Rights Project, 280
workfare program, 351
workforce, women in, 4, 7–8, 13, 200–201
work-related benefits, 352
World War I, 19, 35
World War II, 5, 19, 68, 356; economic growth after, 28; European integration after, 76; golden age after, 83; population transfers with, 47; private health-insurance systems after, 152; welfare expansion after, 21–22, 27, 28, 34, 67

Young, Whitney, 285

zero-tolerance policies, 208